The Selected Works of

MAULANA

ABUL KALAM

AZAD

Volume IV
(1949-50)

Chief Editor

Dr. Ravindra Kumar

ATLANTIC PUBLISHERS AND DISTRIBUTORS

Published by
ATLANTIC PUBLISHERS AND DISTRIBUTORS
B-2, Vishal Enclave, New Delhi - 27
Phone: 5413460

Sales office
4215/1, Ansari Road, Darya Ganj
New Delhi - 110002
Phone : 3273880

Typeset at
APD Computer Graphics
B-2, Vishal Enclave, N. Delhi - 27

Printed in India at
Mehra Offset Press
New Delhi

TO

MOTHER INDIA

Preface

Dr. Ravindra Kumar is an admirer of Maulana Abul Kalam Azad. This is nothing unusual. Maulana Azad had numerous admirers in the course of India's struggle for freedom. The number increased appreciably after India attained freedom. Partition of India was the heavy price India paid for this freedom. Maulana Azad had throughout his whole political life opposed forces which encouraged separatist trends in our national life. It was in the partitioned India that people realised more vividly the soundness of the views Maulana had expressed on the communal problem.

Maulana Azad was among the major figures in our unique struggle for freedom waged under the leadership of Gandhiji. The selected works which Dr. Ravindra Kumar has edited bring out the greatness of Maulana Azad in several fields of life. He was most assuredly an outstanding scholar, a great journalist, a matchless orator but with equal ease he was also a great statesman who played a significant role in every crisis which India and, in particular, the Indian National Congress faced from time to time in its struggle to make our country free and independent.

He had also his due share in shaping India's destiny in her first decade of Independence. He was an outstanding member of the Union Cabinet but what was more important was the mature advice he made available to his comrade and fellow warrior Pandit Jawaharlal Nehru as the latter sought to grapple with India's difficult and daunting problems in the first crucial phase of her independence.

Dr. Ravindra Kumar may not yet be a mature scholar but the enthusiasm he has shown in portraying the intellectual and political life of Maulana Azad deserves commendation. The country is still faced with problems which greatly exercised the Maulana's mind. What he thought and said on these problems would still be a source of inspiation and enlightenment to his countrymen in the difficult days through which we are all passing.

Sadiq Ali

Introduction

I

Maulana Azad always thought in terms of national unity, integrity, solidarity and secularism within the form of Indian society and Indian political and Indian religious conditions. It was his greatness that he both before and after independence worked according to this thought. He has been source of guidance and inspiration in the matter of communcal unity and national cohesion. Today our thoughts go back to Maulana Abul Kalam Azad's ideas, and beliefs in these vital matters. And it is my firm belief that it is only by adopting Maulana's ideas that we can rid overselves of those separatist, communal and religious tendencies that are eating into the vital of India's body-politic. The concept of secularism developed by him, in letter of national unity and integrity which was important in his time and also highly significant for modern time constitute the subject matter of this Volume 4 of the Selected Works of Maulana Abul Kalam Azad covering the period 1949-50.

II

In this Volume Maulana Azad's speeches, statements and other documents apart from his correspondence with Sardar Vallabhbhai Patel, Pandit Nehru, Rajendra Babu and others have been included. His work as a Union Minister of Education is an important part of this volume which certainly adds to the contemporary social, political, economic, cultural, historical and parliamentary informations on the one hand and can inspire for devotion and dedication to the coming generations on the other.

Like the previous Volumes several important documents relating to the main events (1949-50) and pertaining to Maulana Azad's multi-dimensional personality have been included in appendices.

III

Maulana Azad's views on educational matters were very clear. He had made an appeal to exercise caution for a country like India where a number of languages are spoken. He believed in a common script for India in the matter of languages; obviously there is validity in this argument. Even so he gave support to making Hindi our national language and thus he advocated nationalist course. But he was opposed to religious education in universities and colleges. He put forward a number of suggestions in the matter of language and education policy for the country. It is clear from the documents included in this volume.

He always laid great stress on national approach to resolve the differences between Hindus and Muslims. For the cause of United India he believed that we should look more to the past than to some intellecutal thinking at the present moment. In order to strengthen the unity of the country we should strike a balance between circumstances and consequences.

In conclusion we can say that it is only by going deep into Maulana Azad's ideas on national unity, integrity and secularism that we can build a solid foundation of Indian nationalism.

I am grateful to the staff of National Archives of India specially to its Director General Dr. Rajesh Parti, Assistant Director Shri P.R. Malik, Mrs. Manju Sehgal and Mrs. Meena Kapoor, President, Shri Sadiq Ali and other staff of Gandhi National Museum, New Delhi, staff and officials of Sardar Vallabhbhai Patel National Memorial, Ahmedabad, Shri Jitendra Thakorebhai Desai, Managing Trustee, and other staff of Navjivan Trust, Ahmedabad, Director Dr. Ravinder Kumar and Shri A.K. Awasthi of Nehru Memorial Museum and Library, Teen Murti House, New Delhi and the staff of several other institutions and Archives providing me the all important literature in their possession.

I am greatly indebted to his excellency, Dr. Shankar Dayal Sharma, Vice-President of India, His Holiness Maulana Syed Abul Hasan Ali Nadvi, Rector, Nadwatul Ulama, Lucknow, Dr. (Mrs.) Najama Heptullah, Deputy Chairperson, Rajya Sabha, Dr. Karan Singh, Shri A.J. Jalali and Mr. S.G. Mohiuddin, Dr. Akbar Ali Khan, President, Azad Institute, Hyderabad, Shri V.N. Gadgil, His Excellency, Shri B. Satya Narayan Reddy, Governor of U.P. and others for their kind encouragement and guidance in preparation of this volume.

My thanks are due to Mrs. Kamlesh Ravindra Kumar, Prof. K.L. Malik and Dr. (Mrs.) Malti Malik for their kind co-operation in many ways.

My special thanks are due to Dr. K.R. Gupta and Shri Manish Gupta of the Atlantic Publishers and Distributors, New Delhi for undertaking the publication of the selected works of this great son of Mother India courageously.

Ravindra Kumar

Abbreviations

A.I.C.C.	:	All India Congress Committee
A.I.E.C.	:	All India Educational Conference
A.L.C.	:	Asiatic Language and Culture
A.P.I.	:	Associated Press of India
C.A.B.E.	:	Central Advisory Board of Education
C.A.I.L.	:	Constituent Assembly of India (Legislative)
C.E.B.	:	Chairman Education Board
C.G.E.P.	:	Central Government Educational Programme
C.I.E.	:	Central Institute of Education
C.I.H.R.	:	Commission on Indian History Records
D.D.D.E.	:	Deputy Director of the Department of Education
E.D.	:	Education Department
E.M.	:	Education Ministry
I.P.C.	:	Inter-Provincial Communication
J.M.I.	:	Jamia Millia Islamia
L.A.	:	Legislative Assembly
L.M.C.	:	Lucknow Muslim Conference
L.P.G.B.	:	Labour Party in Great Britain
M.I.B.	:	Ministry of Education and Broadcasting
M.L.	:	Muslim League
N.E.	:	National Education
N.G.	:	National Government
N.M.	:	Nationalist Muslims
O.S.S.	:	Overseas Scholarships Scheme
P.G.	:	Provincial Government
P.S.	:	Parliamentary Secretaries
R.E.P.S.	:	Religious Education to Private Sources
R.S.	:	Roman Script
R.S.C.	:	Report of the Security Committee
S.C.	:	Scheduled Castes
S.C.L.E.	:	Standing Committee of the Legislative on Education
S.W.A.E.	:	Social Welfare and Adult Education
T.H.R.C.	:	The Historical Records Commission

U.K.	:	United Kingdom
U.S.A.	:	United States of America
V.C.	:	Vice-Chancellor
W.C.	:	Working Committee

List of Documents

Contd.

S. No.	Document	Date
12.	Replies to the questions asked in connection with the Scheduled Caste candidates returned after foreign studies.	22.02.1949
13.	Replies to the questions asked regarding the Expansion of Primary Education in Ajmer-Merwara.	22.02.1949
14.	Replies to the questions asked about the Education of the Blind.	22.02.1949
15.	Replies to the questions asked in the Indian Legislative Assembly about the revision of District and State Gazetteers.	22.02.1949
16.	Replies to the questions asked about the compulsory Primary Education.	22.02.1949
17.	Replies to the questions raised in the Constituent Assembly of India (Legislative) in connection with the new scheme for award of scholarships for studies abroad.	25.02.1949
18.	Maulana Abul Kalam Azad's replies to the questions asked in connection with the Basic Education Scheme in Delhi Province.	25.02.1949
19.	Answers to the questions asked in connection with the facilities for Education in Mother Tongue in Primary and Secondary Stages.	25.02.1949
20.	Replies to the questions asked in Legislative Assembly in Connection with the scholars sent abroad for advanced Technical Studies.	25.02.1949
21.	Speech at the Diamond Jubilee Celebration of the Scindia School, Gwalior.	26.02.1949
22.	Speech in the Indian legislative Assembly on General Budget–List of Demands and replies to the questions raised by the Members during the speech.	18.03.1949

Contd.

Contd.

Contd.

Contd.

Contd.

Contents

Document No. 1

LETTER FROM PT. JAWAHARLAL NEHRU TO MAULANA ABUL KALAM AZAD

New Delhi
4 January, 1949

My dear Maulana,

I am very glad to read your statement[1] on the Turkish earthquake.[2] I have just sent a telegram to Rajendra Babu[3] suggesting that he should send £100 on behalf of the Congress to Turkey. I hope it may be possible also for the U.P.P.C.C. to send Rs. 500.

As you know, I spent two days in the Punjab. I think it is felt urgently necessary that you should spend some days there as soon as possible. In spite of the complicated situation there, there are many hopeful signs and good material. I should have liked to see you before you went there. But I shall be away from Allahabad from the 6th to the 14th touring in Aligarh, Meerut, Bulandshahr, Muzaffarnagar, Saharanpur and Moradabad.

Yours affectionately,
Jawaharlal Nehru

---

1. Azad stated that the Congress Party would like to send a small amount as a token of goodwill for the victims of earthquakes in Turkey.
2. There were earthquakes in Turkey in three successive years :1946, 1947 and 1948. Anatolia and Erzerum Provinces suffered severe damage, killing nearly one thousand and destroying a number of villages.
3. Dr. Rajendra Prasad, the then, Chairman Constituent Assembly of India.

Document No. 2

SPEECH OF MAULANA AZAD, DATED 7-1-1949 AT THE MEETING OF THE CENTRAL ADVISORY BOARD OF EDUCATION HELD IN ALLAHABAD

Twelve months have passed since we met last in Delhi. That was the first meeting of the Central Advisory Board of Education held after the achievement of independence. Naturally we were full of enthusiasm and wanted to proceed with our programme of educational expansion as rapidly as possible. It was in this spirit that the Ministry of Education went ahead with its schemes and prepared a programme for realising our long cherished plan of expansion of education for the country.

You are, I am sure, aware of the sudden deterioration in the economic condition of the country which faced us during the latter half of the year. The danger of inflation and a rising spiral of prices grew so great that the Cabinet was compelled to reconsider the position and appoint an Economy Committee. That Committee recommended a drastic cut in the expenditure of all the Ministries and pressed that all development programmes must be suspended or at least slowed down. I realise the importance of economy, but at the same time feel that education is a matter which cannot brook suspension or even delay. Nevertheless, as the economic situation grew graver, the Cabinet was forced to give precedence to the resolution of the financial crisis over all other activities of the Government. Much against my will, I therefore agreed to slowing down the tempo of our educational development but insisted that, as soon as there was some improvement in the situation, education must be one of our first priorities for the resumption of the full development programme.

Even with this slowing down, the present position marks a great improvement on the conditions that prevailed before 1947. Before the attainment of independence the education budget of the Government of India was in the neighbourhood of Rs. 2 crore. The first financial year of independence has been a perceptible expansion in the education budget and the next year's budget–in spite of financial difficulties and drastic economy–will be well over twice the amount of pre-independence days. I am glad to say that the New Year has brought with it a gleam of brighter days. I am hoping that I will soon be in a position to announce that the Government would go full steam ahead with the programme of expanding the National Education in all its stages.

The first and foremost task of the National Government is the provision of free and compulsory basic education for all. In your last meeting, you stressed its urgency. This was reiterated by the All India Educational Conference which met immediately thereafter. You will remember that I pointed out to the Conference that the 40 years' programme laid down in the Report of the Central Advisory Board seemed too long and should be reduced. I also suggested that its programme of construction of school houses required fresh scrutiny in order to bring the expenditure within the limits of our financial capacity. I am glad to say that the Conference accepted both the suggestions and recommended that an expert committee should be appointed to go into the question in order to suggest ways and means for reducing the period and the cost of buildings. Accordingly, a committee of experts under the chairmanship of the Hon'ble B.G. Kher was appointed and it has submitted its interim report. According to this report, universal compulsory basic education can be introduced within a period of 16 years by two five-year and one six-year plans. The first five-year plan will aim at bringing that education to a major portion of the children of the country within the age-group of 6-11. The second five-year plan will extend compulsion to the remaining children of the smae age-group so that at the end of ten years all children between the ages of 6-11 will be under compulsory instruction. The six-year plan will then extend the scope of compulsion to 14 so that at the end of 16 years the programme of 8 years' basic education for children between 6-14, as envisaged by the Central Advisory Board, will be completely realised.

The Committee also went into the question of finances and suggested that the Centre should provide 30 per cent of the expenses while the provinces and local bodies should find the remaining 70 per cent. The following table shows the total expenses that would be, incurred from year to year:

Year	Expenditure of compulsory education	Incidental expenditure	Total expenditure
	Rs.	Rs.	Rs.
1949-50	9,38,38,00	4,69,19,00 50% of col. (2)	14,07,57,00
1950-51	19,03,34,000	7,61,33,600 40% of col. (2)	26,64,67,600
1951-52	29,26,57,000	8,77,97,100 30% of col. (2)	38,04,54,100
1952-53	39,85,66,000	7,97,13,13,200 20% of col. (2)	47,82,79,200
1953-54	50,84,25,000	5,08,42,500 10% of col. (2)	55,92,67,500
1954-55	77,15,88,00	..	77,15,88,00
1955-56	104,73,44,00	..	104,73,44,00
1956-57	133,35,90,000	..	133,35,90,000
1957-58	154,95,58,000	..	154,95,58,00
1958-59	177,87,21,00	..	177,87,21,000
1959-60	202,63,63,000	..	202,63,63,000
1960-61	226,34,00,000	..	226,34,00,000
1961-62	251,25,38,000	..	251,25,38,000
1962-63	263,48,36,000	..	263,48,36,000
1963-64	276,32,49,000	..	276,32,49,000
1964-65	288,36,93,000	..	288,36,93,000

1. These figures take account only of the provinces and exclude the States.

2. Incidental expenses are included to cover (i) the cost of increased salaries of teachers in existing schools, (ii) the cost of educating older children who may join the new schools, and (iii) the other expenses which would follow from the increase in the number of pupils at all stages. This percentage has been reduced year by year for the reason that as more and more students are covered by the compulsory scheme the excess of expenditure is bound to decrease.

3. These figures have been calculated on the basis that compulsion will be applied to 40 per cent of the age-group 6-7 during 1949-50 and advanced year by year so that at the end of the first five years 40 per cent of the age group 6-11 will be under compulsion. The second five-year plan will start with compulsion for the whole of the age-group 6-7 and 40 per cent of the age-group 7-11. Here also compulsion will be extended year by year so that at the end of second five-year plan compulsion will be applied to the whole of the age-group 6-11. During the six-year plan, compulsion will be applied in the first year to 50 per cent of the children in the age-group 11-12 and extended year by year so that at the end of three years there will be compulsion for 50 per cent of all children in the age-group 11-14. The second three years will extend compulsion to the remaining children till in six years all children in the age group of 11-14 are brought under compulsion.

The Ministry of Education have accepted this interim report and tried to provide funds in our next year's budget on that basis. In view of the economic and financial dangers to which I have already referred, it has not, however, been possible to provide for the entire amount. Much against my will, I have been compelled to agree to a proposal to postpone the consideration of this scheme for the time being. One factor which weighed with me was that the Central contribution would be effective only if the provinces are in a position to provide their share of the expenses. The financial position of the country makes one doubt if the provinces can find the necessary funds. It has been decided to consider the question again some time before March to find out how far we can carry out the plan. The Government have, however, provided funds for the training of teachers so that, as soon as the economic situation improves, we can go ahead with the programme of basic education.

We all realise the importance of basic education for the future welfare of the State. Equally important for immediate progress is adult education. In a democracy, the provision of such education is all the more necessary as without an educated electorate democracy cannot perform the functions expected of it. For this, we want not merely literacy, but mental development of the adults so that they can take an intelligent interest in the affairs of their country and the world. The scope of adult education has therefore been extended and to mark this change it is proposed to call it social education in future. The committee which you appointed to prepare a scheme of adult education for the country has submitted its report and has also suggested this change of name. The Government have generally accepted the recommendations of the Committee and I am glad to announce that, in spite of inflation and its attendant financial difficulties, we have been able to provide funds in the next year's budget for the implementation of the plan.

I am also glad to inform you that a beginning has been made in the Province of Delhi with programmes for both basic and social education. Plans for the purpose were approved long ago but for reasons into which I need not enter here they were not carried into effect. The Ministry of Education decided that there should be no further delay and the scheme should be worked out in Delhi to serve both as an example and a challenge to other provinces. Accordingly, the Delhi Provincial Post-War Educational Development Board was formed. I have myself attended almost every meeting of the Board to ensure that programmes are put into effect as early as possible. In order to get over the difficulty of securing a sufficient number of trained teachers, it was decided to take trained refugee teachers from West Punjab and give them a short refresher course at Jamia Millia, Delhi. Two batches of teachers have already received their training and a third batch will soon start its course. Since then we have been able to establish two training institutes – one at Ajmer for men and the other at Delhi for women – and we hope that they will help to meet the demand for trained teachers for new basic schools as they are founded.

The first set of 47 schools was started on July 1, 1948, and the second set of 50 schools from the second half of November 1948. A third group of 50 schools will start from April 1, 1949, and it is hoped that before the end of the financial year 1949-50 the entire area of Delhi Province will be covered by such basic schools.

In order to make the programme of basic and social education one of immediate interest and utility to the villagers, it has been decided that these village schools will not only be places of instruction for the village children, but also centres of community life in the villages. They will provide instruction to children, adolescents and adults and, in addition, serve as places of recreation and sport. It is also proposed to give the villagers practical training in some craft in order to improve their economic status and to organise sports and other forms of recreation for increasing their social and community sense. We have taken the help of the Ministries of Health, Labour, Information and Broadcasting, and Agriculture and prepared a composite syllabus which will be gradually introduced in these schools. The following 12-point programme will give a brief indication of the aims we have in view in the scheme of social and basic education:

(1) The village school will be a centre of instruction, welfare work, sports and recreation for the entire village.

(2) Separate times will be allotted to children, adolescents and grown-ups.

(3) Certain days in the week will be reserved exclusively for girls and women.

(4) A number of motor vans fitted with projectors and loud-speakers are being secured to visit the village schools. Film and magic lantern shows will be given and recorded talks played. It is proposed to visit each school at least once a week.

(5) Schools will be provided with radio sets and arrangements will be made for broadcasting special programmes for school children, adolescents and grown-up people in the light of the scheme of social education sketched above. About 140 sets have already been provided by the Ministry of Information and Broadcasting and more will be supplied as soon as possible.

(6) Popular dramas will be organised in the schools and from time to time prizes given for the best plays produced.

(7) There will be provision for teaching national and community songs.

(8) Arrangements will be made for giving simple instruction in some craft or industry suited to the locality.

(9) Lectures will be arranged in co-operation with the Ministries of Health, Agriculture and Labour to instruct villagers in the simple laws of social hygiene, methods of agriculture, cottage industries and co-operative activities.

(10) In co-operation with the Ministry of Information and Broadcasting, suitable films and slides will be shown from time to time. Arrangements will also be made for visits of public men to speak to the villagers on problems of national importance. The help and assistance of public bodies interested in constructive work will be invited to give effect to the programme of social education.

(11) Arrangements will be made for organising group games. Competitions will be held from time to time between different schools and villages.

(12) Periodic exhibitions, fairs and excursions will be organised.

Only a beginning has been made in our scheme of social and basic education in the villages but this in itself has been a revelation to me and to all those who have seen the scheme at work. For long it has been said that villagers have no realisation of the importance of education. Their age-long inertia, sloth and poverty have been held as obstacles to the introduction of a scheme of National Education. It has been feared that because of their ignorance and superstitions, they may even resist any scheme of compulsory education and force may have to be used to bring education to their children. Experience in Delhi has completely dispelled these fears. I had always held the view that the villager in India has been misjudged in this respect. I have great pleasure in announcing that from the very first day of the programme, villagers in Delhi have responded with an enthusiasm that is beyond all expectations.

One of the methods we propose to use for extending social education as quickly as possible is the holding of educational *melas* or fairs from time to time. It is intended to organise sports during these *melas* as well as arrange visits and lectures of prominent public men. In addition, the villagers will be encouraged to produce dramas of their own as well as exhibit products of local industry and craft. Educational films and radio programmes will be among other features at these *melas*. Two such *melas* have been held in Delhi – one in the month of November and the other only a few days ago. Villages – men, women and children – have responded with an enthusiasm that has been most heartening. Villagers have not been only passive spectators but active participants. Each *mela* has called into activity latent energies of not only the village where it was held but of the entire locality. The experience of these two *melas* has confirmed me in my belief that the Indian villager is on the march today and is thirsting for knowledge. He is ready and anxious for progress and the fault will be entirely ours if we fail to provide him with the means of education on all fronts. I earnestly hope that the provinces will take up the plan and organise at least one *mela* a month in every province.

Since the last meeting of the Central Advisory Board of Education, the whole question of scientific and technical studies has been surveyed afresh. You will remember the scheme of Overseas Scholarships instituted by the old Government for training our scientific and technological personnel. Experience showed that the Scheme required thorough overhauling and I appointed for the purpose a committee with Dr. B.C. Roy as its chairman. I also felt that a general survey of our scientific and technological resources and requirements should be made and entrusted the Scientific Manpower Committee with that task.

Both these Committees have recommended that immediate steps must be taken for strengthening the existing technological institutions in the country and starting new institutions for imparting instruction of the highest standard. They have rightly pointed out that it would be in the interest of the country to provide for such instruction within the country itself. This would gradually obviate the necessity of sending large numbers of students abroad. Till such time, however, as arrangements for imparting instruction up to the highest standard are complete, the despatch of students abroad must not cease.

The Government have generally accepted the recommendations of both these Committees and drawn up a modified scheme of Overseas Scholarships which will aim both at strengthening the teaching personnel in our universities and scientific and technological institutions and providing the necessary staff for carrying through the industrial development of the country. I have no doubt that you have already examined the papers circulated to you and will, if necessary, make constructive suggestions to strengthen our hands in carrying through the above programmes.

I have referred to the great financial difficulty with which the country is faced today. This has compelled us to slow down our programme in many aspects of the educational development of the country. This is a contingency which I cannot but regret and the more so when I remember the extremely inadequate provision made for education of all types in India. When we compare the figures for educational expenditure in India with those in other countries, I cannot help feeling that we have, in fact, not yet made a beginning with a programme of National Education in the truest sense of the term. I have already referred to the extremely meagre educational budgets of the pre-independence days. In spite of the progress made since then, I am sorry to say that the provision for education last year amounted to only Rs. 3,85,00,000 out of a total Central Budget of Rs. 395 crore (excluding the Railways), *i.e.*, less than 1 per cent. During the same year, the total of the provincial budgets shows a figure of Rs. 247 crore of which only about Rs. 30.5 crore were spent on education. Thus, in the case of India as a whole, only a little over 5 per cent has till now been spent for educational purposes and though the budget for 1949-50 will show a perceptible improvement, I must confess that the expenditure is not yet up to my expectations.

These figures may be compared with the amounts spent on education in countries like the U.K. and the U.S.A. In the U.K. the State spends on education £ 214,896,000 out of the total budgeted expenditure of £ 2,975,679,000. This represents about 7 per cent of the total budget, but, in addition, another 4 per cent of the total expenditure is contributed by local bodies. Thus in the U.K., the proportion of expenditure on education to the total budget is about 11 per cent. In the U.S.A. the total national expenditure on education to the total budget is about 11 per cent. In the U.S.A. the total national expenditure on education is the colossal figure of 12,050,000,000 dollars. The total budgeted expenditure of the Federal Government is in the neighbourhood of 40,000,000,000 dollars. Thus, for a population of about 50 millions, the U.K. is spending about £ 300 millions, and for a population of about 140 millions the U.S.A. is spending 12,000 million dollars.

It may also be mentioned that according to the Steelman Report, the U.S.A. proposes to spend by 1957 one per cent of the total national income–not the State Revenue–for purposes of research alone in the universities and industries. This will represent a figure of something like 2,000 million dollars (approximately Rs. 750 crore). In addition, the U.S.A. Government propose to provide a sum of about 300 million dollars (Rs. 100 crore) for equalising the opportunity of secondary and university education for children of comparatively poorer parents. Similarly, Great Britain is spending 76.5 millions (Rs. 110 crore) for fundamental and applied research.

Not content with this, the British Government have now under consideration a proposal for further expanding the facilities for higher education by which from 1951 onward, over ninety per cent of the places in the universities and institutions of higher learning will be free. In other words, the process of compulsory education, which started in Great Britain in 1870 by providing universal free education at the primary stage and has continued since 1902 by the provision of free secondary education in the Grammar and the County Schools, has now been brought to its final fruition by making even university education for all practical purposes free and universal. No one can for a moment suggest that Great Britain has not her own financial and economic difficulties. This has not, however, prevented the implementation of her educational expansion programmes, and I trust and hope that we in India also will not allow considerations of financial stringency to hold up for a day longer than is absolutely necessary the programme of universal compulsory and free basic education which is essential for building up the free and democratic India of our dreams.

I have so long spoken to you about basic and social education. University education is, however, of equal importance for the future progress of the land. The recent World War has raised in every country of the world new questionings about the aims and objects of higher education. Such enquiry is of even greater importance to us in the context of our newly won freedom. I will not, however, go into this question today, as we have appointed the Universities Commission to examine the problem of higher education in all its aspects. You have pressed for the appointment of such a Commission for the last three years, and rightly so, for there has been no comprehensive survey of higher education in India since the Sadler Commission submitted its report. Even the Sadler Commission confined itself primarily to one university but the Indian Universities Commission, 1948, has been charged with an enquiry into the whole structure of our higher education in the universities and other institutions of study and research. I am glad that we have as chairman of the Commission so eminent an educationist as Prof. Sarvapalli Radhakrishnan. He is being assisted by able colleagues from India and abroad. I am particularly happy that distinguished educators of the U.K. and the U.S.A. have offered us their services in this venture. I am hoping that the Commission will submit their report before the end of the year.

Before concluding, I will draw your attention to one other burning problem of the day. You recommended and the Government of India agreed that the medium of instruction in the primary stages must be the mother tongue. All provinces have accepted the principle, but I think you will agree that as yet only the general principle has been laid down. Difficulties have, however, been felt in working out the details and giving a practical shape to the principle. There is no problem where the mother tongue of the pupil is also the State language, but, where this is not the case, doubts have arisen on several points. It has not been clearly laid down at what stage the State language should be introduced as a second language. Nor is it clear when it should replace the mother tongue as the medium of instruction in schools. These and allied questions should be examined in detail; and fair and practicable solutions found so that nobody may have any ground for grievance. The Government of India could have taken a decision themselves, but I feel that your advice in the matter will be invaluable, as you represent not only the provinces and the states but also the enlightened opinion of the country.

I trust that you will give special attention to the problem during this session and define in a clear and unambiguous manner the detailed procedure for giving effect to an agreed principle. By doing so you will not only solve one of our most difficult educational problems but also render a real service to national unity.

Document No. 3

LETTER FROM PT. J.L. NEHRU TO MAULANA ABUL KALAM AZAD

New Delhi
January 10, 1949

My dear Maulana,

It is rather odd for me to write to you to suggest a grant to an institution in view of the big cuts that have been made in your budget. I am doing so with considerable hesitation.

I enclose a letter[1] from Swami Kuvalayananda. This letter was handed to me by Shri B.G. Kher, Premier of Bombay, with his strong recommendation. I think the work that Kuvalayananda is doing is rather unique and might prove to be of great importance.[2] The Bombay Government is supporting it. For the present the question is not of any big grants, but rather of an initial token grant of Rs. 10,000 which would help him in many ways.

There is a great deal of interest in foreign countries now in the scientific aspect of yoga training. Indeed Kuvalayananda has been invited by foreign universities especially in America. I would be very sorry if he left India and started his work somewhere else, because I think that this work should be done in India. As a man Kuvalayananda is capable and attractive and earnest. I have known him for a large number of years and learnt something from him. My father used to consult him also.

---

1. Swami Kuvalayananda had requested Nehru to give at least a token grant that year to encourage the work of yoga in his institution.

2. Swami Kuvalayananda was carrying on scientific research in yoga in Kaivalayadhama at Lonavla.

I mentioned this matter to Dr. Matthai. He said that it would be a good thing for this support to be given by the Government of India. The sum involved was so small that it was hardly worthwhile for the Finance Ministry to make a special grant. It might come out of other normal grants.

Yours sincerely,
Jawaharlal Nehru

Document No. 4

MAULANA'S SPEECH AT THE SIXTH MEETING OF THE CENTRAL ADVISORY BOARD OF ARCHAEOLOGY, HELD IN NEW DELHI ON 7-2-1949

In welcoming you to the annual meeting of the Advisory Board of Archaeology, I wish to share with you certain thoughts about the development of archaeological studies in this country. Our main concern must naturally be with the programmes of future expansion, but it is only right and proper that before we do so we should give some thought to the progress of such studies in India and elsewhere up to now.

It has for many centuries been recognised that outside China, the three most ancient centres of civilisation in the world have been India, Mesopotamia and Egypt. For centuries, scholars all over the world have been interested in their history. It has also been recognised for the last 200 years that archaeology offers almost the only key to the history of ancient times. Paper was unknown in these early days, and even after it was invented, records written in paper perished far more easily than the history written in stone and metal.

Recognition of this fact led to extensive archaeological surveys and excavations in Egypt and Mesopotamia with the result that we have today a fairly satisfactory account of their ancient history. In the case of Egypt, not only have the secrets of her ancient hieroglyphics been deciphered but her history ranging back to 5,000 B.C., with the achievements of her 32 royal dynasties, has also been uncovered. In Nineveh and Babylon, excavations have unfolded to us the history of the ancient civilisation built by the Sumerians and the Akkadians of some five thousand years ago. Entire libraries of books written on earthen tablets and even a dictionary of the language have been found giving us an insight into the life of the times. It is therefore surprising that, so far as India is concerned, no attempt was made to utilise the resources of archaeology to discover her ancient history. It would be literally true to say that the history of India is still concealed in the depths of the soil waiting for the archaeologist who will bring new data to light to reconstruct the history of ancient India.

One reason of this comparative neglect of archaeology in India may be that Egypt and Mesopotamia are on the fringe of the European civilisation. For many centuries, the Mediterranean basin has been the home of European culture and modern European civilisation has obvious affiliation with these areas. Nor can it be forgotten that the Old Testament is full of references to both Egypt and Mesopotamia so that Europe felt a natural interest in their past history. Another reason for European interest in these areas may be that the Arabs had developed the historical science to a high level of excellence. We find that even before the rise of modern Europe, elaborate studies had been undertaken by the Arab historians in the civilisation of Egypt and Mesopotamia. It was therefore natural that European scholars should take to the study of these civilisations and carry out the extensive excavations which have lit up the history of ancient times.

In spite of the facts mentioned above, it still seems somewhat strange that archaeology should have developed so late in India. A European power was paramount in the country for almost two centuries. It saw specimens of architecture and monuments which proclaimed a proud and ancient civilisation. It was also aware that the civilisation here dated back to a dim past of which only fragmentary knowledge was available to the world. Its officers must have come across ruined cities and monuments which promised to be an excavator's paradise. It is on record that as early as the beginning of the nineteenth century, the well-known historians, Elphionstone and Barnes, when they were marching towards Afghanistan, were struck by the moulds they found in the district of Rawalpindi. They also came across Greek coins and speculated whether the moulds they saw contained the ruins of the ancient city of Taxila. In spite of all these incentives to an archaeological survey, hardly anything was done in any part of India till the middle of the nineteenth century.

The Asiatic Society of Bengal was, as in so many other fields, the pioneer of archaeological studies in the country. It decided in 1796 to found a museum for housing collections made by the officers of the East India Company. An impetus to the study of Indian archaeology was given by the discovery in the second quarter of the nineteenth century of the key to Brahmi and Kharoshti scripts by James Prinsep. In 1848, General Alexander Cunningham impressed upon the Government of

India the necessity of preserving the ancient monuments by the appointment of a suitable officer. His suggestion was accepted and in 1860 Lord Canning established the Archaeological Department with Cunningham as the first Archaeological Surveyor of India. To Prinsep and Cunningham, India owes an incalculable debt for the preservation of her monuments.

I do not wish to go into the details of the chequered history of the department since then. In 1866, the department was sought to be abolished, but it was revived in 1870 under the pressure of public opinion. The work of the survey was extended to South India only in 1874. There was a further impetus to the development of the department under Lord Lytton and the Indian Treasure Trove Act VI of 1878 was passed. After 1889 there was again a disruption in the department and for several years the work was in a state of complete abeyance. The department was reconstituted after 1895, but it was only with the arrival of Lord Curzon that it received a fresh lease of life. Lord Curzon regarded the promotion of archaeological study, the encouragement of research and the preservation of the relics of the past as part of the "Imperial Obligation to India" and re-established the department with Sir John Marshall as Director General of Archaeology in 1902. It was at the instance of Lord Curzon that the Ancient Monuments Preservation Act VII of 1904 was passed by the Indian Legislature. In 1921, Archaeology, including the Epigraphic Branch, was taken over as a central subject and since then it has continued as such even though the activities of the department were seriously curtailed during the retrenchment campaign of 1931.

During recent years, the department has undertaken important works of excavation, of which the most notable are the Khokrakot Excavation, District Rohtak, East Punjab, in 1937; the Sardhari Excavation in N.W.F.P., in 1938; and the Ahichchhatra Excavation in Bareilly, U.P., during 1941-43. Some work was also done in 1940 in Rajghat, Banaras. In 1944, the Excavation Branch was reconstituted by the Government of India and excavations were undertaken in 1944 at Taxila, in 1945 at Arikamedu near Pondicherry, in 1946 at Brahmagiri and Chandravalli in Mysore State, in 1947 at Harappa and in 1948 at Sisupalgarh. The exploration of megalithic sites in the Madras presidency was also started in 1946. The survey of the Chitaldurg district has now been completed and some work also done in Cochin. There are several new sites which the department propose to take up as soon as the work at Sisupalgarh has been completed, and its report is published. These include sites at Amaravati in Guntur and Rajgir in Bihar.

Up to now, not much work of excavation has been done in the Indian States. Such work, especially in Bikaner and Jaisalmer, has, however, attained a new importance since the partition of India. Most of the sites explored with a view to having a clear idea of the Indus Valley civilisation have fallen within the boundaries of Pakistan. Bikaner and Jaisalmer were, however, important centres of that civilisation in the past. It is therefore hoped that a thorough exploration of the sites in these areas may throw new light on the history of civilisation connected with the Indus Valley.

The department has no provincial centres but in order to carry out archaeological work in the provinces, it has been divided into the following seven circles :

(1) Northern Circle, Agra.

(2) Central Circle, Patna.

(3) Eastern Circle, Calcutta.

(4) South-Eastern Circle, Visakhapatnam.

(5) Southern Circle, Madras.

(6) Western Circle, Poona.

(7) Delhi Circle, New Delhi.

The department has helped societies and bodies, whether governmental or private, in carrying out excavations. It is now helping Allahabad University in the excavations at the well-known site of ancient Kausambi. It has also offered assistance and advice to various local societies and research institutions.

The work of the department is divided into four branches, namely, Epigraphical Branch, Chemical Branch, the Excavation Branch and the Museums Branch. Another important activity of the department is the publication of the results of excavation and other research work. The publications of the Archaeological Survey of India have at times assumed different forms and represented various degrees of scholarship and merit, but they have on the whole constituted a noble mine of information for any future historian of India.

It is now proposed to revive the publication of the *Archaeological Memoirs* which was suspended during the war. Material for two volumes is already in hand. In addition, the department proposes to issue a series of short guides to archaeological monuments and inscriptions. It is also proposed to publish picture post-cards, albums of monuments and museums in addition to the regular journals like *Ancient India, Epigraphia Indica, Epigraphia Indo-Moslemica* and the various annual reports.

The publication policy of the department requires revision and expansion. Until recently, almost all our publications were in English. The time has now come when publications in important Indian languages must be undertaken in order to make the results of research available to an average citizen. I propose to make a beginning in this respect as soon as possible.

I have referred to the desirability of the issue of albums and picture post-cards in order to popularise the work of the department with the general public. This must be done on a far wider scale than has been the case till now. Two types of albums should be produced. There should be albums for presentation – at a somewhat higher price – which could be used not only by the lovers of art in India and outside, but also by schools, colleges and other educational institutions for prizes to deserving students. A second type of cheaper album should also be placed in the market to bring it within the reach of the general public. At the same time, the department should discuss with the Ministry of Communications advisability of issuing picture post-cards by post-offices throughout the country. A far wider public would thereby be reached than by any other method.

I feel that we must also explore the possibility of utilising the film in order to present our archaeological and architectural monuments to the people of our country and the world outside. Well-produced films would not only bring out the beauty of such buildings but also make them alive and interesting to a vast number of our people. Other countries have used films as a media for the education of the people in the ancient history of the land. Here, in India also, a provision could be made, by which every cinema would be required to show for at least 10 minutes films depicting some aspect of Indian history and culture.

I have pointed out to you that our history is still concealed beneath the surface of the earth. A fresh start of exploration and excavation on a much larger scale is necessary to unearth that history. This requires strengthening of the staff in all branches and a complete re-organisation of the department. I am also convinced of the necessity to provide permanent training facilities for students outside the department. Such training is essential for successful archaeological work and you will be glad to hear that we have recently sent two officers for advanced training in the U.K. I have not lost sight of the urgency of a properly equipped National Museum for India. A beginning has already been made, and I am doing all that is possible to bring the scheme to a successful conclusion as early as possible.

You will, however, realise that in view of the present financial difficulties, it may not be possible to do all that is desirable or necessary. Nevertheless, archaeology is so important for a proper appreciation of our history that something must be done in spite of the present difficulties. I can assure you that the Government of India will do whatever is possible within the limitations of finance. You must also advise the Government as to how best to utilise our limited resources during the period of stringency and prepare a long-term programme of work which can be undertaken as soon as the economic position improves.

Document No. 5

MAULANA AZAD'S REPLIES IN THE CONSTITUENT ASSEMBLY OF INDIA (LEGISLATIVE) DATED 9-2-1949 TO QUESTIONS ASKED IN CONNECTION WITH THE INDIAN HISTORICAL AND ART RELICS IN FOREIGN COUNTRIES

Seth Govind Das: (a) Will the Honourable Minister of Education be pleased to state whether Government are aware of the desire among Indians to get back their historical and art relics taken away by foreigners?

(b) Is it a fact that Government propose to appoint a Committee to prepare a list of such relics in various countries?

(c) What steps do Government propose to take to bring such relics back to India?

The Honourable Maulana Abul Kalam Azad: (a) Yes, Sir.

(b) and (c) Government have before them the plan to have full and correct information about the historical and sculptural relics which are in the Museums of the foreign countries or which may be in the possession of individuals there. Government will take necessary action in the matter.

Seth Govind Das: Is the Honourable Minister aware of the fact that when I had put this question on the previous occasion I was given the same reply. In the circumstances may I know when the Government Report would be ready?

The Honourable Maulana Abul Kalam Azad: It is expected that the deliberations of the Committee will be finished within this year.

Seth Govind Das: On the last occasion the reply was given that as far as the British Museum is concerned with these things someone is to be sent from here so that he may bring these things back to India.

The Honourable Maulana Abul Kalam Azad: Yes, but later on this proposal was postponed, as it was thought that the work was a stupendous one and involved many countries. So it would be better to appoint a committee of 2-3 members for this purpose.

Shri H.V. Kamath: Do the Government propose to establish a museum of all these historical things?

The Honourable Maulana Abul Kalam Azad: Yes.

Shri H.V. Kamath: Will some part of the Government House at Delhi utilized for this purpose?

The Honourable Maulana Abul Kalam Azad: For the present nothing can be said in this respect.

Shri Deshbandhu Gupta: Will the Honourable Minister utilising his personal influence try to bring the doors of the Somnath Temple back to India?

The Honourable Maulana Abul Kalam Azad: These doors have once been brought back to India and are probably still lying in the Agra Fort.

Mr. Tajamul Husain: As the questions regarding historical things lying in foreign countries are being put I wish to ask the Government whether the Government have taken any action for retrieving the famous diamond Kohinoor?

The Honourable Maulana Abul Kalam Azad: No, no action has been taken.

Mr. Tajamul Husain: I wish to ascertain why no action has been taken?

Mr. Speaker: Order, order. Reply has been given.

Document No. 6

REPLIES OF MAULANA AZAD TO QUESTIONS ASKED IN THE CONSTITUENT ASSEMBLY OF INDIA (LEGISLATIVE) BY SETH GOVIND DAS AND OTHERS DATED 9-2-1949 ABOUT THE REGIONAL LANGUAGE IN DEVANAGARI SCRIPT AS UNIVERSITY LANGUAGE

Seth Govind Das: (a) Will the Honourable Minister of Education be pleased to state whether the attention of Government has been drawn to the resolution passed by the All India University Teachers' Convention held in Delhi in the first week of December 1948, on the use of the regional language in Devanagari script as the University language?

(b) If so, what steps do the Government of India propose to take to implement the resolution of the Convention?

The Honourable Maulana Abul Kalam Azad: (a) The All India University Teachers' Convention did not send to this Ministry copies of any of the resolutions passed by them, but the Ministry are aware of the resolutions that were passed.

(b) In view of the fact that the Universities Commission is engaged in looking into all aspects of University Education, the Central Advisory Board of Education at their last meeting have recommended that a decision on this matter may be deferred till the Commission has submitted their report.

Seth Govind Das: When the Report of the Commission is expected?

The Honourable Maulana Abul Kalam Azad: It is expected that the commission would take nine months to complete its work.

Seth Govind Das: I wish to ascertain that if the Report of the Commission is not expected before nine months then will the matter referred to in part (a) of the question be kept pending.

The Honourable Maulana Abul Kalam Azad: I have just submitted that the Advisory Board has recommended that this matter would be settled when the said report is out. So naturally the report will be awaited.

Seth Govind Das: Is the Honourable Minister aware of the fact that as far as this question is concerned the Advisory Council has made no such recommendations?

Mr. Speaker: The honourable member is going into argument.

Mr. Frank Anthony: Is it not a fact that at a Vice-Chancellors' meeting held some time back, it was unanimously agreed to defer any change in the media of instruction for a certain number of years?

The Honourable Maulana Abul Kalam Azad: Yes, the recommendation was that for five years the medium of instruction in the University stage should be English, and change may be made afterwards.

Mr. Frank Anthony: Are the Government aware that hasty policies on the part of certain provincial Government are causing considerable hardships to linguistic minorities?

Mr. Speaker: Order, order.

Shri O.V. Alagesan: Will Government make it clear that they have no intention of abolishing the Provincial scripts and set at rest all doubts in the matter?

The Honourable Maulana Abul Kalam Azad: Government will thoroughly go into the question. It is clear that there are many aspects of this problem. The Government will take into consideration every aspect.

Shri Deshbandhu Gupta: Has the Honourable Minister received any recommendations in this connection from the Chief Commissioner's Advisory Council?

The Honourable Maulana Abul Kalam Azad: No, I am not in receipt of any such recommendations.

Shri O.V. Alagesan: May I have a translation of the answer given to my question?

Mr. Speaker: He will get in due course.

Dr. Mono Mohon Das: May I know, Sir, whether it is a fact that the Central Government do not like to interfere in the regional languages and scripts so far as administration and education in Universities are concerned?

The Honourable Maulana Abul Kalam Azad: The question of interference does not arise because the Central Advisory Board consists of representatives of all the Provinces and whatever decisions would be arrived at will be with their consultation.

Document No. 7

REPLIES BY MAULANA ABUL KALAM AZAD DATED 9-2-1949 IN THE CONSTITUENT ASSEMBLY OF INDIA (LEGISLATIVE) TO THE QUESTIONS ASKED IN CONNECTION WITH THE PAY OF LANGUAGE TEACHERS IN DELHI PROVINCE

Seth Govind Das: (a) Will the Honourable Minister of Education be pleased to state whether it is a fact that the Government of India, in sanctioning new grades of pay for teachers in Delhi Province, have shown discrimination between Hindi-Urdu teachers, Sanskrit-Persian teachers and English teachers in Higher Secondary schools?

(b) Do Government propose to give the new grades of pay sanctioned for the three categories of teachers?

(c) In view of the growing importance of Indian languages, do Government propose to consider the advisability of removing any such discrimination in the grades of pay of language teachers?

The Honourable Maulana Abul Kalam Azad: (a) No. The scales of pay prescribed for different categories of teachers are based on their qualifications. A statement showing the revised scales of pay is laid on the table.

(b) Yes. The scales prescribed will be applied to the different grades.

(c) The question does not arise as there is no discrimination in the grade pay of teachers.

Statement showing scales of pay prescribed for different categories of staff in Government schools, Delhi Province

	Name of Post (1)	Existing scale (2)	Prescribed scale (3)	Remarks (4)
1.	Principal of Higher Secondary School	200—10—40	350—25—500—30 590	Same as notified in the *Gazette of India*, dated 16-8-1947.
2.	Headmasters and Headmistresses of High Schools	150—10—200—10—250	(i) 200—10—300 (ii) 300—20—400 (iii) 400—20—500	Do.
3.	Headmasters and Headmistress of Veracular and A.V. Middle Schools	80—4—100—4—160 *plus* special pay Rs. 20 (men) & Rs. 100—5—140—5—160 *plus* special pay Rs. 10 (women) and Rs. 140—10—190.	140—10—200—EB—10-300 (for more than six classes) 100—8—140—10—200 upto six classes.	Do.
4.	Teachers in High School with the qualifications M.A., B.T. or M.A. with 3 years experience in a college.	Various Scales	200—10—250—15—400.	
5.	Teachers in High Schools with the qualifications B.A., B.T.	Various scales	80—5—120—8—200—10 300 (with initial start of Rs. 120 p.m. for B. Ts. & L.T.s.	

(1)	(2)	(3)	(4)
6. Graduates with Junior Training qualification *viz*.., S.V., J.A.V. or J.V.	45—2—65	80—5—120—8—200—10/2—220.	Same as notified *in the Gazette of India,* dated 16-8-1947.
7. Matric (J.A.V.) Prabhakar, Shastri, Munshi Fazil & Adib Fazil.	Various Scales	68—4—120—5-—70	..
8. S.V. (Matric or Middle)	Various Scales	68—4—120—5—170	Same as notified in the *Gazette of India*, dated 16-8-1947.
9. Arts & Handicrafts teachers, Smithy teachers and Carpentary teachers.	Various Scales	68—4—120—5—170	..
10. Junior Oriental teachers (Vernacular non-Matric) teachers.	20—1—25	50—2—60—3—90	..
11. Untrained teachers	20—1—25	35—1—40—2—60	Same as notified in the *Gazette of India*, dated 16-8-1947.
12. Laboratory Assistants	20—1—35	30—1—50	
13. Matron in Govt. Training School for Women.	Rs. 50/-	55—3—85—4—125—5—130	
14. Librarians	60—4—100	(i) 55—3—85—4—125—5—130	(i) if untrained

		(ii) 68—4—120—5—170	(ii) if trained	
15.	Clerks	Various scales	55—3—85—4—125—5—130.	Same as notified in the *Gazette of India*, dated 16-8-1947.
16.	Bus Drivers	Rs. 40	Rs. 60—5/2—75	..
17.	Peons, Sweepers, Chawkidars Malis, Caller-women, Waterman, etc.	Rs. 13	Rs. 30—1/2—35	Same as notified in the *Gazette of India*, dated 16-8-1947.
18.	Inter (Honours in Oriental Classical Languages).	Various scales	Rs. 80—5—120—EB—8—200—10/2—220.	
19.	Inter (Honours in Vernacular Languages).	Do.	68—4—120—5—170 (with initial start of Rs. 76 p.m.)	
20.	Oriental Teachers (Shastries etc.) non-matriculates, but teaching in High and Middle Departments.	Do.	68—4—120—5—160	
21.	Junior Vernacular teachers	Do.		
	(a) Matriculates.		68—4—120—5—170	
	(b) Non-Matriculates		50—2—60—3—90	

(1)	(2)	(3)	(4)
22. Drawing Masters with the qualifications :	Do.		
(a) Matriculation and 2-year course in Art	Do.	68–4–120–5–170	
(b) Intermediate with 2-year course in Art	Do.	68–4–120–5–170 (with initial start of Rs. 76 p.m.)	
23. Physical Training Instructor with the qualifications:			
(a) Matriculation and certificate in Physical Education	Do.	68–4–120–5–170	
(b) B.A. and Diploma in Physical Education	Do.	80–5–120–8–200–10–300 (with initial start of Rs. 120 p.m.)	
24. Domestic Science Teachers with the qualifications:			
(a) Matric and Home Science Diploma	Do.	68–4–120–5–170	
(b) Inter and Teachers Training Diploma in Domestic Science.	Do.	80–5–120–EB.–8–200–10/2–220	
25. Music Teachers		68–4–120–5–170	
26. Librarian:			
(a) Untrained		55–3–85–EB–4–125–5–130	
(a) Graduate with Diploma in Librarianship		100–8–140–10––250.	

Document No. 8

MAULANA ABUL KALAM AZAD'S REPLIES IN THE CONSTITUENT ASSEMBLY OF INDIA (LEGISLATIVE) DATED 14-2-1949 TO THE QUESTIONS RAISED BY S.R.K. CHAUDHURI AND OTHERS ABOUT THE ARCHAEOLOGICAL EXCAVATIONS

Srijut Rohini Kumar Chaudhuri: Will the Honourable Minister of Education be pleased to state:

(a) whether any excavation has been conducted by the Archaeological or Anthropological Department of the Government of India for purposes of research and discovery within recent years and if so, when and with what result; and

(b) whether any assistance, monetary and otherwise, has been given by the Government of India to Kamrup Museum in Gauhati for this purpose and if so, what?

The Honourable Maulana Abul Kalam Azad: (a) Yes; the following excavations were carried out by the Department of Archaeology during the past four years of which the results are briefly indicated below:

1945. During April-June, 1945, excavations were conducted at a site called Arikamedu near Pondicherry, the capital of French India. Here an Indo-Roman trading station belong to the 1st-2nd centuries A.D. was brought to light. Of the structures discovered, a ware-house and a large factory-area deserve special notice. The excavations helped a great deal in chronologically classifying the local ceramic industry.

1946. During April-June, 1946, excavations were conducted at the well-known site of Harappa in the Punjab. Here a citadel of outstanding importance was brought to light. Besides, a cemetry belonging to the Harappa culture was also discovered.

1947. During March-May, 1947, excavations were undertaken at sites called Brahmagiri and Chandravalli in the Northern part of the Mysore State and it was here for the first time that the local megaliths were dated from circa 200 B.C. to the beginning of the Christian era.

1948. During April-June, 1948, the site of Sisupalgarh near Bhuvaneshwar in Orissa was excavated and a squarish fort measuring about 3/4ths of a mile each way, with an excellent lay-out and elaborate system of gateways ranging in date from circa 200 B.C. to A.D. 300 was brought to light.

(b) No monetary assistance for purposes of research has been given by the Government of India to Kamrup Museum in Gauhati which is a provincial museum. The Department of Archaeology has, however, made always available such advice as was possible for the development of the Museum. The Museum has also been presented with a representative set of Mohenjodaro antiquities and a representative set of painted potsherds from Harappa.

Srijut Rohini Kumar Chaudhuri: I would like to get this answer translated into English as it is in Urdu.

Mr. Speaker: Not necessary, I believe the honourable member understand Hindustani.

Srijut Rohini Kumar Chaudhuri: No, I did not understand some of the words, such is 'Khudayagaya' 'Jamana', etc.

Mr. Speaker: It seems to me, we are turning the occasion of the questions for a controversy about Hindi, Urdu and all that. I do not propose to allow it. If the honourable member has not really understood the answer, then of course, I would request him to study the same.

Srijut Rohini Kumar Chaudhuri: I could understand the answer in a way, but not fully.

Mr. Speaker: Then we may proceed with the supplementary questions.

Srijut Rohini Kumar Chaudhuri: Sir, I want to know whether since the establishment of the two Departments, any excavations has been done by the Archaeological Department in the province of Assam?

The Honourable Maulana Abul Kalam Azad: No.

Srijut Kuladhar Chaliha: After the discovery made by Dr. Hutton, has any scholar been deputed to carry out investigations in Assam in the field of anthropology?

The Honourable Maulana Abul Kalam Azad: I would like to have notice of that question.

Shri O.V. Alagesan: Will Government consider the desirability of taking under the control of the Archaeological Department, in addition to important ancient monuments, important sites also like the birth place of Shri Krishna in Mathura?

Mr. Speaker: The honourable member need not proceed with the question, because it is a suggestion for action.

Shrimati G. Durgabai: May I know from the Honourable Minister whether all the articles which have been converted from these five places have been collected at one place; and if so, from what place?

The Honourable Maulana Abul Kalam Azad: The work in this direction is already in progress at different places. No final arrangements in this respect could however, possibly be made by this time.

Srijut Rohini Kumar ChaudhuriL: Is it a fact that Dr. Girja Shankar Guha visited Assam and he had reported that there was a large field for research in anthropology in Assam?

The Honourable Maulana Abul Kalam Azad: This is not within my knowledge. I would like to have a notice for that.

Shri H.V. Kamath: Has the Honourable Minister in view any such proposal for the postponement of all these excavation works and utilize the amount thus saved for the provision of food and clothing for the masses?

Mr. Speaker: It is only a suggestion for action.

Shri H.V. Kamath: The question is, whether there is such proposal before Government?

Mr. Speaker: Whatever the form of it, in substance it is a suggestion for action.

Document No. 9

MAULANA ABUL KALAM AZAD'S REPLIES, DATED 17-2-1949 IN THE CONSTITUENT ASSEMBLY OF INDIA (LEGISLATIVE) TO THE QUESTIONS, RAISED BY MR. V.C.K. RAO AND OTHERS IN CONNECTIONWITH THE UNIVERSAL BASIC EDUCATION

Shri V.C. Kesava Rao: (a) Will the Honourable Minister of Education be pleased to state what progress has been made in the introduction of universal basic education?

(b) Are the Government of India incharge of the whole scheme or is it to be eventually entrusted to the Provincial Governments?

The Honourable Maulana Abul Kalam Azad: (a) Almost all the Provincial Governments have opened Basic Schools for children of 6-11. Some of the Provinces, for example Bihar, have also started Senior Basic Schools for 11-14 age group. Several Provinces have made arrangements for training of teachers in Basic system.

In regard to Centrally administered Areas, during 1948-49, about 100 new Basic Schools were started in the rural areas of Delhi Province. Two Training Institutions for Basic Teachers, one in Delhi and the other in Ajmer, were started. Coorg has deputed three candidates for training in Basic Education to the Training College, Allahabad. After their return, Training College for Basic Teachers and Basic Schools for children will be started in Coorg.

Some of the States namely, Mysore, Rampur, etc. are also taking steps to introduce Basic system of education.

(b) The Provincial Governments are directly responsible for Basic Education in their respective areas, though they are following the general outline of the Basic System laid down by the Central Advisory Board of Education in their Report of 1944 as modified by the Board during 1948-49. All the Provincial Governments, however, get grants for Basic Education from the Centre.

The Centre's responsibility, however, does not end with giving grants to the Provinces. The Ministry of Education have prepared an All-India Scheme for introducing compulsion among all children of 6-11 in a period of 10 years as against a period of 40 years, previously envisaged by the Central Advisory Board of Education. This scheme has been accepted by the Board at its last meeting in January and immediate implementation of it will be discussed at a Conference of all Provincial Education Ministers to be held this month. The main difficulty in implementation of the scheme is lack of funds but in spite of this, it is hoped that a beginning can be made in the coming academic year.

Shrimati Renuka Ray: In view of the fact...

Shrimati Dakshyani Velayudhan: I want translation.

Mr. Speaker: Let her put the question.

Shrimati Renuka Ray: In view of the fact that provincial governments spend a very small proportion of their Budget on education, has the Central Government taken steps to emphasize on them the necessity of allocating more funds for education and also refusing to give Central subsidies if they do not keep in touch with the programme of the Central Advisory Board and spend more money on education ?

Dr. P.S. Deshmukh: On a point of order. The honourable Lady member on this side of the House was asking for a translation of the replies before any supplementaries were put. I think her request should be considered.

Mr. Speaker: That is not a point of order. I have heard that request and in due course of time, after seeing how the supplementaries are developing, I will see whether that request should or should not be granted. The difficulty, honourable members will realize, is this, that, if on account of the request of any single individual member, I were to allow the translation of every question, then the proceedings must absolutely be conducted in English and there can never be any turn-over to Hindustani. So I request the honourable members to see that they try to follow Hindustani, particularly the replies of the Honourable Maulana Saheb which are in very simple Hindustani in this case, and for all the most important things, English words are used by him, but that is another matter. It is a matter of opinion.

Shri Ramalingam Chettiar: May I suggest that the Honourable the Education Minister may have a Deputy to him to answer in English ?

Shrimati Renuka Ray *rose* —

Mr. Spearker: Order, order. Let us allow her to put her question.

Shrimati Renuka Ray: Have Central Government emphasized on the provincial governments the need for coming into line with the C.A.B. schemes and spending more money on education in provincial budgets and if they do not do so, will the Central Government be prepared not to give them subsidies for development schemes?

The Honourable Maulana Abul Kalam Azad: The Central Government does its best, but there is no such thing before it on account of which it should stop giving grant to any Provincial Government.

Mr. Speaker: Mr. Chettiar. He wanted to put a question.

Shri T.A. Ramalingam Chettiar: Not a question. I suggested with reference to the difficulties expressed regarding translation....

Mr. Speaker: That has been noted.

Shrimati G. Durgabai: May I know if a sufficient number of qualified hands is available for employment in the basic Schools opened both by the Central and Provincial Governments? Are any figures available? And what efforts are being made by Government in this respect?

The Honourable Maulana Abul Kalam Azad: Every effort is being made in this direction. But I cannot give its full details at the moment.

Shri V.C. Kesava Rao: How many teachers were given training in basic education during the last financial year?

The Honourable Maulana Abul Kalam Azad: I would require notice for that.

Shri H.V. Kamath : Will the Honourable Minister of Education please state how much amount was spent by the Government during the past year on the introduction of basic education in Delhi, Ajmer-Merwara and Coorg?

The Honourable Maulana Abul Kalam Azad: A notice for that is required.

Dr. Y.S. Parmer: May I know whether any basic school has been opened in Himachal Pradesh, and any teachers sent for receiving training?

The Honourable Maulana Abul Kalam Azad: No, as far as I am aware this work has not been taken up there on these lines.

Shri Moturi Satyanarayana: May I know that considering the importance of basic education, the money spent upon higher education should be spent towards basic education?

Mr. Speaker: Order, order. This is a suggestion for action.

Begum Aizaz Rasul: May I know which of the Provinces are in receipt of grants from the Centre, and what are the basis on which the amount of these grants has been fixed?

The Honourable Maulana Abul Kalam Azad: Grant is being given to almost all the Provinces.

Shri Deshbandhu Gupta: Is it not a fact that the requirements of the basic schools opened in Delhi were not met with for a long time and even at present these are not working satisfactorily?

The Honourable Maulana Abul Kalam Azad: Many difficulties were felt which were the outcome of various reasons. Every effort is being made to remove these as early as possible.

Seth Govind Das: Will Government also try to keep it in view that this basic education is made uniform in all the Provinces and that the opinion of the Provinces should also be obtained in this respect?

The Honourable Maulana Abul Kalam Azad: Action is being taken on these very lines.

Shri Kishorimohan Tripathi: May I know from the Honourable Minister the total number of schools opened in the different provinces and the amount of money spent towards them?

The Honourable Maulana Abul Kalam Azad: I would require notice.

Shrimati Dakshayani Velayudhan: How many candidates trained in basic education are unemployed at present?

The Honourable Maulana Abul Kalam Azad: I would require notice for that.

Shrimati G. Durgabai: Sir, May I know whether any grant is being given by this Government to all the basic schools opened under the auspices of the Kasturba Trust, and if not, will it consider over the matter?

Mr. Speaker: Order, order. This is a suggestion for action.

Dr. P.S. Deshmukh: May I know if there were any experiments carried on with regard to the suitability of the basic education in any part of India; if so, what where those places and with what success were the experiments carried out?

The Honourable Maulana Abul Kalam Azad: I think the matter has passed this stage. At present this is no longer an experiment. On the contrary it has been admitted that basic education should be developed further throughout the whole of the country.

Document No. 10

MAULANA AZAD'S REPLIES TO THE QUESTIONS ASKED BY PT. M.B.L. BHARGAVA IN THE LEGISLATIVE ASSEMBLY OF INDIA DATED 17-2-49

PRIMARY EDUCATION IN DELHI AND AJMER-MERWARA

Pandit Mukut Bihari Lal Bhargava[1] : (a) Will the Honourable Minister of Education be pleased to state the approximate number of boys and girls between the ages of 5 and 14 in the Provinces of Delhi and Ajmer-Merwara?

(b) What is the approximate number of boys and girls of the above age group receiving education in the various institutions in these areas?

(c) Has any primary education expansion scheme been prepared for these Provinces and if so, by which year will Government be able to arrange for primary education of all such boys and girls?

(d) Have Government any intention to introduce free and compulsory primary education in these areas and if so, by what time and in what stages?

(e) Do Government intend to introduce legislation for the purpose, and if so, when and if not, why not?

The Honourable Maulana Abul Kalam Azad: (a) On account of influx of the refugees it is not possible to give accurate figures pending the undertaking of fresh census.

(b) Approximately 72,000 in Delhi and 30,000 in Ajmer-Merwara.

(c) Yes. As regards Delhi Province all pupils of the age group 6-11 in the rural area are scheduled to be in school by the year 1951-52. In Ajmer-Merwara the scheme is to be implemented from July 1949 in certain selected areas. The whole area is proposed to be covered within a period of five years.

(d) The scheme referred to in (c) above aims at giving free and compulsory basic education by 1951-52 in rural areas of Delhi and by 1954-55 in Ajmer-Merwara.

(e) The Punjab Compulsory Education Act with certain modifications has already been extended to the Delhi Province. Similar steps are proposed to be taken for Ajmer-Merwara in due course.

1. Answer to this question laid on the table, the questioner having exhausted his quota.

Document No. 11

CONVOCATION ADDRESS BY MAULANA AZAD DATED 20-2-1949 AT THE MUSLIM UNIVERSITY OF ALIGARH

In accepting the invitation extended so cordially by your Vice-Chancellor to come and address the annual convocation of Aligarh University, it was but natural that my thoughts should turn to the occasion when I first came in contact with it. That was 36 years ago and took place in circumstances which represented me to many as an opponent of this institution.

The facts of the case were, however, entirely different. It was a time when the Indian Muslims not only stood aloof from all political movements of the day but were inclined to oppose the country's struggle for emancipation. The single largest factor responsible for such political inertia of the Indian Muslims was the lead which the late Sir Syed Ahmed, founder of this institution, had given in the last quarter of the 19th century. The Aligarh Party which continued his policy tried to keep the Muslims out of the Indian National Congress and was generally successful except in the case of a few distinguished individuals.

It was in this background that I brought out the *Al Hilal* in 1912. From the beginning of my political life, I was convinced that the Indian Muslims must participate in the movement for emancipation and work towards that end through the National Congress. It was inevitable that I should criticise the political lead which the late Sir Syed Ahmed had given and which represented the policy of the Aligarh Party. I therefore came into a clash with this party on the political issue. This was, however, regarded by its members as opposition not only to the founder's political policy but to the institution itself. In fact, some of them went so far as to look upon me not only as an opponent but an enemy of Sir Syed Ahmed and Aligarh.

Nothing was, however, farther from the truth. It is true that I regarded the political lead of Sir Syed Ahmed as a grave blunder but at the same time I had the highest admiration for the educational and other reforms which he carried out. I regarded, and still regard him as one of the greatest Indians of the 19th century. His achievements in the field of education and social reform could not, however, blind me to the wrong lead he gave to the Indian Muslims in the field of politics. Thirty-six years have passed since then but as I survey the course of events during this period, I find no reason to revise my judgment on this issue. I then held and still hold that Sir Syed was a great reformer in the educational and social fields, but the wrong lead he gave in politics has been responsible for many of the evils from which we have suffered. It is, however, not my purpose to discuss the political role today but to pay my tribute to the memory of Sir Syed Ahmed Khan, the educational reformer, who laid the foundation of modern education among the Indian Muslims.

Today, Western education has become part of our national life and we naturally think of it when we use the term 'education'. It is therefore difficult to realise the opposition and struggle which, a hundred years ago, faced the reformers who wanted to introduce this new education in India. They had not only to blaze a new trail but had to contend with obstacles and difficulties at every step. They had to face all those forces which any movement for reform has to face. The prejudices and superstitions of ages clouded the minds of the people. Accepted beliefs and age-old sentiments were both against such a change. The cry of religion supplied the opponents of progress with one of their most potent weapons. The path of religion is not in fact opposed to that of reason and knowledge but unfortunately this has often been represented to be so. The usual cry was that Western education was opposed to the teachings of religion and those who held religion dear must therefore adhere to the old education.

Human thought has had to face this conflict at different times in different countries. Europe went through this struggle in the 17th and 18th centuries while the Eastern countries faced this conflict in the 19th century. The Hindus of India faced this struggle earlier and ended it quickly. Among the Muslims, it took a longer time but in the end the inevitable happened. The forces of change triumphed and the new order had to replace the old. So far as the Muslims of India are concerned, one can assert without any fear of contradiction that the man who played the most important role in this struggle is the presiding spirit of this University. The battle was fought here in Aligarh and Aligarh is a visible embodiment of the victory of the forces of progress.

Some of our writers have compared Sir Syed Ahmed Khan with Raja Ram Mohan Roy. To a large extent the comparison is valid. What Raja Ram Mohan Roy did for Bengal was done by Sir Syed Ahmed, 40 years later, for Northern India and especially for the Muslims of the country. The only difference between the two is that the main reforms of Raja Ram Mohan Roy were in the field of religion while those of Sir Syed were in the field of education. They have, however, left the stamp of their personality in all spheres of intellectual activity. Religion, education, social life, language, literature and journalism bear witness to their spirit of reform and creative energy.

We have also to remember that even though Sir Syed Ahmed was opposed to the political movement of the Congress, there was not the least tinge of communal politics in his attitude. His activities even in the political field comprised both Hindus and Muslims. He was throughout his life a believer in Hindu-Muslim unity. He opposed whatever was in any way likely to cause dissension or difference between them. In his speeches, he again and again used the beautiful metaphor that Hindus and Muslims were the two eyes in Mother India's face.

We can form some idea of his outlook on Indian nationalism from the significance he gave to the term 'Hindu.' In addressing an association of Hindus in Lahore he said, "I am sorry that you have restricted in this manner the application of the term 'Hindu'. You have applied it to a particular religious group. But to my mind this application is wrong. I count as Hindu all those who are the inhabitants of this country whatever be their religion or race. This is the reason why I take pride in the fact that I am a Hindu." If the Hindus and Muslims of India had understood the spirit of this teaching and followed it, the whole course of recent events would have taken a different turn.

Sir Syed Ahmed laid the foundations of this educational institution with a specific object. He had been impressed by the spirit of English education and realised that its excellence lay not merely in imparting instruction but in training of a special kind. The peculiarity of this training was that it developed the character of young men and women and gave them a distinct stamp. He also felt that along with European education, the Muslims must have religious instruction and training. He knew that without such provision the new education would not be popular among the Muslims. He realised that his objects could not be achieved without a special institution for the purpose. He therefore dedicated the remaining years of his life to the creation of the Aligarh College. We must remember that this was the first institution in India which sought to create the atmosphere of a British Public School.

The scheme he had in mind initially was the establishment of a residential university on the lines of Cambridge. He had, however, to content himself with the establishment of only a college. Considering the prevalent conditions, this was no mean achievement. The movement for the University was started after his death as a memorial to him and was accomplished after hard labour of some 20 years.

Sir Syed had established in Aligarh not only a college but an intellectual and cultural centre in tune with the progressive spirit of the times. The centre of this circle was Sir Syed himself and he attracted round him some of the best intellects of the day. Perhaps no journal in India has ever had such influence upon the mind of the generation as his *Tehzib-ul-Akhlaq*. Sir Syed founded this journal after return from his tour in England. He and his colleagues were its main contributors. In fact, this journal laid the foundation of modern Urdu literature and so developed the language that today it is capable of expressing the highest and most abstruse thoughts. Perhaps, there was not a single literary figure among the Muslims of the day who was not influenced by his circle. The best Muslim authors of the modern age were nourished here. Here developed the new schools of research, interpretation and reconstruction of Muslim thought. Though modern Urdu poetry was born in Lahore, it was here that it found the atmosphere most conducive to its growth. Poems of a new style were composed and read at the sessions of the Mohammcdan Education Conference. This was also the first forum of Urdu oratory. All the important speakers of the day were created or nurtured on this platform.

The 19th century was for India, as for other regions in the East, a transitional age. The old forms of life and thought were being demolished and new ones set up in their place. The old earth of India was being moulded into a new form. So far as the Indian Muslims are concerned, one can say that it was in Aligarh that these movements of reform were consummated. It was one of the regions which took the lead in the creation of a new India. The 19th century marked a period of renaissance for the Indian spirit and Aligarh was one of the centres of such renaissance.

It is true that with the death of Sir Syed Ahmed Khan, Aligarh lost many of its distinctive features. Though the College was raised to the status of a University, it could not revive the traditions of its early glory. Nevertheless, you must remember that this glorious heritage is yours, and it is for you to revive the past splendour of Aligarh. The inscriptions which have been carved on the walls of your Strachy Hall may fade with the passage of time, but the inscriptions which Aligarh has written on the modern period of Indian history can never fade. Future historians will discover in Aligarh one of the main sources which have contributed to the evolution of modern India.

An educational institution which has such a glorious past must necessarily hold the promise of an equally glorious future. I am not aware what the state of your minds is today, nor in what colours the future appears to you. Does it bring to you the message of closing doors or of opening gates that introduce you to new vistas of experience? I do not know what visions are before you, but I will tell you what visions I see. You perhaps feel that doors that were open have been closed. I see that doors that were locked have now opened. In the words of the Persian Poet,

Tafawut ast main-i-shanidan-i-man-o-to
Tu bastan-i-dar, o, man fatahe-bab me shanwam.

What you and I hear are different. You hear the sound of closing doors but I of doors that open.

I want that I should speak to you frankly and without mental reservations and I am sure that this is what you would expect of me. If I thought that you were still living in that atmosphere of communal politics which was prevalent before the 15th of August, 1947, I would without hesitation say that your future does not hold that promise which, as an Indian Muslim, I would like you to have. I am glad that there has been a profound change since then and the signs of a new era are becoming clearer every day. You have realised in good time what the intellectual atmosphere of this institution must be in the changed circumstances of today. You have responded to the call of the new times and created conditions which are in conformity with the changed outlook. I have no hesitation in saying that by conforming to the spirit of the times, you have rendered a great service not only to this Institution but to all Muslims of the Indian Union. For this, I extend to you my sincere congratulations.

I would like to describe to you briefly the Central Government's plan and programme of national education and the place which an institution like Aligarh University will have in that new scheme. I think you will agree that the educational set-up for a secular and democratic State must be secular. It should provide for all citizens of the State the same type of education without any distinction. It should have its own intellectual flavour and its own national character. It should have as its aim the ideal of human progress and prosperity. The Indian Union has set before itself such a scheme of common education for all without distinction or discrimination in favour of any community or group.

At the same time, it recognises that there is scope for educational institutions which emphasise certain special types of learning. Their doors should, however, be open to all who are interested in such studies. This is the sphere of national education in which your institution can find its proper place in conformity with the spirit of the times. In this way, you will, in spite of your special characteristics, be a part of the general scheme of education and serve a special function in it. For this you must, however, display the widest catholicity of spirit. It is said that Plato had the following text inscribed on his Academy: "Those who do not know Geometry, have no place here." Your Institution must not have even such a restricting clause. Your motto should be that you will welcome both those who "know Geometry" and those who "do not."

I am aware that the governing principle in your Institution has been from the very beginning wide and liberal. When your College was founded, the very first batch of students included Hindus as well as Muslims. Your staff has also been recruited from all communities. The names of certain Hindu professors have become part of your Institution's history. I am sure that these traditions will be broadened and further enriched in the course of time.

Study and research in Islamic learning and Islamic history have been part of your tradition. I must say that, after the death of Sir Syed, it no longer displayed the vigour it had during his days. Even after the University was established, old hopes were not fulfilled. Your duty today is to revive those old traditions and to create in your University an atmosphere of research and enquiry into all the spheres of knowledge.

I have already reminded you that Aligarh was the place where modern Urdu literature developed. This is an achievement of which your University can be rightly proud. It is your duty to cherish this heritage and further enrich it. I must, however, remind you that your literary efforts must have a wider field than in the past. You should take an equal interest in Hindi literature. Muslims have been noted for their interest in different langauges and literatures. Hindi literature has the same claim on the Muslims as on the Hindus of India. Both the communities have contributed equally to the development of Urdu and Hindi literatures. The new literature in Brij Bhasha which commenced in the Mughul period was the result of the patronage of rulers like Akbar and Jehangir and the contributions of writers of genius like Mohammad Jayesi, Khan Khannan and Abdul Jalil Bilgrami. We find that, up to the end of the 18th century, the number of Muslim poets who wrote in Brij Bhasha is considerable. The time has come when you must revive that old tradition. I desire that this Institution should produce a large number of writers who are equally at home with Hindi and Urdu literatures.

The question of script is one of the controversial problems of today. You know what the opinion of Gandhiji was in this respect. His sincere desire was that every Indian should know both the Urdu and the Devanagiri scripts. That is why he founded the Hindustani Prachar Sabha and made it an essential condition that its workers should know both the scripts. This has also been my opinion for years. I feel that this is the only solution which is possible in the present circumstances. I hope that the lovers of Urdu literature will not wait to find out the reactions of the advocates of Hindi literature, but will themselves do what they regard as conducive to the best interest of the country. In every other sphere of life, one may wait to see what others do, but in the field of learning we can wait for others only at the risk of detracting from our credit. If others are content to know only one script, we need not be sorry that we have learnt two. My sincere desire is that every Muslim in India should learn both the scripts, and thus set an exmaple before the country. This was the message of Mahatma Gandhi, and I am confident that Muslims will act up to it with enthusiasm.

I am glad to find that there is already a recognition of the importance of such work on all sides, and that books have been written in Urdu which make it easy to learn Devanagiri script and become familiar with Hindi literature. Some organisations have been set up in different parts of the country for this purpose. They have already started their activities. I am sure that you have realised the importance of this work and your Institution will be recognised as one of its most active centres.

I will now conclude with a few words of advice to the young graduates who have taken their degrees today and are entering into the responsibilities of life. You yourselves have, no doubt, felt the tremendous changes which have taken place since the days you entered the portals of this University. When you first joined this Institution, you were members of a subject nation. Today you are leaving this University as free citizens of an independent India. I am not sure whether all of you appreciate fully the extent of this tremendous change. As members of a subject nation, you suffered many disabilities. As citizens of a free State, you enter into new responsibilities. The widening of opportunities which freedom has brought has aslo necessarily brought with it the need for greater loyalty and devotion to your State. Today there are no limits to what you can achieve but this very fact imposes upon you the duties which freedom brings.

You are the citizens of free India–a State which is determined to develop its political and social life on secular and democratic lines. The essence of a secular and democratic State is freedom of opportunity for the individual without regard to race, religion, caste or community. As members of such a State, you have therefore the right–provided you have the necessary qualities of character and attainment –to expect all doors to open to you, whether in the fields of politics, trade, industry, service or the professions. There is no gainsaying the fact that in the past many of the alumni of this Institution looked to nothing but employment under the Government. Freedom must bring in a widening of the mind and an enlargement of your ambitions. You must therefore look forward in a free India to the utilisation of your talents in the manner best suited to the needs of the Nation.

I have no doubt in my mind that if you can imbibe this spirit of progressive nationalism which is the motto of our secular democratic State, there will be no position in any field of life that will be beyond your reach. I would therefore urge upon you to develop and strengthen your character and acquire knowledge that will fit you to play your rightful part for the future progress and prosperity of the country.

Document No. 12

REPLIES BY MAULANA AZAD IN THE CONSTITUENT ASSEMBLY OF INDIA (LEGISLATIVE) DATED 22-2-1949 TO QUESTIONS ASKED IN CONNECTION WITH THE SCHEDULED CASTE CANDIDATES RETURNED AFTER FOREIGN STUDIES

Shrimati Dakshayani Velayudhan: (a) Will the Honourable Minister of Education be pleased to state how many Scheduled Caste candidates sent on Central Government scholarship have returned after completing their studies abroad?

(b) What were the subjects in which they were sent to specialise?

(c) How many of the candidates have been absorbed in the Government of India services?

(d) Is it a fact that these scholars were sent abroad to get technical training in subjects prescribed by the Government of India?

(e) Is it a fact that candidates who were sent for training in Public Health Engineering and who were sponsored by the Ministry of Health were told that there was no such line in the Health Ministry?

The Honourable Maulana Abul Kalam Azad : (a) Twenty-one.

(b)			
(b)	Agriculture	...	3
	Research in Animal Nutrition	...	1
	Mechanical Engineering	...	2
	Radio Engineering	...	2
	Public Health Engineering	...	1
	Fuel Technology	...	1
	Textile Chemistry	...	1
	Meteorology	...	1

Social Science	...	1
Teachers' Training	...	8
Total	...	21

(c) Three.

(d) Only seven of these were sent abroad to get technical training in the lines prescribed by the Government of India. The remaining 14 were sent under the Scheduled Castes Scholarship Scheme for 1945-46 and the courses of studies were published to suit the students in particular keeping in view the requirements of the country in general.

(e) No. Public Health Engineering is one of the subjects for which the scholarships are awarded by the Ministry of Health.

Shrimati Dakshayani Velayudhan : I want the English translation of the answer.

(The Honourable Shri Satyanarayan Sinha read out the English translation of the answer)

Shri H.V. Kamath : What are the countries in which these Harijan students were sent for receiving training in different subjects?

The Honourable Maulana Abul Kalam Azad : I would like to have notice for that.

Shrimati Dakshayani Velayudhan : How many of the candidates who came back were sent to the provinces?

The Honourable Maulana Abul Kalam Azad : I would like to have notice for that too.

Shri Ajit Prasad Jain : Have Government any such record showing as how many candidates returned from abroad have been absorbed here; and how many are still out of employment?

The Honourable Maulana Abul Kalam Azad : I have just stated in my reply to the honourable member that there are seven scholars who were sent on Central Government scholarship. Out of these, three have been absorbed, an offer has been made to another and efforts are being made for the remaining ones.

Shri S. Nagappa : May I ask what will happen to the other 14 that have returned from foreign countries after having the necessary qualifications?

Mr. Speaker : What will happen!

Shri S. Nagappa : Whether the Government are going to absorb them in the Centre or in the provinces?

The Honourable Maulana Abul Kalam Azad : Government are not responsible for this. But this has come within the knowledge of Government that they have been able to secure employment in different provinces and private firms.

Shrimati Dakshayani Velayudhan : How many out of these 21 are unemployed at present?

The Honourable Maulana Abul Kalam Azad : Out of the seven scholars sent by the Government of India, three have since been employed; and an offer has been made to one. The remaining fourteen scholars are those who have been employed by the various Provincial Governments and firms.

Shri H.V. Kamath : May I know if roughly speaking the number of Scheduled Caste candidates is not at least the half of the Non-Harijans?

The Honourable Maulana Abul Kalam Azad : How does it arise out of this question?

Shrimati Dakshayani Velayudhan : Since how long have these three candidates been unemployed?

The Honourable Maulana Abul Kalam Azad : I cannot specify the exact period. I think these people will be employed during the course of this very year.

Document No. 13

REPLIES OF MAULANA ABUL KALAM AZAD DATED 22-2-1949 IN THE CONSTITUENT ASSEMBLY (LEGISLATIVE) TO THE QUESTIONS RAISED BY MR. M.B.L. BHARGAVA AND MR. HARI VISHNU KAMATH

Expansion of Primary Educaiton in Ajmer-Merwara

Pandit Mukut Bihari Lal Bhargava : (a) Will the Honourable Minister of Education be pleased to state whether the Government of India have received any schemes for the expansion of primary education within the Muncipal limits of Ajmer and Beawar from these Municipalities and if so, what action has been taken thereon?

(b) Do Government intend to make any provision for recurring and non-recurring expenditure for the expansion of primary education in these areas in the next year's budget?

(c) Have Government taken any decision in the matter of taking over primary and secondary education into their own hands from the Municipalities and Local Boards in the Province of Ajmer-Merwara? If so, in what stages will it be done and by which time is the scheme likely to be completed, and if not, why not?

The Honourable Maulana Abul Kalam Azad :(a) to (c) A scheme for the expansion of primary education within the Municipal limits of Beawar was received from the local Municipal Committee and is under consideration. The Governemnt of India propose to introduce universal compulsory basic education by stages throughout Ajmer-Merwara as part of their post-war educational development plan. Details are being worked out and it is expected that the scheme will come into operation from the beginning of the next financial year. The question of taking over primary and secondary education from the hands of the Municipalities and Local Boards is being exmained in this connection and is still under consideration.

Shri H.V. Kamah: Will the Honourable Minister please state whether Governemnt have under consideation any scheme for the introduction in the near future of compulsory primary education in the Provinces of Delhi, Ajmer-Merwara and Coorg?

The Honourable Maulana Abul Kalam Azad : Yes. Efforts are being made. This has already been started in Delhi.

Shri H.V. Kamath : And what about Ajmer-Merwara and Coorg?

The Honourable Maulana Abul Kalam Azad : This will be introduced with effect from the ensuing financial year.

Document No. 14

REPLIES TO QUESTIONS OF MR. V.C. KESHAVA RAO, ASKED ON 22-2-1949 IN THE LEGISLATIVE ASSMEBLY, BY MAULANA ABUL KALAM AZAD

EDUCATION OF THE BLIND

Shri V.C. Kesava Rao: (a) Will the Honourable Minister of Education be pleased to state what steps have been taken to educate the visually handicapped?

(b) How many institutions are being run by the Government of India for this purpose?

(c) What are the trades which are being taught to them and how many are usefully employed at present?

The Honourable Maulana Abul Kalam Azad : (a) To further the cause of the education of the blind in India, a common Braille Code for major Indian Languages, known as Uniform Indian Braille has been drawn up, and its use has been recommended to all the Institutions for the Blind in India. To publish suitable literature and text-books for the blind, a Central Braille Printing Press is being set up. Expert advice is being given, whenever necessary, to all the existing institutions for the blind. Attempts are being made for giving grants-in-aid to all the institutions for the blind for transcribing books in Braille, pending the establishment of the Press.

Deepavali, a periodical, devoted to the education and welfare of the blind, is being published in Braille as well as in ink-print and is being distributed to all the institutions free of charge.

Tangible apparatus and appliances imported by the public institutions for the blind, for the use of their trainees, have been exempted from the payment of Customs Duty.

(b) At present there is no institution for the blind run by the Government of India. The Government of India, are, however, considering the question of provincializing the existing Institution for the Blind in Ajmer-Merwara as early as possible. Besides, the establishment of a National Centre for the Blind in Dehra Dun, is making good progress.

(c) Trades, such as cane-weaving, basket-making, coir-making, carpet-making, loom-weaving, elementary carpentry, elementary book-binding, broom-making, etc., are taught in almost every institution. From available information, approximately 1,000 blind men who have received training in the existing institutions are usefully employed.

Document No. 15

REPLIES OF MAULANA AZAD IN THE LEGISLATIVE ASSEMBLY TO QUESTIONS ASKED ON 22-2-49 BY MR. M.V. THAKKAR AND MR. H.V. KAMATH

Revision of District and State Gazetteers

Shri A.V. Thakkar[1] **:** (a) Will the Honourable Minister of Home Affairs be please to state whether Government have in contemplation or under consideration the revision of all District and State Gazetteers in the country?

(b) If not, do Government propose to consider the matter?

The Honourable Shri Satyanarayan Sinha : This question has been referred to the Minister of Education and he will give the reply in due time.

Shri H.V. Kamath : When?

The Honourable Maulana Abul Kalam Azad: With your permission, Sir, I shall answer this question.

Mr. Speaker: Yes. The Honourable Minister may do so.

The Honourable Maulana Abul Kalam Azad:(a) and (b). The last edition of the Imperial Gazetteer of India was published by the Clarendon Press, Oxford, in 1908. The District Gazetteers were also published about that time by the Provincial Governments. Efforts to revise them seem to have been made from time to time but abandoned on grounds of economy. As soon as Government find an opportunity the matter will be considered.

Shri H.V. Kamath : Have the present Government ever considered over this?

The Honourable Maulana Abul Kalam Azad: No. Government have had no time to consider it so far.

Shri H.V. Kamath: Do Government contemplate to consider over it.

The Honourable Maulana Abul Kalam Azad: When the proper time comes Government will see to it.

1. An eminent Gandhian; was closely assoicated with the constructive works and to the Servants of India Society.

Document No. 16

MAULANA AZAD'S REPLIES IN THE LEGISLATIVE ASSEMBLY TO THE QUESTIONS ASKED BY MR. A.V. THAKKAR AND MR. TAJAMUL HUSSAIN ON 22-2-1949

COMPULSORY PRIMARY EDUCATION

Shri A.V. Thakkar[1]**:** (a) Will the Honourable Minister of Education be pleased to state whether Government have in contemplation any scheme for the introduction of compulsory primary education in (i) the Centrally Administered Areas, (ii) the Provinces; and (iii) the State Unions or single States of the Union of India, in the year 1950 or in the following year?

(b) If not, when are they likely to take this into consideration?

The Honourable Maulana Abul Kalam Azad: (a) and (b). The scheme of compulsory primary education is already in operation. For details the honourable member's attention is invited to the reply given on the 17th February, 1949 to starred question No. 454 by Shri V.C. Kesava Rao.

Mr. Tajamul Husain: Will this compulsory primary education be given free?

The Honourable Maulana Abul Kalam Azad: Surely.

---

1. A well known Social reformer of Gujarat and a close associate of Mahatama Gandhi.

Document No. 17

MAULANA ABUL KALAM AZAD'S REPLIES TO THE QUESTIONS RAISED IN THE CONSTITUENT ASSEMBLY OF INDIA (LEGISLATIVE) DATED 25-2-1949 BY MR. R.K. SIDHVA AND OTHERS IN CONNECTION WITH THE NEW SCHEME FOR AWARD OF SCHOLARSHIPS FOR STUDIES ABROAD

Shri R.K. Sidhva : (a) Will the Honourable Minister of Education be pleased to refer to the answer to starred question No. 404 asked on the 23rd August, 1948 regarding scholarships awarded for studies abroad and state whether the new scheme for award of scholarships has since been formulated.

(b) Have any new students been sent in 1948 overseas under the Overseas Scholarship Scheme and if so, how many?

(c) How many of the students who have returned after theoretical education in foreign countries have been absorbed either in service or in business?

(d) Has any effort been made to give practical education to these students after they passed out from Colleges and Universities?

The Honourable Maulana Abul Kalam Azad: (a) Yes; the lines on which the Overseas Scholarships Scheme is to run in its revised form from 1949 onwards have been decided. Arrangements for fresh selections for 1949 are already in progress.

(b) No, except 52 scholars who had already been selected in previous years but could not be sent earlier for want of admission or passing facilities.

(c) Out of 220 Central Scholars so far returned from abroad, 109 have been employed; out of 133 returned Provincial scholars, 64 have been employed.

(d) Practical training forms generally an integral part of the overseas studies and is imparted to the students, wherever necessary and available, according to the recommendations of the sponsoring authorities.

Shri R.K. Sidhva:I want to enquire from the Honourable Minister that as he has stated that the new scheme has been approved, so, when the applications for this will be invited ?

The Honourable Maulana Abul Kalam Azad: I think that probably the applications will be invited in the month of October.

Shri R.K. Sidhva: In answer to part (d) of the question, the Honourable Minister has stated that there is a great necessity of practical education. I wish to ascertain if any arrangements for this have been made in India?

The Honourable Maulana Abul Kalam Azad: In the new scheme that will be introduced it has been decided that the scholars who may be selected may be given a special training for some time before being sent.

Shri Mohan Lal Gautam : It is alleged that out of 220 students only 109 have been employed. Out of those who have returned 111 are still unemployed. What thought the Government is giving to them?

The Honourable Maulana Abul Kalam Azad: Fifty have been offered posts and called for interview. Efforts are being made for the rest. But the honourable member must bear this in mind that the scheme was launched by the previous Government and there is no doubt that it was not launched with better planning, with the result that difficulties are cropping up. But the present Government is making fullest efforts.

Shri Deshbandhu Gupta : Is it not a fact that after their return these 111 students have not been given the same work for which they were best suited or for which they were sent abroad?

The Honourable Maulana Abul Kalam Azad: No, it is not so, so far as I am aware.

Shri Deshbandhu Gupta: Anything contrary to this?

The Honourable Maulana Abul Kalam Azad: No. As far as Ministry of Education is aware they have been mostly employed on the duties for which they were sent. It is just possible that some of them may not have been appointed at their proper posts but appointed on other work. It is just possible it may be so, but this I can say that a majority of them have been appointed at their proper places.

Shri Mahavir Tyagi: Have they been appointed on Government posts or in private firms?

The Honourable Maulana Abul Kalam Azad: Only 17 have been employed in private firms, the rest have been given Government service.

Shri Mahavir Tyagi: Have the Government met from its treasury all the expenses incurred on their education by the students sent abroad?

The Honourable Maulana Abul Kalam Azad: Certainly. This scheme was introduced with this very arrangement.

Shri Mahavir Tyagi: Have the Government made any arrangement that those students who after receiving education have not been appointed on Government posts be made to refund the money spent on their education from their pay or the firms where they are employed be asked to refund the money?

The Honourable Maulana Abul Kalam Azad: No, there was nothing like this in the scheme.

Shri Ajit Prasad Jain: Will the Honourable Minister be pleased to mention the salient features of the new scheme and how far these differ from the old one?

The Honourable Maulana Abul Kalam Azad : I cannot give the full details just now. I require notice for this.

Shri Raj Bahadur : Will the Honourable Minister be pleased to state that out of these 220 students how many come from States?

The Honourable Maulana Abul Kalam Azad : Notice is required for this.

Shri Deshbandhu Gupta: Has a provision been made in this new scheme that all the students who will be sent abroad will be employed, lest it may come out to be as happened in the time of the previous Government.

The Honourable Maulana Abul Kalam Azad : The defects that cropped up in the previous scheme were mainly due to the fact that a proper plan had not been drawn up. So difficulty is being felt in providing suitable work to the persons who return from there after finishing their studies. Now in this new scheme this fact has been taken into consideration that only as many persons be sent abroad as could be employed immediately after their return.

Babu Ramnarayan Singh : Can the Honourable Minister foretell the time when India may have such facilities that our students may not be obliged to go abroad but students from other countries may come here instead to get their education?

The Honourable Maulana Abul Kalam Azad : The new scheme that has been introduced is based on this very principle. A major portion of the money that was being spent on the previous scheme will now be spent on the institutions in this country, so that they may be strengthened and a time may soon come when there may not be any necessity of sending students abroad.

Shri R.K. Sidhva : Will the Honourable Minister be pleased to state that is it a fact that the Indian students in Scotland held a meeting in which the President Mr. J.C. Gupta stated as follows:

"We have received 15 letters from returned State Scholars who are walking on streets of New Delhi and seeking for jobs."

If this fact is correct, then what efforts the Government are making for these students?

The Honourable Maulana Abul Kalam Azad : I have just stated that we cannot be held responsible for the shortcomings of the previous scheme. Whatever we could do is being done. We have formed a Special Board for this and special efforts are being made so that not a single scholar may remain unemployed.

Mr. Deputy Speaker : I have heard for the past two days similar letters read out by Mr. Sidhva. It will be better, as we have popular Government functioning, if he writes to the Government with regard to these details and avoids questions here on the matters. There are many questions on the Order Paper to be gone through during the question hour.

Shri Mohan Lal Gautam : Will the Government make a provision in the new scheme that the students who are sent abroad may receive all the education that they can get here in India?

The Honourable Maulana Abul Kalam Azad : Fullest attention has been paid to this.

Document No. 18

REPLIES BY MAULANA AZAD DATED 25-2-1949 IN THE LEGISTLATIVE ASSEMBLY TO THE QUESTIONS ASKED BY MR. R.K. SIDHVA, MR. H.V. KAMATH AND OTHERS IN CONNECTION WITH THE BASIC EDUCATION SCHEME IN DELHI PROVINCE

Shri R.K. Sidhva : (a) Will the Honourable Minister of Education be pleased to state whether Government have started a Basic Education Scheme in Delhi Province and if so, how many schools under this scheme have been opened and how many boys have ben admitted?

(b) Is the scheme confined to rural areas only or to urban areas also and if it is confined to rural areas, what is Government's plan for its extension to urban areas?

(c) What is the number of children in the Delhi Province of the ages of 6 to 11 in rural and urban areas respectively?

The Honourable Maulana Abul Kalam Azad : (a) The Basic Education Scheme has been introduced in the rural area of the Delhi Province. About 100 schools have been opened already and 50 more will be opened in April, 1949.

The number of pupils (boys and girls) in these schools is 4,000 approximately.

(b) Yes. At present the scheme is confined to rural area only. Facilities for Basic Education are being expanded by stages and at present the Government have no plan for introducing Basic Education in the urban area of Delhi. It may be added for information that the Delhi Municipal Committee has 10 Basic Schools.

(c) As the last Census was taken in 1941 and many changes have taken place since then, only approximate figures can be given. The number of children inclusive of refugees in the Delhi Province of the ages of 6-11 is in the neighbourhood of 1,25,000 of which about 40,000 are in rural area.

Shri H.V. Kamath : What is the number of boy and girl students in these schools for basic education?

The Honourable Maulana Abul Kalam Azad : I have just stated the number in replying to you. The number of children in these schools is about four thousand, which includes both boys and girls.

Shri H.V. Kamath : What out of them are the numbers respectively for boy and girl students?

The Honourable Maulana Abul Kalam Azad : Notice is required for this. I cannot give figures just now.

Mr. Deputy Speaker : Mr. Poker.

Several Honourable Members *rose*-—

Mr. Deputy Speaker : I cannot allow all the members to stand at the same time, and any honourable member putting a question before he is asked to do so. There must be some amount of order maintained in the House. I have called Mr. Poker.

Mr. B. Poker : May I just suggest that in view of the importance of this question, you may be pleased to ask the honourable Minister for Education to give the substance of his answer in English, if he is so pleased, or otherwise to make arrangements to have it inerpreted?

Mr. Deputy Speaker : That is nothing new. The honourable member was not here when such an arrangement was agreed to. Every time the honourable member comes, he puts forward this claim. I know that whenever an honourable member wants an answer, the Honourable Minister has made arrangements for translating his answers in English and if the honourable member had only asked me, I would have asked the honourable minister to read the translation.

Mr. B. Poker : I did ask you, Sir.

Mr. Deputy Speaker : He must have done so earlier.

Shri Mahavir Tyagi : We wanted to put supplementary questions, but the honourable member raised a point of order, therefore we did not stand up.

Shrimati G. Durgabai : Sir, you have just stated in reply to (b) that there was a conference of the Education Ministry. As regards its recommendations may I know if any recommendation was made for the extension of the scheme to the urban area or not?

The Honourable Maulana Abul Kalam Azad : I have just told you that this is not the kind of job that could be accomplished at once. We can go step by step. The Ministry of Education felt that for the present work among the rural population was the most important. So, it has been taken up. We have no special plan for Delhi city before us yet. The Delhi Municipality has started this work and 10 schools have already been opened in the city. We should have to wait for some days.

Shrimati G. Durgabai : May I also know if any Government grant will be available for these basic schools which are being started in the villages?

The Honourable Maulana Abul Kalam Azad : The question of grant does not arise. The entire responsibility for the basic education scheme rests upon the Government. It is the Government that is opening these schools and bearing the entire expenditure.

Shri Deshbandhu Gupta : May I enquire if any arrangements have also been made for adult education under this basic education (scheme)?

The Honourable Maulana Abul Kalam Azad : Certainly. The scheme has been started with just such a plan in view, but things have not taken that shape yet when adult education could be imparted to a full extent. We have made a beginning in some areas and are extending it day by day.

Shri Mahavir Tyagi : What industries are taught under this basic education?

The Honourable Maulana Abul Kalam Azad : This requires notice.

Shri Mahavir Tyagi : May I enquire whether this scheme has any regard for the fact, as desired by Mahatma Gandhiji, that these schools should be in a position to pay their own way with the help of the income from these industries?

The Honourable Maulana Abul Kalam Azad : No. The Government gave their full consideration to this scheme. It came to the conclusion that these industries are very useful for education but it should not be expected of them that they should be able to meet their entire expenditure.

Mr. Tajamul Husain : May I enquire, in view of the fact that Mahatma Gandhiji's advice with regard to the bringing into operation of this scheme was that the income obtained from the industry should be expended thereon, how much of the annual expenditure on these schools will have to be borne by the Government?

The Honourable Maulana Abul Kalam Azad : I cannot give the amount just now, but the expenditure would be considerable.

Document No. 19

ANSWERS OF MAULANA AZAD DATED 25-2-1949 IN THE LEGISLATIVE ASSEMBLY OF INDIA TO QUESTIONS ASKED BY MR. G.S. GUHA AND OTHERS IN CONNECTION WITH THE FACILITIES FOR EDUCATION IN MOTHER TONGUE IN PRIMARY AND SECONDARY STAGES

Shri G.S. Guha : Will the Honourable Minister of Education be pleased to state:

(a) whether it is a fact that at the recent meeting of the Central Advisory Board of Education, it has been decided that facilities for instruction in the mother tongue, where it is different from the State language, should be provided if there are at least 40 children in a Junior basic school and also in the secondary stage if there are sufficient pupils to justify the existence of a separate school;

(b) whether it is a fact that these recommendations were adopted unanimously with the participation of representatives from all the Provincial Governments;

(c) whether the attention of Government has been drawn to complaints against the violation of these recommendations by certain provincial Governments in respect of the langauges of the minorities within their territorial jurisdiction; and

(d) what are the principal languages spoken in the different provinces and the population speaking each of those languages in them?

The Honourable Maulana Abul Kalam Azad : (a) and (b). Yes. Attention is drawn to this Ministry Resolution No. D. 3791/48-D.I., of the August, 1948 which is placed on the table.

(c) Yes. This Ministry have been receiving, from time to time, complaints against the violation of the rights of the linguistic minorities in several Provinces.

(d) In this connection honourable member's attention is invited to Statistical Handbook No. 2, parts II and III.

No. D. 3791/48-D.I.

GOVERNMENT OF INDIA

MINISTRY OF EDUCATION

New Delhi 3, dated the ..... August, 1948

RESOLUTION

SUBJECT :- *Medium of Instruction in Educational Institutions*

The principle that a child should be instructed, in the early stage of his education, through the medium of the mother tongue has been accepted by the Government. All educationists agree that any departure from this principle is bound to be harmful to the child and therefore to the interests of society. Unfortunately the application of this educationally sound principle in practice raises some difficulties. One question is what is to be considered as the mother tongue through which education has to be imparted. As is well known in every Region, Province and State in India a number of dialects are spoken. Children learn these dialects at home; are they to be all adopted as media of education? Unfortunatley their number is large and most of them are without literature and therefore without necessary pabulum to nourish education. There are, however, about a dozen languages more or less developed which possess literatures and which seem to be marked out to become such media.

Here a second difficulty arises. Although in some Province one of these languages is predominant, in others speakers of two, three or four of them live together, and there is hardly a province in which besides a principal language there are not considerable number of inhabitants speaking other languages.

In the Madras Province four principal languages are used, *viz.*, Tamil, Telugu, Malayalam and Kanarose and in the city of Madras there are numerous speakers of both Telugu and Tamil. Similarly in the Bombay Province there are Marathi, Gujarati and Kanarose speaking people, and in the city of Bombay a mixed population of Marathi, Gujrati, Urdu and Hindi speakers. In Bihar and U.P. there are certain district and cities where along with Hindi, Bengali is spoken by many. Calcutta again is a sort of cosmopolitan town with a mixed population speaking a number of languages. In Orissa, Oriya is the main language but in some parts Telugu is used. The Central Provinces have large areas of Marathi and Hindi speaking inhabitants. Nagpur is a city of mixed speakers of Hindi and Marathi. East Punjab has two languages Hindi and Punjabi.

Conditions like these make it impossible for any State or Province to adopt any single language as the medium of instruction. An attempt to adopt one language in a Province where groups of people speaking different languages reside, and to impose it on all is bound to lead to discontent and bitterness. It will affect inter-provincial relations and set up vicious circles of retaliation. Provincialism will grow and Indian nationalism will suffer.

The History of European countries is a warning. England sought to impose English on Ireland, Germany on Poles, Eastern European countries their particular languages on pockets of inhabitants speaking foreign languages. In every case the results have been disastrous.

In the case of India there does not exist any justification for adopting a policy which Europeans followed to their discomfuture. All Provincial languages are Indian languages and there is little reason why any Province in India should seek to deprive children inhabiting that Province of their fundamental right to receive education through the medium of the mother tongue.

It is obvious that if a Province has adopted any particular language as the language of administration, it will be to the interest of those whose mother tongue is different, to learn it in order to claim participation in the life and privileges of the people of the Province.

The principle of teaching through the mother tongue then is of general application, but practical consideration suggests two limitations.

In the first place the principle applies mainly to the first stage of education, *i.e.* the stage of compulsory primary education, or to the group of children at the junior basic stage from the ages of 6 to 11, for the reason that at the stage of compulsory education children should not be forced to study a language which is not their mother tongue. In the higher stages after the junior Basic it will be necessary for pupils to learn the language of the Province.

Secondly, employment of the mother tongue for the education of the children whose numbers are extremely small will create administrative and financial difficulties; hence it is desirable that a minimum number should be fixed for the use of their languages. The Provincial or State

Government should not only refrain from forcing any particular language on such groups, but should place the same facilities of education at their disposal as it does for the other children.

The Government of India is of opinion that in the larger interests of the country it is desirable that the policy enunciated above should be followed by all Provincial and State Governments.

TARA CHAND,
Secretary

Dr. Mono Mohan Das : May I know whether it is a fact that the Tejpur Local Board in Assam has stopped the grant to the Bengalee Girls School there, because the medium of instruction was Bengalee and not Assamese?

The Honourable Maulana Abul Kalam Azad : I cannot say anything about this particular incident but complaints have reached the Ministry about the Bihar Government.

Shri H.V. Kamath : For the secondary stage, mentioned in part (a), what should be the requisite number in those schools to enable education to be imparted in the mother tongue?

The Honourable Maulana Abul Kalam Azad : I would require notice.

Shri H.V. Kamath : Mr. Deputy Speaker, my question was what should be the requisite number in the secondary stage, just as it is to be 40 in the case of primary education?

The Honourable Maulana Abul Kalam Azad : With regard to this the Central Advisory Board decided at their Allahabad meeting that if there is a sufficient number of such boys who wish to continue their education at the secondary stage in some particular languge they too should be afforded the opportunity to do so, but no set number has been fixed.

Shri Biswanth Das : May I know whether the Honourable Minister has received any complaint from the district of Singhbhum especially from Tatanagar and other areas also, to the effect that even students at the primary stage are forced to learn Hindi as against Oriya?

The Honourable Maulana Abul Kalam Azad : I have just stated that complaints have been received from several provinces. Now I cannot say anything about the particular instance mentioned by the honourable member but the Government of India have drawn the attention of those provinces, from which complaints have been received, to those complaints.

Shri Arun Chandra Guha : Arising out of part (c) of the question what has been the reaction of the defaulting provinces to the protests sent by the Government of India to these provinces? Some provinces have violated the instructions of the Government of India and the Government of India has sent protests or circulars to those provinces. What action has been taken by these provinces on those circulars?

The Honourable Maulana Abul Kalam Azad : All that the Government of India can do in this respect is to draw the attention of the provinces and wait for the result.

Shri Arun Chandra Guha : What action have those provinces taken on those circulars of the Government of India?

Mr. Deputy Speaker : They are considering them.

Shri H.V. Kamath : What is the mother tongue in Delhi Province and the East Punjab?

The Honourable Maulana Abul Kalam Azad : Whatever has been the mother tongue in those areas will be regarded as such.

Shri Santanu Kumar Das : Two states, Serai Kalan and Khuraswan, have merged with Bihar. Why are the Oriya children there not allowed to read Oriya?

Mr. Deputy Speaker : How does any honourable member expect the Honourable Minister to remember the details of every place? He may put a specific question for answer on the floor of the House or he may write a letter to the Honourable Minister to elicit his reply.

Shri H.V. Kamath: Out of the hundred schools in the Delhi Province, in how many of them instruction is imparted in Hindi and in how many in Urdu?

The Honourable Maulana Abul Kalam Azad : This requires notice.

Maulana Hasrat Mohani: May I enquire if the Honourable Minister has also received any such complaint from U.P.? There they are not prepared to agree to any proposal from any other quarter.

The Honourable Maulana Abul Kalam Azad : Yes, complaint has also been received from U.P.

Document No. 20

MAULANA ABUL KALAM AZAD'S REPLIES DATED 25-2-1949 IN THE LEGISTLATIGE ASSEMBLY TO THE QUESITONS ASKED BY MR. MAHAVIR TYGI AND OTHERS IN CONNECTION WITH THE SCHOLARS SENT ABROAD FOR ADVANCED TECHNICAL TRAINING

Shri Mahavir Tyagi: (a) Will the Honourable Minister of Education be pleased to state the number of scholars sent abroad for advanced technical training by Government during the years 1945-47?

(b) What is the estimate of average expenditure on each such scholar?

(c) How many of them have completed their course of training and returned?

(d) Out of those who have returned, how many have been absorbed in Government employment?

The Honourable Maulana Abul Kalam Azad : (a) 736, out of which 415 are Central Scholars and 321 are Provincial Scholars.

(b) The average estimated expenditure on each scholar calculated on a 2½ years basis is Rs. 28,000 (Rupees twenty-eight thousand only) for the United States of America, Rs. 19,000 (Rupees nineteen thousand only) for the United Kingdom and Rs. 14,000 (Rupees fourteen thousand only) for Australia and New Zealand. The expenditure on Central Scholars is borne entirely by the Government of India, whereas the expenditure on Provincial Scholars is shared by them equally with the Provincial Governments.

(c) 353, comprising 220 Central Scholars and 33 Provincial Scholars.

(d) 156, namely 92 Central Scholars and 64 Provincial Scholars.

Shri H.V. Kamath: Were any of our scholars sent to other countries of the world other than the United Kingdom, United States of America, Australia and New Zealand?

The Honourable Maulana Abul Kalam Azad : The figures which I have just given relate to the old scheme. Now under the new scheme to be enforced, it is proposed to send them to many other places.

Shri Ram Chandra Upadhyaya : May I know if it consists of states scholars also?

The Honourable Maulana Abul Kalam Azad : No. This comprises of only Central and Provincial Government scholars. There is a separate number of scholars sent from the states.

Shri Raj Bahadur: Will any scholars be sent to Russia also?

The Honourable Maulana Abul Kalam Azad : This all depends uspon the nature of the various subjects for which the scholars may have to be sent abroad during the next year and the particular countries in which they would have to undergo training.

Shri H.V. Kamath : May I know in what particular subject, in the opinion of the Honourable Minister, Russia has advanced?

Shri Mahavir Tyagi : Since the Government are spending about Rs. 28,000 on each scholar, will they keep it in view that in future such a huge amount is spent in respect of those scholars only whom the Government are in a position to employ under them?

The Honourable Maulana Abul Kalam Azad : This has been kept in view while preparing the new scheme.

Shri Ram Chandra Upadhyaya : Have the Government any means at their disposal by which they can know whether or not the scholars who have gone are studying; and if they have made any progress or not?

The Honourable Maulana Abul Kalam Azad : The honourable member should know that the Government do not cease to take interest after sending the scholars abroad. The Government have got their Officers there who have been sepcially deputed to look after this job.

Document No. 21

MAULANA'S SPEECH AT THE DIAMOND JUBILEE CELEBRATION OF THE SCINDIA SCHOOL, GWALIOR ON 26-2-1949

I am very glad of this opportunity of visiting the Scindia School at Gwalior founded fifty years ago by the late Maharaja of Gwalior, Sir Madhava Rao Scindia. The manner in which the School has developed since then and established for itself an all-India position is eloquent testimony to the interest taken by him and his successors. I am confident Your Highness will continue to take the same interest in its future growth and development.

A good school is a national asset of the highest value at any place or at any time. Schools are the laboratories which produce the future citizens of a State. The quality of the State therefore depends upon the quality of such laboratories. In the context of modern India the importance of good schools is even greater. On the one hand, we have vast illiteracy and on the other, almost unbounded opportunities. The achievement of independence has opened to the people new vistas and we can achieve all that we have hoped for, provided the human material in the country can meet the challenge demanded of them. In spite of the vastness of our resources and opportunities, it is an unfortunate fact that the number of good schools in this country is all too rare. The obligation of a school like the Scindia is therefore all the greater.

I have been very glad to learn of the manner in which the Scindia School has grown through a synthesis of Indian and British traditions. You have in this school rightly proved that there is in this country an ancient tradition of residential schools which shared many features in common with the modern Public Schools. You have, as is only right and proper, taken from the English Public School system whatever was good in it but you have grafted in on what is basically an Indian Institution. A school like yours, in which equal emphasis is placed on academic work, physical and health organisation, creative activity and training in responsibility and integrated behaviour, can serve a most useful purpose in the present transitional phase of Indian life. I am particularly glad to see that, apart from the emphasis the usual Public School activities found in British schools, you have made provision for the development of the spiritual aspect of the boys in your charge.

It was perhaps inevitable that when the School started, it was meant to be exclusive and had a distinct military bias for a considerable time. I am glad that you have given up that exclusiveness and turned the School into an all-Inida Public School drawing boys from all parts of India and from all major social and religious groups. This is a move in the right direction and is in keeping with the spirit of the times. If there is any one feature which distinguishes modern India, it is the growth of the spirit of democracy which seeks to give equality of opportunity to all its citizens. All past barriers based on birth, privilege, caste or wealth are breaking down. As a secular democratic State, we are pledged to the widening of opportunities and equality of chances for all. I am very glad to learn that your Highness has taken a leading part in the breaking down of such barriers. I am confident that the same wise statesmanship will guide you in widening still further the services which the Scindia School can offer to the rising generations of free India.

In the past, exclusive schools like yours served two main purposes. They were established either to cater for the needs of princely families or they were founded by Europeans to offer education according to European models. Whatever opinion we may have about their exclusive character, it cannot be denied that they rendered a geat service in introducing education of the British Public School type to India. This system of residential education with its emphasis on the growth of character and leadership has much to offer to India, and both types of schools to which I have referred deserve well of the country, having brought the benefits of this system to young Indians.

This is the reason why after the attainment of independence, the Ministery of Education in considering the future of such schools decided that with certain changes they could render great service to free India. After the 15th of August 1947, there was no longer any room for schools of an exclusive type, but once their exclusive character was removed, the former Chiefs' Schools and European Schools could be fitted into our scheme of National Education. Not only so, their special characteristics in developing discipline and corporate life make such schools more necessary for training the future leaders of independent

India. The Ministery of Education have therefore decided to put under their direct supervision both schools like the Chiefs' College at Ajmer or Raipur and the European Schools like those at Lovedale and Sanawar associated with the name of Sir Henry Lawrence. Their exclusive character have been removed and their doors thrown open to all without regard to birth, status or province. They have thus become for the first time Public Schools in the real sense of the term. I am glad to find that here at Gwalior you have developed along the same lines and converted your school into an all-India school which is open to all without distinction.

I am glad to find so many distinguished representatives of the princely order of India present here. May I take this opportunity of saying how greatly I have appreciated the manner in which you have helped in breaking down the barrier between what were the provinces and the states during the British days? By your action in breaking these barriers and bringing your states within the orbit of the Indian Union, you have acted wisely and well. You have also acted wisely and well in transferring power to the hands of representative bodies and thus placing the administration on a level with that of the rest of India. These are great services and I am sure that the country appreciates the spirit in which you have rendered them.

There remains, however, one question that I would ask of you. Till yesterday you were rulers; today you have given up the reins of power. Do you feel that by giving up power in this manner, you have still a function to perform on the stage of modern India? Some of you may feel that now that administration is in the hands of popular bodies, you have nothing further to do. Such a feeling is, to my mind, unjustified, for there is one function you can perform that no one can take from you. You will agree with me that just as a ruler has power over his people, he has also the opportunity of serving them. His power may disappear but no one can take away his capacity for service. You have acted wisely in responding to the challenge of the changed times and divesting yourselves of your administrative work. You will act even more wisely if you train yourselves to serve the country in keeping with the spirit of the new age, and I can assure you that should you decide to do so, you will have in future India a position even more exalted than the one you had occupied in the past. For, in the past, your position was based on power and fear; in the future, your position will be built on service and love.

We are living today in an age of democracy. There are men who think that there is no scope for aristocracy in such a context. This is, however, not my opinion. When aristocracy is opposed to democracy, it may be cast aside by the present age, but when aristocracy serves as an adjunct to democracy and seeks to fulfil its purposes, aristocracy can render a service to democracy which nothing else can. Aristocracy develops a width of vision and a far-reaching imagination which is not usually found outside its orbit. Such vision and imagination cannot be acquired by training in a school. Book learning is no substitute for the vision which develops from generation to generation. Your family traditions and the art of leadership which you have developed through the training of generations can therefore help in supplying qualities which we need to build the India of our dreams. My appeal to you is therefore to rise to the occasion and prepare yourselves in a spirit of service in order to take your right place in the growth and development of free India.

Document No. 22

SPEECH OF MAULANA AZAD DATED 18-3-1949 IN THE INDIAN LEGISLATIVE ASSEMBLY ON GENERAL BUDGET– LIST OF DEMANDS AND HIS REPLIES TO QUESTIONS, RAISED BY THE MEMBERS DURING THE SPEECH

The Honourable Maulana Abul Kalam Azad (Minister of Education) : Sir, as I am not feeling well therefore I think you would kindly allow me to speak while sitting.

At the very outset I would submit a few words about the time that has been allotted this year for Education Budget. It has generally been complained that very little time has been allotted and not only for Education but for Health and Labour Ministries also an acute shortage of time has been felt. I am fully in favour of this complaint. Without the least doubt it is essential that we may take more active interest in those matters that pertain to the nation-building activities and be able to scrutinise the matter in more details. I assure you that the treasury benches also, from where I am speaking, have also felt this necessity. We have decided that from next year one full day will be set apart for Education. As regards Labour and Health also I hope more time will be allotted.

Shri B.L. Sondhi (East Punjab: General) : For Transport also.

The Honourable Maulana Abul Kalam Azad : Yes, sufficient time should be allotted for this also. In this connection only 6 speeches have been made. The object of the first speech, as far as I have been able to understand, was that while planning the scheme of national education we have not to copy the western education only but have to plan our own particular scheme of education. I think that it is such an acknowledged fact that there can be no two opinions about it. Without doubt we cannot refrain ourselves from imparting instruction in modern sciences and knowledge. We have to go forward on the way of learning. We have not to recede. But besides this we have to keep in mind certain other facts also. We cannot forget them in any way. India has got a definite civilization of her own. India has a history of her own and has well developed philosophy and metaphysics. She has her own traditions about mental and spritiual life. She has taken a conspicous and splendid share in the devleopment and diffusion of human knowledge and civilization. Hence it is essential that we should preserve our splendid heritage and draw up such a scheme of our national education, in the outline of which the influence of Indian Culture and Spiritualism may be fully apparent. The outline of our national education should be modern but the spirit must be Indian. I will assure this House that the Education Ministry has before her such a plan and as far as this aim is concerned the Government is wholeheartedly with them.

My honourable friend has drawn attention towards one more point. He acknowledges the fact that for higher studies in scientific and technical subjects Indian students should be sent to foreign countries. But he likes this work to be done in such a manner whereby our objective may be achieved at the earliest and then after that we may not stand in need of sending any more students to foreign countries. I am fully in support of this viewpoint. I would like to assure them that the Government have drawn up the new overseas scholarship scheme with this very objective in view and this scheme has to come into force from the new financial year. Under this scheme the Government wish to send every year a certain number of Indian students to foreign countries. But the object of sending them to foreign countries is that necessity of sending students abroad may at the earliest come to an end. For attaining this object it was essential to investigate the educational facilities that are available in all the existing institutions of the country and to ascertain their weak points also. Then in order to substantiate those aspects that may prove to be weak, particular educational subjects be selected, and for those subjects only students be sent to foreign countries. Besides this special help may be given to the existing institutions for making suitable arrangements for higher technical education and as far as possible new institutions also be started at the earliest. So the Education Ministry is working in this manner and the details you have read in the report of the Ministry.

As you know the overseas scholarship scheme was started by the previous Government in 1945 and some batches of students had been sent to the foreign countries. But when I took charge of the Education Ministry on 15th January, 1947 then at once I came to know that the scheme has not been worked on proper lines and some defects of fundamental character are working therein. The first and foremost defects of fundamental character are working therein. The first and foremost defect has been that the scheme was not planned in such a way whereby efforts may have been made to take into consideration all these important aspects. Special emphasis was laid on the fact that maximum number of students be sent to foreign countries for technical subjects but sufficient attention was not paid for the selection of the subjects for training for which students were to be sent abroad so that they might properly make up our present needs and deficiencies in the educational institutions. The result was that the sphere of benefit accruing from this scheme was considerably narrowed down and as much benefit the country was to have could not be had.

One more mistake was committed whereby a new type of complication has been produced namely a great difficulty is being felt in giving immediate employment to all the students–who are returning from foreign countries after completing their studies. An honourable member has just given out in his speech that he has come to know of the case of a certain gentleman who was sent abroad under the overseas scholarship scheme. He has now returned after completing his studies but is sitting idle. The honourable member has come to know only of one such case, but I would like to tell him that more than one such cases have come within my knowledge and I fear that in future more such cases will come to our knowledge, but this is the inevitable result of the defects of the previous overseas scholarship scheme. As far as possible we are trying to improve the situation but we cannot escape the consequences of the past mistakes.

In that scheme it was decided that the various departments of the Provincial and Central Governments may be consulted as to what kind of persons they would require for their work in future and for which technical subjects they want students to be sent to foreign countries. So the Education Department of the past did likewise and questionnaires were sent to the different departments. It was war-time and it was generally thought that the development schemes would surely be started after war and for these schemes technical experts would be required. Keeping this imaginary plan of hope and expectation before them every department selected a number of subjects and referred them to the Education Department. The Education Department announced those very subjects and the selection board after selecting the students sent them to foreign countries. In the meantime the war came to an end but the financial and political condition of the country assumed such a trend that the development schemes, whose imaginary plans had been drawn up, could not be started and even now it cannot be said whether they can be started or not. The result is that when these state scholars return after finishing their courses of studies of 2-3 years then a majority of them come to know that the projects for which they had been sent have not so far been started and so they cannot be given immediate employment.

Now one more obstacle has also sprung up, about which no one could have the slightest doubt or suspicion, namely, the division of the country took place and a large number of Government servants migrated to this country from Pakistan. Besides this a huge influx of refugees had to turn its face towards India. It was the foremost duty of the Government to provide employment to these unfortunate persons. So we had to come to the decision that the refugees should be given first preference while making appointments for all those posts that might fall vacant. The result was that the vacancies that could be created for these state scholars in Government service, were to a great extent filled.

From what I have said to you I do not mean to say that the present Government wants to shirk its responsibility by laying the fault on the previous Government. The Government cannot do so. The Government are fully conscious of its responsibilities. The Government are making all possible efforts to give employment to these state scholars so that the maximum benefit of their education could be had. So a greater number of the state scholars, that have so far returned from foreign countries, have been given employments and the remaining ones also will be given employment in the very near future. Of course, the Government expects at least so much that it may not be held responsible for the state of affairs that has been created.

I am in full agreement with the motive behind the things upon which stress has been laid by Shrimati Durgabai. No programe of national education can be appropriate if it does not give full consideration to the education and advancement of one-half of the society, that is the women. The Central Government is doing whatever it can in this connection and is going to do it with an even greater speed. But with regard to those matters which concern the provincial governments or the universities I cannot say anything with absolute confidence at this time. The Central Government can give them its advice and can also exert pressure to a certain extent but the final decision has to be made by them. At any rate, I should assure her that the Government would certainly make whatever endeavours it can in that direction.

The Honourable Pandit Hirday Nath Kunzru has drawn attention to the fact that the scheme to shift the Delhi colleges to the university grounds has not been put into practice yet and the matter has constantly been deferred. In so far as matters have come to my notice I can say that the responsibility for that state of affairs does not lie with the Government. Matters had taken such a turn that the scheme could not be put into effect immediately. The scheme had been planned out several years back. The circumstances changed completely after the war. A building that could then he built at an expense of *one lakh* rupees cannot now be constructed even at a cost of *five lakhs*. Then the difficulties that have arisen in the matter of procurement of building material are also known to everybody. The necessity arose that a plan of the entire scheme be prepared anew and the case of each college judged afresh. At any rate, I would assure him that there would be no negligence on the part of the Government in this behalf. Full efforts will be made that the scheme be put into effect at an early date and that it should not remain in abeyance for long.

Shri Deshbandhu Gupta (Delhi) : Sir, may I interrupt the honourable Minister? Is it not a fact that the hostel building of the Hindu College, Delhi has remained as it is for the last three years and the Government has paid no attention to it?

The Honourable Maulana Abul Kalam Azad : In so far as matters have come to my notice I can say that a case is going on in court in regard to this building and the Government cannot do anything until this case is decided.

Shri Deshbandhu Gupta : No, Sir. Is it not a fact that the Government has paid no attention to it so far, nor have they appointed any enquiry committee?

The Honourable Maulana Abul Kalam Azad : I can say nothing in that connection.

Shri Deshbandhu Gupta : I would enquire whether the Vice-Chancellor has been asked about it. How far is Government responsible for it? Have rupees *three lakhs* been spent in this connection?

The Honourable Maulana Abul Kalam Azad : Has this matter been brought to the notice of the Education Ministry?

Shri Deshbandhu Gupta : No, Sir.

The Honourable Maulana Abul Kalam Azad : If this matter has not been brought before the Ministry of Education what is the honourable member complaining about? Whatever I have come to know is just this much that a case about the building is pending in court and its decision is being waited for.

An honourable member has mentioned some irregularities of the Delhi University and has, in that connection, referred to a pamphlet. I feel that the facts have not come before him in their true perspective. When the true position comes before him he will be satisfied. The matter relates to that meeting of the Delhi University Council that was held in November last for the election of the Vice-Chancellor. The matter was brought to my notice on the very day this meeting was to be held. I made an inquiry without delay and duly called for a written reply from the University. The facts that emerged as a result of the inquiry did not contain anything so objectionable as to call for intervention on the part of the Government. The result was that the matter ended at that stage. I fail to understand what necessity has arisen now after four months to reagitate this matter all over again.

May I tell the House what the true position is? According to the rules of the University Principals of colleges are appointed members of the Executive Council. The objection has been raised that the Principal of the Agriculture College was not called in his capacity as a member of the Council. The Vice-Chancellor, however, states that the Agriculture College has not yet become a recognised University College, that correspondence is going on in this connection between the University and the Ministry of Agriculture and that until this matter is decided and the college attains the status of a recognised institution its Principal cannot take part in the meeting of the Council in the capacity of a member. In reply to this statement it has been said that the ex-Principal of the Agriculture College did participate in the Council meeting. In reply to this the Vice Chancellor has stated positively that he was not called in the capacity of a member but by special invitation and that, at any rate, he did not take part in the voting. Now the question is are both these facts true or not? If they are correct no irregularity of any kind is proved. No such thing has come to the notice of the Government as might cause them to doubt the correctness of these two facts and hence there appears to be no reason why it should interfere in the internal administration of the University.

Another case cited is that relating to the election of the Dean of Medicine. It has been alleged that his election was not conducted in a proper manner. I regret my time is over and I cannot therefore go into this matter in greater detail. The Vice-Chancellor's version is like this. The Committee consists of six members and that there is no specified quorum. Two of the members have already recorded their vote in favour of the candidate before the meeting and made a plea that they could not participate in the meeting. There was only one candidate. The question of a contest between more than one candidate did not arise. There was a meeting of the remaining members who gave their vote in his favour and elected him. Now, I should like to know, in view of this statement, what was the objectionable part of the business on the score of which the Government might have decided to intervene.

This fact should be kept in view that the University is an autonomous body, and so long as concrete instances are not brought to the notice of the Government, they cannot interfere in its internal administration.

The Honourable member should consider the statement made by me in respect of these two points. If he has got any further information that would give a clear proof of the irregularities in the existing management of the University, then he should bring it to the notice of the Government. The Government can never suffer the presence of any sort of irregularities in the administration of the Delhi University, and that they should keep quiet over it.

Shri Deshbandhu Gupta :I would ....

Mr. Speaker : The time is already up for the other demands and let us not prolong this by further discussion.

Shri Deshbandhu Gupta: On a point of personal explanation.

Mr. Speaker : The honourable Member has already distributed the pamphlet.

Shri Deshbandhu Gupta : I only want to ask whether the honourable Minister has himself gone into the matter and whether he is satisfied.

The Honourable Maulana Abul Kalam Azad: I have myself made necessary enquiries and even if it is found that whatever I have stated is incorrect, then I am prepared to institute further enquiries.

The honourable Member Begum Aizaz Rasul has drawn attention towards the necessity of imparting primary education to the children in their mother tongue and urged the Government of India to lay down a clear-cut policy in this respect. I would like to tell her in this connection that this question has already been decided once for all and there is nothing more to be done. The medium of basic education should be the mother tongue, because this is the natural and appropriate medium for imparting education. The Government of India have already emphasized upon his principle through their Resolution of August, last year and this fundamental principle has generally been accepted. As a matter of fact, the difficulty arises only at that time when there is a difference between the language spoken by one group of people and the State language of the Province concerned, *e.g.*, in Bihar there are Bengali speaking classes. In such a case, the Central Advisory Board have proposed that the medium of primary education should be the mother tongue, and after the fifth class the State language should be taught. But the medium of education should strictly be the mother tongue.

Maulana Hasrat Mohani (U.P. : Muslim): Why should not the entire education from the lowest to the highest be given in the mother tongue?

The Honourable Maulana Abul Kalam Azad: If the language spoken by a certain group of people is not the same which has been adopted by the Provincial Government concerned, then in such a contingency it shall have to be admitted that every inhabitant of the Province should learn the State language, otherwise he will himself suffer. This is also obvious that the University education cannot be given through the medium of different languages. One language only shall have to be adopted and that shall be the State language. Except this, there cannot be any practical solution of this problem.

In this connection, I shall also admit that complaints are regularly pouring in from certain provinces to the effect that this fundamental principle is not being fully acted upon. If these complaints are correct, then I must admit that his is really a deplorable state of affairs and it is most essential that it should be remedied. The Government of India are already in correspondence on this subject with certain Provincial Governments, and it is very likely that a conference of the Provincial Education Ministers may be convened in this connection. In any case, I shall assure the honourable Member, Begum Aizaz Rasul, that the Government are fully alive to the importance of this matter, and they shall do their utmost to remove genuine complaints.

Now, I shall say a few words with regard to the last speech delivered by my honourable friend Mr. A.V. Thakkar. As a matter of fact, the point raise by him is the crux of the entire subject of education. If the problem of education is treated as the fundamental basis for the uplift of the nation, then is it not necessary that more money should be earmarked out of the revenues of the Central Government for this purpose than what is being spent at present? The previous Government used to spend Rs. 2 crores at the most for the purposes of education which did not form even one per cent. of the Central Budget. It was hardly 5 per cent. After having put in strenuous efforts for the last two years, I have been able to get it raised to Rs. 5 crores, and now it can be said that 1 per cent. of the Central Budget shall be spent for the purposes of education. But I would like to know whether this amount is adequate for a country whose literate population does not exceed 15 per cent. even. And should our conscience feel satisfied after spending this amount.

Today, there is no other matter which more vitally affects the country than this problem. When will we be able to confer upon 85 per cent. of the subjects of the Indian Union their birth-right of learning 3 R's? The Sargent Scheme had contemplated a period of forty years. But I do not think that today anyone of us shall be prepared to wait for such a long period. On my assuming charge of the Ministry of Education, I devoted myself towards this aspect; and prepared a fresh scheme for imparting basic education in the junior standards by means of which the basic education upto this standard can be made universal and compulsory during a period of ten years at the most. 'Kher' Committee was set up to consider this scheme. This Committee considered all the aspects of the matter and prepared a comprehensive scheme covering a period of sixteen years, *viz.*, 10 years for junior basic education and again six years more for senior basic education. The Ministry of Education were eager to implement this scheme from the beginning of the new financial year. A sum of Rs. 5,40,00,000 was needed for this purpose. I am deeply constrained to say that this could not be arranged and the implementation of the scheme has had to be postponed.

I was rather much pleased to find that my honourable friend Mr. Thakkar shares with me in my present predicament, and other members too have seriously felt the paucity of funds. But I would like to tell you that this is not quite sufficient. You should realize your responsibility in right earnestness and think over as to how to remedy this state of affairs. Certain friends have complained against the Ministry of Finance and drawn their attention for attaching more importance to the nation-building programme. But I will dare say that the mere complaint against the Ministry of Finance cannot solve the problem. As a matter of fact, the real solution of the problem lies in your treasury own hands. The Ministry of Finance merely maintains an account of your, while you have got full powers to spend it. If you really feel that more amount should be spent under 'Education', then you should accept a plain and well-balanced proposal in this House that at least 10 per cent of the Central revenues should be allocated to this head. So long as no such action is taken, the Gordian knot of the national education shall never be disentangled.

Shri H.R. Guruv Reddy (Mysore State): Sir, we could not follow a syllable of what the honourable Minister said. It seems to be a very interesting reply, and we have to ask for a translation of his speech.

Mr. Speaker : He will get it, in due course.

Now, what is the position about the çut motion of Pandit Kunzru? Does he want it to be put to vote?

Pandit Hirday Nath Kunzru : With the permission of the House I wish to withdraw it.

Mr. Speaker : Has the honourable Member leave of the House to withdraw his cut motion?

The cut motion was, by leave of the Assembly, withdrawn.

Mr. Speaker : I now put the Demands to the House.

The question is:

"That a sum not exceeding Rs. 33,76,000 be granted to the Governor General to defray the charges which will come in course of payment during the year ending the 31st day of March, 1950, in respect of 'Ministry of Education'."

The Motion was adopted.

Document No. 23

MAULANA ABUL KALAM AZAD'S REPLIES DATED 24-3-1949 IN THE CONSTITUENT ASSEMBLY OF INDIA (LEGISLATIVE) TO THE QUESTIONS ASKED ABOUT THE RETURN OF HISTORICAL DOCUMENTS AND ANCIENT BOOKS FROM FOREIGN COUNTRIES

Seth Govind Das: Will the Honourable Minister of Education be pleased to state:

(a) whether Government are aware of the resolution passed by the Historical Records Commission on the 24th December, 1948 regarding the return of historical documents and ancient books from Britain, France, Holland and Portugal;

(b) whether these Governments have been approached in connection with this matter; and

(c) what steps are being proposed to be taken by Government to get back India's historical documents and ancient books?

The Honourable Maulana Abul Kalam Azad : (a) The Resolution passed by the Research and Publication Committee, an adjunct of the Indian Historical Records Commission, at its last session in Delhi in December, 1948 does not envisage the return of any original historical documents and ancient books from Britain, France, Holland and Portugal, but recommends that arrangements should be made with the Governments of Holland, Portugal and France for obtaining copies of all such records in their possession as may have any bearing on India.

(b) The Resolution has not yet formally been received by the Government. The National Archives of India, are, however, in touch with the principal record repositories in Europe and elsewhere and have already procured microfilm copies of the Palk Manuscripts in the custody of Exeter City Library and Major Browne's correspondence with Warren Hastings in the custody of the India Office.

(c) The Government have before them a plan to have full and accurate information about the Indian treasures and historical documents and ancient books which are in foreign respositories.

The Director General of Archaeology and the Director of Archives have been asked to take necessary action in the matter.

Seth Govind Das : Is it not a fact that the Government had formulated a plan some days ago that so far as London is concerned, some persons should be deputed to go there to find out as to how many documents as may have any bearing on India are available there; and they should also be entrusted to make efforts to obtain all such records?

The Honourable Maulana Abul Kalam Azad : This plan was considered not only in respect of England, but for all other countries. But the Government thought that first of all we should have full record of all such documents, and then only it would be advisable to set up any Committee. Until and unless we are able to ascertain the names of the various places to which the particular documents were sent, we cannot take any decisive action in the matter.

Seth Govind Das : How long do the Government expect to take to have such record got ready?

The Honourable Maulana Abul Kalam Azad : It is difficult to specify the exact time, but we are doing our best to get this record ready in the least possible time.

Dr. Bakhshi Tek Chand : Will the Honourable Minister please state whether any such action is being taken in respect of Pakistan also? A lot of such record is lying in the University Library and Public Library in Lahore. Is any action being taken in this direction also, or is it confined to other countries only?

The Honourable Maulana Abul Kalam Azad : This is not applicable to Pakistan. So far as the question relating to Pakistan is involved, a Partition Council was set up and the assets are being divided in accordance with the decisions of this Committee.

Mr. Homi Mody : Have Government taken any special steps for the purpose of obtaining books, manuscripts and other precious things from the India Office?

The Honourable Maulana Abul Kalam Azad: Government have already carried on negotiations, in the matter so far as it relates to India Office. These are within our possession. All that is wanting is that the issues relating to India and Pakistan have got to be decided. We shall soon be taking necessary action in this matter.

Shri Deshbandhu Gupta: Is it a fact that many people in this country are in possession of very valuable prescriptions and no efforts to procure these are being made? Are Government prepared to take any such steps by which these are procured ?

The Honourable Maulana Abul Kalam Azad : I will just elucidate this matter while replying to another question.

Shri H.V. Kamath : Have Government any intention to secure original documents wherever these are available instead of artificial ones?

The Honourable Maulana Abul Kalam Azad : Certainly.

Document No. 24

MAULANA ABUL KALAM AZAD 'S REPLIES IN THE CONSTITUENT ASSEMBLY OF INDIA (LEGISLATIVE) DATED 1-4-1949, TO THE QUESTIONS RAISED BY MR. TAJAMUL HUSAIN IN CONNECTION WITH THE PUBLICATION OF PAMPHLET, GUIDE OR BOOK ON BODH GAYA

Mr. Tajamul Husain : (a) Will the Honourable Minister of Education be pleased to state whether any pamphlet, guide or book has been published by the Archaeolgoical Department on Bodh Gaya?

(b) If the answer to part (a) above be in the negative do Government propose to publish a pamphlet, guide or book on Bodh Gaya?

The Honourable Maulana Abul Kalam Azad : (a) No, Sir. But under the auspices of the late India Office, London, General Alexander Cunningham, the first Archaeological Surveyor of India, published his Mahabodhi containing an exhaustive research on the Maha Bodhi temple at Bodh Gaya.

(b) The Bodh Gaya temple is not a protected monument, and the Archaeological Department of the Government of India does not publish Guides on monuments which are not under its control.

Mr. Tajamul Husain : May I know from the Honourable Minister that in case the Bodh Gaya temple is not under the control of the Archaeological Department of the Government of India, then under whom is it? And whether or not the Government contemplate to publish any guide or book in connection therewith, just like the one on the Nalanda University?

The Honourable Maulana Abul Kalam Azad : These things have altogether a separate entity, and are directly under the control of the Archaeological Department. Just as I have already informed the honourable member, the Bodh Gaya temple is not under the control of the Government. It is protected by its Private Trust.

Document No. 25

ANSWERS OF MAULANA AZAD DATED 1-4-1949 IN THE CONSTITUENT ASSEMBLY OF INDIA (LEGISLATIVE) TO QUESTIONS RAISED IN CONNECTION WITH THE EXCAVATION OF VIKRAMSHILA IN BHAGALPUR DISTRICT OF BIHAR

Mr. Tajamul Husain : (a) Will the Honourable Minister of Education be pleased to state whether Government propose to excavate the great University of Buddhist times Vikramshila, in Bhagalpur District of Bihar?

(b) If so, when and if not, why not?

The Honourable Maulana Abul Kalam Azad : (a) Yes.

(b) The Excavations Branch of the Department of Archaeology, as constituted at present, has very limited technical staff and funds at its disposal. A scheme for strengthening its staff is under the active consideration of Government. If it is sanctioned and sufficient funds are available, exploration is proposed to be undertaken to determine the comparative importance of known sites. If exploration shows that the site of Vikramshila is of greater importance than others, priority will be given to it for excavation in the programme of the field work.

Mr. Tajamul Husain : In view of the fact that the condition of this Buddhist University in Bhagalpur is fast deteriorating, as the people are removing its bricks and stones for the purpose of constructing their own houses; does not the Government consider it necessary to take up this matter?

The Honourable Maulana Abul Kalam Azad : Government have already taken action in this matter.

Shri M. Tirumala Rao : May I know if Government is making full use of the knowledge of one Swami Pranavananda who has made a special study of this Vikramshila University?

The Honourable Maulana Abul Kalam Azad : No. I cannot say anything in this respect at the moment.

Shri K. Hanumanthaiya : What is the amount required for this excavation?

The Honourable Maulana Abul Kalam Azad : It is difficult to specify this at the moment. But a large amount of funds is required for such purposes which has not been placed at the disposal of the Archaeological Department?

Shri K. Hanumanthaiya :I did not follow the answer.

Mr. Speaker : It requires a large amount of funds and the Archaeological Department has not got the funds at its disposal. I believe this matter was discussed in the Education grant and he mentioned the sum of Rs. 50,000.

Shri B.P. Jhunjhunwala : Has Government taken any action to find out whether any prior action is required before the excavation of Vikramshila at Bhagalpur?

The Honourable Maulana Abul Kalam Azad : Yes; just as I have stated now, the Archaeological Department's circles in Bihar and Patna are taking necessary action in the matter. This is also under the consideration of the Central Government, and action has been taken to protect the site which has been explored in Bhagalpur and is considered to be the original one. Further, this matter has not as yet reached that stage when work in respect thereof may be undertaken without any delay.

Shri H.V. Kamath : Is it very necessary to find such a large amount for this excavation from the point of view of national development and prosperity?

Mr. Tajamul Husain : Do Government contemplete to excavate the old capital of the King Asoka which is in Patliputra?

The Honourable Maulana Abul Kalam Azad : Government keep many such things in view, but the primary question is the availability of funds.

Document No. 26

ELECTION TO ALL INDIA COUNCIL FOR TECHNICAL EDUCATION (SPEAKER'S ANNOUNCEMENT DATED 1-4-1949 REGARDING THE MOTION MOVED BY MAULANA ABUL KALAM AZAD)

The Honourable Maulana Abul Kalam Azad (Minister of Education) : Sir I beg to move:

"That the Members of this Assembly do proceed to elect in such manner as may be approved by the Honourable the Speaker, five persons from among their number to be members of the All India Council for Technical Education for a period of three years to be reckoned from the date of reconstitution of the Council under the provisions of the Resolution of the Government of India in the Ministry of Education No. F.16-10/44-EIII, dated the 30th November, 1945, as subsequently amended."

Shri Mahavir Tyagi (U.P. General) : Sir, may I know what will be the functions of this Technical Education Committee and what are the provisions of that Resolution under which this has been set up? What are the terms of reference of this Committee and what would be its functions? Who would besides the Members of this Assembly be the membes of this Committee and nominated from what bodies?

Mr. Speaker: He is not answering any question.

Motion moved:

"That the Members of this Assembly do proceed to elect in such manner as may be approved by the Honourable the Speaker, five persons from among their number to be members of the All India Council for Technical Education for a period of three years to be reckoned from the date of reconstitution of the Council under the provisions of the Resolution of the Government of India in the Ministry of Education No. F. 16-10/44-EIII, dated 30th November, 1945, as subsequently amended."

The Honourable Maulana Abul Kalam Azad : It is not necessary to give full details at the moment because the Resolution has since been published in the Government Gazette and all these details are available therein. The object of the constitution of this Council was that a high class agency should be set up for the purpose of developing the technical education at a high standard. Its constitution provides for the nomination of five Members of the Assembly; the Educational Adviser to the Government of India; one representative from each of the Provinces; five representatives from States and fourteen members representing the Industry, Commerce, Labour etc.; two members of the Central Board of Education, one number of the Inter-University Board and two more members are to be nominated by the Government of India who represent other interests. This is the constitution of this Board.

Mr. Tajamul Husain(Bihar: Muslim) : Sir, there are two motions before the House; one as moved by the honourable the Minister for Education, and the other as read out by you. We want to know, Sir, which of the two is the original.

Mr. Speaker : Both are originals.

Shri Mahavir Tyagi : Sir, I would suggest that this election should not be made so soon and before doing this, it would be better if a report of the activities of this Board is brought up before the House, because this is quite a new subject for me and I think that since it consists of many representatives from the Provinces; it should also be considered whether it will not be proper that each Provincial Government should spend money towards this direction and they should themselves manage these affairs and we should not incur this heavy expenditure by setting up such a large Committee at present. It would be better if the honourable Minister agrees to postpone this for a couple of days so that we may consider these aspects and the House could acquire an adequate knowledge as to what work has been done by this Committee heretofore, and, what sort of work will be signed to this Committee, and thus enable us to elect the Members amongst ourselves after keeping all this in view.

The Honourable Maulana Abul Kalam Azad: I do not think if this can be postponed at this stage. The tenure of the previous Committee will expire on 29th of April and after that date a new Committee should be set up. The question before the House is not that whether this Council should be reconstituted or not. But the question is that it should elect five Members representing its quota.

Mr. Tajamul Husain: What expenses will be incurred by the Government in the constitution and working of this Board?

The Honourable Maulana Abul Kalam Azad: I cannot say. But the membes are paid an allowance in accordance with the rules and regulations framed in this connection.

Mr. Speaker: I am putting the motion to the House.

The question is:

"That the Members of this Assembly do proceed to elect in such manner as may be approved by the Honourable the Speaker, five persons from among their number to be members of the All India Council for Technical Education for a period of three years to be reckoned from the date of reconstitution of the Council under the provisions of the Resolution of the Government of India in the Ministry of Education No. F.16-10/44-EIII, dated the 30th November, 1945, as subsequently amended."

The motion was adopted.

Document No. 27

A MOTION OF MAULANA AZAD, MOVED IN THE ASSEMBLY ON 5-4-1949 ABOUT THE ELECTION TO THE CENTRAL ADVISORY BOARD OF ARCHAEOLOGY

The Honourable Maulana Abul Kalam Azad (Minister of Education): Sir, I beg to move:

"That this Assembly do proceed to elect, in such manner as the Honourable the Speaker may direct, two members to serve on the Central Advisory Board of Archaeology in India constituted by the Government of India *vice* Shri R.R. Diwakar and Shri T.A. Ramalingam Chettiar resigned from the Board."

Mr. Speaker : The question is:

"That this Assembly do proceed to elect, in such manner as the Honourable the Speaker may direct, two members to serve on the Central Advisory Board of Archaeology in India constituted by the Government of India *vice* Shri R.R. Diwakar and Shri T.A. Ramalingam Chettiar resigned from the Board."

The motion was adopted.

Document No. 28

MAULANA'S SPEECH DATED 9-4-1949 AT THE INAUGURATION OF THE NATIONAL COMMISSION OF UNESCO, NEW DELHI

I have great pleasure in welcoming you to this inaugural meeting of the National Commission of Unesco. This is in some ways a memorable occasion, for the constitution of the National Commission gives concrete shape to our efforts for international co-operation in the fields of education, science and culture. It would therefore perhaps be appropriate if I should describe in some detail the aims and objectives of Unesco and the manner in which it has attempted to carry out its purposes.

After the experience of two world wars within the course of barely twenty-five years, thinking men and women all over the world realise, as never before, that there must be a change in the outlook of man to avert the calamity of a future disaster. It was out of this universal desire to find an instrument for the settlement of disputes without resort to war that there arose the United Nations with renewed hope for afflicted humanity.

All conflicts have their ultimate origin in the mind of man and it was felt that unless the causes of fear, suspicion, distress and jealousy could be eradicated from human minds no efforts by politicians and statesmen could remove the possibility of future wars. At the time of the preliminary discussions for setting up a United Nations Organisation, it was therefore decided that there should also be an organisation for promoting closer collaboration among different people of the world in the fields of education, science and culture. Accordingly, Unesco was set up to achieve these ends.

At the time of the constitution of Unesco, it was realised that co-operation and understanding among nations could be built only if there was co-operation and understanding among the different elements within the nation itself. If within a nation itself there were divergent elements whose differing points of view had not been fully co-ordinated, such a nation could hardly serve as a harmonious unit in the international setting. Experience showed that there was not only colossal ignorance about different nations but in many cases members of the same nation were ignorant of one another's attitudes, beliefs, customs and faith. This was an experience which was almost universal except in the case of a very few small and homogeneous nations. Further, it was felt that closer co-operation between different elements in our national life would lead to a pormotion of activities in all the fields of education, science and culture. The constitution of Unesco therefore provided that every nation should set up as soon as possible a National Commission or co-operating body for furthering the aims and objects of Unesco within the national unit. It was also felt that such activities could be carried out better by a non-official agency than by the Government or anybody set up directly under the Government auspices.

The constitution of Unesco provides that only States can be members. This guarantees that there will be no possibility of adding to international complications through its activities. There is, however, another aspect of the question which cannot be ignored. The nature of education, science and culture is such that their cause can be served better by private and voluntary agencies. This is the reason why Unesco constitution insists that there should be voluntary bodies or National Commissions to perform its functions in the national field.

Unfortunately, the experience of the last three years has not fully justified the hopes which were raised by the establishment of the United Nations Organisation. In spite of the initial agreement with which it started, it has today become the arena for struggles between rival blocks. It is true that the struggle is yet only a cold war. This is, however, little consolation to those who seek peace on an enduring basis. It is tragic that even today nations have not given up the old attitudes which so often led to war.

The one gleam of hope offered in this dark picture today is the manner in which Unesco, an allied organisation of the United Nations, has been attempting to establish better relations among human beings in the fields of education, science and culture. It is obvious that in the realm of material clash of interests, compromise is difficult while in the fields of the creative spirit, co-operation and compromise are not only possible, but are the natural law. The division of material wealth leads to a diminution in quantity while the distribution of spiritual wealth leads to mutual enrichment. Unesco has also rightly recognised that all conflicts, even in the material field, have their ultimate origin in the mind of man. It was therefore felt that unless the causes of fear, suspicion, distress and jealousy could be eradicated from the human mind, no efforts by the politicians and statesmen alone could remove the possibility of future conflicts. This is the justification of Unesco as well as the reason why it has become a rallying ground for the faith and hope of all who want to avert the disaster of a third world war.

In its brief life of three years, Unesco has already made considerable progress towards the achievement of its objects. The very fact of associating together a large number of people of different nations with marked differences in language, background, social habits and outlook is a considerable achievement. The obligation under the constitution of holding the General Conference in a different country each year has added to the burdens of the Secretariat but in spite of such initial difficulties, the progress achieved holds promise of still greater achievements in the future. In three years, the membership has increased to 44 while national commissions are either in operation or about to be inaugurated in about 35 countries. A large number of international conferences and seminars have been held under its auspices. Of the various activities in these fields, one which deserves special mention is the establishment of the Institute of Hylean Amazon. Another is the establishment of pilot projects in fundamental education in Haiti. The development of the educational section as a clearing house for ideas and experience in different parts of the world is also proving extremely helpful. The constitution of a new Division of Arts and Letters with Dr. Lin Yutang as head has also contributed to a greater exchange in cultural matters between the Asian and European countries. Recently, it was decided to set up a special centre for the Middle and Near East. It has also been decided to promote the establishment of an Institute for Arid Zones and another for the study of conditions in high altitudes.

Unesco has also tried to contribute to a clearer analysis and understanding of the philosophical concepts as the basis of modern civilisation. A volume on human rights is already in the press and one on the concept of democracy is under preparation. A specialised journal, *Museum*, and an official organ called *The Unesco Courier* are among its regular publications.

Unesco has helped in the organisation of work camps for both reconstruction and education in war devastated areas. It has arranged for the exchange of students and voluntary works. During 1948, over 50 million dollars were distributed in educational relief by voluntary organisations largely through its efforts. In its last conference at Beirut it decided to extend the field of reconstruction from the war devastated areas to the undeveloped or underdeveloped areas of the world in order to help in the achievement of more uniform standards throughout the world. It is expected that a concrete programme for the achievement of this end will be one of the main items before the next General Conference.

Unesco has also been helping the exchange of books by Book Coupons for countries which have a shortage of dollars. It has also helped in making scientific equipment available to countries short of such material. A Field Science Co-operation Office has recently been established in Delhi for South Asia. The East Asia Science Co-operation Office has undertaken the responsibility of allocating and distributing in that region two million dollars worth of education and engineering equipment collected by Unrra.

Another project undertaken by Unesco is the translation of great books in order to make the cultural heritage of different countries available to one another. Considerable progress has been made in exploring the possibilities of the production of cheap books. Another valuable contribution to international understanding is the project of studying the causes of tensions between different people and communities with a view to finding out methods of eradicating them. Its most ambitious venture in this field is the project to produce a scientific and cultural history of mankind.

Members will be glad to learn that ever since the foundation of Unesco, India has been playing an important part in its deliberations. She is one of the founder members and helped in the shaping of its aims and purposes. In spite of the political and other disabilities under which she then laboured, and the extremely restricted size of her delegations, she played a leading role in both the first and the second conferences. She has been on the Executive Board from the very beginning and her representatives have made valuable contributions in almost every sphere of Unesco's activities.

During the last year, several achievements and projects of special interest to India have been undertaken. The election of Prof. Radhakrishnan as the Chairman of the Executive Board has brought an Asian to the Head of the Organisation for the first time. The Indian Delegation at the third Conference played a very important role and made valuable contributions in almost every decision taken there.

Some of the Indian experts who have been associated with the special activities of Unesco during the last year may be specially mentioned. Dr. Zakir Hussain attended a meeting on Fundamental Education of Experts in Paris in April 1948, and Mr. N.K. Sidhanta attended a meeting of experts for the translation of great books. Mr. Humayun Kabir of this Ministry was invited to contribute a chapter to Unesco's volume on Human Rights as a result of the International Symposium. Mr. Lakshmanan, Director General of All India Radio was invited to attend the Technical Needs Commission Expert Committee and Mr. Kirpal of this Ministry to survey the educational and cultural needs of the refugees in the Middle East. Dr. S.K. Banerjee attended the International High Altitude Research Conference and Mr. M.S. Sundaram of this Ministry represented India in the Preparatory Conference of the universities of the World.

During the last General Conference of Unesco, there was a proposal to hold a Far Eastern Seminar on Education. The object originally considered was 'Education of War-handicapped Children,' but at the instance of India, the subject finally chosen was 'Adult Education' which is the most pressing problem facing all the Asian countries. Unesco has accepted India's invitation to hold the seminar in India. This will be its first seminar to be held in Asia and is to take place during November.

For reasons which are known to every one, it has not been possible to set up the Indian National Commission of Unesco earlier. As members are aware, the problems created by partition demanded all the energy and attention of the Government till about the middle of 1948. As soon as things started settling down, the Government appointed a Committee to consider the setting up of a Commission and after its report had been approved by the Central Advisory Board of Education in January this year, the Government did not allow any lapse of time in setting up this Commission. It is expected that this Commission will serve as a focus of educational, scientific and cultural activities of the Nation and will contribute to the enrichment of national life in all these fields as well as better co-operation and understanding with other countries.

Document No. 29

SPEECH OF MAULANA AZAD ON THE OCCASION AT THE LAYING OF FOUNDATION OF THE CENTRAL INSTITUTE OF EDUCATION ON 18-4-1949 IN NEW DELHI.[1]

Immediately after I assumed charge of the Ministry of Education in January 1947, I looked into the development projects which had been accepted in principle but not carried out in practice. Of these, one of the most outstanding was the scheme for a Central College of Training for Teachers. The Central Advisory Board of Education had, in 1944, recommended the establishment of two training colleges–one for men and the other for women, each providing for an intake of 200 students for the service of the Centrally Administered Areas and the smaller provinces and states. On grounds of economy the Government of India modified that recommendation and decided to establish one college for both men and women, with a capacity of 300. Provision was accordingly made in the budget of 1946-47 for the establishment of the college.

When I took office, I was therefore surprised to find that the whole programme had been held up on the ground of shortage of building materials. I was aware of the difficulties in securing steel and cement and other equipment and I could understand the delay in the implementation of the building programme. I could not, however, understand why this led to a postponement of the entire scheme. Even if buildings were lacking, the institute could have been started in temporary structures or hired houses, but here, as in so many other cases, programmes of educational development were held up on the ground of lack of accommodation. This undue stress upon buildings has always seemed to me to be an instance of confusing ends with means. Buildings are only a means of which the end is education, and yet it seemed to me that many of our educational planners were so engrossed

1. Foundation of the Institute was laid by Pandit Jawaharlal Nehru.

with building projects that they could not conceive of carrying on educational work in their absence. I therefore decided forthwith that the institution must be started immediately with whatever accommodation was readily available.

The period was an exceedingly difficult one and all the attention of the Government was concentrated first on the disturbances in the Punjab and later on the impending division of the country. Even then, a small house was secured in the Delhi University area in July 1947. I realised that this was not adequate for our needs and the work of the institute even on the smallest scale could be carried out only by the additional accommodation provided in tents. In spite of our anxiety to get the institute working, a further period of delay was enforced by the division of the country and the extension of disturbances of Delhi itself, and for several months all normal activities had to be totally suspended. As soon, however, as the situation was brought under control, on the 19th of December, 1947, the Central Institute of Education was formally opened by Lady Mountbatten and it started to work in one hired building and several tents.

It is hardly necessary for me to relate at length the importance of an institute of this kind. With literacy figures so low as only 15 per cent. the paramount importance of expanding the facilities of education is obvious. The acceptance of democracy as the pattern of our State has, if anything, added to the urgency of the problem. It is also self-evident that the first step towards expanding the facilities of education is to provide for an increase in the number of trained teachers. Equally necessary is an institution to assess the results of educational methods followed till now and devise improvements, demanded in the changing circumstances of today.

It will be noticed that the institution, which was started in December 1947, was the Central Institute of Education and not the training colleges which had originally been planned in 1944 and 1945. This meant not merely a change in nomenclature, but a considerable expansion in the purpose and functions of the institution. I felt that changes were necessary in two directions. First, it should not be merely a college for training teachers but also an institution for research in the fields of education. Secondly, its services should not be restricted to the Centrally Administered Areas but should extend to the whole of India.

The Central Institute will therefore both train teachers for higher and secondary schools and also carry on research on the problems of basic and secondary education. The stage at which a child should be introduced to a craft as distinct from activity, the relative emphasis on craft and academic subjects and their correlation, the production of a new type of school literature to bring out the social functions of all human activity, the degree of abstraction possible in the earlier stages of education, the stage at which there may be some bifurcation between academic subjects and crafts, the grouping of children according to aptitude, taste and ability, the place of art in the school curriculum – these are only a few of the many problems which arise out of a new conception of basic education and require constant and careful study in a research institution.

There are also problems relating to adult education which demands fresh and careful scrutiny. It is a commonplace that the methods which are suitable for children cannot without modification be applied to adults. No doubt, a good deal of work in this connection has been done in other countries of the world but each country has its own peculiar problems arising out of its social and economic background and its political history. We will have to devise the quickest methods of liquidating adult illiteracy. Equally important is the maintenance of a continued service of literature to prevent relapse into illiteracy. Thus alone can we provide adult literates with the knowledge to discharge their functions as citizens of a democratic state.

I could go on referring to many other problems which require immediate attention if we are to make our education truly creative. The system of examinations is itself being studied all over the world. The problem of textbooks which will provide useful and interesting information and at the same time develop a truly human outlook on world affairs is also engaging the attention of many countries. The aim and purpose of secondary education also require a re-examination. It is my hope that the Central Institute of Education will be our laboratory for examining all these important questions under controlled conditions and offering suggestions as to the best methods for their solution.

I have already stated that we did not allow the lack of buildings to delay the starting of the institution and I am glad that, in spite of these difficulties, the institution has made good progress. Nevertheless, I felt that now that the Institute has started to work, we must provide suitable buildings for it as soon as possible. When the plans were made in 1945, the estimated expenditure for buildings was Rs. 18 lakh, but the sharp rise in the cost of construction is bound to lead to an increase in expenditure. I am, however, glad that, notwithstanding the difficulties, we are today in a position to take in hand the building programme of the Institute and I hope that it will, in the near future, have all the buildings it needs.

A library of over 5,000 books has been built up at cost of approximately forty thousand rupees. We are hoping that when completed, the Institute Library will be comparable with similar research libraries elsewhere. I am also hoping that we shall, in the course of the next year or so, attach to the Institute a Psychological Section to carry out experiments in aptitude tests, selection methods, vocational guidance and other services.

We are conscious that only a beginning has been made and all that we propose and hope to accomplish is still in the realm of the future. Foundations truly laid are, however, a guarantee of future success, and no one, Mr. Prime Minister, is more aware than yourself of the need of imaginative planning and bold execution in order to achieve our objects. It is for this reason that we requested you to lay the foundation of this Institute, so that this new institution may, from its very inception, be inspired by that broad humanism and width of culture which have distinguished your actions in public and private life. I have, Mr. Prime Minister, great pleasure in requesting you to lay the foundation-stone of this Institute.

Document No. 30

LETTER FROM DR. TARA CHAND TO RAJAJI

New Delhi
30 May, 1949

Dear Shri Rajagopalachariji,

I am enclosing a note concerning the appointment of a committee to investigate the affairs of the Banaras Hindu University with a view to suggesting what changes (if any) may be made in the Act, statutes and regulations of the university and for the improvement of the working of the University.

I am not sure whether the fourth paragraph regarding the Universities Commission and the first three lines of the fifth paragraph should be included in this.

According to the Act of the Banaras Hindu University, Section 19 vests certain emergency powers in the Governor-General in Council. I am enclosing a copy of the Section. The procedure laid down seems to require that the Governor-General-in-Council should first indicate to the Council the matter in regard to which he desires explanation and if the Council either fails to offer any explanation within the time prescribed or offers an unsatisfactory explanation, then he may issue such instructions as appear to him to be necessary. I do not know whether the Government can without following this procedure straightaway appoint a committee. I hope you will kindly look into this matter and advise as to what should be done.

Yours sincerely,
Tara Chand

His Excellency Shri C. Rajagopalachari

Enclosure I

Banaras Hindu University

NOTE ON THE APPOINTMENT OF A COMMITTEE TO INVESTIGATE THE AFFAIRS OF THE BANARAS HINDU UNIVERSITY

The Banaras Hindu University Act was passed in 1915. It was amended in minor respects in 1922 and 1930. Since then the authorities of the university have drawn the attention of the Government of India from time to time to its pressing needs, and the time has come to examine closely the working of the Act and the administration of the university with a view to adapting the constitution thereof to present-day conditions and to attain a more efficient management of this, one of the most important universities in India and one which is the direct responsibility of the Central Government. It has therefore become necessary to appoint a small committee consisting of the following members to examine the working of the university:

Shri Rustom Masani[1]

Bakshi Tek Chand

Dr. C.R. Reddi, and

The Vice-Chancellor of the Banaras Hindu University.

The committee will generally review the work of the Banaras University and to that end hear such evidence as they deem necessary and scrutinise any paper or document which they consider relevant and useful. The committee will, in particular, consider –

(a) how the administrative machinery of the university has functioned;

(b) how the finances of the university have been managed, what are its sources of income and its expenditure;

---

1. Sir Rustom Pestonji Masani: Former Vice-Chancellor of Bombay University.

(c) how the standards of teaching, examination and discipline have been maintained, whether the university should continue Intermediate classes and maintain all the present departments and subjects; and

(d) how the affairs of the University have been conducted in furtherance of the objects and purposes of the university.

The committee will also enquire into the relations of the university with the provincial and Central Governments and examine its present needs and its requirements in the immediate future.

The committee will, after considering all the material before it, recommend such changes in the Banaras University Act, 1915, or in the statutes and regulations made thereunder as they deem necessary and such measures for improvement in the structure and working of the university as in their opinion should immediately be undertaken.

Enclosure II

SECTION 19 OF THE BANARAS HINDU UNIVERSITY ACT XVI OF 1915

19. (1) If, at any time, the Governor-General-in-Council is of opinion that special reasons exist which make the removal of any member of the teaching staff desirable in the interest of the University, or that, as a special measure, the appointment of a certain examiner or examiners to report to him is desirable to maintain the standard of University examinations, or that the scale of staff of the University is inadequate, or that in any other respect the affairs of the University are not managed in the furtherance of the objects and purposes of University or in accordance with this Act and the Statutes and Regulations, he may indicate to the Council any matter in regard to which he desires explanation, and call upon that body to offer such explanation as it may desire to offer, with any proposals which it may desire to make, within such time as he may prescribe.

(2) If the Council fails to offer any explanation within the time prescribed, or offers an explanation or makes proposals which, in the opinion of the Governor-General-in-Council, is or are unsatisfactory, the Governor-General-in-Council may issue such instructions as appear to him to be necessary and desirable in the circumstances of the case, and the Court shall give effect to such instructions.

Document No. 31

LETTER FROM RAJAJI TO MAULANA AZAD

New Delhi

7 June, 1949

My dear Maulana Sahib,

I place a letter dated 30 May 1949[1] from Dr. Tara Chand[2] about the appointment of a committee to look into the working of the Banaras Hindu University, and its enclosure. I assume you have already been consulted in the matter.

Section 19 of the Banaras University Act, 1915, which confers certain emergency powers on the Central Government and prescribes steps and conditions therefor is no bar to the appointment of a committee for the purpose in view. What is intended now is that a thorough examination of the working of the university should be undertaken with a view to promoting necessary amendments in the Act and for more efficient management of the institution. A Government resolution constituting the committee, on the lines of the enclosed draft, should, I think, suffice, and if you see no objection, I could send it to the Prime Minister as Lord Rector of the University for securing the approval of the Cabinet.

Yours sincerely,
C. Rajagopalachari

The Hon'ble Maulana Abul Kalam Azad
Minister for Education

---

1. See previous Document.
2. Secretary and Adviser, Union Ministry of Education, 1948-51; Ambassador to Iran, 1951-56.

Document No. 32

LETTER[1] FROM MAULANA AZAD TO PT. NEHRU

Camp "Chashm-e-Shahi"
Srinagar
9 June, 1949

My dear Jawaharlalji,

Please refer to your letter of 31 May about the selection of nurses for overseas scholarships. I agree with you that for the present the work of the selection of nurses may be left with the Ministry of Health. I have issued necessary instructions to the Joint Secretary in this connection.

Dr. Tara Chand sent me a summary of the conversation he had with you and Rajaji regarding the Hindu University. There is no doubt that the affairs of this university have been deteriorating and if no steps were taken at an early date to remedy the defects, they might get worse and much of the dirty linen might be washed in public. The question for decision all along had been when action should be taken and in what form. I considered the matter from its various aspects and had reached the conclusion that we should wait for the report of the University Commission which, as you know, has particularly been asked to look into the working of the three universities under the control of the Central Government and submit its report after taking all the relevant factors into consideration. Therefore, I thought it would be better if we had this report before us and in the light of which action could be taken.

Dr. Tara Chand, however, informs me that Rajaji and you have agreed to the formation of a three-man committee which will submit its report after examining the general administrative and educational condition of the university. The terms of reference for the committee will be in general and no reference to the Vice-Chancellor will be made. The names of Masani, Tek Chand [and] Reddy have been suggested for the committee. I agree with all this. I now feel that a detailed report from this committee will help us to consider in its true perspective the report which will be submitted by the University Commission. If the committee is established soon and starts its work immediately on its establishment, it is hoped it will be able to submit its report to Government by the end of September next.

The other consideration which has weighed with me in coming to the above agreement is that there is a fear that after the summer vacations are over the student community of the University, who were found restless before the vacations started, might resort to doing some unpleasant things. The formation of the committee will, in all probability, have a good effect on the students and stop them from taking things into their own hands.

I have sent a note about the committee to Dr. Tara Chand and my approval for its formation. If you feel that this note should be submitted to the Cabinet, it will be sent to the Cabinet Secretariat. Personally I do not think there is any need for its being submitted to the Cabinet. If the latter be the case, the Education Ministry will write to the Chancellor or the Rector to appoint a committee as above.

Yours sincerely,
A.K. Azad

The Hon'ble Pandit Jawaharlal Nehru

1. This letter was sent to Sardar Vallabhbhai Patel by Pandit Nehru on 13-6-1949 to inform previous views to Maulana Azad.

Document No. 33

LETTER FROM PT. JAWAHARLAL NEHRU TO MAULANA AZAD

New Delhi

13 June, 1949

My dear Maulana,

Your letter of 9 June.

I think it will be desirable to have a three-man committee as you have suggested. The names mentioned in your letter are Masani, Tek Chand and Reddy. I presume you mean the elder Masani, who was Vice-Chancellor of Bombay University. I mention this, as I think the younger Masani would not be suitable.

I do not think this matter need be put up before the Cabinet. But I think that the Governor-General and Sardar Patel should be informed of it, as they have taken interest in the Hindu University affairs. I am writing to both of them.

Yours sincerely,
Jawaharlal Nehru

The Hon'ble Maulana Abul Kalam Azad

Document No. 34

LETTER FROM MAULANA AZAD TO RAJAJI

Srinagar

18 June, 1949

My dear Rajaji,

I thank you for your letter of 7 June 1949. Dr. Tara Chand had written to me to say that he had a talk with you and Pandit Nehru regarding the Hindu University and it had been agreed that a three-man Committee might be formed in order to go into the working, administrative as well as educational, of the university. I had agreed to this and thought that the proposed committee consisting of Rustom Masani, Bakshi Tek Chand and C.R. Reddy would prove useful for the work. But, from the draft resolution which you have sent with your letter it appears it has now been proposed to include the Vice-Chancellor of the university into this Committee. I feel that if the present Vice-Chancellor of the university was included in it, would not be regarded by many as desirable and whoever is conversant with the present affairs of the university would take very lightly the formation of such a Committee.

I am, therefore, of the opinion that either no committee may be formed for the present or if one was to be formed in the interests of the university, the present Vice-Chancellor should have no place on it.

I intend to stay here till the end of this month and hope to be in Delhi some time during the first week of July.

Yours sincerely,
A.K. Azad

His Excellency Shri C. Rajagopalachari
New Delhi.

Document No. 35

LETTER FROM RAJAJI TO MAULANA AZAD

20 June, 1949

My dear Maulana Sahib,

I thank you for your letter of 18 June about the Banaras Hindu University. I think when you return we shall one day personally discuss the question and settle matters.

I am going to Simla tonight and shall return to Delhi on 1 July.

Yours sincerely,
C. Rajagopalachari

The Hon'ble Maulana Abul Kalam Azad
Srinagar

Document No. 36

LETTER FROM DR. RAJENDRA PRASAD TO MAULANA ABUL KALAM AZAD

1, Queen Victoria Road,
New Delhi

The 24th June, 1949

My dear Maulana Saheb,

There is a large number of manuscripts of great value lying about in various places in the country and in the neighbouring countries like Nepal, Tibet, etc. These have a great historical interest for our country and should as far as possible be collected, preserved and catalogued. A great deal of such literature has gone away to England and other countries but what remains should be preserved. I believe, many of the States have got such collection of historical material but as valuable material may deteriorate. I would, therefore, suggest that steps may be taken by the Government to collect and preserve them. Steps should be taken for the preservation of even such as have to be left where they are. A catalogue is absolutely essential. May I therefore request that the Government may depute some of its officers to do this work of national importance? The archaeological department or the department which is in charge of the archives might undertake it and if necessary a few special appointments may be made in this connection. As it is matter of public importance I thought it necessary to draw your attention to it, although I know that you are also interested in it.

Yours sincerely,
Rajendra Prasad

The Hon'ble Maulana Abul Kalam Azad
Minister for Education
New Delhi.

Document No. 37

LETTER FROM SARDAR PATEL TO MAULANA AZAD

New Delhi

23 July, 1949

My dear Maulana Sahib,

With reference to the discussion we had the other day on Banaras Hindu University, Rajaji tells[1] me that he has not agreed to your proposals and has, in fact, pressed his original position. I feel myself that Rajaji's proposals were the best in the circumstances and would again ask you to reconsider whether those proposals should not be accepted.

Yours sincerely,
Vallabhbhai Patel

The Hon'ble Maulana Abul Kalam Azad
New Delhi

---

1. See appendices for more details.

Document No. 38

SPEECH, DELIVERED BY MAULANA AZAD DATED 19-8-1949 AT THE PROVINCIAL EDUCATION MINISTERS' CONFERENCE HELD IN NEW DELHI

We have as one of the items for discussion today a problem which raises fundamental issues of law and justice. Till now, the State has looked upon an offence as a crime for which the offender must expiate. Such offences, whether you call them crimes or sins, were regarded as evil and attracted as their inevitable consequence punishment. Punishment was therefore regarded as a consequence of crime and justified in itself. The classic exposition of this view is in the principle "An eye for an eye, a tooth for a tooth."

Later ages, however, raised the question of the utility or justification of punishment. Critics arose who asked how a murdered person benefited by the slaughter of his murderer. In fact, the only result was the loss of life of two individuals instead of one. Punishment was therefore sought to be justified on grounds of its deterrent character, but even this did not satisfy critics who pointed out that, as a matter of fact, punishment did not deter. A new school of thought arose, which approached the problem of punishment from the point of view of reform of the offender. Instead of a retributive theory of punishment, we thus find the emergence of an educative and reformatory theory of punishment.

This dispute between the different theories of punishment has not yet been settled, but on one point there is almost unanimous agreement among both theorists and practical men of affairs. All are ageed that in the case of juveniles there must be a change of outlook with regard to punishment. For one thing, young persons, without maturity of judgment, cannot be held fully responsible for their actions. For another, experience has shown that confinement of such juveniles in jails confirms them into criminals. In fact, children who may have committed some crime through want to knowledge or on the impulse of the moment, become habitual criminals if they are once sent to jail.

Recognition of this fact had led many countries to provide separate establishments for juveniles. In India we have had reformatories and houses of correction in different provinces, but it must be admitted that even these have not fully met the purpose. The provision of such reformatories or juvenile jails has, no doubt, separated the juvenile offenders from the confirmed criminals, but as they themselves have been miniature jails, the educative and reformatory aspect has not found a proper emphasis.

Apart from the inadequacy of existing institutions in India, we have to recognise the fact that their development in the different provinces has been unequal. Bombay, which has gone farthest in the matter, passed its Children's Act in 1924 and revised it in 1948. It has 17 Remand Homes and uses a large number of Probation Officers to look after juvenile delinquents. Thirty-two such officers have been appointed by the Government in addition to 150 working on a voluntary basis and seven appointed by non-official bodies. Bombay has 28 Certified Schools and 12 Associations which attend to the after-care of the children. No other province has gone so far, though Madras, under its Children's Act of 1920, has set up five Juvenile Courts and six Certified Schools. The C.P. passed an Act in 1928 and has 32 Probation Officers and one Certified School. West Bengal has a Children's Act, passed in 1922, and recently the West Bengal Government has initiated action to change the character of administration in respect of juvenile crime. East Punjab has an Act before the Assembly, while the U.P. Government are drafting a Bill for the purpose. We have no information of such Bills in either Assam, Bihar or Orissa.

The position with regard to the care and management of juvenile delinquents is thus obviously unsatisfactory. In the first place, not all the provinces that have Children's Acts on their statute-books are working them adequately. The work is chiefly confined to bigger cities and even there it leaves much to be desired. The Probation Officers have not the requisite training; nor have the magistrates of the Juvenile Courts the required qualifications. The Certified Schools are not working properly and after-care is all but non-existent.

A little consideration will show that in a matter like the problem of juvenile delinquency and the proper methods of dealing with it, there must be uniformity among the different provinces. It is also desirable that the practice of this country should conform, as far as possible, to that of other enlightened countries of the world. In the U.K., the persons between the age of 8 and 17 are regarded as juveniles and are tried by special Juvenile Courts. Panels of magistrates are selected from Justices of Peace and, according to present regulations, these panels consist of two or three persons selected every three years. In metropolitan courts one of the magistrates must be a woman, while outside London this practice is observed as far as possible. The administration of the courts is under the Home Officer, but special Advisory Committees were set up in 1910 in order to make the attitude of the administration more progressive. In the past, punishment for the juvenile delinquents was in proportion to the gravity of the offences but in recent times, the trend is towards the reclamation of the future citizen rather than the punishment of an offender.

The change-over from punishment to education is almost complete in the U.S.A., and in some of the European countries. In the U.S.A., the upper age-limit for juvenile delinquents is 21. Up to the age of 18, the offender is under the exclusive jurisdiction of the Juvenile Courts, but from 18 to 21 these courts exercise a concurrent jurisdiction with the ordianary courts. The trend of legislation is to make the Juvenile Courts independent of the ordinary system of criminal justice. In addition to the special magistrates, the U.S.A. provides for references to assist in the hearing and disposition of the cases. Where the delinquent is a girl, it is the practice to associate a properly qualified woman referee with the Court. The U.S.A. has no advisory bodies, perhaps because social service agencies play an important part in all cases before the Juvenile Courts.

One feature which is common to both the U.K. and the U.S.A. is the effort to retain the child in his or her own surroundings. The U.S.A. has the largest provision for institutional care, but even there the trend of theory is away from institutional care to the education of the delinquent in his or her own home atmosphere. The following table gives an idea of the results of the disposition of cases in the Juvenile Courts in the U.K. and the U.S.A. :

	U.K.	U.S.A.
Put on probation	51%	43%
Discharged after charge proved or bound over with supervision	32%	29%
Committed to Schools	9%	16%
Fined	6%	6%
Probation to non-official persons	} 2%	2%
Placement with board department or agency ..		3%
Other care		1%

The examples of the U.K. and the U.S.A. therefore indicate that the most progressive opinion in the world today favours that the juvenile offender must be regarded as a subject for education rather than punishment, and where it is necessary to send him to a reformatory, the character of such juvenile institutions must change. They should be educational institutions in the best sense of the term and not "houses of correction or penalty." These progressive countries have also found by experience that the best method of dealing with juvenile delinquents is to provide for their instruction without removing them from their homes. This requires a close co-operation with their families.

As I have already stated, there must be uniformity among the provinces with regard to measures for dealing with juvenile delinquency. It seems that this can best be achieved by means of central legislation with an enabling clause which will permit provinces to make such minor modifications as may be necessary. Notice of a private member's bill for dealing with some aspects of juvenile delinquency has already been given by Dr. Panjabrao Deshmukh and is likely to come up during the next legislative session of the Constituent Assembly. After this Conference has decided on the main lines which such legislation should take, one of the two procedures may be followed. Either we may accept Dr. Deshmukh's bill with such modifications as may be necessary or, in the alternative, we may introduce a more comprehensive bill as a Government measure.

I will briefly mention some of the points for consideration in this context. I have already referred to the fact that the trend of progressive opinion in Western countries favours the retention of juvenile delinquents in their homes. We have to consider whether in the prevailing conditions in India, juveniles will benefit more by being trained at home or by receiving instruction in special hostels established for the purpose.

Another point which the Conference will have to consider is the question of institutions dealing with juvenile delinquency. While Juvenile Courts may remain in the administrative charge of the Home Department, assisted by the Education Department, it appears to me that the homes and schools for the juvenile delinquents must be directly administered by the Department of Education itself.

The Conference should also advise on the nature of instruction to be provided in such schools and homes. It is obvious that in addition to instruction in letters, there must also be a provision for training in some craft or trade. The provision of moral instructions seems to me to be equally important. This need not be narrow or sectarian, but wide ethical teaching of a universal type that will help in building up the character of the inmates.

The final point for consideration is the question of setting up an Advisory Committee in every province. These committees should be small and compact and should include Education Ministers, representatives of the Law and Home Departments and some social workers.

The second big problem before this Conference is the question of the medium of instruction at different stages of school education. The basic principle in this matter is not in dispute. The claims of the mother tongue are accepted by all but in spite of this, there are complaints that this principle is not always observed in practice. On the contrary, a language other than the mother tongue is sought to be imposed on the minorities.

India is a vast country with many languages. We must accept unreservedly that all these langauges are Indian languages and deserve the same treatment. Where a province is linguistically homogeneous, there is no difficulty in acting on this principle, but even where the languages transcend provincial barriers, this should not affect our attitude to the problem. Since all the langauges are Indian languages, what objection can there be if a minority in a particular province speaks or learns a language other than that of the majority? One thing is certain. Even if our aim is unity, it cannot be achieved by compulsion or imposition. Experience has shown that the only way to achieve unity in cultural or linguistic matters is to accept the existing differences. Any attempt to iron out the differences only leads to greater conflict and bitterness.

A constructive approach to this problem cannot but lead to an amicable settlement. It is therefore a matter for gratification that the C.A.B. of Education, which is representative of all the provinces, has decided unanimously that primary instruction should, provided there is the minimum number of pupils available, be invariably given in the mother tongue, and that even in the secondary stage, instruction should be provided in the mother tongues if a sufficient number so desire. It is obvious that the mother tongue of the pupil means the language which is described as such by the guardian of the pupil. How can any one, except the parents, decide what is the mother tongue of the child?

The conflict is not about the principle but about its application to concrete cases. Recently, the Congress Working Committee discussed the problem in all its aspects and, after a thorough examination of all the issues involved, passed a resolution which you have no doubt seen. I am myself convinced that the attitude adopted by the Working Committee is the right one, and I hope that you will be of the same opinion and approach this problem with clear vision and without any mental reservations. I am sure that if this is done, all causes for grievance will be removed. We can then solve this problem once and for all, so that there may be no future complaints from any minority.

A satisfactory solution of the problem of languages is more important in the context of our newly-won freedom. We have only now achieved our freedom and it is essential that every effort must be made to develop a sense of solidarity among the nation. If we allow grievances to grow over basic things like the question of the mother tongue, I am afraid that the consequences will affect all aspects of our national life. I need hardly stress this point before you as you are equally alive to the necessity of a satisfactory settlement of this question. I would only appeal to you that we should approach this question with large-hearted generosity and try to meet the wishes of the minorities in a manner which will leave no ground for dissatisfaction or complaint.

Document No. 39

MAULANA AZAD'S ADDRESS DATED 21-8-1949 AT THE CONFERENCE FOR CULTURAL COOPERATION BETWEEN INDIA AND ASIAN COUNTRIES, HELD IN NEW DELHI

I am grateful to you for having accepted, at such short notice, my invitation to attend this preliminary meeting for the setting up of an orgnisation for cultural co-operation between the different Asian countries. I have, for a long time, felt that we must take steps to increase and strengthen such cultural contacts. From the earliest period of recorded history to almost the last days of the Moghul Empire, India's relations with her neighbours–both to her West and to her East–have been cordial and intimate. We remember the religious and cultural missions that went to countries so far flung as China and Japan on the one hand, and Egypt and Asia Minor on the other. We also remember the close trade relations which brought Indian traders and commercial men to the Byzantine courts or led them to colonise and develop outposts of Indian culture in the south-eastern regions of Asia. When we recall that all this was done at a time when the means of communication were meagre, if not primitive, we wonder even more at the closeness of contacts established then. With the loss of political independence, these ties were loosened and for over a century contact with our neighbours has been slight and occasional. I was convinced that we must take early steps for removing this lacuna and immediately on the attainment of our independence I decided to take action in the matter.

Following a Goodwill Mission from Iran, and Indo-Iranian Scoiety was set up about four or five years ago. This was a move in the right direction, but it was not enough. We want to deepen our friendship and contact not only with Iran but also with Turkey and the countries of the Middle-East and China and our neighbours in South-East Asia. Such co-operation is also necessary from an international point of view. If we can create large blocks of goodwill in different areas of the world, grounds for suspicion and hatred will be removed and we can contribute to increased international understanding and amity.

Experience has proved that cultural contacts are far more effective in uniting nations than political alliances. Political alliances are based on a spirit of bargaining while cultural contacts deepen mutual understanding. Such understanding is more necessary today in view of the new awakening which is taking place throughout the Eastern world. We have today, throughout the Orient, a movement for educational and cultural regeneration which demands close attention and sympathetic study.

For various reasons, India in recent years has been brought into contact with the countries of Europe and America in varying degrees. The need today is for a greater understanding with countries outside that orbit. The need of an organisation to promote such cultural contacts is obvious, but I must confess that I have found some difficulty in choosing an appropriate name for such a body. One body to cover all these regions may well prove unwieldy, and I can think of no suitable name to cover all of them. Geography itself has determined the lines on which such associations can be built. We must, on the one hand, establish closer contacts with Turkey, Afghanistan and the Middle-East countries, on the other we should also develop closer relations with China, Japan and the countries of South-East Asia. A solution which strikes me at first sight is to have two bodies and call one India-Middle-East Association, and the other India-South-East-Asia Association. Even this is not fully satisfactory as Turkey and Afghanistan would not be included in a Middle-East Association. Similarly, an India-South-East Asia Association would leave out countries like China, Japan and Korea. It seems that the only way of overcoming this difficulty is to describe the organisation as an Indian Council of Cultural Co-operation. This body would have two different sections–one for the Western group of countries including Afghanistan, Turkey and Egypt, and the other for the second group, including Korea, Japan and China.

Obviously, the main object of such a Council will be to maintain and increase cultural contacts between India and these countries. It should act as an agency for the exchange of information and literature as well as personnel. Short visits of professors and students from India to these countries and from these countries to India would go a long way to increase mutual understanding. The Council should, I feel, also maintain a library and a reading room and arrange for the publication of magazines and other periodical literature.

A non-official organisation, if it is representative of the intelligentsia of the land, is, from the nature of the case, best suited to perform functions of this type. If we consider how such an organisation is to be set up, I think, you will agree with me that the best method would be to frame a constitution by which all the Indian universities and appropriate cultural societies may send three or four representatives to the proposed Council. In addition, the Council should include eminent men who have distinguished themselves in the field of art, letters or the humanities.

These are, however, matters of detail, which cannot be settled in this preliminary meeting. I have been considering how this Council can be set up most expeditiously, and have consulted others interested in the project. The best method seems to be as follows:

We should set up, today, an interim body which will define the aims and objects of the Council, draft its constitution and carry on other preliminary work. I would therefore request you to form a 'Provisional Committee' and appoint out of your numbers a sub-committee to work out the details of the scheme. This sub-committee should start work immediately and be instructed to complete its labours by October. The Council can then be formally inaugurated early in November, with representatives from the universities and cultural bodies from all over India.

Document No. 40

LETTER FROM MAULANA AZAD TO RAJAJI

New Delhi

22 August, 1949

My dear Rajaji,

As you had advised me, I asked the Chairman of the University Education Commission to let me have an advance copy of the Commission's report on the Central Universities. He has sent me two copies of the Chapter concerned. I am sending one copy to you; the other I have kept with me.

I enclose herewith a 'Confidential' note by the Commission on the Banaras Hindu University. The two notes will help you to have a clear picture how things stand in this university.

Yours sincerely,
A.K. Azad

His Excellency Shri Chakravarti Rajagopalachari
New Delhi

Enclosure

BANARAS HINDU UNIVERSITY

EXTRACTS FROM NOTE BY THE UNIVERSITY EDUCATION COMMISSION

The discipline of the university for some months past has been unfortunate.

The report of the officer of the Ministry of Finance deputed to scrutinize the accounts has pointed out many irregularities and asked for radical changes in financial management, etc.

There is a sense of insecurity and nervousness on the part of the teachers.

The working of the university bodies like the Court, the Council, and the Syndicate, has not perhaps been on sound or academic lines.

There have been complaints about victimisation of teachers and students.

Document No. 41

MAULANA'S INAUGURAL ADDRESS DATED 22-8-1949 AT THE ALL INDIA CONFERENCE ON ARTS HELD IN CALCUTTA

I am glad to welcome you to this first All India Conference on Arts to be held under the auspices of the Central Government. In the past, India made valuable contributions to the cultural world, especially in the fields of literature, religious philosophy, architecture and the fine arts. While these achievements were due to the innate genius of the people, the encouragement and support extended by enlightened kings and other lovers of art and culture should not be overlooked. The great traditions of the past still remain, but, for reasons which are known to you, the patronage which was extended by the State to the fine arts and other expressions of culture, has been largely missing since India lost her independence. A situation has now been reached where, unless prompt steps are taken to preserve, develop and enrich the heritage of our cultural traditions, they may be damaged beyond repair. With the attainment of independence, the need for encouragement to the different forms of Indian culture has become even more insistent.

I may recall to your memory the steps which have been taken in recent years to ensure the preservation and enrichment of our cultural heritage. About four years ago, the Asiatic Society of Bengal put forward proposals for the establishment of a National Cultural Trust which would be entrusted with the task of stimulating and promoting the culture of the country in all its apsects and represent the various cultural elements in our country. They proposed that the Trust should function as an autonomous and independent body predominantly non-official in its constitution and should operate through appropriate agencies. There should for the purpose be three Academies, namely, an Academy of Letters to deal with Indian languages, literature, philosophy and history, an Academy of Arts (including graphic, plastic and applied art) and Architecture, and an Academy of Dance, Drama and Music. The object of these Academies would be to develop, promote and foster studies in the subjects with which they deal, with a view to maintaining the highest possible standards of achievement. The Trust should have the following additional functions in addition to those performed by the Academies :

(*i*) to encourage cultural education and research with particular reference to the preservation and development of traditional Indian culture in relation to such subjects as literature, architecture, sculpture, painting, dancing, dramatic art and music;

(*ii*) to acquire for the State sites, monuments, manuscripts, pictures or other objects of importance from the point of view of Indian culture;

(*iii*) to advise the Government of India and the Provincial Governments in regard to cultural matters;

(*iv*) to co-operate with the universities in the development of activities in the purely cultural fields;

(*v*) to co-operate with the learned societies of India in order to encourage and expand the cultural aspects of the work now performed by them;

(*vi*) to publish suitable popular literature on cultural matters;

(*vii*) to maintain close touch with all parts of India (including states) by holding periodical conferences;

(*viii*) to organise archaeological and other cultural missions to foreign countries and generally to develop and extend existing cultural contacts between India and other countries.

It was also proposed that the Trust should be financed by an endowment of four crores of rupees, which would make it independent of annual grants from the Central or the Provincial Governments. The Committee of the Central Advisory Board of Education which considered the proposals of the Asiatic Society of Bengal were of the opinion that such endowment was necessary if the trustees were to function properly. The Committee recommended that the Central Government should contribute half the amount while the Provincial Governments and the Indian States should contribute the balance in equal proportions.

The Government of India accepted the principle underlying the recommendations of the Central Advisory Board of Education and arrangments were made to bring the Trust into existence as soon as possible. A sum of rupees eight lakh was therefore proposed in the budget for 1947-48, but the partition of the country and the disturbances which followed prevented the execution of the plan. During 1948-49, the proposal was again considered, but in view of the financial difficulties from which the country is now suffering, the establishment of the Trust had to be postponed. Nevertheless, a sum of Rs. 1 lakh was provided in the budget for 1949-50 to carry on the preliminary work in connection with the foundation of the Trust.

Instead of spending the major portion of this inadequate amount for the setting up of a secretariat for the Trust, we considered it more advisable to utilise the money, as far as possible, in schemes for the promotion of art in the country. I therefore decided that we should have three conferences during the year, the first with representatives of the visual arts, the second with men of letters and the third with representatives of dance, drama and music. It is in accordance with that programme that the present Conference is being held and I look forward to this gathering of representative artists from all over the country to offer advice to the Government in respect of some of the most urgent issues before us. I may, however, draw your attention to the fact that when the Asiatic Society of Bengal originally proposed the establishment of a National Cultural Trust and even when the Government of India first accepted the principle underlying that recommendation, we did not have in our view the proposed Indian National Commission for co-operation with Unesco. Now that this Commission has been established, I feel that we should re-examine the whole issue and consider whether much of the work which was originally to have been performed by the Trust cannot be performed by one of the Sub-Commissions or sections of the National Commission. You are aware that the National Commission is divided into three Sub-Commissions, namely, the Sub-Commission for Education, the Sub-Commission for Culture and the Sub-Commission for Science. Much of the work which the Cultural Trust was to have done would be co-terminus with that to be performed by the Sub-Commission for Culture. In fact, the three Academies of the proposed Cultural Trust, namely, the Academy of Letters, the Academy of Dance, Drama and Music and the Academy of the Visual Arts could very easily be formed under the aegis of the Cultural Sub-Commission of the National Commission. This, however, is a matter which requires further consideration, and I would at this stage only request all members to keep in mind the possiblity of such integration of work under the

National Commission. This will not only make for simplicity, but also save considerable expense in money, men and energy.

Whether the work of promoting the artistic and cultural life of the country is to be carried out through a Trust or through the National Commission, the most important point is that there should be facilities for their preservation and development. Members of this Conference are perhaps aware that the Government of India have, as a first step towards the encouragement of Indian Music, promoted the establishment of two academies–one of Hindustani Music at Lucknow and the other of Karnataka Music at Madras. The object of these academies will be to promote advanced studies and research in these branches of Indian Music. The Government have also tried to encourage young painters and sculptors by the award of suitable scholarships. In 1947-48, six scholarships each of the value of Rs. 2,500 were given to promising young artist, and this year we have offered eight scholarships of equal value to young artists who are prepared to devote their talents to the revival and development of art in the context of social education in rural areas. The selection of scholars will be made by a committee of experts consisting of the principals of recognised art schools, and the works of the candidates are being displaced in an exhibition organised in connection with this Conference. It is also proposed to establish an Artists' Travelling Fund to encourage amateur artists. The Government of India have provided an amount of Rs. 15,000 and requested the provinces to make contributions to the fund. I fully realise that these are extremely inadequate measures, but we must recognise the grave financial difficulties through which we are passing. The fact that we have not allowed these difficulties to stand in our way and have made a beginning, even though on a meagre scale, should serve as an earnest of the future policy of the Government of India in promoting the development of our art and culture.

You are also aware that the Government of India are contemplating the establishment of a National Museum where the finest exhibits of Indian art will be collected and preserved for the nation. The entire collection of Amrita Sher Gil's paintings has been purchased, and, in addition, the Government have acquired valuable exhibits from several well-known private collections in the country. As part of this programme, it is proposed to attempt to secure such of our heritage as has gone out of the country and may be available on reasonable terms. You are, no doubt, aware that some of the finest specimens of our art, sculpture and miniature, went out of the country long ago. Some of these are in national museums in foreign countries and it may be difficult, if not impossible, to bring them back. There are, however, other objects in the possession of private collectors or museums which come into the market from time to time and may be regained. I think you will agree that we should try to get back such objects wherever possible, and where the originals cannot be secured we should, at any rate, obtain copies made by competent artists, so that our representation of Indian art may not remain incomplete.

Before, however, any steps in this direction can be taken it is necessary to have full knowledge about the number of such objects and their distribution. We have some knowledge of exhibits in public museums and galleries. There are records also of some of the private collections, but there are many objects of art of which we have no information at all. I have already written to all our representatives abroad to inform us as early as possible about the number, description and location of art objects scattered within their respective areas. I, however, feel that non-official advice from experts is essential for the purpose, and I would ask you to consider whether this Conference may set up a small committee to make an inventory of such art objects as are at present abroad and advise the Government on the best possible methods to secure either the originals or their copies.

Another important question which requires the attention of this Conference is that of the relation of art to education in general. It is a sad commentary on our present system of education that art has either no place or plays a very minor role in our general education. One reason for this is, of course, the very one-sided view of education we have had in the past. Till now our education has aimed at developing only the intellect of the child. Even this is perhaps an over-generous estimate.

The present system of education has not always been conducive to the development of the whole intellect, but only encouraged the growth of linguistic efficiency among our pupils. This is one reason why there are so many people who display all the external signs of high education and at the same time exhibit in their attitudes, beliefs and conduct a totally uneducated mind.

It is today realised that no education can be complete which does not pay proper attention to the development and refinement of the emotions. This can be done best through the provision of facilities for training the sensibilities by the practice of one of the fine arts. Apart from the general question of developing the finest aspects of personality through artistic education, there is also the immediate utility of such education in developing our manual skill and perceptive sensibility. It is recognised today that education at pre-primary or nursery stage can be best imparted by training the child in the matching of colours, shapes and sizes. This releases the creative instinct in the child and thus diverts his superfluous energy from merely destructive channels into those of social behaviour and decorum. Thus, whether from the point of view of training of the emotions or refinement of sentiments or development of manual skill and creative urge, the importance of art as an element of education cannot be over-emphasised.

The obvious implication of this is that a society is healthy and well-balanced if training in and appreciation of arts are widespread among its members. The modern malaise of society in which individuals are torn and divided and society riven with a hundred conflicts is the result of the fact that the arts have been divorced from intimate contact with life at a thousand points. I may recall to your minds that there was no distinction recognised between art and craft in the past. In the olden days, the craftsmen who produced objects for the use of society were also simultaneously artists. On the other hand, artists took pride in the excellence of their craft and never hesitated to take their full share in social production. One of the unfortunate results of the Industrial Revolution and the development of the capitalist system of production has been the divorce between art and craft. The result is that the artists tend to look down upon the craftsmen as mere artisans. The labourers who produce goods for consumption are, on the other hand, equally suspicious of the social and seemingly useless activities of the artists. In the sequel, both art and craft have suffered, so that art is today divorced from our immediate requirements while craft has degenerated into a mechanical manipulation from which all joy of creation has disappeared.

It is for the artists to attempt to bridge this gulf. You may remember the efforts of William Morris to overcome this breach by ensuring that even commercial products must have the highest artistic qualities. This would immediately result in an improvement of taste throughout society and thus enrich the life of the common man. It would, on the other hand, be of equal service to the artist himself. He could in such a context depend upon the support of society as a whole instead of a handful of rich patrons here and there. Much of the insecurity and poverty from which the artist suffers today is due to lack of social support. The moment he re-establishes contacts with society, the causes of insecurity disappear and the results would be of advantage to art and craft and to society at large.

In a growing democracy the need of this closer relation between the artist and the average man has become even more important. It is the standard of the common man which determines the standard of society. If therefore the life of the common man is poor and devoid of artistic qualities, there is no possibility of a rich and flourishing art. Artists must therefore play their full part in the education of the people, and it is for this Conference to suggest to the Government how best this could be achieved through museums, art galleries, travelling exhibitions and any other methods that may be necessary.

This Conference may also appoint a small committee of experts who may advise the Government on the selection of some of the finest specimens of Indian art which would then be reproduced and made available to the people at large. It is obvious that the finest masterpieces will never be accessible to all individuals. Even if they are collected in the museums, only those who live in the cities where these museums are situated or those who have the means of travelling there, will enjoy such masterpieces. If, however, these masterpieces are made available in suitable copies at prices within the reach of everybody, one of the greatest obstacles to a general spread of art appreciation throughout the community will be removed.

I will conclude by drawing your attention to one other point. In the past, great artists enjoyed patronage of kings, courtiers and other men of affluence. In the modern world where democracy is the order of the day, the artist must look to the State for patronage. In the present stage of development of art appreciation among the people, this, however, involves a danger that the most original and talented artists may not receive that recognition which is their due. Excellence in art, as elsewhere, can be properly appreciated only by those who have in them the same excellence. However much we may desire that the standard of excellence must be high throughout the community, we must confess that this is not yet the case. In order therefore to ensure that the most powerful and original genuises among the artists get their proper recognition, I would suggest for your consideration the establishment of an Academy of Art more or less on the lines of the world famous French Academy.

You will remember that the French Academy has only a handful of members and academicians. Its membership is the highest honour that can fall to the lot of a Frenchman. Many are the scholars, artists or scientists who have worked for this honour throughout their life and have not been admitted to the distinguished company of the academicians. Such exclusiveness has given to the membership of the French Academy a distinction which has few equals anywhere else in the world. I would therefore be happy if in India we could establish an Academy of Arts, with a membership of not more than 30, confined only to people who by their creative work have established their position beyond dispute. It is not necessary that the Academy now, I cannot see how more than a dozen members can be elected straightaway. Whatever be the number of academicians so elected, they alone should have the right to elect their fellow members and once the full quota is complete, no one would be admitted to the Academy till a vacancy had occurred through death or resignation. If standards are once laid down, I have no doubt that membership of the Academy will serve as an incentive to the highest endeavours in the field of Art.

These are some of the problems which this Conference must consider. I hope we will be able to arrive at judicious and balanced decisions, so that the cause of art in independent India may flourish and we may recapture and enhance the glories of the Gupta and the Moghul periods.

Document No. 42

MAULANA'S INAUGURAL SPEECH DATED 2-11-1949 AT THE UNESCO SEMINAR ON RURAL ADULT EDUCATION, HELD IN MYSORE

On behalf of the Government and the people of India, I extend a most cordial welcome to all of you. We appreciate the spirit in which you have accepted our invitation, for in spite of the difficulties imposed by distance and by pre-occupations in your own countries you have responded to our call. I also wish to place on record my thanks to Unesco for having acceded to our request to hold its first Asian Seminar in our country and extending to us assistance and co-operation in all possible ways.

You have met here today to discuss what is perhaps the most important and vital problem for all Asia. The welfare, progress and prosperity of any State depend upon the quality of its citizens, and this in turn depends upon the education which moulds their character and shapes their thoughts. Important as a sound system of education is for all countries, it is still more important for the countries of Asia. Here we are witnessing a new awakening after centuries of slumber and quiescence. The past glorious traditions of the Asian countries demand that this new awakening must bring to the world a new message even as our ancient civilisations sent forth to the farthest corners of the globe, for Asia gave to the world its religions, philosophies, cultures and civilisations.

The challenge of our ancient traditions and the spiritual poverty of our immediate past both require from the peoples of Asia an exceedingly great effort for the reconstruction of their lives in all spheres. This involves a basic reconstruction of our modes of education, for without such education we cannot fulfil our hopes. Ours is essentially a democratic age and the spirit of equality, fraternity and liberty is sweeping over all the peoples of the world. The Asian countries must reconstruct their polity and their society in conformity with this spirit.

It is universally recognised today that education of the future citizens is one of the prime duties of the State. On such education depends our prosperity and welfare. Of even greater urgency is the problem of educating the adult population. They determine the present which in its turn will shape our future destiny. Education of the future generations can only be planned if the present generation recognises the importance of such education. Material prosperity or spiritual welfare cannot be achieved unless the citizen of today accepts the challenge of these values. An educated electorate is, thus, essential for the survival and proper functioning of modern democracy.

When we contrast the demands which democracy makes upon citizens of a State with the actual condition of education in the different countries of Asia, the picture is one of grave and anxious concern. It is true that in some exceptional cases the problem has been largely mastered. We have Japan which according to figures available for 1946 has a literacy figure of 99 per cent and illiteracy of only 1 per cent. Lebanon in the Middle East is also reputed to have a high literacy figure. In 1945-46, literacy in Turkey was 60 per cent in the towns and 40 per cent in the villages. The Philippines with its figure of 52.6 per cent is also comparatively well-placed. The same remarks would apply to Ceylon, Thailand, Burma and China. We cannot, however, gauge the magnitude of the problem by percentages alone. China has a literacy figure of over 50 per cent. If we take the total population of China to be 450 millions, this would give an adult population of about 225 millions. It is unlikely that the percentage of literacy will be the same for adults as for children and adolescents. Even if this questionable assumption is granted, the number of adult illiterates in China would be some 125 millions.

If we take the figures for India, we find that in pre-partition India the total number of literates, according to the 1941 Census, was 37 millions. Assuming that the number of adult literates is about 40 per cent of the total number of literates, this gives a figure of a little over 15 millions. This refers only to the prepartition Indian provinces. Partition meant a loss of about 26 per cent of the total population and assuming that the reduction in the number of literates was in the same proportion and allowing for fluctuations owing to normal process of birth and death, we may put the figure for adult literates in the Indian provinces after partition at roughly 11 millions. To this we have to add the number of adult literates in the states. This is estimated to be about 6 millions. The number of adult literates in India on the basis of 1941 Census is therefore approximately 17 millions against a total adult population of about 180 millions, which gives a literacy percentage of slightly less than 10 for adults. This is not only unsatisfactory but positively disturbing. Naturally, the Government of India propose to give the first priority to a programme of social education in its schemes of educational development for the country.

You have met here today to devise ways and means for solving this colossal problem. As I have already said, this is the problem of problems for Asia. I would go further and say that this is the problem of problems for all countries of the world. Scientific progress and technical achievement have today unified the world into one community without creating the psychological conditions in which men and women all over the world can live in peace and amity. The conquests of science have led to a situation where disaster threatens mankind unless we can conquer hatred, suspicion and distrust among peoples. I have no doubt in my mind that all governments of the world desire peace and yet it is a strange paradox that all of them adopt measures whose inevitable consequence is a world conflagration. How is one to explain this seeming contradiction between the intentions of intelligent people and the course of action followed by them?

I have pondered deeply over this question and to me it seems that the reason for the paradox is to be sought in the mechanism of the State, which proves at times too powerful for even the most gifted individual. Governments are composed of men who follow certain forms and traditions. Even though the men are often well-intentioned, they inherit a legacy of governmental procedure and commitments which ties their hands. The inertia of the machine proves stronger than the energy of the individual. We find in consequence that while most political leaders talk in terms of peace, their actions are guided by considerations of defending and safeguarding vested interests. If mankind is to overcome this impasse and achieve conditions where peace and tranquility can become a reality between individuals and nations, the common people of the world must assert themselves. They have made no commitments and are not tied down by any governmental procedure. If they take an intelligent interest in the affairs of the world and demand that the governance of man must be in the interest of peace, then and then alone can the different governments of the world be compelled to pursue policies which will lead to peace instead of war.

This is where the need for adult education – in our country we have termed it Social Education – becomes imperative. By social education we mean an education for the complete man. It will give him literacy so that the knowledge of the world may become accessible to him. It will teach him how to harmonise himself with his environment and make the best of the physical conditions in which he subsists. It is intended to teach him improved crafts and modes of production so that he can achieve economic betterment. It also aims at teaching him the rudiments of hygiene both for the individual and the community so that our domestic life may be healthy and prosperous. The last but not the least, this education should give him training in citizenship so that he obtains some insight into the affairs of the world and can help his Government to take decisions which will make for peace and progress.

You will, no doubt, examine all the implications of such a programme of social education for the masses, but there are several outstanding issues which readily come to my mind. The first is the problem of arousing and maintaining the interest of the adult illiterate. It is obvious that his psychology is different from that of the child. He may be illiterate but his mind is mature. The approach which may be suitable for children would, in many cases, repulse him. His books must therefore avoid childish subjects and yet at the same time deal with problems affecting him in a language simple enough for him. The effort of learning the script must also be lessened so that his interest does not flag. I am sure that the Seminar will examine various methods of making him literate and suggest the use of suitable modern devices – psychological or visual – to overcome the inertia of age and the innate pride of the adult.

Our programme of social education must, however, be more than a mere literacy drive. This is a point which I need not labour. What I would like the Seminar to examine is the best method of teaching the adult illiterate subjects which are of vital interest to him. We must largely depend on oral teaching, but oral instruction has certain limitations. The experts assembled in this Seminar will, I hope, indicate to the participating countries the emphasis to be given to oral instruction, the use of books, demonstrations, the use of visual aids, lectures of exhibitions in teaching different subjects like hygiene, elementary arithmetic, elements of citizenship, or simple problems of business and commerce.

Another peculiar problem which faces all Asian Countries and therefore also India is the problem of finding the requisite number of teachers for a programme of social education. It is, I believe, generally agreed that adults require greater personal care and attention than children. The ratio of teacher to taught must therefore be higher in their case than with minors. We require in India about a million teachers to deal with children of school age who constitute only about 12 ½ per cent. of the total population. For adult illiterate who will constitute almost 50 per cent. of the population, we would, even on the same basis, require about 4 million teachers. If, in addition to this, we make allowance for the higher ratio necessary in their case, the number of teachers required may amount to almost 5 millions. Against this, we can, of course, balance the factor that the adult education courses will be of short duration and perhaps last for about 3 months at a time for giving them the first stage of literacy. Even then, the number of teachers to be continually employed on the adult education drive will be over a million.

To find the million teachers for school children is difficult enough; but if in addition we have to find another million for our programmes of adult education, the problem becomes almost insuperable. We are considering in India the possibility of utilising the basic school teacher for our programme of social education. We are also examining a proposal to use some kind of social conscription by which all educated persons will be required to contribute to this national service for a specified period. If all students after matriculation are compelled to teach for even six months, it would, of course, go some way towards helping the solution, but even then the gap to be overcome would be considerable.

There is also the question how far the basic school teachers or young collegians will prove suitable for such a programme of National Education. The teaching of small children requires in the teacher certain habits and attitudes which he may not be able to shed when addressing adults. Similarly, it is a problem whether young men and women just out of school will have the necessary patience and insight to be successful teachers of adults. I would therefore urge you to examine the different aspects of this intricate question and make recommendations that may be of use to us and other Asian countries.

There are numerous other problems, but I will mention only one more. It has been our unfortunate experience – and I have no doubt other countries must have faced the same situation – that many people who have learnt to read and write in schools lapse into illiteracy. If this were not so, all children who had once been to school would have remained literate. The percentage of literacy in all countries would then have been appreciably greater. The distinguished educationists assembled in this Seminar must advise us how best to prevent this relapse into illiteracy. There is the problem of suitable literature for new literates, of continuation classes, of extension lectures, of visual aids and exhibitions, films and picutres and other devices which may be used. All of them, however, involve money and it is common experience that there is not enough money for the purpose. I hope therefore that the Seminar will suggest priorities in the use of such aids and also draw up a scheme which will enable the best possible utilisation of our limited resources.

I am glad to find that you have chosen for the Seminar subjects for study which cover almost all these aspects. I have no doubt that the distinguished assemblage of educators and experts from all over the world will make valuable contributions in dealing with all these problems. As far as I can see, there is no difference in our ideals. The difficulty arises in defining the methods through which those ideals are to be attained. I am confident that the deliberations of the Seminar will yield fruitful results and suggest to the different Asian and non-Asian States how best to achieve the ideals we have set before ourselves.

It is not my purpose today to offer any opinion as to what recommendations this Seminar should make to Unesco and its member states in order to fulfil the objectives which Unesco has set before itself. Unesco has rightly pointed out that all conflicts begin in the mind of man and therefore the root of conflict must be weeded out of his mind. I have no doubt that the Seminar will make recommendations to this effect and I am as anxious as all of you that our joint deliberations will enable us to suggest concrete measures for the attainment of these ends.

I would, before I conclude, like to draw the attention of the distinguished participants in the Seminar to the lesson of Indian history. India had been at her best when her doors were wide open to all who came from abroad. She freely partook of whatever lessons the world had to teach and equally freely gave the world her best. The acceptance of unity in diversity has been her motto throughout the ages. The essence of this principle is a large and wide-hearted toleration in which differences are recognised and given their due. The Indian genius has always recognised that truth has many facets, and conflict and hatred arise because people claim a monopoly of truth and virtue.

This was the lesson of India in the days of her glory. This is the lesson which Mahatma Gandhi has taught anew in the context of the modern age. His message to the Indian people was one of toleration, goodwill and love for all. Hatred, he said, is born of weakness and fear and he therefore exhorted his countrymen to shed fear. He believed in a new education which would reshape the character of man. Its aim is to eradicate the impulse to exploitation, violence and ill-will from the individual and the society. He not only preached the need for love and toleration for all but laid down his life to vindicate these eternal values. If we can instil in our private and public conduct his spirit of tolerance and large-hearted humanity so that divergences can exist side by side without conflict, we will have solved one of the most difficult problems of the modern world.

I have to meet you again on the 4th of December. You will, in the meantime, have examined many of these problems and framed tentative recommendations. I expect to keep in touch with your work and hope that on that occasion I will have some concrete suggestions to make for the implementation of your findings. I am convinced that this Seminar, jointly planned by Unesco and the Government of India and built up through the co-operation of nations from all over the world, will attain its objectives and mark an important mile-stone in the history of the development of adult education throughout the world.

II*

It is just over a month ago that we had assembled to participate in the inauguration of this Unesco Seminar on Rural Adult Education. We had then met with high hopes and intentions and I am glad that though only a month has passed we can now look back with satisfaction on the work accomplished. I must sincerely congratulate the Director, the Consultants, the Chairmen of the Groups, the delegates and other participants of the Seminar for the energy and competence with which they have carried out their important task. I have every hope that all the

---

* Address at the closing session of the Unesco Seminar on Rural Adult Education, Mysore, December 4, 1949.

countries participating in this Seminar will benefit by the recommendations you have made and carry out your constructive suggestions for solving one of the most pressing problems of the world. I can assure you that so far as India is concerned, we shall examine every one of your recommendations with care and sympathy in order to give effect to them as far and as soon as may be possible.

I cannot naturally go into any details regarding your various recommendations. They are the result of hard work and careful thought and deserve close attention before any judgment is passed on them. I must, however, express my sense of satisfaction for the way in which you have set down to work and divided the different aspects of a colossal problem for study by special groups. The provision of literacy may not by itself be enough for the education of adults, but there is no denying that it is the basis of all real education.

The first Study Group which dealt with different methods of teaching reading to adults has made suggestions which will be of value to all countries. The second Group dealing with specific problems of health and family life has discussed questions which are vital for any scheme of social welfare. No community can flourish until and unless the individuals constituting it are happy and no individual can be happy without health and a satisfactory home life. Women have a special role to play in this and I am glad to hear that your Group has not overlooked the imperative necessity of securing to women and adequate knowledge of home-craft and health. The third Group dealing with the economic aspects of rural adult education has attacked what is perhaps the most immediate concern to all rural adult educators. Unless the economic conditions of the villagers can be immediately improved, there is little hope of attracting and still less of retaining adults in any literacy course. Your suggestions about methods of extension work and securing the help of Unesco in the preparation of posters and other illustrated material will, I have no doubt, receive the consideration of every participating country. The fourth Group deals with the intangible but real problem of citizenship and the role of the rural community in society and the State. The valuable sociological data secured from different countries are in themselves a material gain, but still more fruitful results may follow from the suggestion of setting up working camps in the rural areas to provide scope for co-operative activities in various fields.

I must not, however, anticipate the action which different Governments may take on your various recommendations. So far as India is concerned, I can say that I am greatly impressed by a suggestion made for the setting up of some centralised agency to guard against the possible dissipation of energy, enthusiasm and competence through unnecessary duplication of efforts. I have felt that some such agency is necessary to advise the states and the provinces of the Indian Union, not only on the general principles of education, but also on the co-ordination of steps, procedure and methods in order to achieve the best results at the minimum cost.

Another topic discussed in the Seminar which has appealed to me and which I propose to pursue in our country is the setting up of some machinery to carry out a vocabulary study of the different Indian languages with a view to finding out what words are most commonly used in different parts of the country. I may tell you that even though there are 13 main languages recognised in our Constitution, these languages cannot by any means be regarded as completely alien to one another. They have large common vocabularies and if allowance is made for the mutations due to the factors of space, time and pronunciation, the number of common words will be larger still. I have for some time had in mind a plan for the collection of common Hindi words which are found in all the other Indian languages. I am convinced that when this work has been accomplished, the non-Hindi speaking people of India will find that they already possess a large vocabulary of Hindi words, and with the addition of a few more common Hindi words they can acquire without difficulty a working knowledge of Hindi. I feel that the textbooks in Hindi for the non-Hindi speaking people should be prepared on the basis of such graded vocabularies. The Government will take the necessary steps in this respect, but I must pay my tribute to the many non-official agencies which have been carrying out valuable work on these lines for many years.

People all over the world are beginning to recognise that one of the surest ways of securing international peace is fundamental education for the peoples of the world on the lines envisaged by Unesco. Unesco has already begun this programme, but much more remains to be done and I hope that its service will be available to all the member and even non-member States by the provision of charts, visual aids, posters and other illustrated material to impart social education in the fullest sense of the term. The language of pictures is universal and can overcome the barriers created by differences of verbal languages. Linguists can therefore help to prepare posters on questions of health, hygiene, home and simple arts and crafts which can serve the interests of the people all over the world. Equally valuable to me is the suggestion to follow up this Asian Seminar by regional seminars in the different parts of the country. I recognise the value of studies carried out in such seminars where comparative detachment from political and administrative stress and the preoccupations of day-to-day routine will enable educators to study problems in their proper perspective. So far as India is concerned, we shall take advantage not only of the experiences gained in this Seminar but also utilise these experiences for the organisation of further seminaras for the different linguistic areas.

Before I conclude, I must once again thank the Director of the Seminar, the consultants, the delegates and other participants, for the devotion and energy with which they have worked. I must make special mention of Dr. S.Y. Chu who came and joined us in spite of the political vicissitudes of his country. He could not stay till the end, but the very fact that he came is evidence of his devotion to the cause of education and Unesco.

I hope your stay in our country has been pleasant and has led to the formation of friendship and contacts that may be of mutual value. I must also thank the Mysore Government for the generosity and efficiency with which they have helped us in making this, the first Unesco Seminar on Asian soil, such a success.

Document No. 43

REPLIES OF MAULANA ABUL KALAM AZAD DATED 21-2-1949 IN THE CONSTITUENT ASSEMBLY OF INDIA (LEGISLATIVE), TO THE QUESTIONS RAISED BY MR. HARI VISHNU KAMATH, SETH GOVIND DAS AND OTHERS IN CONNECTION WITH THE EXCHANGE OF STUDENTS WITH RUSSIA

Shri H.V. Kamath : Will the Honourable Minister of Education be pleased to state:

(a) whether the attention of Government has been drawn to a report appearing in the *Hindu*, dated the 13th October, 1948 (on page 8, column 5 thereof) under the caption "Exchange of students with Russia";

(b) whether the report is correct; and

(c) if so, the reasons for the recommendation of the Home Ministry, as a consequence of which the scheme for exchange of students between India and Russia had to be abandoned?

The Honourable Maulana Abul Kalam Azad: (a) Yes.

(b) and (c) The report which appeared is not fully correct. What actually happened was that some Indian students wanted to know whether the necessary facilities would be available to them if they proceeded to Russia for further studies. Government made enquiries into the matter and it was learnt that for the present it could not be said definitely whether the rquired facilities would be available. The students concerned were informed accordingly.

Shri H.V. Kamath : Has any such 'Exchange Scheme' been agreed upon with any other country?

The Honourable Maulana Abul Kalam Azad : Yes, we are in touch with certain countries where educational facilities are available.

Shri H.V. Kamath : With how many countries has this scheme been agreed upon?

The Honourable Maulana Abul Kalam Azad : I cannot reply this offhand. I would like to have notice for this.

Shri M. Ananthasayanam Ayyangar : Is it not a fact that even without any particular course of studies in any of these subjects, students who are sent there to study various subjects, leave those subjects and study only communistic principles even there?

The Honourable Maulana Abul Kalam Azad : The honourable member can form an opinion in this connection according to the enquiries made by him.

Shri Mahavir Tyagi : May I know that when the students were informed by the Government that the requisite training facilities could not be made available there, what were the difficulties that stood in the Government's way?

The Honourable Maulana Abul Kalam Azad : The main difficulty is in respect of language. The medium of instruction in vogue in all the Russian Universities is the Russian language from the lowest to the highest standard. Our students who could go there, knew English only. Apart from this, there is a great difficulty of living there; and there are many other difficulties.

Seth Govind Das : May I know the names of the countries with whom the Government are in touch at present with regard to the exchange of students?

The Honourable Maulana Abul Kalam Azad : The Russian Government have not been addressed on this subject.

Seth Govind Das : What I wanted to know is which of the countries have been addressed on this subject?

The Honourable Maulana Abul Kalam Azad: So far as I am aware of, no such talks are in progress with any particular country. Our Board will sit and decide this matter as regards the various subjects and the particular countries to which the students should be sent for receiving training therein. It is then only that this could be decided.

Shri Brajeshwar Prasad : Was the Russian Government approached through the Russian Ambassador in India to provide facilities for those applicants?

The Honourable Maulana Abul Kalam Azad : I cannot answer this at the moment.

Seth Govind Das : Are Government also considering this that the students should be sent abroad for training in those subjects only for which facilities are not available in India?

The Honourable Maulana Abul Kalam Azad : Yes. This is the policy of the Government.

Shri H.V. Kamath : May I know who initiated this exchange of students with Russia, whether India or Russia?

The Honourable Maulana Abul Kalam Azad : Just as I have informed you, the question with regard to exchange had not arisen. The only thing that came up before us was that an enquiry should be made for the sake of those students who wanted to go there.

Mr. Tajamul Husain : The Honourable Minister has just now stated that there are many difficulties there. Is it also not one of the difficulties existing there that food is scarcely available; milk is altogether out of question and even eggs are not available, and these difficulties are particularly experienced by the Indian students?

Shri Mahavir Tyagi : Is it not so that the Russian Government would not have desired to send their students to this country; and we might have either refused or put difficulties in their way?

The Honourable Maulana Abul Kalam Azad : No; there is nothing like this.

Shri Mahavir Tyagi : Are any of the Russian students studying here at present?

The Honourable Maulana Abul Kalam Azad : So far as I am aware of there is none.

Shri H.V. Kamath: Is English not at all taught in the Russian Universities?

The Honourable Maulana Abul Kalam Azad : So far as I am aware of English is not the medium of instruction in any of the Institute there?

Shri S.V. Krishnamoorthy Rao : Are there any arrangements in any of the Indian Universities to teach Russian to those students who wish to go to Russia? If not, such arrangements should be made.

The Honourable Maulana Abul Kalam Azad : Yes, efforts have been made to teach foreign languages. So far as the Russian language is concerned, I understand that the Delhi University is trying to arrange for it.

Document No. 44

MAULANA ABUL KALAM AZAD'S REPLY DATED 2-12-1949 TO THE QUESTIONS RAISED BY R.K. SIDHVA AND OTHERS IN THE C.A.I. (L) IN CONNECTION WITH THE OVERSEAS SCHOLARSHIPS

Shri R.K. Sidhva: (a) Will the Honourable Minister of Education be pleased to state the number of scholars sent overseas and the names of places they were sent overseas and the names of places they were went to, during the current year?

(b) How many are for technical and practical training and what stipends have been offered to them?

(c) Are these scholars given training in such industries which are likely to grow in India in near future?

(d) Has the new scheme for sending scholars to foreign countries for study which was announced by Government during the last session materialised? If so, what are the details thereof?

The Honourable Maulana Abul Kalam Azad: (a) Forty-four scholars out of whom thirty-five have been sent to the U.S.A., eight to the U.K. and one to Switzerland.

(b) The overseas scholarships scheme is essentially an educational one but technical and practical forms an integral part of it and is imparted where necessary. The majority of the students have courses of technical and practical training included in their programme of study.

The rate of stipend for U.K. and Switzerland is £ 400 per annum for all institutions except Oxford and Cambridge where the rate is £ 460 per annum. For the U.S.A. the rate is $ 1,920 per annum. These figures exclude the actual tuition fees which are paid direct to the institutions concerned.

(c) These scholars were selected and sent abroad against the specific needs of the various Ministries of the Government of India, the Provincial Governments and the Indian States Governments, and not particularly with a view to manning Indian Industries, although some of them are actually receiving training in subjects useful for industrial development.

(d) All preliminaries of the New scheme had been settled and the selection of the candidates was about to commence, but due to financial difficulties the work had to be stopped.

Shri R.K. Sidhva : May I know from the Honourable Minister how many of the scholars completed their Course?

The Honourable Maulana Abul Kalam Azad : I cannot say without making necessary equiries.

Sardar Bhopinder Singh Man : Have those scholars who were sent abroad been fixed up against suitable posts on their return or not?

The Honourable Maulana Abul Kalam Azad : A large number have been provided with jobs.

Sardar Bhopinder Singh Man : What was the number of scheduled-caste scholars out of this?

The Honourable Maulana Abul Kalam Azad : I require notice for this.

Shri Jainarain Vyas : Will the Honourable Minister please state whether the number referred to in part (b) also includes the scholars sponsored by the States and States Union?

The Honourable Maulana Abul Kalam Azad : Yes. The scholars from the Indian States may have been included in this figure.

Shri Jainarain Vyas : Does this figure include the scholars whose expenses are borne by the States or not?

The Honourable Maulana Abul Kalam Azad: The scholars from Indian States were also included in the Overseas Scholarships Scheme.

Seth Govind Das: Will the Honourable Minister please say whether this has been kept in view that scholars should be sent abroad for training in those subjects only for which no arrangements exist in India?

The Honourable Maulana Abul Kalam Azad: The Honourable Member is very well aware that the old Overseas Scholarships Scheme was introduced by the previous Government. It contained many obvious defects which the present Government felt and it was for this reason that this scheme had to be abandoned. One of the defects was that even in respect of those subjects in which training could be easily arranged in India, scholars were sent abroad. But the number which I have stated in my reply does not include any scholar who has been sent for receiving training in any subject arrangements for which are at present available in India.

Shri Ajit Prasad Jain: What is the method of selecting these students? Are they selected on the recommendations of the University or the Government make the final selection on their own responsibility?

The Honourable Maulana Abul Kalam Azad: The scholars are selected through the selection boards.

Shri Deshbandhu Gupta: Is any record maintained of the scholars who have gone to receive training in technical and other subjects in foreign Countries? Have Government decided to give them any facilities in view of their increased expenses as a result of devaluation?

The Honourable Maulana Abul Kalam Azad: The question of giving facilities because of devaluation does not arise. The question that arises is one of saving.

Shri Deshbandhu Gupta: I am referring to those students who would be faced with difficulties on account of the dollar.

The Honourable Maulana Abul Kalam Azad: No such difficulty has as yet been brought to the notice of the Ministry. If and when it is brought to the notice, it will be considered.

Shri Deshbandhu Gupta: May I know from the Honourable Minister whether or not scholars will be sent abroad for receiving education under the new scheme that has been started after the old scheme has ceased to operate?

The Honourable Maulana Abul Kalam Azad: The new scheme was being acted upon, but it had to be stopped because the question of economy cropped anew. The result is that so far the selection of candidates has not started.

Seth Govind Das: While framing the new scheme, will this be kept in view that scholars are sent for training in those subjects only for which arrangements do not exist in India?

The Honourable Maulana Abul Kalam Azad: Certainly. This thing has been kept in view under the new scheme.

Mr. Tajamul Husain: May I know whether there are such scholars who were given stipends and on their return went away to Pakistan?

The Honourable Maulana Abul Kalam Azad: No such case has come within the knowledge of the Government.

Shri S.V. Krishnamoorthy Rao: How many scholars who had gone abroad and returned to India still remain to be absorbed by the Government or industries in the profession?

The Honourable Maulana Abul Kalam Azad: Just as I have already stated, a very large number have been employed. I cannot tell the number of those for whom arrangement has not yet been made.

Ch. Ranbir Singh: Is the Honourable Minister aware of the fact that scholars were also sent abroad for receiving training in agriculture, and now on their return they have not been provided with any jobs?

The Honourable Maulana Abul Kalam Azad: A large number have been provided with employment. There still remain some such men for whom efforts are being made.

Document No. 45

MAULANA AZAD'S REPLIES TO QUESTIONS ASKED IN THE CONSTITUENT ASSEMBLY OF INDIA (LEGISLATIVE) ON 7-12-1949 REGARDING THE LOCAL ADVISERS FOR INDIAN STUDENTS IN U.K. AND U.S.A.

Shri R.K. Sidhva: (a) Will the Honourable Minister of Education be pleased to state whether Government have appointed local advisers for Indian students in the U.K. and U.S.A.?

(b) If so, what will be their functions?

(c) What are the names of these advisers?

(d) What will be the expenditure involved in these appointments?

The Honourable Maulana Abul Kalam Azad : (a) Government has not appointed any advisers for Indian students in the U.K. and U.S.A. Government has appointed Educational Officers in both countries for educational and cultural work.

(b) to (d) Do not arise.

Shri R.K. Sidhva : May I know what are the functions of those who have been engaged for cultural work?

The Honourable Maulana Abul Kalam Azad : There are educational works of various nature. We have to find out in which of the Universities seats can be available and in which not. And so are other cultural and educational works.

Sjt. Kuladhar Chaliha : May I know whether it is the duty of these advisers to find out the dollar requirements of the students?

The Honourable Maulana Abul Kalam Azad : This is not the special duty assigned to them. But the requirements of the students, of whatever nature, if brought to their notice, are surely looked after.

Shri Deshbandhu Gupta : Do they ever come into contact with the students?

The Honourable Maulana Abul Kalam Azad : Whenever necessity arises, they do meet them.

Shri R.K. Sidhva : Are they whole-time officers?

The Honourable Maulana Abul Kalam Azad : Yes, Sir.

Shri Deshbandhu Gupta : Is there any officer amongst them who received his education in any of the Universities in the U.S.A. and is conversant with the conditions prevailing there or possesses experience in the affairs of that country?

The Honourable Maulana Abul Kalam Azad : Government have not considered it necessary to prescribe this qualification for them.

Sardar Bhopinder Singh Man : What is the expenditure involved on the employment of these officers?

The Honourable Maulana Abul Kalam Azad : I cannot give this information at the moment.

Document No. 46

REPLIES OF MAULANA AZAD DATED 7-12-1949 TO THE QUESTIONS ASKED BY MR. S.C. SAMANTA AND OTHERS IN THE CONSTITUENT ASSEMBLY OF INDIA (LEGISLATIVE) IN CONNECTION WITH THE SCHOLARSHIP FOR TRAINING ABROAD

Shri Satish Chandra Samanta : (a) Will the Honourable Minister of Education be pleased to state the number of students sent abroad to have training in Agriculture and allied subjects in the years 1948 and 1949?

(b) How many of them received scholarships and help from (i) the Government of India and (ii) other Governments?

The Honourable Maulana Abul Kalam Azad : (a) Twenty-nine students, comprising sixteen during 1948 and thirteen during 1949.

(b) (i) Nine of these received scholarships from the Government of India, and (ii) four were sponsored by the Provincial Governments and sixteen by the Indian States Governments.

The expenditure on the Provincial sponsored students was borne by the Provincial Governments except in the case of one where it was shared by the Government of India with the Provincial Government in the ratio of 50:50.

The expenditure in respect of the States sponsored students was borne entirely by the States concerned.

In addition to the above twenty-nine scholars two private students who went on their own responsibility were given financial assistance in the form of a loan from the Government of India.

Mr. Tajamul Husain : May I know whether Government have got any such scheme under which the total amount, that has been spent over the education of those scholars who have since returned after receiving their training abroad and have been provided with jobs, could be recovered from their salaries on some percentage basis till such time the entire amount is repaid. If not, why not?

The Honourable Maulana Abul Kalam Azad: No. No such condition had been laid down in the scheme.

Shri O.V. Alagesan: At least the Honourable Minister might give the figures in English so that we may be able to follow him.

Shrimati G. Durgabai: May I know whether, besides arranging for their training, Government also take upon themselves the responsibility to provide them with jobs?

The Honourable Maulana Abul Kalam Azad: Government do their best to provide them with employment and a large number have been employed.

Seth Govind Das: Are these scholars sent abroad for receiving education in those subjects for the teaching of which no arrangments exist in India? I would like to know what are those subjects in which training cannot be imparted here and for which they are sent abroad?

The Honourable Maulana Abul Kalam Azad: The Honourable Member is aware that they were sent under the old scheme. The present Government are not responsible for any of the defects that existed in the old scheme.

Shri H.J. Khandekar: May I know what is the number of those scholars who have since returned to India after receiving education in Agriculture and have not as yet been provided with Government jobs?

The Honourable Maulana Abul Kalam Azad: I cannot say this at the moment. I would like to have a notice of it.

Shri H.J. Khandekar: Are Government aware that the two Harijan scholars from C.P. who were sent for receiving education in Agriculture have not as yet been provided with any employment?

The Honourable Maulana Abul Kalam Azad: I cannot say anything unless details are made available.

Shri O.V. Alagesan: How many of these students belong to the scheduled castes?

The Honourable Maulana Abul Kalam Azad: I cannot say this just now.

Shri Mahavir Tyagi: Have all these persons been given training for the sake of employment?

The Honourable Maulana Abul Kalam Azad: It is not necessarily so.

Ch. Ranbir Singh: Is the Honourable Minister aware of the fact that all those posts for which these persons were sent to receive training have already been filled up six months ago?

The Honourable Maulana Abul Kalam Azad: No such case has come to the notice of Government.

Sjt. Rohini Kumar Chaudhuri: Is any undertaking taken from the scholars, who are sent overseas for training in technical subjects, to the effect that they will serve the Government after return.

The Honourable Maulana Abul Kalam Azad: This condition has been prescribed. But along with this, provision has been made that in case they are not provided with service within a period of three months, they would be permitted to undertake any private employment that they might secure.

Document No. 47

MAULANA AZAD'S REPLIES TO THE QUESTIONS ASKED BY DR. M.M. DAS AND OTHERS IN THE CONSTITUENT ASSEMBLY (LEGISLATIVE) ON 7-12-1949 IN CONNECTION WITH THE WARDHA SCHEME

Dr. Mono Mohon Das : (a) Will the Honourable Minister of Education be pleased to state whether Government have taken into consideration the 'Wardha Scheme of Education' of Mahatma Gandhi?

(b) If so, what steps have been taken by Government in this connection?

The Honourable Maulana Abul Kalam Azad : (a) and (b). The Honourable Member's attention is invited to the replies already given to the starred question No. 454 by Shri V.C. Kesava Rao on 17th February, 1949 and to starred question No. 829 by Shri Basanta Kumar Das on 3rd March, 1949.

The following is the gist of the replies given before. The main principle of the Wardha System of Education of Mahatma Gandhi which is 'learning through activity' has been accepted by the Government of India. The Basic System of Education recommended by the Central Advisory Board of Education and generally accepted by the Central and Provincial Governments mainly conforms to the Wardha System of Education, the chief point of difference being that it has not yet been found possible to achieve complete economic self-sufficiency as advocated by the Wardha Scheme.

All the Provinces have implemented the scheme of Basic Education and have included it in their development plans for which they receive some block grants from the Centre.

The Centre is also taking steps for the production of literature for Basic School children and teachers.

Dr. Mono Mohon Das: What financial help are the Central Government giving to the provinces in which basic education has been introduced?

The Honourable Maulana Abul Kalam Azad : I have just stated that the block grant which is given by the Central Government is also utilized for this purpose.

Dr. Mono Mohon Das : What arrangements have been made for training teachers to impart this basic education in the provinces?

The Honourable Maulana Abul Kalam Azad : Training Schools have been opened in different Provinces and effort is being made to increase the number thereof.

Dr. Mono Mohon Das : What is the number of students in the schools?

Mr. Speaker : It is more or less a provincial subject.

Shri Arun Chandra Guha : Is the scheme adopted by the Government of India, the Sargent Scheme or the Wardha Scheme?

The Honourable Maulana Abul Kalam Azad : The scheme which is now in force cannot be exactly described as the Sargent Scheme. This embodies the main principle of the Wardha Scheme.

Shrimati G. Durgabai : What is the total number of schools based on the scheme which are directly working under this Government and what is the total amount of expenditure on these?

The Honourable Maulana Abul Kalam Azad : I cannot give this information at the moment.

Shri Mihir Lal Chattopadhyay : May I know whether any Central Institute for the training of teachers has been opened by the Central Government?

The Honourable Maulana Abul Kalam Azad : Yes, Sir.

Shri Mihir Lal Chattopadhyay : Where is it situated?

The Honourable Maulana Abul Kalam Azad : In Delhi.

Shri S.V. Krishnamoorthy Rao: Is it the intention of the Government to replace the present system of education by the Wardha System of education and if so, in how many years?

The Honourable Maulana Abul Kalam Azad : Government are doing their best. But it is difficult to say at present how long it will take to complete this task because due to financial stringency so many avenues have been closed.

Shri H.V. Kamath : What is the number of schools in Delhi Province in which basic education is being imparted in conformity with this scheme?

The Honourable Maulana Abul Kalam Azad : I cannot give this number at the moment.

Document No. 48

MAULANA AZAD'S REPLIES IN THE LEGISLATIVE ASSEMBLY TO THE QUESTIONS ASKED ON 12-12-49 BY DR. M.M. DAS AND OTHERS REGARDING THE INVITATION OF THE GOVT. TO DR. FRANK C. LAUBACH TO TOUR INDIA

Dr. Mono Mohon Das: (a) Will the Honourable Minister of Education be pleased to state whether Government invited Dr. Frank. C. Laubach the well-known American literacy expert to tour India during March and April 1949?

(b) If so, has Dr. Laubach submitted any report or made any suggestions regarding the literacy drive of the Government and if so, what are they?

The Honourable Maulana Abul Kalam Azad : (a) Dr. Frank C. Laubach was not invited by the Government of India. However, the Government utilized offer of his services during his last tour (March-April, 1949) to arouse interest and enthusiasm for literacy campaign in India.

(b) After his visit Dr. Laubach wrote a letter to Prime Minister giving his impression and suggestions, which included:

(i) The levying of a tax on those who do not teach or learn.

(ii) Mobilization of students and Government servants for literacy work.

(iii) Franchise to be limited only to literate adults etc.

Dr. Mono Mohon Das: May I know whether Mr. Laubach worked in an honorary capacity or he was paid for his services?

The Honourable Maulana Abul Kalam Azad: Honorary.

Shri S. Nagappa: May I know how many of these recommendations have been implemented by Government?

The Honourable Maulana Abul Kalam Azad: Government felt that it could not possibly implement a majority of his recommendations.

Mr. Tajamul Husain: May I know what amount has been spent by the Government of India on his account?

The Honourable Maulana Abul Kalam Azad: I have just stated that he did not come on the invitation of the Government of India. He came of his own accord. The Government of India have not incurred any expenditure on his account.

Document No. 49

MAULANA ABUL KALAM AZAD 'S REPLIES TO THE QUESTIONS RAISED ON 15.12.1949 BY MR. R.K. SIDHVA AND OTHERS IN THE CONSTITUENT ASSEMBLY (LEGISLATIVE) REGARDING THE IMPORTED MACHINERY LYING IN THE INDIAN NATIONAL ARCHIVES BUILDING

Shri R.K. Sidhva : (a) Will the Honourable Minister of Education be pleased to state whether it is a fact that machinery worth more than two lakhs of Rupees, imported from hard currency areas and brought to India about 18 months ago under the highest priority is lying stacked in the Indian National Archives Building in New Delhi?

(b) If so, what is the nature of this machinery and for what purpose was it imported?

(c) Why has there been such delay in utilising this machinery?

(d) What is the condition of this machinery at present?

The Honourable Maulana Abul Kalam Azad : (a) The machinery is not lying stacked: its installation is in progress.

(b) The machinery is meant for the (i) Vacuum fumigation of insect infested records, (ii) mechanical repairing of old and brittle documents with cellulose acetate foil, and (iii) microfilming and photo-duplication of documents.

(c) The delay in installing the machinery has been due to lack of funds. Some funds have, however, now been made available and the machinery is being installed.

(d) The present condition of the machinery is sound and no major damage has taken place. The extent of the actual damage and defects, if any, would, however, be known only when the machinery has been properly installed and worked.

Shri R.K. Sidhva : May I ask the Honourable Minister as to when the machinery arrived, when was it installed, and what was its price?

The Honourable Maulana Abul Kalam Azad : The machinery was received in Delhi in October, 1948.

Shri R.K. Sidhva : In other words, it arrived in 1948 and was also installed.

The Honourable Maulana Abul Kalam Azad : No. The installation work could only be undertaken long after.

Shri R.K. Sidhva: If it is correct that it took a long time to instal it, then may I know how much damage was thus caused to the machinery?

The Honourable Maulana Abul Kalam Azad: I have myself seen all the parts of the machinery and found that no major damage has taken place.

Shri Krishna Chandra Sharma: What is the number of books which have been damaged and require to be repaired?

The Honourable Maulana Abul Kalam Azad: There must be many such books which shall have to be protected from being infested by insects. I cannot quote the exact number thereof at the moment.

Document No. 50

REPLIES OF MAULANA AZAD TO THE QUESTIONS ASKED IN THE CONSTITUENT ASSEMBLY OF INDIA (LEGISLATIVE) DATED 15-12-1949 ABOUT THE HIGHER SECONDARY SCHOOLS

Seth Govind Das: Will the Honourable Minister of Education be pleased to state what has been the effect of the new system of education in Delhi University, *viz.*, opening of higher secondary schools with 11 years course followed by three years' degree course?

The Honourable Maulana Abul Kalam Azad: The system of Higher Secondary Education by which a student leaves the school after an eleven year course has been in operation for a period of five years only. Government is however, considering the recommendations of the Central Advisory Board of Education to appoint a Secondary Education Commission which will after an enquiry into all matters connected with Secondary Education and surveying the systems prevalent in India, make a report to the Government of India.

Seth Govind Das: Is it not a fact that the experiment made during these five years has proved to be successful?

The Honourable Maulana Abul Kalam Azad: The report of the Local Government is that this experiment has proved a success. This is also the opinion held by the Vice-Chancellor, Delhi University.

Seth Govind Das: If this experiment proves a success, will Government write to different Provinces that they should also make provision to this effect.

The Honourable Maulana Abul Kalam Azad: Because other aspects of this matter have also been brought before the Government, it has, therefore, been considered expedient that a Higher Secondary Commission should be appointed which may study all the points so that proper action may be taken in this matter.

Maulana Hasrat Mohani: Is it a fact that all Vernacular Schools have been closed, and if so, why?

The Honourable Maulana Abul Kalam Azad: I do not understand how does this arise out of this question?

Shri Raj Bahadur: Will the Honourable Minister be pleased to state how and in what form the experiment has proved to be a success?

The Honourable Maulana Abul Kalam Azad: The report of the Local Government says that by increasing one year the standard of ability has been raised, and those students who go to the University, are better prepared. Apart from this, there are other things also.

Begum Aizaz Rasul: Will the Honourable Minister please state whether any report has been received from Provinces that experiments in this system of Higher Secondary Education have been started there?

The Honourable Maulana Abul Kalam Azad: No. No such report has been received and so far as Government are aware this experiment has not perhaps been made in other Provinces.

Sardar Bhopinder Singh Man: In view of the fact that this system of Higher Secondary Education has proved a success, so far as ability is concerned, may I know what are the other points which have necessitated the appointment of this Commission?

The Honourable Maulana Abul Kalam Azad: This sytem has not been introduced in other Provinces. Of course, if any student comes to Delhi from outside or goes from here to some other Province, difficulties do arise.

Shri Raj Bahadur: The Honourable Minister has stated that the standard of ability is raised. May I know what is the criterion or method of judging that?

The Honourable Maulana Abul Kalam Azad: I have just stated that this matter has got manifold aspects. One thing which has come before us during the period of five years is that it has yielded good results. The University Commission have, however, recommended that the period should at least be twelve years, they want to increase one more year, and wish to make it twelve instead of eleven. All these aspects are of such a nature that these should be carefully considered by a Commission. An opinion could only be formed at then.

Shri O.V. Alagesan: Has the University Commission made any recommendation in regard to this matter? If so, will the Report of the Commission be made available to Honourable Members of this Assembly?

The Honourable Maulana Abul Kalam Azad: This is difficult as only a limited number of copies of the Report of the University Commission have been printed and it will not be possible for the Government to distribute them.

Shri Sita Ram S. Jajoo: Will the Honourable Minister please state whether such Boards will be set up in those Provinces and States Unions where new Boards are going to be constituted?

The Honourable Maulana Abul Kalam Azad: Government are not aware of any such thing.

Shri Satish Chandra Samanta: Has this new system of education been accepted by any other University in India?

The Honourable Maulana Abul Kalam Azad: No, so far as Government are aware.

Babu Ramnarayan Singh: May I know, Sir, what is the necessity of appointing another Commission after experiments have been made and their success proved? What are the reasons for not enforcing this in those places where experiments have been made and success achieved?

The Honourable Maulana Abul Kalam Azad : The Commission is not being appinted to consider over this particular aspect only. Just as the University Commission was appointed in connection with the University education, similarly the necessity to constitute a Commission to consider *de novo* the question of secondary education has been felt. The Commission will also *inter alia* consider over this matter.

Shri Arun Chandra Guha : Has the Government received any representations from any secondary school or other institution seeking financial help as this system has involved them in great cost?

The Honourable Maulana Abul Kalam Azad: No. No such representation is at present under the consideration of the Government. But surely the expenditure has been increased, and every educational reform is bound to raise the expenditure.

Shri Sita Ram S. Jajoo: Will Government of India advise the Provinces, where new Boards are likely to be set up, to constitute similar Boards?

The Honourable Maulana Abul Kalam Azad: Government of India will consider over these aspects after the receipt of the report of the Secondary Education Commission.

Document No. 51

MAULANA ABUL KALAM AZAD'S ANSWERS DATED 15-12-1949 TO THE QUESTIONS ASKED IN THE CONSTITUTENT ASSEMBLY OF INDIA (LEGISLATIVE) IN CONNECTION WITH THE HINDI ACADEMY

Seth Govind Das : Will the Honourable Minister of Education be pleased to state if in view of the fact that Hindi has been declared to be the State Language, an Academy is going to be established which may be engaged in research and improvement of the proposed State Language by (i) compiling suitable dictionaries; (ii) publication of literature in subjects which do not have sufficient books; and (iii) publication of popular books on culture at cheap rates for the masses of India?

The Honourable Maulana Abul Kalam Azad : This Ministry has under active consideration a scheme to prepare a dictionary of Scientific Terminology for Hindi and other Modern Indian Languages and another to prepare text books in the Federal Language. It is also proposed to publish this Ministry's periodical *Deepavali* devoted to the 'education and welfare of the blind', both in English and Hindi. There are other schemes also before the Government which they intend to implement provided the financial position allows.

Seth Govind Das : Are Government aware that similar efforts are also being made in some of the Provinces especially in the Central Provinces, and if these different attempts are made, many kinds of new things will come into being? Will not the Government of India do anything in this matter?

The Honourable Maulana Abul Kalam Azad : This matter is under the consideration of the Government. Government desire that a Central body should be constituted to look after the work so that uniform action is taken throughout the country.

Seth Govind Das : Are Government also considering that the advice of old institutions like the Hindi Sahitya Sammelan is sought in this connection?

The Honourable Maulana Abul Kalam Azad : Government will surely consider it.

Shrimati G. Durgabai : May I know, Sir, what step Government are taking to enrich this language, namely, Hindi, which has still to be developed by absorbing words which are in common use from other Provincial languages? Is it the function of this Academy to concern with that matter also?

The Honourable Maulana Abul Kalam Azad : Yes. This is an essential work. But so far Government had no opportunity to take practical steps. Government will make every effort and so far as circumstances permit, action will be taken to achieve this end.

Seth Govind Das : The Honourable Minister has stated that action in this matter will be taken provided the present financial position allows. Will Government also consider the aspect that despite the present financial position the work is most essential and should be undertaken?

The Honourable Maulana Abul Kalam Azad : Government will certainly consider. But it is quite obvious that unless funds are made available, what can we do to meet the demands?

Seth Govind Das : Will Government then consider the desirability to appropriate funds from other items of expenditure and to utilize them for this purpose?

The Honourable Maulana Abul Kalam Azad : I associate myself with this desire of the Honourable Member.

Shri S.V. Krishnamoorthy Rao : Has the Government examined the debates of the Constituent Assembly on the resolution for adoption of Hindi as the national language? If so, how is Government going to implement that resolution? Will they associate experts in other non-Hindi languages with this Academy?

The Honourable Maulana Abul Kalam Azad : The Government of India will surely take steps to implement the decision arrived at in this connection by the Constituent Assembly and do their utmost in the matter.

Shrimati G. Durgabai : Are the Government aware where there are other institutions also which concern themselves with the propagation of Hindustani will their advice be sought?

The Honourable Maulana Abul Kalam Azad : Government will certainly keep this in view.

Shri O.V. Alagesan : In view of the valuable work already done in this field by the Dakshina Bharat Hindi Prachar Sabha, Madras, will Government consider giving financial assistance to that body?

The Honourable Maulana Abul Kalam Azad : It is difficult for me to hold out any promise in this connection.

Sardar Bhopinder Singh Man : May I expect that action which will be taken by the Government with regard to Hindi shall also be taken in respect of other similar languages, such as Hindustani?

The Honourable Maulana Abul Kalam Azad : Yes. Government will keep all the aspects in view.

Document No. 52

MAULANA ABUL KALAM AZAD'S REPLIES TO THE QUESTIONS RAISED IN THE PARLIAMENT, DATED 15-12-1949 BY MR. D.S. SETH IN CONNECTION WITH THE RURAL ADULT EDUCATION

Shri Damoder Swarup Seth: Will the Honourable Minister of Education be pleased to state:

(a) what percentage of rural adult population were able to receive the benefit of education during the last two years in the various Provinces of India;

(b) whether Government have calculated the approximate total amount needed for adult education in the country; and

(c) the source or sources contemplated to be tapped for this purpose?

The Honourable Maulana Abul Kalam Azad : (a) In 1947-48 and 1948-49, 0.22 per cent and 0.33 per cent. respectively of rural adult population were receiving education.

(b) The Government of India have estimated that a ten year scheme for education of illiterates within the age group 12-40 would cost Rs. 206 crores.

(c) The Provincial and Central governments are sharing the expenditure on adult education between themselves. Some municipalities are also meeting a part of expenditure on adult education work within their jurisdiction. The provincial governments are also encouraging voluntary organisations to make their contributions to adult education.

Document No. 53

MAULANA AZAD'S REPLIES DATED 15-12-1949 IN THE PARLIAMENT TO THE QUESTIONS ASKED BY SETH GOVIND DAS AND OTHERS IN CONNECTION WITH THE CHILDREN'S PARKS

Seth Govind Das: Will the Honourable Minister of Education be pleased to state the number of children's parks opened in Delhi?

The Honourable Maulana Abul Kalam Azad: The number of Children's Parks in Delhi is ten.

Sardar Bhopinder Singh Man : Will the construction of the sports stadium which is proposed to be built in Delhi affect any of the existing children's parks in Delhi?

The Honourable Maulana Abul Kalam Azad : I cannot reply to this offhand.

Shri Deshbandhu Gupta : May I know whether Government feel that there should be more such parks?

Sardar Bhopinder Singh Man : May I know whether it is a fact that under the building programme many of the children's parks which existed in Delhi have disappeared?

The Honourable Maulana Abul Kalam Azad: This has not come to the knowledge of the Government.

Document No. 54

MAULANA AZAD'S REPLIES DATED 15-12-1949 IN THE PARLIAMENT TO THE QUESTIONS RAISED BY MR. DAMODAR SWARUP SETH REGARDING THE ADULT EDUCATION

Shri Damoder Swarup Seth: Will the Honourable Minister of Education be pleased to state:

(a) the amount which the Government of India and the Provincial Governments together at present spend annually on adult education and on all items of education; and

(b) the percentage of revenue annually spent by the Government of India and the Provincial Governments separately on education as a whole?

The Honourable Maulana Abul Kalam Azad: (a) and (b). The total budget provision for education in 1949-50 was Rs. 6 crores which comes to 1.16 per cent. of the total budget of the Central Government. As a result of recent cut however the education budget has been reduced approximately to Rs. 4.51 crores which is .89 per cent. of the total budget.

Information from the Provinces is being collected.

Document No. 55

LETTER FROM DR. RAJENDRA PRASAD TO MAULANA AZAD

Camp: Bajajwadi, Wardha
December 24, 1949

My dear Maulana Sahib,

I spoke to you about Mr. Cherian Thomas who is an Indian Christian belonging to Malabar. He has been working in the All India Congress Committee office for the last 3 years or so. He is a man with capacity for organisation and is much interested in social welfare activities. He is a candidate for the United Nations Organisation Social Welfare Fellowship for 1950, which has been offered through the Ministry of Education. He will be a suitable person and will prove of great service to the country, if he gets this further training.

This is just to request you to consider his case when it comes before you.

Yours sincerely,
Rajendra Prasad

The Hon'ble Maulana Abul Kalam Azad
Minister for Education
Government of India
New Delhi.

Document No. 56

MAULANA AZAD'S SPEECH DATED 8-1-1950 AT THE MEETING OF THE CENTRAL ADVISORY BOARD OF EDUCATION HELD IN CUTTACK

This is the third meeting of the Central Advisory Board of Education since India attained her independence. It is now necessary in the light of experience we have gained in the last three years to consider carefully and dispassionately our hopes and plans for the education of free India in the coming years. It was but natural that after the attainment of freedom we should have considered ambitious programmes for the expansion of our national education. This was necessary as education is one of the most important of our nation-building activities. We had also to make special efforts to wipe out the deficiency in education created by over a hundred years of foreign rule. It was in this spirit that the Ministry of Education prepared a programme of work for the next ten years.

It was obvious that we had to build our educational structure from its very basis and improve it both qualitatively and quantitatively. The number of our literates was and is lamentably low. Even the literacy that is imparted is not of the highest quality. In view of the demand for an all-round expansion and improvment, it became necessary to fix an order of priorities, so that our limited resources were not frittered away in attempting too many things simultaneously. You will remember that it was with this object in view that the Ministry of Education, with your general support, proposed that our immediate objectives should be four, namely:

(i) the provision of basic education on a universal, free and compulsory basis for all our school-going children;

(ii) the provision of adult education in order to wipe out the colossal illiteracy of our masses;

(iii) the improvement and expansion of technical education in order to solve the problem of manpower for industrial and technical development; and

(iv) the reorganisation and improvement of university education from a national point of view.

The Post-War Development Plan laid down that it would take 40 years to implement a scheme of basic education and cost the nation a sum of Rs. 8,000 crore at the rate of about Rs. 200 crore a year. You will remember that after the attainment of independence we all felt that the period was too long and exigencies of our national economy demanded a reduction in the cost. Nor was this all. We realised that lack of finance was not the only obstacle in our way. A truly national system of education demanded the creation of a new spirit among our educated men and women, so that they would regard the spread of education as a national obligation for all. The question of buildings had also to be faced from a new angle, for if we waited for the construction programme envisaged in the Post-War Plan, the introduction of compulsory, universal and free education would be deferred indefinitely. We therefore felt that we must utilise whatever accommodation was available in the land and employ the entire educated personnel of the land either on a voluntary basis or through some form of social conscription. It was with this end in view that we prepared a plan of junior basic education to be implemented in ten years and at a greatly reduced cost.

In the field of adult education, we revised our programme so that it became one of social education for training in citizenship and aimed at making at least 50 per cent of illiterate adults literate in the course of the next ten years.

You considered these reports last year and generally approved of the recommendations. I agree with your views and feel that in the light of the modifications suggested, we may prepare our programmes on the basis of co-operation between the State and the people, so that the State may extend the necessary facilities and services on the one hand and the people on the other supplement on a voluntary basis the efforts of the State.

To improve our standards of technical education, the programme that we had envisaged was the establishment of four higher technological institutes in addition to the strengthening of existing institutions. Considerations of finance did not permit us to start with all the four, but we thought that at least a beginning should be made. The Eastern

Higher Technological Institute near Calcutta was taken in hand without even waiting for the construction of all the necessary buildings. The scheme is in progress and I hope that the next academic year will see the first batch of teachers and students working in this Institute. Simultaneously, it has been our aim to strengthen the existing institutions by improving their quality and increasing their capacity.

In the field of university education, the Indian University Education Commission under the Chairmanship of Professor Radhakrishnan was asked to submit its report within nine months. You will be glad to know that it has already done so. The Report is before you and one of the main functions of this meeting of the Board will be to consider the recommendations of the Commission.

I have even at the risk of some repetition recapitulated these points, so that we may be in a position to judge where we are. You will appreciate that so far as planning is concerned, the Ministry is ready with its programme in all the four fields mentioned by me. I would therefore like to draw your attention to the obstacle which stands in the way of their immediate implementation.

You will remember that in 1947 the problem of refugees from Western Pakistan absorbed almost all the energy and a major portion of the finances of the nation. There was therefore no hope of adequate funds being available for educational expansion in the immediate future, but in spite of these difficulties, the budget for 1948-49 saw an increase in provision for education. During 1948-49, our scheme for educational reconstruction reached a suitable stage for implementation. It was my hope that the 1949-50 budget would enable us to make a beginning with the programme.

In spite of our best efforts, we were, however, unable to provide sufficient funds even for the very modest programme of expansion which we had framed. Our intention was to provide for an amount of Rs. 11 crore for 1949-50, as this would enable us to start the basic education programme and undertake the preliminary work for social education. Our financial position, however, allowed us to provide only about Rs. 6 crore. We accepted the situation, as we hoped that at least during 1950-51, conditions would improve sufficiently to enable us to carry out the scheme which had been carefully prepared and repeatedly revised in order to cut down cost.

To our great disappointment even this expectation is now belied. Within six months of the adoption of this year's budget, we have had to face a financial crisis of such magnitude as to force a reduction of ten to twenty per cent in the already approved budgets. This was followed by devaluation and still further difficulties with the result that our current year's budget has been severely curtailed. Instead of going ahead as we had originally planned, we suddenly realised that we had to retreat. For 1949-50, we had to surrender about Rs. 153 lakh out of a total budget of about Rs. 588 lakh. The result is that a country with a population of almost 350 millions and with hardly 14 per cent literates cannot provide more than Rs. 4.5 crore from its Central revenues for education !

The problem before us today is not what schemes we should prepare for national education. These are already there. We have to consider whether we can take any forward step at all in the immediate future. It is true that edcuation is a Provincial subject, but, in the existing circumstances, the problem of education cannot be solved unless the Centre assumes appropriate responsibility for its expansion and growth. We are as keenly conscious of this as all of you and this makes the present situation even more painful to us. There are no two opinions about the need for the provision of education on an expanded and improved scale. The programmes are also ready, but, in spite of the urgency, we cannot go ahead because of the shortage of funds.

I may bring to your notice the policy which the British Government have adopted in a similar situation. In a recent circular, the Ministry of Education of that Government have said:

"Local education authorities will be aware that the economic difficulties of the country have called for a close review of Government expenditure. They will also have noted the announcements that the Government do not contemplate any major change in policy which would result in a reduction in the scope of the services for which the Minister of Education is responsible.

The Minister wishes to make it clear in particular that:

(a) there is to be no going back on reforms already instituted or on the plans by which the number of teachers in primary and secondary schools will be increased with the increasing school population;

(b) there is to be no cut in the extent of the building programmes already approved to meet the increasing number of children, the needs of new housing estates and of technical education.

Every effort, however, must be made to reduce costs. A separate circular is being sent to the authorities on these points and on the measures which have to be taken to reduce capital investment for other educational purposes;

(c) schemes for further education, including plans for county colleges, not yet completed should be proceeded with and submitted in due course;

(d) arrangements for maintaining an adequate number of university awards should proceed concurrently with termination of the Further Education and Training Scheme, and discussion between universities and local education authorities on the adoption of a new procedure for local awards based on paragraph 34 of the Working Party's Report should continue.

There is, however, no point in merely discussing these difficulties and obstacles. What we have to do is to devise ways and means so that funds may be found for education and other constructive projects. There is no immediate prospect of a large increase in our revenues. Funds can therefore be found only by diverting a larger proportion of our available resources to education and other nation-building activities. As you are aware, the main burden on our finance today is due to the expenditure on the import of food, the rehabilitation of refugees and defence. It is obvious that welfare services cannot be expanded till these burdens are lightened. There is every hope that the expenses on the food account will be diminished and ultimately disappear. The expenditure for rehabilitation cannot be curtailed till our displaced people have been re-established on a sound basis, but it is diminishing with the flux of time. There remains Defence. During the British regime, we have always complained that the Defence expenditure was excessive. After the attainment of freedom, it was therefore natural to expect savings in this field, but circumstances took a turn, where in spite of all our efforts, the expenditure on Defence had to be further increased. The Government are, however, keenly alive to the situation and I can assure you that we are examining every possible avenue of saving and economy.

The need for education is accepted in principle by every one. It is necessary to wipe out the illiteracy of 150 years and make our people efficient, productive and responsible citizens of a democratic State. The new Constitution gives power to the people, but if this power is to be exercised with wisdom and foresight, it is necessary that the people must have the requisite knowledge. Even from the point of view of increasing the economic and industrial efficiency of the people, it is essential that our educational facilities must be expanded. As a famous economist has said, there are no poor or rich countries but only countries in which the people use their resources and countries in which the do not. Some parts of Africa are among the richest in the world in natural resources and yet because the people are illiterate and ignorant, they are poor and suppressed. There are other parts of the world, poor in natural resources, which have been developed and enriched through the knowledge and industry of their people. India will have to decide to which category her people should belong.

Document No. 57

SUPL. QUESTIONS ASKED BY MR. M. TYAGI DATED 13-2-1950 IN CONNECTION WITH THE STUDENTS FROM COUNTRIES OVERSEAS AND THEIR REPLIES BY MAULANA AZAD

Mr. Tyagi: What is the approximate estimated expenditure being incurred on these 53 students from countries overseas?

Maulana Azad: I said it just now that a sum of Rs. 200 per month per student has been fixed in such cases. I am not in a position to give the total amount. The students who are here under the Exchange system, come from the countries different from those to which these 53 belong.

Shri Tyagi: Is it so that the students coming here on mutual exchange belong to the countries different from which these 53 come?

Maulana Azad: Students coming on exchange basis come under a different scheme. It is just possible that from one and the same country students should have come under the general scheme as also under the exchange scheme. The purpose behind the general scheme is that mutual educational relations should be created between India and other countries of the East and also that the children of the Indians living in other countries should have an opportunity of coming over to India and receiving education here.

Shri Tyagi: Is the choice of subjects for which they come here to receive education made by us or by the Government of the students' own country?

Mr. Chairman: The question hardly arises. The main question relates to Philippines and exchange of students does not relate to it.

Shri Tyagi: I want to know whether we are giving them education in subjects of our choice or whether they choose the subjects themselves. In giving our scholarships, are we trying to disseminate our culture?

Mr. Chairman: I do not say the question is not important, but it does not arise out of this.

Document No. 58

REPLIES OF MAULANA AZAD DATED 13-2-1950 IN THE PARLIAMENT TO THE QUESTIONS ASKED BY S. HUKUM SINGH AND OTHERS IN CONNECTION WITH THE STUDENTS FROM THE PHILIPPINES

Sardar Hukam Singh: (a) Will the Minister of Education be pleased to state whether it is a fact that under the Students Exchange Scheme some Philipino students had come to India for studies?

(b) What was the number of these students and which are the Universities or Institutions to which these students were attached?

(c) Did these students stay in India for the full course of their studies and if not, why not?

(d) What was the understanding or the basis on which these students were invited to this country?

The Minister of Education (Maulana Azad): (a) No Philippine student came to India under the exchange scheme, though one Philippine student came under the General Scholarship scheme of the Government of India.

(b) One, University of Calcutta.

(c) No. The student, Mr. Banito F. Reyes from Philippines, left without taking up his course at the University because immediately on his arrival in India he asked for a substantive increase in his scholarship. Government could not agree to his request.

He then asked for financial assistance for his return passage. The Government of India could not agree to this request also, as, like the former, this request too was outside the scope of the scholarship scheme under which he had been selected for studies in India and no exception could be made in his case.

(d) The details of the understandings given by Government may be seen in the Memorandum of Instructions placed on the Table of the

House. (See *Appendix I, annexure No. 24*). It was made clear to all students before they left their respective homes that no increase in their scholarship could be considered in any circumstance, nor would the Government of India bear any part of their passage expenses. While in India, they are to be paid a fixed stipend of Rs. 200 P.M. out of which they are required to meet expenses for games, libraries, hostel and other miscellaneous fees, as also their normal medical charges and expenses during vacations etc. The Government of India have, in addition to the fixed stipend of Rs. 200 per mensem, undertaken to pay their tuition fees, examination fees and capitation charges if any, direct to the Institutions where they study.

Sardar Hukam Singh: May I know if any of our Indian students were sent to Philippines?

Maulana Azad: To my knowledge, no Indian student was sent.

Sardar Hukam Singh: Is the hon. Minister aware of the propaganda carried on in the Philippines Press that students from there had to return because of the refusal of the Government of India to extend certain facilities to them?

Maulana Azad: I have stated the facts. If any propaganda is being carried on in this connection we may regret it. I would say with all emphasis that nothing has been left undone by the Government of India in this connection.

Sardar Hukum Singh: Has there been correspondence with the Government in this connection?

Maulana Azad: None, as far as I know.

Shri Kamath: What is the number of countries with which the Government has entered into an Exchange Scheme of this type?

Maulana Azad: I have just said that the students in question were not here under the Exchange Scheme but under the General Scholarship Scheme. Under this General Scheme 53 persons are receiving education at present.

Document No. 59

REPLIES OF MAULANA ABUL KALAM AZAD DATED 21-2-1949 IN PARLIAMENT TO THE QUESTIONS ASKED BY PROF. K.K. BHATTACHARYA AND OTHERS IN CONNECTION WITH THE ALLEGATIONS AGAINST DELHI UNIVERSITY VICE-CHANCELLOR

Prof. K.K. Bhattacharya: (a) Will the Minister of Education be pleased to state whether his attention has been drawn to certain articles which appeared in the *Organiser* dated the 2nd November 1949, 23rd November 1949 and 14th December 1949 and in the *Indian News Chronicle*, dated the 18th December, 1949?

(b) If so, what steps do Government propose to take to enquire into the truth of these allegations?

(c) Has there been a complete audit of the accounts of the University in recent years including money spent on building operations?

(d) Has the attention of the Government been drawn to the auditors' notes in the last audit and what action are Government taking in the matter?

(e) What is the total amount granted to the University under the General Expansion Scheme of the University, including money for buildings?

(f) Have Government verified that the buildings put up are really of the value for which they have been built?

The Minister of Education (Maulana Azad): (a) Yes Sir.

(b) I am informed by the Vice-Chancellor that one of the complaints is *sub-judice*. All the allegations made do not indicate that any Rules and Regulations of the University have been infringed. These are matters of internal administration which are within the competence of the various bodies of the University.

(c) Yes, the last audit report was on the accounts of the University for the year 1947-48.

(d) Yes; the University's accounts are audited by Government auditors, and the audit objections have been dealt with by the University to the satisfaction of Government.

(e) A sum of Rs. 7.36 lakhs recurring and Rs. 47.05 lakhs non-recurring has been paid to the University during the period 1946-47 to 1948-49 towards development and the construction of various buildings.

(f) The Buildings are constructed on the plans approved by the Government and subject to inspection by the Chief Engineer, Central Public Works Department.

Prof. K.K. Bhattacharya: Is the hon. Minister aware that four Chevrolet buses purchased by the University of Delhi have used petrol coupons without doing any appreciable running, and is he going to institute an enquiry in regard to the disposal of the petrol coupons or the petrol itself?

Maulana Azad: The hon. Member is aware that the University is an autonomous body, and the Government cannot interfere in its administration. The Government can, of course, interfere if the University have in any way infringed its Constitution and Regulations; but no such thing has been brought before the Government.

Prof. K.K. Bhattacharya: Is the hon. Minister in a position to say whether the election of the Vice-Chancellor itself was a nullity...

Mr. Speaker: Order, order. I do not think the hon. Member can go into that question.

Prof. K.K. Bhattacharya: Is the hon. Minister in a position to substantiate that honorary degrees are being conferred by the University on some employees of the University?

Mr. Speaker: The hon. Member is going into the autonomous sphere of the University.

Shri Deshbandhu Gupta: May I know whether any such incidents have been brought to the notice of the hon. Minister that the contracts for the construction of the buildings were given without inviting the tenders, and these contracts involved a huge amount, and the Auditor raised an objection to this? If any such instance has been brought to his notice, may I know what action has been taken by him in the matter?

Maulana Azad: No, no such thing has been brought to the notice of the Government.

Shri Sidhva: The hon. Minister has stated that there are many complaints and one of them is *sub-judice*. May I know from him which is that complaint?

Mr. Speaker: If the hon. Member will refer to the copy of the newspaper, he will find that two suits have been filed.

Shri Gautam: May I take it that the Audit Report did not contain any such item from where it could be revealed that there has been some irregularity in maintaining the accounts?

Maulana Azad: No such thing has come within the knowledge of the Government.

Shrimati Velayudhan: What is the answer to (e) and (f)?

Mr. Speaker: He has already read it out. It is some Rs. 46 lakhs and 7 lakhs.

Shri T.N. Singh: I want to know whether the expenditure exceeded the grant sanctioned for the building operations, and if so, what is the amount involved?

Maulana Azad: I cannot say this at the moment.

Document No. 60

MAULANA'S REPLIES DATED 21-2-1950 IN PARLIAMENT TO THE QUESTIONS ASKED IN CONNECTION WITH THE PHYSICAL EDUCATION IN SCHOOLS

Shri Ethirajulu Naidu: (a) Will the Minister of Education be pleased to state whether Government have any scheme for imparting physical education to students in schools and colleges in the Centrally administered areas?

(b) What is the rough percentage of students whom physical education reaches under the present arrangements in those areas?

(c) What is the type and how many hours are devoted for such education in a week?

(d) Do Government propose to consider the advisability of making physical education compulsory in schools and colleges in the Centrally administered areas?

The Minister of Education (Maulana Azad): (a) The Government intend shortly to set up a Board of Physical Education, one of whose tasks will be the preparation of such a scheme.

(b) and (c) The information is being collected and will be supplied to hon. Member when received.

(d) Government will take decision after it has received the report of the Board of Physical Education mentioned in part (a) above.

Shri Ethirajulu Naidu: Within what time is the Board likely to be constituted?

Maulana Azad: Efforts are being made to set up the Board as early as possible.

Shri Ethirajulu Naidu: Do the Central Government give any directives or advice to State Governments in educational matters?

Maulana Azad: Yes, on different occasions such directives have been issued. But the Government have felt that this work can be properly done only when a practical scheme is prepared and action will be taken in consonance therewith.

Shri Ethirajulu Naidu: What will be the territorial scope, if I may say so, of the Board? Will it be restricted to the Centrally Administered Areas or extend to the entire Union?

Maulana Azad: No. The object of the Board contemplated to be set up will be that we may be able to render advice to the entire country and prepare such a scheme which can be extended to the whole country.

Shri Kamath: Which of the schemes will remain in force till a new one is formulated by this Board?

Maulana Azad: There is no particular scheme.

Shri Kamath: Is there no particular scheme before the Government?

Mr. Speaker: That is what he says.

Document No. 61

REPLIES DATED 21-2-1950 IN PARLIAMENT BY MAULANA AZAD TO THE QUESTIONS RAISED REGARDING THE GRANTS OF LOCAL BODIES

Shri Kannamwar: Will the Minister of Education be pleased to state whether Government propose to consider the advisability of making provision for grants to Local Bodies in the Centrally administered areas to enable them to revise the scales of pay of Primary Teachers according to the recommendations of the Pay Commission?

The Minister of Education (Maulana Azad): Government are already paying grants-in-aid to Local Bodies in Delhi and Ajmer in respect of the expenditure incurred by them on Primary Education. The expenditure incurred by the Local Bodies on the introduction of the Government scales of pay to their teachers is considered as approved expenditure for purposes of Government grant.

Shri Kannamwar: According to what rule is the grant being paid?

Maulana Azad: According to the Pay Commission.

Document No. 62

MAULANA ABUL KALAM AZAD'S REPLIES DATED 21-2-1950 IN PARLIAMENT TO QUESTIONS ASKED IN CONNECTION WITH THE STUDENTS IN U.S.A. AND U.K.

Shri Karmarkar: (a) Will the Minister of Education be pleased to state what is the number of Indian students studying in the United States of America and the United Kingdom and other foreign countries?

(b) How many of them are Government scholars?

(c) What is the arrangement for looking after the interests of Government scholars and non-Government scholars, in the respective countries?

The Minister of Education (Maulana Azad): (a) Approximately 3,150. A statement showing the distribution of the students in the U.S.A., the U.K. and other foreign countries is laid on the Table of the House. [See *Appendix I, annexure No. 52.*]

(b) 651 of them are Government scholars.

(c) The Education Department attached to the Indian Embassy in the U.S.A. and the High Commissioner's Office in the U.K. look after the welfare and educational interests generally of these students in these countries. In other countries where the number of scholars is small these duties have been entrusted to the diplomatic missions there.

Seth Govind Das: Is this thing kept in view that no fresh student shall now be sent abroad till the return of these scholars?

Maulana Azad: So far as the Government's Overseas Scholarship Scheme is concerned, the hon. Member is aware that it was discontinued after the year 1947. And the number which I have just referred to consists of only 651 Government scholars and a large majority thereof are private scholars. In any case, the Government of India have got no such scheme at present under which the scholars are being sent abroad.

Thakur Lalsingh: Have the Government compensated for the loss sustained by the scholars who were sent to the United States of America or those who are private, consequent on the devaluation of the rupee and increase in the value of the Dollar?

Maulana Azad: They were being paid in the form of Dollars and hence they have not been affected. Government have made special arrangements to meet with the difficulties faced by the private students.

Prof. Ranga: Have Government received any complaints from the Indian students who are in America or who have returned from America about the inability or unhelpful attitude of the Education Department of our Embassy to help them adequately?

Mr. Speaker: To help them, in what manner?

Prof. Ranga: In the manner in which they are expected to help them.

Maulana Azad: Government shall not accept this. Government have carefully considered this matter and we are fully satisfied that necessary help is being given.

Shri Karmarkar: Is it a fact that the Education Officers specially posted for this purpose in Washington consider it their duty to keep in contact only with Government scholars, and not with other students? If the hon. Minister is not in possession of the answer to this question, will he make enquiries?

Maulana Azad: So far as Government are aware, the Education Department not only looks after the Government scholars but all the students and keeps itself in contact with them. No such complaint has been brought within the knowledge of the Government.

Shri Lakshmanan: May I know for what careers the majority of the Scholars are preparing?

Maulana Azad: I cannot say this at the moment.

Shri D.D. Pant: Is there any arrangement for giving practical training in the factories to the non-Government Scholars after they come out of the Universities?

Maulana Azad: Yes.

Shri Sonavane: May I know, Sir, how many out of 651 Government scholars are Harijans?

Maulana Azad: I cannot say this offhand.

Shri Syamnandan Sahaya: Will the hon. Minister of Education be pleased to state what arrangements have been made by the Government to counteract the difficulties which are being faced by non-Government scholars on account of devaluation? You had just stated that some arrangement has been made in this direction. I would like to know what arrangement has been made for them ?

Maulana Azad: What I had stated was in respect of Government scholars. It is obvious that the Government cannot accept any responsibility for the expenses of private scholars. But if any particular case is brought to our knowledge, we try to help them as far as possible.

Document No. 63

REPLIES DATED 21-2-1950 BY MAULANA AZAD IN THE PARLIAMENT TO THE QUESTIONS ASKED BY MR. B.K. PANI REGARDING THE GRANTS TO UNIVERSITIES

Shri B.K. Pani: Will the Minister of **Education** be pleased to state:

(a) the Central grants given to each of the Universities for development and research in Science and Technology in each of the years 1947-48 and 1948-49; and

(b) whether the Utkal University has applied for any grant in these years and the reason why no grant was allotted?

The Minister of Education (Maulana Azad): (a) A Statement showing grants given to the Universities in India for development and research in Science and Technology in each of the years 1947-48 and 1948-49 is laid on the Table of the House. [See *Appendix I, annexure No. 54.*]

(b) The Utkal University applied in 1949 for a grant for the construction of University buildings, equipment of its Library, and Research in Science and Archaeology. The proposal could not be considered as grants to state Universities for such general schemes are not normally made from Central Revenues.

Document No. 64

REPLIES BY MAULANA AZAD DATED 24-2-1950 IN PARLIAMENT TO THE QUESTIONS ASKED IN CONNECTION WITH THE PRIMARY AND SECONDARY EDUCATION IN CENTRALLY ADMINISTERED AREAS

Pandit M.B. Bhargava: (a) Will the Minister of Education be pleased to state the number of primary and secondary schools in the Centrally Administered States of Delhi and Ajmer and how many of these are Government aided?

(b) Have Government any intention of giving aid to the institutions, which depend wholly on voluntary efforts and if not, why not?

(c) What progress, if any, has been made so far by the Government of India to take over the primary and secondary institutions run by the Municipalities in the said States?

(d) Whether the Punjab Compulsory Education Act which has already been extended with certain modifications to the State of Delhi has been enforced in Ajmer as well and if not, why not?

The Minister of Education (Maulana Azad): (a) Necessary information is given in the statement placed on the Table of the House. [See *Appendix III, annexure No. 12.*]

(b) Such of the private institutions, whose Managements apply for Government recognition and grant and satisfy the prescribed conditions will be given grant-in-aid.

(c) In 1947, all Secondary Schools run by the Delhi Municipal Committee were taken over by Government. From next year, it is proposed to provincialize all Primary and Secondary Schools now run by Local Bodies in rural areas of Delhi. There is no intention, at present, of taking over the schools run by the Delhi and the New Delhi Municipal Committees in respect of Education. In Ajmer State in rural areas the Primary Schools are run by Government. The Management of the Betham Municipal High School, Kekri, was taken over by Government in 1945. The question of taking over all Primary Schools run by Local Bodies in Ajmer is, however, under consideration by Government; but pending a final decision in the matter, Government have sanctioned a grant-in-aid to these Local Bodies at 90 per cent of the net expenditure incurred by them on Education, subject to the condition that the Local Bodies spend not less than 7½ per cent. of their total income each year on primary education.

(d) The question of extension of the Punjab Compulsory Education Act to Ajmer-Merwara is under consideration.

Document No. 65

MAULANA AZAD'S REPLIES DATED 24-2-1950 IN THE PARLIAMENT TO THE QUESTIONS ASKED IN CONNECTION WITH THE HISTORY OF INDIAN PHILOSOPHY

Shri Barman: (a) Will the Minister of Education be pleased to state the names of the persons appointed to compile the History of Indian Philosophy?

(b) How far have they completed or, advanced with, their work?

The Minister of Education (Maulana Azad): (a) An Editorial Board consisting of the following was appointed for writing a comprehensive History of Indian Philosophy:

(1) Dr. Sarvepalli Radhakrishnan (Chairman)

(2) Prof. A.R. Wadia, Principal, Gwalior College, Gwalior.

(3) Prof. D.M. Datta, Professor of Philosophy, Patna University.

(4) Prof. Humayun Kabir, Joint Secretary to the Government of India, Ministry of Education (Secretary).

(b) The Editorial Board is now engaged in preparing for the press the chapters submitted by the various experts. It is expected that the material will be handed over to the publisher in June.

Shri Tirumala Rao: Sir, may I know whether there is a proposal to associate with this Committee anyone well versed in oriental studies, say, a pandit well-versed in Sanskrit and philosophy?

Maulana Azad: The persons whose names were included in the list were supposed to possess profound knowledge of this subject, and so it was thought that as these Scholars are there so there is no necessity of having other people also.

Shri Tirumala Rao: Is any one of them an oriental scholar knowing Sanskrit?

Maulana Azad: I think that it has universally been accepted that Dr. Radhakrishnan is a great Sanskrit Scholar.

Shri R.K. Chaudhuri: I wish to enquire why the name of the Educational Adviser to the Government of India was not included in the Committee?

Maulana Azad: It was not at all essential to nominate the Educational Adviser to this committee also. He cannot find time for all sorts of work.

Shri Tyagi: In which language will this book be published?

Maulana Azad: In English.

Shri Raj Bahadur: May I know if besides Dr. Radhakrishnan any other Sanskrit Scholar also took part in the proceedings of the committee?

Maulana Azad: The Board, we had to constitute could not have been a very big one. Four such persons were nominated to this committee who could have collectively accomplished the task in the best possible manner.

Khwaja Inait Ullah: Will the Government publish the translation of this book in other languages also?

Maulana Azad: For the present efforts are being made to publish the book. After the publication it is just possible that the question of translating the book may be taken into consideration.

Dr. M.M. Das: I want to know the expected time when this work will be completed and also the estimated expenditure that will be incurred?

Maulana Azad: I have just stated that we hope that the book would be given to the publisher by the month of June. Then it would take some time to print the book. As far as the question of setting up of this Board and the necessary expenditure is concerned, 20,000 rupees were set apart for this work, but so far the actual expenditure done has been far less, and it is hoped that the total expenditure would be less than twenty thousand rupees.

Dr. V. Subramaniam: Have Government any idea of appointing a committee to investigate the possibilities of writing a book on a subject allied to Indian Philosophy, namely the History of Indian Medicine?

Mr. Speaker: Order, order. The hon. Member need not pursue the question.

Maulana Azad: No, no such proposal is before the Government at this time.

Shri Gautam: Have the Government any intention of setting up any other committees for subjects other than Philosophy?

Maulana Azad: No.

Thakur Lalsingh: How many members of this Board know Pali and Prakrit?

Maulana Azad: It is just possible that some other persons also might be knowing Pali, but I know that Sir Radhakrishnan is much interested in Pali. It was practically impossible to have scholars of all the ancient languages on this committee.

Shri Raj Bahadur: Will the hon. Minister for Education be pleased to state if for this work any authority or verdict or any other help of other Sanskrit scholars was also sought by this Board or not?

Shri Kamath: Whether the committee has authority to co-opt other members also may they be Pandits or Maulvis?

Maulana Azad: No, it was not considered to be at all essential. This committee was set up to edit a book so that the persons possessing expert knowledge could be asked to write the different chapters of the book and then to edit the same.

Document No. 66

REPLIES DATED 24-2-1950 BY MAULANA AZAD IN PARLIAMENT TO QUESTIONS ASKED BY LALA-RAJ KANWAR IN CONNECTION WITH THE ARCHAEOLOGICAL SURVEY OF AGROHA

Lala Raj Kanwar: Will the Minister of Education be pleased to state:

(a) whether it is a fact that the small town of Agroha in the Hissar District of the Punjab on the Delhi-Sirsa Road contains extensive ruins of a great city;

(b) whether Government have carried out any archaeological survey of this site or intend doing so as part of the programme of the Archaeological Survey of India; and

(c) if a survey has been carried out, whether a detailed report thereof has been published?

The Minister of Education (Maulana Azad): (a) Yes, Sir.

(b) A partial excavation was done at the site in 1937-38. It is not proposed to restrart excavation on the site in the near future owing to the fact that much more important sites call for attention and funds and technical staff necessary for excavation are limited.

(c) No detailed report has yet been published, for the report submitted by the excavator was intended for publication in the Annual Report of the Archaeological Survey of India, the publication of which was suspended during the war and has not yet been resumed. The publication of the Agroha report in *Ancient India* which is at present the only publication of the Archaeological Department is under consideration.

Document No. 67

QUESTIONS ASKED REGARDING THE UNIVERSITY COMMISSION IN PARLIAMENT DATED 24-2-1950 AND THEIR ANSWERS BY MAULANA ABUL KALAM AZAD

Shri B.K. Das: (a) Will the Minister of Education be pleased to state whether Government have considered the recommendations of the University Commission?

(b) If so, what steps have been taken for the implementation of their recommendations?

(c) Has any University given effect to any of their recommendations?

The Minister of Education (Maulana Azad): (a) and (b). The Report was circulated to the Governments of the different States and the Universities in the Union, for eliciting comments. It has also been referred to the Central Advisory Board of Education and the Inter-University Board, and it is expected that their views will be available in April. Meanwhile a preliminary examination of the Report has been undertaken by the Ministry to prepare the ground for necessary action immediately after the views of the States, the Universities and other bodies referred to have become available.

(c) Does not arise.

Document No. 68

MAULANA ABUL KALAM AZAD'S REPLIES IN PARLIAMENT DATED 24-2-1950, TO QUESTIONS ASKED BY DR. DESHMUKH IN CONNECTION WITH THE BASIC EDUCATION

Dr. Deshmukh: (a) Will the Minister of Education be pleased to state the date from which Government accepted Basic Education Scheme?

(b) What are the stages in which it has so far been introduced?

(c) Is it proposed to be confined to the primary stage or to be extended to the middle and higher stages also?

(d) What is the expenditure incurred on Basic Education including conferences held for the purpose, or contributions made to other organisations each year, from the time Basic Education Scheme received the support and approval of the Government of India?

(e) What was proposed to be spent on Basic Education from the Centre in the year 1950-51?

(f) Has this amount been reduced on account of the drive for economy and if so, by how much?

The Minister of Education (Maulana Azad): (a) The outline of Basic Education was laid down by the Central Advisory Board of Education in their Report on Post-War Educational Development in India, 1944 which was accepted in principle by Government on the 19th November, 1945.

(b) and (c). Basic Education as accepted by the Government of India is an integrated course of eight years for children from six to fourteen years of age. For practical and administrative purposes, however, while preserving its essential unity, the course has been divided into two stages. The first Stage, the Junior Stage, covers a period of five years and the Second Stage, the Senior Stage, a period of three years.

Junior Basic Schools have been started in all the Provinces except Punjab. A few Senior Basic Schools have also been started in Bihar, the Central Provinces and Bombay.

(d) As Block Grants are given to the Provinces for all development purpose, it is not possible to state the exact amount given by the Centre for Basic Education to the Provinces. The Ministry of Education have so far spent an amount of Rs. 19.1 lakhs approximately on the Centrally Administered Areas of Delhi and Ajmer, for training of Basic Teachers in Jamia Millia and Shantiniketan and for organising Committees in this connection.

(e) and (f) The budget estimates for 1950-51 are under consideration and it cannot therefore be stated now what will be the provision for Basic education in that Budget.

Document No. 69

REPLIES OF MAULANA AZAD DATED 24-2-1950 IN THE PARLIAMENT TO THE QUESTIONS RAISED BY SARDAR B.S. MAN AND OTHERS IN CONNECTION WITH THE CENTRAL ADVISORY BOARD OF EDUCATION

Sardar B.S. Man: (a) Will the Minister of Education be pleased to state whether a meeting of the Central Advisory Board of Education was held to decide the medium of instruction at the University stage?

(b) If so, what is its decision?

(c) What other subjects were placed before the meetings and what are the results arrived at?

The Minister of Education (Maulana Azad): (a) The Report of the Committee on Medium of Instruction at the University Stage was first placed before the Central Advisory Board of Education at their 15th meeting held in January 1949. The Board deferred decision on the Report in view of the appointment of the University Education Commission, which were to examine *inter alia* the medium of Instruction at the University Stage.

The Report of the University Education Commission together with the Report of the Committee on Medium of Instruction were placed before the Central Advisory Board of Education at their last meeting held in January 1950. In deference to the wishes of the members that more time be given to them to study in detail the University Education Commission Report, decision on the Report was deferred for a few months more. It is now proposed to call a special session of the Board in April 1950 to consider the University Education Commission Report and also the Report of the Committee on Medium of Instruction at the University stage.

(b) Does not arise.

(c) A copy of the Agenda of the meeting is laid on the Table of the House [See *Appendix III, annexure No. 11.*]

Proceedings of the meeting when finalised will as usual be communicated to the hon. Members.

Sardar B.S. Man: May I know whether at that meeting any set policy was arrived at so far as overseas scholarships are concerned, as well as scholarships for backward classes are concerned?

Maulana Azad: This Committee had no connection whatsoever with this thing. This Committee was set up to report about the medium of instruction.

Sardar B.S. Man: Sir, I want to draw your attention to part (c) of my question wherein I had stated that the Board had other points also under consideration.

Maulana Azad: No Sir, no other points were under consideration.

Shri Deshbandhu Gupta: Is it a fact that the agenda of this meeting was issued a month earlier and this meeting was called for the purpose to give a decision after taking into consideration the recommendations of the University Commission made in this connection, but this matter was not at all taken into consideration and the entire money spent on calling a meeting in this way was wasted?

Mr. Speaker: That is an expression of opinion. I find...

Shri Deshbandhu Gupta: Sir, I want to know whether on the agenda...

Mr. Speaker: He must ask for information and not express an opinion. I find many Members expressing opinions and making inferences instead of asking for information, and that makes the answering of the question very difficult. I do not propose to allow those questions, in which opinions are expressed.

Shri Deshbandhu Gupta: Perhaps the opinion is shared by the hon. Minister. Sir, I only want to know whether it is a fact that the agenda was issued one month before the consideration of the recommendations?

Maulana Azad: I cannot tell just now how long back this was published.

Shri Tirumala Rao: Sir, may I know if Government have considered the report of the University Commission and the recommendations made therein with regard to the medium of instruction at the university stage?

Maulana Azad: The Government is taking into consideration the said report. But as the report has been sent to the Provincial Governments and all the Universities and as the Central Advisory Board and the Inter-University Board also have to take this report into consideration. Therefore the Government is awaiting their opinions. When all the opinions are received then the Government would take the final decision.

Shri R. Velayudhan: Sir, may I know how many members are there on this Central Advisory Board of Education, and whether they are being paid travelling allowance by the Central Government for attending the meetings of the Board?

Mr. Speaker: No, that does not arise.

Shri Gautam: Is the Government confident of the fact that the expenditure incurred thereupon was proper and justified?

Mr. Speaker: It is a matter of opinion.

Shrimati Velayudhan: Who are the members of this Central Board of Education. I mean this Central Advisory Board of Education?

Maulana Azad: I cannot give this information just now. The Reports of the various Boards are available in the Library of the House and these reports contain the names of the members also.

Shri Kamath: Sir, on a point of order. Do not questions on the printed list take precedence over questions in the supplementary list? There is question No. 497 in the printed list which Dr. Deshmukh had authorised me to put, but...

Mr. Speaker: Unfortunately I had no information of that.

Shri Kamath: The Secretary has, I believe, a copy of the authorisation.

Mr. Speaker: If I had got any idea of it, I should certainly have come to that question. But I had no intimation of it, and office does not say that it has received any such notice or copy.

Document No. 70

REPLIES OF MAULANA ABUL KALAM AZAD IN THE PARLIAMENT DATED 24-2-1950 TO THE QUESTIONS RAISED IN CONNECTION WITH THE BASIC EDUCATION

Shri Jnani Ram: Will the Minister of Education be pleased to state:

(a) the names of States which have started Basic Education; and

(b) the total number of students, boys and girls, trained or under training in the Centrally Administered areas?

The Minister of Education (Maulana Azad): (a) Basic Schools have been started in all the States hitherto known as Provinces (except Punjab) and in the Centrally Administered Area of Delhi. Hon. Member's attention is invited to the reply given to the Starred Question No. 454 asked by Shri V.C. Kesava Rao on 17th February 1949.

(b) According to the information available in the Ministry the number of students trained and under training in the Centrally Administered Areas is roughly speaking 1,300.

Shri Jnani Ram: Will the hon. Minister be pleased to state that taking into consideration the speed with which Basic Education is being imparted, how much time would it take to spread it throughout the length and breadth of the country?

Maulana Azad: We aspire to spread it at the earliest but the conditions are such that we will have to wait for a long time.

Giani G.S. Musafir: The hon. Minister has just given out that such schools have not been opened in Punjab, then when is it intended to open such schools in Punjab?

Maulana Azad: The hon. Member is perhaps aware of the fact that after partition the condition in East Punjab had deteriorated very much. It was difficult for the East Punjab Government to open these new Basic Education Schools.

Shri R.K. Chaudhuri: May I know if it is a fact that some basic education trainees from Assam have been asked to withdraw and they have left this place for want of funds?

Maulana Azad: No, no such case has come to my notice.

Shri Jnani Ram: In the Centrally Administered Areas education up to what standard is being imparted?

Maulana Azad: Education up to junior basic standard is being imparted.

Dr. R.S. Singh: Will the hon. Minister be pleased to state as to what amount of money per year is being spent per student in respect of this basic education and what ratio this amount bears to the money spent per boy in other schools?

Maulana Azad: I cannot give this information at present.

Lala Achint Ram: Will the hon. Minister be pleased to state as to how many institutions have been started to impart basic education to the teachers?

Maulana Azad: Perhaps the hon. Member wants to know the total number of these institutions in all the provinces. I cannot give this information just at present.

Lala Achint Ram: What is the number in Delhi and other Centrally Administered Areas?

Maulana Azad: In Delhi 1086 pupil teachers are receiving education in the teachers training schools; in Ajmer 110; in Coorg 3, in Himachal Pradesh 74 and in Cutch 23. The total is 1296.

Shri Kamath: Have special inspectors been appointed for these basic education schools in the Centrally Administered Areas?

Maulana Azad: Yes.

Document No.71

REPLIES OF MAULANA ABUL KALAM AZAD DATED 24-2-1950 IN THE PARLIAMENT TO THE QUESTIONS ASKED BY PROF. N.G. RANGA AND OTHERS ABOUT THE REMOVAL OF FINDS FROM NAGARJUNAKONDA

Prof. Ranga: Will the Minister of Education be pleased to state:

(a) whether any of the 'finds' were removed recently from Nagarjunakonda in Guntur District to Delhi and other places;

(b) if so, how many and to what places; whether temporarily or permanently;

(c) whether it is not the practice to make 'replicas' for the "original finds" and distribute them to various Museums while keeping the 'originals' in the principal place;

(d) whether Government are aware that there is a museum at Nagarjunakonda; and

(e) whether Government propose to return these finds to Nagarjunakonda and if so, when?

The Minister of Education (Maulana Azad): (a) and (b) Yes. 10 sculpture pieces were removed to the National Museum, New Delhi.

(c) No.

(d) There is a sculpture shed built on the site by the Department to protect from weather the antiquities collected or excavated from the site.

(e) No, not at present.

Prof. Ranga: May I know why the Government do not propose to return the finds to Nagarjunakonda?

Maulana Azad: If the hon. Member thinks that the things excavated from a particular place must not be removed to other places then there can be no National Museum.

Prof. Ranga: Will Government later on supply the information as to which of the finds have been removed from there to Delhi?

Maulana Azad: Ten things have been removed from there, but I cannot tell the details just at present.

Shri Tirumala Rao: Have Government any proposal for replacing the originals by replicas at least, so that the collections there may be complete?

Maulana Azad: No. I would like to draw the attention of the hon. Member towards the fact that things from that place only have not been removed to the National Museum but articles from Calcutta and other provinces also have been brought there. If we were to accept the principle that in no case things would be removed from their original places then no National Museum can be created.

Shri Tirumala Rao: My question has been misunderstood. I only wanted to know whether such of the finds as were removed from Nagarjunakonda would be replaced by replicas made from the originals?

Maulana Azad: No, for the present there is no such intention.

Prof. Ranga: Are these finds major or minor ones?

Maulana Azad: No, I cannot give this information just now.

Prof. Ranga: Why were they taken from there secretly without anybody knowing anything about it and removed in special cars all the way from that place?

Mr. Speaker: That is an insinuation.

Prof. Ranga: That is why I have not used the word 'stealthily'. I said they were secretly taken away.

Shri R. Velayudhan: What were those finds?

Prof. Ranga: My question has not been answered.

Mr. Speaker: He has stated that he cannot give the information without notice.

Shri Kamath: On what basis these things were considered fit for the National Museum?

Maulana Azad: Because it was thought that the things are such as ought to have been in the National Museum.

Document No. 72

MAULANA AZAD'S SPEECH IN PARLIAMENT DATED 15-3-1950 DURING THE DISCUSSION ON GENERAL BUDGET (LIST OF DEMANDS) AND HIS REPLIES TO QUESTIONS RAISED IN THIS CONNECTION

Maulana Azad: I am thankful of those hon. friends of mine who have taken part in the budget discussions. It was highly gratifying to note that they are full conscious of the difficulties that are being faced by the Ministry of Education. I do not want to conceal my feelings from you. I am not at all happy with the present state of affairs. I think the present state of affairs to be highly regrettable. But besides this I also see that the matters are taking such a shape and have so paralysed us that we cannot make any progress. It is third year since I assumed charge of this Ministry. The first was the year 1947, and as you all well know that was a year full of calamities and misfortunes. Such a violent commotion of misfortunes and calamities came to pass that it shook the entire country. My heart was also moved. I thought it to be a passing tide all the time thinking as it has come so it would vanish in the due course of time. But we wish to put the schemes, that we have before us into operation with all possible promptness so that we may be able to make definite progress.

Till that time our schemes had not been finalized. Special Committees had been set up for those matters that we had taken upon ourselves to accomplish thinking them to be of highest importance. Last year these Committees finished their deliberations and all our important schemes were finalized. Now the time had come to give these schemes a practical shape and rapid progress made, but at the time of the last year's budget some such difficulties cropped up that we were compelled to think of postponing these schemes for one year more, and to complete only the preliminaries of the more important ones. Therefore I did so. Till now my hopes were high and I had not even thought of any discomfiture, but I like to tell you that when some six months back a crisis came to pass we came to know that the budget was having a deficit of some 40 crores of rupees, and we were to make up this deficit anyhow. In the meantime devaluation and such other things occurred, and the result was that the amount of money that was allocated for Education in the budget had to be reduced by ten per cent. I did not very readily agree for this cut. My friends, who are not here this time, know it full well that I continued to wrangle for two weeks on end but when the actual facts faced me then I also had to acknowledge that except this there was no other way out, and only then was I constrained to accept this cut. The result was that out of the budgetted amount a sum of Rs. 1 crore and 53 lacs had to be given back. The result was that we had to shelve our schemes and to put a stop to those undertakings that we had begun, and one of them was to distribute a sum of Rs. 1 crore to the various provinces during the year. In the Conference of the Provincial Education Ministers it was decided that out of this sum of money grants would be allocated to the various provinces. In the Provinces also some preliminaries had been completed. The result of this ten per cent. cut was that the sum of one crore 53 lacs of rupees, that had been placed at the disposal of this Ministry, had to be returned and we were compelled to give out that only 60 lacs of rupees should be spent on this work.

The provinces protested against this cut but we were helpless and we had no other way out. Then the question arose about the coming year's budget. On making a study of the same I came to the conclusion that I should better dismiss even the last flickering rays of hope that I had longingly cherished so far. After taking into consideration the entire situation I came to the conclusion that what to say of the coming year for two or three years to come no hopes could be entertained that the Government would be able to find and allocate money out of the Central Revenues for education. The result was that I became down-hearted. Such a state of affairs came to pass for the reason, as you all well know, that the economic condition of the Central Government was not sound. Taking into consideration the difficulties that the world had to face as a result of the World War our economic condition was quite sound, our income was quite sufficient. But this also you know that rather unfortunately such things came to pass that we had to spend a huge amount of money on such items of expenditure that could not be postponed, for example you well know the amount of money that we spend on food imports or on rehabilitation of those thousands of homeless persons, who have come here after losing their hearths and homes. Last year 29 crore of rupees were allocated for the rehabilitation of these refugees and this year 20 crores have been set apart for this purpose. Besides this you know that the condition in the country have taken such a turn that we cannot make even the slightest cut in the Defence Budget.

I do not know whether you know it or not that in 1947 when our country had not been partitioned then we, the Central Cabinet, had fully taken into consideration the fact as to how much money should we allocate to all the three services of Defence Forces. After much deliberations and fully taking into consideration the fact that we must not make drastic cuts in the Defence expenditure but should reduce it gradually, it was decided that at the maximum we should allocate a sum of Rs. one hundred crores for all the three services of the Defence Forces. This decision ,was for the undivided India. Then came the partition, and what was the result of this partition? The result was that one third of our country was sliced away and thus the burden of this one third part of the country was shifted off shoulders of the bigger portion. But in spite of this you well know how much we are spending on the Defence of the country. We were spending 170 crores of rupees. This year 168 crores of rupees have been set apart for Defence. Before the partition we had decided to spend at the maximum 100 crores but now we are spending 170 crores and for the next year we have planned to spend 168 crores. Out of this amount 68 crores have been set apart to give training to the State's Forces. In this way the Defence budget amounts to 168 crores. This money we are not spending all willingly. But you well know that the conditions are such and the circumstances have forced our hands to do so and hence we cannot reduce the defence expenditure. The result is that there is now left no channel wherefrom money could be had for the general welfare work. Then from where money could be had? The result was that I had to become helpless and so I made an unconditional surrender. There was no other alternative even. When the new Government assumed charge then the Education budget of the Central Government did not exceed two and a half crores of rupees. I made strenuous efforts and increased it to six crores. But for the important things that we have to do even these six crores of rupees are just like a paltry sum of six rupees, they are just like a drop in the ocean. If we were to allocate at least 15 crores of rupees for education from the Central Government budget then, no doubt this sum also is not quite sufficient, with this money we can complete the more important of our schemes.

According to the new scheme of Basic Education, as has been recommended by Kher Committee, we seek to spread Basic Education both of junior and senior standards throughout the country in 16 years' time and want to make it universal and compulsory. The junior standard would be ten years and the senior of six years. If we were to launch that scheme then the Central Government should have to contribute 30 per cent. of the expenses, and the rest 70 per cent. would be contributed by the States. If we were to launch this scheme then in the very first year we require four crores of rupees to complete the Centre's quota, and in the next year we would have to contribute seven crores and some lacs towards this.

Similar is the case of the Adult Education Scheme. The entire adult population would be divided into two batches of five years' duration. Fifty per cent. of the adult population would be made literate in five years' time and the rest 50 per cent. in the succeeding five years. This scheme was to be completed in ten years' time. In this scheme the burden of expenditure was equally divided between the Centre and the various States. Fifty per cent. of the expenditure was to be borne by the Centre and the rest 50 per cent. by the States. This scheme also we could not launch. For this we had allocated a sum of Rs. one crore in the last budget, but after a few months only more than half of this sum had to be returned. You well know the position of this year's budget. The position in this budget is that if money could be found for basic education, training of teachers and adult education then the amount would be nearly 15 lacs only. You all can well imagine to what use this paltry sum of 15 lacs can be put. This sum of money cannot even meet the expenditure on education in Delhi alone. Therefore the thing that I wish to submit is that I am very unhappy. I do not see any cure of the canker that is eating into my heart. If I were to know that this scarcity and difficulty is to last for so much time and after that we would not be constrained to restrict our activities, then at least this thought would have relieved much of the pinch of the pricking. But I do not see any such way out and I have been forced to think that this affair is a very very deep seated one. This matter is not such that at the time of Demands for Grants some of my hon. friends table a few cut motions and hold discussions for two or three hours. This matter is far more deep seated than this. We should conclusively think from where the money, that we wish to take from the Centre for Education, would come. There is no doubt about the fact that difficulties are there, and as I have just submitted before you I did not see any such way out whereupon I would have insisted and pointed out that money for education should be had from this source. Yet still the matter is such that if we were to hold a council together and pay fullest possible attention to this problem with the intention that we have to find this money anyhow, then it is not at all impossible to find a sum of 15 crores of rupees per year for education provided we pay attention and have a will to do. I wish the House to pay attention to this and after pondering over the whole matter should try to evolve ways and means whereby this affair could be given a final consideration. If some Committee would be set up for this then the Ministry of Education would give it its whole-hearted support and I hope that the Ministry of Finance also, as far as possible, would surely be willing to give all possible help.

Anyhow the thing that I wished to submit before you is that as far as the matters of Education are concerned the condition is quite deplorable and no reasonable and responsible person can feel satisfied or even happy on this state of affairs. But the pity is that the affairs have taken such a shape that I do not see any effective solution or way out of this *impasse*.

Some of my hon. friends have drawn my attention to certain things. Shrimati Durgabai has laid stress on the fact that these days we are facing an acute shortage of funds. But many such national institutions and national organizations do exist in our country which are rendering useful service, and if they are given some help and patronage then they can render a good deal of service to the country. I quite agree with the views expressed by her and I would like to assure her that the scheme of Basic Education, that the Ministry of Education has placed before it, could not have been completed by the Government alone. Many elements had been incorporated in this scheme, one of them was that of national organisation and this included the scheme of seeking co-operation of the educational men and women of this country. It was planned that they would be asked to take up this national service and their enthusiasm and talents would be utilized to the best possible advantage. But when the original scheme was shelved then this also had to be postponed. I assure her that I have not left that scheme for good. I still have that under my consideration and most probably I would try to implement that scheme very soon.

Some of my hon. friends have complained that adequate efforts do not appear to have been made, as they ought to have been, for the spread of the Hindi language and for making its learning popular.

I fully agree with the views held by them, that the provision that we have laid down in the Constitution, that for the coming 15 years English would be used in the Centre, must not for one minute mean that we should not begin our efforts in this direction from now from this very minute. If we would not make efforts to popularize Hindi throughout the country from today from this very minute, and give all possible aid and help for the spread of education in the country, then we must not expect that after the lapse of 15 years the country would be in a position to conduct the entire work of the State in Hindi, I fully agree with their views on this point. I think that this work could be done quite satisfactorily if the Governments of the States would try for this end, and the Centre also taking a part in the efforts made. But I wish to assure you that as far as these things were concerned, such as that Governments of the States would draw people's attention towards this, would create facilities for learning Hindi, then I wish to inform you that this task is being done with all possible speed and is decidedly showing satisfactory results. As far as the question of the Central Government taking any direct step in this direction is concerned, then I beg to inform you that all possible efforts are being made in this direction.

The most difficult task facing us is of finding technical terms. If in place of English we wish to make Hindi and other State languages the medium of instruction in the University stage of Education, then we would have to face the most difficult problem of the scientific and technical terms. Till we would not resolve this difficulty our education of Hindi would not make any progress. The Ministry of Education has decided to set up a Board for this purpose. Some money has been allocated for this purpose. It is expected that this Board would include experts of the subject and they would be able to take the various aspects of this problem into consideration. This Board would compile a dictionary and would complete this task after taking into consideration all the aspects of the problem. Besides this it is also necessary to compile after careful deliberations a Text Book of Hindi for schools. For this purpose also some money has been set apart in the Budget. For this purpose also we wish to set up a Board, but this work only is not comprehensive enough by itself and so we wish to begin our work on bigger scale, but in this matter also we are facing the self-same obstacle, that we have been encountering in all our efforts. And this obstacle is that of money or financial help. The result is that no schemes can be completed and no tasks undertaken.

We have called a meeting of the Central Advisory Board in the month of April to discuss the Report of the University Commission and to give its opinion on it. But what would happen afterwards, and if it is decided to implement and put into practice the various recommendations of the University Commission then the question of adequate funds automatically crops up.

Just now an hon. friend was saying something about the rural universities. There is no doubt about the fact that rural universities are things of utmost importance, and especially for the life in India, where 80 per cent. of the population is rural such universities are very essential so that by their cultural atmosphere these universities should give lead to the rural population. But for this also the problem of money faces us.

Just now an hon. friend has given out that for secondary education a Board is being set up and would soon come into existence. But for this Board also money is required and there are certain other schemes also in this very connection, but for all these money is required.

Shrimati Durgabai: I wish to enquire one thing. Would it not be better first to ensure availability of funds before setting up Boards for preparing educational schemes? Because though money is spent on the deliberations of the Board yet funds are always wanting for implementing the recommendations of the Board.

Maulana Azad: If we would adopt this procedure, that till funds are not available we would not proceed with any schemes, then all our activities would come to a dead stop. Therefore I think that the Board should be set up and it may be asked to present its report at the earliest. But besides all this the thing of basic importance is the question of money, and till no satisfactory arrangements are made to this effect, it is difficult for us to make any progress in any direction, whatsoever.

My hon. friend Shri Jaipal Singh has complained that the amount of money, which is given as scholarships to the backward classes, is very inadequate. One criterion of judging the relative importance of the various tasks can be that it should be planned to do a particular work in a particular manner and then see if that standard is achieved or not. Another test can be to ascertain whether a particular work, which is being carried on under certain circumstances, would be able to produce maximum output or not. When the present Government assumed the reins of the Government then there was only one scheme for giving scholarships to the scheduled castes, and some two and a half to three lacs of rupees had been set apart for this purpose. Only this scheme was in force. The next year when I took charge of the Ministry then I, after making strenuous efforts, allocated a sum of 50 thousand rupees for giving scholarships to backward classes. Later on this sum of 50 thousand was increased, at one stroke of pen, to four lacs and you must take into consideration the circumstances and conditions under which this work was being carried on. I increased this sum from 50 thousand to four lacs, and the sum set apart for scheduled castes I raised from five lacs to ten lacs. Now remains the question of giving them more and more impetus, well, this would surely be taken into consideration.

Shri Sonavane (Bombay): The share allotted to scheduled castes is not even according to their population. A reasonable share due to them is not allotted to them. It is much less than that.

Maulana Azad: I would like to draw the attention of the hon. Member towards the fact whether the education here is being imparted on the population basis?

An hon. friend made a mention of the Saugor University. Saugor University and such other Universities are the concern of the State Governments. Efforts were made in this connection. The Development Grants, that are being given to the various States, include a sum of money exclusively meant for educational purposes. It was expected that the Madhya Pradesh Government would give a grant to the Saugor University out of this Development Grant. But as a result of the financial difficulties the Development Grant, that was being given to the States, had to be stopped. But I hope that the munificent legacy, that the late lamented Dr. Gour has very generously left for the University, will in a way put an end to all the difficutlies faced by this University.

Anyhow I am very grateful to you for your kindly realizing the difficulties of the Ministry of Education. I have placed before you the real facts and conditions. I am not at all satisfied with the state of affairs resulting from the difficulties that are in our way. It is hoped that a time would soon come when we would be able to develop the cause of education to our entire satisfaction.

Shri B. Das (Orissa): I wish to enquire one thing. In the Constituent Assembly while we sat discussing we expected the Government will soon establish an Indian Academy for the propagation of Hindi culture and Hindi language. I want to know whether Government of India have come to any consideration about the foundation of Hindi Academy.

Maulana Azad: The Government had a proposal of calling a Conference for this purpose, but on account of financial difficulties this proposal was shelved. There are other matters also of this type and if funds would be forthcoming then I can get this thing also done.

Shri Chattopadhyay: A very interesting suggestion was put by Shrimati Durgabai that the education of girls should be specially entrusted in the Primary and Secondary forms to women only and no reply has been given on that point by the hon. Minister.

Maulana Azad: This suggestion needs no reply. As far as my opinion is concerned I fully agree with her in this matter.

Document No. 73

REPLIES BY MAULANA AZAD DATED 29-3-1950, IN THE PARLIAMENT TO QUESTIONS ASKED ABOUT THE FEDERAL LIBRARY IN NEW DELHI

Seth Govind Das: Will the Minister of Education be pleased to state whether it is proposed to set up a federal library at the capital of India for purposes of research and education like the one in Calcutta?

The Minister of Education (Maulana Azad): Yes. Government have before them a Scheme for establishing a Central Reference Library in Delhi with a Copyright Section attached to it. The Expert Committee appointed to work out the details thereof has not yet completed its deliberations.

Seth Govind Das: Are the Government thinking of transferring the books of the National Library of Calcutta also to this Library?

Maulana Azad: No, this is a self-contained and separate scheme altogether. The object of this scheme is to start a Library at Delhi.

Seth Govind Das: Has the Committee of the Experts constituted for this purpose started its deliberations? And if so, when the recommendations would be received by the Government?

Maulana Azad: A meeting of this Committee was held in January 1950, but as yet the Committee has not formulated its recommendations.

Seth Govind Das: When the recommendations should be expected? Have the Government fixed any time limit for the submission of the recommendations?

Maulana Azad: No, no time limit has been fixed. It is expected that no sooner the deliberations would finish the Committee would submit its recommendations.

Dr. Deshmukh: May I know if this Library will be opened in the present Capital of India or in the future Capital of India?

Mr. Speaker: Order, order.

Shri Bhatt: Will the Library be opened in this very year?

Maulana Azad: This all depends upon the extent to which the financial position of the Government permits.

Shri Kishorimohan Tripathi: What amount of money would be spent on the scheme that has been drawn up for starting a Library at Delhi?

Maulana Azad: No amount of money has been fixed for this purpose as yet. A decision in this connection would be made when the report of Expert Committee set up for this purpose is received.

Shri Raj Bahadur: When was this Committee of Experts set up?

Maulana Azad: This committee was set up on 5th November, 1947.

Shri Raj Bahadur: May I know the reason why no meeting of this committee was convened from 5th November 1947 to 25th January 1950?

Maulana Azad: We should expect that the members of the Committee would finish their work at the earliest. I would like to draw the attention of the hon. Member towards the fact that taking into consideration the financial difficulties that are embarrassing the Government, very little hopes can be entertained that money for such things could be found immediately. Suppose we get the report of the Committee today, yet still we would not be able to find money for this Library immediately.

Giani G.S. Musafir: Who are the members of this Committee?

Maulana Azad: This Committee has six members:

1. Educational Adviser, Government of India–*Chairman*.
2. Dr. S.N. Sen, Director of Archives.
3. Dr. P.N. Joshi, Director of Archives, Government of Bombay.
4. Dr. S.R. Ranganathan, Delhi University.
5. Prof. D.S. Kothari, Secretary, National Institute of Science.
6. Librarian, National Library, Calcutta.

Document No. 74

REPLIES BY MAULANA AZAD DATED 29-3-1950 IN PARLIAMENT TO THE QUESTIONS ASKED BY SETH GOVIND DAS IN CONNECTION WITH THE GRANTS TO UNIVERSITIES

Seth Govind Das: Will the Minister of Education be pleased to lay on the Table of the House a statement showing the amounts of grant given to various universities and educational institutions for the year 1950-51, and state whether any provision has been made to provide Chairs for Hindi where none exists at present?

The Minister of Education (Maulana Azad): A statement is laid on the Table of the House. [See *Appendix VI, annexure No. 4.*] This would show the amounts of grants sanctioned by this Ministry to the various educational institutions for 1948-49 and 1949-50. It also shows the budget provisions for 1950-51. Establishment of special Chairs in various Universities for particular subjects is not such a thing for which specific grants may normally be made by the Government.

For the information of the hon. Member I wish to say that as far as the question of spreading and promotion of learning of Hindi language is concerned the Ministry of Education has received some suggestions in this respect. The special meeting of the Central Advisory Board of Education that is to be held on 22nd April will take these suggestions into consideration and it is expected that after this we would be able to give a practical shape to these suggestions.

Seth Govind Das: As Hindi has now become the National language then so far as the founding of Chairs for Hindi are concerned are the Government taking this proposal into consideration that in those States where Hindi is not generally spoken and specially in the Universities of such States, Chairs for Hindi be founded and the Government should give them help?

Maulana Azad: All these matters are before the Ministry of Education, and these very things would be brought to the notice of the Advisory Board at its next meeting.

Seth Govind Das: Are Gurukul Kangri of Hardwar, Kashi Vidyapity and Shanti Niketan of Bolpur among the educational institutions whom the Government have given help.

Maulana Azad: If the hon. Member would take the trouble of going through the Statement then he would come to know of these things. Help has been given to Gurukul Hardwar.

Seth Govind Das: And to Kashi Vidyapith?

Maulana Azad: No.

Document No. 75

REPLIES OF MAULANA AZAD DATED 29-3-1950 IN THE PARLIAMENT TO THE QUESTIONS ASKED BY DR. DESHMUKH AND OTHERS IN CONNECTION WITH THE INDIAN STATISTICAL INSTITUTE

Dr. Deshmukh: (a) Will the Minister of Education be pleased to state the year in which the Indian Statistical Institute was established?

(b) Is it a private, Government or semi-Government Institute?

(c) What is the annual expenditure of the Institute since 1945 and what are the grants and donations given by the Central and State Governments since 1945 up-to-date?

(d) What is the total grant proposed to be given to the Institute in the year 1950-51?

(e) Is it proposed to take over the Institute under complete Government management if not already under such management?

(f) What are the sources of income of the Institute apart from grants given by the State and Central Government, if any?

(g) Are there any proposals for the re-organization of the Institute?

The Minister of Education (Maulana Azad): (a) 1932.

(b) It is a private body registered under the Societies Registration Act, 1860.

(c) A statement giving the necessary information is laid on the Table of the House. [See *Appendix VI, annexure No. 6.*]

(d) Rs. 4,50,000

(e) No, Sir.

(f) The Institute mainly depends on Central and State grants. But other income is from membership fees, interest on investments, Training and Examination fees and Contributions from Certain Scientific Bodies.

(g) In 1948 the Government agreed to give a block of Rs. 5 lacs per annum for 3 years to the Institute on the condition that the Institute was reorganised on certain lines acceptable to Government. The proposals provided for the representation of the Central Government on the various bodies, *viz.*, Governing Body, Finance Committee and Selection Committee of the Institute. The adoption of the scheme by the Institute is yet awaited.

Dr. Deshmukh: May I know how many students are studying here at present and how many would be able to study therein in future?

Maulana Azad: I cannot tell the number just now.

Dr. Deshmukh: When will this reorganisation be completed? Have all the terms and conditions for its reorganisation been settled?

Maulana Azad: Yes, but we are just waiting. The final decision of the Institute has not yet been communicated to us.

Shri Tyagi: Does this Institute teach the subject of statistics or simply collects and compiles the statistical figures?

Maulana Azad: It does both these things. It imparts instruction as well as collects and compiles the statistics.

Shri Tyagi: Do the Government according to its requirements ever send instructions that statistics on a particular subjects be collected and compiled?

Maulana Azad: Yes.

Document No. 76

MAULANA AZAD'S INAUGURAL SPEECH DATED 9-4-1950 AT THE INDIAN COUNCIL FOR CULTURAL RELATIONS, NEW DELHI

I have great pleasure in welcoming you to this inaugural meeting of the Indian Council for Cultural Relations. You will remember that we met last year on the 21st August, when we decided to set up a Council for the establishment of closer cultural relations between India and her neighbours in the east and west. On that occasion, I described to you how during the war years the Indo-Iranian Cultural Committee had reopened one of the doors that had been shut some centuries ago. I also drew your attention to the need of re-establishing all our old cultural contacts in the context of a free India. In that meeting it was agreed to set up a Provisional Committee to define the aims and objects of the Council and draw up its constitution, and also appoint a small sub-committee to do the necessary work in that behalf.

The Provisional Committee met on November 27, 1949, and, after making some notable changes, accepted the draft constitution which had been prepared by the sub-committee. Of these changes, the most important was the removal of all the territorial or geographical limitations on the activities of the Council. The Provisional Committee recommended that the Council should aim at establishing closer contacts between India and all other countries of the world whether in Asia or outside. While we welcome this extension in the scope of the activities of the Council, I think you will agree that it would be more practical to proceed towards that aim step by step. We therefore propose to set up for the present two sections of the Cultural Council, *viz*., a Middle-East and Turkey Section, and a South and East Asian Section. The Middle-East and Turkey Section has accordingly been set up and will work towards the establishment of closer relations with all the countries of the Middle East, Turkey, Afghanistan and Pakistan. Since India and Iran have always had special relations with each other, there will be a special sub-section for the promotion of Indo-Iranian relations. I hope that within the next year or so, we will be able to set up the South and East Asian Wing of the Council to promote closer contacts with the countries in that region.

You will be glad to hear that our first steps towards the setting up of this Council have met with warm welcome from different foreign countries. Egypt and Syria, Lebanon and Iraq, Iran and Afghanistan, Burma and Ceylon and the Republic of Indonesia, have all expressed strong support for the proposal. I hope that now that the Council is established, our cultural relations with these countries will continually expand and we will secure the full co-operation of the universities and other cultural and learned societies of India and these countries for the furtherance of our objects.

I have already referred to the limitation of our resources which compel us to proceed step by step. Nevertheless, action has been initiated and I can report to you some of the things already done:

(a) The headquarters of the Council have been established at Hyderabad House. In the headquarters, we are building up a library which will provide facilities to scholars for the study of the history and culture of these countries.

(b) To make a beginning with the library, I have presented to the Council my personal library and I hope that soon these books, which are being despatched from Calcutta, will be available to users here.

(c) The Ajit Ghosh collection which has been purchased for the Council possesses many rare and valuable books on Indian art and architecture.

(d) The reading room is being set up in the headquarters where newspapers, magazines and journals of all these countries will be available as well as the publications of universities and cultural societies.

(e) We also propose to arrange for periodic meetings where specialists will discuss particular aspects of the culture and civilisation of India and these countries.

(f) One of the functions of the Council will be the exchange of professors between India and these countries. We have already sent a professor of Sanskrit to Anjuman-e-Iran-Shinasi, Teheran. The Council also arranged for the lectures of Professor Nafisi, a well-known Iranian scholar, in some of the Indian universities.

(g) The Council also propose to publish two Quarterlies, one in Arabic to interpret Indian culture and civilisation to the Middle-East countries, and another in English for the exchange of information and knowledge between India and South and East Asian countries. The first number of the first Quarterly is in press and will soon be available, while preparations for the second Quarterly will be taken in hand at an early date.

I will not, however, go into further details of the programme which will be decided by the executive body that will be set up for the purpose.

I would, before I conclude, like to draw your attention to a practical question which is of some interest for the proper working of the Council. This Council which seeks to create better understanding among peoples of different countries must necessarily concern itself with the language of its transactions. At one time French was the language of international intercourse. Nowadays that position is being gradually taken by English. We will therefore have English as the major language for the transactions of the Council but it is our intention to provide also for French as an alternative medium as soon as possible. At the time, I hope, that the work of this Council will encourage the study of Sanskrit, Arabic, Persian, Chinese and other oriental langauges which have contributed to the development of human culture and civilisation.

Document No. 77

REPLIES TO QUESTIONS IN PARLIAMENT DATED 14-4-1950, BY MAULANA AZAD, ASKED ABOUT THE CULTURAL MISSIONS TO ASIAN COUNTRIES

Prof. S.N. Mishra: (a) Will the Minister of Education be pleased to state whether Government propose to send Cultural Missions to some of the Asian Countries in near future?

(b) If so, what are the names of the countries to which such missions are proposed to be sent?

The Ministry of Education (Maulana Azad): (a) At present there is no proposal to send Cultural Missions to any Asian countries in the near future.

(b) Does not arise.

Prof. S.N. Mishra: Have invitations been received from Asiatic countries requesting that Cultural Delegations be sent there?

Maulana Azad: As far as the question of sending Cultural Delegations is concerned we have received no special invitation from any foreign country. As also we have not written anything to any country in this respect.

Prof. S.N. Mishra: Was it intended some time back to send a cultural mission to Bali?

Maulana Azad: I think the hon. Member is alluding to that Mission which was to be sent there by the Archaeological Department. As far as I remember the Mission had gone there and has since returned after completing its work.

Sardar B.S. Man: Different cultures are found in India. When those Cultural Missions go to other countries then thinking which culture to be superior to all others they try to propound?

Maulana Azad: The culture that we call Indian Culture.

Document No. 78

REPLIES TO QUESTIONS ASKED REGARDING THE CULTURAL RELATIONS COUNCIL, DATED 14-4-1950 IN THE PARLIAMENT

Prof. S.N. Mishra: (a) Will the Minister of Education be pleased to state the functions of the Cultural Relations Council?

(b) Do Asian Cultural Relations fall within its ambit?

The Minister of Education (Maulana Azad): (a) The function of the Indian Council for Cultural Relations is to revive or establish and strengthen cultural relations between India and other countries and take all steps conducive to that end.

(b) Yes. The hon. Member's attention is drawn to the Constitution of the Council of which a copy is placed on the Table of the House. [See *Appendix VII, annexure No. 21.*]

Prof. S.N. Mishra: Have its branches been established in Egypt, Turkey and Iraq?

Maulana Azad: No. The council has just been set up. It is just possible that its branches may be established in the long run. But for the present no branches have been established.

Shri Gautam: Is the Council going to adopt such measures that would help to improve our relations with the other countries of Asia?

Maulana Azad: As I just said the Council would gradually make efforts to put into practice such things that would be considered essential for this purpose. For the present a professor of Sanskrit has been sent to Iran on behalf of the Council. At its headquarters the Council has set up a library and is going to open a reading room. Soon the Executive Body would hold its meeting and would discuss and chalk out the future programme.

Shri Kamath: For improving the cultural relations between the Asian countries how much amount of money has been sanctioned under this scheme for the next year?

Maulana Azad: A sum of Rs. one lakh has been allocated for the next year.

Shri R. Velayudhan: How many members are there on the Council and on what basis have they been selected or nominated?

Maulana Azad: The constitution has been laid on the Table of the House. If the hon. Member would take the trouble of going through it then he would come to know of the details. The Council has been constituted in the manner that all the universities and cultural societies have been given representation on the Council and 30 members have been nominated by Government of India.

Shri Borooah: May I know whether the Government propose starting a school for the proper study of the languages and culture of the Asian countries, so that the work of Council may be facilitated?

Maulana Azad: No, for the present this is not included in the programme of the Council. This thing relates to the Ministry of Foreign Relations. If that Ministry would deem it necessary then such a school would be established.

Shri A.P. Jain: May I know if the Council intends to work according to a well settled scheme or would take such steps as would be deemed necessary to meet the needs of the situation that may arise?

Maulana Azad: No, a scheme would be chalked out. But it is quite clear that the Council would enlarge the field of its activities after taking into consideration the amount of money at its disposal and the duties it has to perform.

Babu Ramnarayan Singh: This work is to be accomplished with the cooperation of other countries. If no branches are established in the foreign countries then how the work would proceed?

Mr. Speaker: You are entering into argument.

Babu Ramnarayan Singh: I am asking the ways and means of securing co-operation of the other countries.

Maulana Azad: The cooperation would be secured in this way that professors from those countries would be invited to come here and those of this country would be sent there. These are the methods with which we can improve our cultural relations with other countries.

Document No. 79

REPLIES TO QUESTIONS DATED 14-4-1950 BY MAULANA AZAD IN PARLIAMENT ASKED ABOUT THE FRENCH STUDENTS

Shri P. Basi Reddi: Will the Minister of Education be pleased to state:

(a) the number of scholarships awarded to French students for study in India;

(b) the number of scholarships awarded by French Government to Indian students for a similar purpose; and

(c) the expenditures involved for both the Governments separately on account of these scholarships?

The Minister of Education (Maulana Azad): (a) Nine Fellowships have been awarded to French scholars for the year 1949-50. So far only one has arrived in India.

(b) The French Government has awarded so far 37 scholarships to Indian students as under:

Year	Awards
1945-46	3
1946-47	4
1947-48	9
1948-49	11
1949-50	10
Total	37

(c) (i) The Government of India have no information about the expenditure incurred on this scheme by the French Government.

(ii) Approximately Rs. 900 have been spent by the Government of India on the scheme during the financial year 1949-50. A budget provision of Rs. 30,600 has been made for expenditure on the same scheme during 1950-51.

Shri P. Basi Reddi: Has the Government awarded scholarships to students of any other country?

Maulana Azad: Yes, these have been awarded to certain other countries also.

Shri P. Basi Reddi: What are the countries?

Maulana Azad: I cannot give the list thereof at present.

Shri Sonavane: What are the subjects for study for the students who are awarded these scholarships and sent abroad?

Maulana Azad: I cannot say this offhand.

Shri Deshbandhu Gupta: What is the number of boys and girls, among the students of foreign countries who have been awarded scholarships?

Maulana Azad: I am afraid I cannot reply this offhand.

Document No. 80

MAULANA AZAD'S REPLIES DATED 14-4-1950 IN PARLIAMENT TO THE QUESTIONS ASKED IN CONNECTION WITH THE ANCIENT MONUMENTS IN SIBSAGAR IN ASSAM

Shri Buragohain: Will the Minister of Education be pleased to state:

(a) the names of ancient monuments preserved in Sibsagar district in Assam;

(b) the nature of conservation work done and expenses incurred in preserving the said monuments in the year 1949-50; and

(c) what steps if any are taken to repair the golden dome of the Sibdole Temple at Sibsagar?

The Minister of Education (Maulana Azad): (a) and (b) Two statements, one giving a list of protected monuments in the district of Sibsagar and the other showing the nature of work done and expenditure incurred on the various monuments during 1949-1950 are placed on the Table of the House. [See *Appendix VII, annexure No. 22.*]

(c) Due to non-availability of a suitable local gilder, repairs to the golden Kalasi (final) of the Sibdole temple could not be attended to. It is proposed to bring down the Kalasi to Calcutta this year as soon as the parcel booking on the New Assam Rail link is restored.

Shri Buragohain: With regard to (a) and (b), may I know when the list of monuments of national importance was first prepared and whether it has since been brought uptodate?

Maulana Azad: The list gives full details of 19 places, and last year a sum of Rs. 7,720/- was spent over its repairs.

Shri Buragohain: But when was the list first prepared and has it since been brought uptodate?

Maulana Azad: This list was prepared at the time when the hon. Member gave notice of this question.

Shri R.K. Chaudhuri: May I know what amount has been set apart for the repair of this dome?

Maulana Azad: No. I cannot say this offhand.

Maulvi Wajed Ali: May I know when the work for repairing this Kalasi shall begin?

Maulana Azad: I cannot exactly tell this to the hon. Member, but I think that as soon as it is brought down to Calcutta, its repairing work shall be immediately undertaken and efforts made to carry out the repairs without any delay.

Shri Satish Chandra: According to item 67 of the Union List of the Constitution, a few particular ancient monuments in this country should be declared by law to be of national importance. When do the Government expect to bring forth legislation in this connection before the House?

Maulana Azad: Action is being taken in this direction.

Shri Kamath: May I know what is the criterion for distinguishing as to which of these monuments are 'ancient' and which of these are 'modern'?

Maulana Azad: The first test is history. Those which are modern are 'modern' and those which are old are 'old'.

Shri Buragohain: Is there any officer of the Archaeological Department posted in any part of Assam to look after these monuments?

Maulana Azad: There are Circle Superintendents and such officers are posted in Assam also.

Shri R.K. Chaudhuri: May I take it from the hon. Minister that he will have no hesitation in giving as much money as is required for the repair of this dome?

Maulana Azad: Yes, I shall certainly assure the hon. Member that as much money as is required shall be spent for its repairs.

Document No. 81

LETTER FROM SARDAR PATEL TO MAULANA AZAD

New Delhi
3 June, 1950

My dear Maulana Saheb,

The PIO, Mr. B.L. Sharma, has just now shown me, as he was bound to, the statement which you propose to issue to the Press. I myself feel that it would have been better if you had left the matter to be dealt with by the Prime Minister as he thought best. It is quite clear from Dr. Matthai's statement that the matter is rather personal between him and the Prime Minister. As it is, I do not like the controversy which has been started by Dr. Matthai's second statement. However, he has issued a statement and I think the Prime Minister is the most suitable person to deal with it, as constitutionally he should. Apart from this, I feel that for an individual Minister to issue a statement of this kind would be rather inappropriate, particularly if it contains some factual inaccuracies which, as I would show later, have occurred in your statement. If these inaccuracies remain, it might provoke some counter-reply from Dr. Matthai or some of our ex-colleagues, who were present in the Cabinet at the time, and even present colleagues. I should certainly like to avoid all this in the interest of the good name of our own Cabinet no less than with the intention of leaving the Prime Minister a free hand to deal with the matter as he likes. I am arranging for the whole statement to be wirelessed to him on board ship. The inaccuracies to which I have referred above are as follows:

(a) During the time that the 20 per cent. cuts were imposed, the Prime Minister was away in America. Dr. Matthai knows it and could easily contradict you and say that the whole thing was completed before the Prime Minister returned from there; and

(b) It is not correct to say that Dr. Matthai did not oppose the [Nehru-Liaquat Ali] Pact during its discussion in the Cabinet. I recall several times when Dr. Matthai did express his opposition in emphatic language. In fact, we were all surprised at Dr. Matthai taking so much interest in the discussion over this issue.

2. My advice to you would, therfore, be that you should not issue this statement and leave it to the Prime Minister to deal with the statement as he likes. I do not think the delay would very much matter. If, however, you feel that you must do so, although I would regret this decision of yours, I feel that you should correct the inaccuracies to which I have referred above. I have asked Sharma to await your instructions.

Yours sincerely,
Vallabhbhai Patel

The Hon'ble Maulana Abul Kalam Azad
Minister for Education
New Delhi.

Document No. 82

LETTER FROM MAULANA AZAD TO SARDAR PATEL

New Delhi

4 June, 1950

My dear Vallabhbhai,

Many thanks for your kind letter of yesterday. Had the statement of Dr. Matthai been limited to personal affairs between him and the Prime Minister there could have been no reason for a third party to interfere. But he has discussed the appointment of the Planning Commission and has not only held it useless but has tried to prove it injurious as well. We have appointed the Commission and have raised hopes in the public mind that it would be helpful in removing the present troubles of the country. Personally, I consider it to be a very important work and I am deeply hurt if any one tries to ridicule it. Dr. Matthai has undoubtedly a right to put his point of view before the public and similarly those who differ from him must also get a chance to speak out their mind. I have said nothing new in my statement. I have only expressed my views about the Planning Commission. I thank you for the advice which you have kindly given to me. I have always valued your advice and shall do so in future, but you should excuse me if I have felt the need of putting my idea before the public in this connection.

In regard to financial control, you have written that when the 20% cut was decided, the Prime Minister was in America. I think full facts have not come to your notice in this connection because you were probably out of Delhi at that time. The proposal of 20% cut had come up before the Cabinet in the presence of the Prime Minister. It was hotly discussed in two successive meetings. Dr. Mookerjee, Kidwai and Rajkumari strongly objected to it. I too was not prepared for the cut. On the contrary, Pandit Nehru supported the Finance Minister with all emphasis and requested all the Ministers to support the Finance Minister during the present financial crisis.

After that it was decided that you and the Finance Minister would call for details from all the Ministers and give a final decision. Accordingly you gave the decision. So whatever I have written is not incorrect. Had I got even the least doubt in its accuracy I would never have liked to refer to it.

I may also mention here that the procedure adopted by Mr. B.L. Sharma was not proper. If he considered the publication of a Minister's statement inadvisable, he could bring it to the notice of his Minister. The Minister could then have a talk with me in this regard, or he could bring it to your notice as the acting Prime Minister (as he did later on). The matter would have ended there and then. But he himself chose to object to the statement and advise me personally in this matter. This could in no way be proper. He is a publicity officer. He is not the adviser of Ministers. You can well imagine my reactions to his lecturing. The first question I put to him was whether he was speaking to me on behalf of his Minister or on his own behalf. He replied that he had not mentioned it to anyone up to that time; but he considered it necessary to advise me on his own behalf. Naturally my reply could be none other than that I did not need his advice, and that he should not dare advise Ministers.

I hope he would be directed to bring such matters to the notice of his Minister, who would take whatever action he would deem necessary.

Yours sincerely,
A.K. Azad

The Hon'ble Sardar Vallabhbhai Patel
Acting Prime Minister
New Delhi

Document No. 83

LETTER FROM SARDAR PATEL TO MAULANA AZAD

Dehra Dun

6 June, 1950

My dear Maulana Sahib,

Thank you for your letter of 4 June, 1950 which I received this morning.

2. Like you, I myself did not like Dr. Matthai's statement. When I said that the matter had been treated by Dr. Matthai on a personal plane with the Prime Minister, I referred to the fact that he was giving the points on which he had differed from the Prime Minister personally and I still feel that the best reply could have come from the Prime Minister himself. Nor did I feel it necessary that any of us should intervene in this matter because I anticipated – and my anticipations have come true – that the Press and the public would react adversely to Dr. Matthai. On the whole this has been so. I still regard your intervention most unfortunate. Dr. Matthai's statement has been rightly called 'unedifying'. It was hardly necessary for any of us in that case to follow it up. There was also another reason. I felt that it would have added to the prestige of the Cabinet as well as to the position of the Prime Minister if he had spoken on behalf of the Cabinet Ministers rather than individual Ministers aired their own views. You issued the statement as a Member of the Cabinet and I tendered to you my advice as Deputy Prime Minister. This was not as if we were dealing with this statement as Congressmen. I feel – and to be quite frank I am quite sore about it – that my advice to you given as Deputy Prime Minister should have been constitutionally accepted.

3. As regards the point about emergency cut, the 20% cut was not accepted before the Prime Minister left for America. I am quite clear about it because I was present at the Cabinet meetings before he left when Dr. Matthai gave an account of the financial position and

suggested his remedies. All that happened before the Prime Minister left was that the Prime Minister felt that cuts and economy were essential. As to of what order it should be was left to the committee of which he, I and the Finance Minister were members. He left for America immediately after and the whole burden of imposing cuts and implementing them fell upon me and the Finance Minister. Dr. Matthai told me himself that before the Prime Minister left for America he had written to him seven or eight letters pleading for some costly scheme or other. After his return also Dr. Matthai got some letters from the Prime Minister. My apprehension was and still is that Dr. Matthai might issue a rejoinder to you giving these instances which would rather compromise the statement which you have made and might embarras the Prime Minister in dealing with Dr. Matthai's statement with full freedom. It was this contingency which I wished to avoid.

4. As regards the procedure adopted by Mr. B.L. Sharma, he saw you himself because his own Minister was away at Hubli and the Secretary, I & B. Ministry, was touring Jammu and Kashmir. In these circumstances, he was the only one who could tender advice to you and I think in publicity matters he is entitled to tender it. I have not discouraged him from tendering advice to me also. After all, he is in touch with the Press. He knows the people. He knows also the mechanism and art of publicity. Nevertheless, when he went to you and failed, I realised the handicap from which he was suffering in the absence of his Minister and Secretary. Not being able to come myself because of the late hour at which I came to know of it, I tried to contact Sir Girja Shankar Bajpai and Dharma Vira to ask them to see you and dissuade you from issuing the statement. Sir Girja Shankar was reluctant and hesitant although he agreed with my view that the statement should not issue. Dharma Vira could not be contacted as he went out to dinner to a place which had no telephone.

5. I think the PIO knows full well that normally he must approach an honourable Minister through his own Minister and in view of the circumstances which I have explained, I think no such direction, as you have suggested, is necessary.

Yours sincerely,
Vallabhbhai Patel

The Hon'ble Maulana Abul Kalam Azad
New Delhi

Document No. 84

LETTER FROM MAULANA AZAD TO SARDAR PATEL

Camp Chashma Shahi
Srinagar
17 June, 1950

My dear Vallabhbhai,

Your letter of 6 June was received here in Srinagar on 12 June. I am replying it today. The delay is deliberate as I did not want to write to you under any immediate reaction on the receipt of your letter. I wanted to consider the matter with a cool mind and this naturally meant that some time was necessary for it.

You have said in your letter, "I feel and to be quite frank I am quite sore about it that my advice to you given as Deputy Prime Minister should have been constitutionally accepted." I will assure you not for one moment did I see the matter in that light which is now disclosed by your letter nor could I ever imagine that you would so feel about it. Let me refer you to your first letter in this connection. I had no idea that you were objecting even to my statement being released at all. What I felt after the receipt of your letter was that you would prefer that the matter was left to Pandit Nehru to deal with but if I considered its publication necessary I was free to make my choice. In that case you thought it would be better if no mention was made about the 20% cut as it related to a matter which could be contradicted by Dr. Matthai.

Naturally I thought you wanted me to say those things only which you felt could not be contradicted and the portion that could be contradicted you had drawn my attention to it. I re-read that portion and I felt that as far as the real point of Dr. Matthai's statement was concerned I had not said in my statement anything which may be regarded as not in accordance with facts. Therefore, I let this portion remain as it was. I could not have any notion that you were objecting to the very idea of the publication of such a statement.

Let me put the matter in another way. As soon as Mr. Sharma got the statement he should have gone to you with it. My relationship with you is not only as a member of a Cabinet but it goes much deeper. You could have phoned to me and advised me against its being released. I would certainly have expressed my feelings about it and perhaps I might have persisted in my arguments for it. But if you had stuck to your views about it, surely I would have given up the idea of its publication altogether. It was an ordinary matter, not affecting any fundamentals. In matters like this, without going into arguments, one gives preference to one's colleague's opinion and should have no hesitation in following his advice.

In your second letter you have said, "All that happened before the Prime Minister left for America was that the Prime Minister felt that cuts and economy were essential." What I have said in my statement is that the Prime Minister was with the Finance Minister in the latter's demand for cuts and economy of expenditure. I am afraid I do not find anything more than this in my reply to Dr. Matthai. Nevertheless, if you feel that this portion of my statement does not interpret the facts rightly, I am prepared to correct my statement in this behalf in accordance with what you think about it and to say that what actually happened was that though the Prime Minister had expressed himself in favour of cuts and the need for general economy, the final decision in this connection was made by the Deputy Prime Minister and the Finance Minister after the Prime Minister had left for the United States and the programmes of the various Ministries had been carefully scrutinised.

But, as far as I am concerned, the matter does not end there. What I feel about your second letter I should be frank with it and should tell you what it is.

The Indian Cabinet is not yet three years old but our relationship with each other is of more than thirty years. We were brought together very close on account of the Indian National Congress and the leadership of Mahatmaji. We struggled together like members of the same family for the freedom of our country. We spent together our hours of joy and together we drank the draughts of bitterness. We shared with one another our joys and our sorrows. If we were together for the meetings of the Congress Working Committee, the Indian jails also found us together to spend our days there. We had our disagreements on many an occasion and we had our quarrels. But, as our unity was that of brothers, so were our disagreements and quarrels. If we quarrel among ourselves, soon we were to unite once again.

After we had achieved freedom we formed ourselves into Government. But, here also we did not enter from different doors. We came in by only one door and found ourselves bound together in unity of outlook and goal. Soon we were faced with extraordinary happenings and difficult problems and it was not easy to work in unison in those stupendous moments. Yet these hard trials could not break the strong bonds of comradeship that had existed among us for many years past. We marched on hand in hand and faced the extraordinary together.

From our old comrades many have left us for good. Those of us who are still alive have almost reached the journey's end. As far as I am concerned, I regard three of my friends as my old comrades and in no circumstances am I prepared to sever my close ties with them. They are Jawaharlal, yourself and Rajendra Prasad. I will never allow that our relationship be ever strained for a moment, particularly when this relationship is now thirty years old and has got behind it the whole history of this long period.

From your letter it appears you have felt strongly over the publication of this statement of mine. You have said, "I feel and to be quite frank I am quite sore about it..." As I have said above I am sorry I do not find anything in it which should have agitated your mind to this extent. However, in matters like this argument is of little avail and I would not like to go into it. I am prepared to resign from the Cabinet without any bitterness on my part. It is not necessary I should serve my country from inside the Government only. Perhaps I may serve her better for the remaining days of my life from outside of it. To me the most important question is that I cannot stay in a place where I may be the cause of any worry to my comrades of 30 years.

I hold more dear the continuance of the relationship that has existed between us than the membership of the Cabinet.

I hope you will excuse me for this long letter.

Yours sincerely,
A.K. Azad

The Hon'ble Sardar Vallabhbhai Patel
Deputy Prime Minister

Document No. 85

LETTER FROM SARDAR PATEL TO MAULANA AZAD

Dehra Dun

21 June, 1950

My dear Maulana Sahib,

Thank you for your letter of 17 June, 1950.

I was unhappy about the whole thing because I was placed in an embarrassing position. The matter was referred to me as Deputy Prime Minister. At the same time, my relations with you are more 'unofficial' than 'official'. If I did not act I might have been committing a dereliction of duty and, if I did and you did not accept my advice, it would place me in an embarassing position *vis-a-vis* others. It was in this quandry that I wrote to you hoping that you will accept the advice tendered; at the same time, in order not to hurt you in view of the relations which subsisted between us, I left the choice to you. My first letter was directed against the very question of your making a statement. I only pointed out that in two particular matters I thought your impression was not correct.

I understand that Dr. Matthai, as was to be expected, was not quite happy about your statement, but restrained himself from adding to the controversy; otherwise, the controversy would have probably been unending and led to bitterness and might even have affected the atmosphere about the Indo-Pak Agreement which is now prevailing. It is all this that I wanted to avoid.

This does not mean that our relations are in any way affected. They transcend official contacts and are based on years of comradeship in freedom's struggle and the conduct of affairs of a great and noble organisation. You can dismiss any thought from your mind that on this account our relationship has in any way been strained.

With kind regards,

Yours sincerely,
Vallabhbhai Patel

The Hon'ble Maulana Abul Kalam Azad
Srinagar

Document No. 86

MAULANA AZAD'S INAUGURAL ADDRESS DATED 25-12-1950 AT THE INDIAN HISTORICAL RECORDS COMMISSIONS' CONFERENCE HELD IN NAGPUR

We are meeting after a year to discuss our common problems. As you are aware, the Indian Historical Records Commission deals with all kinds of historical records. The scope of our deliberations is therefore wide and extensive. It will, however, be of advantage to confine ourselves to matters of first concern, and I am sure you will agree that these relate to questions affecting the National Archives. In all countries the National Archives are the treasure-houses of their historical wealth, and we in India can justly take pride for the extent and magnitude of our riches in this field.

Our national Archives contain a vast collection of records, but systematic series begin from 1672. Some of the latest records are as late as 1949. They therefore tell the story of nearly 300 years of a most interesting and momentous period of India's history. If what remains of the scattered records of the Moghul period are added to these collections, we can say that our records go back to the 15th century. There are not many countries which can claim records which go so far back. From the point of view of quantity also ours is one of the biggest collections not only in Asia, but in the world. I cannot give you the exact number of our records, for much work of indexing and cataloguing still remains to be done, but to give you some idea of the extent of the collection, I may say that if all these records are assembled in one place, there is no building in India big enough to contain all of them.

It is hardly necessary for me to stress before the present audience the importance of national records. Such records are the basis of history and can alone give authenticity to our knowledge of the past. When we read of the past, we are often troubled by the fact that our knowledge is neither complete nor adequate. Contemporary historians hardly ever leave accounts which satisfy succeeding generations, and in fact, they are often not in a position to judge what should be recorded and what left out. If, however, complete records are available, the annals of the past can be reconstructed, but, in most cases, such records of the past do not exist. We know that during the Moghul period, India had all the instruments of civilised government and that full records were kept of all official decisions and happenings. Unfortunately, most of these records were destroyed during the troubled period of the 18th century. In consequence, we have lost some of the most valuable sources of our knowledge of the age. It is, however, fortunate that the histories written by Abul Fazl, Abdul Hamid Lahori, Khafi Khan and others, based on official records, are available to us. Even though they were written from an official point of view, their use of records makes them a valuable source material for us.

During the 19th century, the European States adopted the convention that all State records should be opened to the public after a lapse of 50 years. The records of the Napoleonic era were thus released to the public in about 1870. The Napoleonic era was a period of great progress in different fields, and it was described contemporaneously by many well-known historians. In fact, all the known methods of history writing were used in making the Napoleonic period vivid to the public of the day, but even then, when the official records became available in 1870, it was found that our knowledge of the period was both enriched and altered. Much new light was thrown on obscure incidents and happenings. Many old opinions had to be revised in the light of the new information.

Similarly, the official papers relating to the so-called Indian Mutiny of 1857 were released in 1907. The Government of India published a three-volume history of the Mutiny based on these records. It is true that this book was written from the British point of view, and did not therefore do full justice to the Indian participants. It is therefore necessary that these records should be examined afresh, and a true account of the period written in as objective a manner as possible. Even then the official history which was based on these records revealed many facts that were previously unknown and corrected many of our wrong ideas about the different characters who participated in these momentous happenings.

These two examples show how essential records are for a true interpretation of history. If, however, the records are to be utilised to the fullest extent, it is necessary that they should not only be preserved, but also arranged and classified systematically. There must also be a sufficient number of scholars with the necessary knowledge and scientific attitude to take full advantage of the information contained in them. In our National Archives, we have an immense store-house of such records but two things have stood in the way of our utilising them fully :

(1) We have not been able to make arrangements for all the records to be kept in one place.

(2) We have not been able to appoint the staff necessary for the completion of the work of classification and indexing of the available records.

In 1948, I had intended that the Government of India should undertake this task at an early date, and, accordingly, a scheme was drawn up for the improvement of the tempo and the quality of the work. This demanded an increase in the staff of the Archives to cope with the additional work, but, unfortunately, financial stringency prevented the implementation of even this modest scheme.

I would like to give the members of the Commission some idea of the magnitude of the task which faces the National Archives today. In 1939, it was little more than a medium size depository, with a limited body of records. These were, however, fairly well organised though they were not open to students for research. Today, it is one of the leading archival institutions in the world, and is certainly the largest in Asia. It is also mechanically one of the best equipped. Our holdings in the last ten years have greatly grown in bulk, especially since December 1948. It was then decided that all records prior to August 15, 1947, of the Residencies and Political Agencies of the Government of India would be transferred to the National Archives. The increase since then has been almost phenomenal. The number of Residencies and Political Agencies which then went out of commission was 15 and 14 respectively. Of these, the National Archives have already received the records of 14 Residencies and 3,581 bundles, and cover a period from 1672 to 1949 A.D.

Apart from the sudden accession to our collections, we are also getting an increasing number of records from different Ministries and their attached and subordinate offices. With growing consciousness, both in the Government and among the people, of the value of records, the destruction of records has now become out of the question. Besides, the increasing function which the Government are undertaking and the necessity of written instruments in a democratic government make it inevitable that the number of records will continue to grow. This will accentuate the problems of space and maintenance of records for each government department, and it is inevitable that offers of transfer of records from the different governmental agencies will continually become more pressing. It is also proposed to legislate in order to ensure complete and regular transfer of all records to the National Archives.

Further problems have been created by the fact that the material which is now coming to the National Archives is often in a chaotic condition. When it was decided to transfer the records of the Residencies and Political Agencies it was also decided to transfer all existing inventories and indexes to these records. This was essential if the National Archives were to check these records, arrange them in their proper order and supply them to the Government or to research scholars on requisition. It is, however, unfortunate that many of the Agencies either did not maintain working lists or indexeds of their records, or their records became considerably disarranged during the transfer. As a result, it is difficult to find documents as and when required. These records have therefore to be listed, re-arranged in their original order and properly indexed. Only then can these records tell correctly the story of the transactions of which they are the evidence. Unless restored to their original order, the documents will remain isolated pieces, disconnected, meaningless and unreliable. The phenomenal increase in the production of records in the departments themselves, and their indifferent maintenance in the current and semi-current stages have also added to the difficulties which the Archives have to face. I may cite one example. One series of the Political Department records from 1880 to 1930 which has just been transferred to the Archives does not possess even a check list.

The physical condition of a large bulk of these records also presents a serious problem. Owing to various reasons, many of these series are in a very bad state of preservation and require immediate rehabilitation in order to ensure their continued existence. To give the members some idea, I may mention that about 3,000 volumes of the Residency records require major and another 4,000 require minor repairs and reconditioning immediately. This task of restoration is very urgent as the climate of New Delhi accelerates the physical deterioration of the records. In order to cope with the situation, the processes of rehabilitation have now been mechanised.

The member of the Commission are also aware that the records have now been thrown open for research. At first, only records up to

1880 were available for inspection, but now all records up to 1901 have been brought under this category. More recent records will also be thrown open in the years to come. In addition, the Archives have undertaken an extensive programme of analysis, indexing, condensing, editing and publication of records in order to facilitate the work of research and reference. The Historical Records Commission has also increased the scope of the work of the Archives as the Records Survey Committees in the different States work directly under the Commission. The interest in the archives and archival work is consequently growing. At the same time, the demand for information from various sources has grown and is still growing.

Thus, on the one hand, we have increasing pressure of work and growing interest on the part of both the Government and the public and, on the other, we know that the prevailing financial stringency will not permit an adequate expansion of the Department in the next few years. In this situation the only way of meeting the shortage of staff is to seek the co-operation of the universities and learned societies. If a sufficient number of scholars take up the task and assist the existing staff in the classification and cataloguing of the material which has been collected, much can be done in spite of the inadequacy of public funds. The universities can also help by allotting the task to post-graduate students of history. If the universities agree to recognise such work as part of the normal training of a post-graduate student, this will not only benefit the students themselves but it will also be a real national service. It is only through the co-operation of professors, lecturers, scholars and research and post-graduate students that the vast material we have can be utilised properly. I understand that our Director of National Archives had approached the universities once but the response was not satisfactory. I would like to take this occasion, when so many distinguished schoalrs are present, to press once more that this work of urgent national importance should be undertaken by all the universities and learned societies without further delay. I have every hope that with your co-operation, we can overcome the difficulties created by financial stringency and create conditions in which the Archives can perform their proper function and serve as a treasure-house of information for all students of history.

APPENDICES

Appendix-1

Document No. 87

LETTER FROM RAJAJI TO SARDAR PATEL

New Delhi

25 April, 1949

My dear Vallabhbhai,

Please read these papers about the Banaras Hindu University. Maulana Azad seems to be keen on having an enquiry. This is the first I hear of financial irregularities. As for (ii) and (iii) of his letter dated 23 April, anything can be brought under these heads and I do not know how an enquiry will help. It will only lead to allegations of all kinds being reduced to writing. The main point is discipline of students which now seems to have receded into the background in Maulana's letter.

I am sure you will be able to give some advice either to Maulana Azad or to me.

Yours sincerely,
C. Rajagopalachari

The Hon'ble Sardar Vallabhbhai Patel
New Delhi

Appendix -2

Document No. 88

LETTER FROM SARDAR PATEL TO RAJAJI

New Delhi
26 April, 1949

My dear Rajaji,

Thank you for your letter of 25 April regarding the Banaras Hindu University.

I entirely share your doubts about the enquiry suggeted; in fact, I think that such an enquiry would harm the university and will defeat the very object which we all have in view. The irregularities etc. about which the enquiry will be held relate to the past, *i.e.* during the period when Dr. Amarnath Jha, Dr. Radhakrishnan[1] and others were Vice-Chancellors. Whatever defects will be noticed will be nailed at their doors. Along with them the present Vice-Chancellor may also share the blame, but the fact remains that they will not escape. I do not know about the state of discipline in the university, but I doubt if other universities can point to a clean record. You know what is happening in Delhi and what has happened in Lucknow and Allahabad. Public enquiry of this kind will, if anything, worsen the financial situation of the university. Those who might be prepared to give donations will withhold their hands. Others who might be giving annual donations may postpone them. The result may be a complete financial breakdown.

If the object is to bring out other defects in the administration of the University, I am doubtful if this is the right way of approaching the matter. As you say, all kinds of allegations will be reduced to writing and the enquiry would be the forum of mutual mud-flinging. We, as

Government, will hardly be able to come out of it without criticism of some sort. To me, by far the best procedure would seem to be to ask the Vice-Chancellor for an explanation of such defects as may have been noticed. Government can then think of how to dispose of the matter.

Yours sincerely,
Vallabhbhai Patel

H.E. Shri C. Rajagopalachari

1. Dr. Sarvapally Radhakrishnan.

Appendix -3

Document No. 89

LETTER FROM PANDIT JAWAHAR LAL NEHRU TO SARDAR VALLABHBHAI PATEL

New Delhi

13 June, 1949

My dear Vallabhbhai,

I enclose a copy of a letter from Maulana Azad about the Hindu University. I think the proposal to appoint a three-man committee is a good one and the three names suggested might suit. Masani, of course, is the elder Masani who was the Vice-Chancellor of Bombay University.

I do not think the matter need be put up before the Cabinet. But perhaps you could inform Maulana of your views on the subject. I enclose a copy of my reply to him.

Yours,
Jawaharlal Nehru

The Hon'ble Sardar Vallabhbhai Patel
New Delhi

Appendix -4

Document No. 90

LETTER FROM RAJAJI TO SARDAR PATEL

New Delhi

15 June, 1949

My dear Vallabhbhai,

I enclose copies of correspondence between me, Maulana Azad and Pandit Nehru about the Banaras Hindu University.

Yours sincerely,
C. Rajagopalachari

The Hon'ble Sardar Vallabhbhai Patel
Dehra Dun

Appendix -5

Document No. 91

LETTER FROM RAJAJI TO PT. NEHRU

New Delhi

16 June, 1949

My dear Jawaharlalji,

I have just read your letter of 16 June, 1949 about the Banaras Hindu University and I think I should explain at some length what has happened.

The original proposal of Dr. Tara Chand was that we should order an enquiry into the present state of things in the Banaras Hindu University, that is to say, an enquiry over Govind Malaviyaji's administration. I had my doubts as to the effects of such a step and whether it might not make matters worse instead of better. I explained my doubts to Dr. Tara Chand and also wrote to Maulana Sahib. I communicated also with Vallabhbhai who replied to me on 26 April as per copy enclosed. The matter rested there. On 28 May Dr. Tara Chand again called on me and discussed the position. I suggested that instead of an enquiry against the present Vice-Chancellor, it may be useful, if Maulana Sahib desired an enquiry, to appoint a committee with larger terms of reference with a view to amending the Banaras Hindu University Act. Dr. Tara Chand thereupon sent me his letter of 30 May enclosing a note by his Ministry, a copy of which I enclose.

I noticed in these discussions that section 19 of the Banaras Hindu University Act had been misunderstood and that the reference in the section to the Governor-General had not been correctly appreciated. Any emergency steps by way of administrative orders should be taken by the Government of India and not by the Governor-General in his capacity as Lord Rector.

After considering Dr. Tara Chand's fresh proposal I wrote to Maulana Sahib my letter of 7 June, 1949, a copy of which I have sent you with my letter of 15 June, 1949 when I got your letter of 13 June.

My suggestion that the scope of the enquiry should cover larger ground is therefore in accordance with Dr. Tara Chand's own final proposal and meets Vallabhbhai's and my own doubts as to the kind of enquiry originally proposed. It is now for you, Vallabhbhai and Maulana Sahib to decide as to what course to follow. My own view is that if the Minister of Education feels strongly that there should be an enquiry, it should be an enquiry with a view to amending the Act and not to review Govind Malaviyaji's administration over a short period. If the Education Minister can be induced to drop the idea of an enquiry altogether I have no objection.

I am sending a copy of this letter to Vallabhbhai in reply to a letter from him to me dated 15 June in which he desires to know what the position is so that he may reply to you.

Yours sincerely,
C. Rajagopalachari

The Hon'ble Pandit Jawaharlal Nehru

Appendix -6

Document No. 92

LETTER FROM SARDAR PATEL TO PT. JAWAHARLAL NEHRU

Dehra Dun

19 June, 1949

My dear Jawaharlal,

Thank you for your letter dated 13 June, 1949 about the Banaras Hindu University. I am sorry for the delay in replying, which was due to the fact that I wanted to have all the material from Rajaji. As he has written to you, he has sent me the whole correspondence.

I have carefully gone through the matter and entirely agree with the advice which he has tendered to you. I do not think we can single out just one regime for enquiry. From what I know, it seems that some other regimes in the past have been also to blame. I would, therefore, advise that we avoid any enquiry into personal direction of the affairs of the university and should have a general enquiry which Rajaji suggests.

Yours sincerely
Vallabhbhai Patel

Appendix -7

Document No. 93

LETTER FROM PT. JAWAHARLAL NEHRU TO RAJAJI

New Delhi

21 June, 1949

My dear Rajaji,

Thank you for your letter of 20 June on the Banaras Hindu University and the papers enclosed. I have now come round to your view about this matter except for one thing. I still do not think that the *de facto* Vice-Chancellor should be a member of the committee of enquiry.

Yours,
Jawaharlal

His Excellency Shri C. Rajagopalachari
New Delhi

Copy to the Hon'ble Sardar Vallabhbhai Patel

Appendix -8

Document No. 94

LETTER FROM RAJAJI TO PT. JAWAHARLAL NEHRU

Governor-General's Camp
Simla

24 June, 1949

My dear Jawaharlalji,

Thank you for your letter dated 21 June 1949 about the Banaras Hindu University. I met Dr. Zakir Hussain[1] here and have casually learnt from him that the University Commission will bring its Report out in about a month's time and that the Report will deal, among other things, with proposals for the better administration of the three Central universities, including Banaras. This also has to be taken into account when dealing with the Education Ministry's present proposal.

Yours sincerely,
C. Rajagopalachari

The Hon'ble Pandit Jawaharlal Nehru

---

1. Vice-Chancellor of Jamia Millia, 1926-53; Vice-Chancelllor of Muslim University of Aligarh: Governor of Bihar, 1962; Vice-President of Indian Union, 1962-67; President of Indian Union, 1967-69.

Appendix -9

Document No. 95

LETTER FROM SARDAR PATEL TO RAJAJI

New Delhi

20/21 July, 1949

My dear Rajaji,

Maulana saw me this morning and told me that you had agreed to his proposal regarding the committee of enquiry and to the omission of Govind Malaviya. I had accepted your proposals and am, therefore, surprised to know that you had modified your views; but if you have done so, please let me know.

Yours,
Vallabhbhai Patel

His Excellency Shri C. Rajagopalachari
New Delhi

Appendix -10

Document No. 96

LETTER FROM RAJAJI TO SARDAR PATEL

New Delhi

26 August, 1949

My dear Vallabhbhai,

The Education Ministry has not done with the Banaras University question yet! The University Commission have now sent a confidential note on the Banaras University which Maulana Sahib has sent to me for consideration. I am enclosing a copy of the note as also a copy of Maulana Sahib's letter. Charges have been made in the confidential note and the Commission have recommended that those charges should be enquired into.

What would you advise me to do in view of our previous discussions and conclusion?

I hope you are now better.

Yours sincerely,
C. Rajagopalachari

The Hon'ble Sardar Vallabhbhai Patel
Camp Bombay

Appendix -11

Document No. 97

QUESTIONS AND ANSWERS IN THE INDIAN PARLIAMENT DATED 14-8-1950 IN CONNECTION WITH THE VISIT OF HON. MAULANA ABUL KALAM AZAD TO MIDDLE EAST COUNTRIES

Shri Hanumanthaiya:
Shri Channiah:

(a) Will the Prime Minister be pleased to state whether it is a fact that the hon. Maulana Abul Kalam Azad, Education Minister to the Government of India, intended to go on a Goodwill Mission to the Middle East countries?

(b) Are Government of India sponsoring such a mission and if so, what is its purpose?

(c) What are the countries which the hon. Maulana Abul Kalam Azad would be visiting and for how long will the visit last?

(d) What is the expenditure involved?

(e) Who are accompanying him?

The Deputy Minister of External Affairs (Dr. Keskar): (a), (b) and (c) There have been longstanding invitations from various countries of Western Asia for hon. Maulana Abul Kalam Azad to pay a visit of goodwill and friendship. Government have been anxious that he should pay such a visit at the earliest convenience. It was proposed that he should visit Iran and Turkey last July. Owing, however, to the unfortunate accident early last month from which hon. Maulana Abul Kalam Azad has not yet recovered, the visit has been postponed.

(d) and (e) Government is unable to indicate the approximate expenditure or the composition of the Delegation until plans have been finalised for the next date of his visit.

Who's Who

Abbas, Tayabji : Former Judge, Baroda State, joined national liberation movement (1916); became President of Kaira District Congress Committee.

Anney, M.S. : Reputed nationalist leader, some time member of Viceroy's Council; was elected President of the first Session of All India Hindu League, held at Lucknow in 1935.

Azad, Abul Kalam : Nationalist and front ranking freedom fighter; was the Editor of 'The Vakil of Amritsar' Al-Hilal', 'Al-Balagh'; was elected President of Indian National Congress in Delhi (1923) and in Ramgarh (1940); was appointed Education Minister in free India's first Cabinet (1947) headed by Jawaharlal Nehru.

Beasant, Annie : A leading social reformer; was the founder of Indian Home Rule League; elected twice President of Indian National Congress.

Benarji, W.C. : Liberal Congress leader of Bengal; was elected first President of Indian National Congress (1885).

Bhopatkar, L.B. : A Prominent Congress Worker of Poona.

Boulay, James De : Member Incharge of Home Department Political, Government of India (1918-20).

Curzon, Lord : Governor-General of India (1905), was responsible for the division of Bengal.

Das, C.R. : Renowed Swarajyaist leader of Bengal; was elected President of Indian National Congress at Gaya in 1922.

Desai, Bhulabhai J. : Leader of Congress Party in Indian Legislative Assembly (1946); was appointed a Member of Congress Working Committee several times between 1934-46; marvellously pleaded for I.N.A. Convicts (1946). His parleys with Liaqat Ali Khan, when the Congress leaders were in Jail, regarding the future set up for national government had been one of the reasons for Congress High Coomand's cool attitude towards him.

Despande, G.R. : A close devotee of B.G. Tilak and prominent figure of Maharashtra.

Gandhi, Kasturba : Devoted wife of Mahatama Gandhi, the father of Nation.

Gandhi, M.K. : Supreme leader of national liberation movement (1920-47); was elected President of Indian National Congress (1924); was the Editor of 'Young India' and 'Navjivan' (1920-1930), 'Harijan' (1933-48), Harijan Sewak (1933-1948) and author of 'Hind Swarajya'; participated in the Second Round Table Conference held in London in 1931.

Gokhale, D.V. : An eminent Parliamentarian of Maharashtra.

Gokhale, G.K. : One of the founder leaders of the Indian National Congress (1885); was nominated to the Central Legislative Council (1906); was founder of Servants of India Society; visited England in 1906 to discuss the Education Policy for India; was elected President of Congress in 1905.

Hakim Ajmal Khan : Veteran freedom fighter and Congress leader of Delhi; was a prominent figure of Non - cooperation and Khilafat Movement (1920); was appointed a Member to the Working Committee of Indian National

		Congress (1920, 1923 and 1925); was elected President of Congress, in 1921 at Ahmedabad.
Jaykar, M.R.	:	A moderate leader of Bombay and leading lawyer; was an expert in Constitutional matters.
Jinnah, Mohammad Ali	:	First Governor-General of Pakistan (1947); was the Vice-Chancellor of Osmania University; elected a Member to the Indian Legislative Assembly in 1930 and 1934.
Kelkar, N.C.	:	A close associate of B.G. Tilak and well known Swarajyaist leader; was elected to the Indian Legislative Assembly in 1924.
Khaparde, G.S.	:	An ardent follower of B.G. Tilak; was a member of Imperial Legislative Council; became Vice - Chairman of Indian Home Rule League in 1918.
Kher, B.G.	:	A leading Congressman of Bombay, became the Premier of the state in 1937 and the Chief Minister in 1946.
Liaqat Ali Khan	:	A Prominent leader of United Provinces Muslim League; was appointed Finance Member in the Interim Government (1946) headed by Jawaharlal Nehru; elected leader of All India Muslim Parliamentary Party (1946) and became first Prime Minister of Pakistan in 1947.
Malviya, M.M.	:	Front ranking Congress leader was elected President of the Indian National Congress in 1919.
Mavalankar, G.V.	:	Leading freedom fighter of Gujarat; was a Secretary to Gujarat Sabha (1920), became President, Indian Legislative Assembly (1946), and Speaker, Lok Sabha (1958).
Mehta, Firozeshah	:	Founder leader of Indian National Congress; was elected President in its Surat Session held in 1907.

Minto, Lord	:	British Viceroy to India since 1908; became popular for his reforms scheme of 1909 which was known as Marley-Minto Reforms; introduced Separate Electorate System for Hindus and Muslims.
Misra, Gokaranath	:	Prominent Congress leader of U.P. 1916-20 and General Secretary of the Party in 1919-20.
Mohammad Ali	:	Prominent figure of Non-cooperation and Khilafat Movement (1920); was elected President of Indian National Congress at Kokanada in 1923; Edited 'Comrade' and 'Hamdard' newspapers (1910-20); presided over the Session of All India Jamiat Ulama - i -Hind (1929); was appointed Inspector of Schools of Rampur (1903-1904); was the author of 'Political Problem of India'.
Mukhtar Ahmed Ansari	:	Patriot and nationalist; was a front ranging Congress leader of Delhi; elected President of Indian National Congress in 1927; participated actively in the Non-cooperation and Khilafat Movement (1920) and Salt Satyagraha (1930); was nominated to the Working Committee of Indian National Congress in 1919, 1922 and 1930.
Nehru, Jawaharlal	:	Noted freedom fighter, was President of Indian National Congress (1929, 1936 and 1946), became first Prime Minister of free India (1947); was the founder of All India Kisan Sabha, Bharat Krishak Samaj and a number of organisations.
Nehru, Motilal	:	A well known Barrister of Allahabad; was a prominent figure of Congress Party, was elected to the Indian Legislative Assembly in 1924 and also President of Indian National Congress in 1928.
Pal, B.C.	:	Prominent Congress Swarajyaist leader from Bengal; was the Editor of 'New India' (1901) and 'Bande Mataram' (1904).

Patel, Vallabhbhai : Great freedom fighter; was organiser of 'Nagpur Flat Satyagraha' (1923), Borsad Movement (1924) and Peasants Agitation of Bardoli (1928); was elected President of Indian National Congress at Karachi in 1931; became Deputy Prime Minister in the first Cabinet (1947) of free India, headed by Nehru; was elected Chairman of Congress Parliamentary Board in 1934, 1937 and 1946.

Patel, Vithalbhai J. : Top ranking Congress leader of Gujarat; was a Barrister of Bombay High Court (1908 – 1914); was elected to the Legislative Council of Bombay (1913), Imperial Legislative Council (1919) and the Indian Legislative Assembly (1924); became President of Bombay Municipal Corporation (1924) and the first Indian Speaker to the Indian Legislative Assembly (1925 – 30).

Plato : Great Greek Philosopher (about 500 B.C.), was author of the 'Republic', 'The Laws' and 'The Statesman'.

Prasad, Rajendra : A prominent Congress leader and constructive worker of Bihar; was elected President of Indian National Congress (1935); was appointed a member to the Working Committee of Indian National Congress several times between 1922 and 1949, Congress Parliamentary Board (1937 and 1947), Food and Agriculture Minister in the Interim Government headed by Nehru (1946); was elected Chairman of Indian Constituent Assembly (1947) and the President of Indian Republic in 1950, 1952 and 1957.

Rai, Lajpat : Popularly known as 'Punjab Kesari'; was elected President of Indian National Congress in Calcutta in 1920, a front ranking Congress leader from Punjab and social reformer.

Rajagopalachari, C. : Front ranking Congress leader of Madras and a Gandhian thinker, twice premier of Madras State (1937 and 1946); was appointed Governor for West Bengal (1947), Governor-General of India (1948) and Minister of Home Affairs in 1950; was well known for his suave diplomacy and cruditness; founder of Swatantra Party of India.

Raj Bahadur : Noted freedom fighter of Rajasthan, was appointed a Minister in the Cabinet by Mrs. Indira Gandhi.

Ramatirtha, Swamy : A prominent scholar of Hindu philosophy; was a follower of Adventism; visited United States and other Western countries several times.

Roy, M.N. : Thinker and well-known freedom fighter from Bengal; was a Congress leader who participated in Communist International held in Moscow in 1920; was defeated by Maulana Abul Kalam Azad for Congress President's election in 1940 at Wardha.

Saminullah Khan : Prominent Citizen of Dacca and the founder of All India Muslim League in 1905.

Shauqat Ali : Elder brother of Maulana Mohammad Ali; was a prominent figure of Non-Cooperation and Khilafat Movement; was appointed to the Working Committee of Indian National Congress between 1920 and 1930.

Shibli, Nomani : Well-known spiritual leader from Lucknow; was a scholar of Islamic philosophy.

Shivaji Maharaj : A Great Maratha Sardar of 17th Century.

Spoor, Ben C. : A member of British Parliament in 1918.

Swamy Dayanand Saraswati	:	Founder of 'Arya Samaj' and the author of 'Satyartha Prakash' ; was a great reformist and scholar of Vedic Philosophy.
Syed Ahmed Khan, Sir	:	Muslim reformist and the founder of Scientific Society of Ghazipur and the Muslim College of Aligarh; was the editor of 'Tahzeeb-ul-Akhlaq'; was nominated to the Indian Legislative.Council (1878); was author of a number of books including 'College of 'The Indian .Revolt', 'The Asbab Bagawaat-e-Hind', 'Present State of Politics' and 'Loyal Mohammadans'.
Tara Chand	:	Noted educationist; was secretary and adviser, Union Ministry of Education; was appointed Ambassador to Iran in 1951.
Tegore, Devendra Nath	:	Father of Ravindra Nath Tagore and a well-known Social reformer of Bengal.
Thakkar, A.V.	:	Noted Gandhian and constructive worker of Gujarat, was closely associated with the Servants of India Society.
Tilak, B. G.	:	Great Congress leader from Maharashtra; was a prominent figure of Swadeshi Movement (1905); was the editor of 'Maratha' and 'Kesari' and was imprisoned several times during national liberation movement of India.
Tyagi, Mahavir	:	Prominent Congress of U.P. ; was appointed a Minister of State in the Union Council of Ministers by Pandit Nehru.
Vivekananda, Swamy	:	Great thinker, scholar of Adventism and Hindu Philosophy ; was a staunch follower of Swamy Ramkrishna 'Paramahansa' and founder of the 'Ramakrishna Mission', visited U.S.A. several times.
Vyas, Jaynarayan	:	Leading Congressman of Rajasthan; was the Premier of the State in 1946.

Glossary

Ahimsa	: Non-violence, Mahatma Gandhi's weapon of love for mass action.
Ashram	: Literally, hermitage, a place for penance and spiritual pursuit.
Begar	: Forced labour.
Bhagvadgita, The	: The song celestial, highly philosophic poem laying emphasis on the selfless views of life and action.
Bhakta	: Devotee, disciple.
Brahmin	: One belonging to the priestly class.
Chaddar	: Bedspread
Chawl	: Locality.
Civil Disobedience Movement	: Satyagraha Movement of Mahatma Gandhi to resist British rule in India.
Constructive Programme	: Eighteen-fold programme of Mahatma Gandhi for resurgence of India.
Dal	: Pulse cooked or uncooked
Kaira Satyagraha	: No-tax campaign of the Peasants of Kaira District in 1918 against the Bombay Government, it was the second campaign (after Champaran) of Mahatma Gandhi in India against the British Rule and the first of Sardar Vallabhbhai Patel.
Karma Yogi	: Believer in the path of Karma action with selflessness.
Khadi	: Hand spun and hand woven cloth.
Kshatriya	: One belonging to warrior class.

Lathi	: Cudgel, wooden stick.
Maharaja	: The ruler of a former Indian State of bigger territory.
Mahatma	: Literally, high-souled person, a title bestowed on Mahatma Gandhi by Indians.
Mhahavidyalaya	: A Centre of higher education, College.
Namaskar	: Respectful salutations.
Resolution on forced labour	: This resolution was passed in the first Gujarat Political Conference, held at Godhra in October 1917 under the Presidentship of Mahatma Gandhi. In the resolution "It was the custom of Government Officers when touring in the district to extract work from certain section of the people, and often not to pay for it. The village carpenter, for instance, would be called upon to make the wooden pegs for the officers' tents, the potter to provide earthen vessels and even to fetch water in them, the barber to tidy up and to do the lamps, the sweeper to sweep and to take and fetch message, the grocer to supply all foodstuffs, and the peasants to arrange bullock carts for transporting the Saheb's luggage from one camp to another. The petty officers of the village had to remain in attendance throughout the period of the officer's stay and in addition, to look after the needs of the shrishteder (the judicial clerk) and other clerks. It was rarely that all this work and supplies were paid for and on top of it all, all these men had to remain in attendance for hours, and sometimes for days, on end. After the Home Rule League was established, vigorous agitation was started to an end to this pervicious system." Lokamanya Tilak was also present in the Conference.
Rowlatt Bill	: In this Bill the Government had been provided a number of special powers for arresting and detaining, without trial, persons suspected of anti-government activities.

Satyagraha : Literally, insistence of truth, Mahatma Gandhi's weapons of truth and love for mass action.

Servants of India Society : A band of people pledged to serve the country in a constitutional way. This society was organised by the Great Leader of Maharashtra Mr. Gopal Krishna Gokhale.

Swadeshi : Country made.

Swaraj : Self-rule, according to Mahatma Gandhi's conception, social, economic and political independence in the true sense of term.

Swarajist : Term used for those who wedded to Council Entry Programme after Civil Disobedience and the Khilafat Movement.

Talati : The Talati is a village revenue officer, concerned with collection of land revenue.

Taluka : Taluka or Tahsil is an administrative unit of varying sizes, but usually extending over a few hundred square miles in area and containing a number of villages and one or two towns of population exceeding 10,000.

Talukdar : A land-holder.

Vad : The Second half of Indian month.

Veth : Forced free labour.

Vishnu : The second among the trio of gods symbolizing protective facet of the supreme.

Yogi : One who practises Yoga, *i.e.* spiritual, mental and bodily discipline for self-realization.

Zamindar : Absentee landlord.

Chronology of Events
(1949-1950)

1949	Jan.	7	: Presided over the meeting of the Central Advisory Board, held at Allahabad.
	Feb.	2	: Delivered welcoming speech at the sixth annual meeting of the Central Board of Archaeology, held in New Delhi.
		9	: Clarified position in the Legislative Assembly about the regional language in Devanagari script as University language.
		20	: Delivered convocational speech at the Muslim University of Aligarh.
		26	: Addressed the Diamond Jubilee Celebration of the Scindia School at Gawlior.
	March	18	: Speech delivered in the Indian Legislative Assembly on General Budget – List of demands for 1949-50 year.
	April	1	: Made clarification in L. A. about Bodh Gaya Pamphlet.
			: Speaker (I.L.A.) announced the motion moved by Maulana Aabul Kalam Azad regarding the election to All India Council for Technical Education.
		5	: Motion Moved in the Assembly about the election to the Central Advisory Board of Archaeology.
		9	: Inaugurated session of the National Commission of UNESCO in New Delhi.
		18	: Delivered speech on the occasion at the laying of foundation of Central Institute of Education in New Delhi. Foundation of the Institute was laid by Pandit Jawaharlal Nehru.

	June	7	: Wrote to Rajaji about the proposed Amendment Bill on Banaras Hindu University.
	August	8	: Addressed the Provincial Education Ministers' Conference held in New Delhi.
		21	: Delivered speech at the Conference for Cultural cooperation between India and Asian Countries.
		22	: Placed report of the U.E.C. on Banaras Hindu University.
			: Inaugurated All India Conference on Arts in Calcutta.
	Nov.	2	: Delivered inaugural Speech at the UNESCO Seminar on Rural Adult Education, held in Mysore.
1950	Jan.	8	: Presided over the meeting of the Central Advisory Board of Education held in Cuttack.
	Feb.	13	: Clarified position in the Indian Legislative Assembly regarding the Students from the Philippines.
	March	15	: Delivered Speech in Parliament during the discussion on General Budget – List of Demands for 1950-51 year.
	April	9	: Inaugurated the session of the Indian Council for Cultural Relations, held in New Delhi.
		14	: Clarified position regarding the cultural Missions to Asian countries.
	June	4	: Wrote to Sardar Vallabhbhai Patel regarding Matthai's differences with Pandit Jawaharlal Nehru.
		6	: Appreciated views of Maulana Azad by Sardar Vallabhbhai Patel about statement.
	Dec.	25	: Delivered inaugural speech at the Indian Historical Records Commissions' Conference, held in Nagpur.

Index

E

F

G

H

I

N

O

P

Q

R

V

W

Y

Z

The Selected Works of MAULANA ABUL KALAM AZAD

Volume III
(1947-1948)

Chief Editor
DR. RAVINDRA KUMAR

ATLANTIC PUBLISHERS & DISTRIBUTORS

Published by
ATLANTIC PUBLISHERS AND DISTRIBUTORS
B-2, Vishal Enclave, New Delhi - 27
Phone: 5413460

Sales office
4215/1, Ansari Road, Darya Ganj
New Delhi - 110002
Phone : 3273880

Typeset at
APD Computer Graphics
B-2, Vishal Enclave, N. Delhi - 27

Printed in India at
Mehra Offset Press
New Delhi

To

MOTHER INDIA

FOREWORD

I have gone through with great interest the Volume Third of the Selected Works of Maulana Abul Kalam Azad (1947-48), edited by Dr. Ravindra Kumar, and feel privileged to write its Foreword.

Fair deal politics, thought of freedom and equality for all, secularism, nationalism, Hindu-Muslim Unity, discipline, clear speakingness and many other qualities were the most important aspects of Maulana Azad's versatile personality.

In 1947 he became the Minister for Education in the Union Cabinet, headed by Pandit Jawaharlal Nehru and died in harness on February 22, 1958. This was the period when the obstinies of the country were in the making and education had to play an important role. Under his unique guidance the Ministry met the challenges and under his stewardship rapid expansion took place in all fields of education, particularly on the technical side. He always stressed the need of coordinated efforts and unity of purpose, various institutions, commissions and organizations were set up to examine the educational problems and requirements and the possibilities to achieve them, and it was mainly due his vision and efforts that educational planning was set on a sound footing in the country.

I am sure that this Volume would be warmly welcomed by the reading public and researchers in our country and abroad.

I wish Dr. Ravindra Kumar a success.

Hitendra Desai

PREFACE

Dr. Shri Ravindra Kumar is an admirer of Maulana Abul Kalam Azad. This is nothing unusual. Maulana Azad had numerous admirers in the course of India's struggle for freedom. The number increased appreciably after India attained freedom. Partition of India was the heavy price India paid for this freedom. Maulana Azad had throughout his whole political life opposed forces which encouraged separatist trends in our national life. It was in the partitioned India that people realised more vividly the soundness of the views Maulana had expressed on the communal problem.

Maulana Azad was among the major figures in our unique struggle for freedom waged under the leadership of Gandhiji. The selected works which Dr. Ravindra Kumar has edited bring out the greatness of Maulana Azad in several fields of life. He was most assuredly an outstanding scholar, a great journalist, a matchless orator but with equal ease he was also a great statesman who played a significant role in every crisis which India and, in particular, the Indian National Congress faced from time to time in its struggle to make our country free and independent.

He had also his due share in shaping India's destiny in her first decade of Independence. He was an outstanding member of the Union Cabinet but what was more important was the mature advice he made available to his comrade and fellow warrior Pandit Jawaharlal Nehru as the latter sought to grapple with India's difficult and daunting problems in the first crucial phase of her independence.

Dr. Ravindra Kumar may not yet be a mature scholar but the enthusiasm he has shown in portraying the intellectual and political life of Maulana Azad deserves commendation. The country is still faced with problems which greatly exercised the Maulana's mind. What he thought and said on these problems would still be a source of inspiration and enlightenment to his countrymen in the difficult days through which we are all passing.

Sadiq Ali

CONTENTS

INTRODUCTION

I

Maulana Abul Kalam Azad was one of those great freedom-fighters, educationist, nationalist and intellectualist who sacrificed their all for the cause of the nation before and after the dawn of independence from the British Imperialism. In fact he was a true son of Mother India.

In the Words of Pandit Jawaharlal Nehru, Maulana Abul Kalam Azad was a man of luminious intelligence and mighty intellect with an amazing capacity to pierce through a problem to its core. This evaluation of Maulana Azad's mind remains with posterity as from perhaps the foremost world thinker of the time. It is an appraisal which must be given due weightage in any estimate of the true value of the ideas and thoughts that emanated from Maulana Azad and went on to influence the national environment.

Now I am glad to write introduction to the third volume of the Selected Works of Maulana Abul Kalam Azad covering the period 1947-48. In this volume all importance statements (Document 23, 24, 63 and 68), interviews (Document 1, 20 and 81), speeches (Document 6, 17, 30, 40, 41, 44, 46, 67, 81, 94, 97, 98 and 99) and correspondence with Mahatama Gandhi (Document 10 and 14), Pt. Jawaharlal Nehru (Document 4, 5, 11, 15, 16 and 31), Dr. Rajendra Prasad (Document 45, 80, 82 and 84), Sardar Vallabhbhai Patel (Document 2, 3, 7, 9, 18, 33, 34, 35, 36, 37, 38, 39, 51 and 55) and several other stalwarts (Document 42 and 83) have been incorporated which will be bringing out all facts of his great life into limelight.

II

Maulana Abul Kalam Azad was also a great Parliamentarian and Policy-maker. His work in the Constituent Assembly of India and in the Indian Legislative Assembly (1947-1948) are the important and interesting part dealt with in this volume for the first time (Document 8, 12, 13, 14, 17, 19, 21, 22, 25, 26, 27, 28, 29, 48, 49, 50, 52, 53, 54, 56, 57, 58, 59, 60, 61, 63, 64, 65, 66, 69, 70, 71, 72, 73,

74, 76, 77, 78, 79, 86, 87, 88, 89, 90, 91, 92, 93, 94, and 95) which certainly add to the contemporary social, political, economic, historical, cultural and Parliamentarian (Legislative) informations on the one hand and can inspire certainly the generations to come on the other.

Several important documents relating to the main events of the period (1947-48) and pertaining to Maulana Azad have been included in appendices (Document 97, to 100).

III

Maulana Azad always talked in term of a broad-based nationalism embracing all religions and communities in a country like India where there has been great diversity in the matter of language and culture. He had a firm faith in a balanced mind representing a composite nationalism which is all inclusive. In spite of basic unity of all religion there have been occasion of conflict and controversies and quite often emotions get the letter of reason. It was Maulana Azad's voice which asserted itself, in 1923, at Delhi Session of Indian National Congress in favour of a broad-based humanitarian nationalism. It is such a concept of truly comprehensive nationalism which is the need of hour in our country.

In this volume I have tried to give a brief account of his life and works and it is my belief the coming generations especially historians, political scientists, statesmen, researchers and the general people of the country can lay a peep into his towering personality.

His life and works are the source of inspiration and teachings of clean and fair deal politics, being up from all the differences for the cause of the nation and live to be open-eyed for the interest of national welfare, unity and integrity. By this point of view, the readers will be benefited.

I am grateful and thankful to the staff of National Archives of India specially to its Director General Dr. Rajesh Patri and Asstt. Director Mr. P.R. Malik, Chairman, Mr. Sadiq Ali and other staff of Gandhi National Museum and Library, New Delhi, staff and officials of Sardar Vallabhbhai Patel National Memorial Ahemdabad, officials and staff of Nehru Memorial Museum and Library, Teen Murti House, New Delhi and officials and staff of Navjeevan Trust, Ahemdabad, Provincial Archives of U.P., Lucknow, Maharashtra, Bombay and Bihar, Patna.

I am greatly indebted to His Holiness, Maulana Syed Abul Hasan Ali Nadvi, Rector, Nadwatul Ulama, Lucknow, Dr. Hari Dev Sharma, Deputy Director, N.M.M.L., Mr. A.J. Jalali, Mr. S.G. Mohiuddin, Dr. Akbar Ali Khan, President Abul Kalam Azad Oriental Research Institute, Hyderabad, Mr. V.N. Gadgil, and Mr. Z.R. Ansari for their kind encouragement and guidance in preparation of this volume.

My thanks are due to Mrs. Kamlesh Ravindra Kumar, Mr. Lakhmendra Khurana, Mrs. Meena Kapoor, Mr. Achal Kumar Awasthi, Mrs. Manju Sehgal, Dr. Hari Singh and Mr. Anil Juneja for their kind cooperation in many ways.

My special thanks are due to Dr. K.R. Gupta and Mr. Manish Kumar Gupta of Atlantic Publishers and Distributors, New Delhi for undertaking the publication of the Selected Works of Maulana Abul Kalam Azad courageously.

Ravindra Kumar

ABBREVIATIONS

A.I.C.C.	:	ALL INDIA CONGRESS COMMITTEE
A.I.E.C.	:	ALL INDIA EDUCATIONAL CONFERENCE
A.L.C.	:	ASIATIC LANGUAGE AND CULTURE
A.P.I	:	ASSOCIATED PRESS OF INDIA
C.A.B.E.	:	CENTRAL ADVISORY BOARD OF EDUCATION
C.A.I.	:	CONSTITUENT ASSEMBLY OF INDIA
C.E.B.	:	CHAIRMAN EDUCATIONAL BOARD
C.G.E.P.	:	CENTRAL GOVERNMENT EDUCATIONAL PROGRAMME
C.I.E.	:	CENTRAL INSTITUTE OF EDUCATION
C.I.H.R.	:	COMMISSION ON INDIAN HISTORY RECORDS
D.D.D.E.	:	DEPUTY DIRECTOR OF THE DEPARTMENT OF EDUCATION
E.D.	:	EDUCATION DEPARTMENT
E.M.	:	EDUCATION MINISTRY
I.P.C.	:	INTER-PROVINCIAL COMMUNICATION
J.M.I.	:	JAMIA MILLIA ISLAMIA
L.A.	:	LEGISLATIVE ASSEMBLY
L.M.C.	:	LUCKNOW MUSLIM CONFERENCE
L.P.G.B.	:	LABOUR PARTY IN GREAT BRITAIN
M.I.B.	:	MINISTRY FOR INFORMATION AND BROADCASTING
M.L.	:	MUSLIM LEAGUE
N.E.	:	NATIONAL EDUCATION
N.G.	:	NATIONAL GOVERNMENT
N.M.	:	NATIONAL MUSLIM
P.G.	:	PROVINCIAL GOVERNMENT
P.S.	:	PARLIAMENTARY SECRETARIES
R.E.P.S.	:	RELIGIOUS EDUCATION TO PRIVATE SOURCES

R.S.	: ROMAN SCRIPT
R.S.C.	: REPORT OF THE SECURITY COMMITTEE
S.C.L.E.	: STANDING COMMITTEE OF THE LEGISLATURE ON EDUCATION
S.W.A.E.	: SOCIAL WELFARE AND ADULT EDUCATION
T.H.R.C.	: THE HISTORICAL RECORDS COMMISSION
U.K.	: UNITED KINGDOM
U.S.A.	: UNITED STATES OF AMERICA
V.C.	: VICE-CHANCELLOR
W.C.	: WORKING COMMITTEE

LIST OF DOCUMENTS

Contd.

Contd.

Contd.

No.	Subject	Date
50.	Reply to the questions asked in the Legislative Assembly about the Technical Training of Indian Students in foreign countries	05-02-1948
51.	To Vallabhbhai Patel	09-02-1948
52.	Reply in the Legislative Assembly to the questions raised about the shifting of constituent colleges of Delhi University to University site.	09-02-1948
53.	Reply in the Legislative Assembly to the questions raised about the shifting back of Ramjas College Delhi and continuance of Agricultural College at Anand Parbat	09-02-1948
54.	Reply in the Legislative Assembly to the questions asked regarding the post-war plans for training of technical personnel and facilities to Andhra University	09-02-1948
55.	From Vallabhbhai Patel	11-02-1948
56.	Answers in the Legislative Assembly to the questions asked about the educational institutions under Ministries other than Health and Agriculture	23-02-1948
57.	Answers in the Constituent Assembly of India (Legislative) to the questions asked regarding the Institutions affiliated to All India Council for Technical Education and Various Syllabuses	23-02-1948
58.	Answers in L.A. to the questions raised regarding the affiliation of Delhi Polytechnic to Delhi University	23-02-1948
59.	Replies in the Constituent Assembly of India (Legislative) to the questions asked in connection with the publication of South Indian Inscriptions collected by Archaeological department.	23-02-1948

Contd.

No.	Subject	Date
60.	Answers in L.A. to questions asked about the terms of Service of Director General of Archaeology	23-02-1948
61.	Replies in L.A. to questions raised regarding the Government proposal of a National Museum for India	23-02-1948
62.	Resolution moved in the Constituent Assembly of India in connection with the Election to Standing Committee for Ministry of Education.	01-03-1948
63.	Reply to the questions asked in the Constituent assembly of India (Legislative) about the Recognition of Indian Degrees in Arts, Medicine, Engineering etc. in U.K. and U.S.A.	04-03-1948
64.	Answer in L.A. to the questions asked about the Universities in Indian Dominion	04-03-1948
65.	Replies in the Legislative Assembly of India to the questions asked about the Post of Joint Director General of Archaeology	08-03-1948
66.	Reply to the question asked in the Legislative Assembly regarding the Maintenance of Archaeological Gardens by Archaeological Department	08-03-1948
67.	Speech in connection with the General Budget – List of Demand for the year 1948-49	11-03-1948
68.	Statement of Policy in connection with the cut-motion on the Budget proposals for 1948-49 as circulated to Honourable Members	11-03-1948
69.	Reply to the questions asked in the Legislative Assembly regarding the place of Music in proposed Cultural Trust of Government	19-03-1948

Contd.

Contd.

No.	Subject	Date
82.	To Rajendra Prasad	02-07-1948
83.	From Basantalall Murarka	27-07-1948
84.	To Rajendra Prasad	29-07-1948
85.	From Rajendra Prasad	30-07-1948
86.	Reply to the questions asked in the Indian Legislative Assembly in connection with the grant of Tata School of Social Sciences	10-08-1948
87.	Reply to the questions asked in the Legislative Assembly about the admission of students in and grant to Laxmi Narain Institute of Technology at Nagpur	10-08-1948
88.	Replies in the Legislative Assembly to the questions asked in connection with the Policy of the Government concerning excavation work carried out under the auspices of the Archaeological Department	10-08-1948
89.	Reply to the question asked in the Constituent Assembly of India (Legislative) in connection with the Relics of Indian Art in British Museum	13-08-1948
90.	Answers to the questions asked in the Legislative Assembly regarding the Preservation of Indian Archives	13-08-1948
91.	Answers to the questions asked in the Legislative Assembly regarding the Allotment of Machine Tools to Madras Institute of Technology	13-08-1948
92.	Replies in connection with the improvement of Stupa and Monastery at Kushinagar, Deoria District (U.P.), to the questions raised in the Indian Legislative Assembly	13-08-1948
93.	Answers in L.A. to the questions asked about the exclusive admission of Caste Hindus in Lakshminarayan Technical Institute, Nagpur	13-08-1948

Contd.

Document No. 1

MAULANA AZAD'S INTERVIEW TO THE A.P.I.

CALCUTTA
10-1-1947

Maulana Abul Kalam Azad, former Congress President who is shortly to take charge of the Education portfolio at the Centre told the Associated Press of India in an interview on 10th January, 1947, that he had agreed to enter the Interim Government because he felt that India's future depends on solving her difficulties in a spirit of wise statemanship. Maulana Azad said:

> "Friends and colleagues as well as the public are aware that when the Interim Government was first formed, I was pressed to join the Cabinet. The pressure increased at the time of the reshuffle of the Cabinet on account of the entry of the Muslim League. For various reasons I was reluctant to do so and felt that I could serve the country better from outside...My friends and colleagues, however, think otherwise, Gandhiji as from the very beginning anxious that I should join and he also holds that I can render greater service to my country from within than from outside. In face of their united pressure, I now feel that I must yield. When Gandhiji and all my friends and colleagues hold that my joining the Cabinet will strengthen it and enable it to face better the difficult problems ahead, I cannot allow personal inclination to stand in the way."

"For some time past I have felt that the development of Indian politics has reached a stage when our problems require a new approach of constructive statesmanship. The present balance of international forces demands such reorientation of our policy and the rise to power of the Labour Party in Great Britain has in my opinion created conditions favourable for such change. Ever since I came out of Ahmadnagar Fort Jail in June, 1945, I have tried to work in the light of the changed circumstances and I feel that events have on the whole justified my attitude. This does not mean that our difficulties have been overcome. On the contrary, great difficulties still exist, and our future depends on solving them in a spirit of wise statesmanship. It is to serve that end that I have agreed to enter the Interim Government and work for the goal of independence for which we have fought and suffered so long. In conclusion, I would like to take this opportunity of thanking the many friends all over India who have sent their messages of good wishes and kind thoughts."

Document No. 2

LETTER FROM MAULANA AZAD TO SARDAR PATEL

26 January, 1947

My dear Vallabhbhai,

Some friends told me about two weeks ago, before my departure for Calcutta, that a new scale was proposed for the ratio of Urdu and Hindi in All India Radio. Pandit Jawaharlal dropped in to see me that very day. I suggested that it would be inadvisable to alter the existing position for the present and better to keep the proposal pending. I went to Calcutta and do not know what happened. I now understand that Mr. Liaquat (Ali Khan)[1] wrote to you on the subject and you are in correspondence also with the Viceroy on this point.[2]

I would request you to drop the matter and it should be postponed for some more suitable occasion. You perhaps know that the committee set up by All India Radio to tackle this question was sponsored by me. I regret that it could not come to any agreed decision. I have given the matter careful thought and come to the conclusion that we can settle the question on some future date in a way to which there would be no opposition from any quarter whatsoever. I would strongly suggest that the question may be kept pending.

I will discuss the matter fully with you when we meet.

I hope you are progressing in health.

Yours sincerely,
A.K. Azad.

The Hon'ble Sardar Vallabhbhai Patel

---

1. See Appendices
2. See Appendices

Document No. 3

LETTER FROM MAULANA AZAD TO SARDAR PATEL

New Delhi,

27 January, 1947.

My dear Vallabhbhai,

I understand that a case has been drawn up about the riot which took place in the Mach Jail (Baluchistan). The real responsibility for this was that of the Inspector General of Prisons. Influences are at work which make it probable that the local courts will not be able to maintain their impartiality. Non-residents may therefore be convicted even without justification. The accused apprehend that they will not receive justice from the local court. They have therefore appealed to the local Government that the cases be transferred to some other province. I am forwarding to you a copy of the original application. I hope you will look into the matter and, if there is no bar in law, order that the case may be transferred to some court in the Punjab.

Yours sincerely,
A.K. AZAD

The Hon'ble Sardar Vallabhbhai Patel

Document No. 4

LETTER FROM PT. JAWAHARLAL NEHRU TO MAULANA ABUL KALAM AZAD

New Delhi

29th January, 1947

My dear Maulana Sahib,

I enclose a letter from Dr. Tara Chand. In this he refers to the Science Department of the Allahabad University. This Department has done very good work in the past and has at present one of our best scientists, Dr. Krishnan, in charge of it. Unfortunately, work suffers tremendously, because of lack of money. I do not know what can be done in this matter, but I should like to bring it to your notice.

Yours sincerely,
Jawaharlal Nehru

Document No. 5

LETTER FROM PT. JAWAHARLAL NEHRU TO MAULANA AZAD

New Delhi

31 January, 1947

My dear Maulana,

You asked me yesterday for names for a committee to consider the question of sending Indian students abroad. As you know there has been considerable dissatisfaction both in regard to the choice of these students and the arrangements made for their study abroad. English and American universities are over-full of men returning from the Armed Forces and it is difficult to get admission to good universities. The result has been that many of our students have had to wait long and then have joined second-rate universities which do not provide any very special training.

2. I think that we should not send any person abroad who can get the training he wants or is capable of absorbing in India. It is far better to start training establishments in India or to expand those already existing than to send a few students abroad.

3. Those who go abroad should be specially selected for specific purposes connected with our industrial and technical development. They might even be chosen with a view to helping some of the big projects we have in hand. With this end in view persons with some experience should be chosen so that they might specialize in a particular subject in a year or six months and come back to take charge of the work in hand or help in training others in India. No hard and fast line can be drawn, but generally speaking the choice should be made on the principle indicated abo e.

4. Our urgent need is foı technicians, statisticians, engineers, etc. Higher training in some of these subjects cannot easily be obtained in India. If we send more or less junior students abroad, they waste much of their time in learning things there which they can learn here. We cannot take advantage of their services for a considerable

time and our immediate needs are not met. I do not think it is necessary to send any student abroad on behalf of Government for what might be called literary studies, important as these are. There are plenty of individuals who go privately for these studies and Government should, therefore, concentrate on choosing its scholars for specific industrial, scientific or technical training which we lack so much.

5. It is desirable, therefore, that the Committee you constitute should consist of men acquainted with scientific and technical training. I am suggesting four names for your consideration. All four are good and have taken special interest in technical and scientific education. These four names are: Prof. M.N. Saha, F.R.S., Prof. P.C. Mahalanobis, F.R.S., Dr. Homi Bhabha, F.R.S., and Colonel Sir S.S. Sokhey.[1]

6. Mahalanobis is at present, I believe, in America, but he is likely to come back before long.

Yours sincerely,
Jawaharlal Nehru

1. Major-General Saheb Singh Sokhey (1887-1971); joined Indian Medical Service, 1913; Director, Haffkine Institute, Bombay, 1932-49; Assistant Director-General, World Health Organization, 1950-52; nominated member of Rajya Sabha, 1952-56; awarded International Lenin Peace Prize, 1953.

Document No. 6

ADDRESS TO THE PRESS CONFERENCE

New Delhi

3-2-1947

Maulana Abul Kalam Azad, Addressing his first press conference as member for Education and Arts, on Feb. 3, 1947 appealed both to the public and to the selected scholars to treat the system of overseas scholarships as a sacred trusts by which the foundation of India's future educational, industrial and technical development were being laid. The scholars who go abroad, he urged, "must go in a spirit of service and dedication".

It was proposed, said Maulana Azad, to strengthen the organisation in the U.K. and U.S.A. for dealing with the student's problems as quickly as possible. In the U.K. particularly, a separate welfare branch would be set up in the Education Department of the High Commissioner's office to help the students in regard to accommodation and also their welfare generally. Government had already set up at considerable expense two hostels for Indian students, one in London and the other at Edinburgh, and it was now proposed to establish another hostel in London to serve as a reception and transit camp.

The scholarships awarded unde the scheme had till now been confined exclusively to technical and scientific subjects. The necessity for a large personnel of trained scientists and industrial technicians was obvious. At the same time it must be realised that a balanced system of national education required also workers in the fields of pure science and the humanities. He therefore, intended that in future a percentage of scholarships should be earmarked for study in such cultural subjects. The numebr of women who had secured scholarships under the scheme had been very small. The main reason had been that scholarships were confined to technical and industrial scientific subjects. The expansion of the scheme to include both pure science and the humanities would allow women scope. "The future development" of education in India demands that a large number of women scholars should go abroad and study such subjects. If the expansion in the list of subjects for the award of scholarships serves this purpose, well and good, otherwise I will consider the desirability of earmarking a percentage of scholarships for women.

Maulana Azad realised the necessity of looking into the problem of selection and for this purpose a committee would be formed shortly to make recommendations in the light of the experience of the past three years. The committee might not be purely departmental. Experts might be taken from outside also.

> "The method of selection followed till now," he said "has been satisfactory. As however, the scholars are required to sign a bond to serve under government, it is considered desirable to associate the Federal Public Service Commission with the selection. The department is considering alternative methods for doing so."

> "I feel that the time has also come to consider the terms of the bond which students have till now executed. They are required to pledge themselves to serve government for a period of five years after completion of their training. Such bonds may at times prove harsh on a scholar if the Government is not in a position to offer him employment, as no period is laid down to define the termination of his obligation. Possible solution would be to fix a period during which the Government would have the first call on the services of the trained scholar. If the Government are unable to find him suitable during this period, the scholar would be privately accept employment elsewhere. I will soon announce my decision on this question."

There had been some misunderstanding of the scope and functions of the scheme of overseas scholarship carried out by Government since 1945. There had also been public criticism in respect of the utility of the scheme and the manner and method of training and accommodation secured for selected scholars. He was satisfied that selection was entirely on merits and there were no grounds for complaints. Some attempt at convassing were made in 1945 but hardly any in 1946. It had been the policy of the Department from the very outset to look immediately into any complaints that were made.

The experience had been that most of them were unfounded or exaggerated and only few justified. All cases of unsatisfactory arrangements were, however, looked into at once and had since been remedied. The Deputy Educational Advisor (Overseas) who went abroad this year visited many of the Universities where Indian students were studying and he had almost invariably received satisfactory reports about them. The criticisms which had been made had rarely mentioned any specific case. In view of this, he was satisfied that the criticisms were not justified.

The position in respect of accommodation had been very bad and had been steadily worsening. Particularly in the U.K. life was far from comfortable in regard to food and other necessities. These difficulties and discomforts could not be helped because they were inherent in the existing conditions. Every endeavour had, however, been made to warn students repeatedly of the difficult conditions, "Indian students who go abroad must go in a spirit of pioneers and be prepared to rough it with the people of the land.

There is no evidence that these hardships are peculiar to Indians. While there are still people in the U.K. who suffer from colour prejudice, there has been considerable improvement in this respect lately and it would not be fair to make a general statement that Indian students are discriminated against."

The scheme initiated during the war did not allow much opportunity of sending students to countries other than the U.K. and U.S.A. but the whole position was not being surveyed and a small committee was likely to be appointed to go into the whole question. The Department was even now trying to place students in other countries like Australia, Sweden and Switzerland.

Asked whether Govt. had awarded any scholarships purely on grounds of war service, Maulana Azad said that cases of war service candidates were considered but there was no question of giving any scholarships purely as a regard for one's personal or family services.

Asked whether the Department was considering the question of training teachers to implement the basic education scheme. Maulana Azad said that he desired to call a conference of Provincial Ministers as well as representatives of Universities to discuss this question as early as possible.

"I selected the education portfolio because of my special interest in the problems of education and because I regard reconstruction of our educational system as the foundation of a new national life" said Maulana Azad. "I propose to give an outline of my views on the subject at an early date."

Document No. 7

LETTER FROM SARDAR PATEL TO MAULANA AZAD

New Delhi

7 February, 1947

My dear Maulana Sahib,

Please refer to your letter dated 27 January 1947 regarding riot in the Mach Jail in Baluchistan. The matter concerns the External Affairs Department, and I am sending a copy of your letter with its enclosures to Jawaharlal.

Yours sincerely,
V.J. PATEL

The Hon'ble Maulana Abul Kalam Azad
Member of Education
New Delhi.

Document No. 8

RESOLUTION, DATED 10-2-1947, MOVED BY MAULANA AZAD IN THE LEGISLATIVE ASSEMBLY IN CONNECTION WITH THE ELECTION OF A MEMBER TO THE COURT OF THE DELHI UNIVERSITY AND HIS REPLIES TO THE QUESTIONS RAISED IN THIS REGARD

The Honourable Maulana Abul Kalam Azad (Member for Education and Arts): Sir, I move:

> "That in pursuance of Clause (xiv) of sub-section (1) of Section 18 of the Delhi University Act, 1922 (VIII of 1922) as amended by the Delhi University (Amendment) Act, 1943 (XXIV of 1943), read with clause (5) of Statute 2 of the Statutes of the University set out in the Schedule to the latter Act, the elected members of this Assembly do proceed to elect, in such manner as may be approved by the Honourable the President, one person from among their own number to be a member of the Court of the University of Delhi *vice* Honourable Mr. Liaquat Ali Khan resigned."

Honourable Members of the House are aware that Delhi University Act, 1922 entitles the Central Legislatures to elect a few members to the Court of the Delhi University. Accordingly, on the 20th February last year the Honourable Mr. Liaquat Ali Khan was elected. He has now resigned and a member should be elected in this place for the rest of the term.

Mr. Ahmed E.H. Jaffer (Bombay Southern Division: Muhammadan Rural): What about translation to the European Group?

Mr. Deputy President: Order, order. Motion moved:

> "That in pursuance of Clause (xiv) of sub-section (1) of Section 18 of the Delhi University Act, 1922 (VIII of 1922) as amended by the Delhi University (Amendment) Act, 1943 (XXIV of 1943), read with clause (5) of Statute 2 of the Statutes of the University set out in the Schedule to the latter Act, the elected members of this Assembly do proceed to elect, in such manner as

> may be approved by the Honourable the President, one person from among their own number to be a member of the Court of the University of Delhi *vice* Honourable Mr. Liaquat Ali Khan resigned."

Haji Abdus Sattar Haji Ishaq Seth (West Coast and Nilgiris: Muhmmadan): Have I to speak in Urdu, so that my Honourable friend may understand?

Mr. Deputy President: If any Honourable Member is acquainted with English to the extent that he can talk in English and he has been talking in English, then he should make his speech in English. If he cannot speak English, then he is quite at liberty to speak in whatever language he chooses.

Haji Abdus Sattar Haji Ishaq Seth: I want to ask a question of my Honourable friend. I want to know whether he will understand it.

Mr. Deputy President: I understand that the Honourable Member does understand English so much that he will be able to follow the question but he may not be able to speak in English.

Khan Abdul Ghani Khan (North West Frontier Province: General): Chaudhari Sri Chand used to speak in Hindustani, although he knew English very well.

Haji Abdus Sattar Haji Ishaq Seth: The Honourable Member said that a member is to be elected for the balance of the period that was to be served by the Honourable Mr. Liaquat Ali Khan: What is the balance of the period?

The Honourable Maulana Abul Kalam Azad: The Honourable Mr. Liaquat Ali Khan was elected a member of the Delhi University Court for three years on the 20th February 1946. He has now resigned.

Mr. Deputy President: The question is:

> "That in pursuance of Clause (xiv) of sub-section (1) of Section 18 of the Delhi University Act, 1922 (VIII of 1922) as amended by the Delhi University (Amendment) Act, 1943 (XXIV of 1943), read with clause (5) of Statute 2 of the Statutes of the University set out in the Schedule to the latter Act, the elected members of this Assembly do proceed to elect, in such manner as may be approved by the Honourable the President, one person from among their own number to be a member of

the Court of the University of Delhi *vice* Honourable Mr. Liaquat Ali Khan resigned."

The motion was adopted.

Mr. Deputy President: I have to inform Honourable Members that the following dates have been fixed for receiving nominations and holding elections, if necessary, for the purpose of election of a member to the Court of the University of Delhi.:

Date of nomination – 12th February, 1947.
Date for election – 14th February 1947.

The nominations will be received in the Notice Office upto 12 noon on the date mentioned for the purpose. The election, which will be conducted in accordance with the Regulations for the holding of elections by means of the single transferable vote, will be held in the Assistant Secretary's room in the Council House, between the hours of 10.30 A.M. and 1 P.M.

Document No. 9

LETTER FROM MAULANA AZAD TO SARDAR PATEL

New Delhi

10 February, 1947

My dear Vallabhbhai,

I have been able to make time to listen to the broadcasts of All India Radio for the last two weeks and want to suggest to you two things that I have noticed.

The first is in respect of Indian music. You perhaps do not know that I have always taken a keen interest in Indian music and at one time practised it myself. It has, therefore, been a shock to me to find that the standard of music of All India Radio broadcast is extremely poor. I have always felt that All India Radio should set the standard in Indian music and lead to its continual improvement. Instead, the present programmes have an opposite effect and lead one to suspect that the artistes are sometimes chosen not on grounds of merit.

The second thing is in respect of the overseas broadcasts of All India Radio in Arabic, Persian and English. These were instituted during the war and have been somewhat curtailed after the cessation of hostilities. They can, however, serve as a useful vehicle of our national interests and represent the Indian point of view abroad. Unfortunately the present broadcasts do not fully serve either purpose. They are not only inferior from the point of view of language and style but, what is worse, the contents of the broadcasts and their point of view leave much room for improvement.

I know you are extremely busy and it is hardly possible for you to attend to these details. If, however, you desire, I am willing to help in any way possible. I do not know the exact position but if there be no insuperable objection, would you ask your Secretary for Broadcasting to come and see me about the programme on these two points *viz.* music and overseas programmes in Arabic and Persian? I shall find time to advise him from time to time and keep you informed. If I have any further suggestions to make on these two questions, I shall either write to you or discuss with you when we meet.

Yours sincerely,
A.K. AZAD

The Hon'ble Sardar Vallabhbhai Patel
New Delhi.

Document No. 10

EXTARACT FROM THE LETTER OF MAHATAMA GANDHI TO MAULANA ABUL KALAM AZAD

February 12, 1947

If the ahimsa[1] about which I have written so much and which I have striven to realize in practice all these years does not answer in a crisis, it ceases to have any value in my eyes. Your affection prompts you to say that if only I were near you, all would be well[2]. The truth however is that so long as I cannot make good here, I can be of no use anywhere.

---

1. Non-violence
2. The addressee had suggested to Mahatama Gandhi to make Calcutta his headquarters if he could not go and stay at Delhi.

Document No. 11

LETTER FROM MAULANA AZAD TO PT. JAWAHARLAL NEHRU

New Delhi

13-2-1947

Dear Jawaharlal,

I do not think there is anything in the statement[1] I have prepared which requires consideration by the cabinet. I am, however, sending it to you all the same for your perusal.

Yours sincerely,
Abul Kalam Azad

---

1. See appendices

Document No. 12

ANSWERS BY MAULANA AZAD DT. 14-2-1947 IN THE LEGISLATIVE ASSEMBLY IN CONNECTION WITH THE ALL-INDIA TECHNICAL INSTITUTE TO THE QUESTIONS RAISED BY SETH GOVIND DAS AND OTHERS

Seth Govind Das : (a) Will the Honourable Member for Education be pleased to state whether it is a fact that a committee was appointed to consider the question of setting up of an All India Technical Institution on the lines of the Massachusetts Institute of Technology?

(b) Has any report been submitted by the said Committee; and if so, what steps are Government taking to implement the Committee's recommendations?

The Honourable Maulana Abul Kalam Azad : (a) Yes. With a view to ensuring an adequate supply of technical personnel for post-war industrial development in the country, an *ad hoc* committee (Sarkar Committee) was set up by the Education Department in the beginning of 1945, to consider the establishment of high grade technological institutions in India on the lines of Massachusetts Institute of Technology.

(b) The Committee have submitted an interim report in which they have recommended that:

(i) Not less than four Higher Technical Institutions, one in the North, one in the East, one in the South and one in the West will be necessary to satisfy India's post-war requirements.

(ii) The one in the East should be set up in or near Calcutta at an early date.

(iii) Establishment of the Western Institution which should be in or near Bombay should be taken in hand concurrently with the Eastern Institution or failing that as soon after as possible.

(iv) To satisfy the immediate needs for Engineers generally

and for those with specialised training in Hydraulics in particular, the engineering nucleus of the Northern Institution should be set up without delay.

(v) To ensure the proper planning of buildings, equipment and courses of study, the Principal and Heads of the Main Department of these institutions should be appointed and the services of an architect with experience in the planning of technical institution secured at a sufficiently early stage.

A copy of the report is placed on the table of the House.

The recommendation of the Sarkar Committee in regard to the establishment of the four Higher Technical Institutions has subsequently been endorsed by the All-India Council for Technical Education, which has been set up to advise the Government on matters relating to higher technical education. The advisory council, however, recommended that the exact location of these institutions should be decided by the Council itself after taking into consideration the facilities available in the locality, the existence of engineering, Technical and Technological Institutes, University Colleges, and research facilities and the particular industries existing in the area concerned. The Government have accepted these recommendations in general and are taking necessary steps to establish the Eastern and the Western Higher Technical Institutions with the least possible delay. Possible sites for the institutions have been inspected and their final selection and acquisition will be expedited as much as possible. Nucleus staff for planning of both the institutions has also been sanctioned and necessary financial provision for construction of buildings for the Eastern Institute is being included in the budget estimates for 1947-48.

Seth Govind Das : The Honourable Member has just said that it was under consideration to establish four institutions.....

Sreejut Rohini Kumar Chaudhari: On a point of order, Sir, You had passed a ruling that if a Member has once spoken in any language, he should continue to speak in that langauge. My Honourable friend Seth Govind Das knows English and he speaks in English. Why should he speak in Urdu? Does he mean to say that the Honourable Member for Education does not understand English?

Mr. President : As I said before, this is a matter which requires consideration and when the Honourable Member for Government is speaking in Hindustani....

An Honourable Member : It is not Hindustani.

Mr. President: Whatever it is, I would call it Hindustani. If any Honourable Member wishes to put a question, he must make himself easily understandable to the Honourable Member for Government. I can see the difficulty that some Honourable Members may not be able to follow the questions and answers. I do not claim to understand fully every word that has been spoken.

Dr. G.V. Deshmukh : I do not understand a word of it.

Mr. President : That is unfortunate. But if an Honourable Member of this House has got the liberty of speaking in his own language, I find it difficult immediately to come to the conclusion that any Honourable Member who wishes to put a question to such an Honourable Member should not be permitted to address that Honourable Member in that particular language. But, as I said, this matter requires consideration and the whole question of the language of the House is under the consideration of this very House, on a question raised. So, I should not like to complicate the situation further by giving any ruling on the legal position as it stands today. After all, if the rules of the House are going to be changed, it will be an advantage to have this practice for some time in order to realise how far than change will, on the whole be, conducive to the conduct of the proceedings in this House. That is why I said that I would like to postpone the consideration of this subject for some time, till the question of the amendment of the rules is decided by this House itself. But I can do one thing. The number of supplementaries will be much shorter.

Dr. G.V. Deshmukh : May I make one request and it is this? Many of us who do not come from northern parts of India do not know what language is this that is spoken here, whether it is Hindustani or Urdu. Some of us would like to study the language in view of what the decision of the House may be, but we should know exactly what language is this. Those who understand it say that it is Hindustani; others say that it is Urdu; I do not know that language it is. Therefore, if we are told what language it is, we will make an effort to understand it and ask question in that language in which the Honourable Member speaks. In fact, we should try to put question in our own language which we do understand. You will realise the difficulty of some of us who want to put questions.

Mr. President: There is nothing in the name. I style it Hindustani.

The Honourable Member can try and pick up such a language if he likes. It will take him a long time to study the language if he wants to put supplementary questions in that language.

Seth Govind Das: I was saying that the Honourable Member had just said that it was under consideration to establish four institutions – one in the North and one in the East. Of the other two, will the Honourable Member please consider of establishing one in Central India, particularly in Jubbulpore inasmuch as there are so many Government and non-Government factories there and there is no place more important than Jubbulpore in Central India.

The Honourable Maulana Abul Kalam Azad : There is nothing against considering this point.

Document No. 13

(ANSWERS BY MAULANA AZAD DT. 14-2-1947 IN THE LEGISLATIVE ASSEMBLY TO QUESTIONS ASKED REGARDING THE NUMBER OF STUDENTS SENT ABROAD FOR STUDIES IN HIGHER ECONOMICS AND STATISTICS UNDER THE CENTRAL GOVERNMENT OVERSEAS TRAINING SCHEME)

Mr. Vadilal Lallubhai: (a) Will the Honourable Member for Education please state how many students have so far been sent abroad for higher education under the auspices of the Central Government Overseas Training Scheme?

(b) How many of these students have been sent for studies in Higher Economics and Statistics and how many applications were received by the Government for studies in these subjects?

(c) Is it a fact that for 1947-48, Government do not propose to send any students for studies in Higher Economics and Statistics?

(d) Is it a fact that Government did send some students for studies in these two subjects in previous years?

(e) If so, on what grounds have Government decided to drop these subjects from the list of subjects for overseas scholarships in the year 1947-48?

(f) Do Government propose to employ all the students sent abroad under the auspices of the Government Overseas Training Scheme after their return from abroad or are they to find employment for themselves? Have Government any scheme in this respect, if so, what is its nature?

The Honourable Maulana Abul Kalam Azad: (a) 407 scholars have so far been sent abroad for higher education under the Central Government Overseas Scholarships Scheme.

(b) Six scholars have been sent for Statistics, one for Agricultural Statistics and eight for Economics. It is not possible at this stage to give the total number of candidates who applied for Economics or Statistics but the number of those with first class or near first class applications was 208 for Economics and 321 for Statistics.

(c) No Sir, Two Scholarships are scheduled to be awarded for Statistical Economics in 1947-48.

(d) Yes.

(e) In view of (c) the question does not arise. It may, however be mentioned that Central Overseas Scholarships are awarded in accordance with the requirements of the different Departments of the Central Government.

(f) The attention of the Honourable Member is invited to the reply given this morning to starred question No. 300 by Seth Govind Das on this aspect of the Overseas Scholarship Scheme.

Mr. Manu Subedar : Will the Honourable Member examine the position whether by their own efforts private parties will not send their sons for higher education and Government will not secure the necessary recruits for their Departments and whether it is necessary to spend such large sums as Government have been spending in sending students for any and every type of subjects?

The Honourable Maulana Abul Kalam Azad : As I have already said in reply to question the department is considering it and it is very soon appointing a committee to reconsider the whole question of the overseas scholars.

Mr. Vadilal Lallubhai: I could not follow the reply to part (b).

The Honourable Maulana Abul Kalam Azad : Six scholars for Statistics, eight for Economics and one for Agricultural Statistics.

Lala Deshbandhu Gupta: Will the Honourable Member please state the number of scholars from Delhi out of the 407 scholars sent overseas?

The Honourable Maulana Abul Kalam Azad: Notice is required.

Document No. 14

(ANSWERS BY MAULANA AZAD DT. 14-2-1947 TO THE QUESTIONS ASKED IN L.A. ABOUT THE UTILIZATION OF STUDENTS AFTER TECHNICAL TRAINING)

Seth Govind Das : (a) Will the Honourable Member for Education please state how many students sent abroad by Government at Government expenditure for technical training have up to now returned after completion of their studies?

(b) How do Government propose to utilize the valuable knowledge acquired by them.

The Honourable Maulana Abul Kalam Azad: (a) None of the overseas scholars sent abroad by Government have so far completed their studies.

(b) All the overseas scholars are expected to be employed on their return by Central and Provincial Governments concerned in gazetted posts on some suitable work connected with the various plans of development.

Seth Govind Das : Will the Government please state how many of the scholars sent abroad are expected to return soon?

The Honourable Maulana Abul Kalam Azad: Notice is required to answer that question.

Shri D.P. Karmarkar : Is the Honourable Member aware of the fact that in the case of some subjects, for instance, micro-films, there are no corresponding facilities in India for utilizing the services of the scholar after his return?

The Honourable Maulana Abul Kalam Azad: Notice is required to answer this question also.

Mr. Siddiq Ali Khan : Will the Honourable Member please state whether the ratio fixed for the minorities was taken into consideration when the scholars were sent abroad?

The Honourable Maulana Abul Kalam Azad : I have been informed by the Department that the same ratio, as is commonly observed in the services that is 25 per cent, has been observed here also.

Sardar Mangal Singh : Will the Honourable Member please state if all the scholars who return from abroad will be provided with jobs?

Shri A.C. Vellingiri Gounder : I want your ruling on this point. I raised this point before. The Government Member may talk in Hindustani but the other members who know English should speak in English. I should like to have your ruling.

Mr. President : The matter requires further consideration so far as the position of the rules goes. The Honourable Member is aware that there was a suggestion in the form of a question in this House in the last session to amend the rules and that matter is under consideration. So, I do not think I should commit myself to this or that view, till a final decision is taken by this House as regards the language which is permissible.

Shri V.C. Vellingiri Gounder : May I submit, Sir, that until those rules are framed, a translation may be made of these supplementary questions and answers which are put in Hindustani?

Mr. President: That translation will be printed in the debates.

The Honourable Maulana Abul Kalam Azad: It is hoped that all will be provided with jobs. I will, however, draw the attention of the Honourable Member to my statement given a few days ago to the Press Conference. The Department is also considering to create some further facilities in this connection.

Shri Sri Prakasa : Will the Honourable Member please take the trouble to state the number of scholars who were granted scholarships but could not be sent abroad because no arrangements could be made for them?

The Honourable Maulana Abul Kalam Azad : I gladly take the trouble to state that owing to difficulties met with in England and America some of the scholars could not be sent but they were warned of the obstacles that were to come in their way.

Shri Sri Prakasa : What could be the number of such scholars?

The Honourable Maulana Abul Kalam Azad: I want notice to answer that question.

Seth Govind Das : Will the Honourable Member please state whether or not proper arrangements for the boarding and lodging of scholars sent abroad could be made when food situation in those countries had so much deteriorated? If scholars were sent abroad without giving due consideration to this fact it is possible they may have to be called back.

The Honourable Maulana Abul Kalam Azad : The Department has given full consideration to the point and a committee is to be set up to further consider it.

Document No. 15

LETTER FROM PT. JAWAHAR LAL NEHRU TO MAULANA AZAD

New Delhi

14 February, 1947

My dear Maulana,

Thank you for sending me the note you have prepared for your press conference on the 18th. I have read it carefully. There are some matters in it which are likely to raise controversy. For instance, with reference to imparting religious instruction in schools you yourself say that there is a great deal of difference of opinion among experts on this point.[1] Without going into the merits of any such proposal, it is clear that opinions differ widely and if this is so, it would be unwise to say something on behalf of the Government without references to the Cabinet and without some kind of a decision on the subject. It would raise a controversy in the public also, and when we have so many controversies it hardly seems desirable to add to them.

2. Of course you are entitled to give your personal opinion, although the personal opinion of a Minister in regard to his department cannot wholly be personal.

3. Another matter, which is highly controversial in India at present, is the encouragement of the Roman script.[2] Personally I am not at all opposed to it, though I am not clear in my mind as to how far we can go. Gandhiji, as you know, is very much against it, and he has only recently written about it.[3] I am quite sure that the great majority of our people are opposed to it at present and are likely to remain so at least so long as any vestige of British rule remains here. In this state of affairs no proposal to use the Roman script officially or semi-officially is likely to be approved of. It will only result in controversy.

4. The proposal to set up a National Museum should fit in with an actual proposal on that subject which has been made by a

committee specially appointed.[4] It is true that the Museum is supposed to deal chiefly with art, archaeology etc.

5. The reference to the British Museum is perhaps not very appropriate because this Museum contains the collection not of British works of art etc., but rather foreign specimens. The chief British thing it has is a huge library.

6. You refer to the Jamia Millia and Shantiniketan. As you know, substantial grants have been made to both recently.

7. If I may say so, parts of your statement for the press are very good, but they are more in the form of an essay than of a press statement. The fairly long account of missionary effort is very interesting, but I doubt if it will be particularly relevant in the present context.

8. I am returning your note.

Yours affectionately,
Jawaharlal Nehru

---

1. As religious instruction imparted in private institutions in India, in many cases, instead of broadening the outlook and promoting a spirit of toleration and goodwill, had produced the opposite results, Azad felt that religious instruction could be imparted more effectively if the State took charge of that question.
2. Azad favoured the use of Roman script as supplementary to Devanagari and Urdu, but added that this question should be considered by educationists all over India.
3. In a press statement on 24 January 1947 Mahatma Gandhi said that the Roman script should not be allowed to replace "the two Indian scripts"; "let it not be said of India that it is so degraded as to become the blotting sheet of civilisation."
4. The Central Advisory Board of Education proposed the setting up of a National Cultural Trust as the first step to setting up a National Museum.

Document No. 16

LETTER FROM PT. JAWAHARLAL NEHRU TO MAULANA AZAD

New Delhi

14 February, 1947

My dear Maulana,

I have received your note on Parliamentary Secretaries which I have read. I have also been thinking about the Council of State nominations. Apart from certain present difficulties in carrying out these proposals, there is a major difficulty. We are now in the midst of a very severe crisis which is likely to affect the whole constitution of the Government. No one knows what may happen within the next week or ten days. It is almost certain, however, that things will not remain where they are, and some decision this way or that way will have to be taken. It is at least a possibility that we may not remain in Government. In such a state of affairs it seems to me undesirable to make any fresh proposals which are in the nature of innovations or which may lead to controversy. I think we should allow matters to rest where they are till we know definitely what is going to happen. Because of this, I have for several weeks refrained from making several proposals in my department which I might otherwise have done.

2. There are some other considerations also which make me doubt the advisability of considering these matters. Any nomination to the Council of State should not be made without reference to the Leader of the Council, namely Nishtar. It is obvious that Nishtar will object to many of our nominations. We can hardly take this matter to the Cabinet and decide by a majority.

3. If any one Parliamentary Secretary is appointed, it will inevitably follow that the Muslim League Members will demand such secretaries for themselves. That will increase the Government in its wider sense and produce more confusion by bringing in non-

cooperative elements in it. Parliamentary Secretaries will have access to confidential files. Nothing will remain private.

4. We shall be on very weak ground if we make a major issue of appointments and nominations in such a way. If our proposal is accepted, the League will have full right to do the same. There will also be considerable heart-burning among our own people in the Assembly.

5. Charges of nepotism might be brought against us. These, no doubt, will be untrue, but they will still be believed. We have been very careful in this matter since we took charge of Government. Indeed I have appointed nobody to my departments although a change is needed.

6. Yesterday I heard, to my surprise and dismay, that Rajendra Babu had appointed Jugal Kishore Khanna as a Deputy Secretary in his department. Such an appointement of a leading Congressman in Delhi to a Deputy Secretary's position seems to me full of danger. It will give a big handle to our opponents and it will do no particular good to us. Apart from its effect upon us and the Government, it will, I think, adversely affect the Congress where there will be personal rivalries as to who should be appointed. The Congress organization, which is in a bad way today, will become worse. I am writing these brief points for your consideration.

7. I am returning your nc

Yours affectionately,
JAWAHARLAL NEHRU

Document No. 17

MAULANA AZAD'S ADDRESS IN THE PRESS CONFERENCE DATED 18-2-1947

It is universally recognised today that a system of national education is one of the fundamental tasks which faces any government. Not only is the existing condition of society determined by the quality of individuals composing it but its future as well. Nothing has a more important bearing on the quality of the individual than the type of education imparted. A truly liberal and humanitarian education may transform the outlook of the people and set it on the path of progress and prosperity, while an ill-conceived or unscientific system might destroy all the hopes which have been cherished by generations of pioneers in the cause of national freedom.

India is today on the threshold of freedom. It is therefore imperative that we survey the prevalent systems of education in order to find out how far they meet our national requirements. There can be no denying that the existing system of education was shaped by non-nationals in non-national interests. Macaulay is primarily responsible for our existing educational methods and ideals. He never concealed the fact that his chief aim was to create in India men who in training, outlook and loyalties would be devoted to the interests of Great Britain. Nevertheless, the great services which the existing system of education has rendered to the Indian people need not be denied. It opened to them a new world of science and modern technology. It inculcated a progressive spirit and brought Indian educational standards in line with the standards obtaining elsewhere. It has led to a re-awakening of the national spirit and a growth of modern and progressive outlook in all affairs of the world. There is equally no denying that this system has led to the creation of a small intelligentsia separated from the mass of the Indian people. It has also at times tended to divorce the educated class from the currents of India's traditional life. Dazzled by the achievements of the West, it has at times encouraged a tendency to disown or look down upon our national heritage. It has also tended to encourage fissiparous tendencies. The greatest charge against the present system of education is that it has not led to the development of a national mind.

Macaulay's contempt for oriental studies is well known. History has not justified the sweeping condemnation which Macaulay extended to them. Nor can history justify the method which Macaulay adopted for the promulgation of learning in this land. Macaulay's contention that Sanskrit and Persian were unsuited to be the medium of instruction in India is no doubt correct, but English could serve the purpose no better. It is true that the different Indian Provincial languages were not at the time sufficiently developed to serve as the medium of instruction but there can be no doubt that a National Government would have taken these languages in hand and gradually developed them to serve the purpose. In any case, the Indian languages today have attained a development where they can serve as the medium of instruction up to the highest stage. The experiment of imparting instruction in the mother tongue up to the Matriculation standard has already been tried with success and the time has come when the process must be extended further and all education in the land made accessible to the people in their own language.

All such development, however, presupposes a sound system of basic education. If the foundations have not been truly and firmly laid, no abiding superstructure can be built. The whole edifice of education and culture ultimately rests upon the teaching imparted in the early stages. In India this has been unfortunately neglected in a way which cannot be too strongly condemned. Education has often been left in the charge of persons who do not possess the minimum qualifications for it. Nor can they be blamed, for the profession of teaching has been debased against the best traditions of the land. In the past the status of the teacher in Indian society was an exalted one. He might not have been wealthy but his comparative poverty was compensated by the need of respect and prestige which the profession of teaching carried with it. Today unfortunately all this has changed, and the teacher, especially in primary stages, is considered as hardly better than an inferior servant. Any programme for reconstruction of education must therefore place in the forefront the task of improving the status and condition of teachers, and I am confident that the new National Government of India will recognise this as one of its first and foremost tasks.

It is not necessary to go into the details of the scheme for reorganisation of basic education as that has already been sufficiently discussed in the press and on the platform. It will suffice to say that the basic scheme of education will go a long way towards meeting some of the points indicated above. This report popularly known as the Sargent Report not only ensures an improvement in the status of teachers in all stages but also lays down the criteria along which education for citizenship should proceed. The emphasis on the development of education through the mother tongue has also been sufficiently recognised in that scheme. It is a matter for pleasure that the Provinces are making arrangements for giving immediate effect to the scheme and have requested co-operation from the Centre. The Educational Adviser has received invitations from most of the Provinces and is shortly going out on tour. I propose to call a conference of Provincial Ministers and representatives of universities in order to plan out a comprehensive programme of work.

One question on which the report has not come to any definite conclusion is that of religious instruction in schools. I know that there is a sharp difference of opinion among experts on this question. Two committees appointed by the Central Advisory Board of Education have submitted contrary reports. In the past a majority of educationists placed the emphasis on purely secular education. This was true of Great Britain and in Russia, after the Soviet Revolution, there was a positive anti-religious temper in educational policy. Those who hold a different view emphasise that experience tends to prove the futility of education from which religion has been divorced. Today in Great Britain a system of education has been evolved under the supervision of the State. It is reported that Russia also has in the recent past recognised the value of religious instruction and taken steps to that effect.

The Government will have to give proper weight to both these points of view and come to a decision on the question. One thing, which, however, has to be remembered, is that in India the emphasis on religion has been and is greater than in other countries. Not only the past traditions of India but also the present temper of the people tend to emphasise the importance of religious instruction. If the Government decide that religious instruction should be included in education, it seems imperative that the religious instruction offered should be of the best type. The religious instruction often imparted in India in private institutions is of a kind which instead of broadening the outlook and inculcating a spirit of toleration and goodwill to all men produces exactly the opposite results. It is likely that under

State supervision even denominational teaching can be imparted in a more liberal spirit than under private control. The aim of all religious teaching should be to make men more tolerant and broad-minded and it is my opinion that this can be more effectively done if the State takes charge of the question than if it is left to private initiative. I will indicate the decision of the Government on this question at an early date.

Another point on which I want to express my opinion is in respect of the educational activities of missionary societies. Friends from England have sent me cuttings from papers in which this question has been raised. There is no doubt that missionary societies have played a very important part in the dissemination of modern education and the development of the modern outlook. This is true not only of India but of other countries of the East as well. I can speak with personal knowledge of the Middle East countries. Before 1907 the only institution imparting modern higher education in Turkey was Robert College run by the American Mission and its contribution to the awakening of Turkey can never be forgotten. Modern education in Syria was largely the work of missionaries who founded three colleges in Beirut of which the most famous was the American Missionary College (Al Kulliatus-Suria). Higher education in Iraq is similarly indebted to 'Kulliya Qudais Yusuf', *i.e.*, St. Joseph's College. The same story is repeated in Egypt. It is true that Mohammad Ali the Great founded in the first quarter of the 19th century overseas scholarships for Europe under the name of 'Israliat' but most of the important personalities in Egyptian renaissance are products of the Missionary College of Beirut. The well-known modern Arabic author, George Zaidan, whose *History of Islamic Civilisation* has been translated into English by Nicholson, was a student of the Missionary College of Beirut. The Sarroof Brothers, well-known editors of 'Al Muqattam' and 'Al Moqtataf' also received their education and their inspiration of service from the same missionary college.

These missionary societies helped not only in the spread of modern education but, what is more, contributed greatly to the development of indigenous languages. They were also in many cases the pioneers in oriental research and scholarship. Vondyke came as an American missionary to Beirut when he was only 18 and devoted himself to the development of modern education in Syria. The Scientific series which he published under the name of 'An Naqsh Fil Hajar' is one of the best scientific works in Arabic of the 20th century. Perhaps the best modern book on Astronomy in Arabic is his work entitled 'Al Haiat.' I do not want to dilate here on the services they have rendered in China, Japan and other South-East Asian countries.

New education in India also began with the work of the missionary societies. The East India Company had at first been in favour of oriental education and it was through the efforts of the Serampore Mission that the foundations of European Education in India were laid. Since that time missionary societies have kept up their educational work and brought learning to millions who, but for their help, would have remained immersed in illiteracy and ignorance.

Their work in the development of Indian languages has also been of the greatest value. One of the first standard works in Urdu prose is a translation of the Bible that they completed in the beginning of the 19th century. Urdu has made tremendous strides in the last 150 years and yet this early translation of the Bible remains a standard of Urdu prose.

With such valuable examples of the work done by the missionaries in the past, there is no reason why their work on the same humanitarian lines should not receive equal appreciation in the future. It is only in respect of one problem that difficulties arise at times. This is on the vexed question of conversions and especially conversions *en masse*. World opinion has undergone great changes on the question and responsible missionaries have themselves come to recognise that mass conversions are in reality no conversion at all. Christ himself emphasised the baptism of the spirit rather than formal baptism by water, and missionaries would be true to the spirit of Christ if they preached His message of humanity instead of attempting to convert people to the dogma of a Church. If all missionary societies adopt this enlightened outlook, there is no reason why independent India should in any way hesitate to accept the services which it is theirs to offer.

I would like to say a few words about another problem. The Deputy Educational Adviser (Resettlement) informs me that during the war two million soldiers were made literate by the Army through the use of the Roman script. Experience showed that they could acquire a working knowledge of Hindustani in three to six months' time. I am told that this would have been impossible to achieve if the Devanagri or the Urdu script had been used. Roman has thus solved the problem of finding alternative scripts for men of different provinces. If these men who have been made literate during their service in the Army are not to lapse into illiteracy, we must provide them with suitable literature in Roman Hindustani. There is a great demand for such literature and the Department is considering how to meet this demand.

It is desirable that every Indian should learn both Devanagiri and Urdu scripts. This will, however, take time and till this is achieved, it would be worth considering whether the use of Roman as a supplementary script, in addition to Devanagri and Urdu, in central educational publications may not be a temporary expedient. There are millions of Bengalees, Madrasis, Oriyas, Assamese and men speaking other languages who can understand Hindustani and pick it up quickly but find an impediment in their progress because of the script. This, however, is a question which ought to be considered by educationists all over the land.

I will now indicate some of the main items which may be taken up in the near future:

1. The time has come for setting up a National Museum where the finest representations of Indian philosophy, literature and art may be preserved. The first step in this direction will be the setting up of a National Cultural Trust as proposed recently by the Central Advisory Board of Education.
2. There should be provision for fundamental research work, and for this, definite sums should be allocated every year. It is obvious that there can be no advance in either industry or technology without fundamental research work. The scope of such research should, however, be extended and cover not only the scientific subjects but also the humanities including philosophy, the social sciences, anthropology, etc. The Co-ordination Committee of the Cabinet has approved, in principle, of a grant of Rs. 75,00,000 for fundamental research work in the next five years.
3. (a) There is also a proposal for the appointment of a committee to prepare a Guide for Teachers for the new scheme of education. While the Central Government do not wish to impose uniformity but to leave the greatest possible margin of freedom to the Provinces, there should be some indication of the general lines on which this education is to be imparted.

(b) The question of preparing some kind of a generalised curriculum may also be considered. Any fixed curriculum has the tendency of imposing rigid uniformity and therefore the preparation of this curriculum should be undertaken with the greatest possible care.

4. The Government of India are considering the quesiton of making grants to educational experiment institutions without waiting to verify the rsults of such experiments. There are not many institutions of this kind and most of them have been unable to give their best as financial difficulties have hampered them from the very outset. It is not suggested that the Government of India should be lavish or careless in making grants but wherever genuine efforts of this kind are in evidence, the Government should come to the help of the institution at the initital stages so that lack of funds may not hinder the institutions from carrying out their experiments. Two institutions of this type which have recently received Government help are the Jamia Millia University, Delhi, and Santiniketan in Bengal. It is, however, obviously impossible to mention all such institutions.

5. Another field which requires immediate attention is the development of archaeological studies in India. We have as yet no complete history of India and it will have to be reconstructed from the monuments and other archaeological remains which are scattered all over the land.

6. Disraeli very rightly recognised that a democracy has not future unless it educates its masses. In India, the problem arises with even greater intensity. The problem of mass education here is of vast proportions and will require time for its solution. It cannot, however, wait and modern science has placed in our hands effective insturments in the form of broadcasting and the film. I am considering schemes by which they may be utilised to the fullest extent for broadening the mind of the masses and opening up a new world of knowledge to them.

I will conclude by stressing once again the imperative necessity of reforming and expanding our system of education, Education should have the highest priority in our national budget and shoud take its place immediately after food and clothing. In fact, a proper system of education is necessary in order to tackle satisfactorily even these problems. I have every hope that we shall be able to make up our leeway by a determined and concerted effort and place education in India on a par with education in other civilised countries of the world.

Document No. 18

LETTER FROM SARDAR PATEL TO MAULANA AZAD

New Delhi,

20 February, 1947

My dear Maulana Sahib,

Many thanks for your letter of the 10th instant, in which you were good enough to make some suggestions regarding the improvement of music and overseas broadcasts of All India Radio.

2. I am glad to know that you are taking so much interest in these matters, and I am always at your disposal in regard to any suggestions that you might have to make for the improvement of these broadcasts. While I make no apology for such defects as exist in the quality of these broadcasts, I think it would be a mistake to ignore the patent fact that the artistic talent at the disposal of each radio station is limited, and that they have to make the best of whatever talent is available to them. We have also to take note of the fact that the remuneration which we cân give to these artistes is not sufficiently attractive, and having regard to the present financial difficulties, of which you are no doubt aware, it does not seem possible to make any improvement in that respect.

3. The limited availability of talent in foreign languages is even more marked.

Yours sincerely,

Vallabhbhai Patel

The Hon'ble Maulana Abul Kalam Azad
22, Prithviraj Road
New Delhi.

Document No. 19

ANSWERS DATED 24-2-1947 BY MAULANA AZAD TO THE QUESTIONS ASKED IN THE CONSTITUTENT ASSEMBLY OF INDIA (LEGISLATIVE)

INTRODUCTION OF VERNACULARS AS MEDIUM OF INSTRUCTION IN DEGREE COLLEGES

Mr. Madandhari Singh: Will the Honourable Member for Education be pleased to state:

(a) the names of Universities where Vernaculars have been introduced as medium of instruction in Degree Colleges;

(b) the names of Universities who are contemplating to introduce vernaculars as medium of instruction in Degree Colleges; and

(c) whether there is any University which has not yet done any thing to introduce vernaculars as the medium of instruction in Degree Colleges; if so, the reasons therefor?

The Honourable Maulana Abul Kalam Azad: (a) to (c). The Osmania University, Hyderabad (Deccan) has adopted Urdu as the medium of instruction. The Government of India have no official information in respect of other Indian Universities but it has been reported that the Lucknow University has introduced Hindi and Urdu as medium of instruction for B.A., B.Sc., and LL.B., Classes from July 1946 and the Nagpur University has permitted from 1945 the introduction of Indian Languages in the Central Provinces as media of instruction in the Colleges in Nagpore and Wardha. It is also reported that Patna University had decided to introduce Hindustani as medium of instruction for non-language subjects at Intermediate and Bachelor stages of Faculty of Arts, Science and Commerce from July 1947 and Nagpur University has decided to introduce Hindi, Urdu and Marathi as medium of instruction. The Government of India have been fully alive to the importance of the issue raised in the question and I propose to summon at an early date a Conference of representatives of Universities and the Provincial Governments to survey the whole position.

Lala Deshbandhu Gupta: Will the Honourable Member please state, so far as the Delhi University is concerned, whether it has taken into consideration the question of making Hindustanti as the medium of education?

The Honourable Maulana Abul Kalam Azad: The Government has no information about it.

Lala Deshbandhu Gupta: Will the Honourable Member make a move in this connection?

The Honourable Maulana Abul Kalam Azad: As I have already told the Honourable Member that it is under consideration to call a conference in this connection.

Dr. Zia-ud-din Ahmad: Is the Honourable Member aware of the fact that the United Provinces Government invited a Committee to consider this question but that Committee never met and it was postponed at the last minute?

The Honourable Maulana Abul Kalam Azad: In any case, the question should not be asked from me.

Document No. 20

MAULANA AZAD'S INTERVIEW TO THE A.P.I. DATED 25-2-1947

Maulana Azad in an interview to the A.P.I. said that Mr. Attlee's statement on India had evoked mixed feelings in his mind. He was, on the one hand, gratified to find that the reading of the situation, he adopted in June 1945 had been justified by events. At the same time he could not help a feeling of regret that Lord Warvell, who was the initiator of new chapter in the history of relation between India and England, was retiring from the scene.

Recalling the atmosphere of the country at the time of his release in June 1945, Maulana Abul Kalam Azad said:

"There was on all hands suspicion and distrust of British intentions at the time I confess that I was myself prejudiced and the events of the last three years had left in my mind a legacy of bitterness. It was in that mood that I went to Simla to participate in the proposed conference but when I met Lord Wavell, I experienced a sudden change of mind. I found him a rugged, straightforward soldier void of verbiage and direct both in approach and statement. He was not devious like the politician but came straight to the point and created in the mind an impression of great sincerity which touched my heart. Therefore, I felt it my duty to advice the country to adopt a constructive method for achieving its political objective and since then in spite of a general atmosphere of doubt and opposition, I have never deviated from that course. It is common knowledge that since the first Simla Conference at least on four different occasions there were attempts both from within and outside the Congress to precipitate a movement and force Congress to resort to direct action but I was convinced that in view of the conciliatory attitude of the British Government such a course would be ill-advised.

I exerted all my influence to keep the Congress course steady, and to-day I feel justified that my reading of the situation was not wrong. The Simla Conference had failed, but soon after, the general elections were held in England and the Labour Party came into power. They declared that they would carry out in practice their former professions about India. Events have since then proved that their declaration was sincere.

Cripps' Mission Recalled

I do not know what communications passed between Lord Wavell and H.M.G. in the last two or three weeks. Obviously there were some differences which led to his resignation. We may differ from his appraisement of the situation. But we cannot doubt his sincerity or integrity of purpose. Nor can I forget that the credit for the changed atmosphere in Indo-British relations to-day must be raced back to the step which he so courageously took in June 1945. After the failure of the Cripps Mission Mr. Churchill's Government had made up their mind to put the Indian question in the cold storage for the duration of the war. Indian opinion could also find no way out and the events after 1942 had further increased the bitterness. To Lord Wavell must belong the credit for opening the closed door and in spite of initial opposition from the Coalition Government, he was able to persuade them to agree to make new offer to India. The result was the Simla Conference which indicated a way out of the impasse. The Simla Conference did not succeed but everything that has followed since then has been a logical development of the courageous step which he took.

I am confident that India will never forget this service of Lord Wavell and when the time comes for the historian of independent India to appraise the relations of England and India, he will give Lord Wavell the credit for opening a new chapter in those relations.

Document No. 21

ANSWERS DATED 27-2-1947 BY MAULANA AZAD TO THE QUESTIONS ASKED IN THE LEGISLATIVE ASSEMBLY OF INDIA

DIFFICULTIES EXPERIENCED BY INDIAN STUDENTS IN ENGLAND

Sri R. Venkatasubba Reddiar: Will the Honourable Member for Education be pleased to state:

(a) whether Government are aware of the difficulties experienced by Indian students in England and their representation to the India House;

(b) whether it is a fact that students sent from this country find it difficult to get admission into efficient institutions and also accommodation;

(c) if the answer to part (b) is in the affirmative, the steps Governmenvt propose to take to secure admission and accommodation for these students; and

(d) the steps that are proposed to be taken to prevent such difficulties arising in future?

The Honourable Maulana Abul Kalam Azad: (a) Yes.

(b) Yes. The position with regard to the admission and accommodation of Indian students in the United Kingdom is very difficult. British Universities have been and are likely to be far some time extremely overcrowded on account of rush of demobilised personnel to educational institutions. As 90 per cent. of the available seats have been reserved for British *ex*-servicemen and women, very few seats are left in the British Universities and Institutions for other students. It is therefore, inevitable that out of the very large number of Indian students, both private and Government Scholars, now going to the United Kingdom for studies, some do not succeed in obtaining admission to the best institutions.

Similarly with regard to accommodation there is a general shortage in the United Kingdom and the authorities concerned, in spite of their best efforts, are unable in all cases to make satisfactory arrangements, particularly for those students who reach the country without notice or at very short notice.

(c) and (d) Arrangements already exist in the Education Department of the High Commissioner's Office in London for helping students to secure admission and accommodation. It is now proposed to strengthen the organization and to set up a separate Welfare Branch to deal with the problem of accommodation. Last year one hostel for Indian students in London and another in Edinburgh were purchased and the proposal to set up a Reception and Transit Camp in London is now under consideration.

Sri R. Venkatasubha Reddiar: Sir, I have not understood the Hindustani reply to my question.

Mr. President: A translation of the reply will be supplied to the Honourable Member later on.

Sri R. Venkatasubha Reddiar: I want to put supplementary questions.

Shri D.P. Karmarkar: With regard to part (d) of the question may I know whether Government are taking steps to create more and more facilities in India itself for tuition in faculties for which people are sent abroad?

The Honourable Maulana Abul Kalam Azad: Yes, every effect is being made in this respect. The new Committee will consider this question *de nove*.

Mr. Tamizuddin Khan: Will the Honourable Member please state whether Government scholars also find it difficult to secure admission in any British Universities after going to the United Kingdom?

The Honourable Maulana Abul Kalam Azad: Yes, this difficulty is being encountered.

Mr. Tamizuddin Khan: Will the Honourable Member please state why the admission of Government scholars is not previously arranged before they go to the United Kingdom?

The Honourable Maulana Abul Kalam Azad: Owing to War, this sort of arrangement could not be made; but, so far as my information goes, scholars, who were sent abroad, were fully warned of the conditions in these countries and of the difficulties that they would have to face there.

Sri R. Venkatasubha Reddiar: Will the Government consider the desirability of discontinuing the awarding of scholarships till sufficient accommodation is secured for the scholars in the United Kingdom?

The Honourable Maulana Abul Kalam Azad: As I have already brought it to the notice of the Honourable Member a new Committee has been set up who will consider this question afresh.

Mr. Muhammad Nauman: I want to know if arrangements have been made to increase the stipends of the scholars who are at present proceeding abroad or they are being paid at the old rate?

The Honourable Maulana Abul Kalam Azad: I want notice to answer this question.

Shri Mohan Lal Saksena: May I know the number of the members of this Committee.

The Honourable Maulana Abul Kalam Azad: It will be announced very soon.

Document No. 22

ANSWERS DATED 27-02-1947 BY MAULANA AZAD TO THE QUESTIONS ASKED IN THE LEGISLATIVE ASSEMBLY

ANCIENT MONUMENTS AND TEMPLES AT AIHOLI AND PATTADKAL IN BIJAPUR DISTRICT

Shri D.P. Karmarkar: Will the Honourable Member for Education be pleased to state:

(a) the number of ancient temples at (i) Aiholi, and (ii) Pattadkal in the Bijapur District?

(b) whether Government are aware that these monuments are of importance from the point of view of History and Art;

(c) whether Government are aware that these temples are not well looked after by the Archaeological Department;

(d) the number of care-takers on the spot in charge of these monuments;

(e) whether it is a fact that there are no good roads from the nearest Railway Station to these places; and

(f) the steps Government propose to take to keep these monuments in order and make them easily accessible to the visiting public?

The Honourable Maulana Abul Kalam Azad: (a) the number of ancient temples at (i) Aiholi, is sixty and at (ii) Pattadkal, ten.

(b) Yes.

(c) No. Such repairs as are necessary in the light of archaeological requirements, are carried out to these temples from time to time.

(d) Two care-takers are employed at Aiholi and one at Pattadkal.

(e) Maintenance of roads is the responsibility of the Provincial government. The approach paths to these monuments belong to private owners of the land on which they are situated.

(f) The monuments are being kept in good repair but to make them more accessible than they are at present, would require acquisition of vast areas of private land.

Shri D.P. Karmarkar : With reference to answer to part (f) of the question, may I ask whether the Honourable Member is aware that in spite of the care that has been taken or perhaps on account of the care that has been taken many of the temples are dilapidating fastly?

The Honourable Maulana Abul Kalam Azad : government is not aware of such a state. In any case it will be investigated.

Shri D.P. Karmarkar : Is the Honourable Member aware that these monuments belong to a type of architecture which is peculiar to the tract and therefore they require special attention at the hands of the Archaeological Department?

The Honourable Maulana Abul Kalam Azad : The Government will consider it.

Mr. Ahmed E.H. Jaffer : Is the Honourable Member aware that in this very district of Bijapur and particularly in Bijapur City itself there are several mosques and Idgahs where there are latrines near about with the result that they cause a great nuisance to those who go there to pray? Will he take the trouble to see that these latrines are removed without delay?

The Honourable Maulana Abul Kalam Azad : Investigations will be instituted in this connection.

Document No. 23

STATEMENT IN THE PRESS CONFERENCE

27-2-1947

Maulana Abul Kalam Azad in a Statement in the press conference today said,

"The form in which my speech at the conference of the Committee of Arabic and Persian studies in Lucknow has been reported is likely to cause misunderstanding. The reports say that I had stated that the medium of instruction, should be the mother tongue and that knowledge of English was necessary only to the extent of being able to read and write the language. My remarks were confined to Arabic students and in that context I had said that students should acquire at least a working knowledge in English. So far as general studies are concerned, it was never my intention to suggest that there should be any failling in the standard of English taught.

"150 years of intimate contact has made English an integral part of our educational system and this cannot be changed without injury to the casue of one of the major languages of the world and Indians can neglect its study only at the risk of loss to themselves, I am convinced that in the future as well, the standard of teaching English should be maintained at as high a level as possible but the medium of instruction must from the very nature of the cause, be the mother tongue."

Document No. 24

STATEMENT IN THE PRESS CONFERENCE

New Delhi

27-2-1947

"Education should have the highest priority in our national budget and should take the place immediately after food and clothing. In fact the proper system of education was necessary in order to tackle satisfactory even those problems," said Maulana Abul Kalam Azad, Education Member, Government of India, at a press conference on Feb. 27, 1947.

The Central Government's educational programme, Maulana Azad said, included the setting up of a national museum, allocation of fund for fundamental research work, development of archaeological studies and the use of broadcasting and films for the purpose of mass education.

Replying to a question regarding his views on communal Universities the Maulana said: "Communal Universities have been harmful to the country and I hope in future there should not be Universities on communal basis."

Surveying the present system of education he agreed that it had been shaped by non-nationals in non-national interests and that it had not led to the development of a national mind. Nevertheless, he added, the services which the existing system of education had rendered to the Indian people need not be denied. "It had opened a new world of science and modern technology to the Indian people. It had inculcated a progressive spirit and had brought the Indian educational standards into line with the standards obtaining elsewhere."

The education member revealed that the two committees appointed by the Central Advisory Board of Education had submitted contrary reports on the question of religious instruction in schools and that the Government would have to give proper weight to both the reports before coming to decision. "If the Government decide that religious instruction offered should be of the best type. The religious instruction often imparted in India in private institutions is of a kind which instead of broadening the outlook and inculcating a spirit of toleration and goodwill to all men poduces exactly the opposite result," he said.

Communal Universities

Referring to the existence of communal universities, Maulana Azad declared that Government was opposed to the establishment of such universities as they have harmed the country greatly. The Government would, however, have to go on subsiding them till strong public opinion prevailed against them and they were replaced by national universities, he added.

Acknowledging the valuable work done by missionary societies in spreading modern education and in contributing referred to the question of mass conversions carried on by these societies and said, "Responsible misssionaries have themselves come to recognize conversion at all. If all missionary societies adopt this enlightened outlook, there is no reason why independent India should in any way hesitate to accept the service which it is theirs to offer."

Roman Hindustani

Maulana Azad emphasised the need of producing literature in Roman Hindustani for the benefit of nearly two million soldiers who were made literate by the army through the use of Roman script. "If those men who have been made literate during their service in the army are not to lapse into illiteracy, we must provide them with suitable literature in Roman Hindustani. There is great demand for such literature and the Department is considering how to meet this demand." He remarked that every Indian should learn both Devanagri and Urdu script line same that were the line he suggested that the use of Roman in addition to Devanagri and Urdu, in central educational publications may be considered as a temporary expedient.

Research Work

The Government he said, proposed making provisions for fundamental research work and for this definite sums would be allocated every year. The Co-ordination Committee of Cabinet had approved, for principle, of a grant of Rs. 7,500,000 for research work in the next five years. The Government also had under consideration the questions of giving grants to educational experimental institutions and preparing some kind of generalised curriculum.

"I have every hope that we shall be able to make up our leaway by a determined and concerted effort and place education in India on a par with education in other civilised countries of the world," he concluded.

Document No. 25

ANSWERS OF MAULANA AZAD DATED 5-3-1947 TO THE SHORT NOTICE QUESTION, IN THE CONSTITUENT ASSEMBLY OF INDIA (LEGISLATIVE) GIVEN BY PANDIT M.B.L. BHARGAVA.

GRIEVANCES OF AJMER-MERWARA SCHOOL TEACHERS

Pandit Mukut Bihari Lal Bhargava : Will the Honourable Member for Education be pleased to state:

(a) whether Government have received a representation from the Teacher's Association, Ajmer-Merwara, claiming similar interim relief as has been provided to the teachers of Delhi Province;

(b) whether this Association has served a strike notice;

(c) whether Government and the Association have recently carried on any negotiations to find out a solution satisfactory to all parties concerned; and if so, what is the result; and

(d) what steps, if any, are being taken by Government to avert the strike and to improve the lot of the teachers?

The Honourable Maulana Abul Kalam Azad : (a) A Copy of a Resolution passed at an extraordinary General meeting of the Ajmer-Merwara Teachers' Association, held on the 17th January, 1947, demanding similar relief as has been provided to the teachers of Delhi Province was received by the Government of India through the Local Administration on the 17th February, 1947;

(b) No Official communication of a final decision to go on strike has been received by the Government of India;

(c) The teachers had placed their grievances before the Local Education Department, Ajmer-Merwara, who referred the matter to the Government of India for decision;

(d) The Government of India have agreed to grant the same concessions as sanctioned to teachers in Delhi Province to teachers in Ajmer-Merwara. The Local Administration have been informed of this decision on the 1st March, 1947 and have been asked to submit details for expenditure sanction immediately.

Document No. 26

ANSWERS BY MAULANA AZAD IN THE LEGISLATIVE ASSEMBLY DATED MARCH 17, 1947 TO THE QUESTIONS OF PT. SHRI KRISHNA DUTT PALIWAL ON THE PROVISION OF FACILITIES TO DIPLOMA HOLDER OF DELHI POLYTECHNIC

Pandit Sri Krishna Dutt Paliwal : Will the Honourable Member for Education be pleased to state: (a) If the students of the Delhi Polytechnic after passing the Polytechnic senior course are eligible for going abroad for further studies; and

(b) The facilities which Government intend to provide to the Diploma holders of the Polytechnic as compared to the graduates of other Universities for further studies abroad?

The Honourable Maulana Abul Kalam Azad : (a) The Polytechnic Senior courses leading to All-India Diplomas are recognised for the award of Central Government Overseas Scholarships under the scheme sponsored by the Education Department.

(b) The Diploma holders are treated on par with the graduates of other universities and Government do not contemplate extending sponsored by the Education Department.

Document No. 27

(MAULANA AZAD'S CLARIFICATION IN THE LEGISLATIVE ASSEMBLY, DATED 17-3-1947 IN CONNECTION WITH THE DEMAND OF THE ALL INDIA DIPLOMAS

THE HONOURABLE MAULANA ABUL KALAM AZAD: (a) The main demand of the students was the recognition of the All-India Diplomas or in the alternative affiliation of the Polytechnic to the Delhi University. The Federal Public Service Commission have now provisionally recognised the All-India Diploma in Electrical Engineering as a sufficient qualification for admission to the Combined Engineering Services Examination for recruitment to Superior Engineering Services under the Central Government. This recognition will be made absolute after the Institution of Engineers (India) accept this qualification for purposes of exemption from Section 'A' and 'B' of their Associate Membership Examination. A Committee of the Institution of Engineers (India) recently inspected the Polytechnic and the Institution's decision is awaited.

The All-India Diploma in Commerce with Auditing as a special subject has been recognised an equivalent to first R.A. Examination for purposes of Rule 61(2) (iv)(b) of the Income-tax Act. The Diploma with Auditing and Accountancy as special subject has been accepted as equivalent to a degree of an Indian University for purposes of employment in the Office of the Auditor General in India.

All All-India Diplomas have been recognised for recruitment to teaching posts under the Central Government and for overseas scholarships.

The other grievances of the students relate to laboratories, staff and hostels and these have been removed to a considerable extent.

(b) An application has been made to Delhi University for affiliation of some of the Technical Departments of the Polytechnic. A scheme for instituting Honours Degree Courses in Technology is under consideration.

Document No. 28

ANSWERS BY MAULANA AZAD DT. 25-3-1947 TO THE QUESTIONS RAISED IN THE LEGISLATIVE ASSEMBLY IN CONNECTION WITH THE EXCAVATION ON AGROHA MOUND IN HISSAR DISTRICT FOR ARCHAEOLOGICAL PURPOSES

Pandit Thakur Das Bhargava: (a) Will the Honourable Member for Education kindly state if the Agroha mound in the Hissar District of the Punjab was excavated for archaeological purposes?

(b) Have any valuable articles been discovered? if so, what?

(c) Is there any proposal to start the excavations again? If so, when?

(d) Was any research made to find out the age of the articles found at Agroha? If so, what was the result?

The Honourable Maulana Abul Kalam Azad: (a) Yes, in 1937-38.

(b) About 400 antiquities were brought to light in trench up to a depth of 12 feet, comprising pottery, terracotta and copper objects, fragments of stone sculptures, plaques, grinding stones, beads, shell bangles, iron implements and other objects including an inscribed clay die, a burnt brick-bark manuscript and a clary seal.

Two pits sunk at the extreme east of the mound, yielded a well made of terracotta rings, and 120 portable antiquities comprising pottery and two small hoards of coins; one containing five silver coins belonging each to Antialkidas, Appollodotes, Starto, Amyntas and one punch-marked coin with solar and tree symbol; and the other containing 55 mostly rectangular copper coins with an inscription Agodaka Agacha Janapadasa.

(c) Yes, as soon as possible; but it will, however be appreciated that funds available for excavation are limited.

(d) Yes, the recovery of Indo-Greek and the Agodaka coins have established the antiquity of the place to about the 2nd century B.C.

Pandit Thakur Das Bhargava : Have these coins been found to bear any connection with Raja Ugra Sen?

The Honourable Maulana Abul Kalam Azad : I want notice to answer this question.

Seth Govind Das : Will the Honourable Member consider that in addition to this place Muttra and Ajodhya are two other places where Suraj Bansi and Chander Bansi dynasties ruled? Will it be taken into consideration in connection with archaeological survey that such work is started at those places at an early date.

The Honourable Maulana Abul Kalam Azad: As I have already said our means are very limited and we have been little fund for the work, yet the proposal will receive consideration.

Document No. 29

REPORT DATED 24-4-1947 OF THE COMMITTEE APPOINTED BY THE CONSTITUENT ASSEMBLY OF INDIA TO NEGOTIATIVE WITH THE STATE NEGOTIATING COMMITTEE WITH MAULANA AZAD AS A MEMBER

By a resolution of the Constituent Assembly passed on the 21st December 1946, the following members, *viz.*

(1) The Hon'ble Pt. Jawaharlal Nehru

(2) The Hon'ble Maulana Abul Kalam Azad

(3) The Hon'ble Sardar Vallabhbhai J. Patel

(4) Dr. B. Pattabhi Sitaramayya

(5) Mr. Shankarrao Deo

(6) The Hon'ble Sir N. Gopalaswami Ayyangar

were appointed as a Commitee to confer with the Negotiating Committee set up by the Chamber of Princes, and with other representatives of Indian States, for the purpose of

(a) fixing the distribution of the seats in the Assembly not exceeding 93 in number, which in the Cabinet Mission's Statement of May 16, 1946, are reserved for Indian States,

(b) fixing the method by which the representatives of the States should be returned to the Assembly,

and thereafter to report the result of such negotiations. By a further resolution passed on the 21st January, 1947, we were empowered to confer with such persons as we thought fit, for examining the special problems of Bhutan and Sikkim, and to report to the Assembly the result of such examination. This report deals only with the negotiations conducted by us in pursuance of the resolution of the 21st December.

2. The first series of our joint meetings with the States Negotiating Committee were held on the 8th and 9th February, 1947. The discussion largely centred on the scope of subjects to be negotiated between the two committees. It was urged by the States Negotiating Committee

that there had been no decision yet on the part of the States to enter the Constituent Assembly, and that it would not be possible for them to decide this issue till they received satisfactory assurances on a number of points mentioned in the resolution adopted on the 29th January, 1947, by the General Conference of Rulers (Appendix A). On the other hand, we pointed out that most of those points could only be discussed by a fully constituted Constituent Assembly including the representatives of the States; they were in any case clearly beyond our competence as a Committee, our own functions being limited to the matters laid down in the resolution of the Constituent Assembly passed on the 21st December, 1946. But while we were not prepared as a committee to discuss matters going beyond our mandate, we raised no objection to discussing, in a friendly and informal manner, as individuals, certain difficulties, and to removing certain misappre hensions which seemed to be causing concern to the Princes. The more important of the points cleared up in the course of these discussions were summarised by Pandit Nehru as follows :

> "The first thing to be clear about is to proceed with the full acceptance of the Cabinet Mission's Statement. Apart from the legality of the Statement one thing also seems to me obvious, namely, that the scheme is essentially a voluntary one, where no compulsion, except, as I said, compulsion of events, is indicated. No doubt, so far as we are concerned, we accept it as a voluntary scheme where people may join as individuals, as groups, or Rulers or otherwise. We are not trying to force any to join if they do not want to. It is a matter for negotiation throughout....
>
> "Now, to go back, apart from the acceptance of the scheme which is basic, some points were raised yesterday. One was about the monarchical form of Government. That question has not arisen at all in the Constituent Assembly nor, so far as we can see, does it arise at all from the Statement. But is has been repeatedly stated on our behalf in the Constituent Assembly as outside that we have no objection to it we accept that, and we do not want to come in the way of the monarchical form of Government at all. This has been made perfectly clear.
>
> "Another point that we raised in our discussion yesterday

was about some apprehension about territorial readjustments. I tried to point out that the Resolution passed by the Constituent Assembly had no reference in the minds of those who framed the Resolution or who proposed it there, to any change regarding the States. It has no relation to the States. It was an indication that there will be provision made in the constitution or in the process of re-grouping units, etc., where some changes may have to be made. It had no reference to changing boundaries. I can concede territorial boundaries being changed for economic reasons, for facilitating governmental purposes, etc., but any such territorial readjustments, we are quite clear, should be made with the consent of the parties concerned, and not be forced down. I say, for the moment we are not thinking in terms of any such thing, but if this question arises, it should be essential that the parties concerned should consent to it.

"The scheme, as has already been stated, is a voluntary one, and whether in regard to the entry into the Constituent Assembly or subsequently when the Constituent Assembly decides and comes to conclusions, there will be no compulsion, and the States will have the right to have their say at any stage just as anybody else will have the right to have their say at any stage. So the coercive factor must be eliminated from that.

"In regard to some confusion which has possibly arisen in regard to subjects and powers, we go on what the Cabinet Mission's Statement specifically says. The Cabinet Mission's Statement said: "The States will retain all subjects and powers other than those ceded to the Union." That is perfectly clear, we accept that statement, we accept that entirely. Generally speaking, those are the matters that came up yesterday in the course of discussion, and perhaps we might proceed on that basis and consider matters now."

We further explained that the Constituent Assembly could not possibly take up the position that they were not prepared to discuss matters with States not represented on the Chamber of Princes Negotiating Committee; or with representatives of States peoples, as that would involve an element of compulsion which was contrary to their conception of the scheme.

3. A general understanding having beein arrived at, as a result of the above exchange of views, the States Negotiating Committee proceeded to consider the two matters on which we had been asked to negotiate by the Constituent Assembly. After a preliminary discussion, it was decided that the question of the distribution of the 93 seats should be referred to the Secretariats of the Constituent Assembly and the Chamber of Princes, and their recommendations placed before the next meeting of the two committees on the 1st March, 1947.

4. In the meanwhile, the Dewan of Baroda had asked for direct negotiation with us on the representation of Baroda in the Constituent Assembly. We accordingly met Sir B.L. Mitter on the 9th February. In the course of our discussion, he made it clear that it was the decision of the Baroda State, both the Ruler and the people, to give the fullest co-operation to the Constituent Assembly in its work and that they were prepared to take steps forthwith for the selection of representatives so that these could take part in the work of the Assembly at the earliest possible date. It was agreed between us and the Dewan that Baroda should, having regard to its population, send three representatives and that these should be elected by the Dhara Sabha (the State Legislature) on the principle of proportional representation, by means of the single transferable vote, and that only its elected and nominated non-official members should take part in the election.

5. The next joint meeting of the two committees was held on the 1st March, 1947. At this meeting we urged that H.M.G.'s declaration of the 20th February had introduced an additional element of urgency in our task and that it would be greatly to the advantage of the States no less than to the British Indian representatives in the Constituent Assembly if State's representatives could join the Assembly during April session. We pointed out that there was nothing in the State Paper of the 16th May which operated as a bar against States doing so. We also suggested that it would be to our mutual advantage if State's representatives could function forthwith on some of the committees set up by the Constituent Assembly, particularly the Union Powers Committee and the Advisory Committee on fundamental rights, etc. The States Negotiating Committee, however, expressed their inability to take these steps in the absence of a mandate from the General Conference of Rulers whom they promised to consult at an early date.

6. The discussion then turned on the method of distribution of the 93 seats allotted to the States. The Committees approved of the distribution as proposed by the two Secretariats (Appendix B) and authorised the making of such minor modifications as are considered necessary by the parties concerned.

7. After this, we discussed the method of selecting representatives. Various proposals were made and discussed in a joint sub-committee set up for the purpose. Eventually, after a consideration of the sub-committee's report, the following formula was accepted by both Committees, *viz.*, that not less than 50 per cent. of the total representatives of States shall be elected by the elected members of legislatures or where such legislatures do not exist, of other electoral colleges. The States would endeavour to increase the quota of elected representatives to as much above 50 per cent. of the total number as possible.

This formula has since been ratified by the General Conference of Rulers held on the 2nd April. A copy of the resolution passed by the Conference is attached (Appendix C).

We pointed out that in regard to two States, *viz.*, Hyderabad and Kashmir elections to their legislatures had been boycotted by important organisations representing the people of the States concerned and the legislatures therefore could not be considered to represent the people as they were intended to do. In the cases of these two States, we suggested that a suitable method of electing representatives for the Constituent Assembly should be devised. The Chancellor said that he would communicate the suggestion to the States concerned.

8. A Committee consisting of the following members: (1) Dr. Pattabhi Sitaramayya; (2) Sir N. Golpalaswami Ayyangar; (3) Sir V.T. Krishnamachari; (4) Sir Sultan Ahmed; (5) Sir B.N. Rau; (6) Mir Maqbool Mahmood; (7) Mr. H.V.R. Iengar, was set up to consider the modifications referred to in para. 6 above and other matters of detail that might arise from time to time and to report, if necessary, to the two Negotiating Committees.

We have been informed that the States of Baroda, Jaipur, Jodhpur, Rewa, Cochin and Bikaner have already selected their representatives in accordance with the agreement arrived at. These representatives have been invited to take their seats at the forthcoming session of the Assembly. The seats of Patiala, Udaipur, Gwalior and Bhavnagar have also announced that they will take part in the work of the Constituent Assembly.

JAWAHARLAL NEHRU
A.K. AZAD
VALLABHBHAI PATEL
N. GOPALASWAMI
SHANKARRAO DEO
B. PATTABHI SITARAMAYYA

NEW DELHI;
24*th April*, 1947.

Document No. 30

OPENING SPEECH OF MAULANA AZAD IN THE SESSION OF S.C.L.E.

Simla

22-5-1947

Maulana Abul Kalam Azad, Education Member, Interim Government in his inaugural address at the session of the Standing Committee of the Legislature on education in Simla today on May 22, 1947, said that the Interim Government should have given their highest priority to problem of education but political situation in the country had not been easy and most of them had been preoccupied with constant changes in the political scene. He felt that he had not been able to do all that he wanted though he had certain definite schemes and all that was necessary was to put them into execution.

Maulana Azad said, "Things are however coming to a head and we are all hoping that in a few weeks time the political problem will be decided finally. We can then apply our undivided attention and energy to the fulfilment of our educational plans. The most important task before the National Government is to set up a new programme of National Education. Although we have not achieved all that we wanted a new spirit is already in evidence."

Maulana Azad added, "Education is a provincial subject. Provinces will, therefore, carry the actual work but it is the task of the Centre to set a standard for national education, I do not for a moment suggest any encroachment on provincial autonomy but if we are to get the most desirable results it is necessary that there should be one common pattern and here the Centre is of very great importance.

Whatever may be the decision in the political field it is therefore necessary that this department should continue for some time to come. In this way alone would it be possible for the provinces to work together in cooperation, coordinate all necessary measures and avoid duplication."

Maulana Azad said that they need not discuss the omissions and commissions of the system of education obtaining for the last 150 years. Now the whole outlook was changing, new responsibilities and new demands had come and old standards must give place to new.

Referring to the changes since the Cabinet Mission's arrival in March 1946, Maulana Azad said: "Now independence is within our grasp. The problem to-day is not so much as conquest of power as its proper use."

Document No. 31

LETTER FROM PT. JAWAHARLAL NEHRU TO MAULANA AZAD

New Delhi

1 August, 1947

My dear Maulana,

I am writing to you rather formally to invite you to join the new Cabinet. This is hardly necessary, but still I felt that certain formalities should be observed.

As you know, all the existing Members, excepting those who have gone to Pakistan, will continue minus Rajaji who will become a Governor.

The question of portfolios will be finally determined later. But I take it that you would like to continue with the Education portfolio.

We shall have very difficult problems to face. The only way we can do so is to work as a joint team sharing each other's burdens. The old department system of work will have to give way to joint consultation on all important matters.

Yours sincerely,
Jawaharlal Nehru

Document No. 32

SPEECH DELIVERED BY MAULANA AZAD AT JAMA MASJID OF DELHI ON 23-10-1947

My brethren

You know what has brought me here today. This congregation at Shahjehan's historic mosque is not an unfamiliar sight for me. Here, I have addressed you on several previous occasions. Since then we have seen many ups and downs. At that time, instead of weariness, your faces reflected serenity, and your hearts, instead of misgivings, exuded confidence. The uneasiness on your faces and the desolation in your hearts that I see today, reminds me of the events of the past few years.

Do you remember? I hailed you, you cut off my tongue; I picked my pen, you severed my hand; I wanted to move forward, you broke off my legs; I tried to turn over, and you injured my back. When the bitter political games of the last seven years were at their peak, I tried to wake you up at every danger signal. You not only ignored my call but revived all the past traditions of neglect and denial. As a result the same perils surround you today, whose onset had previously diverted you from the righteous path.

Today, mine is no more than an inert existence or a forlorn cry; I am an orphan in my own motherland. This does not mean that I feel trapped in the original choice that I had made for myself, nor do I feel that there is no room left for my *aashiana*(nest). What it means is that my cloak is weary of your impudent grabbing hands. My sensitivities are injured, my heart is heavy. Think for one moment. What course did you adopt? Where have you reached, and where do you stand now? Haven't your senses become torpid? Aren't you living in a constant state of fear? This fear is your own creation, a fruit of your own deeds.

It was not long ago when I warned you that the two-nation theory was death-knell to a meaningful, dignified life; forsake it. I told you that the pillars upon which you were leaning would inevitably crumble. To all this you turned a deaf ear. You did not realise that fleet-footed time would not change its course to suit your convenience. Time sped along. And now you have discovered that the so-called anchors of your faith have set you adrift, to be kicked around by fate. Their understanding of the word fate does not correspond with the lexicon of your belief. For them, fate is another name for lack of courage.

The chessboard of British gamesmanship has been upturned. Those pawns called 'leaders' which you had carved and installed, have disappeared overnight. You believed that the chessboard had been spread forever and forever, and the worship of those pawns was the *summun bonum* of your existence. I do not want to lacerate your wounds, or aggravate your agony. However, if you look into the past you will find that through hindsight you can unravel several mysteries.

There was a time, when exhorting the need for achieving India's Independence, I had called out to you.

No nation, however depraved, can stop the inevitable turn of events. A revolutionary political change has been inscribed in India's book of destiny. The twentieth century maelstrom of freedom is about to break India's chains of slavery. If you falter and fall behind the march of the times, if you remain inert and lethargic, the future historian will record that your flock, a cluster of seven crores, adopted an attitude towards freedom, which was characteristic of a community heading towards extinction. Today, the Indian flag has been hoisted in all its majestic splendour. This is the very same flag which evoked sneers and contemptuous laughter from the rulers of the time.

It is true that time did not accede to your wishes; instead, it bowed in deference to a nation's birthright. This turn of events has struck fear in your heart. Perhaps, you believe that something good has been taken away from you, and has been substituted with something evil. Yes, you are restless because you had not prepared yourselves for the good, and believed that the evil was, in fact, manna from heaven. I refer to your years of slavery under a foreign rule, under which you were treated as play puppets. There was a time when our nation had plunged herself in pitched battle to overthrow the foreign rule; and, today, the outcome of that struggle is causing you consternation. How should I berate you for your unbecoming haste? Hardly have we completed our journey that you are showing signs of going astray.

My brothers! I have always attempted to keep politics apart from personalities, thus avoiding those thorny valleys. That is why some of my messages are often couched in allusions. But what I have to say today, needs to be direct and to the point. *The partition of India was a fundamental mistake*. The manner in which religious differences were incited, inevitably, led to the devastation that we have seen with our own eyes. Unfortunately, we are still seeing it at some places.

There is no use recounting the events of the past seven years, nor will it serve any good. Yet, it must be stated that the debacle of Indian Muslims is the result of the colossal blunders committed by the Muslim League's misguided leadership. These consequences however, were no surprise to me; I had anticipated them from the very start.

Now that Indian politics has taken a new direction, there is no place in it for the Muslim League. Now the question is whether or not we are capable of any constructive thinking. For this, I have invited the Muslim leaders of India to Delhi, during the second week of November.

The gloom cast upon your lives is momentary; I assure you we can be beaten by none save our own selves! I have always said, and I repeat it again today; eschew your indecisiveness, your mistrust, and stop your misdeeds. This unique triple-edged weapon is more lethal than the two-edged iron sword which inflicts fatal wounds, which I have heard of!

Just think about this life of escapism that you have opted for, in the sacred name of *Hejrat*. Get into the habit of exercising your own brains, and strengthening your own hearts. If you do so, only then will you realise how immature your decisions were.

Where are you going and why? Raise your eyes. The minarets of Jama Masjid want to ask you a question. Where have you lost the glorious pages from your chronicles? Was it only yesterday that on the banks of the Jamuna, your caravans performed *wuzu*? Today, you are afraid of living here! Remember, Delhi has been nurtured with your blood. Brothers! Create a basic change in yourselves. Today, your fear is as misplaced as your jubilation was yesterday.

The words *coward* and *frenzy* cannot be spoken in the same breath as the word Muslim. A true Muslim can be swayed neither by avarice nor apprehension. Don't get scared because a few faces have disappeared. The only reason they had herded you in a single fold was to facilitate their own flight. Today, if they have jerked their hand free from yours, what does it matter? Make sure that they have not run away with your hearts. If your hearts are still in the right place, make them the abode of God. Some thirteen hundred years ago, through an Arab *ummi*, God proclaimed, "Those who place their faith in God and are firm in their belief, no fear for them nor any sorrow." Winds blow in and blow out: tempests may gather but all this is short-lived. The period of trial is about to end. Change yourselves as if you had never been in such an abject condition.

I am not used to altercation. Faced with your general indifference, however, I will repeat that the third force has departed, and along with it, its trappings of vanity. Whatever had to happen has happened. Politics has broken out of its old mould and a new cast is being prepared. If your hearts have still not changed and your minds still have reservations, it is a different matter. But, if you want a change, then take your cue from history and cast yourself in the new mould. Having completed a revolutionary phase, there still remains a few blank pages in the history of India. You can make ourselves worthy of filling those pages, provided you are willing.

Brothers! Keep up with the changes. Don't say, "We are not ready for the change." Get ready. Stars may have plummeted down but the sun is still shining. Borrow a few of its rays and sprinkle them in the dark caverns of your lives.

I do not ask you to seek certificates from the new echelons of power. I do not want you to lead a life of sycophancy as you did during the foreign rule. I want to remind you that these bright etchings which you see all around you, are relics of the *Qafilas* of your forefathers. Do not forget them. Do not forsake them. Live like their worthy inheritors, and, rest assured, that if you do not wish to flee from this scene, nobody can make you flee. Come, today let us pledge that this country is ours, we belong to it and any fundamental decision about its destiny will remain incomplete without our consent.

Today, you fear the earth's tremors; once you were virtually the earthquake itself. Today, you fear the darkness; once your existence was the epicenter of radiance. Clouds have poured dirty waters and you have hitched up your trousers. Those were none but your forefathers who not only plunged headlong into the seas, but trampled the mountains, laughed at the bolts of lightning, turned away the tornados, challenged the tempests and made them alter their course. It is a sure sign of a dying faith that those who had once grabbed the collars of emperors, are today, clutching at their own throats. They have become oblivious of the existence of God as if they had never believed in Him.

Brothers! I do not have a new prescription for you. I have the same old prescription that was revealed to the greatest benefactor of mankind, the prescription of the Holy Quran:

> "Do not fear and do not grieve. If you possess true faith, you will gain the upper hand."

The congregation is now at an end. What I had to say, I have said, briefly. Let me say once again, keep a grip on your senses. Learn to create your own surroundings, your own world. This is not a commodity that I can buy for you from the market-place. This can be bought only from the market-place of the heart, provided you can pay for it with the currency of good deeds.

May God's grace be on you.

Document No. 33

LETTER FROM MAULANA AZAD TO SARDAR PATEL

New Delhi
27 November, 1947

My dear Vallabhbhai,

The position of Muslims, especially the business community, in Delhi has become very precarious. In Chandni Chowk only three or four Muslim shops are left. From reliable reports received by me, it appears that non-Muslims go to the shopkeepers daily and threaten them with naked swords if they still refuse to evacuate and even snatch away their goods. One shopkeeper, Mohd. Shafi, who has been a genuine Congressman for the last fifteen years and who was boycotted by the Muslim Leaguers, is one such sufferer. This poor man at least expected to be given some protection and special consideration, looking to his political affiliation; but unfortunately even his shop is visited daily by these gangs, and when he appeals to the police, nothing is done.

I should be grateful if you could kindly let me know what advice in these circumstances I can give to these Muslim shopkeepers of Chandni Chowk.

Yours sincerely,
Abul Kalam Azad

The Hon'ble Sardar Vallabhbhai Patel
New Delhi.

Document No. 34

LETTER FROM MAULANA AZAD TO SARDAR PATEL

New Delhi

1 December, 1947

My dear Vallabhbhai,

I had written a letter to you on 27 November, 1947 about the position of the Muslim shopkeepers in Chandni Chowk. I should be grateful if you could kindly let me know what has been done in this matter.

The second matter which I would like to bring to your notice is the question of Khaksar prisoners who are in Delhi jails. The relatives and friends of these prisoners have written to me to say that they are being ill-treated and that if they are released they will go to Pakistan. I know nothing about the details of their cases, but you may now like to consider the desirability of sending them to Pakistan rather than detaining them here.

Yours sincerely,
Abul Kalam Azad

The Hon'ble Sardar Vallabhbhai Patel
New Delhi.

Document No. 35

LETTER FROM MAULANA AZAD TO SARDAR PATEL

New Delhi

2 December, 1947

My dear Vallabhbhai,

Government employees were given a period of six months in which to decide finally their choice of the dominion in which they wanted to serve. Recently, I have been receiving a number of enquiries in this connection. One such enquiry I am enclosing.

Will you please let me know the decision of the Partition Committee in this matter?

Yours sincerely,
A.K. Azad

The Hon'ble Sardar Vallabhbhai Patel
New Delhi

Document No. 36

LETTER FROM SARDAR PATEL TO MAULANA AZAD

New Delhi

3 December, 1947

My dear Maulana Sahib,

Thank you for your letter dated 27 November 1947 regarding the position of Muslims. I am having enquiries made and will write to you again as soon as possible.

Yours sincerely,
Vallabhbhai Patel

The Hon'ble Maulana Abul Kalam Azad
Minister for Education
New Delhi

Document No. 37

LETTER FROM SARDAR PATEL TO MAULANA AZAD

New Delhi

5 December, 1947

My dear Maulana Sahib,

In continuation of my letter dated 3 December 1947, I am enclosing a copy of the report[1] which I have received from the Superintendent of Police, Delhi, on the situation in Delhi with particular reference to the case of Mr. Mohd. Shafi. I also give below a copy of the forwarding remarks of the DIG Police:

> "I am enclosing hereiwth a copy of a report submitted by Fairhall who, as you know, is Superintendent of Police in-charge Delhi city. Fairhall has rather put the matter strongly, but I agree with him on facts, and cannot think of any reason why Mohd. Shafi did not approach him while Fairhall is present within 300 yards of Mohd. Shafi's shop.
>
> "Regarding the general position in Chandni Chowk and other places in the city, there has been a great improvement during the last few weeks. But it is impossible to ensure that no crime is committed in a big city. What I want to prevent is a general feeling of lawlessness and I am glad to say that this has been checked to a great extent."

I have nothing to add to these remarks.

Yours sincerely,
Vallabhbhai Patel.

The Hon'ble Maulana Abul Kalam Azad
New Delhi.

---

1. see Enclosure.

Enclosure:

REPORT OF THE SUPERINTENDENT OF POLICE, DELHI, ON THE SITUATION IN DELHI

I have to report as follows:

1. In my opinion, bearing in mind the cirucumstances prevailing, the position of the Muslims, especially the business community in Delhi, is on the whole satisfactory. It is certainly better than could be expected and this is due to the police department's superhuman efforts to be sincere executors of Government's policy.

2. It is completely false that Muslim shopkeepers are daily threatened with naked swords etc. Naturally non-Muslim refugees, who have lost their all, resent the comparative prosperity of the Muslims in Delhi; when occasionally this resentment shows any tendency to lawlessness, the police immediately restore the situation.

3. Mohammed Shafi of Chandni Chowk has been, and is still being, given every police protection. It is not only false but completely mischievous for him to state that when he appeals to the police nothing is done. Since I have been i/c City I have personally noticed a picket permanently outside his shop. Moreover he has never cared to complain direct to me although my office is only 300 yards from his shop. Nor have I received any complaints from him through the DIG. Apparently it is Mohd. Shafi's policy to go straight to the highest places with complaints which do not bear inspection.

4. For the future I have advised Mohd. Shafi to come direct to me at the Kotwali if he has any complaint, and I have assured him of every assistance.

5. In conclusion I must record that it is most discouraging to have complaints of this nature when the Police Department is putting forth its sincerest efforts to protect minorities under extremely difficult circumstances.

C.H. Fairhall
Supdt. of Police
City, Delhi.

DIG
4-12-1947

Document No. 38

LETTER FROM SARDAR PATEL TO MAULANA ABUL KALAM AZAD

New Delhi

6 December, 1947

My dear Maulana Sahib,

Thank you for your letter dated 2 December, 1947 regarding options given to Government employees to serve in either of the two dominions. The case which you have referred to me is that of final choice and not provisional choice which could be altered within a period of six months. The Partition Council decision has been that once a final choice is made it should be adhered to. I could see no prospect, therefore, of the gentleman, whose application you have sent me, being allowed to change his option now.

Yours sincerely,
Vallabhbhai Patel

The Hon'ble Maulana Abul Kalam Azad
Minister for Education
New Delhi.

Document No. 39

LETTER FROM MAULANA AZAD TO SARDAR VALLABHBHAI PATEL

New Delhi,

10 December, 1947

My dear Vallabhbhai,

Thank you for your letter of 5 December and for the note of the Superintendent of Police, Delhi, which was enclosed with it. The conditions as depicted in the note are encouraging, but, unfortunately, looking to the tension which still prevails, I wonder how much value we can really place on this note.

Yesterday, for instance, a Muslim was stabbed in the Custodian's office while he was there in connection with his case. The assailant got away, and as far as my information goes, no effort was made to arrest him. If the police really wanted to take strong preventive measures such incidents could hardly take place in broad daylight in a Government office.

Yours sincerely,
Abul Kalam Azad

The Hon'ble Sardar Vallabhbhai Patel
New Delhi.

Document No. 40

SPEECH DELIVERED BY MAULANA AZAD AT THE OPENING OF THE CENTRAL INSTITUTE OF EDUCATION DATED, 19-12-1947

India which has taken its place in the comity of free nations of the world has to march forward in every field of her national life with alacrity, but you will agree that none of these fields is as important as the educational field. At present, the percentage of literacy in India is only 14.7, that is, out of every hundred nearly 85 persons are totally illiterate. Not counting the population of the provinces which have ceded from the Indian Union, the remaining population, according to the last census, is in the neighbourhood of 24,02,54,500. Of these, 2,93,72,000 are school-going children – between the ages of six and eleven. These statistics show that even if we ignore persons above the age of eleven we have still to make immediate arrangements for the education of about 3 crores of school-going children between the ages of six and eleven.

I am sure you will agree with me that this state of affairs is most deplorable and no civilised Government can tolerate it. If we are unable to make arrangements for the primary education of about 30 millions of our children, all our nation building schemes will, *ipso facto*, become valueless. The only way out therefore is to try and lift millions of these children from the depths of neglect and ignorance immediately.

The question is how best to solve this problem. The greatest hurdle facing us is the lack of trained teachers. Supposc, we take three teachers per 100 children, we will require a minimum of 9 lakhs of trained teachers for 30 million school-going children. If we want to break this vicious circle, we should not postpone our educational schemes simply because there are not sufficient trained teachers. Rather we should mobilise as teachers all the educated persons available, and at the same time carry on the training of teachers with the greatest possible speed, so that trained teachers can be made available in sufficient numbers in the shortest possible time.

The former Government of India had set up a Central Advisory Board of Education which the present Government has continued. This Board had in the year 1944 submitted a detailed report on the post-war educational development. One of the basic recommendations in this report was the establishment of new training institutions for teachers both by the Central and the Provincial Governments. Accordingly, all the Provincial Governments as well as the Central Government while formulating their five-year post-war programme had this recommendation in view. A number of such training institutions have already been opened and are still being opened in the various parts of the country.

The educational plan of the Central Government included a proposal to establish a Central Institute of Education located at Delhi. In 1945, the details of this scheme were finalised and Rs. 18,00,000 for its buildings and Rs. 2,45,000 for equipment, etc., were set aside. It was proposed that the building of the Institute should provide class-room accommodation for 300 students of both sexes and hostel accommodation for 150 students. It was also decided to have the Institute within the University grounds and regard it as a Faculty of Education of the Delhi University. It is estimated that when the scheme is in full operation, its annual recurring expenditure will be in the neighbourhood of Rs. 2 lakh. This sum has been sanctioned by the Government.

It was decided in 1945 that this scheme should start from 1946-47, but it could not be taken in hand and a full year was thus wasted. The building programme was held up owing to the non-availability of building materials. This year, however, it was decided to start the institution in a rented building. Accordingly, the house in which we are at present assembled, was acquired in July last; but we could not proceed with this work earlier owing to the recent unfortunate disturbances in Delhi. However, I am now happy that we have surmounted all our difficulties and that today this Insitute is being opened by Your Excellency.

The teachers trained at this Institute will naturally be employed in the teaching institutions in the Centrally Administered Areas. But while gauging the real importance of the Insitute, we should not give undue importance to this aspect of the Institute. The function of the Institute is something greater than this. It will turn out teachers who will be 'model teachers' for provinces but over and above all this,

this Institute will be a research centre for solving new educational problems of the country and will be a beacon light for the training institutions of the country. The problems facing the Institute will be: how to correlate the different systems of basic education; how to reform the present system of examinations; and how to mould the primary education of a child so that he is given full opportunity to develop his individuality and also to equip himself to keep abreast of world affairs. This and similar other problems will come before the Institute and it will have to find ways and means of solving them.

We have had to start this Institute in a building which is hardly suitable for it but there was no alternative owing to the acute shortage of suitable houses. This house, as Your Excellency can see for yourself, is not big enough for our requirements even with the two tents which we have had to pitch to supplement this accommodation. Because of this limited accommodation, our work and progress will necessarily be greatly hampered and restricted. We have every hope, however, that these difficulties will not hamper our progress for long and that soon this Institute will blossom forth and take its rightful place.

Your Excellency, we are fully aware of the keen interest which you have evinced in the social and educational activities of this country. We are deeply grateful to you for the zeal, the promptness and the personal interest which you have shown in dealing with the relief of the unfortunate and afflicted people from the Punjab. To show our appreciation it was only natural that I should have asked you to perform the opening ceremony of this Institute. I am thankful to you for your kindness in accepting my invitation. I will now request Your Excellency to perform the ceremony of opening the Central Institute of Education, Delhi. By pressing the electric button you will open the doors of the Institute. May the gates of darkness and ignorance which have prevented light from reaching the millions of my countrymen be thrown open very soon in the same manner.

Document No. 41

MAULANA AZAD'S CONVOCATION ADDRESS AT PATNA UNIVERSITY ON DECEMBER 21, 1947

Last year the Chancellor of your University invited me to come here and deliver the Convocation Address. Your able Vice-Chancellor too pressed me for it. I would have certainly agreed to your request but my ill-health stood in my way and I had to beg leave to be excused. But this year again when I was approached I could not venture to offer an excuse. Now I am here, and thank you for the opportunity you have given me to place my views before you.

Perhaps this is the first time in the history of the Indian universities when English is being replaced by an Indian language for delivering a Convocation Address. I do not know what your reactions would be to my speaking in Hindustani. Do you think it is necessary for me to offer an apology for breaking with the past? No doubt it is a departure from the old established practice and whenever a tradition is given up it is customary to offer an excuse. But I do not think you require an explanation from me. Whatever I am doing is no doubt an innovation, but I may be permitted to say that it is neither improper nor inopportune. Therefore, there is no need for an apology. Standing as I do before an audience entirely composed of Indians and within the precincts of an Indian university what could be more natural for me than to speak in an Indian language? Indeed, if an apology was needed, it was only for the adoption of a language forced upon us by the course of historical events. Even in our own country we were made to give up our own languages and adopt the language of a foreign country. Today we find ourselves in the unenviable predicament of offering explanations. The rest of the world naturally wants to know why we are without a national language in spite of our independence. How is it that this unnatural state of affairs has come to exist that we have no Indian language for running our government and our education?

Now the question arises how this unnatural state of affairs came to pass. There can be only one answer to this question. Our educational system was not introduced by us. It was founded and controlled by foreigners. Whatever they decided to teach us was right, but their method of imparting education was wrong.

It is already known to you that during the regime of the East India Company when the question of introducing Western education in India first arose, the British officials were divided. One group was of the opinion that the old indigenous system of education should be encouraged while the second group was in favour of Western education. Ultimately, it so happened that the second group had its way. The famous Minute of Lord Macaulay bears upon this controversy. So far as this Minute deals with the introduction of Western learning, it was correct and we have nothing to say against it. But the method of teaching adopted by them was entirely unsuited to the life and needs of our countrymen. No Indian language but English which was foreign to us was made the medium of instruction. The result was that modern education in India began to be imparted in an un-Indian way. The Indians had to shape their minds in artificial and not in natural moulds. Not only they had to change their language but also their minds. Their whole approach to different branches of learning was through the medium of a foreign tongue. Now it became necessary for every Indian child to shape an artificial mind and to tackle every aspect of learning from an unnatural angle of vision. He could not enter the sacred precincts of learning with a natural mind.

His whole energy which should have been entirely devoted to learning is now divided, and he is forced to spend a great part of it in learning and mastering a foregin language.

Another great harm that accrued from it was that the development of our languages was impeded. If the Indian languages had been made the media of instruction a hundred and fifty years ago they would have come in line with the progressive languages of the world.

Supposing this educational revolution had been brought about by our own hands, we should have certainly done what other countries of Asia and the East did in the nineteenth century. Egypt, Syria, Turkey, Persia, China and Japan all felt the need of having western education. They established schools and colleges for modern learning, but none of them had the experience of undergoing the artificiality of giving up their own language and receiving education through the medium of a foreign language.

It cannot be denied that the conditions prevailing in India were certainly different from those of other eastern countries and it was not easy to decide which language of the country should be the medium of instruction. At that time three classical languages, Persian, Arabic and Sanskrit, were taught in India. They were capable of becoming the media for western education but none of them could become the medium of instruction in India. Sanskrit was not a spoken language and its teaching was confined only to a few. Arabic too was in the same category so far as India was concerned. It was known only to a limited number of scholars. Persian, no doubt, was generally studied and was the official language of the country for about 600 years. But that too was not an Indian language. No Indian could speak Persian without learning it in the first instance. Evidently, only those languages could be adopted as the media of instruction which were spoken in the various parts of India. But all these languages had not fully developed, and they were not so refined or polished that they could serve the purpose of higher education. Under the circumstances they were brushed aside. Persian was disposed of simply by saying that it would not do for India. Thus ended the whole controversy.

But it may be remarked here that the difficulties which India had to face in the matter of language also presented themselves to some of the other Asian countries. Indeed, Egypt, China and Persia had their own classical languages. But Turkey and Japan were linguistically more or less in the same position as the Indian languages were in the nineteenth century. Their whole literary wealth was only poetical, but they had little prose literature. Still, unlike India they did not adopt a foreign language for purposes of education. They made their own languages the media of instruction and the result is before the world. Today in all the universities of Turkey and Japan education is imparted through the language of the country. There is no field in any branch of learning where their national languages are not advancing.

Had the educational policy of India been in the hands of Indians they would have adopted the same course as was done by Turkey and Japan. India today in that case would not have had to face a situation when I have to think of making excuses for delivering an address in our own language.

But friends, there are always two sides to a picture in this pictorial world of ours. Whatever I have said up to now is one aspect of it. Justice demands that we should examine the other side of the medal as well.

Howsoever wrongly the English language made its way into our life, the fact remains that it has influenced our mental and educational outlook for the past one hundred and fifty years. This state of affairs though harmful in some ways has also benefited us in many ways. We have to acknowledge it without reservations. The greatest advantage that we gained from the adoption of English was that many of the obstacles were automatically removed from our newly born national life. It has led to the unification of the whole of the country. All the different parts of the country were brought together in spite of distances and different languages. In this respect it can be said that English has played the same part in cementing and uniting India as did Persian in Moghul times. Our country is a sub-continent and every part has its separate entity. But the English language has been responsible for creating a bond of mental fellowship among all educated Indians from Kashmir to Cape Camorin. It is a connecting link between all the Provincial Governments, Universities, Legislative Assemblies, public platforms and national organisations. It was this state of affairs that led to the birth of the Indian National Congress in 1885 which created political awakening and gave a new national life to the country.

Then we have been benefited in another direction also. Through English India cultivated direct intellectual relationship with Europe and America. Her voice reached the outer world without any intermediary. I do not feel the slightest hesitation in saying that India's position and recognition in the international world are greatly due to our having recourse to the English language both written and spoken.

Any way whatever opinion we may hold about English, we find it influencing all aspects of our national life. Now a basic problem confronts us. What is to be our attitude in future towards English? As the Ministry of Education in the Government of India has been entrusted to me, naturally you will want to know my views on education and language. I have given ample expression to my ideas before but I will utilise this occasion and invite your attention to an important aspect of this question.

One thing is quite clear and definite, and I have no doubt that any Indian will disagree with me. The position that English occupies today in our educational and official life cannot be sustained in future. It is but essential that Indian languages should find their legitimate position. But we have to decide after mature deliberation how to bring about this change. Obviously there are two courses open to us. We may either take an immediate and sudden step or we may proceed gradually measuring our way and considering the pros and cons of our steps. I wish to make it quite plain to you that after having considered all the aspects of the question I have come to the conclusion that it is the second alternative alone that can suit us. If we are precipitious and take hasty steps without due consideration, we may endanger our national fabric.

Surely you cannot be unaware of the fact that no Indian would be more anxious than myself to see that Indian languages should replace English. You are also aware of the fact that I am not indebted to English college or school. As a student I was not even for a day in any college or schoool. I was brought up in a family where the old traditions of Indian learning and culture prevailed and there could not be the slightest trace of English education. Whatever education I received as a student was Arabic and Persian and was imparted in the old style. I came to learn English much later by self-study only. From this it will be clear to you that my educational connection with English is not of the same type as yours. You need not therefore suspect that I am in any way influenced in my opinion by my English education. I can make bold to say that my opinion is perfectly unbiased. I am not one of those who are the products of English type of universities. I am entirely disconnected with them and as such can take a detached point of view and understand your needs and requirements.

I find that from various parts of the country voices have been raised that we should at once banish English from our government offices. In some provinces decisions have been taken to the effect that from the New Year the Government Gazette will not be published in English. I have not the slightest doubt that this kind of precipitancy will retard the government machinery. It is correct and essential to instal provincial languages in place of English. But howsover essential and desirable a thing may be, any hurried step, instead of helping us, may prove harmful. Even a good thing, if done in haste, may stand in our way.

Supose you decide today in your province that after six months in all government offices English will be discarded. Just imagine what will come to pass in that case. Today English is serving the purpose of an inter-provincial language. The Central Government is being run with the help of English. What language is going to take the place of English? What will be the connecting link between Bengal and Madras? How will Assam and Bombay communicate with each other? How will the Central Government correspond with the provinces? You will naturally say we shall have a common language instead of English. But I put to you where is that language as yet? Will that language suddenly replace English? Ample time will be required for an Indian language to develop so as to become a vehicle of thought among all the peoples of India and serve as the official language of the country. If you suddenly displace a language which is holding its own for the past one hundred and fifty years and instal in its place a language which needs some time to develop, you will not be able to solve the problem of language. On the other hand, you will create chaos and confusion in all your affairs.

We should remember that so long as the British were the rulers in India there was the danger that we might be swept away by all those influences which were the direct outcome of British rule. Now that we are a free nation, that danger is past. But then again there is the danger of going to the other extreme. We may become anti-everything that is English. I may warn you against this new danger. If you are not on your guard it may again thwart your national aspirations.

We have yet to evolve our national life. It can be perfected only when our languages come to occupy their natural position. We should first make a well thought out plan and proceed step by step.

After carefully considering all the implications of this question I have come to the conclusion that the problem of language has two aspects – one concerns government offices and the other education.

For government offices we should chalk out a programme on the following lines:

(1) The Central Government and the Provincial Governments should decide that in all government offices in future an Indian language will be used side by side with English. But in so far as English is the official language, the *status quo* will be preserved for five years.

(2) During these five years the Indian language will have to be so developed as to adapt itself to the offiical language. Its use may be encouraged gradually so that in the sixth year it may completely replace English.

In other words in the next five years there will be two official languages – one Indian language and the other English. In the sixth year only one language will be left. English will naturally lose its place except in some special departments.

So far as education is concerned, the following should be the programme:

(1) We should decide that the medium of instruction throughout will be the regional language.

(2) So far as elementary and secondary education is concerned there is no obstacle in our way. But we have to make provision for higher education. We have to make a start straightaway. Here, too, we shall have to fix a time-limit of five years. In this period we have to so advance that in the sixth year all branches of higher education should be handled through our own regional languages.

(3) By making the Indian languages the media of instruction it should not be understood that there will be no room left for English in our educational system. In order to keep ourselves in direct touch with the achievements of Europe and America a large section of our people will have to depend on English. English at present occupies an honoured place in the curricula of studies in Asia and the East. It is serving a useful purpose in creating contacts for us with foreign countries. We have connections with countries such as China, Japan, Indonesia, Burma, Ceylon, Egypt, Mesopotamia, Syria, Persia, Turkey only through English. English is an international language today. It is in our interest that we should make the best use of our knowledge of English and continue its study in our educational institutions. But it goes without saying that with the adoption of an Indian language it can be given the place of an important second language. English will be one of the special subjects for post-graduate studies.

As the problem of language and education is equally important for all the provinces, the best method for its consideration will be for the representatives of provinces to assemble together and deliberate on it. The Central Government will help them as much as it can. It was one of the objects for which an Educational Conference was to be called by the Government of India in July 1947 but it had to be postponed on account of the political conditions prevailing then. Now it has been decided to hold it in January 1948. It is hoped that we will fully consider this problem on that occasion.

In this connection there is another thing to which I shall invite your attention. Man is always inclined to go to extremes in realms of thought and action. It is very seldom that he steers a middle course, and it is where he stumbles. He is like the watch of which the regulator has gone wrong. It goes either too fast or too slow. It never keeps right time. It is not many years when our educated young men had lost themselves in imitating the English, in their language, dress, manners, etc. They wre not mindful of their own heritage. Some of them felt ashamed to talk to their own countrymen in their language. They were ever ready to quote Shakespeare, Milton, Goethe and Wordsworth but they felt no love for Valmiki, Kalidasa, Khusro or Anis. Then there came a time when under the leadership of Mahatma Gandhi the national movement took a new turn and the craze for imitating the British began to wane. But now I notice that a number of my countrymen are on the verge of making another mistake. Previously they were on one brink of the precipice and now they want to jump over to the other extreme. By Indian nationalism it is now meant that we should forget the English language and literature and that we should have nothing to do with Milton or Shakespeare. From certain quarters I hear that in order to be true nationalists we should have no tinge of modern civilisation in us. I believe there is nobody here who holds these views. But if there is any I must remind him that just as the previous position was wrong, this latter position will also be in the same category. In the ineffaceable words of the Buddha via media is the only tangible reality. Just as it was not proper for you to lose yourself in the slavish love of western civilisation or literature to the extent that you might forget the grand and proud civilisation of your own country, similarly it would be wrong to put yourself in a cage so that no ray of the light of western learning and civilisation may enter it. Do not forget that you can seal all your worldly possessions within national and geographical limits but no seal can be put on learning and civilisation. They are outside the pale of boundaries, and seals are of no avail there. For them there are no territorial limits. They are above nationalities. They are free from the stains of race, colour or fractions. They might have originated in any part of the world but they are now the common heritage of mankind and are the joint property of all countries and nations. No doubt Shakespeare was born in England but the immortal works of Shakespeare are for all countries. Even if England wants it she cannot keep Shakespeare to herself. Do you think that the dramas of Kalidas were also Indian nationals just as Kalidas was? Do you think no foreigner has a claim on them?

Friends, in the advancement of nations there is no greater hindrance than narrow-mindedness. It is our duty to keep ourselves free from this disease in this new era of independence which has just begun. There is no other disease so dangerous for the healthy growth of national life. It makes its appearance in every field of thought and action. Like an actor it masquerades in disguise. In the domain of religion it appears in the form of blind faith and wants to deceive us in the name of orthodoxy. In politics it wants to overpower us in the guise of nationalism. In learning and culture it makes an appeal to us in the name of our nation and country. It behoves us not to be taken in by these fictitious names. We must remember that the root cause of all this is nothing but narrow-mindedness.

We have to keep in mind that the nationalism propagated in the nineteenth century Europe is all shattered and the world is sick of the bounds of narrow nationalism. It is anxious to break those shackles. Instead of small cooped up nationalities the world wants to build supernationalism. Obviously there is no room for narrow-mindedness in this modern age. We shall find a secure place in the comity of nations only if we are international-minded and tolerant.

It is possible that other nations may have to learn new lessons for broadening their outlook and for cultivating a spirit of tolerance. But so far as India is concerned we can say with pride and glory that it is the main trait of our ancient civilisation, and that we have been steeped in it for thousands of years. In other countries differences of thought and action led to mutual warfare and bloodshed but in India they were resolved in a spirit of compromise and toleration. Here every kind of faith, every kind of culture, every mode of living was allowed to flourish and find its own salvation.

From the dawn of history Indian mind has been comprehensive, and tolerant of every kind of thought. It admitted every kind of faith and accommodated all shades of opinion. It was ready to offer hospitality to every new-comer. New caravans of various peoples and cultures arrived here and found their resting places. Its orbit of social life was not shut on any creed or religion. The highest school of Vedantism

with the budget estimates for 1948-49. Both the things were sent on the 3rd of June, 1948.

I have given all these details to show that our case has been before your Department for more than 16 months. I have personally seen you twice to emphasis the points contained in our representation. In the meantime, many educational and cultural institutions have received grants-in-aid from the Central Government. We do not grudge these grants but we feel worried and disappointed because our claim has not been admitted so far. The Gurukula Kangri is perhaps the oldest institution imparting education on purely national lines, without asking any help from the foreign Government. Against odds, we have worked for about 48 years with a hope that when freedom comes this national institution will get automatic recognition. Our hope has been fulfilled insomuch as many Provincial Governments have recognised the degree of the Gurukula University but unfortunately our case has so far failed to persuade the Central Government. Many of the Ministers of the Central Cabinet (Pandit Jawaharlal Nehru, Sardar Patel, Shri Shanmukham Chetty and others) besides prominent leaders such as Mahatma Gandhi and Dr. Rajendra Prasad have visited the institution more than once and have expressed their appreciation of the work and the principles on which it was founded.

I hope you will excuse me for the length of this letter. As my object in writing this letter was to draw your attention towards our application, I have had to refer to the long and protracted correspondence held between the Gurukula and the Education Department. I am sure you will give personal attention to our case so that the Gurukula may get the advantage of securing grants-in-aid for the last (1947-48) as well as the current (1948-49) years.

Yours sincerely,
Vice-Chancellor
Gurukula University, Kangri (Hardwar)

The Hon'ble Maulana Abul Kalam Azad
Minister for Education
Government of India
New Delhi.

Document No. 43

LUCKNOW MUSLIM CONFERENCE WITH AZAD AS PRESIDENT

The Indian Muslim Conference, held at Lucknow on the 27th and 28th of December, was a step in the right direction. In his presidential address, the first thing which Maulana Abul Kalam Azad Emphasized was that all political organizations formed on communal lines should be liquidated. The Maulana was only addressing the seventy thousand Muslims who had gathered to follow his lead. But the truth of his remarks applies equally to all communal organizations – Hindu, Muslim, Sikh or any other. As the Maulana rightly pointed out, nobody can object to organizations which merely look to the religious or cultural progress of a particular community. So long as we do not regard all life and property, without regard to religion, as equally sacred, we can neither have peace in this country nor maintain the glory and dignity of our respective creeds. All communal distinctions defeat the very object of religion and spell ruin to the entire society.

While expressing his well-known views on the partition of the country and on the two-nation theory, and advising all the Musalmans of India to join the Indian National Congress, the Maulana, in a gathering held with a particular objective, wisely refrained from raking up better memories or straying into the field of controversial politics.

The Conference, in its resolutions, unanimously accepted the lead given by the Maulana. The resolution on communal organizations could well have been passed by any national gathering, with a few verbal changes. Maulana Ahmad Saheed, while moving the resolution, deplored the sad consequences of the propagation of the two-nation theory. Dr. Syed Mahmood rightly warned the Hindus and Sikhs that if any one community was finished, it could inevitably mean the ruin of all. Several speakers like Syed Abdulla Brelvi, Prof. Humayun Kabir and Maulana Hifzur Rahman suggested that the Musalmans should join the Indian National Congress *en masse*, also to help that body to maintain its truly national character.

Sundarlal

New Delhi
11-1-48

Document No. 44

SPEECH OF MAULANA AZAD AT THE 14TH SESSION OF THE CENTRAL ADVISORY BOARD OF EDUCATION, HELD IN NEW DELHI ON JANUARY 13, 1948

On the occasion of this fourteenth session of the Central Advisory Board of Education I accord my sincere welcome to you. Historically speaking, it is the fourteenth session as thirteen have alrady been held. But to be more accurate, I think we should call at the Inaugural Session of the Board, since the first thirteen took place during British rule which on August 15, 1947, came to an end and with it a long chapter of Indian history. Today we are assembled in a new India which has yet to make its history.

I believe it will not be out of place to mention that the change in the political situation has greatly affected the temper and nature of the work which we have undertaken. The scales in which the educational problems were weighed by this Board until now have grown out of date. New scales with new weights will have to be substituted. The dimensions of the national problems of the day cannot now be judged by the measurements which have been employed so far. The new aspirations of the New India will require fresh outlook and new measures to tackle its problems.

With whatever depth of vision and sympathetic imagination the Board might have tackled the educational problems in the past, it could not escape the fact that there was no free National Government to support it. In spite of its desire to have the fullest scope it had to keep itself somewhat in restraint. Now things have changed. The nation, about the educational problems of which you are going to deliberate, has its own government at your entire disposal. The Government in its turn expects that you, too, offer your deliberations with the same tenacity of purpose and breadth of vision as are guiding the administration today.

But if we want to adopt new measures with fresh determination and redoubled efforts, it should not mean that we do not acknowledge the past services of the Board. Its lengthy reports covering thousands of pages are a record of the zeal and ability with which the task was handled in the past thirteen years and the present day educational activities of the country bear testimony to it. Probably the most valuable service rendered by the Board was the preparation of the scheme of Basic Education in 1944. It was the first occasion in the history of British India when the problem of elementary education was presented in its true aspect. A scheme was then initiated which contained the elements of broad outlook and bold action, the two things which were least expected in the then prevailing circumstances. The name of Sir John Sargent who was our Educational Adviser is intimately connected with the scheme because of the prominent part he took in framing it. I am glad that he will continue to remain in our country though at the moment he is away and unable to be present at this session.

Now we have to think how far this scheme can be adapted to suit the changed circumstances and how soon obstacles in our way can be removed. But I will not discuss this question at this time, as an educational conference which is to tackle such problems has been called to meet here as soon as this session is over. We shall have ample opportunity of taking up these questions there.

But there is a particular aspect of the question to which I shall invite your attention. In connection with the scheme of the Basic Edcucation the question of religious instruction had cropped up at thc time. Two committees of the Board pondered over it but they were unable to come to an agreed decision. I should like this question to be reconsidered in the light of the changed circumstances. For our country this question has a special importance.

It is already known to you that the nineteenth century liberal point of view concerning the imparting of religious education has already lost weight. Even after the World War I a new approach had begun to assert itself and the intellectual revolution brought about in the wake of the World War II has given it a decisive shape. At first it was considered that religions would stand in the way of the free intellectual development of a child but now it has been admitted that religious education cannot altogether be dispensed with. If national education was devoid of this element, there would be no appreciation of moral values or moulding of character on human lines. It must be known to you that Russia had to give up its ideology during the last World War. The British Government in England had also to amend its educational system in 1944.

So far as India is concerned, the problem presents itself in an entirely different shape. Europe and America felt the need of religious education as it was observed that without religious influences people became over-rationalistic. But in so far as they are working in Indian life we have to face the other side of the medal. We have no fear that people will become ultra-rationalists. On the contrary we are surrounded by over-religiosity. Our present difficulties, unlike those of Europe, are not creations of materialistic zealots but of religious fanatics. If we want to overcome them, the solution lies not in rejecting religious instruction in elementary stages but in imparting sound and healthy religious education under our direct supervision so that misguided credulism may not affect the children in their plastic stage.

It is obvious that millions of Indians are not prepared to see that their children are brought up in an irreligious atmosphere and, I am sure, you, too, will agree with them. What will be the consequence if the Government undertake to impart purely secular education? Naturally people will try to provide religious education to their children through private sources. How these private sources are working today or are likely to work in future is already known to you. I know something about it and can say that not only in villages but even in cities the imparting of religious educations is entrusted to teachers who though literate are not educated. To them religion means nothing but bigotry. The method of education, too, is such in which there is no scope for broad and liberal outlook. It is quite plain, then, that the children will not be able to drive out the ideas infused into them, in their early stage, whatever modern education may be given to them at a later stage. If we want to safeguard the intellectual life of our country against this danger, it becomes all the more necessary for us not to leave the imparting of early religious education to private sources. We should rather take it under our direct care and supervision. No doubt, a foreign government had to keep itself away from religious education. But a National Government cannot divest itself of undertaking this responsibility. To mould the growing mind of the nation on the right lines is its primary duty. In India, we cannot have an intellectual mould without religion.

But if religious instruction is to be a part of basic education, what will be its proportion? How is it to be managed? These are questions which are to be thoroughly considered. Indeed, there will be difficulties in the way. A solution will have to be found. But I need not go into details. If the main issue is settled, details can be tackled later on. In any case I request you to appoint a committee to go into the question *ab novo*. It may be authorised to send its recommendations directly to the Government.

There is another problem on which you have to take a final decision now. What is to be the medium of instruction in our educational institutions? I am sure there are two things with which you will agree. First, that in future English cannot remain the medium of instruction. Secondly, whatever the change may be in this direction, it should not be sudden but gradual. In my opinion, so far as higher education is concerned, we should come to the decision that the *status quo* may be preserved for five years. But along with it a provision may be made by the universities for the coming change. I should like you to make your suggestions to the Government after due deliberation.

But in this connection a fundamental question arises with regard to Indian languages. How is the change to be brought about? Is university education to be imparted through a common Indian language or the provinces may be given an opportunity to have their own regional languages for university teaching? English was a foreign language. We were greatly handicapped by having it as our medium of instruction. But we were also greatly benefited in one way that all the educated people in the country thought and expressed themselves in the same language. It cemented the national unity. It was such a great boon to us that I should have advocated its retention as the medium of instruction, had it not been fundamentally wrong to impart education through a foreign language. But obviously I should desist from offering this advice. I put it to you, if only till recently a Madrasi or a Punjabi or a Bengalee felt no difficulty in receiving education through a foreign language, why he should be handicapped if he were to be educated through one of the Indian languages. If instead of English we adopt an Indian language, we shall certainly be able to retain the same intellectual unity which was created for us by the English language. But if we fail to substitute an Indian language for English our intellectual unity will certainly be affected.

The alternative course before us is to have regional languages for university teaching and one common compulsory language for the Central Government and for inter-provincial communication. Anyhow it is but necessary that you should come to a final decision on this point after discussion and deliberation.

Document No. 45

LETTER FROM DR. RAJENDRA PRASAD TO MAULANA ABUL KALAM AZAD

1, Queen Victoria Road
New Delhi

14th. January, 1948

My dear Maulana Sahib,

I wrote to you some time ago requesting you to make a suitable grant to the Bharatiya Itihas Parishad (Indian Academy of History) and you were good enough to tell me that the matter would receive your consideration but that I should send you some details.

The Bharatiya Itihas Parishad was established some years ago with the special object of getting a history of India written by the best scholars in the country from the Indian point of view. Sir Jadunath Sarkar was made the Chairman of the Editorial Board and I was made the President of the Council of the Parishad. The Parishad has planned to bring out the history in 20 volumes of which one volume has alrady been published and another is in the press. The scheme for several other volumes is ready and scholars are engaged and they are in various stages of preparation. The volume which has already been published has been well received by scholars. We had raised funds which have so far been utilised but they are exhausted now. The work has been somewhat delayed on account of the political movement of 1942 and no volume could be published till 1946 although work had been started on several of them. It is estimated that the cost in bringing out all the volumes will be something between 2 and 3 lakhs of rupees. The history will be published in English as also in Hindi and, if possible, in other Indian languages also. The Parishad has been fortunate in securing the cooperation of some of the best known historians in the country and I hope it will be possible for the Government to give adequate financial assistance so that it may be expedited. It is estimated that it will take some 4 to 5 years to bring out all the volumes.

I shall be obliged for an early reply.

Yours sincerely,
Rajendra Prasad

Document No. 46

MAULANA AZAD'S OPENING ADDRESS AT THE ALL INDIA EDUCATIONAL CONFERENCE, HELD IN NEW DELHI ON JANUARY 16, 1948

It is exactly a year ago that I assumed charge of this Ministry on January 15, 1947. It was then my intention to summon immediately an educational conference of representatives of Provincial Governments, the States and the universities in order to chalk out our future programme of action. In fact, dates had been announced for such a conference twice, but circumstances over which we had no control intervened on both occasions. I need not go into the reasons for these postponements as they are well known to you and will only say that I have spared no efforts to summon the conference as early as possible. In any case we have met today and I have every hope that the combined wisdom of all who are present today will enable us to formulate schemes that will meet adequately the educational requirements of this ancient land. I extend to you my cordial welcome and thank you all for your response to my invitation.

The agenda is already before you. You will find that it contains only the most pressing problems that confront us today. The first issue refers to the provision of basic education for every citizen of the State. It is accepted on all hands that without such education a modern democratic state cannnot flourish or perform those functions which are expected of it. The scheme of Post-war Educational Development prepared by the Central Advisory Board of Education has been accepted by the Central and the Provincial Governments. Steps have already been taken to set on foot the programme of action according to a five-year plan, but I must point out that all these have been done according to old methods and on the old scales. After the attainment of our independence, we cannot, however, be content with programmes which were considered adequate for the old regime. Thus, no one will for a moment tolerate today that 40 years must elapse before the full scheme of basic education for all the inhabitants of this land can be implemented. In fact, even half that period will seem to many to savour of delay and procrastination.

We must therefore devise measures by which the educational progress of this country can be so accelerated that we reach our objective within a much shorter time.

I know the many difficulties and obstacles which face us. I know that on account of the happenings in the recent past, the attention of the Government and the people has often been diverted from constructive work. After full consideration of all these factors, I would still assert that education cannot wait. Even if other nation building activities of the Government have to be slowed down or deferred on account of such difficulties, education, at any rate, must be pushed forward as rapidly as possible. We must not, for a moment, forget that it is the birthright of every indiviudal to receive at least the basic education without which he cannot fully discharge his duties as a citizen.

In talking of basic education, we have to deal separately with the problem of providing education to school-going children and to adults. The population of India today, after partition, is roughly 24 crores, if we leave out of account the people of the States. The school population will therefore be about 2,93,72,000 if we consider the age-group of 6 to 11 years. If we calculate on the basis of even three teachers for every hundred pupils, this would require about nine lakhs of teachers for teaching about three crores of boys and girls. I will not raise here the question whether we should discourage single-teacher schools, though the best educational opinion favours at least two teachers for a school. In any case, the provision of nine lakhs of trained teachers immediately seems an altogether impossible task and nothing that the Government can do remedy this defect overnight. In fact, this seems to be one of the main reasons why 40 years was regarded as the minimum period which must elapse before educational facilities can be provided for all citizens of the land.

We have, however, already seen that we cannot wait for such a long time and therefore my appeal will be to all educated men and women of this country to come forward to meet this deficiency. I would urge upon every educated man and woman to regard it as a sacred national service to come forward and serve as a teacher for at least two years. They should regard it as a sacrifice to the national cause and accept for their services whatever allowance the State may afford. We may also consider some kind of conscription for the purpose. If every matriculate is required to put in one year's and every graduate two years' service in education before he or she obtains his or her certificate, we would get a large supply of teachers for our purpose. If two lakhs of educated men and women come forward every year, we can in five years have the minimum number of teachers necessary for fulfilling our plans. This will, however, be an emergency measure and cannot continue indefinitely. We must therefore devote these five years for the greatest possible expansion in the provision of facilities for training teachers, so that, by the end of that period, we may gradually replace volunteer teachers by teachers who have taken up teaching as their vocation.

Another great obstacle towards the immediate provision of educational facilities for all is the financial implication of constructing the necessary school houses and other buildings. This, however, need not and should not deter us. I would go so far as to say that we need not just now make any provision for building expenses at all. India is a country where for nine months in the year pupils can work in the open without any difficulty or injury to their health. In villages, if necessary, educational work can be carried on under the trees and even where structures have to be put up whether in town or village these can be built with bamboo and mud at a much lower cost than a pucca building would cost. In addition, we must never forget that in India there have already been voluntary contributions towards the establishments of schools and I have no doubt that if we can tap fully the resources of private munificene, the problem of meeting the cost of educational structure will at least be partially met.

Another chief obstacle to the immediate fulfilment of the Basic Education Plan is the problem of finance. For basic education alone we require at least nine lakhs of teachers. The Pay Commission recommended a scale of Rs. 30-50 for such teachers. I realise that this is hardly enough to attract the best type of candidates, but as I have stated earlier, my appeal is to educated men and women to regard this educational service for two years as a sacrifice in the cause of the nation. They must therefore agree to work on this meagre pay and look at it more in the nature of an allowance than wages for their labour. I have suggested that we should have at least two lakh volunteers every year which will give four lakhs of such volunteers at a time from the second year of the enforcement of the scheme. Even on the basis of pay suggested in the Pay Commission's Report, this would mean a wages bill of Rs. 2 crore per month or Rs. 24 crore per year for the next five years. The amount actually spent on primary education by the Provinces and the Centre as shown in the budget for the year 1945-46 is as follows:

Name of Province	Expenditure on primary education by various provinces during 1945-46
Assam	21,66,186
Bihar	2,09,820
Bombay	1,71,22,281
C.P. & Berar	23,60,391
Madras	2,89,28,403
Orissa	16,77,017
United Provinces	57,52,008
Total	5,82,16,106
Bengal (Undivided)..	74,10,142
Punjab (Undivided)..	57,66,474
Total	1,31,76,616
Total of all Provinces	7,13,92,722
Centrally Administered Areas	
Ajmer-Merwara	2,29,634
Civil & Military Stations	
Bangalore	1,03,958
Coorg	47,430
Delhi	2,72,564
Minor Administrations	1,49,960
Total	8,03,546
Grand Total	7,21,96,268

The above figures have been taken from the Provincial General Educational Table. Since then there have been considerable increases in the provision for Education in the Central and Provincial Budgets, but figures are not at present available for the years 1946-47 and 1947-48, except in the case of the Centre. In the Centre, the Budget provides for a little over Rs. 11 lakhs for 1947-48. We may, however, ignore these variations as well as the variation that has been caused by the partition of the Provinces of Bengal and the Punjab.

We would therefore have to find additional funds to the extent of about Rs. 16 crores for the next five years. In Bengal, an attempt has been made to find money for educational purposes by the imposition of an educational cess. It is for you to consider whether some such method may not be applied to other provinces in order to meet part of this gap. You have also to suggest what further steps the Central Government can take in addition to what it has already done.

I now come to the problem of providing for the education of adults who are illiterate. Its importance need hardly be emphasised, especially to a body of educational experts like you. It is obvious that with the extension of democracy, the problem of adult education has become even more important than it was in the past. As you know, some work for adult education has been started in the provinces since 1938 but this was on a very small scale and must be incresed and expedited manifold, if we are to obtain the desired result. Adult education has two aspects, *viz.*, (a) arrangements for making the adults literate, and (b) the provision of measures to enlarge their minds and enable them to take an intelligent interest in the affairs of the country.

I will take up the question of education in the second sense first, as obviously this is more important in the case of adults than mere provision of literacy. Such expansion of the mind of the adults can largely be effected today through the use of scientific methods and machinery which has made our task in this respect much lighter than it was before. There is experience of countries like Russia and the U.S.A. where open-air drama, the film and the radio have been used to very great effect. Russia has, in fact, succeeded in carrying out her successive five-year plans largely through the use of such scientific methods and machinery. We should benefit by the experience of these countries and draw upon the vast stores of educational films which have been built up in Russia and the U.S.A. At the same time, it has to be remembered that our conditions differ in many respects and their experience will have to be modified to meet our requirements.

I am glad to inform you that the Education Ministry has recently established a Department of Social Education which will take up this problem. The expansion of the Department is, however, necessary in order to make it possible to provide such dramas, films and radio programmes in all Indian languages. I hope that very soon the Ministry will be able to publish complete plans and schemes for this purpose.

The problem of imparting literacy to adults must be taken up along with that of providing basic education to school-going children. For this purpose, we must not only depend upon the teachers who are engaged in such schools, but also call upon government employees of all categories to render such voluntary service as may be possible. This would be necessary, especially in the rural areas where it would not be possible to provide any alternative machinery for adult education. Government employees can render great help both in their spare time by working in night schools and Sunday schools, and also by their example in introducing a 'drive' for literacy among their own subordinates who are illiterate. A time must soon come when literacy will be made one of the conditions for any employment under the Government, and in the meantime, the Government are considering methods by which illiterate government servants may be encouraged to become literate.

I now come to the second broad problem which we have to discuss in this Conference today. This concerns the medium of instruction in the schools and colleges. You are already aware of my views on this question. I hold that there is no place for English *as a medium of instruction* in future India, but at the same time there should be no precipitate action that may damage the cause of education. I hold that the replacement of English as a medium of instruction should be gradual and stage by stage so that there is the least possible interruption or interference with the process of education in the country.

I think it is not necessary to raise the question of the medium of instruction in the primary and secondary stages. Opinion is unanimous that instruction in these stages can be imparted only through the mother tongue. Differences arise only when we come to the stage of education in the universities. Two sharply divided schools of thought hold the field. There are on the one hand those who want one common language as the medium of instruction for all the universities in India. There is another school that holds that education in the universities should be imparted through the regional language. I realise that there are weighty arguments in favour of both the alternatives. The Central Advisory Board, which has just completed its session, had discussed this question and decided to appoint a committee of experts to go into it and submit recommendations. I have been asked to nominate the members of the committee and I will announce the names as soon as this Educational Conference is over.

I placed my own views before the Central Advisory Board and said that we should not change the medium of instruction in the university suddenly but allow a period of five years during which we can prepare for the gradual replacement of English by an Indian language. This would mean that by the sixth year, English would no longer be necessary as the medium of instruction in the universities and an Indian language could take its place. I am glad to inform you that the Board is in full agreement with this view.

One important problem in this connection is in respect of scientific terms, but the Central Advisory Board has tried to solve it by declaring that scientific terms are international, and it would be a serious mistake to try to translate them. I agree with the view of the Board and believe that this is the only rational solution of the difficulty.

I may here refer to the experience of other eastern countries which have already made the experiment of coining new words for scientific and technical terms or importing them from ancient classics. In Egypt the question of scientific terminology became important in the 19th century when she took to modern European education on a large scale. Egypt, as you are aware, has a rich classical langauge from which it can derive most of the scientific terms. In fact, Arabic possessed many terms in Astronomy, Chemistry, Physiology and other Sciences which have since been incorporated into the European languages. It was therefore easy for modern Egypt to coin new Arabic terms in the old moulds and one group in Egypt sought to adopt these Arabic terms for current use in Egyptian education. Many words were thus derived from the Arabic Classics and many new words coined, but experiment soon proved that this was not the happiest solution of the problem. With experience, the Egyptians were convinced that the scientific terms in current usage in modern Europe should be adopted, as they have become international and do not now belong to any particular nation or country. Turkey and

Iraq have also come to the conclusion that in matters of science and knowledge there should be no narrow nationalism but a truly international approach. Similar has been the experience of China and Japan. It must, however, be admitted that for certain technical terms, especially in Philosophy, Logic and Mathematics, many terms are already available in the Indian classical languages and we should certainly use them, especially as in their case there is not the same universal agreement as in the case of scientific terms.

The next problem I want you to consider is the question of reforms in university education. As I have already stated, there can be no question of narrow nationalism in the field of knowledge, but at the same time we must see that there is no wrong perspective of a nation's past history and culture nor a failure to encourage the highest ideals in national character and civilisation. Unfortunately, this has happened in India and I will draw your attention by way of example to the two particular instances of Philosophy and History.

To take up Philosophy first. Greek Philosophy was revived in Europe through the agency of the Arabs who were its commentators and critics during the Middle Ages. It was only during the Renaissance that direct translations were made from Greek and Latin. The result is that in Europe, even the general history of Philosophy starts with the Greeks and ends with modern European Philosophy, touching merely the fringe of Indian and Chinese thought. This is the history of Philosophy which the universities teach in India. But you will all admit that this does not represent the true facts of the development of philosophical thought in the world. No one today can deny the supreme achievements of the Indian mind in the realms of metaphysics and philosophy. It is true that recently Indian Philosophy has been introduced as one of the subjects of study in the Indian universities, but it has not yet gained the position which it deserves in the general history of the philosophy of the world.

One of the earliest schools of Greek Philosophy is that of Pythagoras. The tradition of his visit to India may or may not be true, but his philosophy shows unmistakable marks of the influence of Indian thought. There is little doubt that the Indian mind had already advanced beyond the stage reached by Pythagoras. In fact, almost every school of Greek Philosophy has its counterpart in India. In addition, there are flashes of insight which we do not find in Greek Philosophy. I think that with the exception of two specific branches of learning, the Indian mind has shown itself superior in every respect to the achievements of the Greeks. The only two exceptions are in Logic and Astronomy. Aristotle's 'Logic' is superior in structure and scope to Indian 'Nyaya', while in Astronomy Ptolemy's 'Majestic' is superior to Brahma Gupta's 'Siddhanta' and the work of Aryabhatt. We therefore need a new history of Philosophy in which Indian Philosophy may find its rightful place.

Similary in the field of History. Up to the time of Vincent Smith, there has been no reasonably true or correct History of India in English. Even Smith's History is defective and in many respects out of date. All histories used in our universities today reflect these defects. They suffer from both lacunae and distortions. Nothing is more important today than the reorientation of historical studies from the primary to the highest stages. This is a task which the universities must immediately undertake. The most practical method would be to prepare books in English which can then be translated into all the Indian languages. This would not only mean economy in labour but also give a uniformity in tone and treatment of the subject. I would therefore appeal to all the Indian universities to help in this noble task, and I can assure them that the Central Minister will extend to them every possible help.

Another important question that I would like the Conference to consider is the study of the oriental langauges and culture. We must admit that this has been most inadequate till now. I am sure there will be no difference of opinion that in the future we must make ample provision for remedying this defect. For this, two things are immediately necessary. We must, on the one hand, have a reform and simplification in the methods of teaching and, on the other, we must afford both encouragement and facility for such studies.

Even where oriental subjects have been taught in the universities, they have been treated in a most ravalier fashion. If we look at the plight of Sanskrit or any other of the classical languages in the universities, we cannot deny that this has been done in a most half-hearted fashion in spite of the fact that such studies are essential for a true appreciation of Indian history and culture. What applies to Sanskrit, applies also to the study of Arabic and Persian.

I would like to draw your attention to the provision of facilities for the study of other oriental languages as well and especially of Tibetan and Chinese. It is well known that many of the Buddhist scriptures and literature are preserved in Tibetan, though the original in Sanskrit has been lost. For instance the *Tarka Bhashya* of Mokshankar Gupta could not for long be obtained in Sanskrit but a Tibetan translation was available and till recently that constituted the only source of our access to his thought. It is only lately that the original has been found and published in the Gaekwar Oriental Series.

The accounts of Chinese travellers are similar sources of illumination in respect of ancient India. Other treasures lie hidden in the Chinese language and literature for the interpretation of our ancient history, if only they were accessible to us. For these reasons it is essential that our universities must provide adequate facilities for the study of these oriental languages. We must not forget that in the past India was a centre where the currents of Asiatic thought met and from which flowed out streams which spread to the farthest corner of the Asiatic continent. To appreciate Ancient India truly it is therefore essential to have a knowledge and understanding of other Asiatic languages and cultures as well.

Document No. 47

EXTRACTS FROM THE REPORT OF THE SPEECH OF MAULANA AZAD IN DELHI

17-1-1948

Addressing a gathering of three hundred thousand people in Delhi, on January 17, Abul Kalam Azad said: "Before coming here I went to Gandhiji again and asked him what we should do so that he may break his fast. He gave me seven tests which should be fulfilled by the people. Assurances on these points, he said, must come from responsible people who can guarantee the proper fulfilment of these conditions....No false assurance should be given." The conditions were as follows:

Complete freedom of worship to Muslims at the tomb of Khwaja Qutub-ud-Din Bakhtiar and non-interference with the celebration of the Urs which was due to be held there within a week.

Voluntary evacuation by non-Muslims of all the mosques in the city which were being used for residential purposes or which had been converted into temples.

Free movement of Muslims in areas where they used to stay befor the disturbances.

Full safety to Muslims while travelling by train.

No economic boycott of Muslims

Full discretion to Muslims to invite non-Muslims to live in areas occupied by them and freedom to Muslim evacuees to come back to Delhi if they so desired.

Document No. 48

REPLY DT. 30-1-48 IN THE LEGISLATIVE ASSEMBLY BY MAULANA AZAD TO THE QUESTIONS ASKED ABOUT THE MONETARY GRANTS TO DELHI BRANCH OF HINDUSTAN SCOUT ASSOCIATION

Mr. R.K. Sidhva: (a) Will the Honourable Minister of Education please state whether it is a fact that in reply to a supplementary question raised on started question No. 557 asked on 3rd December, 1947, it was stated that the application of the Delhi Branch of Hindustan Scout Association for a grant was receiving attention?

(b) If so, has the application been considered and the grant passed?

(c) If so, what is the amount of the grant?

(d) Do the Government of India pay annual grant to the All India Hindustan Scout Association (Allahabad)?

(e) If so, what amount?

(f) If not, have Govenment at any time received application from them for such a grant?

(g) What is the amount of grant given to the Boy Scout Association in Delhi and its all India organization?

(h) Is it a fact that the Hindustan Scout Association was started by Indian Leaders and the Boy Scout Association by foreigners?

The Honourable Maulana Abul Kalam Azad: (a), (b) & (c) When I said, Sir that the question of a grant-in-aid to the Hindustan Scout Association was under consideration I meant the application of the central organisation of the Association.

(d), (e) and (f) The application of the Central Organization of the Hindustan Scout Association for a grant has been considered and subject to the vote of the Assembly a sum of Rs. 15,000 has been provided in the budget for 1948-49.

(g) The Delhi Branch of the Boy Scouts Association is in receipt of a grant of Rs. 2,700 from the Local Administration. The Central Organization of the Boy Scouts Association receives a grant of Rs. 15,000 from the Government of India.

(h) The answer is in the affirmative, but eminent Indians are also associated with the latter.

In view of the changed circumstances however, I think that it would be better if both these organisations were to amalgamate. I hope the office bearers concerned will consider this suggestion.

Mr. R.K. Sidhva : You have stated that the Delhi Branch of the Hindustan Scouts Association is in receipt of a grant of Rs. 400 from the Local Administration. The Boy Scouts Association has been granted Rs. 2,700. I would like to know what he Hindustan Scouts Association has been given a relatively lesser amount?

The Honourable Maulana Abul Kalam Azad: You may put this question to the Delhi Administration. The grant which the Delhi Branch of the Association receives has been sanctioned by the Local Administration. The Government of India is not concerned in the matter. There is no doubt that there is difference between the amounts of the grant-in-aid that have been allotted to these associations.

Shri Deshbandhu Gupta: Will the Honourable Minister please issue necessary instructions to the Delhi Administration that the amount of grant to the Delhi Association may be raised to Rs. 2700?

The Honourable Maulana Abul Kalam Azad: This is being considered.

Shri H.V. Kamath : Will the Honourable Minister please state if the Girl Guides also form part of the Boy Scouts Association?

The Honourable Maulana Abul Kalam Azad: I cannot say this..

Mr. R.K. Sidhva: Is it a fact that the Boy Scouts Association owe their allegiance to the King and the Hindustan Scouts Association to the country?

The Honourable Maulana Abul Kalam Azad: Anyway, so far as the allegiance to the King is concerned, that also still applies to the Indian Dominion.

Mr. R.K. Sidhva : Is it not a fact that even up till now the Boy Scouts Association owe their allegiance to the King and the Hindustan Scouts Association to the country?

The Honourable Maulana Abul Kalam Azad: I have just stated that these organisations were started under the circumstances existing in the past and we should now endeavour that both these should be amalgamated.

Seth Govind Das : Is the Honourable Minister aware of the fact that so far as the Delhi Administration is concerned, all questions relating thereto are asked in the floor of this House and the responsibility for answering them devovles on the Ministers in this Assembly?

The Honourable Maulana Abul Kalam Azad : What I mean to say is that I am not aware of the circumstances under which the Local Government sanctioned the grant of Rs. 400 to the Delhi Branch. Moreover I do not know the details which led to this decision. But the question as to why a lesser amount was granted to them is already receiving attention.

Mr. R.K. Sidhva: Is it not a fact that efforts were made by the Government previously that both these should be amalgamated? But the Members of the Boy Scouts Association do not want to abjure their allegiance to the King. What steps do the Government of India propose to take under these circumstances? Do the Government intend to suspend payment of the grant and insist on their renouncing allegiance to the King?

The Honourable Maulana Abul Kalam Azad : We should try that both these should be amalgamated.

Shri Deshbandhu Gupta : Is it a fact that the Delhi Scouts Association submitted a representation to the effect that they should also be granted the same amount as was given to the Boy Scouts Association.

The Honourable Maulana Abul Kalam Azad : I cannot give any reply to this. I do not know.

Document No. 49

REPLY DT. 30-1-48 IN THE LEGISLATIVE ASSEMBLY BY MAULANA AZAD TO THE QUESTIONS ABOUT THE POLICY RE-ADOPTION OF ONE INDIAN LANGUAGE IN PLACE OF ENGLISH AS OFFICIAL LANGUAGE IN CENTRE AND PROVINCES

Mr. R.K. Sidhva : (a) Will the Honourable Minister of Education please state whether it is a fact that he stated at the last convocation address of the Patna University that a limit of 5 years time be fixed for continuing the English Language alongwith an Indian language and that at the sixth year only one Indian language be used as the official language, in Central and Provincial Government?

(b) Is that the decision of the Government of India?

(c) If so, has any province discarded the English language altogether for official business and adopted only one Indian language?

(d) If so, which are those province and do Government propose to issue instructions to these provinces to continue English language alongwith an Indian Language for official purpose for 5 years?

The Honourable Maulana Abul Kalam Azad: (a) Yes.

(b) No. This is my personal opinion, and I hope that when the time comes, Government will pay the necessary attention to this point of view.

(c) As far as Government is aware, no Province has done so up till now.

(d) Does not arise.

Seth Govind Das : Is the Honourable Minister aware of the fact that the linguists in India believe that there is obviously no necessity to continue teaching in the English language in the country for five years?

The Honourable Maulana Abul Kalam Azad : This is a matter of opinion.

Maulana Hasrat Mohani : So far as the U.P. Government is concerned, I would like to tell the Honourable Minister that they finished with the English language from the very start. At present no business is concerned in U.P. in any other language except Hindi. The Government Gazette is also printed in Hindi. And moreover all the circulars are issued in this language. They have discarded English for all purposes.

Mr. Speaker : The Honourable Member will see that it is for the Minister to give information and he should put a question.

Maulana Hasrat Mohani : This is with reference to part (c) of the question.

Is the Honourable Minister aware of the fact that U.P. government have altogether done away with the English language and introduced the Hindi language so that the people who know Urdu only may not be able to understand anything?

The Honourable Maulana Abul Kalam Azad : It is within the knowledge of the Government of India that in U.P. the Government Gazette is published in English also.

Document No. 50

ANSWERS BY MAULANA AZAD, DT. 5-2-1948 TO THE QUESTIONS ASKED IN THE LEGISLATIVE ASSEMBLY ABOUT THE TECHNICAL TRAINING OF INDIAN STUDENTS IN FOREIGN COUNTRIES

Mr. R.K. Sidhva : (a) Will the Honourable Minister of Education please state how many scholars are intended to be sent to the United Kingdom, the United States of America and other foreign countries for technical training in the year 1948?

(b) Are the selections made province-wise or otherwise?

(c) Has the attention of Government been drawn to a statement issued on the 12th December, 1947 from London by Miss Shanti Ranga Rao, the Indian Educationist, who was sent to the United Kingdom on special Government deputation.

(d) Are Government aware that she deprecated the idea of sending students to foreign countries for training?

(e) Are Government aware that she strongly recommends to Government the building and development of Universities in India without any further delay?

(f) Do Government propose to accept the suggestions made by her?

(g) If not, what is Government's future policy?

The Honourable Maulana Abul Kalam Azad: (a) The question is still under consideration in the light of the interim report submitted by the Overseas Scholarships Committee, which was appointed to examine the overseas scholarships in all its aspects.

(b) Some scholars are selected by Provinces and others by the Central Government directly according to whether they are intended to serve a Provincial Government or the Central Government on their return.

(c) Yes. Miss Ranga Rao was sent to London in May 1947 for six months to provide temporary assistance in the High Commissioner's Education Department, which was inadequately staffed.

(d) & (e) Yes, as far as her views are indicated by the press report referred to by the Honourable Member.

(f) & (g) It is Government's policy to give every possible assistance to the expansion and improvement of facilities for University Education in the country, but Government have been advised by the Expert Committee, referred to in part (a) that it is necessary for some time yet to send selected students abroad for advanced studies and training.

Mr. R.K. Sidhva : I want to enquire from the Honourable Minister for Education what is the annual expenditure?

The Honourable Maulana Abul Kalam Azad: The expenditure incurred during the current financial year is Rs. 27,50,000 and Rs. 28,50,000 have been provided for the ensuing year.

Mr. R.K. Sidhva : Is it a fact that scholars are being sent to foreign countries for taking in subjects for which training facilities are available in India ; or they are sent for training in those subjects only for which no arrangements exist here?

The Honourable Maulana Abul Kalam Azad : The scheme which is being approved after careful consideration will provide that for subjetcs for which arrangements can be made in India, scholars will not be sent abroad.

Mr. R.K. Sidhva : Is it a fact that training for nurses is given abroad which facilities for such training exist in India. Moreover they are not able to secure admission into the University Hospitals there?

The Honourable Maulana Abul Kalam Azad : Some scholars were sent for this purpose during the year 1945-46, but the Government will consider this matter for future.

Shri Gokulbhai Doulatram Bhatt : Is any selection made from States as well while selecting scholars?

The Honourable Maulana Abul Kalam Azad : The selection is made from Provinces and the Centre. No separate circulars are issued for States.

Seth Govind Das : Will the Honourable Minister please see that first of all only those scholars should be sent to foreign countries who have uptil now been selected, and until all of them have been sent, no fresh scholars should be selected.

The Honourable Maulana Abul Kalam Azad : This has been stopped.

Mr. Tajamul Hussain : I would like to know if the Government have got any such scheme under which the entire amount that is spent over the training of scholars may be recovered from them when they return after completion of their training.

The Honourable Maulana Abul Kalam Azad: No provision to this effect was made in this scheme. This scheme was introduced with a view to spend more money on education so as to increase the resources of the country. In future the Government will consider over this matter which is already under consideration.

Shri H.V. Kamath : Will the Honourable Minister please state if apart from England and America, some scholars will also be sent to other European countries such as Russia and France?

The Honourable Maulana Abul Kalam Azad : I have just informed you that this scheme is being considered *de novo*. I cannot give any detailed information in the matter at the moment.

Prof. N.G. Ranga : Are any steps being taken to see that these scholars on their return to India after the completion of their studies are suitably employed in Government Departments?

The Honourable Maulana Abul Kalam Azad : The selection is made after keeping this thing in view. The scholars are sent from Provinces as well. The subjects in which they want training are considered over by the Centre before they are sent abroad.

Mr. R.K. Sidhva : Is it a fact that the British Universities have decided that out of the total vacancies, ninety per cent thereof should be allotted to ex-servicemen.

The Honourable Maulana Abul Kalam Azad : This is correct. Such a decision has been arrived at there. The Government will consider over it in future in this light.

Seth Govind Das : Will the Honourable Minister please consider that when Rs. 27-28 lacs is annually spent over this work and a major portion of which is given to the Universities for opening of new departments not already existing there, these scholars should be provided with necessary training facilities here instead of being sent abroad.

The Honourable Maulana Abul Kalam Azad : It is already receiving attention of the Government.

Shri M. Ananthasayanam Ayyangar : Sir, is it not a fact that in the recent conference of the Central Board of Education it was urged that instead of sending raw graduates or students from here for further studies, persons who are all employed in technical and other professions in this country and have had some experience may be sent instead for getting some further experience by way of refresher courses in foreign countries so that they may be useful?

The Honourable Maulana Abul Kalam Azad : Just as I have stated the whole matter is before the Government and receiving consideration.

Shri M. Ananthasayanam Ayyangar : May I know, Sir, whether in the Selection Board sufficient representation was given to Members of this House so that they also sit along with them and evolve or carry out any schemes based on the suggestions made on the floor of this House?

The Honourable Maulana Abul Kalam Azad: The Government will consider over it.

Document No. 51

LETTER FROM MAULANA AZAD TO SARDAR PATEL

New Delhi

9 February, 1948

My dear Vallabhbhai,

The Education Ministery has been trying to absorb most of the refugee teachers from Pakistan areas, who were in Government service and who have now migrated to Delhi. Now, however, I find that a number of refugee teachers from certain Indian States, such as Bahawalpur, are coming to Delhi. These teachers were in State service in the States, but as rules stand at present, we cannot classify them as Government servants for the puroses of Government service here. My personal opinion is that these refugee teachers, who were in State service, should be accorded the same treatment as refugee teachers who were in Government service. Unless this is done, it will be difficult to absorb these State service teachers in Government institutions.

I should be glad to have your opinion as to how we should classify these refugee teachers from the Indian States which they have had to leave on account of communal disturbances.

Yours sincerely,
Abul Kalam Azad

The Hon'ble Sardar Vallabhbhai Patel
New Delhi.

Document No. 52

ANSWERS BY MAULANA AZAD, DT. 9-2-1948 TO THE QUESTIONS ASKED IN THE LEGISLATIVE ASSEMBLY ABOUT THE SHIFTING OF CONSTITUENT COLLEGES OF DELHI UNIVERSITY TO UNIVERSITY SITE

Shri Deshbandhu Gupta : (a) Will the Honourable Minister of Education be pleased to state whether Government still adhere to their declared policy of shifting the Constituent Colleges of the University of Delhi to the University site?

(b) What are the financial implications of the scheme and how long will it take to implement this policy?

(c) Are Government aware that it entails heavy expenditure to Government and the managements of the colleges concerned and add to the difficulties of the students in regard to expenditure and convenience?

(d) If so, do Government propose to consider the desirability of dropping the Idea?

The Honourable Maulana Abul Kalam Azad: (a) Yes, Sir,

(b) The Government of India have still under consideration the question of the grant that may have to be given to the colleges to enable them to shift to the University enclave. It is hoped that it will take about two years to implement the first phase of the move of the colleges to the University enclave.

(c) & (d) The shifting of the colleges to the University enclave does involve expenditure but this expenditure would be necessary in the interest of co-operative teaching.

Shri Deshbandhu Gupta : Will the Honourable Minister please state whether he has received any representation which contains a proposal to drop this scheme?

The Honourable Maulana Abul Kalam Azad : No.

Shri Deshbandhu Gupta : Is it not realised that this scheme has been in existence for several years past and the colleges have still to extend their buildings? How can, under such circumstances the colleges be expected to carry this scheme out for extending their buildings in the future?

The Honourable Maulana Abul Kalam Azad : The Honourable Members are not unaware of the difficulties experienced in the construction of buildings. But it is hoped that this scheme will be enforced early.

Shri Deshbandhu Gupta : Will any priority be given to the Colleges for purchasing the building material, so that they may be able to secure the material without any difficulty and construct the buildings?

The Honourable Maulana Abul Kalam Azad : Efforts will certainly be made.

Document No. 53

ANSWERKS BY MAULANA AZAD DATED 9-2-48 TO THE QUESTIONS ASKED IN THE LEGISLATIVE ASSEMBLY ABOUT THE SHIFTING BACK OF RAMJAS COLLEGE, DELHI AND CONTINUANCE OF AGRICULTURAL COLLEGE AT ANAND PARBAT

Shri Deshbandhu Gupta : (a) Will the Honourable Minister of Education be pleased to state whether Government are aware of the fact that Ramjas College, Delhi was shifted from Anand Parbat to Daryaganj when Anand Parbat was requisitioned by the Government of India, in 1942?

(b) Are Government further aware that at present Ramjas Higher Secondary School is handicapped for want of sufficient accommodation for day scholars as well as for resident students?

(c) Are Government aware that Ramjas College authorities have provided hostel accommodation for some of their students at Anand Parbat which is four miles from the College?

(d) Do Government propose to consider the advisability of allowing Ramjas College to shift back to Anand Parbat?

(e) How long do Government intend to continue the Agricultural College at Anand Parbat?

The Honourable Maulana Abul Kalam Azad: (a) Yes Sir.

(b) & (c) No, Sir.

(d) As the Government of India desire that the College should soon shift to the Delhi University enclave it is not desirable to allow the Ramjas College to shift to the Anand Parbat. The buildings at the Anand Parbat do not belong to the Ramjas College Society which runs this College, but belong to the Ramjas Trust with which the College has no concern.

(e) The Agriculture College at Anand Parbat will be shifted as soon as suitable land is made available in or near Delhi and the necessary buildings are put up.

Shri Deshbandhu Gupta: Will the buildings at the Anand Parbat be returned to the Ramjas College when the Agricultural College shifts to its own buildings?

The Honourable Maulana Abul Kalam Azad : The Government have not considered over this matter.

Document No. 54

ANSWERS BY MAULANA AZAD DT. 9-2-1948 IN THE LEGISLATIVE ASSEMBLY TO THE QUESTIONS RAISED REGARDING THE POST-WAR PLANS FOR TRAINING OF TECHNICAL PERSONNEL AND FACILITIES TO ANDHRA UNIVERSITY

Shri V.C. Kesava Rao : Will the Honourable Minister of Education be pleased to state:

(a) Whether there are any post-war plans for training an adequate number of men in mechanical, electrical, highway, civil and marine engineering.

(b) The facilities Government propose to grant to the Andhra University to train this kind of personnel; and

(c) The number of Andhra students sent to overseas universities for higher training in the subjects mentioned in part (a) above?

The Honourable Maulana Abul Kalam Azad:

(a) Yes. Government have been sending students abroad for higher studies in various branches of Engineering under the Overseas Scholarships Scheme.

With regard to facilities for training Engineers in India, Government propose, to start with, to establish as early as possible within the next three years or so, two regional Higher Technical Institutions near Calcutta and Bombay. There is also a scheme for strengthening and improving the existing technological institutions in India.

(b) The All India Council for Technical Education, appointed by Government, has recommended that a recurring grant of upto 70,000 and a capital grant of upto Rs. 5½ lakhs should be made from the Central Revenues for the improvement of Chemical Technology Department of the Jaipur Vikram Dev College of the Andhra University. This proposal is being given urgent consideration by Government.

(c) So far as the Central Scholars are concerned, the information is not available as the candidates are required to indicate in their applications only the Province or State and not its particular part to which they belong. With regard to Provincial Scholars, the Government of Madras may perhaps be able to give the information desired by the Honourable Member, but the information with the Government of India is incomplete.

Shri M. Ananthasayananm Ayyangar : How many students are proposed to be sent for any of these courses overseas during the ensuing year?

The Honourable Maulana Abul Kalam Azad : The overseas scholarships Scheme has been discounted this year. The Government are considering over the recommendations made by Doctor Rai's Committee so that this work may be started on new lines in future.

Shri V.C. Kesava Rao : May I know the number of Andhra graduates undergoing training in foreign universities at the present moment?

The Honourable Maulana Abul Kalam Azad : I have already stated this that it is not possible for the Centre to give this information, because Andhra is not a separate Province. It is a part of the Madras Province. So far as I have been able to ascertain probably eight or nine scholars from Andhra were definitely sent for undergoing training in technical education.

Dr. B. Pattabhi Sitaramayya : The Honourable Member who has put the question does not understand the language in which the question has been answered and hence he is repeating his question. If possible you may, Sir order the answer to be rendered either into Telugu or English.

Mr. Speaker : That may be done after the question hour is over.

Shri M. Ananthasayanan Ayyangar : Arising out of the answer to clause (a) of the question, may I know what post-war plans are for training an adequate number of students in mechanical, electrical and other kinds of engineering? At what stage is the proposal to open technological institutions in four places in India, *viz.*, Bombay, Calcutta, Delhi and one in the South? Has anything been done in this direction and if so, what progress has been made?

The Honourable Maulana Abul Kalam Azad : The technical Council had recommended that four higher technical institutions should be opened, two of which should be located at Bombay and Calcutta. The work is in hand and it is hoped that both these will start functioning within three years.

Shri M. Ananthasayanam Ayyangar : May I know what is going on in Madras?

The Honourable Maulana Abul Kalam Azad : The matter concerning the South has not yet been taken in hand as it was not possible to set up all the four institutions simultaneously.

Shri M. Ananthasayanam Ayyangar : Why has it not been taken in hand?

The Honourable Maulana Abul Kalam Azad : I have already answered this.

Shri M. Ananthasayanam Ayyanagar : When will this be taken up?

The Honourable Maulana Abul Kalam Azad : The Government will try to take this up soon.

Shri V.C. Kesava Rao : In view of the fact that the Andhra Province will be separated soon, will Government consider the question of training more men of Andhra for the efficient administration of the future Government?

Mr. Speaker : That is more or less hypothetical today?

Shri Biswanath Das : While deciding to start technological institutions in Bombay, Calcutta, Delhi and in Madras may I know how the Government propose to cater to the needs of provinces which are less developed and want more technological institutions?

The Honourable Maulana Abul Kalam Azad: The provinces cannot be kept in view while starting such institutions. The Council had recommended that these should be established at four places and four separate circles set up for this purpose.

Document No. 55

LETTER FROM SARDAR PATEL TO MAULANA AZAD

New Delhi
11 February, 1948

My dear Maulana,

Thank you for your letter of 9 February 1948 regarding Bahawalpur State employeers.

The question which you have raised has been considered by me a number of times, but I have found it impossible to agree to the proposal made. The Transfer Bureau is intended exlusively for Government employees who had to flee from Pakistan, and have sought refuge here or who were formerly Government employees in Pakistan who opted for service in India. Apart from the fact that we have more than enough already, and it would be physically impossible to accept any more commitments from non-Government employees, once we open the door to outsiders there would be practically no reason whatsover to exclude many other categories of employees, as for example, District Board and Port Trust employees. We have also felt that, while we do owe a moral responsibility to refugees in general, including Bahawalpur State employees and others whom I have mentioned above, Government owes a special obligation to take into service, as far as possible, former Government employes in Pakistan.

In the circumstances, I much regret it is not possible for me to agree that Bahawalpur State employees should be treated on a par with Government servants. I would have no objection, however, to their being considered after our commitments in regard to Government servants are fulfilled.

Yours sincerely,
Vallabhbhai Patel

The Hon'ble Maulana Abul Kalam Azad
Minister for Education
New Delhi.

Document No. 56

ANSWERS DATED 23-2-1948 IN THE CONSTITUENT ASSEMBLY OF INDIA TO THE QUESTIONS ASKED IN CONNECTION WITH EDUCATIONAL INSTITUTIONS UNDER MINISTRIES OTHER THAN HEALTH AND AGRICULTURE BY MAULANA AZAD

Shri V.C. Kesava Rao: (a) Will the Honourable Minister of Education be pleased to state whether any Ministries other than those of Health and Agriculture are in charge of Educational Institutions engaged in higher training of technical personnel?

(b) What are the reasons for dividing the responsibility in the matter of higher technical education among different Ministries?

The Honourable Maulana Abul Kalam Azad: (a) The only other Ministry concerned with Higher Technical Education is the Ministry of Works, Mines and Power who have the responsibility for administering the Indian School of Mines, Dhanbad.

Various other Ministries of the Government of India *e.g.*, (i) Ministry of Works, Mines and Power, (ii) Ministry of Communication, and (iii) Ministry of Transport, arrange for the practical training of personnel to meet their special requirements.

(b) This is the old arrangement and for the present it is being continued. If Government feels that any change is necessary in the interest of higher education, Government will examine it in due course.

Shri V.C. Kesava Rao: I want a translation.

Mr. Speaker : It is rather difficult. Well, he may have it later on.

Shri H.V. Kamath: He is asking for a translation for putting supplementaries.

Mr. Speaker: It is unfortunate.

Document No. 57

(ANSWERS TO THE QUESTIONS ASKED IN THE CONSTITUENT ASSEMBLY OF INDIA (LEGISLATIVE) BY MAULANA AZAD ABOUT THE INSTITUTIONS AFFILIATED TO ALL INDIA COUNCIL FOR TECHNICAL EDUCATION AND VARIOUS SYLLABUSES ON 23-2-1948)

Shri Mohan Lal Saksena: (a) Will the Honourable Minister of Education be pleased to state how many institutions have so far been affiliated to the All-India Council for Technical Education?

(b) Have the All-India Board of Studies prepared the syllabuses for different All-India Diploma courses? If not, why not?

(c) Are Government aware of the hardship which students experience in the absence of proper syllabuses?

The Honourable Maulana Abul Kalam Azad: (a) So far 7 institutions have been affiliated to the All-India Board of Technical Studies in Commerce and Business Administration. The Delhi Polytechnic, is in addition affiliated to the All-India Boards of Technical Studies in: (i) Architecture and Regional Planning, (ii) Chemical Engineering and Chemical Technology, and (iii) Engineering and Metallurgy.

(b) So far the syllabuses for the following All-India Diploma courses have been prepared: (i) Commerce, (ii) Chemical Engineering, (iii) Engineering (Civil, Electrical and Mechanical), and (iv) Architecture.

Syllabi for the other All-India Diploma courses, *viz.*, Textile Technology and Applied Art are still in draft form and will be approved by the appropriate All-India Boards in due course.

I should, however, mention that the syllabus in Engineering and in Chemical Engineering are being revised.

(c) It is difficult to see what hardship the Honourable Member is referring to as no examinations are conducted for the courses for which no syllabi have been prepared.

The Honourable Maulana Abul Kalam Azad: I have just now referred to those schools for which syllabi have been prepared, and to those also for which they are being prepared. It is quite possible that some changes were being made, but so far I have no information.

Shri Mohan Lal Saksena: Is the Honourable Minister aware that the Syllabi for most of the classes in Polytechnic School are not ready. Some are ready and some have been altered.

Shri Mohan Lal Saksena: May I request the Honourable Minister to make further enquiries in this matter. I have some information and have come to know from students that there are two or three such schools whose syllabus has been changed twice and still the students do not know under which syllabus they will be examined?

The Honourable Maulana Abul Kalam Azad: So far as I know, no such thing has happened, but all the same an enquiry will be made.

Document No. 58

ANSWERS DATED 23-2-1948 BY MAULANA AZAD TO THE QUESTIONS ASKED IN THE LEGISLATIVE ASSEMBLY

AFFILIATION OF DELHI POLYTECHNIC TO DELHI UNIVERSITY

Shri Mohan Lal Saksena: (a) Will the Honourable Minister of Education be pleased to state whether Government are aware of the assurance given by Government to the Legislative Assembly in 1946 that the Delhi Polytechnic will be affiliated to the Delhi University? If so, why has it not been so far affiliated?

(b) Have any steps taken in that direction and when is it likely to be affiliated to the Delhi University?

(c) Are Government aware that the delay in affiliation has been causing inconvenience and financial loss to the students?

The Honourable Maulana Abul Kalam Azad: (a) I am afraid that the Honourable Member is not quite correct in stating that an assurance was given to the Legislative Assembly in 1946 that the Delhi Polytechnic would be affiliated to the Delhi University.

A statement was however made to the effect that when the contemplated development of the Delhi Polytechnic has been completed, it was anticipated, that the Polytechnic would be recognised as the Technological Department of the Delhi University.

(b) The Government have formulated certain development plans some of which are now well on the way. An application for affiliation to the Delhi University was made in October, 1946. The Governing Body of the Polytechnic which was constituted early in 1947, have, after examining the development programme and reviewing the progress made so far recommended on the 22nd October, 1947, the affiliation of the Engineering Department of the Delhi Polytechnic immediately and of certain other departments thereafter. The University has already appointed a Sub-Committee of the Executive Council. This Sub-Committee is understood to have made certain recommendations to the Executive Council.

(c) The Government do not agree that the delay in affiliation is causing inconvenience and financial loss to the students since the students now undergoing to the courses of instruction were admitted to the Diploma courses offered at the Institution.

Shri Mohan Lal Saksena: Is not the Honourable Minister aware that at the time of making appointments this fact is kept in view that only people with University Degrees are appointed and no heed is paid to the Diploma of that Institution?

The Honourable Maulana Abul Kalam Azad: This Institution was opened for diploma classes. It has a special procedure and the same procedure is being followed uptil now. It is expected that it shall be affiliated to that.

Seth Govind Das: Do Government consider that so far as Government services are concerned no distinction shall be made between such degrees and University degrees?

The Honourable Maulana Abul Kalam Azad: Government are considering this matter.

Shri Deshbandhu Gupta: Do Government consider that the educational standard also of students should be raised? It should not be merely a concern of Universities.

The Honourable Maulana Abul Kalam Azad: However, it is so intricate matter that it shall be considered in future. No promise can be made in this connection at present.

Shri Deshbandhu Gupta: Do Government keep in view that it is very essential to make arrangements for imparting practical engineering training in factories to students, to whom no opportunity has been provided so far?

The Honourable Maulana Abul Kalam Azad: Certainly this aspect of the matter requires serious consideration, and it will be considered.

Document No. 59

ANSWERS DATED 23-2-1948 BY MAULANA AZAD TO THE QUESTIONS ASKED IN THE LEGISLATIVE ASSEMBLY OF INDIA

PUBLICATION OF SOUTH INDIAN INSCRIPTIONS COLLECTED BY ARCHAEOLOGICAL DEPARTMENT

Shri S.V. Krishnamurthy Rao: (a) Will the Honourable Minister of Education be pleased to state the approximate number of South Indian inscriptons so far collected by the Archaeological Department?

(b) How many of these have been published *in extenso*?

(c) When are the rest likely to be published?

(d) When was the last report on South Indian Epigraphy published and why have further reports not been issued?

(e) What are the reasons for the delay?

(f) How far is this delay due to the Government Press not being able to print in time?

(g) Is the Department allowed to print their publications in non-Government presses?

The Honourable Maulana Abul Kalam Azad: (a) 29,500.

(b) 8,300.

(c) The rest are likely to take about 10 years for publication.

(d) The last Report on South Indian Epigraphy was issued for the years 1937-38, and the last volume of South Indian Inscriptions was published in 1941. Further reports and volumes could not be issued due to the fact that the Government of India placed restrictions on the printing of such publications for the duration of war. Now that the restrictions have been removed, two Reports on South Indian Epigraphy and one volume of South Indian Inscriptions are in the press.

(e) and (f) In the case of the Report, the Government Press is not responsible for the delay. This is due to the circumstances explained above. In the case of the volume of South Indian Inscriptions which was sent to the Madras Government Press in 1940, pressure has already been brought to bear with a view to expediting the volume.

(g) Only when it is absolutely essential to do so. In the case of Epigraphy, however, the difficulty is that a majority of the non-Government presses are unable to supply the necessary fonts.

Shri T. Channiah: Sir, may I know the reason why the Honourable Minister of Education is determined not to give his replies in English?

Mr. Speaker: That does not arise out of this question.

Shri K. Santhanam: Even those of us who have picked up a little Hindi are unable to follow him.

Mr. Speaker: I will give Honourable Members a translation of the reply.

(English translation of the reply was then read out.)

Shri T.T. Krishnamachari: May I know if the reply to part (c) is due to the fact that Government want to emphasise the antiquarian value of these relics and therefore they are allowing ten years to elapse before they are published?

The Honourable Maulana Abul Kalam Azad: Honourable Members are aware that they are a large number of them and only eight thousands out of twenty-nine thousands have been published so far. This work is of such a nature that it cannot be easily accomplished. It has been estimated that it will take about ten years or less to publish all of them.

Shri H.V. Kamath: Is the Honourable Minister in a position to state to which age the oldest of the twenty-nine thousand five hundred and ten inscriptions belongs?

Mr. Speaker: Order, order; that will be going into the contents of these things.

Shri Deshbandhu Gupta: Is it a fact that all the proceedings of the Archaeological Department are published in English, and will Government consider publishing them in Hindi?

The Honourable Maulana Abul Kalam Azad: Yes. This matter will be considered. So far all the proceedings of Government of India have been carried on in English.

Shri R.R. Diwakar: In view of the importance of these inscriptions, will the Government consider the publication of a summary of the epigraphic records that have been collected?

The Honourable Maulana Abul Kalam Azad: Yes, it will be considered and at least separately in future.

Shri S.V. Krishnamurthy Rao: Should any of the private presses come forward to print these reports to the satisfaction of Government, will the Government re-consider the position to entrust some of this work to the private presses?

The Honourable Maulana Abul Kalam Azad: Government will certainly consider it.

Document No. 60

ANSWERS DATED 23-2-1948 BY MAULANA AZAD TO THE QUESTIONS ASKED IN THE INDIAN LEGISLATIVE ASSEMBLY

TERMS OF SERVICE OF DIRECTOR GENERAL OF ARCHAEOLOGY

Shri S.V. Krishnamurthy Rao: (a) Will the Honourable Minister of Education be pleased to state who is the present Director-General of Archaeology and when his term is expiring? Did he opt to go to Pakistan and if so, why could he not go?

(b) Is his term being extended and if so, why?

(c) Is it the policy of the present Government not to entertain non-Indians in key positions?

(d) If so, is that policy being followed in the case of this appointment?

(e) If not, why not?

The Honourable Maulana Abul Kalam Azad: (a) Dr. R.E. Mortimer Wheeler is the present Director General of Archaeology. The term of his appointment is due to expire on the 23rd April, 1948. He did not express any preference for service either in India or Pakistan. The Partition Council, however, decided that as the Pakistan Government did not need his services, he should be retained in India till the expiry of his term of contract.

(b) No.

(c) The appointment of non-Indians to civil posts under the Government of India is made in very exceptional circumstances and on a contract basis for short periods.

(d) Yes. The question of appointing an Indian to succeed Dr. Wheeler is under consideration.

(e) Does not arise.

Mr. R.K. Sidhva: Has the Director General personally applied or not for going to Pakistan?

The Honourable Maulana Abul Kalam Azad: I have said just now that at the time of establishment of the Partition Council no application from Dr. Wheeler here?

Shri T.T. Krishnamachari: May I ask the Honourable Minister if it is a fact that the Pakistan Government probably finds it beneficial for them to keep Dr. Wheeler here?

Mr. Speaker: That is a matter of opinion.

Document No. 61

ANSWERS DATED 23-2-1948 BY MAULANA AZAD TO THE QUESTIONS ASKED IN THE LEGISLATIVE ASSEMBLY OF INDIA

NATIONAL MUSUEM FOR INDIA AND PROVINCIAL MUSEUMS

Shri S.V. Krishnamurthy Rao: (a) Will the Honourable Minister of Education be pleased to state whether it is a fact that the Government propose to have a National Museum for India? If so, what is its general plan?

(b) Is it going to be located in some central place in India? If not, why not?

(c) Are there Provincial Museums in different Provinces? If so, in how many provinces?

(d) Do Government propose to encourage Provincial Museums by lending expert hands and by giving adequate grants?

(e) What special steps do Government propose to take in order that those museums may be of the maximum educative value?

The Honourable Maulana Abul Kalam Azad: (a) The Government have accepted in principle the Scheme for the establishing of a Central National Museum of Art, Archaeology and Anthropology in India. The general plan of the Museum is embodied in the report *of the Committee, a copy of which is placed on the table.

(b) It is proposed to locate the Museum in New Delhi.

(c) There are provincial museums, or museums of similar status, in all provinces except in the newly created province of the East Punjab.

(d) It is intended that aprart from being an exhibiting institution, the new National Museum will provide expert assistance, advice and training for the museum-service for India as a whole. As for grants to provincial Museums, the Central Advisory Board of Archaeology at their meeting held at Baroda in September 1947, appointed a

---

* Not printed in these Debates. A copy has been placed in the Library of the House – *Ed of D.*

Museum Committee to go into the whole question of the principles of State-aid to provincial museums. Government will take necessary decision in the light of the recommendations of this Committee, which are still awaited.

(e) The development of local museums is primarily the concern of the Provincial Governments but on the establishment of the National Museum. Government will be prepared to render such help as training for museum service, expert advice and temporary loan of experts, etc.

Shri S.V. Krishnamurthy Rao: May I have the reply in English?

Mr. Speaker: It will not be possible in every case to give a translation. The Honourable Member should make an effort to understand Hindustani. That is the best course.

Haji Abdus Sattar Haji Ishaq Seth: Before the Honourable Members are able to follow this, the Government should make some arrangements. They have their Assistant Whips and their Whip. I certainly r sent your being asked to read the answers every time.

Shri H.R. Guruv Reddy: In cases like this would it not be possible for the Minister concerned to answer in English the particular member who has put the question?

Mr. Speaker: That will lead to supplying the answers to the members beforehand. I am afraid that practice will not be a very desirable or proper one. Sometimes this difficulty will arise and when I find that a question is important, I will read the translation; not otherwise. This should not be taken as a practice necessarily to be followed by the Chair.

Shri H.R. Guruv Reddy: Would you permit us to put questions in our own mother tongue?

Mr. Speaker: Yes. The Honourable Member may put such a question but if it is not understood by the Honourable Minister, the Honourable Member will not have a chance of having it translated. He will be at liberty, of course, to put his questions.

Shri K. Hanumanthaiya: When every other Minister answers in English, this Honourable Minister may also do so.

Mr. Speaker: The Honourable Members are not aware as to what passed in this House before the 15th August. Even then it was considered essential for national self-respect that our proceedings should be conducted in Hindustani and as far as possible. The situation has much changed since 15th August and it is up to Honourable Members to see that they try to pick up the language.

The Honourable Pandit Jawaharlal Nehru: I am perfectly prepared to answer questions in Hindustani in future.

Dr. B. Pattabhi Sitaramayya: That does not solve the difficulty. It is all easy for one whose mother tongue is Hindustani to impose on others his mother tongue. But it is a real difficulty which must be faced by the House and I wish the Speaker would give this his attention and also the Government of the day, instead of forcing people to remain silent in their ignorance. Some arrangement must be made simultaneouly to present these answers. I do not feel the grievance so much because I understand something of the language. But even I do not feel equal to the highly Arabised and Persianised Hindustani of the Maulana. Even ten years hence, I guarantee that South Indians who learn Hindustani will not be able to follow such Hindustani.

Prof. N.G. Ranga: I do not think it would be derogatory to our national dignity and uniformity if we were to make it convenient for speakers speaking in Hindi to have their speeches translated into English and for people speaking in English to have their speeches translated into Hindi. In most of the Assemblies in other parts of the world wherever there are these bi-lingual or tri-lingual and multi-lingual needs such facilities are made and especially in international gatherings......

Mr. Speaker: I do not think any further arguments is necessary. While I have indicated that it is not quite proper to insist that answers be given in English, I have already tried to help members by giving translations when the question is an important one. At the same time I made a request to those people who do not understand Hindustani to make an effort: because in the new set up of things, we are going in the direction of having the proceedings in the common language. Whether what is spoken it is in Persianised Urdu or Sanskritised Hindi, it is a different matter. I do not wish to have any further discussion. I shall give the translation as the question seems to be of some importance. But I will leave it to myself to decide as to whether a question is so important as to deserve to be translated.

Pandit Lakshmi Kanta Maitra: What about the supplementaries to be raised on that?

Mr. Speaker: I cannot translate each and every answer.

Pandit Lakshmi Kanta Maitra: Therefore, at least so far as this particular portfolio of this particular Honourable Minister is concerned, he may be kindly allowed to permit some of his Secretaries to read out the replies, for it is not a matter of joke.

Mr. Speaker: That point has been solved. No Secretary can come into the House. No further argument is necessary. Order, order. I may state that whenever an Honourable Minister uses a special expression, he tries to give the English equivalent.

Order, order. The reply to the question is as follows:

(English translation of the reply was then read out.)

Seth Govind Das: Are Government aware that the Calcutta Museum is a Provincial Museum? It was built at the time when Calcutta was Capital. Do Government consider, now that the All India Museum is to be established in Delhi all the selected articles from the Calcutta Museum will be removed from that place and brought to Delhi.

The Honourable Maulana Abul Kalam Azad: So far Calcutta Museum is the Indian Museum. The proposal will be considered at the time of execution of National Museum Scheme.

Shri H.V. Kamath: Who were the members of the Committee which was formed in 1945 and whose report was laid on the table of the House?

The Honourable Maulana Abul Kalam Azad: Their names are: Sir John Sargent, Mr. H.A.N. Medd, Mr. V. Narhari Rao, Mr. H.V.R. Iyengar, Mr. G.S. Bozman, Dr. R.I. Mortimer Wheeler, Dr. H.N. Sen, Dr. B.S. Guha, Dr. D.M. Sen and Dr. N.P. Chakravarti.

Shri K. Santhanam: May I know, Sir, if the Honourable Minister will consider the desirability of covering the present Government House into a museum?

Mr. Speaker: That is a suggestion for action.

The Honourable Maulana Abul Kalam Azad: Yes. It needs a building. At the time of the execution of this scheme a building will be constructed.

Shri S.V. Krishnamurthy Rao: The Honourable Minister told us that the Museum will be located in Delhi. May I know, Sir, why a more central place for the whole of India cannot be chosen?

The Honourable Maulana Abul Kalam Azad: In a way Delhi is a central place and is Capital also.

Giani Gurmukh Singh Musafar: Is there any scheme for the construction of a National Museum for the East Punjab also?

The Honourable Maulana Abul Kalam Azad: It is a matter for the consideration of the Provincial Government.

Document No. 62

ELECTION TO STANDING COMMITTEE FOR MINISTRY OF EDUCATION DATED 1-3-1948

The Honourable Maulana Abul Kalam Azad (Minister for Education): Sir, I move:

> "That this Assembly do proceed to elect, in such manner as the Honourable the Speaker may direct, one member to serve on the Standing Committee to advise on subjects dealt with in the Ministry of Education, until the end of the financial year 1948-49, *vice* Shri S. Radhakrishnan resigned."

The Standing Committee of the Ministry of Education was elected in November last. Shri S. Radhakrishnan was also one of its members. He has now tendered his resignation; saying that his engagements are such that it would not be possible for him to devote sufficient time to the Standing Committee. A vacancy has therefore occurred and it should be filled up.

Mr. Speaker: Motion moved:

> "That this Assembly do proceed to elect, in such manner as the Honourable the Speaker may direct, one member to serve on the Standing Committee to advise on subjects dealt with in the Ministry of Education, until the end of the financial year 1948-49, *vice* Shri S. Radhakrishnan resigned."

Shri M. Ananthasayanam Ayyangar (Madras: General): May I request the Honourable Minister to inform us if there have been any meetings of the Standing Committee for Education till now?

The Honourable Maulana Abul Kalam Azad: No, not yet. After consultation with the members it was decided to hold the meeting in March, and so it will be held at the end of March.

Shri M. Ananthasayanam Ayyangar: In view of the fact that Prof. Radhakrishnan continues to be a member of this Constituent Assembly and he is one of the eminent scholars, cannot the Honourable Minister persuade him to be a member of this Committee, especially in view of the fact that a number of meetings of this Committee have not been held till now, so that he can attend one or two of its meetings?

The Honourable Maulana Abul Kalam Azad: It depends upon the opinion of the House. If the House desires, I will again write to him, though he has submitted his resignation.

Mr. Speaker: The question is:

> "That this Assembly do proceed to elect, in such manner as the Honourable the Speaker may direct, one member to serve on the Standing Committee to advise on subjects dealt with in the Ministry of Education, until the end of the financial year 1948-49, *vice* Shri S. Radhakrishnan resigned."

The motion was adopted.

Mr. Speaker: I have to inform Honourable Members that for the purpose of election, by means of the single transferable vote, of a member to the Standing Committee for the Ministry of Education the programme of dates will be as follows:

Nomination to be filed in the Notice Office upto 12 noon on Wednesday, the 3rd March.

Election, if necessary, will be held on Friday, the 5th March, in the Assistant Secretary's room (No. 21) in the Council House between the hours of 10.30 A.M. and 1 P.M.

Document No. 63

REPLY DATED 4-3-1948 BY MAULANA AZAD TO THE QUESTIONS ASKED IN THE CONSTITUENT ASSEMBLY OF INDIA (LEGISLATIVE)

RECOGNITION OF INDIAN DEGREES IN ARTS, MEDICINE, ENGINEERING ETC. IN U.K. AND U.S.A.

Shri V.C. Kesava Rao: Will the Honourable Minister of Education be pleased to state whether Indian degrees in arts, medicine, engineering and other technological subjects have been recognised in foreign countries, especially in the United States of America and the United Kingdom?

The Honourable Maulana Abul Kalam Azad: In most foreign countries, including the U.S.A., degress and diplomas awarded by the Indian Universities and Institutions are not recognised formally, but each application from an Indian student is considered on merits and the qualifications acquired by the student in India are taken into account. The Ministry is pursuing the question of a general recognition of Indian degrees by American Universities.

A statement is laid on the table giving the latest information available regarding the recognition of Indian degrees and diplomas by British Universities.

Statement

Showing the latest information available regarding the recognition of Indian degrees and diplomas by British Universities

As a general rule, all Universities in the U.K. accept a degree of the Indian University as exempting from the Matriculation Examination and certain universities accept also the Intermediate Examination of an Indian University. The following statement gives the detailed position according to the latest information available in regard to each University separately:

1. *Birmingham University* – (a) holder of a Bachelor's degree of an approved Indian University, or an Intermediate certificate of an Indian University is eligible for admission to the Degree course.

(b) Graduates of Indian Universities may apply for exemption from the first year course and examination. This examination is usually decided on the merits of each application.

2. *University of Bristol* – (a) A holder of an Intermediate certificate of a recognized Indian University is eligible for admission to the Matriculation course.

(b) No definite regulations for exmeption in the faculties of Arts and Science have been laid down but consideration is given to individual applications.

In the faculty of Engineering of this University exemption from the first year course is usually given to candidates who have obtained the Diploma of Thompson Civil Engineering College, Roorkee.

3. *Cambridge University* – (a) A holder of a First Class Intermediate or a First or Second Class Bachalor's degree of an approved Inidan Univeristy is eligible for admission to the University without passing the 'Previous' Examination.

(b) Exemption from any portion of the courses or period of residence prescribed for the Bachelor's degree are only granted to affiliated students. A student who has been a member of an Associated Institute for not less than three years, and who, before matriculation at this University, has graduated, or done all that is necessary for graduation at that Associated Institution is entitled to be approved as an affiliated student.

The Indian universities at present approved as *Associated Institutions* are : Agra, Aligarh, Allahabad, Bombay, Calcutta, Delhi, Lucknow, Madras, Mysore, Osmania and Patna. The old Punjab University was also approved, and it is hoped that the East Punjab University will now be approved.

4. *Durham University* – (a) A holder of an Intermediate certificate of an Indian University is eligible under certain conditions for exemption from the Matriculation Examination of this University.

(b) Exemption is granted from the first year of study, provided that an equivalent course of study has been pursued at some approved institution and exemption is obtained from the first year examination, provided an equivalent examination has been passed elsewhere.

An Indian Graduate may be a admitted to the status of an advanced student in order to study for the Ph.D. Degree, provided his qualifiations justify such admission.

5. *Leads Univeristy* – (a) A holder of a Bachelor's degree of an approved Indian University, or an Intermediate certificate of an Indian University is eligible for admission to the Degree course.

(b) The University has not found it possible to draw up a scheme of exemption for students from Indian Universities but is prepared to consider each application on its merits.

6. *Liverpool University* – (a) A holder of a Bachelor's degree of an approved Indian University, or an Intermediate certificate of an Indian University is eligible for admission to the degree course.

(b) The University has not found it possible to draw up a scheme of exemption for students from Indian Universities but it is prepared to consider each application on its merits.

7. *University of London* – (a) A holder of a Bachelor's degree of an approved Indian University is exempted from the Matriculation Examination.

(b) External Students are not entitled to any exemption from examinations above the Matriculation.

Internal Students who are graduates of other Universities may proceed as candidates for a Bachelor's degree without taking the Intermediate Examination, after they have pursued an approved course of studies as Internal Students.

8. *University of Manchester* – (a) A holder of a Bachelor's degree of an approved Indian University, or an Intermediate certificate of an Indian University is eligible for admission to the Degree course.

(b) This University has never laid down any general scheme for exemption and each application for exemption is dealt with individually and on its merits.

9. *Oxford University* – (a) A holder of a Bachelor's degree of an approved Indian University obtained after a course of study extending over three years only, with uninterrupted success at all examinations and certificate of satisfactory progress is exempted from 'Responsions' (*i.e.* Matriculation Examination) and is eligible for admission as a member of the University.

(b) Exemption from any portion of the prescribed courses or period of residence for the B.A. Degree is only granted to students of Senior Status. Students who have obtained a Bachelor's degree at a University in the British Dominion or Colonies or in India or in Great Britain and North Ireland or at a foreign University are admitted to the status and privileges of a Senior student, provided that they have pursued at that University a course of study extending over at least three years.

10. *Sheffield University* – (a) A holder of a Bachelor's degree of an approved Indian University, or an Intermediate certificate of an Indian University is eligible for admission to the Degree course.

(b) At this University exemption of one year is usually granted for courses in the various Faculties to degree holders of approved Universities.

11. *Aberdeen University* – (a) A holder of a First Class Intermediate certificate of an approved Indian University with English and either Mathematics or Science is eligible for admission to the course of a study qualifying for graduation.

(b) With the exception of the Preliminary Examination, this University does not make any exemptions or concession in virtue of Degrees or courses obtained or pursued at Indian Universities unless a special application has been submitted and approved by the University court.

12. *Edinburgh University* – (a) A holder of a First Class Intermediate certificate of an approved Indian University with English and either Mathematics or Science is eligible for admission to the course of a study qualifying for graduation.

(b) Each application is considered on its merits and exemption is granted from attendance or from both attendance and examination.

13. *Glasgow University* – (a) A holder of First Class Intermediate certificate of an approved Indian University with English and either Mathematics or Science is eligible for admission to the course of study qualifying for graduation.

(b) Students from India who have attended Degree courses at a recognized Indian University may receive exemption from class attendence in certain courses at this University, but they are required to pass the Degree Examination.

14. *St. Andrews University* – (a) A holder of First Class Intermediate Certificate of an approved Indian University with English and either Mathematics or Science is eligible for admission to the course of a study qualifying for graduation.

(b) Exemption from part of the curriculum or examinations is granted to students who have given attendance or passed examination at other Universities recognized by the University.

15. *University of Wales* – (a) A holder of an Intermediate certificate of an approved Indian University is exempted from the Matriculation Examination.

(b) Graduates of an Indian University may enter upon a scheme of research or advanced study in one of the Constituent College without having first to qualify for the degree of Bacealaureus.

Seth Govind Das: Will the Honourable Minister issue orders that the degrees of those Universities of America and U.K. will not be recognised in India, which do not recognise Indian Universities Degrees?

The Honourable Maulana Abul Kalam Azad: So far as I know Indian Universities are also not recognising them.

Shri V.C. Kesava Rao: Is it a fact, Sir, that our degrees are not recognised by the foreign Universities because they are not given practical training?

The Honourable Maulana Abul Kalam Azad: No, I do not think so. But the Ministry is taking up the question of recognition by American Universities of Indian Universities degrees. We will see what should be our policy in this connection in future?

Shri V.C. Kesava Rao: What steps are Government taking to give sufficient practical training in the Indian Universities?

The Honourable Maulana Abul Kalam Azad: I do not think the question of practical training arises. Students who are sent abroad do not have to face any practical difficulty at all, and our work is running smoothly. But I admit that this point should be settled as a matter of principle.

Mr. R.K. Sidhva: Is there any country where Indian Universities degrees are recognised?

The Honourable Maulana Abul Kalam Azad: Some British Universities have recognised them.

Shri Rohini Kumar Chaudhuri: Is it a fact that various complications arise on account of the present system of using the name of the Province after the degree and if so, do Government propose to use only the wo·d 'Hind' instead of using the name of different Provinces like B.A. (Mad.), M.A. (Cal.) etc.?

The Honourable Maulana Abul Kalam Azad: I do not think we are experiencing any difficulty on account of the addition of the name of the Province.

Document No. 64

ANSWERS DATED 4-3-1948 BY MAULANA AZAD TO THE QUESTIONS ASKED IN THE INDIAN LEGISLATIVE ASSEMBLY

UNIVERSITIES IN INDIAN DOMINION

R.B. Lala Raj Kanwar: Will the Honourable Minister of Education be pleased to state:

(a) the names of the Universities in the Indian Dominion together with the years in which they were established; and

(b) the amount of the annual or recurring grant, if any, made by the Government of India to each University?

The Honourable Maulana Abul Kalam Azad: (a) A statement showing the names of the Universities in the Indian Dominion incorporated by Law and the years in which they were established is laid on the table of the House.

(b) The Government of India give recurring grants to the three Central Universities only.

A statement indicating the recurring grants paid to these Universities during the year 1946-47 is also laid on the table of the House.

Statement

Showing the Names of Universities in the Indian Dominion and the years in which they were established

	Name of University	*Year*
1.	Agra University, Agra (United Provinces)	1927
2.	Aligarh Muslim University, Aligarh (United Provinces)	1920
3.	Allahabad University, Allahabad (United Provinces)	1887
4.	Andhra University, Waltair (Madras)	1926
5.	Annamalai University, Annamalainagar, Chidambaram (Madras)	1928

6. Benaras Hindu University, Benares (United Provinces) 1915
7. Bombay University, Bombay (Bombay) 1857
8. Calcutta University, Calcutta (Bengal) 1857
9. Delhi University, Delhi 1922
10. East Punjab University, Solan (Simla Hills) 1947
11. Gauhati University, Gauhati (Assam) 1947
12. Lucknow University, Lucknow (United Provinces) 1921
13. Madras University, Madras (Madras) 1857
14. Mysore University, Mysore (Mysore State) 1916
15. Nagpur University, Nagpur (Central Provinces and Berar) 1923
16. Osmania University, Hyderabad Deccan 1918
17. Patna University, Patna (Bihar) 1917
18. Rajputana University, Jaipur 1947
19. Travancore University, Trivandrum (Travancore State) 1937
20. Utkal University, Cuttack 1943
21. University of Saugar, Saugar (Central Provinces) 1946

Recurring grants paid to the Central Universities 1946-47

University	*Grant*	*Remarks*
Benares Hindu University	7,02,168	Includes a sum of Rs. 3 lakhs as an advance against the grant of Rs. 4 lakhs recommended by the University Grants Committee in a full financial year.
Aligarh Muslim University	6,30,265	Includes a sum of Rs. 2,25,000 as an advance against the grant of Rs. 2,50,000 recommended by the University Grants Committee in a full financial year.
Delhi University	5,77,398	Includes a sum of Rs. 1,95,000 as an advance against the great of Rs. 3,64,000 recommended by the University Grants Committee in a full financial year.

R.B. Lala Raj Kanwar: May I know which University receives the highest grant?

The Honourable Maulana Abul Kalam Azad: This is given in the statement. I can give to the House the figures for the last two years:

	RS. A.P.
Banaras Hindu University	702168-0-0
Aligarh Muslim University	630000-0-0
Delhi University	577000-0-0

Shrimati G. Durgabai: Will the Honourable Minister be pleased to state whether the Prayag Mahila Vidyapith and Kharve University in Bombay are full-fledged Universities in the sense that they are recognised as such by this Government?

The Honourable Maulana Abul Kalam Azad: Notice is required for this.

Shri B.P. Jhunjhunwala: May I ask the Honourable Minister if there is any basis on which the grants are given for different educational Universities?

The Honourable Maulana Abul Kalam Azad: There is a Universities Grants Committee which deals with it. All cases of grants are referred to it.

Shri B.P. Jhunjhunwala: On what basis do they consider the different cases?

The Honourable Maulana Abul Kalam Azad: The Universities Grants Committee takes its decisions in the light of the development schemes, and the requirements of the Universities.

Shri H.V. Kamath: Will Government consider the desirability of discontinuing grants to merely communal Universities?

The Honourable Maulana Abul Kalam Azad: These grants are being given at present. The question of communal universities is altogether different. The Government will, however look into it.

Shri Rohini Kumar Chaudhuri: May I know why the Assam University has not been given any grant?

The Honoruable Maualana Abul Kalam Azad: The Assam University has just started.

Prof. N.G. Ranga: Have Government any proposals, Sir, to see that these Universities to which Government are making these grants are converted into non-communal universities at the earliest possible moment?

The Honourable Maulana Abul Kalam Azad: The scheme which is before the Government in this connection will be considered in due course.

Shri Biswanath Das: Arising out of the replies given to some of the supplementary questions may I know whether the Honourable Minister incharge of the Department has considered the need of suggesting to these Universities to change their names suitably so as to take away the communal sting which now attaches to their name, especailly in view of the fact that the Hindu University, though the name 'Hindu remains is not at all a communal University?

The Honourable Maulana Abul Kalam Azad: When the question comes up before the Government for consideration, all these matters will be kept in view.

Shri Biswanath Das: May I request Government to consider the need for suggesting if they think proper, to name it in the name of Pandit Malaviya...

Mr. Speaker: Order, order. We cannot make any suggestions. I do not propose to allow that question.

Document No. 65

ANSWERS OF MAULANA AZAD DT. 8-3-1948, IN THE LEGISLATIVE ASSEMBLY TO THE QUESTIONS ASKED ABOUT THE POST OF JOINT DIRECTOR GENERAL OF ARCHAEOLOGY

Shri Jaspat Roy Kapoor: (a) Will the Honourable Minister of Education be pleased to state when the post of Joint Director General of Archaeology was created, and for what period?

(b) What were the reasons for the creation of this post?

(c) Is it proposed to abolish this post after the termination of the present period, or is it proposed to continue it or to make it permanent?

The Honourable Maulana Abul Kalam Azad: (a) The post of the Joint Director General of Archaeology was first created temporarily from 28th December 1945 to 28th February, 1947, but the tenure of the post was subsequently extended upto the end of June, 1948.

(b) The reasons for the creation of the post of Joint Director General of Archaeology were:

(1) It was considered necessary to have at headquarters during the general re-organisation of the Archaeological Department an Officer with extensive experience to assist the Director General of Archaeology in his task, relieve him of a number of exacting administrative duties which prevented him from carrying out his primary and urgent task of training new entrants and re-modelling the Circles, and to enable him to maintain sufficiently close contact both with work in field throughout India and with the Government at New Delhi.

(2) It was false economy to bring out as a short-term Director General of Archaeology an Officer with special technical qualifications and experience and then to compel him to devote the greater part of his time to administrative duties.

(3) The Woolley Report of 1939 strongly stressed the need for a larger departmental headquarters.

(c) A final decision will be taken shortly.

Shri Deshbandhu Gupta : Is it a fact that the appointment of Joint Director was not made according to the seniority list?

The Honourable Maulana Abul Kalam Azad: On the basis of the information, available to me at the moment, I am not in a position to say 'yes' I want notice of this question.

Shri H.V. Kamath : Will the Honourable Minister be pleased to state what work has been taken in hand after the excavations at Mohenjadaro and Harappa?

The Honourable Maulana Abul Kalam Azad : But this has no reference to the question.

Document No. 66

ANSWERS BY MAULANA AZAD, DT. 8-3-1948 TO THE QUESTIONS ASKED IN THE LEGISLATIVE ASSEMBLY REGARDING THE MAINTENANCE OF ARCHAEOLOGICAL GARDENS BY ARCHAEOLOGICAL DEPARTMENT

Shri Jaspat Roy Kapoor : Will the Honourable Minister of Education be pleased to state whether it is proposed that the Archaeological Department should assume responsibility for the maintenance of Archaeological gardens which have hitherto been maintained by the Provincial Governments?

The Honourable Maulana Abul Kalam Azad : The Government of India have already accepted in principle the responsibility for the maintenance by the Department of Archaeology of gardens attached to ancient monuments which at present rests with the Provincial Governments. The date from which the Archaeological Department should assume this responsibility has not yet been determined.

Prof. N.G. Ranga : Is it a fact that this post was created after a European came to be appointed as a Director-General in order to help him?

Mr. Speaker : That relates to another question.

Document No. 67

SPEECH OF MAULANA AZAD DT. 11-3-1948, IN THE LEGISLATIVE ASSEMBLY IN CONNECTION WITH THE GENERAL BUDGET — LIST OF DEMAND FOR 1948-49

The Honourable Maulana Abul Kalam Azad (Minister for Education) : Sir, General complaints have been made about the shortage of time. I share this view. The allotted time, however, cannot be changed and I shall try to have my say within the time permitted. For the information of Honourable Members, I have had a statement circulated which will give them an idea of the complete picture of the work before the Ministry of Education and they can have an idea of the progress than can be possible with the help of the grants provided in the Budget for the new year.

The first cut motion relates to an important matter namely Adult Education. In this connection I fully agree with the object of my Honourable friend. There is no doubt that the problem of adult education is as important as that of child education. The adult education has far greater aims than merely teaching adults how to read and write. It is our duty to impart to adults an education which should develop their thinking faculty so that they are enlightened and enabled to take due interest in the affairs of a demoratic state and society. In no walk of our national life can we progress without the considered and judicious cooperation of millions of our countrymen. Anyhow no body would deny the extreme importance of this work. What we have to see is how this work can be accomplished in the shortest time.

The report submitted by the Central Advisory Board in the year 1944 contained also a scheme for adult education. But this scheme could not be enforced. It was after the last general elections, when the Congress Ministries were re-established in the provinces, that attention was paid to this thing. Work was taken in hand but on too small a scale to meet the demands of the day. After my assumption of office as Education Minister last year the first task that confronted me was the Basic Education and Adult Education schemes. But the political condition of our country at that time was such that no time could be spared for attending to the task of education. Government was over head and ears engrossed with other affairs. I wanted to convene a meeting of the provincial education ministers and representatives of the Universities. Twice a date was fixed but every time it had to be postponed because conditions at that time made it impossible for men to assemble for a conference. Opportunity offered itself at last, and in January meetings of the Educational Conference and the Central Advisory Committee were held. I placed before them a new scheme for Adult Education; and you know that it was approved by both of these bodies. The report of the sub-committee appointed for this purpose by the Standing Committee of the Central Advisory Board was presented and accepted with some modifications. Our scheme is ready now. Its one branch concerns literary education and the other with the developement of mental faculties. The latter provides besides oral lectures the media of radio, films and modern methods of open air dramas. Efforts are being made to secure the best equipment. For this very reason this year money has been earmarked for a film library. Production of educational films is being undertaken. A separate section has been started under the ministry for the purpose of helping in the preparation of necessary literature. The sub-committee appointed by the Advisory Board had stressed the inclusion of certain amount of technical education in this scheme because a majority of the adults receiving education under this scheme would be connected with some profession or art. This suggestion has therefore also been incorporated in the scheme. Opinions of the provincial Governments have been invited in this connection. We intend to introduce this scheme in such a way as should enable the schools of Basic Education to become centres of all activities of the Adult Education as well. In this way we want to create a new intellectual atmosphere in this country.

So far I have told you the story of Adult Education. But mere paper scheme does not do. It requires material and for material the question of money comes first. The House is familiar with the attitude the Central Government have hitherto been adopting in this connection. Government proceeds upto a certain point beyond which it cannot proceed. I wish we could cross these old limits and move along new lines.

I wanted to have double the present grant but due to the emphasis laid by the Ministry of Finance on our limitations for the year I had to content myself with it. The political conditions and especially the misfortunes of the Punjab, have suddenly burdened the finances of the Central Government; and due to this we have been forced to proceed slowly. Nevertheless I admit that other things can afford to wait but not education. It is necessary that somehow or other provision for money for this work must be made. This was also one of the fundamental questions which were raised in the Educational Conference which met on the 16th January. The Conference has appointed a committee to go into this question and to make its recommendation. I hope Government will receive their recommendation by June and we will be able to arrange sufficient funds for carrying out essential schemes of education.

In moving the second cut motion the Honourable Shri Deshmukh has drawn the attention of Government to the necessity for technical education. I may assure him that Government have been doing everything possible in this connection and in our plan for the next year's Budget we have tried to move quickly. If the Honourable Members had glanced through the statement circulated to them, this cut-motion would probably have not been necessary. I will briefly tell to the House what has been done in this connection.

(1) The Government of India have decided to open four Higher Technical Institutions on the model of American Institutes: of these two will be located near about Calcutta and Bombay and work has to be started at once. From the files I find that this matter has been under consideration for the last two years; but so far neither any site has been selected nor any progress made in pushing through the work. I tried to remedy this state of affairs, and to enforce the scheme as soon as possible. The site has now been selected and arrangements for the staff are being made. Each of the four institutes would cost Rs. three crores as capital expenditure and rupees forty four lacs as recurring expenditure and will provide for the training of 3,000 students – 2,000 Under-graduates and 1,000 Post-graduates. The whole scheme is expected to be completed within two or three years.

(2) Four years' development plan for the Indian Institute of Science, Bangalore, has been sanctioned, and the power engineering department is being opened.

(3) Three years' development plan for the Delhi Polytechnic has been sanctioned and the work is being started.

(4) The All India Council for Technical Education recommended to give from the Centre a grant to the existing technical institutions in the country. Accordingly the grant has been sanctioned for five years and it is being given.

(5) The House might be aware of the fact that an Overseas Scholarship scheme was passed by the Central Government in 1944 and scholars from India were being sent abroad for training. When the new Government assumed office it was felt that this scheme was not followed properly. Therefore the first thing was to try to raise the status of the existing institutions to a level so as to train students with much higher qualifications, and then to determine according to the plan the subjects for the study of which scholars should be sent abroad and then to grant scholarship for those subjects only. Accordingly with this object in view a committee called the Scientific Man-Power Committee was set up, to investigate into the country's immediate scientific requirements and to prepare a plan how arrangements can best be made to carry out these requirement earlier. The committee is still functioning. It has submitted its interim report and Government gave their immediate attention to it and have accepted most of its recommendations. The recommendations stressed the need for giving fresh grants to the country's universities and institutions to enable them to augment their resources for imparting educational facilities in scientific and technical subjects. We have started giving grants from this year, and allotment of funds has been made for the three Central Universities.

(6) In addition to these activities of the Central Government the technical education work is also being generally accelerated in all the provinces. The Central Government have this year given handsome amounts to the Provincial Governments to enable them to implement their development schemes quickly. Accordingly:

29 Junior Technical institutions are being organised, and their scope of instructions is being enlarged,

4 Technical High Schools are being opened,

11 Senior Technical Institutions,

140 Junior Technical Schools,

38 Technical High Schools,

16 Polytechnics,

4 Senior Technical Institutions,

will soon begin to function.

These statictics relate to the general Post-War Development Plan.

In moving the third cut motion, the Honourable Mrs. Mehta has drawn our attention to the fact that no rules have yet been prescribed for grants to the universities. And it is necessary that the Central Government should elucidate its policy in this respect. I feel that no such question arises. The practice followed by the previous Government was to give grants to the three Central Universities only and with a view to give these grants a committee called the Univeristy Grants Committee was constituted. The present Government felt that it was desired to raise the standard of education of the entire country to the same level, then the scope of Central Government's help should not be confined to the three Universities only. It should be further expanded. In other words we should open its doors for the distribution of grants to other Universities also. With this object the University Grants Committee was constituted *de novo* and its terms of reference have been framed in such a manner so as to fully conform to this new policy. All the applications which are now received by the Ministry will be passed on to the University Grants Committee. The Government will carefully consider over the recommendations made by the Committee in this respect.

Shrimati Hansa Mehta : It is true that I mentioned in my speech also that the scope of the Grants Committee is extending, but on what basis are we to give grants to other Universities? It should be on the same basis as the Central Universities and there should be no distinction, that is what I said.

The Honourable Maulana Abul Kalam Azad : Honourable Mrs. Hansa Mehta is one of the members of this Committee and she has every opportunity to discuss this matter in the Committee. I cannot say why she thought it necessary to move a cut motion to discuss this point.

She has also referred in her speech to the existence of communal institutions and has stressed the point as to why the word 'Hindu' and 'Muslim' should at all be associated with the names of Benares and Aligarh Universities? I fully agree with the views expressed by her. I do not only agree but I welcome this idea. I extend a hearty welcome to this. No one else than myself will be happier if the words 'Hindu' and 'Muslim' are eliminated from the names of these two Universities. But it is clear that legislation establishing these Universities was passed by this House and until the Acts are amended we cannot make any change.

An Honourable Member : Why can't you amend the Act?

The Government are also in full agreement with the point stressed by Shrimati any Honourable Member of the House can move for an amendment of the Act. In any case this change must be made.

The Honourable Maulana Abul Kalam Azad : The Government are also in full agreement with the point stressed by Shrimati G. Durga Bai. Nothing can retard more the growth of our national life than the encouragement of 'community', 'religion' and 'caste' in the educational sphere and placing of such limitations as would separate one class of people from the other. When we oppose this, it is not our intention that the backward classes should not be provided with facilities for advancement. On the contrary they should be helped in every walk of life and there is no doubt education is the high-road for their advancement. If they have been left behind in the sphere of progress it is not their fault. The society is to be blamed for this. It is all the more necessary therefore that the society which has not uptil now placed them on an equal footing, should help in their advancement. Take the case of our Harijan brethren. If seats can be reserved for them in some institutions it does not mean that they are accorded discriminatory treatment over other classes. The reason is that if such a course is not adopted there is danger that they would be lost and will not be able to receive the benefit of education according to their share. The Governmetn quite agree with the view that there should be no distinction of caste or creed in the sphre of education and whatever policy the Government and universities of the provinces have so far followed in this respect they should now adopt the national policy of the Central Government. The Honourable Member has in particular referred to the Madras Government, but I cannot say what is the actual position there. I shall find out from the Madras Government and will invite their attention to this point.

The last motion was moved by the Honourable Mr. Frank Anthony, pointing out that the Government should have a uniform policy regarding language. If any change has to be introduced it should be done slowly and gradually after full consideration. The change from English to an Indian language should not be sudden as this will distrub the standard of education and will result in harassment to people. I can assure the Honourable Member that this is the policy of the Government who have advised the Provincial Governments to move cautiously and slowly in this matter. It must be known to the Honourable Members that I was first to raise my voice and warn the people against taking hasty steps and to move slowly. In my convocation address at the Patna University I first expressed my view that we should substitute the language in the course of five years and though we should start the process now the English language should continue for five years. This opinion applies not only to matters of education but also to matters of administration. Later on in the month of January when the Central Advisory Board and the Educational Conference met I placed the same view before them and laid emphasis on the point that English should be replaced gradually and after due consideration. I am glad the Central Advisory Board and the Educational Conference both agreed to this view, and I can say with confidence that the general policy of the Government in this connection will be as was indicated by me. Thus the Central Government have, so far as they are concerned laid down a definite and clear policy on this subject and as medium of instruction English will be replaced by one or more Indian languages. We do not want a sudden change but the change should be effected step by step. Our plan is that this should be accomplished in five years and in such a manner that in the sixth year the need for English should vanish.

To put it succinctly the Government policy can be described as follows:

(1) So far as the primary and secondary stage is concerned it has been decided that the medium of instruction will be the mother tongue, and this is being put into practice by all the provinces;

(2) For the University stage it has been decided that English can not continue as the medium of instruction but this change we should bring about in five years so that in the sixth year English will be fully replaced.

This is then the policy of the Government on the language question and the representatives of the provinces who came to attend the Educational Conference also agreed to it. It is, therefore, not correct to say that the Government have no uniform policy in this matter.

Mr. R.K. Sidhva : With your permission I want to ask one question and invite the Honourable Minister's attention to page 102 of the Budget Demand. In this a sum of Rs. 24,500 has been provided for Churches. In respect to this Government has stated that no grant would be given in future and I want to know why is this being continued?

The Honourable Maulana Abul Kalam Azad: I cannot answer this at the moment because the details of this item are not before me. I can only say that this amount is being given to Churches since previous years and it is related to a separate fund.

Shri R.R. Diwakar : Sir, The question about the future national language in the Universities has not been answered.

The Honourable Maulana Abul Kalam Azad: No reply has been given to it because no decision has been taken about it so far. As I have already said it has been decided that the medium of instruction even in the University will be the national language. But we have not decided yet whether we are going to have one or more national languages. The All India Educational Conference which I convened in January last has appointed a Committee to go into this matter and we are awaiting the recommendations of this Committee.

The Honourable Member has specially mentioned the U.P. Government. I cannot say what exactly his point is? In November last I saw a press report to the effect that the U.P. Govenment will stop printing the U.P. Government Gazette in English from the new year. I immediately wrote a letter to the U.P. Premier suggesting that it will not be proper to do away with English so suddenly. In his reply to my letter he assured me that his Government was not in favour of making sudden changes and that he fully concurred in my opinion expressed in my address at the Patna University. Now I am aware that the U.P. Government Gazette is still being published in English as usual.

Shri K. Santhanam : May I enquire from Maulana Sahib whether the English translation of the Persian-couplet appearing in his English statement is correct?

The Honourable Maulana Abul Kalam Azad : The translation is not incorrect but I had better explain the meaning fully. The poet says:

> *"Thou desirest wine? and not only wine but wine that is good and strong, and not only good and strong but in abundance?*

> *Then the poet says : forget not ye, thou art making these requests to a petty wine dealer (a Kalal). He is not the wine server of paradise who can give you what you want."*

I will also tell the House that it is welcome to make as many requests as it pleases matters regarding educational and I will welcome all such requests but it should not forget that I am only a Minister of Education and not an Officer-in-charge of paradise, nor have I a magician's basket with me to produce a full grown tree at a moment's notice.

Shri R.R. Diwakar : Sir, I beg leave of the House to withdraw my cut motion.

Mr. Chairman : Has the Honourable Member leave of the House to withdraw?

The cut motion was, by leave of the Assembly, withdrawn.

Dr. P.S. Deshmukh : Sir, I beg leave of the House to withdraw my cut motion.

Mr. Chairman : Has the Honourable Member leave of the House to withdraw?

The cut motion was, by leave of the Assembly, withdrawn.

Shrimati Hansa Mehta : Sir, I beg leave of the House to withdraw my cut motion.

Mr. Chairman : Has the Honourable Member leave of the House to withdraw?

The cut motion was, by leave of the Assembly, withdrawn.

Shrimati G. Durgabai : Sir, I beg leave of the House to withdraw my cut motion.

Mr. Chairman : Has the Honourable Member leave of the House to withdraw?

The cut motion was, by leave of the Assembly, withdrawn.

Mr. Frank R. Anthony : Sir, I beg leave of the House to withdraw my cut motion.

Mr. Chairman : Has the Honourable Member leave of the House to withdraw?

The cut motion was, by leave of the Assembly, withdrawn.

Mr. Chairman : The question is:

> "That a sum not exceeding Rs. 17,95,000 be granted to the

Governor-General to defray the charges which will come in course of payment during the year ending the 31st day of March, 1949, in respect of 'Ministry of Works, Mines and Power'."

The motion was adopted.

Mr. Chairman : The question is:

"That a sum not exceeding Rs. 86,31,000 be granted to the Governor-General to defray the charges which will come in course of payment during the year ending the 31st day of March, 1949, in respect of 'Ministry of Education'."

The motion was adopted.

The Assembly then adjourned till a Quarter to Eleven of the Clock on Friday, the 12th March, 1948.

Document No. 68

STATEMENT OF POLICY BY THE HONOURABLE MINISTER FOR EDUCATION [1] IN CONNECTION WITH THE CUT-MOTION ON THE BUDGET PROPOSALS FOR 1948-49 AS CIRCULATED TO HONOURABLE MEMBERS

I feel that giving a general outline of the Government's educational policy is necessary in view of the fact that this is the first Budget for a full year of free and independent India. I am, therefore, availing of this occasion to place before the Honourbale Members a statement not only of schemes we have in hand and the moneys involved in their execution, but also a blue-print of our future educational edifice.

2. When the National Government was formed in August 1947, it entered into a heritage which was burdened with many encumberances. There was no clean slate to write upon but a palimpsest on which was scrawled the marks of generations of scribes who had each his own mode and style. For 150 years, there has been in this land a government imposed from above with an attitude, a tradition and a method of work which was largely allien. The first task of the National Government was, therefore, to avoid being wallowed up by the past. It was easy to fall in line with existing tendencies and take the line of least resistance. The National Government resisted that temptation and sought to create new traditions, a new point of view and a new attitude towards our problems and their solution. I do not say that the slate has been wiped clean, for the work of generations cannot be swept away in a day. No efforts have, however, been spared for the reorientation of the policy of Government, and I hope that the House will agree that success in a large measure has been achieved.

3. I assumed charge of what was then the Department of Education on the 15th January, 1947. My task was to survey the schemes, some of which were already in operation, some just started

---

1. Maulana Azad dated 11-3-1948, in the Legislative Assembly.

and others yet in the planning stage. These schemes were, however, all conceived at a time when an alien Government was in the seat of power and I had to examine what modifications were necessary in order to bring them into line with the spirit of the changed time and circumstances. I also conceived it as my duty to undertake new plans in the educational field to enable us to realise the objectives for which the Indian people have been striving for the last 60 years or more.

4. I need not dilate on the difficulties which we have had to face during the last year. There was almost from the beginning political uncertainty and the fate of the country hung in the balance. The Cabinet Mission's plan was in the melting pot and soon after there emerged the plan for a division of the country into two States. In addition, there were, as every member of the House is aware, internal stresses inside the Government itself which made it impossible for us to function as a homogeneous Cabinet and pull our full weight in advancing the interests of India.

5. It is true that after the 15th of August, most of these uncertainties were set at rest and the internal stresses within the Cabinet resolved. There were, however, new and stupendous happenings beginning with the Punjab upheavals when for full three months the Government had to suspend and hold in abeyance almost all its activities and gear the administrative machinery to one and one purpose alone, *viz.* the rescue of those unfortunate countrymen of ours who had been involved in this terrific catastrophe.

6. In spite of all these distractions, the Government have spared no efforts to advance the cause of education in the country. One thing which struck my notice soon after I assumed charge was that even where the Government had formulated well thought-out and beneficial schemes, the execution was so slow that no appreciable results could be expected unless the process was accelerated. I will give you one or two instances of the slowness of the Government machinery when we took over charge. It was decided to establish a Central Institute of Education full two years ago and a budget provision of its 22 lakhs was sanctioned for the purpose. It is true that lack of building material was partly responsible for failure to implement the plan, but in my opinion, this is not sufficient justification for having failed to bring the institute into existence. If necessary, a start might have been made and the institute housed in a temporary or hired building while its permanent edifice was being constructed.

7. Another example to which I must draw your attention is the scheme of basic education for the country. Both the Central and the Provincial Governments had agreed to put into effect immediately the first 5-year plan of the basic education scheme which aimed at providing free and compulsory training to all citizens between the ages of 6 and 14. I feel that the Centrally Administered Areas should have served as a model and even if there were delays elsewhere, these areas should have put the scheme into immediate effect. I regret to say that though huge files of correspondence piled up between the Central Government and the Delhi Local Administration, the work did not start.

8. I now come to schemes which has already started when I assumed charge but not in the spirit and manner that I considered necessary. The scheme of overseas scholarships was conceived in 1944 and a beginning was made during that very year. This was a most important scheme and should have been carried out according to carefully thought out plans. We should have examined what is the capacity of existing institutions in India and how far they can be quickly expanded in order to meet our requirements. Where conditions in the country demanded that students must be sent abroad, it was necessary that great care and thought should be exercised in the choice of scholars and the institutions to which they were sent. We should have considered that the exigencies of war made conditions extremely difficult in both U.K. and U.S.A. Even when war was over, 90 per cent of the seats in most of their universities and technical institutions were reserved for their own ex-service personnel. In addition, there were great difficulties with regard to housing and food for students who would go to the U.K. I am afraid that these factors were not properly weighed, and a decision was taken to send 500 students abroad every year. Two batches had already gone and the selection of a third a most completed when I assumed charge. I did not want to stop this third batch from going abroad but considered that a further survey of the entire scheme was necessary. Accordingly I appointed an Overseas Scholarship Committee which has already submitted its report and the Scientific Manpower Committee which also has submitted an interim report. In the light of their recommendations, new plans are being made and I can indicate the general policy of Government. From now on, more money will be spent on the expansion of Indian institutions and only in exceptional

circumstances will selected candidates be sent for training abroad at Government expense.

9. One of our biggest, and perhaps our most important scheme is the Basic Education Scheme for universal compulsory education. Important and valuable work was done by the Central Advisory Board of Education under the last Government. We could not, however, take their recommendations as they stood and felt that certain important modifications were necessary. According to that plan, the full implementation of the scheme would take 40 years but people of India are not prepared to wait for even half that period. I have said earlier that in my opinion the Centrally Administered Areas should serve both as a pioneer and a model, and accordingly I have set up the Delhi Provincial Education Board, and I am taking steps to see that from the 1st of July this year, the basic education plan starts operating in this area.

10. I felt that we should go ahead with the scheme in other areas of India as well. For this, however, it was necessary to get the fullest cooperation from the Provinces and the States. I, therefore, proposed an All India Educational Conference and had originally intended that this should meet in June 1947. Political uncertainties compelled postponement of this Conference twice but ultimately it was held in January 1948. I suggested to the Conference that instead of 40 years, we should aim at a target of five years for the completion of the plan and in any case see that the plan is fully executed and worked out within a period of ten years. The Conference agreed with me and unanimously resolved that steps should be taken to bring this about. There were the problems of trained teachers and finance. The Conference held that while every effort must be made to increase facilites for training teachers, we cannot wait till a sufficient number of trained teachrs are available but must go ahead with existing material in the country. It was therefore proposed that there should be some kind of educational conscription for five years during which every literate man in the country would be expected to put in a period of service as a teacher of the nation. The finances involved are an additional expenditure of about Rs. 24 crores per year for the next five years. The Conference suggested that a Committee should be appointed to examine all available methods for meeting the financial requirements.

11. I have referred to the Central Institute of Education, the

establishment of which was approved two years ago. I decided that we should not wait because of shortage of building material but go ahead with the scheme with whatever housing was available. Accordingly, the Institute was started in December 1947 and is housed partly in tents and partly in a bungalow in the Cavalry Lines. I am hoping that very soon the foundation-stone of its permanent buildings will be laid.

12. I will now briefly refer to the schemes for which funds are needed during the coming year. You will find that the Tata Institute of Science was given a grant of Rs. 3.5 lakhs non-recurring and Rs. 0.5 lakh recurring in the year 1947-48. Provision for an equal amount had been made during the coming year. Provision has also been made in the budget for 1948-49 for a library of educational and cultural films which will be used to carry out the scheme of adult education. Without simultaneous drive for adult education our schemes for basic education for children of 6-14 years cannot be fully implemented.

13. Provision has also been made for the establishment of a National Museum of Art, Archaeology and Anthropology. Here the amounts provided are less than what are required. The financial stringency compelled us to slow down the rate of progress, but I trust that we will very soon be able to go ahead with the programmes at full speed.

14. You will find that provision has also been made in the budget for helping the universities in schemes of fundamental research. The importance of such fundamental research need hardly be emphasized before so responsible a body as this House. I may only add that with the same end in view, we have also provided moneys for research in Higher Polymer Physics and Chemistry at the Indian Association for the Cultivation of Science, Calcutta, and the establishment of a Power Engineering Department at the Indian Institute of Science, Bangalore.

15. Honourable Members are aware that the Central Government have a special responsibility for the development of the Central Universities, and under this head provision has been made both for implementation of the interim scheme and the execution of the post-war development plans.

16. I have referred earlier to the new poliicy of the Government to expand facilities for training within the country itself instead of sending scholars abroad. In pursuance of that policy, you will find in

the budget provision for improvement and development of existing technical institutions according to the recommendations of the All India Council for Technical Education. The most important porjects in this respect are the establishment of the Eastern and the Western Higher Technical Institutions near Calcutta and Bombay respectively. The site for the Eastern Higher Technical Institute has already been approved and the site for the Western Higher Technical Institute has also been provisionally selected. A start has been made in regard to the recruitment of expert staff and advertisements issued simultaneously in India, U.K. and U.S.A. for recruitment of 1 Director and 8 Heads of Departments for the Eastern Institute. They will also be responsible for the planning work for the Western Institute in the initial stages. Provision has also been made for the establishment of Regional Committees for the All India Council for Technical Education.

17. There is today an extreme emphasis on development of facilities for scientific and industrial training. I, however, feel that a country like India with its age-long traditions can ignore the humanities only at the risk of jeopardising her ancient civilization and culture. Provision has, therefore been made in the budget for the reorganization of the Marris College of Hindustani Music, the establishment of a Central College of Karnatak Music in South India and, most important of all, the establishment of a National Cultural Trust. For the Marris College, a grant-in-aid of Rs. 1,45,000 was sanctioned for the year 1947-48 and an equivalent amount has been provided in the next year's budget. For the Central College of Karnatak Music an amount of Rs. 4,25,000 has been provided in the budget. The establishment of a National Cultural Trust with 3 Academies to cater for Arts, Architecture, Letters, Music, Drama and Dancing will serve to focus the artistic and cultural life of the nation in one common Centre.

18. Schemes have also been formulated for the establishment of a Training College of Physical Education and a sum of Rs. 2,10,000 provided in the budget for the purpose. Provision has also been made for a Training College for Teachers in Domestic Science in cooperation with the Lady Irwin College in New Delhi. Admission will be on an All India basis with provision of scholarships as well as maintenance in deserving cases.

19. I have referred earlier to the necessity of increasing facilities for training of teachers. The two schemes of Training College for Physical Education and for Domestic Science are meant to meet the

requirements from one point of view. For general training of teachers, in addition to the schemes already referred to, provision has been made for expanding training facilities at the Viswabharati. Training in arts and crafts, dancing and music and in basic education will be provided there.

20. Provision has also been made for the establishment of a Central Braille Press for the service of the blind. There are several other schemes which had to be either postponed or slowed down because of financial stringency. I may refer to the proposal for the establishment of a Central Institute of Foreign Languages. With India's expanding contacts with all countries of the world, the need for such an Institute is obvious. A Central Bureau of Psychology is also a pressing need but no provision could be made for it in next year's budget. The matter is, however, under consideration. Another scheme which has had to be postponed is the establishment of an Experimental School in Delhi on the lines recommended by the Central Advisory Board. I trust that after the Basic Education Plan has been put into operation, it will be found possible to revive this project. The establishment of a National Central Copyright Library as well as a Central School of Indian Architecture and Regional Planning had also to be postponed for financial reasons. I would not have, in normal circumstances, agreed to anyone of these schemes being postponed or slowed down, but on account of the extraordinary circumstances of last year and particularly the drain upon the nations resources on account of the Punjab calamity, I have reluctanly agreed to this slowing down. I however, trust that this is purely temporary and we shall soon be able to go fullsteam ahead.

21. I have given some account of the work in hand. I may frankly say that I am not fully satisfied either with the progress achieved or the number of schemes in operation. I would, however, like the Honourable Members to remember that nothing can be done without adequate finances. I will give three further instances of the way in which extremely important work has had to be postponed or slowed down because of shortage of funds. The Honourable Members are aware that the Archaeology Department is one of the most important sources from which we get material for the "Discovery of India". It is well known that the history of India is still a wide and uncovered field, and it will be no exaggeration to say that our real history lies burried underground. Excavations on large scale are necessary to

unearth the relics of the past and reconstruct our history, but mean funds which are not at the moment available.

22. Our National Archives, formerly known as Imperial Records, are a treasurehouse for the history of last 200 years. These records must be carefully preserved for the loss of one record means that one chapter of our history has been lost. Further, once these records are lost, they can never be recovered again. Schemes for air-conditioning and use of modern scientific methods for the preservation of these documents had been planned. We had also planned the classification and arrangement of the records for facility of reference and study, but the lack of funds prevented the provision of any money this year and there is nothing in next year's budget as well.

23. The Royal Asiatic Society of Bengal is also a veritable treasurehouse of Sanskrit, Pali, Arabic, Persian and Tibetan records. The collection there is one of the richest in the world. The climate of Calcutta, however, has led to damage of many old manuscripts. It is essential that immediate steps must be taken to restore and preserve 9000 of such manuscripts. Air-conditioning is indispensable in a climate like that of Calcutta but this again means additional expenditure. I propose to appoint a Committee to report on the best methods of preservation of these records and finding necessary finances for the purpose.

24. There are also new schemes of study which are necesary, if we are to give a proper orientation to our national outlook. There must be a revision of syllabus and courses of study from the primary to the university stage. I will mention only two fields where immediate work in this connection is essential. The history of India is a proud heritage of every Indian citizen. Yet there does not exist as yet any true national history of our land. It is necessary that a history of Indian civilization and culture from the earliest times must be taken in hand at an early date. Honourable Members are also aware that Indian philosophy is one of the proudest possessions of human civilization. In our college histories of philosophy, Indian Philosophy is, however, relegated to an obscure corner. In order to get a true perspective of philosophy, it is necessary that a student should know of the great contributions of India, along with the developments which took place in Greece and modern Europe. I propose to appoint a Committee of eminent philosophers with Dr. Radhakrishnan as the Chairman to write a history of Philosophy in which due and

proper emphasis will be given to these facts. It is my intention to have a similar Committee for supervising the preparation of a history of India.

25. I would like in passing to mention that with a view to providing necessary education for the masses a new Section of Social Education has just been started in the Ministry. I need hardly remind you of Disraeli's famous saying that we must educate our masters, but to serve its real purpose, this education must be not only a teaching of the R's but an education in the structure, traditions and purposes of society.

26. I would also like to inform Honourable Members that we have just started an interesting experiment for encouraging young artists by the award of an honorarium. Six artists have been chosen this year and have been awarded a grant of Rs. 2,500 each. The grant is unconditional but given only to artists who are young, full of promise and in such financial conditions that they require State help to develop their genius. The artists were selected by a Committee of experts of established reputation.

27. I have again and again emphasized the need for providing more funds for education. I would like Honourable Members to consider the proportion of money spent by the Central Government for educational purposes. For the year 1946-47, the total Central budget was Rs. 421,35,86,000. Out of this only Rs. 1,87,13,500 were spent on Education. This represents only 0.4 per cent of the total budget. If the expenditure on Defence, Posts, Telegraphs and Railways is excluded from the budget the percentage of expenditure on Education would work out at 1.3 per cent. This represents an unhappy state of affairs and must be remedied as early as possible.

28. It is true that Education is a Provincial subject but during the present phase of the country's development, it is absolutely imperative that the Centre must take the initiative. I have already referred to the Scientific Manpower Committee. In its interim report, it has urged the necessity of the Centre taking the initiative in the provision of technical education of different grades and types throughout the country. What applies to technical education holds equally true of art, archaeology, anthropology and other sepcialised studies.

29. I know that generally the Treasury Benches want to avoid pressure from Honourable Members and are happy if their proposals are accepted without comment or criticism. I, however, welcome the

constructive suggestions they have made and shall be glad if they put further pressure on me and the Government to do as much as possible for a new expansion of education in this ancient land. I need hardly say that whatever be our programme for industrial, scientific, agricultural, commercial or material progress and development, none of them can be achieved without an improvement of the human material which is the basis of our national wealth. That human material is largely conditioned by the training and education which it receives. It seems to me that whether we think of defence or of food or of industries and commerce we must take every step to see that education is given the first priority among all our national requirements. If this is also the opinion of Honourable Members, and they urge upon the Government to act in that light, no one will be happier than myself, whatever may be said in criticism of the proposals or schemes that I have presented before the House.

30. I know that these schemes are not fully satisfactory. I myself would have liked to present before the House a more ambitious scheme of Educational programme and development. Conditions, were, however, against us and we had to fight against tremendous odds, unprecedented in the history of our land. I would, therefore, plead that the House, should judge us, not by the quantum of results achieved, but by the effort and strain involved in achieving them in the face of stupendous difficulties. Honourable Members are aware of the existence of these obstacles, but perhaps do not always realise their magnitude and extent. The Government have no Alladin's Lamp which can build palaces overnight and must, through days, months and years, strive to erect the edifice which all of us desire. In the words of the Persian poet:

Mai khwahi o tund o tez wangah bisiar
Een badah farosh hast Saqi-e-Kausar nest.

Thou desirest wine : wine that is strong and powerful –

And not only strong and powerful but in profuse and abundant measure. Rememberest thou that here is a vintnex no servitor of Paradise.

31. If you remember our difficulties and also remember what has nevertheless been achieved, I feel confident that you will command the manner in which a beginning has been made. I make bold to say

that though difficulties and obstacles prevented us from completing the house, yet no obstacle, no difficulty, no diversion, no opposition could make us desist from our task. I would submit that though the house has not yet been built, foundations have been laid on true and sound lines.

The 11th *March* 1948.

Document No. 69

REPLY DATED 19-3-1948 BY MAULANA AZAD TO THE QUESTIONS ASKED IN THE LEGISLATIVE ASSEMBLY OF INDIA

PLACE OF MUSIC IN PROPOSED CULTURAL TRUST OF GOVERNMENT

Seth Govind Das: (a) Will the Honourable Minister of Education be pleased to state whether music is proposed to be given any place in the proposed Cultural Trust of Government?

(b) Do Government propose to give any scholarships to suitable candidate for training in music?

(c) Do Government propose to organize an academy of music and dance on the lines of the Royal Academy of Music in the United Kingdom or any other country?

The Honourable Maulana Abul Kalam Azad: (a) Yes.

(b) The question will receive consideration when the proposed Indian Cultural Trust is set up.

(c) The proposed Trust will have three Academies, one of which will be for Music, Drama and Dancing.

Seth Govind Das: Will the Government consider over the desirability as far as possible of imparting training in the arts of Music, Drama, and Dance on the lines of ancient India?

The Honourable Maulana Abul Kalam Azad: Yes. This is one of the main objects of this trust.

Shri H.V. Kamath: Have the Government under consideration any scheme for imparting training in the arts of Western and Eastern Music?

The Honourable Maulana Abul Kalam Azad: This will apply to eastern music only.

Document No. 70

ANSWERS DATED 19-3-1948 BY MAULANA AZAD TO THE QUESTIONS ASKED IN THE INDIAN LEGISLATIVE ASSEMBLY

SCHEDULED CASTE STUDENTS SENT ABROAD ON GOVERNMENT SCHOLARSHIP YEAR-WISE SINCE 1937

Shrimati Dakshayani Velayudhan: (a) Will the Honourable Minister of Education be pleased to state the number of Scheduled Caste students who were sent abroad for higher studies on Government scholarship since 1937 year-wise?

(b) How many were boys and how many girls?

(c) How many of them have returned after completing their study?

(d) How many have returned before completing their course of study due to war or other reasons?

(e) Is any preference given to Scheduled Caste candidates in the selection of sending students abroad for higher studies?

The Honourable Maulana Abul Kalam Azad: (a) The total number of Scheduled Caste students so far sent for advanced studies abroad is 35. Out of these 34 were selected in 1945-46, 22 under the Scheduled Caste Scholarships Scheme and 12 under the Overseas Scholarships Scheme. The remaining one was selected in 1946-47 under the Overseas Scholarships Scheme.

(b) Two girls and thirty-three boys.

(c) Eleven.

(d) One, due to serious illness abroad.

(e) Under the Overseas Scholarships Scheme of the Government of India, the Scheduled Castes are given a proper share of scholarships according to communal ratio prescribed by the Ministry of Home Affairs for purposes of appointments to services, provided suitable candiates are forthcoming. They are thus afforded better chances, with comparatively lower merit, provided they possess the minimum qualifications which would ensure their admission in the already overcrowded foreign universities.

Shrimati Dakshayani Velayudhan: I asked the number of candidates year-wise.

Mr. Speaker: But the question is not very clear on that point.

Shrimati Dakshayani Velayudhan: The original question was all right. I do not know who made it like this.

Mr. Speaker: What does she want to know?

Shrimati Dakshayani Velayudhan: I want to know the number of students from 1937 to 1948 year-wise.

Mr. Speaker: Is it possible for the Honourable Minister to give this information?

The Honourable Maulana Abul Kalam Azad: I want notice for this.

Mr. Speaker: Is there any other question which she wants to put?

Shrimati Dakshayani Velayudhan: I wanted to know only this. But I do not know who has changed the question.

Mr. Speaker: I must refer to the original notice she sent because nobody is interested in amending it.

Shrimati Dakshayani Velayudhan: Why did they amend the question?

Mr. Speaker: Whether the question is amended or not is a matter to be verified. The Honourable Member does not know perhaps that the questions are not amended by the Executive Government. All questions that are sent by members are scrutinised by the Speaker's Office, then they are scrutinised by the Speaker himself and, if necessary, they are amended to bring them within the rules. If she has any complaint about any amendment, she should see me in my Chamber and then the matter will be verified and if there is a mistake, that will be corrected. She cannot discuss in this House what the Speaker has done.

Document No. 71

ANSWERS BY MAULANA AZAD DT. 23-3-1948 TO THE QUESTIONS ASKED IN THE LEGISLATIVE ASSEMBLY REGARDING THE FOREIGN EXPERT INSTRUCTORS TO COACH INDIAN COMPETITORS FOR OLYMPIC GAMES

Shri P. Khunhiraman (on behalf of **Shri V.C. Kesava**) : Will the Honourable Minister of Education be pleased to state whether any representations regarding the necessity of engaging foreign expert instructors to coach the intending competitors for the Olympic games have been received by Government from the participants in the Olympic games held at Lucknow; and, if so, what action Government have taken in the matter?

The Honourable Maulana Abul Kalam Azad : The Government has not received any such representation. The second part of the question therefore does not arise.

Document No. 72.

ANSWERS DATED 23-3-1948 BY MAULANA AZAD TO THE QUESTIONS ASKED IN THE INDIAN LEGISLATIVE ASSEMBLY

PARTITION OF ASSETS OF PUNJAB PUBLIC LIBRARY, LAHORE

Shri Lakshminarayan Sahu: (a) Will the Honourable Minister of Education be pleased to state whether it is a fact that the Punjab Public Library at Lahore was run and maintained by the Government of Punjab?

(b) If so, has it been partitioned like other assets of other institutions of that Provincial Government?

(c) If not, do Government propose to arrange for the transfer of the Sanskrit, Hindi, and Gurmukhi sections to East Punjab?

The Honourable Maulana Abul Kalam Azad: With your permission, Sir, I propose to answer Starred Question Nos. 938-40 together. The Honourable Member's questions pertain to a subject with which the Government of the East Punjab is concerned, to whom the questions have been forwarded.

Seth Govind Das: Will any reply be received from there in this connection?

The Honourable Maulana Abul Kalam Azad: It is hoped that this would receive consideration there.

Shri Deshbandhu Gupta: May I enquire whether these questions do not relate to the Ministry of Relief and Rehabilitation?

Mr. Speaker: That is an argument and not a question asking for information.

Shri Deshbandhu Gupta: I am drawing his attention to the matter and finding out whether he has considered this aspect.

Mr. Speaker: That means argument again. What is the information that he wants?

Shri Deshbandhu Gupta: That is no information.

Mr. Speaker: That is argument.

Document No. 73

ANSWERS DATED 23-3-1948 BY MAULANA AZAD TO THE QUESTIONS ASKED IN THE LEGISLATIVE ASSEMBLY

APPLICATIONS FOR SCHEDULED CASTE SCHOLARSHIPS FOR 1947-48

Shri P. Kunhiraman (on behalf of **Shri V.C. Kesava Rao**): (a) Will the Honourable Minister of Education be pleased to state the total number of applications received by the Scheduled Castes Scholarship Board for scholarships from the Scheduled Caste students during the year 1947-48?

(b) How many of them were granted scholarships?

(c) Were the funds placed at the disposal of the Board adequate to meet the needs of all the applications?

(d) If not, what steps were taken to augment the amount?

The Honourable Maulana Abul Kalam Azad: (a) 1,225.

(b) 590 so far.

(c) Yes, Sir. The funds available have so far been sufficient for awarding scholarship to all the eligible candidates.

(d) The question does not arise.

Document No. 74

ANSWERS BY MAULANA AZAD DT. 23-3-48 TO THE QUESTIONS ASKED IN THE LEGISLATIVE ASSEMBLY ABOUT THE INSTITUTIONS IMPARTING EDUCATION IN MARINE ENGINEERING

Shri Basanta Kumar Das : Will the Honourable Minister of Education be pleased to state:

(a) What institutions are there in India for imparting education in Marine Engineering; and

(b) What steps Government propose to take for increasing the number of such institutions?

The Honourable Maulana Abul Kalam Azad: (a) The I.M.M.T.S. "Dufferin" at Bombay is the only institution in India which imparts instruction in Marine Engineering at present.

(b) The Government of India have set up a committee to enquire into the existing facilities for the training of Mercantile Marine Officers in India and to make recommendations for their expansion. The Committee's final report is still awaited but the Committee in its interim report have recently recommended that the Government of India should set up as soon as possible a Nautical and Engineering College. The recommendation of the Committee is under the active consideration of the Government of India.

Naval Architecture and Marine Engineering is one of the subjects instruction in which up to the degree standard will be imparted at the proposed Western Higher Technical Institution to be located near Bombay.

Shri Basanta Kumar Das : How many students generally come out of that institution?

The Honourable Maulana Abul Kalam Azad: I would require notice for this. I cannot answer at the moment.

Shri Satis Chandra Samanta : When was the Committee formed?

The Honourable Maulana Abul Kalam Azad: I cannot say exactly the time and date when the Committee was appointed, but probably it was constituted about 2 or 3 months ago.

Document No. 75

LETTER FROM DR. RAJENDRA PRASAD TO MAULANA AZAD

Camp: Bajajwadi, Wardha

27th March, 1948

My dear Maulana Saheb,

After the telephone talk I had with you the other day, I had requested Shri Krishna Ballabh Babu to come and see me here in connection with the Zamindari Acquisition Bill in Bihar and he came here to see me today. The present position is this. The Bill which was introduced in the Assembly some months ago was referred to the Select Committee and the Select Committee made its report some time ago. The report of the Select Committee was presented to the Assembly on the 28th February. The third reading of the Bill will begin on the 30th March and the clauses of the Bill will be considered one after another. The Assembly will, it is expected, pass the Bill in a few days after the 30th. The question is whether at this stage the Ministry can postpone consideration of the Bill. There is a strong feeling amongst the members, as also among the public at large, that further progress of the Bill should not be delayed. The Central Parliamentary Board had on a previous occasion convened a meeting of the Revenue Ministers from the various Provinces, and although I had not then taken over charge as the President, I presided over the Conference which you also were good enough to attend for some time. The decision of the Conference was that the Bills should be proceeded with and it was after the Conference that the Select Committee in Bihar sat and with certain amendments prepared its report. So much about the position.

As regards the merits of the Bill, I suppose everybody now accepts the position that zamindari should be abolished and even the zamindars, more or less, have reconciled themselves to it. The only question is about the compensation and the method of paying it. The Bihar Bill has made provision for payment of compensation. The total amount of it, it is calculated, will come to something like 130 crores, may be even 140 crores. That has to be paid partly in cash and partly in bonds which will be negotiable and bear interest at 2½% per annum. As far as I can judge, the Bihar Government has got no cash nor, I am afraid, will it be able to get any cash assistance from the Government of India unless you all could persuade the Finance Minister. On the face of it, it is rather hard on the bigger zamindars that they should get three times their net income as compensation. The net income is arrived at by making certain reductions on account of revenue and collection charges, etc., etc., which comes nearly to about 50% of their gross revenue so that the compensation in their case will come only to 1½ times their present gross collections. The Select Committee made certain changes which favoured the smaller landlords whose scale of compensation has been increased and who have got also a large concession by being allowed to split up their income as members of a joint family and thus bring the income of each member of the family within the scale which pay a higher rate of compensation. This has, on the one hand, added considerably to the Government's liability and added the same amount to the compensation which will be payable to the smaller zamindars. Thus, according to the previous calculation, when the rate payable was lower in the case of the smaller zamindars and the splitting of their incomes was not allowed, the total compensation payable was calculated to be something like 63 or 64 crores. As a result of this Select Committee's amendment, the compensation payable has become more than double and is now calculated to be something between 130 and 140 crores. All this increase will go to zamindars whose income is below 4 lakhs and they will also get something additional from what is taken away from those whose income is more than 4 lakhs, because the minimum payable before was five times the net revenue on incomes of over 50,000. Now it has been reduced to 3 times on incomes of over 4 lakhs, while the compensation payable on incomes between 50,000 and 4 lakhs varies between 7 times and 3 times. The net result of the Select Committee's report has been that the smaller landlords have good reason to be satisfied, but the bigger landlords have no reason to become more dissatisfied than they were before. But, the number of zamindars who will come in the category of zamindars having more than 4 lakhs on which only 3 times will be paid as compensation will be very small. They will practically be only the six States of Darbhanga, Bettiah, Dumraon,

Hathua, Ramgarh and Ratu which would be hit. According to the Bill, as reported by the Select Committee, the total compensation payable to these six States will come to something like 2 crores and 31 lakhs roughly.

I think the Maharaja of Darbhanaga is still there. If you could have a talk with him in the presence of the Revenue Minister, perhaps some way could be found without postponing the Bill to give these six landlords some satisfaction. So far as I can judge, if they are thinking of having the Bill altogether dropped, that will not be possible either for the Ministry or for any of us to do. So the only relief that they can get can be about the compensation. The bill has tried to give higher compensation to the smaller people and the amount will be distributed amongst a large number of smaller zamindars.

At one stage the Select Committee had resolved to fix a ceiling and not to allow more than 25 lakhs as compensation to anyone whatever his income from his zamindari might be. When Sardar went to Patna, he objected to the ceiling put, and so that ceiling has been dropped. If that had remained, the Maharaja of Darbhanaga, whose net income came to, say, 25 or 30 lakhs a year, could not have got more than 25 lakhs as compensation. The bill, as it now stands, will give 75 lakhs or 90 lakhs according as his net income is found to be 25 or 30 lakhs. Similarly, the other five zamindars will also get larger amount than what they would have got if the ceiling of 25 lakhs had been maintained. I am mentioninig all these points for your consideration, so that in the course of conversation, you may be able to point out what has been done so far.

I received a telegram from the Maharaja of Darbhanga two or three days ago in which he complained that another Bill was going to be introduced raising the rate of agricultural income-tax. The Bill has not yet been introduced, but it has been published and is likely to be introduced in April. The effect of this Bill is likely to be to raise the Government's revenue from the agricultural income-tax from 30 lakhs to near about 50 lakhs, that is to say, an additional 15 to 20 lakhs. You might talk about this matter also with Krishna Ballabh Babu.

Yours sincerely,
Rajendra Prasad

P.S. There is another aspect of the acquisition of zamindari problems which requires to be considered from the point of view of the Government. I understand from Krishna Ballabh Babu that he has in mind a plan to pay up the amount on account of compensation at present in negotiable bonds carrying interest at 2½% per annum. The Government will go on paying as also a portion of the principal due on the bonds each year and will thus pay up both principal and interest in 30 years. Interest on 130 crores will be 3¼ crores and if, say, about three crores are paid every year towards principal, the Government will have to pay about 6 crores. Government expenses on account of collection etc. will be about another 3 crores per year. Thus the Government will, within six months of the Act coming into force, incur an annual liability of at least nine crores. They calculate that the rent and other incomes derived from all zamindaris in Bihar comes to about 16 crores a year and they calculate that the Government will be making a profit of 6 or 7 crores a year after meeting the interest and sinking fund charges and renting the cost of collection etc. This calculation is based on the assumption that there will be no reduction in the rent payable by tenants for at least thirty years, that the rent payable by tenants will be realised from year to year without fail, that there will be no demand on the part of the tenants for reduction of rent or for remissions on account of bad seasons as in ryotwari areas where partial or total remission is allowed for various reasons. My fear is that all these assumptions are wrong. There will be a very strong demand on the part of the tenants not only for reduction of rent but for a total abolition of rent and the Government will not be able to resist it. The Economic Committee of the All India Congress Committee recommended and the A.I.C.C. at its last meeting accepted the recommendation that rent should be abolished and should be replaced by agricultrual income-tax. That means that no agriculturist will be required to pay rent, but he will have to pay income-tax like other people having income from other sources. People with small incomes are exempted from the tax. If the present rates of exemption of 2,000 is allowed to agriculturists also as is done to others, then all agriculturists, whose net income is less than 2,000 a year will be free from income-tax also. My idea is that nearly 95 per cent of the agriculturists of Bihar have net income of less than 2,000 a year and thus 95 per cent of the agriculturists will be free from the tax. If this is accepted and rent is abolished, the Government will get a very small amount from agricultural income-tax which will not be able to pay even one-fifth of the interest and principal on the bonds every year. It will be a very serious matter of any Government to issue bonds which it will not be able to redeem. I do not think the Provincial Government has any other source of income to meet this heavy liability of 6 crores a year. After the A.I.C.C. resolution I do not think the Provincial Government will be able to resist the demand for abolition of rent. This applies to all Provinces where there is zamindari, and has to be considered. I do not consider it right or honest to take away the zamindaris today on the promise that compensation will be paid, and then after a short time to turn round and say that because rent is being abolished, the compensation which had been promised at the time of the acquisition cannot be paid. I have always apprehended that the Government will find it most difficult in the present atmosphere to realise the whole amount of rent. Many zamindars are unable to realise it now. The tenants will not easily pay to the Government and its coercive process for realisation will make the demand for abolition more urgent.

The Bihar Bill lays down that all zamindaris will automatically be acquired in six months of the Act coming into force, and the zamindar will be eliminated. The tenant will not get remission or reduction in rent. In fact there is no programme yet ready for giving any kind of relief to the tenant. The only change, so far as the tenant's position is concerned, is that instead of paying the same rent to the zamindar or his tahsildar, he will have to pay it to the Government tahsildar who can enforce payment without going to court by the simple method of issuing a certificate. My fear is that there will be great discontent almost immediately against the Government which cleverer among the idle zamindars will instigate and encourage. This will make realisation progressively more difficult and resistance to abolition of rent impossible.

I have added this long postcript as the question affects not only Bihar but all other Provinces where zamindari has to be abolished like the U.P., Bengal, and the C.P. where no Bill has yet been introduced, and Madras where a Bill is being considered at present by a Select Committee.

Rajendra Prasad
28-3-48

Hon'ble Maulana Abul Kalam Azad
19, Akbar Road, New Delhi.

Document No. 76

ANSWERS BY MAULANA AZAD IN THE LEGISLATIVE ASSEMBLY DATED 28-3-1948 TO THE QUESTION ASKED REGARDING THE TRAINING OF STUDENTS AS TECHNICIANS

Mr. R.K. Sidhva : (a) Will the Honourable Minister of Education be please to state whether Government have revised the policy, as stated in the last budget session, for training of students as technicians in foreign countries?

(b) If so, what are the details?

(c) Have Government considered the necessity of giving such students practical training in workshops and not merely theoretical training?

(d) When is the scheme likely to materialise?

The Honourable Maulana Abul Kalam Azad:

(a) The matter is under consideration in the light of the Final Report of the Roy Committee appointed to examine the Overseas Scholarships Scheme in all its aspects and a decision is expected shortly.

(b) to (d) Do not arise at this stage.

Mr. R.K. Sidhva : What are the recommendations of the Committee?

The Honourable Maulana Abul Kalam Azad: I have already stated in reply to the question, Government are considering the recommendations of this committee and final decision is likely to be arrived at very soon. If the honourable member wants to know its basic recommendations, I can only say at the moment that a major portion of the amount which was previously spent on the old scheme should now be utilized on the public institutions, and a comparatively smaller amount should be spent on sending the scholars abroad.

Mr. R.K. Sidhva : Will this scheme after it is finalized be circulated to the members?

The Honourable Maulana Abul Kalam Azad : The general practice is that whatever decision is arrived at by the Government, it is announced to the public at the proper time. Similar action will be taken in regard to this scheme.

Shri Gopikrishna Vijayavargiya : Will the Honourable Minister please state whether in view of the fact that India is observing a neutral foreign policy with America and Russia, and wants to derive benefit from both the countries, will Government arrange to send stundents to Russia for training?

The Honourable Maulana Abul Kalam Azad : Yes. First of all the subjects for the training of which we have to send scholars abroad will have to be decided. If any of these subjects necessitate that scholars should be sent to Russia, then arrangements will surely be made in this direction.

Shri Ajit Prasad Jain : Will the Honourable Minister please state the amount that the Government are spending on this scheme.

The Honourable Maulana Abul Kalam Azad : I cannot quote complete figures at the moment.

Shri Mahavir Tyagi : Are any recommendations called for from the Governments of Provinces and States in regard to the selection of students who are sent abroad?

The Honourable Maulana Abul Kalam Azad : The old scheme had been designed in such a manner that some scholars were sent by the Central Govenment and some by the Provincial Governments. The Provincial Governments used to make recommendations in respect of the scholars sent by them, and the central Government used to set up a Selection Board for selecting its scholars. No such quota was fixed for the Provinces.

Shri Mahavir Tyagi : Do Government provide any facilities of employment to the scholars who return from abroad after training?

The Honourable Maulana Abul Kalam Azad: Rules were prescribed in this respect. But I will frankly say that no proper arrangement was made in this direction in the old scheme. Difficulties, are however, being experienced in finding employment for those persons who have returned after completion of their studies.

Document No. 77

ANSWERS DATED 31-3-1948 BY MAULANA AZAD TO THE QUESTIONS ASKED IN THE INDIAN LEGISLATIVE ASSEMBLY

POST-WAR SCHEME OF EDUCATION ON ALL-INDIA BASIS

Shri Kishori Mohan Tripathi: (a) Will the Honourable Minister of Education be pleased to state whether any post-war scheme of education on an all-India basis has been drawn up either by the Government of India or by the Government of India and the Governments of the different Provinces jointly?

(b) If so, what are the salient features of the scheme?

(c) If not, do Government propose to draw up such a scheme?

The Honourable Maulana Abul Kalam Azad: (a) Yes. A scheme on post-war education on an all-India basis was drawn up by the Central Advisory Board of Education in January, 1944, main recommendations of which are contained in their Report on Post-war Educational Development in India, popularly known as Sargent Report. These recommendations have been generally accepted by the Government of India and the Provincial Governments.

(b) The Honourable Member may please refer to a copy of the Sargent Report which is available in the Library of the Assembly.

(c) Does not arise.

Shri Kishori Mohan Tripathi: Will the Honourable Minister be pleased to state what steps Government have taken by now to implement that scheme?

The Honourable Maulana Abul Kalam Azad: A meeting of the Central Advisory Board was held in January last, and an all India Conference was also convened for this very purpose. Many schemes were considered in this connection and committees have been set up. The Government is trying to push forward the matter with great speed.

Maulana Hasrat Mohani: Is the Honourable Minister for Education aware of the fact that most of the Provincial Governments are acting quite contrary to the rules framed by the Central Advisory Board? For example, the U.P. Government are not respecting the right of every person to obtain his education in his mother tongue.

Mr. Speaker: What is it that the Honourable Member wants to know?

Maulana Hasrat Mohani: I want to know whether it is a fact that some of the Provincial Governments altogether ignore the directions given by the Advisory Council.

The Honourable Maulana Abul Kalam Azad: The question does not arise.

Mr. Speaker: It is not necessary to answer this question. It is only the opinion of the Honourable Member.

Shri S.V. Krishnamurthy Rao: May I know whether these films will be prepared and supplied to the principal linguistic areas in India

Mr. Speaker: This question does not relate to films. It refers to the Sargent Report.

An Honourable Member: That question comes later on.

Shri S.V. Krishnamurthy Rao: I am sorry, Sir.

Document No. 78

ANSWERS DATED 31-3-1948 BY MAULANA ABUL KALAM AZAD TO THE QUESTIONS ASKED IN THE LEGISLATIVE ASSEMBLY OF INDIA

HELP TO REFUGEE STUDENTS IN RESPECT OF EXAMINATIONS

Shri Kishori Mohan Tripathi: Will the Honourable Minister of Education be pleased to state as to how Government propose to help the refugee students in regard to their examinations in view of the fact that those who have come over to India from Pakistan area may not be in a position to appear at their prescribed examinations ensuing shortly?

The Honourable Maulana Abul Kalam Azad: The Government of India requested all the Provincial Governments and the Indian Universities to afford all facilities to students migrating from the Western Pakistan in connection with their examinations. Statements indicating the concessions given by the Universities of the East Punjab and Bombay, which are the main Universities concerned, are laid on the table of the House.

Statement I

Indicating the concessions given by the East Punjab University to students migrating from the Western Pakistan

The following concessions were extended to refugee students who had to appear in various University examinations to be held in 1947, but who could not take their examinations as a whole or in part owing to the communal disturbances :

(1) They were given the option to put in ten weeks' approved social service at the completion of which they would be eligible for the certificate or degree for which they were studying.

(2) In case any student could not or did not put in social service, he could join the next higher class by taking a qualifying test held by every college in the East Punjab including the Camp College in New Delhi.

Note: While concession 1 above applied to Matriculation, Intermediate (Arts and Science), Degree (Arts and Science) students, concessions 2 applied to Matriculation, Intermediate (Arts and Science) studnets only. Failing 1 and 2 above, students could take the East Punjab University Emergency Examination which was held according to the following schedule:

Matriculation	February, 1948
Intermediate	January, 1948
Degree	February, 1948
M.A.	Commencing on 5th April
M.L.	19th March, 1948
B.T.	29th March, 1948
O.T.	1st April, 1948

(These examinations in normal course would have been held during the period August to September, 1947 by the Old Punjab University). The East Punjab University came into existence on the 1st October, 1947 by an Ordinance and this University announced that the above examinations would be held in December, 1947, but later on changed its decision in view of the difficulties of students.

(4) Concessions to students appearing in examination scheduled to be held in September-October, 1948:

Matriculation, F.A. and B.A. students were given the option to put in ten week's approved social service and thus secure exemption in any one subject only. Besides, on production of evidence that a candidate had passed in one or more papers in any examination held by the Punjab University in Lahore in 1947, he was exempted from appearing in those papers and was allowed to complete the examination by appearing in the remaining papers.

Statement II

Indicating the concessions given by the Bombay University to students migrating from the Western Pakistan

Copy of University of Bombay Circular No. MI of 1948

With a view to clarifying the position arising out of the decision of the University (*vide* Circular No. M-13315/1947) to grant facilities to students who have migrated from Sind (the Punjab and other provinces) on account of disturbances, panic or fear and who are eligible to appear at the Matriculation Examination in the ordinary course, it is hereby brought to the notice of the Heads of recognised schools and the general public that the procedure for admission to the examination will be as under:

(i) Students or ex-students who have migrated from Sind to the Province of Bombay, and have joined a recognised school will be treated as regular students of the school concerned, and will be admitted as such to the examination.

(ii) Students or ex-students who have migrated from Sind to the Province of Bombay, but have not joined any school, will be required to forward their applications, with the accompaniments mentioned in (iii) below, for admission to the examination through the Head of a recognised school. The Head of the recognised school whom the student approaches with a request to forward the application shall be entitled to charge the fee of Re. 1.

(iii) Students or ex-students who have migrated from Sind to other places outside the territorial jurisdiction of the University, will be admitted to the exmaination direct, if found eligible, on production of the Leaving Certificate of the last recognised school attended by them or in its absence an affidàvit made by the student, if major, *i.e.*, over 18 years, the guardian of the student (if below 18) or before a magistrate or a J.P. giving particulars regarding the name of the school last attended, the number of days of attendance in the Matriculation class and the date of birth. The Leaving Certificate or the affidavit shall be attached to the application. It will not be returned under any circumstances. The form of application for admission to the examination and also the fee receipt should preferably be signed in the presence of the person before whom the affidavit is made.

(iv) Ex-students who have joined a school in Sind subsequent to their failure as the last Matriculation Examination and have migrated subsequently will also be admitted to the examination as ex-students falling under categories (ii) or (iii) above, despite the fact that they have lost all the rights of an ex-student since joining a recognised school after their failure under O-156H. Similarly, students who were not sent up last year, but were otherwise eligible, will be admitted to the examination as specified above whether they have joined or not joined a school in Sind during the current academic year.

(v) Students migrating from places other than Sind on account of disturbances, panic or fear will be admitted to the examination as regular students only; such students will not be admitted direct to the examination, though in their cases also the condition regarding minimum attendance for a period of 100 days as laid down in S-202 will be waived, and they will be admitted if they keep an attendance of 50 days in a school recognised by this University.

(vi) Students studying in schools recognised by the University of Sind will not be generally considered eligible for admission to the Matriculation examination of this University, except that those who had left the schools in Sind and have not been able to migrate will be admitted to the examination as laid down in (iii) above.

2. All students who are not eligible for admission to the examination as regular students or ex-students, will be classified as Private candidates. Further, the cases of those regular students who have not been able to keep the attendance prescribed by S-202 will be governed by the foot-note to S-202 in the matter of the condonation of deficiency in attendance and Headmasters are requested to forward cases, if any, to the University for consideration without delay. Headmasters of recognised schools are further requested to insist on a student producing the Leaving Certificate of the recognised school last attended by him or in its absence an affidavit as indicated in clause (iii) above and satisfy themselves that the student is eligible for admission to the examination as laid down and that he has (i) attended a recognised school in Sind for at least 50 days prior to migration; and (ii) has migrated owing to disturbances, panic or fear.

3. Students who apply direct are advised to send the application forms duly filled in with accompaniments as in (iii) above by Registered Post (with acknowledgement due if a receipt is desired). The amount of the fee of Rs. 15 should be sent by Money Order and the necessary

particulars regarding the name, the address and the name of the examination, the languages offered under O-158 and the centre must be supplied in the Money Order coupon. Otherwise the Money Order is likely to be refused. The Money Orders and the letters must be addressed to the Registrar, University of Bombay, Matriculation Department, Bombay 1, to avoid delay. Applications in person will not be accepted, nor will any correspondence in the matter of receipt of applications be attended to.

4. In every case where the admission is granted on the strength of evidence other than the Leaving Certificate of the recognised school last attended, the admission will be deemed provisional and is liable to be cancelled unless confirmed later on by the production of the requisite Leaving Certificate of the recognised school last attended. In all such cases no claim for refund of fees will be admissible, and the candidate concerned will not be entitled to receive the pass certificate if he passes the examination or to any right to appear after failure at any subsequent examination of the University on the more strength of his name being included in the list of candidates appearing at the examination till the confirmation of his admission to the examination.

5. The last date of receipt of applications is Monday, the 19th January, 1948 and the examination is due to commence on Monday, the 15th March, 1948 according to the programme that will be notified in the Bombay Government Gazette in due course. The Seat Numbers of candidates appearing at the examination will be exhibited at the centres concerned one week before the commencement of the examination and candidates are advised to make their own arrangements for ascertaining their seat numbers and the detailed programme of the examination. Queries on these subject from candidates will not be attended to.

6. Those candidates who offer Sindhi as one of the languages under O-158 as also those who require the passage in Sindhi for translation into English in the paper in General English will be required to appear at Bombay or Dadar centres only, as it is not possible to offer them these facilities at other centres. Candidates at any centre will be at liberty to answer questions in Sindhi in papers where the option to answer in the candidates mother-language is allowed.

7. The examination will be held at the centres shown in Circular

No. M-29, dated 16th December, 1947. Students offering a particular language will be allowed to appear only at the centres mentioned against that language in Appendix F (Blue Booklet) and at no other centre.

(Sd.) S.R. DONGERKERY
University Registrar

Bombay, 7th January, 1948

Shri Kishori Mohan Tripathi: Is it that the scope of these concessions is limited to people coming from Western Pakistan only or those coming from Eastern Pakistan can also avail themselves of these concessions?

The Honourable Maulana Abul Kalam Azad: This question arose mainly in connection with students coming from Western Pakistan. The Governments of the East Punjab and Bombay have made arrangements in this connection.

Seth Govind Das: Is it within the knowledge of the Honourable Minister that students have not only come from Western Pakistan but from Eastern Pakistan also? What is being done about their examinations?

The Honourable Maulana Abul Kalam Azad: So far as I know West Bengal Government have made necessary arrangements in this connection, and they are still doing so.

Document No. 79

ANSWERS DATED 31-3-1948 BY MAULANA AZAD TO THE QUESTIONS ASKED IN THE CONSTITUENT ASSEMBLY OF INDIA (LEGISLATIVE)

ABOLITION OF CAMBRIDGE CERTIFICATE OF EXAMINATION FOR STUDENTS IN INDIAN SCHOOLS

Seth Govind Das: (a) Will the Honourable Minister of Education be pleased to state whether it is a fact that the examination of certain schools in this country is held under foreign Universities, such as Cambridge University?

(b) If so, do Government propose to abolish such examinations and how much time will it take to do so?

The Honourable Maulana Abul Kalam Azad: (a) Yes.

(b) The Cambridge Certificate Examinations referred to by the Honourable Member are mostly taken advantage of by Anglo-Indian Schools. Their future is at present under consideration.

Seth Govind Das: Are the Government aware that the medium of instruction in our schools is English in these days, and that the Anglo-Indian students do not know Indian languages. What are the steps the Government propose to take to impart education to the Anglo-Indians in the Indian languages?

The Honourable Maulana Abul Kalam Azad: In this connection, Government have decided that the line of policy to be adopted in future will have to be followed by the schools of all communities.

Document No. 80

LETTER FROM MAULANA AZAD TO DR. RAJENDRA PRASAD

1 April, 1948

My dear Rajendra Babu,

Krishna Ballabh Sahay was here and gave me your letter. I do not know what really the matter is. But Sardar Patel, Maharaja of Darbhanga and Sultan Ahmed – all three of them – had told me that a deputation had called on you and you had promised them that they would be given a chance to clarify their point of view as regards the Bihar Zamindari Bill. If it is really so, they should be given a chance.

You are right in your view that it would be going against popular opinion to stall the Bill now. This should be passed in the Assembly. Krishna Ballabh Sahay was informed accordingly. But there is no harm if, at an opportune time, the deputation of the Bihar Zamindars is given a chance to finally express its views. Krishna Ballabh Sahay had agreed that they may come on 5 April and be heard. But perhaps this date will not be suitable as you may not be able to find time at such short notice. But some date in the 2nd or 3rd week of April, as may suit you, can be fixed. Hope you are perfect all right. Twice I tried to speak to you over the telephone but probably you were not at home.

Abul Kalam Azad

Document No. 81

MAULANA AZAD'S PRESS CONFERENCE IN NEW DELHI ON MAY 31, 1948

Some time ago I made an announcement that a section of Social Education has been opened in the Ministry of Education. This Section is concerned with the preparation of plans for imparting social education to the Indian people. With the introduction of adult franchise the necessity of such education has become even more pressing than before. It is necessary that I should explain to the public the scope and purpose of the programme that we have taken in hand.

There is at present a great deal of confusion about the meaning of the terms Social Education, Social Welfare and Adult Education. In order to remove this the concept of social education must be clearly defined so that we may go ahead with the programmes that have been accepted in this Ministry.

At the outset, let me make it clear that social education is not merely a study of Sociology. Sociology is the science of social phenomena and in its wider meaning covers advanced studies like Economics, Politics, Anthropology, Jurisprudence, etc. Sociology is a branch of theoretic knowledge which systematises a certain type of facts and tries to establish the laws of social inter-actions, relations and developments. By social education is meant something which has an immediately practical bearing.

Nor is social education synonymous with social welfare. Social welfare is primarily an activity directed towards the removal of the many disabilities and evils from which individuals or groups suffer under existing social conditions; thus, the provision of amenities for labour class population or work among drug addicts or attempts to enforce social hygiene are examples of social welfare work. Social education may lead to such activities but must not be confused with them.

Social education may therefore be defined as a course of study towards the production of a consciousness of citizenship among the people and the promotion of social solidarity among them. For this, it is obvious that there must be some knowledge of social conditions, but it is not necessary to have detailed acquaintance with sociological laws which the study of Economics or Politics requires. Its affinity with adult education is more immediate. We may say that adult education has three aspects, namely, (a) the induction of literacy among grown-up illiterates, (b) the production of an educated mind in the masses in the absence of literary education, (c) the inculcation of a lively sense of rights and duties of citizenship, both as individuals and as members of a mighty nation. We may say that social education is synonymous with adult education, but lays more emphasis upon the two latter aspects of education.

For developing a sense of citizenship and producing an educated mind, the following seem essential:

(a) Every citizen must know the meaning of citizenship and the way democracy functions. He should have not only some knowledge of the history and geography of the country but also of its social conditions. In order to fulfil his duties as a citizen, he must also have some acquaintance with the wo:king of the State. With the introduction of adult franchise, it is imperative for every voter to know the meaning of the vote. He should be instructed that in parliamentary democracy, the government is responsible to him, and his vote therefore is not merely a valuable right but also a great obligation. Much of the necessary knowledge in such matters can be imparted by verbal methods. In the case of illiterate adults it is obvious that the emphasis must be on the spoken word rather than on written texts.

(b) There must also be instruction in the laws of personal and public health. True citizenship implies knowledge of and respect for the laws which govern the health of the community. At present, in India, there is often emphasis on certain rituals of personal cleanliness, accompanied by colossal ignorance of and indifference to the laws of social health. One of the main purposes of social education must be to train people in clean and healthy living. This will involve information about ventilation and accommodation in houses, disposal of refuse, some rudimentary ideas of drainage and consideration for the convenience of neighbours and other members of the public.

(c) Social education must also mean the imparting of such information to the people as will enable them to effect some improvement in their economic status. This is necessary not only to rouse an interest among the adult illiterates in the course of study but also from the point of view of the community itself. It is obvious that adults will take a more immediate and active interest in anything which promises improvement in their economic status. Arrangements will therefore be made for training in a craft or the introduction of better techniques in existing crafts, and for improving general efficiency of the men.

(d) Social education, involving as it does the improvement of bodily and mental health, cannot ignore the proper training and refinement of the emotions. Art and literature are the instruments of this training. Folk music, drama, dance, poetry and recreative activities must be included in a scheme of social education.

(e) Social education should also contain an element of instruction in a universal ethic, with special emphasis upon the necessity of toleration of one another's differences in a democracy. In a way, this will be included in the course of training under (a), but, in addition, there should be a special attention devoted to the inculcation of tolerance, mutual appreciation and universal principles of right conduct.

A comprehensive programme of education on these lines will have to be undertaken for the whole of the Indian Union. We cannot, however, overlook that there are financial and other difficulties which make the execution of such a plan extremely difficult. I feel that we should therefore start the experiment in some selected area and, as we gather experience, extend the scope of our programme to other areas. Since it has been decided to start the programme of basic education in Delhi Province from the 1st of July, I propose that the scheme of social education should also first be tried out there. The fact that Delhi is a small province and is also directly administered by the Central Government will make it easier to carry out the experiment in this area.

It is necessary that the basic school buildings and staff should be utilised to the fullest possible extent by serving as schools for children in the morning, adolescent schools and clubs for young people in the afternoon and education centres for adults in the evening. Our programme cannot be completely successful unless the basic schools sponsored by the Government are also centres for the life of the entire village community. It will be necessary to provide a fair proportion of games and group activities for the adolescents as otherwise their interest in instruction is likely to flag. Similarly in the case of adults, the emphasis will be more on social education than on mere literacy, and this will be imparted through visual, aural and oral methods.

The importance of adequate methods of visual and aural education for adolescents and adults need not be stressed. The Government of India intend to encourage the production of folk drama and rural plays by the villagers themselves. Prizes for the purpose may be given from time to time and competitions held between different villages or local units. Films can also play a great part in teaching the lessons of citizenship, social responsibility, personal health, public hygiene, physical drill and other matters of immediate benefit to the community. The radio is also a powerful instrument of aural education, and I have under consideration plans for full utilisation of both the films and the radio.

I need hardly say that all our educational programme will ultimately depend upon the proper education of women. If women take to education, more than half of our problems will be solved. Educated mothers will mean children who can be easily made literate. From the point of view of expense and mangement, it would have been simplest if men and women could be taught through the same agencies. I know, however, that the existing conditions in India will not permit this. At the same time our finances will not allow a complete duplication of the whole apparatus for teaching men and women separately. I would therefore suggest that for the basic schools, that is, for children between the ages of 6 and 11, the institutions might be co-educational. For the adolescents, the solution is to set apart certain days in the week for girls and boys. I would suggest that three days in the week may be reserved for girls when the school centres will be entirely at their disposal. For grown-up women, we may reserve two days in the week for a similar purpose. I know that this is not a perfect solution but in the existing conditions I feel that in this way alone we can meet the demand for the necessary social education to be given to adolescent girls and grown-up women within the limitations of our financial and other resources.

The programme of universal education for Delhi will therefore be as follows:

The programme of universal education for Delhi will therefore be as follows

(1) The village school will be a centre not only of instruction but also of sports and recreation for the entire village.

(2) Separate time will be alloted to children, adolescents and gron-ups.

(3) Certain days in the week will be reserved exclusively for girls and women.

(4) A number of motor vans fitted with projects and loud-speakers are now being secured; these will visit the village school when film and magic lantern shows will be given and recorded talks played. It is proposed that each school will be visited at least once a week.

(5) Schools will be provided with radio sets and arrangements made for broadcasting special programmes for school children, adolescents and grown-up people in the light of the scheme of social education sketched above. About 140 sets have already been provided by the Ministry of Information and Broadcasting, and it is proposed to supply the balance of 150 radio sets as early as possible.

(6) Popular drama will be organised in the school and from time to time prizes given for the best plays produced.

(7) There will be provision for teaching national and community songs.

(8) Arrangements will be made for simple instruction to be given in some craft or industry suited to the locality.

(9) Lectures will be arranged in co-operation with the Ministries of Health, Agriculture and Labour to instruct villagers in the simple laws of social hygiene, methods of agriculture, cottage industries and co-operative activities.

(10) In co-operation with the Ministry of Information and Broadcasting, suitable films and slides will be shown from time to time. Arrangements will also be made for visits of public men from time to time to speak to the villagers on problems of national importance and the help and assistance of public bodies interested in constructive work will be welcomed to give effect to the programme of social education.

(11) Arrangements will be made for organising group games and competitions will be held from time to time between different schools and villages.

(12) Exhibitions and fairs and excursion will be organised from time to time.

Document No. 82

LETTER FROM MAULANA AZAD TO DR. RAJENDRA PRASAD

New Delhi

2nd July, 1948

My dear Rajendra Prasad,

Reference your D.O. letter dated the 25th June 1948 regarding Gurukul Vishwavidaylaya, Kangri. I know that this institution was started about 48 years ago and in spite of the fact that the then Government of India did not help it in any way, it has been carrying on its work uninterruptedly. It did not ask for help from a foreign Government and now naturally it has approached this Ministry for aid. You can well imagine that my sympathies are with this institution and other institutions of like character.

2. The Gurukul Vishwavidyalaya, Kangri, has, as intimated to us, an anticipated deficit of Rs. 1,19,826 for the year 1948-49. In order to help it to bridge the anticipated deficit and in recognition of the past services of this institution, this Ministry has proposed a grant for Rs. 25,000. The file in question is being sent to the Ministry of Finance for its concurrence. This amount will be granted to the institution after the Ministry of Finance has concurred in our proposal.

3. Besides the above, the institution has applied for the following:

(a) A capital grant of Rs. 5 lakhs and a recurring grant of Rs. 2 lakhs for strengthening the existing departments;

(b) a grant of Rs. 10 lakhs for land, building and equipment of a proposed College of Technology.

For the above grants it is necessary that the schemes should be examined by the University Grants Committee and the All India Council of Technical Education, and for this purpose the institution will have to submit an application for a grant along with a copy of their annual report and an audited statement of accounts for the past year. The Ministry of Education will take the necessary action in this matter. But as regards the grants, they will be considered by this Ministry only when they have been examined and recommended by the above two Committees.

4. Needless to say that you can count on my sympathy with all the aspirations of our national universities which in spite of their adverse circumstances somehow pulled themselves on and are now naturally looking to us for help and support.

Yours sincerely,
A.K. Azad

The Hon'ble Dr. Rajendra Prasad
1, Queen Victoria Road, New Delhi.

Document No. 83

TELEGRAM FROM BASANTALALL MURARKA TO MAULANA ABUL KALAM AZAD

Calcutta

27 July, 1948,

MAULANA ABUL KALAM AZAD
SECRETARIAT
NEW DELHI

...OF 180 APPLICATIONS 149 ACCEPTED DESPITE OUR VIGOROUS PROTEST AND OPPOSITION WEST BENGAL. PISEESEE SWAMPED BY EAST BENGAL DELEGATES WHO HAVE NO CONSTITUENCIES HERE PRAY IMMEDIATE INTERVENTION STOP SUGGEST PERMANENT SINDH ANALOGY EAST BENGAL DELEGATES MUST HAVE NO VOTING RIGHT PENDING APPEAL AND FINAL DECISION STAY BIPISEESEE ELECTION.

BASANTALALL MURARKA

Document No. 84

LETTER FROM MAULANA ABUL KALAM AZAD TO DR. RAJENDRA PRASAD

29 July, 1948

My dear Rajendra Prasad

Wires after wires are coming from Calcutta. From Basantalall's wire it appears that 149 applications have been accepted. This was not the decision of the Parliamentary Board. Anyhow, it appears that groupism of Calcutta has entered the All India Congress Committee's office.

Abul Kalam Azad

Document No. 85

LETTER FROM DR. RAJENDRA PRASAD TO MAULANA AZAD

1, Queen Victoria Road
New Delhi

30 July, 1948

My dear Maulana Sahab,

I have received your letters dated the 28th and 29th instant regarding Bengal affair. According to the resolution of the Congress Working Committee 3 persons were appointed to scrutinise the applications of East Bengal members for being taken as members of the West Bengal Provincial Congress Committee. Of these, one was the nominee of the East Bengal members who wanted to be admitted as members; the second was the nominee of the West Bengal members who were opposed to their admission; and the third was Acharya Jugal Kishore who was sort of an umpire to decide where there was some difference. It appears from the accompanying report that the decision was taken by both the parties and Acharya Jugal Kishore had practically no action as an umpire. I do not see how any objection can be raised now.

Yours sincerely,
Rajendra Prasad

Enclosure:

(Report of the Scrutiny Committee)

116, Vivekanand Road
Calcutta

The 28th July, 1948

Dear Friend,

In pursuance of your letter dated 10th July, 1948 we sat as members of the Scrutiny Committee for three days from 24th to 26th

July and examined in all 179 applications received in the Bengal Provincial Congress Committee office. Each and every application was carefully examined in terms of the Working Committee's resolution and of direction issued by the General Secretary, A.I.C.C. in his letter dated 22nd July 1948.

Out of the said applications 48 belonged to category 1 of the aforesaid resolution of the Working Committee, that is, from those who are residents of West Bengal and have been elected from East Bengal constituencies and who have given their West Bengal address according to the Register maintained in the B.P.C.C. office. All these applications were accepted in toto after due scrutiny.

There were 131 applications under category 2 of the said resolution of the Working Committee, that is, from those who have migrated before 30th April last and have already applied for it. Out of these applications 101 applications were passed and accepted after due scrutiny. Of the remaining 30 applications some were rejected for insufficient data and some were voluntarily withdrawn.

Our sincere thanks are due to Acharya Jugal Kishore who sat with us all the days and helped us with his advice and guidance. Our thanks are also due to Shri Kalipada Mukherjee, Secretary, B.P.C.C. and the staff of the B.P.C.C. for their active cooperation and help.

Yours truly,
Members of the Scrutiny Committee

President, A.I.C.C.
New Delhi.

(List of members elected from East Bengal constituencies with permanent address in West Bengal)

District	Name	Address
Barisal	Shri Arun Chandra Guha	32, Upper circular Road, Calcutta.
	Shri Rabindra Nath Bose	32, Upper Circular Road, Calcutta.
	Shri Priya Ranjan Dasgupta	128/3, Bowbazar Street, Calcutta

Contd.

District	Name	Address
Chittagong	Shri Srilal Sewalka	174, Harrison Road, Calcutta
	Shri Adwaita Dutta	8/8/9, Fern Road, Ballygunge, Calcutta
	Mrs. Bina Das (Bhowmick)	17/A, Ekdalia Place, Calcutta
	Shri Radha K. Niyotia	185, Harrison Road, Calcutta
Dacca	Dr. P.C. Ghosh	14/8, Gariahata Road, Calcutta
	Shri Prafulla N. Roy Choudhary	19, Nandaram Sen Street, Calcutta
Faridpur	Shri Pramatha Nath Guha	51, Kalighat Road, Calcutta
	Dr Pratap Ch. Guha, Roy, MLA	51, Kalighat Road, Calcutta
	Shri Jyotish Ch. Maitra	10, Manoharpukur Road, Calcutta
	Shri Prasun Kr. Dasgupta	79, Karbala Tank Lane, Calcutta
	Dr. Suresh Ch. Banerjee	9/A, Mahendra Sarkar Street, Calcutta
Jessore	Syed Nausher Ali	66/1A, Baitakhana Road, Calcutta
Khulna	Shri Rashik Lal Das	32, Upper Circular Road, Calcutta
	Shri Kalidas Ghose	2/1A, Ganga Pd. Mukherjee Road, Calcutta
	Shri Satis Ch. Chakravarti	1/1/6, Nepal Bhattacharjee Street, Calcutta.
	Shri Parikshit Ch. Mukherjee	27B, Creek Row, Calcutta
	Sjta. Kamala Dasgupta	18, Southern Avenue, Calcutta
Mymensingh	Shri Birendra Ch. Bhattacharjee	8/9, Harrison Road, Calcutta
	Shri Hara Prasad Chowdhury	10, Suburban School Road, Calcutta
	Shri Dijendra Ch. Choudhury	35/1, Huzurimull Lane, Calcutta
	Sjta. Pravabati Bose	238/B, Rashbehari Avenue, Calcutta

District	Name	Address
	Shri Suresh Ch. Das	24/4, Russa Road, Calcutta
	Shri Jnananjan Neogi	36, Wellington Street, Calcutta
	Shri Paresh Nath Maitra	1/A, Rajendra Lal Street, Calcutta
	Shri Girija Kanta Chakraborty	10, Suburban School Road, Calcutta
	Shri Bhupendra Ch. Mazumdar	P-440, Kabir Road, Calcutta
	Shri Niharendu Dutt Mazumdar	101-A, Ballygunge Place, Calcutta
Pabna	Shri Upendra Mohan Saha	32, Upper Circular Road, Calcutta
	Shri Jyotish Ch. Bhowmick	117/1, Rash Behari Avenue, Calcutta
	Shri Upendra N. Roy	37B, Peary Mohan Sur Garden Lane, Calcutta
Sylhet	Shri Sudhir Kumar Ghose	17, Bosepara Lane, Calcutta
	Shri Apurba Kumar Das	172/37, Lower Circular Road, Calcutta
	Shri Haripada Dutt	Karimganj, Cachar
	Shri Nabakumar Bhattacharjee	Karimganj, Cachar
Rajshahi	Shri Basantalall Murarka	9, Royal Exchange Place, Calcutta
	Shri Manoranjan Roy Chowdhury	3, Hara Ch. Mallik Street, Calcutta
	Shri Rabindra Nath Sanyal	46, Alipur Road, Calcutta
Rangpur	Shri Satindra N. Guha	54/1/1, Girish M. Road, Calcutta
	Sjta. Bishnupriya Debi	10, Suburban School Road, Calcutta
	Shri Bhal Ch. Sharma	126, Chittaranjan Avenue, Calcutta
Tipperah	Sjta. Labanyalata Chanda	14/8, Gariahata Road, Calcutta
	Shri Harihar Chakraborty	11/C, Indian Mirror Street, Calcutta
Nadia	Shri Jagannath Majumdar	Krishnagar, Nadia
	Shri Tarakdas Banerjee	Krishnagar, Nadia
	Shri Sachindra Mohan Nandy	Nabadwip

(List of B.P.C.C. Members of East Bengal who opted for West Bengal)

District	Name	Address
Bogra	1. Sj. Satis Chandra Sarkar	93/1A, Bowbazar Street, Calcutta
	2. Sj. Anil Chandra Banerjee	44, Manicktolla Main Road, Calcutta
	3. Sj. Birendra Nath Sanyal	Hilli, West Dinajpur
	4. Sj. Rabindra Nath Mukherjee	44, Manicktolla Main Road Calcutta
	5. Sj. Sitaram Biyani	83, Upper Chitpur Road, Calcutta
	6. Sj. Kulada Ranjan Mazumdar	P.O. Nabadwip, Nadia
	7. Sj. Amulya Kumar Saha	135, Bowbazar Street, Calcutta
	8. Sj. Jitendra Nath Bhowmick	Vill. Krishnagar, P.O. Shyamnagar, Nadia
Barisal	9. Sj. Manindra Mohan Das	143/6, Sibpur Road
	10. Sj. Amiya Lal Banerjee	50/4, Harish Mukherjee Road, Calcutta
	11. Sj. Sisir Kumar Dasgupta	5/1F, Bagmari Road, Calcutta
	12. Sj. Sushil Mukherjee	55A, Turf Road, Calcutta
	13. Sj. Rabindra Nath Sen	18/59, Dover Lane, Ballygunge, Calcutta
	14. Sj Sachindra Lal Kargupta	10B, Janak Road, Calcutta
	15. Sj. Amiya Kumar Rai Chowdhury	P-72, Russa Road, South Calcutta.
Dacca	16. Sj. Banamali Bhattacharjee	Konnagar, Hooghly
	17. Sj. Atul Sen	37B, Harish Chatterjee Street, Calcutta
	18. Sj. Nistaran Chakraborty	20/1, Russa Road, Flat No. 6, Calcutta
	19. Sj. Kiron Chandra Sen	10/1, Gariahata Road, Calcutta
	20. Sj. Birendra Chandra Dutta	1, Dr. Bimala Charan Law Road, Bally, Howrah
	21. Sj. Ratul Krishna Ghosh	2M, Cornfield Road, Calcutta
Dinajpur	22. Sj. Abinash Chandra Bose	Balurghat (West Dinajpur)
Faridpur	23. Sj. Radharaman Saha	43/1B, Suri Lane, Calcutta
	24. Sj. Nani Gopal Bhattacharjee	7, Radhamadhab Goswami Lane, Calcutta

District	Name	Address
	25. Sj. Promatha Nath Banerjee	7, Swallow Lane, 1st Floor, Room No. 6, Calcutta
	26. Sj. Indu Bhusan Majumdar	2, Mahesh Choudhary Lane, Calcutta
	27. Sj. Nikhil Ranjan Guha Roy	43/1B, Suri Lane, Calcutta
	28. Sj. Santosh Ranjan Ganguly	108/A, Cornwallis Street, Calcutta
	29. Sj. Bidhu Bhusan Majumdar	Russa, P.O. Tollygunge, Calcutta
	30. Sj. Fazlul Karim Khondakar	10/3, Musalmanpara Lane, Calcutta
	31. Sj. Jitendra Nath Maitra	47, Muktaram Babu Street, Calcutta
	32. Sj. Monoranjan Bhattarjee	1/5/1B, Prem Chand Boral Street, Calcutta.
	33. Sj. Nibaran Chandra Paul	C/o Lister Antiseptic Dressing Co., Cossipore, Calcutta.
	34. Sj. Jibanranjan Sarkar	18, Chore Bazar Lane, Calcutta
Jessore	35. Sj. Nagendra N. Gangopadhyay	Maliporah, Vill. Kaliabaira, Nadia
	36. Sj. Bhujanga Bhusan Roy	Guptipara, P.O. Hooghly
	37. Sjta. Manorama Bose	26, Prasanna Kr. Tagore Street, Calcutta
	38. Sj. Sudhir Kumar Ghose	45, Hara Mohan Ghose Lane, Calcutta
	39. Sj. Ratan Lal Majumdar	72, Sarkarpara Lane, Calcutta
	40. Sj. Sasadhar Acharjee	4, Congress Exhibition Road, Flat No. 5 D., Calcutta
	41. Sj. Kalipada Sarkar	26, Prasanna Kr., Tagore Street, Calcutta.

(List of B.P.C.C. Members of East Bengal who opted for West Bengal)

KHULNA

1. Sukumar Banerji
2. Arabinda Dutta
3. Narayan Samaddar
4. Anil Kumar Mukherjee

5. Bidyut Kumar Bose
6. Parimal Bose
7. Sudev Bhusan Ghosh
8. Rabindra Nath De

MYMENSINGH

9. Dasarathi Chowdhury
10. Bhabani Prasad Chakraborty
11. Kamala Kanta Majumdar
12. Amiya Nath Roy
13. Manindra Nath Sinha
14. Kshitish Ch. Roy Chowdhury
15. Abani Ranjan Ghose
16. Sudhindra Sen Gupta
17. Syamananda Sen
18. Narendra Kishore Dutta
19. Dhirendra Ch. Dutta
20. Sudhansu Bh. Bhattacharjee
21. Sukhamoy Roy
22. Bisheswar Debnath
23. Ramani Mohan Saha
24. Bidhu Bhusan Sen

MALDAH

25. Ramesh Chandra Ghosh
26. Bimal Krishna Sanyal

NADIA

27. Nani Gopal Sinha
28. Sachindra Sinha Roy

NOAKHALI

29. Jagadish Majumdar
30. Parimal Majumdar
31. Subhamoy Sur
32. Pulin Behari Duttagupta
33. Nagendra Kr. Majumdar
34. Ramprasad Majumdar
35. Santimoy Dutta
36. Subodh Ch. Mitra
37. Nagendra Kumar Guha Roy

PABNA

38. Sisir Kr. Chakraborty
39. Makhanlal Maitra
40. Krishnadas Saha
41. Jyotish Chandra Nandi
42. Jogendra Lal Roy
43. Rabindra Nath Bhattacharya
44. Kshitish Chandra Sarkar
45. Bhabesh Chandra Majumdar

RANGPUR

46. Naresh Ch. Choudhary
47. Sudhir Roy Choudhary
48. Gobinda Prasad Kanoria
49. Mohini Mohan Sinha Roy
50. Harish Chandra Choudhury
51. Brajendra Nath Kundu

RAJSHAHI

52. Kshitindra Nath Choudhary

SYLHET

53. Kripesh Ch. Bhattacharjee
54. Probhas Ch. Den
55. Benodebehari Chakravarti
56. Upendra Nath Bhadra
57. Umesh Shyam
58. Manmatha Datta

TIPPERAH

59. Dr. Nripen Bose
60. Janab Habibur Rahman Choudhary

Document No. 86

ANSWERS BY MAULANA AZAD DT. 10-8-1948 TO THE QUESTIONS ASKED IN THE LEGISLATIVE ASSEMBLY IN CONNECTION WITH THE GRANT TO TATA SCHOOL OF SOCIAL SCIENCES

Shri Lakshminarayan Sahu : Will the Honourable Minister of Education be please to state:

(a) The amount of grant sanctioned for the Tata School of Social Sciences, Bombay, and under what conditions;

(b) Whether the proposal to give this grant was placed before the University Grants Committee and approved as grants to other institutions are approved by this body;

(c) If not, whether Government propose to reverse the orders and place the matter before the University Grants Committee; and

(d) Whether Government will consider the cancellation of the grant to Tata School and the diversion of the funds to the building of our own Institute in accordance with the approved needs of the nation?

The Honourable Maulana Abul Kalam Azad: (a) A recurring grant not exceeding Rs. 50,000 in 1948-49, Rs. 70,000 in 1949-50 and Rs. 1,00,000 in 1950-51 (to be finally fixed after scrutinizing the accounts of the Institute) and a non-recurring grant not exceeding Rs. 7 lakhs to meet any uncovered balance of the total cost of the land and buildings (Rs. 20 lakhs) after taking into account all possible donations from other sources like the various Provinces, Indian States, Tata Trust etc. have been sanctioned by the Government of India for the Tata Institute of Social Sciences. The conditions under which the grant has been made have been embodied in a statement which is laid on the table.

(b) No, the grant was not placed before the University Grants Committee because of the following reasons:

(i) The question of giving a grant to this Institute was decided at an Inter-Departmental meeting held on the 5th December, 1947. The University Grants Committee at that time was concerned only with the Central Universities of Aligarh, Benares and Delhi. It was by this Ministry's Resolution of the 16th December, 1947, that the scope of the University Grants Committee was wanted to include other Universities and institutions of higher learning. As such, when the question of grants for the Tata Institute was decided that Institute did not fall under the purview of the University Grants Committee, and it was not necessary to place the question of its grant before the University Grants Committee.

(ii) The University Grants Committee is only a Consultative and Advisory Body (regarding Education, Health and Lands Department Resolution of 4th June, 1945) and it is not obligatory on Government to take its advice on each and every matter.

(c) No. Government of India do not propose to reverse their orders and place the question before the University Grants Committee for reasons already stated above.

(d) The conditions imposed for payment of grants are strict and provide safeguards for the Government. I may add that the Government of India propose to estalish an All-India Council of Social Services to advise Government on all matters relating to social welfare organisations and grant to them from public revenues.

Statement

The conditions under which the grant to the Tata Institute of Social Sciences, Bombay is payable:

1. The Institute should train about 50 candidates a year in Industrial Selections and Labour Welfare subjects.
2. The Institute should train a reasonable number of medical social workers.
3. The Government of India will have the right to nominate if necessary upto a maximum of 15 students every year.
4. The plans and estimate of the buildings proposed to be constructed by the Institute will be submitted to the Government of India for prior approval.
5. The audited account and the annual report of the Institute should be regularly submitted to the Government of India

for the period the Institute is in receipt of grants from the Government of India.

6. The Government of India will have the right to nominate a representative to serve on the Governing Board of the Institute for the period that the Institute is in receipt of grants from the Government of India.
7. Out of the non-recurring grant of Rs. 7 lakhs, a sum not exceeding Rs. 8,50,000 will be paid during 1948-49 subject to conditions 1-6 above but the balance will be paid only when the additional buildings are completed and a certificate to that effect from the Central Works Department is furnished to the Government of India.

Shri Lakshminarayan Sahu : What were the conditions for the payment of grant?

The Honourable Maulana Abul Kalam Azad : I am placing on the table a statement which embodies the conditions under which grant was given it mentions the conditions.

Shri Lakshminarayan Sahju : Will the Honourable Minister please read out the statement for information?

Mr. Speaker : It is no use taking the time of the House.

Document No. 87

REPLY TO THE QUESTIONS ASKED IN THE LEGISLATIVE ASSEMBLY DATED 10-8-1948 BY MAULANA AZAD ABOUT THE ADMISSION OF STUDENTS IN AND GRANT TO LAXMINARAIN INSTITUTE OF TECHNOLOGY AT NAGPUR

Mr. R.K. Sidhva : (a) Will the Honourable Minister of Education be pleased to state whether it is a fact that the Laxminarain Institute of Technology at Nagpur admits students from C.P. and Berar only under the terms of the Deed by the Donor?

(b) Is sufficient number of students available from the C.P. for training in various technical subjects?

(c) Is it a fact that the Government of India contemplate giving a grant to enable the Institute to admit students from all over India.

The Honourbale Maulana Abul Kalam Azad: (a) Yes, but in accepting the Central Government's grant to the institution for 1947-48 the Nagpur University has agreed that the institution will admit students from other provinces in accordance with the quota for each province to be determined by the Central Govt.

(b) The institution admits only thirty students per year and the Province of C.P. and Berar can certainly provide that number.

(c) Yes. The Laxminarayan Institute of Technology, Nagpur, is one of the fourteen technological institutions whom the Government have given or propose to give grants with a view to strengthening and developing them. It is one of the conditions of the grant that the institution will admit students from other provinces, without charging any capitation fees, according to the Provincial quotas to be fixed by the Central Government in consultation with the Provincial Governments and the institutions concerned.

Mr. R.K. Sidhva : What amount of grant does the Çentre give to this institute at present?

The Honourbale Maulana Abul Kalam Azad : I would like to have a notice for this.

Seth Govind Das : As shri Lakshminarayan had while making the donation to the Nagpur University, imposed a condition that students from the C.P. and berar only should be admitted, will Government, therefore please keep this in view that students from other Provinces are admitted only after those from C.P. and Berar have been admitted?

The Honourable Maulana Abul Kalam Azad : Yes. This is receiving Government's attention.

Shri H.V. Kamath : Have Government fixed the quotas for the other Province apart from the C.P. and Berar?

The Honourable Maulana Abul Kalam Azad : While giving the grant for the year 1947-48 a condition was imposed that door should be opened for other Provinces also and the Government had fixed the Provincial quotas.

Shri H.V. Kamath : Have quotas been fixed yet; what is the quota for other Provinces?

The Honourable Maulana Abul Kalam Azad : I cannot say. I require notice.

Shrimati Dakshayani Velayudhan : Is it a fact that this Institute gives admission only to caste-Hindu students?

The Honourable Maulana Abul Kalam Azad : I do not think if any restriction for the admission of caste-Hindus or others have been imposed. The door is open to all.

Shrimati Dakshayani Velayudhan : I could not understand the answer.

Mr. Speaker : It is not restricted to caste-Hindu only.

Shri Ajit Prasad Jain : Are Government also contemplating to increase the number of students from thirty?

The Honourable Maulana Abul Kalam Azad : This entirely depends on the capacity of the institution. Government will try.

Document No. 88

ANSWERS BY MAULANA AZAD IN THE LEGISLATIVE ASSEMBLY DT. 10-8-1948 TO THE QUESTIONS ASKED IN CONNECTION WITH THE GOVERNMENT POLICY CONCERNING EXCAVATION WORK CARRIED OUT UNDER THE AUSPICES OF THE ARCHAEOLOGICAL DEPARTMENT

Shri Lakshminarayan Sahu : (a) Will the Honourable Minister of Education be pleased to state the policy of the Government of India so far as excavation work under the auspices of the Archaeological Department is concerned?

(b) Has Government recognised certain learned bodies who may undertake excavation work on behalf of the Government of India?

(c) Do Government propose to consider the question of according recognition to Kalinga Historical Research Society (Bolangir) (Orissa) and the Orissa Government Museum Committee as learned bodies and allow them to carry on excavation work either on behalf of the Government of India or independently but partly helped and guided by technical advice from the Government of India's Archaeological Department?

(d) Do Government propose to have a record of survey of ancient sites in Orissa?

(e) Do the Government of India propose to authorise or direct the Provincial Governments of the Indian Union to undertake survey work in different Provinces so as to facilitate excavation work in future?

The Honourable Maulana Abul Kalam Azad:

(a) The policy of the Archeological Department in regard to excavation work has for some years past been to proceed from the excavation of site of known archaeological importance, where there is a strong likelihood of digging up objects and monuments which will be of value in the understanding of the past, to less known sites but which are expected to yield good results.

(b) Yes, on the usual conditions and whenever properly trained technical staff approved by the Department of Archaeology if forthcoming.

(c) Yes, when the necessary condtitions have been fulfilled. The Archaeological Department will be glad to give technical advice, but it is not possible for it either to lend technical staff or to give any financial assistance as both the staff and the exploration grant are very limited.

(d) Yes, along with similar surveys of other Provinces.

(e) Government of India would welcome all co-operation from Provincial Governments in this respect. It is the intention of Government of India to address Provincial Governments in this respect in due course.

Seth Govind Das : The decision for the excavation of these sites was taken at the time when the National Government had not been formed. Will Government, therefore, please reconsider what important sites should be excavated especially Mathura and Ayodhya which were the seats of our mighty Empires in the past?

The Honourable Maulana Abul Kalam Azad : Government have already started this work.

Shri B.P. Jhunjhunwala : Will Government take care to see that such sites which are expected to yield good results and have been brought to their notice are protected till the excavation work is undertaken?

Mr. Speaker : The question is "Will Government take care to see that these ancient sites are protected till the excavations take place?

The Honourable Maulana Abul Kalam Azad : Certainly. This is already receiving Government's attention and they are acting on these very lines.

Shri M. Ananthasayanam Ayyangar : When a Provincial Government is authorized to undertake work of excavation and research, may I know either steps are taken to see that it fits into the All-India scheme.

The Honourable Maulana Abul Kalam Azad : Yes, the rules have been framed for this.

Document No. 89

ANSWERS DATED 13-08-1948 BY MAULANA ABUL KALAM AZAD TO THE QUESTIONS ASKED IN THE INDIAN LEGISLATIVE ASSEMBLY

RELICS OF INDIAN ART IN BRITISH MUSEUM

Mr. R.K. Sidhva: (a) Will the Honourable Minister of Education be pleased to state what relics of Indian Art taken from India by Britishers are in the British Museum?

(b) Do Government propose to take steps to bring back those precious relics to India?

(c) If not, why not?

The Honourable Maulana Abul Kalam Azad: (a) Details are not known.

(b) and (c). The matter is engaging the attention of the Government of India.

Mr. R.K. Sidhva: Are any efforts being made to know the number of articles belonging to us lying in the London Museum?

The Honourable Maulana Abul Kalam Azad: I have just now informed the Honourable member that efforts are being made in this direction. Two persons from the Archaeological Department are being deputed to England and they have been entrusted with the task of making necessary enquiries.

Shri Mahavir Tyagi: Are Government aware of the fact that India's 'Koh-i-Noor' Diamond is in England, and that too is our property?

The Honourable Maulana Abul Kalam Azad: Yes. This is certainly within the knowledge of the Government.

Shri M. Tirumala Rao: Some time ago there was a talk that a deputation from the Education Department will be going to England to negotiate and get back our works of art from there but we do not hear anything more about it. May we know what has become of that?

The Honourable Maulana Abul Kalam Azad: The Honourable Member is perhaps referring to the India Office Library. Action in this respect has been postponed for the present.

Babu Ramnarayan Singh: May I know what efforts are being made to bring back the 'Koh-i-Noor' Diamond to India?

The Honourable Maulana Abul Kalam Azad: No efforts are being made in this direction.

Document No. 90

ANSWERS DATED 13-8-1948 BY MAULANA AZAD TO THE QUESTIONS ASKED IN THE INDIAN LEGISLATIVE ASSEMBLY

PRESERVATION OF INDIAN ARCHIVES

Shri Lakshminarayan Sahu: (a) Will the Honourable Minister of Education be pleased to state whether 'Archives' has been made a Central subject like Archaeology?

(b) Have steps been taken to preserve the important archives in different parts of India in view of their historical value?

(c) If not, have Government under contemplation any scheme for protection and preservation of the archives by legislative measures? If so, what?

The Honourable Maulana Abul Kalam Azad: (a) to (c). The points raised by the Honourable Member are already under the consideration of the Government of India.

Document No. 91

ANSWERS DATED 13-8-1948 BY MAULANA AZAD TO THE QUESTIONS ASKED IN THE INDIAN LEGISLATIVE ASSEMBLY

ALLOTMENT OF MACHINE TOOLS TO MADRAS INSTITUTE OF TECHNOLOGY

Shri B. Shiva Rao: Will the Honourable Minister of Education be pleased to state.

(a) whether an application dated 22nd March, 1948 was received by Government from the Madras Institute of Technology for allotment of machine tools required for the College from the surplus stores in order to enable the Institute to start its course in July, 1948;

(b) whether any action has been taken on the application; and

(c) if so, with what results?

The Honourable Maulana Abul Kalam Azad: (a) Yes.

(b) Yes.

(c) The stores in question could not be released to the Institute for two reasons: (i) The disposal of the stores had been banned by the Director of Ordanance; and (ii) Demands for these stores had been received from higher priority indentors also.

Government have now set up a Screening Committee which will shortly meet to consider these demands and finalize allocations to various indentors.

Shri B. Shiva Rao: The application is wrongly stated as having been sent on the 22nd March 1948 – the first application was actually sent on the 26th of October, 1947. Does my honourable friend consider it satisfactory that the Institute of Technology should be made to wait for nine months even to get a reply of a negative character?

The Honourable Maulana Abul Kalam Azad: On the basis of the information before me, I can say only this much that as soon as applications were received, efforts were made, but owing to these restrictions, the demands could not be met.

Shri B. Shiva Rao: Is it not a fact that during this very period over a hundred machine tools were handed over to a private firm in Calcutta.

The Honourable Maulana Abul Kalam Azad: Not to my knowledge.

Shri M. Ananthasayanam Ayyangar: Has the Honourable Minister reviewed the report of the Committee which was appointed for purposes of disposals and also their recommendations that they may be distributed to colleges and technological institutions, and if so may I know what action has been taken?

The Honourable Maulana Abul Kalam Azad: A Screening Committee has been set up for this purpose and it is expected that it will start work within a fortnight.

Document No. 92

REPLIES DATED 13-8-1948 BY MAULANA AZAD TO THE QUESTIONS ASKED IN THE LEGISLATIVE ASSEMBLY OF INDIA

IMPROVEMENT OF STUPA AND MONASTERY AT KUSHINAGAR, DEORIA DISTRICT, U.P.

Shri Satish Chandra: (a) Will the Honourable Minister of education be pleased to state whether Government are aware that the ancient and historical stupa and the surrounding monastery at Kushinagar in Deoria District of the United Provinces, the place of Lord Buddha's 'Nirwan', is treated as a sacred place by Buddhists and Hindus?

(b) Did the Prime Minister of Burma visit this famous site recently?

(c) Do Government, in view of the international importance of the site, propose to improve the sanitary conditions of the locality and develop its surrounding on more aesthetic lines?

The Honourable Maulana Abul Kalam Azad: (a) Yes. Buddhist and Hindus regard this place as sacred.

(b) Yes.

(c) The protected mounds and site are looked after by the Department of Archaeology but the responsibility for the sanitary conditions of the locality and development of its surroundings is that of the local Government.

Shri Satish Chandra: Is the Honourable Minister aware of the fact that it is surrounded by most insanitary conditions on all sides and that high grass has grown up there; which is an eyesore to the visitors when they go to such places?

The Honourable Maulana Abul Kalam Azad: This might be the condition. But it is apparent that the Central Government have got no direct control on that place. This is the duty of the Local Government and the Central Government will draw its attention to this.

Document No. 93

ANSWERS DATED 13-8-1948 BY MAULANA ABUL KALAM AZAD TO THE QUESTIONS ASKED IN THE CONSTITUENT ASSEMBLY OF INDIA (LEGISLATIVE)

EXCLUSIVE ADMISSION OF CASTE HINDUS IN LAKSHMINARAYAN TECHNICAL INSTITUTE, NAGPUR

Shri V.C. Kesava Rao: (a) Will the Honourable Minister of Education be pleased to state whether it is a fact that Lakshminarayan Technical Institute at Nagpur is open only to caste-Hindu students?

(b) Have the Government of India given any grant to this Institution?

(c) What steps do Government propose to take with a view to secure admission of students of all castes and religions into this Institution?

The Honourable Maulana Abul Kalam Azad: (a) No. The Lakshminarayan Institute of Technology is open to all Hindu as well as Sikh students under the terms of the Deed by the Donor.

(b) The Government of India have given to the institution in 1947-48 a capital grant of Rs. 1,10,000 for college buildings and equipment and an interest free loan amounting to Rs. 28,000 for construction of students' hostel.

(c) It has been stipulated, as one of the conditions of the Central Government's grant, that the institution will in future admit students from all Provinces, without charging any capitation fees, in accordance with the quota for each Province to be determined by the Central Government. There will be no restriction as regards castes and religions to which such students may belong, and the Registrar of Nagpur University has in his letter No. 1/V/A/LB/337, dated 21st July, 1948 stated that the Executive Council has agreed to the conditions prescribed by the Government of India.

Shri V.C. Kesava Rao: May I know whether Harijans are allowed to study in this Institute?

The Honourable Maulana Abul Kalam Azad: I have just stated that there are no restriction of religion and caste.

Document No. 94

SPEECH OF MAULANA ABUL KALAM AZAD IN THE CONSTITUENT ASSEMBLY DT. 31-8-1948 ON IMPERIAL LIBRARY (CHANGE OF NAME) BILL AND HIS ANSWERS TO THE QUESTION RAISED BY THE MEMBERS

Sir, I would again like to invite the attention of my honourable friends to what I stated when I moved the motion. The sole object of this Bill is to delete the word "Imperial". One of the honourable friends has pointed out that when no Hindi name could be suggested, why should not the whole matter be postponed? He says that there is no necessity for making this change at present. I would say that there is no necessity for making this change at present. I would say that the necessity is vital? I feel that after August 15 there is no place in India for the words like "Imperial", and the names of all those institutions to which this word is attached should be changed. The Ministry of Education has already made another change for which no Bill was required to be introduced. The word "Imperial" has also been dropped from the name of the "Imperial Records Office". There remains the point as to why the English word "National" has been substituted for "Imperial"? Why could not a Hindustani equivalent found? You are already aware of those reasons. All of our institutions were given English names and until now those very names are there and we could not replace these English names. It was therefore, obvious that the word "National" be substituted for "Imperial" in the name of the library. But this does not mean that the Government have no intention to change the English names and they hesitate to admit this important issue. I have already stated the views of Ministry of Education while moving the motion for the consideration of this Bill. The Ministry thinks that as soon as the task of framing the new constitution is accomplished, various kinds of new problems will crop up before this House and of these questions the most important will be as to what should be the names of all State institutions and Offices in future. It is obvious that in future English names cannot be allowed to continue. It would be necessary to set up a Committee to propose new names and such persons who can be considered experts in this matter should be appointed to this Committee. This Committee would consider overall aspects of the question and will try to find out new names for every English name. The task of finding out names is not so easy as some of my honourable friends think. I had told you that we require a mint for this purpose. Just as a mint is set up for casting of gold and silver coins, exactly a similar mint is also required for the coming of names. You can hammer out sheets of gold and silver, but you cannot make a coin. A mould is required for this purpose which could bring out the fine points of the coin. An honourable friend has just said "You are a great scholar, can't you propose any name for this". The question of scholarship does not arise we have to act after careful consideration. Why should we rush through the matter without any reason? This matter was also considered by us in the Standing Committee but we could not decide as to what should be the most appropriate name. The words "Bhartiya" and "Rashtriya" were also brought up before us at that time, and a doubt was expressed whether these words convey the correct meaning of the implications of the word "National". My honourable friend Mr. Kamath has reminded us that in the translation of the "Indian National Congress" the word "Rashtriya" was substituted for "National". I have a recollection that this was used in translating the name of "All India Congress Committee" into Hindi.

Seth Govind Das : You will excuse me, Sir. The "All India Congress Committee" and the "Congress" were named the "Akhil Bhartiya Congress Committee" and "Rashtriya" respectively.

The Honourable Maulana Abul Kalam Azad : My honourable friends can say this thing more definitely, but I am not opposed to any particular name. It is possible that the Committee which we set up for this purpose may propose these very words, but we should entrust this task to them.

Seth Govind Das : May I submit again that any Hindi-knowing person may be consulted whether "National" means "Rashtriya" only?

The Honourable Maulana Abul Kalam Azad : I have already said that I do not object to any particular word. The only thing to which I would like to draw attention is that we should not press for a change in any particular name for the present. We should entrust the entire task of finding out names to the Expert Committee. The Government thinks that this would be the only proper course to achieve the end. But in any case this House has got full authority to adopt any name it deems proper.

Mr. Speaker : The question is :

"That clause 2 stand part of the Bill".

The motion was adopted.

Clause 2 was added to the Bill.

Clause 1 was added to the Bill

The Title and the Preamble were added to the Bill

The Honourable Maulana Abul Kalam Azad : Sir, I move :

"That the Bill be passed":

Mr. Speaker : Motion moved:

"That the Bill be passed."

Prof. Shibban Lal Saksena (U.P. : General) : I have very attentively listened to the Honourable Minister. I want to ask him one question. He has said that a large number of names have to be changed. I see the difficulty. But I want that the House from henceforth should not add any new English names. A Committee may be appointed afterwards to change the old names but I cannot see any sense in continuing to use English names and of adding new English names. I see we have a legacy of slavery and we have to change all those names. Henceforth we should not go on adding new names in English which will have to be changed again.

Mr. Speaker : I do not think the Honourable Minister desires to say anything more.

The question is :

"That the Bill be passed."

The motion was adopted.

Document No. 95

ANSWERS OF MAULANA AZAD DT. 31-8-1948 IN LEGISLATIVE ASSEMBLY TO THE QUESTIONS RAISED ABOUT THE UNIVERSITIES AT BARODA, INDORE, UJJAIN AND GWALIOR

Dr. P.S. Deshmukh: (a) Will the Honourable Minister of Education be pleased to state whether there is any proposal for the establishment of Universities at Baroda, Indore, Ujjan and Gwalior?

(b) What encouragement and help do the Government of India propose to offer to them?

The Honourable Maulana Abul Kalam Azad: (a) Government have received no official communication from the Government of Baroda, Ujjain and Gwalior for the establishment of Universities in these states.

A communication from the Government of Indore was received in regard to the setting up of a Committee to go into the question of establishing a University at Indore. Nothing further has been heard since.

Part(b) of the question, therefore, does not arise

Shri H.V. Kamath : Will the Honourable Minister please state the total number of Universities, which in his opinion, should be set up in India in accordance with the census figures?

The Honourable Maulana Abul Kalam Azad : How does it arise out of this question?

Shri V.S. Sarwate : Would the Honourable Minister have any objection to have universities both at Indore and at Gwalior?

The Honourable Maulana Abul Kalam Azad : Objection? No; Nothing of the sort.

Shri V.S. Sarwate : Do Government think it desirable to have universities where?

The Honourable Maulana Abul Kalam Azad : This is now the concern of these States. They have now formed into a Union, and got an opportunity to consider over the question of setting up a

University in their jurisdiction. In any way Government will watch the action which the Union takes in the matter.

Seth Govind Das : Does Government consider it advisable to set up Universities in such contiguous areas?

Mr. Speaker : The Honourable member is asking for opinions; next question.

Document No. 96

ANSWERS OF MAULANA AZAD DATED 31-8-1948 IN LEGISLATIVE ASSEMBLY TO THE QUESTIONS RAISED ABOUT THE SCHOLARSHIPS FOR SCHEDULED CASTE STUDENTS

Dr. P.S. Deshmukh : (a) Will the Honourable Minister of Education be pleased to state whether any applications have been invited by the Government of India from Scheduled Caste students for grant of scholarships?

(b) If so, how many scholarships were offered and what was the last date of application?

(c) Has any scholarships been sanctioned so far?

(d) If so, what is the number and how many of them are for studies in India and how many for foreign studies?

The Honourable Maulana Abul Kalam Azad : (a) Yes.

(b) Scholarships of the total value of Rs. 3,85,000 were offered. No number was fixed as it depends upon the expenditure statement of the selected scholars. The last date for receipt of applications was originally fixed as the 30th April, 1948 but later on it was extended to the 31st May, 1948.

(c) The Scheduled Castes Scholarships Board has recently decided upon the principles for the award of scholarships this year. The candidates are being selected on that basis and the scholarships will be sanctioned on receipt of expenditure statements from the selected students.

(d) About 600 scholarships are likely to be sanctioned during 1948-49 for studies in India as decided by the Scheduled Castes Scholarships Board. No foreign scholarships are being awarded this year.

Shrimati Dakshayani Velayudhan : Will the chair please have a translation of the answer read?

(Shri Satyanarayan Sinha read out as above the English translation of the answer).

Dr. P.S. Deshmukh : Is it not a fact that the selection is being done very late? The academic year has started. Is it not a fact that the Department has taken too long to decide the matter?

The Honourable Maulana Abul Kalam Azad : I have just stated that 30th April, was fixed as the last date, but subsequently representations were received requesting for an extension of the period, and as a result of this, the date was extended for one month.

Shri Upendranath Barman : Will the Honourable Minister tell the House whether there were any applicants for foreign scholarships, and if so, why did not the Board consider their applications for such scholarships?

The Honourable Maulana Abul Kalam Azad : During the first year of this scheme, the Board had awarded some scholarships for study abroad. But the result was not satisfactory. The Board, therefore, decided that in future the funds under this scheme should only be utilized for studies in India, and no scholarships should be granted for foreign studies. For studies abroad, the Overseas Scholarships scheme was in existence; and the Scheduled Caste Scholars were deriving full benefit out of it.

Sardar Bhopinder Singh Mann : May I know whether at the time of awarding the scholarships, the Hindu Depressed Classes only are taken into consideration or the Sikhs and Christians also?

The Honourable Maulana Abul Kalam Azad : This is only intended for the Schedules Castes; and by the "Scheduled" Caste are meant those classes only which have after enquiry been admitted by the Government of India as such.

Sardar Bhopinder Singh Mann : Is this Schedule Caste confined to Hindus only or does it include the Sikhs also?

The Honourable Maulana Abul Kalam Azad : This is being done in accordance with the definition of the "Scheduled Caste" as laid down in the Government of India Act, 1935, and I think that the Mazhabi Sikhs do not fall within this Schedule.

Shrimati Dakshayani Velayudhan : May I know the reason for not sending any Scheduled Caste students this year?

Mr. Speaker : He has already replied to that.

Shrimati Dakshayani Velayudhan : I could not understand the reply.

Mr. Speaker : She will get a translation later on.

Dr. P.S. Deshmukh : Have any particular reasons been given by this Board for stopping to send students abroad for training from the Scheduled Castes?

The Honourable Maulana Abul Kalam Azad : During the year 1944, scholarships were awarded to some scholars for study abroad, but this did not yield good results. After having seen this state of affairs, the Board decided that the money under this fund should be utilized only in respect of studies in India. No scholarships should be granted for foreign studies. Those persons who want to go abroad, can do so under the Overseas Scholarships General Scheme. In the opinion of the Board, it would have been more advantageous for the advancement of the community to have undergone training in India in large numbers. It was not worthwhile to incur heavy expenditure by sending few persons abroad.

Dr. P.S. Deshmukh : Are any foreign scholarships being given to non-scheduled caste people this year?

The Honourable Maulana Abul Kalam Azad : No. None has been given. It is hoped that the new scheme which is under the consideration of the Government will be put into operation with effect from next year.

Shri V.C. Kesava Rao : Are the Government aware that the Scheduled Caste candidates for foreign scholarships have not been able to get any seats in the general scheme?

The Honourable Maulana Abul Kalam Azad : The Honourable member should be aware of the fact that the Scheduled Caste candidates have invariably been selected under the General Scheme, and there is no bar in their way. But a new scholarships could be given this year, because this had been stopped for.

Sardar Bhopinder Singh Mann : Will Government consider to award scholarships to Mazahbi Sikhs also like the Scheduled Castes?

The Honourable Maulana Abul Kalam Azad : I had just stated that action is being taken in accordance with the definition of this Caste which is before the Government. In any case if this matter is brought to the notice of the Government, it will be looked into.

Shrimati G. Durgabai : May I know the number of Scheduled Caste scholars who were awarded the scholarships? How many of them were successful and how many unsuccessful?

The Honourable Maulana Abul Kalam Azad : I would like to have a notice for this.

Shri H.V. Kamath : Will Government seriously consider this matter?

The Honourable Maulana Abul Kalam Azad : Government always considers seriously.

Document No. 97

SPEECH OF MAULANA AZAD AT THE OPENING OF THE ART EXHIBITION IN NEW DELHI ON 6-11-1948

I am grateful to you for the interest you have taken in this Exhibition of Indian Art and the readiness with which you accepted our invitation to open it. Organised by the Ministry of Education, this Exhibition is the first of its kind in India. I am sure you will agree with me that no programme of national education is complete unless it can provide an appropriate place to national art. The present Exhibition is a recognition of this fact and marks the first step towards the goal which the Ministry of Education has set before itself.

The most significant characteristic of this Exhibition is that it opens before us a vista of five thousand years of Indian History in all its continuity and wealth. Its value for educational purposes can therefore be easily grasped. It will, I think, be proper to describe briefly the manner in which the exhibits in this collection were chosen.

The Royal Academy of Art in London has been taking a special interest in Oriental Arts since before the War. In 1931, the Academy organised the exhibition of Iranian Art and in 1935 that of the Art of China. After the War was over, it proposed that a similar exhibition of Indian Art should be held. The Government of India warmly welcomed the idea and assured the Royal Academy of every possible help. Accordingly, it was proposed to hold the exhibition of Indian Art in London.

It had been decided that the principle Governing the selection of exhibits should be that they would represent the art of India both from its historical and its artistic aspect. Art objects in India are scattered all over the country. Some are in the possession of the Central Government, some are with the provinces and some in the Indian States. There are in addition many rare specimens in the ownership of private individuals. It was therefore necessary that specialists in art should examine all collections carefully and make their selection. A committee was formed for the purpose with Mrs. Sarojini Naidu (now Her Excellency the Governor of U.P.) as Chairman. Three experts from England came to serve on the Committee. They toured all over the country and after careful examination chose about 1000 exhibits which were sent to England in 239 cases.

The exhibition opened in London at the Burlington House on December 1, 1947, and continued till February 1948.

The Exhibition in London fulfilled the purpose for which the collections had been made, and the time came for the return of the exhibits. The Ministry of Education, however, felt that before the exhibits were dispersed, they should once be exhibited in India. Such a collection of art objects cannot be assembled every day. The London exhibition was held after a selection had been made from all collections of art in the country. It was, in fact, the finest ensemble of specimens of Indian Art and offered most valuable aid to the study of the nation's history. A lesson to refresh our memory about our past has never been more necessary than in the phase through which we are passing today after the achievement of independence. It was therefore decided not to disperse the exhibits till an exhibition had been held in India towards the end of the year.

The next point for decision was the choice of suitable venue for the exhibition. We needed a place where about a thousand art objects of different types could be shown to the best possible advantage. The building also had to be such as would satisfy the requirements of an art exhibition. Inevitably I thought of the spacious State Rooms of Government House. Whenever I see the splendid Hall, the thought that comes uppermost to my mind is: What a wonderful Library or Museum it would make? My feelings find an echo in the words which the Persian poet attributed to the fire-worshipper when he saw Kaaba (the great Mosque of Mecca) and exclaimed:

In Khana Badin Khoobi Atashkadah Bayaste

(What a beautiful house! It should have been a fire-temple)

Your Excellency, I am thankful to you that you responded warmly as soon as the suggestion was made, and placed this section of Government House at the disposal of the Ministry of Education. It is through your courtesy that we are holding this splendid Exhibition in this magnificent Hall.

The Archaeological Department of the Ministry of Education was charged with all the arrangements for the Exhibition. An Executive Committee was formed with the Education Secretary as Chairman and the Director General of Archaeology as Secretary. The work was difficult and arduous and demanded meticulous care. I have great pleasure in expressing my thanks to the various Civil and Defence Departments whose officers have worked so enthusiastically and promptly rendered every service that was demanded of them. I have no hesitation in saying that to them belongs the main credit for the success of this Exhibition.

I will now briefly describe to you the main features of this Exhibition which covers a wide range of art from all over the country from 3,000 B.C. to the 19th century A.D. It has been divided into five sections, *viz.,* Sculptures, Bronze Images, Paintings, Textiles and other minor arts.

The sculpture section includes statuary, domestic objects and jewellery from the time of the Indus Valley civilization right up to the modern age. I may mention the Bull Capital of the 3rd century B.C., a splendid specimen of Asokan Art, and a female chauri-bearer from Patna of the 3rd century, B.C., with bright Mauryan polish, which is a unique specimen of its kind. There are beautiful female figures from Mathura in red sandstone, a magnificent standing Buddha of the 5th century and some beautiful sculptures from the temples of Orissa and Mysore of the 11th-12th century.

The art of Indian bronzes is represented in the Exhibition by first rate specimens available in the country. There is the world famous figure of the 12th century Nataraja or Siva in the cosmic dance. A continuous history of Indian bronzes from the well-known bronze dancing girl of Mohan-jo-daro to figures from Taxila, Bengal, Western India and Madras is also presented here.

The painting section consists of about 350 specimens and represents all the main schools of Indian paintings, *viz.,* the Pala School of Bengal, Gujarati School of Western India, Rajasthani School of Rajputana and Central India, Pahari School of the sub-Himalayan Hill States, the Mughal School and the Deccani School. The Pala School shows several of the earliest palm-leaf manuscripts of the 11th century. The collection of Gujarati paintings includes some rare items. In the Rajasthani paintings are shown a series of Ragamalas in brilliant colours from the collection of Treasurywala, which have already been purchased for the National Museum. These are being exhibited to the public for the first time. The Kangra paintings of the 18th century, the best period of the school, are fully represented by outstanding pictures of the Krishna Lila. Amongst miniatures of the

Mughal School, a very representative selection has been brought together, including a hitherto unknown painting on cloth of the Hamzanama, five paintings from the Razmnama (the Persian translation of the Mahabharata), a page from the Darabnama, two pages of Tarikh-i-Alfi, eight leaves from the Iyari-Danish, all well-known book-illustrations executed in the reign of Akbar. A unique set of Ragamala paintings in mixed Rajput-Mughal style of Jahangir's period, in which Jahangir himself appears, is one of the highlights of the Exhibition. Remarkable portraits of Jahangir, Shahjahan and other grandees are also shown. Several rare manuscripts with excellent calligraphy form part of this section. There is a manuscript with the seal of Hamida Banu Begum, mother of Akbar, and a Quran written in 1781 A.D. for Nawab Asaf-ud-Dawlah of Oudh, lent by the Rampur State Library. Two large-sized paintings showing Chand Bibi and her maidens and Abdullah Qutb Shah in procession are the most outstanding examples of the Deccani School.

Amongst textiles, first-rate specimens of silk saris, embroidered and with gold brocade, have been assembled, including figured cans of Baluchar, Murshidabad, brocade saris of Chanderi, Ahmedabad, Aurangabad, Surat and Tanjore. A very remarkable specimen of tie-and-dye design showing shikargah and garba dance in dotted pattern is a masterpiece of art from Gujarat.

Amongst minor arts two ivory door leaves from Mysore, jade-handled daggers and swords of the Mughal period and a unique shield of Akbar, with a sun symbol in the centre and twelve signs of the zodiac damascened in gold, are of outstanding interest.

Much has been and more will be said about the ancient objects of art. The characteristic which appears most remarkable to me is its historical significance. A nation's art is a visible representation of its history. Annals recorded in writing tell us of the past but cannot make it visible to us. Art, on the contrary, not only tells us of the past but makes it live before our vision. We look at statues and forms, and grasp the history of centuries in minutes. One statue of Apollo or Venus can give us a greater insight into the life and mentality of the Greeks than five thousand pages of writing. You will find in this Exhibition a wonderful standing Buddha of the 5th century. If you stand before it for a few minutes and listen to the silent discourse of the stone, you will learn more about the history of ancient India in a few seconds than you could from hundreds of pages written by the most competent of historians.

There is another aspect of equal importance in an exhibition of this type. Art is an education of the emotions and is thus an essential element in any scheme of truly national education. Education, whether at the secondary or at the university stage, cannot be regarded as complete if it does not train our faculties to the perception of beauty. I must confess that art education has been sadly neglected in our country, whether as a repository of ancient history or an embodiment of the visions of beauty that have moved men. No doubt, students are sometimes taken and sometimes they themselves go to museums like the Indian Museum at Calcutta and other museums in Jaipur, Mysore or Hyderabad. Such visits are, however, perfunctory and occasional, and there is no effort to integrate the study of art into the scheme of our general studies. The Ministry of Education have proposals in hand which will lead to the enrichment of our life through the integration of art in education, both secondary and university, but the implementation of the plans will take some time. I would therefore request you to look upon the present Exhibition as an earnest of our future plans. I hope and trust that this will not only awaken in all of us a more lively sense of our past, and pride and joy in its ancient traditions, but also lead to a quickening of our sensibility so that we may bring more of beauty and grace in the affairs of our daily life.

Your Excellency, I have great pleasure in requesting you to open this Exhibition of Indian Art through the ages.

Document No. 98

INAUGURAL SPEECH BY MAULANA AZAD IN THE ANUAL SESSION OF THE MUSEUM ASSOCIATION OF INDIA

New Delhi
27-12-1948

It gives me immense pleasure this afternoon to be in the midst of you, the custodians of Indian art and culture. You are all engaged in the reconstruction of the country through the monuments of history and art that are housed in various museums in this country. It is true, we have not been able to utilise these resources for the advancement of our education and culture. During the period of about 150 years of foreign domination we had no facilities to attend to the work of our cultural uplift. Now that we are the masters of our own destiny it is our foremost duty to set our house in order, some portion of which is in such ruin that it is beyond repairs, while a few corners are still in a position to be used after repairs. The work that you have before you is to put our old house in proper order.

National education is the most important item of national life. The exhibits that are stored in our museums are a permanent source of knowledge. No scheme of national education can claim to attain perfection unless art education finds a place in it. Unfortunately our art treasures are scattered in various collections and are lying in the most neglected condition. It is therefore absolutely essential to bring together all such art treasures, and display them in a scientific manner. To achieve this aim, we must have a National Museum, supplying a haven for our artistic heritage.

When we glance at the cultural history of the world, we find that most of the countries commence their history not earlier than the 8th or 7th century B.C. India, Egypt, and China, however, can trace their history from most ancient times. Our culture is at least 5000 years old, nay, in some cases we have a story of 7000 years to tell. It is a proud privilege of ours to be the inhabitants of one of the most ancient countries of the world. As a free nation, now it is most essential for us to take care of our national heritage and recognise the importance of our institutions that are doing cultural work. In spite of the attainment of freedom, India is unfortunately passing through critical times. Financial stringency is impeding important schemes of national reconstruction. All the same I may assure you that our Government is desirous of helping all nation building activities like those of yours.

The development of the National Museum is an important part of our nation building programme. As Mr. Gyani has just pointed out, we cannot afford to look upon our museums as mere godowns of antiquities or curio houses. Museology is a highly developed science in other counties. But we, in India, are far behind in this respect. According to my idea a museum must display lifeless relics of the past as living objects presenting a coherent picture of our glorious past.

I would request the organisers of this Conference to keep constantly in view the need of linking up our art heritage with the spread of education. The National Museum can play an important part in educating the masses and the scholars alike. Such a museum should be an imperishable record-house for our ancient history and civilisation. It will tell us the story of our life and culture in the past. We cannot think of a greater source of national pride. We have ben thinking of establishing a national museum for some time. We hoped that it would be possible to go ahead with the scheme after the termination of World War II but unfortunately inflation and an economic crisis of unprecedented magnitude have stood in the way of achieving our objective. Even in these conditions we have been allotting some money for the purchase of exhibits for the proposed National Museum from year to year and we hope to make a further provision for it in the coming budget.

During the past two hundred years, Indian art objects have found their way to foreign countries in very large numbers and we are distressed to note that owing to the poverty and ignorance of the people important art objects and records have gone out of India. We must send a commission to survey and catalogue our national treasures in foreign countries. It is also necessary that art objects in private collections of this country should be surveyed. There is every possibility that even an unassuming cottage may contain treasures important from the historical point of view. Thousands of documents and manuscripts are lying uncared for in this country. Now that the reins of Government are in the hands of our own people, our appeal will certainly reach the masses and create a consciousness among them regarding the importance of protecting and preserving our antiquities. We should appeal to our people from this platform to present such things, if they happen to possess any, to the nation by depositing them in a Provincial or National Museum or to the National Archives if they are records. This will afford the scholars an opportunity to sift unpublished records and find out their historical or artistic importance.

The Government proposes to appoint two commissions to collect art objects in this country, and buy those that have gone out. With a view to attaining the modern standard in museum management I would also like to depute some students to foreign museums. These trained curators can then show us how our museums could best be used for the education of our people. There are many precious things of national importance in the museums of England, France, Holland and other countries. We should try to obtain them if possible. There are also many rare manuscripts and important records in our country that can throw valuable light on our past, that are being destroyed through neglect. They must be saved and preserved in a scientific manner. Let me assure you that your Association can always count upon the fullest support from me and my Department. Your work will not suffer on account of our apathy. I cannot, however, make a long speech and give you high hopes as vague hopes and empty pockets do not go well together.

In the end, I cannot help expressing my great pleasure that a change of outlook has come about in our people and they are becoming more and more aware and conscious of the cultural value of our antiquities. I was most impressed by the response of the people to the Art Exhibition in Government House which had to be extended till the end of March next year on account of popular demand. With the ushering of freedom our minds have also become free. It is therefore the right time for the members of your Association to carry on the task of educating the people through your art galleries. the Government is now your own and you can surely expect the fullest co-operation and encouragement for the laudable efforts of your organisations.

With these few words, I express my gratitude to you for having called upon me to associate myself with the imporatant educational and cultural activities of your Association to inaugurate the proceedings of this Conference.

Document No. 99

PRESIDENTIAL ADDRESS OF AZAD AT THE SILVER JUBILEE SESSION OF THE INDIAN HISTORICAL RECORDS COMMISSION, DELHI, DECEMBER 28, 1948

I have great pleasure in welcoming you to this 25th Anniversary of the Indian Historical Records Commission. During these 25 years, the Commission has done valuable work of which you will find a brief record in the Souvenir prepared by our Director of Archives. I would only like to place on record our appreciation of the services rendered by many colleagues who are no more in our midst and also to welcome new members of the fraternity of historians who preserve our past through their devoted and disinterested work. I am particularly glad that on this occasion we have among us representatives of other countries. The aim of history is to find out the truth about the past. This is a common human quest and the presence of members of different nations is a testimony that such tasks can be carried out only through the co-operative efforts of men and women regardless of race, religion or nationality.

Twenty-five years is not a long period judged by the standard of history and yet the Indian Historical Records Commission has done valuable work in creating a new spirit of research and enquiry among our historians. Members of the Commission have contributed much to our knowledge of Indian past. They have also created a spirit of enthusiasm abroad and we have had in consequence many valuable studies by foreign scholars on various aspects of Indian history. The field, however, is vast and in spite of all our efforts we have been able to accomplish only a fraction of our task. It is therefore essential for us to renew our endeavour and continually make greater efforts so that the resplendent past of India may be discovered to us and the world.

The Historical Records Commission has till now surveyed the problems of history in a general way. Individual authors have contributed important studies in subjects of their choice. Valuable as such work has been, I feel that it would perhaps be of even greater service to the cause of historical research if we frame a programme of work to fill up the gaps in our knowledge of the history of India. No one can deny that many problems are yet outstanding and demand further enquiry and investigation. By way of example, I would draw special attention of the historians assembled here to periods which, in my opinion, should be studied more carefully if we are to appreciate fully all the implications of our heritage.

Our ancient past dates back to pre-history and presents many periods that are only imperfectly known. The relation of the civilisation of Mohenjo-daro to that of Southern India or to lands in the Middle East is yet unsolved. The recent excavations in Bahrein and Kowait have brought to light numerous small tombs which date back to perhaps the second millennium before Christ or even earlier. Some historians find in them evidence of ancient connections between South India and the regions bordering on the Persian Gulf. Some of these problems are no doubt purely archaeological, but there are others which can be solved only by the co-operation of the archaeologists and the historians. The services of Syriology and Egyptology have not yet been full utilised in explaining our ancient past. Nor have we yet explored the materials that have come down to us from the civilisations that flourished in Mesopotamia and the neighbouring lands.

Another period in Indian history which deserves and demands fresh and detailed study is the end of the first millennium after Christ. We have some knowledge of the condition of India up to the 7th and 8th century A.D. and again after the establishment of the Sultanate of Delhi. The intervening period saw the rise of the Ghuznavide power and its expansion into the north-western regions of India, but we have no clear picture of the social and political conditions of India during this time. It is unfortunate that we have not yet been able to lay our hands on all the Persian histories of the period whose names have been handed down to us. Abul Fazal Baihaqi, we are told, wrote a history of the Ghuznavides in thirty volumes, but we have so far found only a fragment of this book. Perhaps new light would be thrown on the Indian history if the lost volumes could be recovered. Some new material has, however, been discovered recently and they are bound to throw further light on our knowledge of this period. It is also somewhat strange that almost all our historical research and studies for even a later period are based on Persian records and entirely overlook material that is hid in the vastness of the Arabian history and literature. Our historians should turn to the field and examine the Arabic sources for information about the trade, commerce and social and political conditions of India during this period.

The decline and fall of the Moghul Empire is a matter of comparatively recent history and yet even this period has not been fully studied or thoroughly understood. One surprising feature of this age is the lack of historians of note within the country itself. The work of foreign historians gives a picture which is full of confusion. To take only one example. Most of the foreign historians speak of the anarchy and lawlessness of the period and yet they are full of praise for the administration of individual rulers. While on the one hand it is said that India was in turmoil and there was neither law nor order, we are on the other hand told that the administration of Alivardi Khan, Zalim Singh or Ahalya Bai compared favourably with that of the European countries of the day. On the one hand there is the condemnation of Hyder Ali as a tyrant and on the other high praise for his achievements in the arts of administration and peace. We are also told that there was free movement of hundies or bills of credit which held currency from the borders of Bengal up to the limits of Central Asia. How is one to explain the financial stability and credit implied in such transactions against the background of political anarchy painted by political historians? Without venturing on any hypothesis, I would be content to say that in spite of plenitude of material the period has not yet been fully studied and will repay the care and attention of scholars.

Another period which we must study afresh is that of British connection with India. The wealth of material for this period is immense and yet it must be admitted that we do not have a fair and balanced study of the period in all its aspects. There have been protagonists of the Empire who have sought to justify everything that the British did and painted the period in golden colours. Political passion has on the other hand sometimes led Indians to condemn the period outright as one of the dark ages of India's history. So long as the political conflict was not resolved, it was difficult to judge the period with the detachment of a true historian. Now, however, the chapter of British dominations is closed and the time has come when Indians must study it without prejudice or passion.

I would now like to say a few words about our National Archives. They are the storehouse of the raw materials of history and the

Historical Records Commission is the agency which should find the best possible use for them. Today only a fraction of our records are available to us in the National Archives, but scattered throughout the land there are family documents, *sanads, firmans* and ancient manuscripts which will be lost unless they are acquired without delay. The present is also the opportune moment to appeal to the public to hand over such documents to the National Government. Such appeal will meet with a readier response now than perhaps at any other time.

Many things must be done to make our National Archives perform their proper functions. Of these, the collection and preservation of records and manuscripts is perhaps the foremost. Records dispersed throughout the provinces and states must be brought to one common centre and steps taken to ensure their proper care. The climate of India is an enemy of all types of documents and air-conditioning is essential if records and manuscripts are to be maintained in a proper state of preservation. The importance of this task can be judged from the fact that once such manuscripts are lost, there is no way of replacing them.

The second task is that of cataloguing and analysis of such records. It is hardly necessary to emphasise to a gathering of historians and archivists the urgency of such work. Without proper use of the manuscripts, they may as well not exist. And yet we have to admit that even the records which are already in our possession have not all been catalogued.

The Government are alive to the importance of both these tasks and the Ministry of Education has been endeavouring to do everything possible to achieve them. You are, however, aware of the financial difficulties through which we are passing at the moment. This may prevent us from carrying out all that we intend, but I may assure you that the Ministry will not spare any effort to achieve whatever is possible in the present difficult conditions and to expand its programme as soon as conditions improve.

The programme of publications has in spite of financial and other difficulties been accelerated. New machinery is being set up and steps are being taken to expand the capacity and scope of our National Archives. We also intend to go ahead as quickly as possible with the installation of the airconditioning plant so that the preservation of the precious heritage of our past may be assured.

I must not, however, go into greater details. It is for you, historians and archivists, to prepare a programme of work. Let your labours yield material for writing a full history of India throughout the ages, in which the story of co-operation and common endeavour, the development of civilisation and culture and the growth of arts, philosophy, religion and humanity will be told in all their wealth. That and not the mere record of wars and conflicts, of dynasties and kings, is the true history of India.

APPENDICES

Appendix - 1

Document No. 100

CONGRESS RESOLUTION ON SOCIAL AND ECONOMIC OBJECTIVES

The AICC which met in November 1947 at Delhi passed an important resolution concerning the social and economic objectives of the Congress. There was much confusion in the public mind as to what exactly was the direction in which the Congress and its Governments were moving in their attempt to reconstruct the economy of India. The Congress resolutions on the subject which have been passed from time to time ever since Gandhiji entered the Congress emphasised aspects which were associated with his advocacy of decentralised economy and self-sufficient village units. The emphasis was plain and yet the Congress did not definitely and unequivocally commit itself to the ideas and doctrines of Gandhiji in the social and economic spheres of our national life.

There was much vagueness in the Congress policies and much legitimate room for doubt and controversy. There has been a growing demand on the part of intelligent Congressmen that the Congress should clarify its economic and social objectives. The advantages of such a clarification were obvious, one of them being that Congress or Congress-controlled governments would more clearly perceive the direction in which they should move in their task of building up a new economy.

The resolution the AICC passed did not contain many words but it laid down briefly and compactly the main principles which should control the future political and social economy of India. The resolution laid down that the democracy which the Congress contemplated was a comprehensive one covering political, economic and social spheres. 'Democracy in the modern age', it said, 'necessitated planned central direction as well as decentralisation of political and economic power, in so far as this was compatible with the safety of the state, with efficient production and the cultural progress of the community as a whole. The smallest territorial unit should be able to exercise effective control over its corporate life by means of a popularly elected panchayat. In so far as it is possible, national and regional economics self-sufficiency in the essentials of life should be aimed at. Large scale industries should belong to the community and they should be so organised that workers became not only co-shares in the profits but were also increasingly associated with the management and administration of the industry. Land and all other means of production, distribution, distribution and exchange must belong to and be regulated, by the community in its own interest.

ECONOMIC PROGRAMME COMMITTEE

With a view to drawing up the economic programme for the Congress in accordance with these principles the AICC appointed the following committee:

(1) Pandit Jawaharlal Nehru,
(2) Maulana Abul Kalam Azad,
(3) Shri Jai Prakash Narain,
(4) Prof. N.G. Ranga,
(5) Shri Gulzarilal Nanda,
(6) Shri J.C. Kumarappa,
(7) Shri Achyut Patwardhan,
(8) Shri Shankarrao Deo.

Appendix - 2

Document No. 101

AZAD'S VIEWS REGARDING THE BRITISH PROPOSALS OF JUNE 3

Maulana Abul Kalam Azad Seconding the resolution disagreed with Pandit Pant that the June 3 statement was superior to the Cabinet Mission's proposals. He had all along held the view the May 16 statement was the best solution of our problems. to that view he continued to adhere.

At his very first meeting with Lord Mountbatten maulana Azad said he was asked if the country could wait for some time so that an agreement could be arrived at. He (Maulana Azad) told the Viceroy that the situation in the country would brook no delay and the question should be settled either way at once. He did not think that the present decision was the right decision but the Congress had no alternative. the choice before the Congress was not which Plan to accept and which to reject, but whether the present state of indecision and drift should continue. There was the unfortunate problem of internal disorder and strife and there was the obstinacy of the Muslim League. Taking into consideration all factors the Congress Working Committee came to the decision and an immediate settlement was urgently required and accepted the June 3 statement

It might be argued, Maulana Azad said, that since the Congress had already accepted to do anything further. but such a stand would hardly be the correct one under the present circumstances. The Congress stood by the ideal of a united India but it was also committed to the principle of self-determination and was against coercing any unwilling areas to join the Union.

Maulana Azad pointed out that even at this stage the State Paper had not been shelved. the peoples of the areas had to decide whether the State Paper proposals should continue or not. If by a majority they decided not to join the Union, then the Congress could not force them into the Union. Whatever might be the result of the Referendum or the decision of the Punjab and Bengal Legislatures, he was sure that those provinces which now sought to cut themselves away from India, would, in the very near future, hurry back to the Union. "the division is only of the map of the country and not in the heart of the people, and I am sure it is going to be a short-lived partition," he said. the Maulana was confident India would soon emerge as a powerful and strong nation.

Having accepted a defective plan it would be our endeavour now to put it into practice in such a way that its defects were minimised, "Our attitude towards our countrymen," he said, "should not undergo any change by the reason of the fact that certain parts had elected to secede."

Appendix - 3

Document No. 102

A meeting of the All India Congress Committee was held in the Constitution Club, New Delhi on February 21 and 22, 1948. Dr. Rajendra Prasad presided. About 200 members were present.

Minutes

The minutes of the last meeting of the AICC held at New Delhi on November 15, 16, and 17, 1947 were confirmed.

The Opening Speech

The Congress President in his opening speech made feeling references to the tragic assassination of Gandhiji. He then briefly dealt with the resolutions which the Working Committee had recommended for their consideration and acceptance and the vital issues they raised.

Condolence for Mahatma Gandhi

The following resolution was moved from the Chair and was passed in solemn silence all members standing for two minutes:

> "The AICC places on record its sense of profound sorrow and shame at the assassination of Mahatma Gandhi."

Communalism and the Congress

Shri Shankarrao Deo then moved the resolution on 'Communalism and the Congress'. It was, seconded by Maulana Abul Kalam Azad. Some six amendments were moved to the resolution. They were followed by a general discussion in which a large number of AICC members participated. The amendments were put to vote and negatived. The following is the text of the resolution, which was put to vote and passed.

"The AICC calls upon all Congressmen in particular and the public in general to exert themselves to the utmost to fight the demon of communalism, which unless immediately checked may destroy our freedom and defeat our objective.

The AICC can never forget the fact that shortly before his soul assasination, Mahatmaji risked his life by undertaking an unlimited fast to fight communalism and to restore peace and harmony between different communities and that the fast was terminated on the sixth day when pledges were given to ensure that Muslims could live with honour and security in India.

The foul deed was therefore all the more reprehensive and condemnable, as it was perpetrated at a time when efforts were being seriously made to eradicate this communal poison, to restore sanity, peace and harmony and to end communal strife.

Though the Father of the Nation is no more physically with us to remind us of our duty and to inspire us with his faith in our mission, the AICC takes this opportunity, of solemnly reaffirming its determination to continue to follow the path he has lighted for us and to do everything possible to fulfil the great task he has left only partially accomplished.

The AICC further approves of the resolution recently passed by the Working Committee at its meeting on 6th February, calling upon the people and the Government to take note of the forces of hatred and violence acting in the open or in the dark to disrupt the roots of social life and to take effective action to counteract them.

The AICC congratulates the Central and the Provincial Governments for having taken speedy steps to ban such communal organisations as were deliberately trying to spread this poison whose propaganda of hatred was responsible for vitiating the minds of some of our misguided countrymen, resulting in the commission of foul deeds.

The AICC further assures the Government of its active support in getting rid of such elements which are responsible or inculcating communal hatred and for encouraging communal strife and disruptive tendencies.

To become an effective instrument for carrying out the heavy and responsible duty which devolves upon the Congress it should set its own house in order and the Committee calls upon Congressmen to purify the organisation even at the risk of shrinkage of the extent of its membership. It should be remembered that during his last days Gandhiji was distressed by the fall in the standard of conduct of

Congress which he expressed in unambiguous language at the time of his last fast. It is up to every worker of the Congress to exercise introspection and help the great organisation which has been built up during the course of years at tremendous sacrifice and to recover and re-establish the standard which Gandhiji had set before it. Possession of power should make Congressmen sober and humble; they should realise their responsibility and turn themselves into fit servants of the people.

The AICC reiterates its faith in the ideal of a secular and democratic state based upon social, economic and political justice, wherein every citizen irrespective of his or her religious profession will be assured equal rights of citizenship, and reaffirms its determination to strengthen the foundation of such a secular state."

Gandhi National Memorial Fund

Dr. Profulla Chandra Ghosh moved the resolution on 'Gandhi National Memorial Fund'. It was seconded by Shri S.K. Patil. The resolution was passed. The following is the text of the resolution:

> "The AICC approves of the action of the Working Committee in starting a Gandhi National Memorial Fund with the object of furthering the constructive, educational, social and cultural ideals and activities with which Mahatma Gandhi was so intimately connected during his life time, and through the implementation of which he hoped to make India a just, healthy, self-reliant, united and democratic nation, as well as to further the cause of world peace and fellowship; and of collecting, preserving and publishing his writings and teachings in various languages."

The AICC endorses the resolution of Working Committee.

The Working Committee in a separate resolution decided that a National Memorial Fund be started with the object of carrying out the constructive programme to which Gandhiji had attached the greatest importance and which was the most effective way in which the nation could honour his memory. The fittest memorial to Gandhiji was of course his own imperishable teachings and achievements which were enshrined in the hearts of his countrymen. The Committee appealed to the people of India to contribute to this National Memorial Fund and suggested that each individual should give at least ten days' income to it. The method of utilising this fund was left to be decided by a representative meeting of those interested in it. They would choose trustees and a managing committee. The Congress President was authorised to take preliminary steps in connection with the fund, including the appointment of a provisional Committee and a provisional Secretary for launching the fund.

The AICC at its meeting in February approved of the action of the Working Committee in starting a Gandhi National Memorial Fund with the object of furthering the constructive, educational, social and cultural ideals and activities with which Mahatma Gandhi was so intimately associated during his lifetime.

The Congress President appointed the follwoing provisional Committee for launching the fund:

Dr. Rajendra Prasa .....*President*
Pandit Jawaharlal Nehru
Sardar Vallabhbhai Patel
Maulana Abul Kalam Azad
Shri C. Rajagopalachariar
Rajkumari Amrit Kaur
Shri Jairamdas Daulatram
Shri Jagjiwan Ram
Acharya J.P. Kripalani...*Secretary*
and Shri J.C. Kumarappa.

Appendix - 4

Document No. 103

A.I.C.C. RESOLUTION, MOVED BY PANDIT NEHRU AND SECONDED BY MAULANA AZAD

1948

The Message

During its long history of struggle for India's freedom, carried on from generation to generation, the Congress expereinced both sorrow and fulfilment and many triumphs and defeats. But under the superb leadership of the Father of the Nation, sorrow was made to chasten and purify the people and every defeat was turned into an incentive for redoubled effort and a prelude to victory.

Two years ago the Congress met in Meerut City at a time of trial and difficulty and again under the inspiration of Gandhiji gave a lead to the nation. These two years have brought fulfilment in a measure, and the independence, for which generations had struggled and suffered, has been achieved. But the cost of that achievement has been heavy indeed, for the Motherland has been cut in two, and following this ill-fated partition, madness descended upon the people and all the great ideals for which the Congress stood seemed for a moment to be eclipsed. That darkness was illumined by the heartening message of Gandhiji, and innumerable sorrowing hearts drew strength and solace from it.

Then came the greatest blow of all, the assassination of him who was the embodiment of love and the gentle unconquerable spirit of India.

Thus the very achievement for which the Congress had laboured and which was a culmination of long struggle, brought no glow of freedom but sorrow and dismay.

In reverent memory of Gandhiji and in homage to his teaching, the country faced these terrible crises, the greatest of which was the crisis of the spirit which had clouded India's mind and made her forget for a while the great lesson which the master had taught.

This Congress, meeting sixteen months after the attainment of independence and nearly eleven months after the passing away of him who fashioned it and gave it life, pays it homage to that great spirit and to his great message, and resolves to continue the service of the people of India and humanity in the light of that life-giving message.

Political freedom having been attained through non-violent action under the leadership of Gandhiji, the National Congress has now to labour for attainment of social and economic freedom so that progress and equal opportunity may come to all the people of India without any distinction of race or religion. This task requires a new and positive approach and a dedication to the service of the Motherland in a constructive spirit.

The people of India have achieved independence: but to enjoy its fruits, they must discharge their responsibilities and obligations. Congressmen must remember that it has been and continues to be their highest privilege to serve the people and to shoulder these responsibilities and obligations, and those who hanker after officer or power forgetting their obligations, do an ill-service to the country.

It was the particular teaching of Gandhiji that service should be directed more specially towards promoting unity and goodwill between all the people of India, abolishing class distinctions and those based on birth or caste or religion, and working for a classless democratic society in a peaceful manner. Above all, the lesson, he taught was the adherence at all costs and in all circumstances, to the moral values which gave meaning to life.

This Congress urges all Congressmen with all earnestness to face the difficulties and crises of today, both national and international, in the light of that message so that India may grow in freedom and moral stature and the great objectives for which this Congress has stood may be fulfilled.

Pandit Govind Ballabh Pant then moved the following Resolution on "Foreign Policy". It was seconded by Shri Harekrishna Mahtab. The resolution was passed unanimously. The meeting adjourned at 8.30 p.m.

WHO'S WHO

Abdulla, Brelvi : Well known Muslim Scholar and one of the chief speakers of Lucknow Muslim Conference, held under the presidentship of Maulana Azad in 1947.

Abdullah, Shaikh Muhamad : A prominent leader of Kashmir Valley, was sent to jail in 1946 by Maharaja; became the head of the Government of State of Jammu and Kashmir(1947) and the Premier since 1948.

Ahmed, Syed : Prominent Muslim Scholar and one of the organisers of Lucknow Muslim Conference held in 1947.

Aney, M.S. : Reputed national leader; some time member of Viceroy's Council; was the president of first session of All India Hindu League, held at Lucknow in 1935.

Anugraha, Narayan Singh : A leading Congressman of Bihar, Finance Minister in the Cabinet of Shri Krishna Sinha in 1946.

Aristotle : A great philosopher of Greek and the father of Political Science.

Asaf Ali : A prominent Congress leader of Delhi, was appointed a Minister in Interim Government in 1946.

Azad, Maulana Abul Kalam : A great freedom fighter and Editor of Al-Hilal, Al-Balagh and the 'Vakil' of Amritsar; was elected President of Indian National Congress in 1940 at Wadha; was

	appointed first Education Minister in Free India's Cabinet.
Bardoli, Gopinath	: Prominent Congress leader of Assam; became the Premier of the State in 1937 and Chief Minister in 1946.
Bhabha, Homi	: Formally Chairman of Indian Atomic Energy Commission and a top-ranking Scientist.
Birla, G.D.	: Well known industrialist and a devotee of Mahatma Gandhi, was president of Harijan Sewak Sangh, became member of Central Legislative Assembly.
Bose, Sarat Chandra	: Prominent Congress leader of Bengal and elder brother of Netaji Subhas Chandra Bose. He was a member of Interim Government, headed by Pandit Nehru in 1946.
Bose, Subhas Chandra	: Great Patriot and front ranking Congress leader of Bengal, elected President of Indian National Congress twice in 1938 at Haripura and in 1939 at Tripuri, founder of Forward Bloc (1939), Indian National Army and Indian National Government during the Second World War, imprisoned several times during National Liberation Movement.
Chowdhary, Khaliquzama	: A Prominent leader of United Provinces Muslim League, was elected to U.P. Legislative Assembly in 1937.
Churchill, W.	: Prime Minister of Great Britain during the World War II.
Das, Nilakantha	: A leading Congressman of Orissa.

Das, Viswanath	:	Leader of Orissa Congress Legislative Party and the Premier of the State in 1937.
Deo Shankarrao	:	A front ranking Congress leader of Maharashtra, was appointed a member to the Working Committee of Indian National Congress by Maulana Azad in 1940.
Deshmukh, R.M.	:	Chief Minister of Bindhya Pradesh (1947-50).
Diwakar, R.R.	:	Well known Congress leader of Karnataka; was appointed a Minister of State in Central Government in 1948.
Gadgil, N.V.	:	A prominent Congress leader of Maharashtra; was appointed a minister in Union Cabinet by Nehruji.
Gandhi, Devadas	:	Youngest son of Mahatma Gandhi and son-in-law of C. Rajagopalachari; was the managing editor of the Hindustan Times.
Gandhi, M.K.	:	Supreme Leader of National Liberation Movement and Indian National Congress (1920-47), President of I.N.A. (1925), Editor, Young India and Navjeevan (1920-31), Harijan, Harijan Bandhuand Harijan Sewak (1933-42), participated in the Second Round Table Conference, held in London in 1931.
Gidwani, Choithram	:	A Congress leader of Sind; President of S.P.C.C. before independence.
Gilani, B.S.	:	Private Secretary to Sardar Baldeo Singh and a Spokesman of Christians.
Ghose, P.C.	:	A Congress leader of Bengal; was the Chief Minister of West Bengal before Dr. B.C. Roy.
Haq, A.K. Fajlul	:	Leader Krishak Praja Party of Bengal and the Chief Minister.
Hasan, S.M.	:	A member in the Central Provinces Ministry in 1937 and again in 1946.

Jairamdas Daulatram	: Congress leader of Sind, member Working Committee (1940-46); Minister in the Union Cabinet, headed by Pt. Nehru, in 1947.
Jinnah, M.A.	: Vice-Chancellor of Osmania University, Supreme leader of Muslim League since 1934; member Indian Legislative Assembly (1924-34); first Governor General of Pakistan.
Kalidas	: Ancient Indian Scholar as well as poet; author of 'Abhigyan Shakuntalam' and 'Meghaduta'.
Khan, Abul Gaffar Khan	: Frontier Gandhi and Organiser of Khudai Khidmatgar in N.W.F.P.; started Red Shirt Movement in the Province (1930); member Congress Working Committee from 1936-47.
Krishnan, Dr.	: A well known Scientist of Allahabad University.
Humayun Kabir	: A close associate of Maulana Azad; was appointed a State Minister in Union Government in 1959.
Khan Saheb, Dr.	: Elder brother of Frontier Gandhi and a leading Congressman; became the Premier of N.W.F.P. in 1946.
Kidwai, Rafi Ahmad	: Prominent Congress leader of U.P.; a nearest friend of Pandit Nehru; became a member in the Union Cabinet in 1952.
Kripalani, J.B.	: A front ranking Congress leader; was appointed the Principal of Gujrat Vidyapeeth; imprisoned several times during the National Liberation Movement, elected President to the Meerut Session of I.N.C. in 1946.
Lal, Sir Manohar	: A leading member of Unionist Party and Finance Minister of Punjab before partition.

Liyakat, Ali Khan	: Prominent leader of U.P. Muslim League, leader Muslim League Parliamentary Party (1946); became the first Prime-Minister of Pakistan in 1947.
Madani, Hussain Ahmed	: President Jamiat Ulema-i-Hind and noted scholar of Islamic Philosophy, founder of Darul Ulum Deoband and a nearest friend of Maulana Azad.
Mahalanobis, P.C.	: A noted Indian Scientist.
Mahtab, H.K.	: Veteran freedom fighter and Congress leader of Orissa; was the Chief Minister of the State from 1946 to 1950.
Misra, Chintamani	: Congressman and Journalist of Orissa.
Misra, D.P.	: Leading Congressman of Central Provinces, Minister in the State Government in 1937 and again in 1946.
Mufti, Kifaytullah	: Scholar and freedom fighter of U.P.
Muhammad Ali Maulana	: Veteran freedom fighter and editor of Hamdard and Comrade; was elected President of Indian National Congress at Cocanada in 1923.
Munshi, K.M.	: A well known barristar and Congress leader of Bombay; was appointed Agent General by Government of India in Hyderabad state in 1948.
Navalrai Lalchand	: A member of Indian Legislative Assembly (1934-37)
Naidu, Sarojini	: Top ranking Congress Worker of Hyderabad, was elected the President of Indian National Congress (1926); become the first Governor of U.P. after independence.
Narayan, J.P.	: Founder Secretary of the Socialist Party of India and a noted freedom fighter.
Narayan, Ram	: Famous Congress worker of Bihar; was an associate of Dr. Rajendra Prasad.

Nehru, Jawaharlal : A leading figure of National Liberation Movement was elected President of Indian National Congress in 1929, 1930, 1937 and 1946; founder, All India Kisan Sabha, Bharat Krishak Samaj and the President of States People organisation; became the first Prime Minister of India after independence in 1947.

Nehru, Moti Lal : Famous barrister of Allahabad and a front ranking Congress leader; was elected President of Indian National Congress in 1919 and again in 1928.

Pandit, Vijaya Lakshmi : Younger sister of Pandit Jawaharlal Nehru, was elected to the Legislative Assembly of U.P. (1937); became the Chairperson of the General Assembly of U.N.O.; appointed Indian Ambassador to the Soviet Union.

Paliwal, S.K.D. : A leading Congress worker of U.P.

Pant, G.B. : Front ranking Congress leader of U.P.; became the Premier of the State in 1937 and the Chief Minister in 1946, elected to the Working Committee of I.N.C. several times between 1936 and 1950; was appointed Home Minister in the Union Cabinet headed by Pandit Nehru.

Patel, Manibehn : Famous social worker and freedom fighter; became the member of Congress Working Committee in 1950, was elected to the Indian Parliament several times between 1952 and 1980. She was the daughter of Sardar Vallabhbhai Patel.

Patel, Vallabhbhai : Popularly known as Sardar, was the organiser of Bardoli Peasant Agitation (1928); elected President of Indian National Congress at Karachi in 1931; became the Chairman of C.P.B. in 1934

	and 1936; appointed Deputy Prime Minister of free India in 1947.
Patwardhan, Achyut	: Noted freedom fighter and socialist party leader.
Prakasham, T.	: Leading Congress man of Andhra Pradesh; became the Chief Minister in 1946.
Prasad, Rajendra	: Top-ranking Congress leader and constructive worker of Bihar; was a colleague of Maulana Azad, Sardar Patel and Pandit Nehru and associate of Mahatma Gandhi; elected President of Indian National Congress (1935); became a member Congress Parliamentary Board (1937); appointed Food and Civil Supplies Minister in the interim Government (1946); elected Chairman Constituent Assembly (1946) and the President of Indian Republic in 1950, 1952 and 1957.
Rajgopalachari, C.	: Gandhian thinker and front ranking Congressman of Madras; became twice Chief Minister of the province; was the first and last Indian Governor-General (1948-50); appointed Minister for Home Affairs in the Government of India in 1950; well known for his suave diplomacy and cruditeness; founder of Swatantra Party of India.
Ray, B.C.	: Renowned doctor and Congress leader of Bengal, became the Chief Minister of W.B. in 1939.
Ray, M.N.	: Well known thinker and freedom fighter of Bengal, participated in Communist International, held in Moscow in 1920, was defeated by Maulana Azad in the election of Congress Presidentship at Wardha in 1940.

Sachar, Bhim Sen	: Prominent Congress leader of Punjab; became a Secretary of P.C.C. in 1921, was elected to State Legislative Assembly in 1936 and 1945. Chief Minister of Punjab in 1952-56.
Shah, M.N.	: A noted Scientist of India
Sahai, K.B.	: A Parliamentary Secretary in Bihar Ministry in 1937.
Sahjanand Swamy	: Leading Public leader of Bihar and the founder of All India Kisan Sabha.
Sanskrityayan Rahul	: A noted freedom figher and progressive writer.
Shah, Shantilal Harjivanlal	: Constructive worker of Gujrat, was a founder member of Indian National Trade Union Congress and Incharge of Congress Election Office in 1945-46.
Saxena, Mohan Lal	: A member of Indian Legislative Assembly (1934-37).
Sarkar, Jadunath	: Eminent historian and the Chairman of Indian Council of Historical Research.
Shakespeare, W.	: A great English Poet.
Sherwani, T.A.K.	: A prominent Zamindar and Congressman of U.P.; was elected President of U.P.P.C.C. in 1929. A nearest friend of Pandit Nehru and Kisan Leader.
Silva, Geogre Da	: Leading Congressman and the Vice-President of Mahakoshal Provincial Congress Committee.
Sinha, Shri Krishna	: A well known Congress leader of Bihar; became the Chief Minister of the province.

Sukhla, R.S.	: A leading Congressman and the Premier of the Central Provinces (1938-39); was again elected as leader of C.P.C.L.P. in 1946.
Sunder Lal	: Eminent freedom fighter of Allahabad and historian.
Syed, G.M.	: A leading Muslim Leader of Sind.
Sitaramaiyya, B. Pattabhi	: Leading Congressman of Andhra; was elected President of Indian National Congress in 1948.
Sriprakash	: Congress leader of U.P.; appointed Indian High Commissioner to Pakistan (1947) ; became Governor of Assam in 1950.
Syed Mahmood	: Formerly Member Parliament and freedom fighter.
Tagore, Ravindra Nath	: Great Bengali Poet as well as the Philosopher; was the founder of Vishwa Bharti University of Shantiniketan. A Nobel Prize Winner, Social reformer and the author of "Geetanjli."
Tarachand	: Eminent historian and former Vice-Chancellor of Allahabad University.
Valmiki	: Author of 'Ramayana' and noted ancient Indian scholar.
Wordsworth William	: A great English Poet.
Zaidan George	: A well known Arabic Scholar of modern age.

GLOSSARY

Ahimsa	: Non-violence, Gandhiji's weapon of love for mass action.
Ashram	: Literally hermitage, a place for penance and spiritual pursuit, here Gandhiji's community of workers engaged in constructive and national work.
Begar	: Forced free labour.
Bhagwadgita, The	: The Song Celestial, highly philosophic poem laying emphasis on the selfless view of life and action.
Bhakta	: Devotee, disciple.
Bhartiya	: Indian.
Brahmin	: One belonging to the priestly class.
Charkha	: Spinning-wheel.
Charkha Jayanti	: Yearly celebration of spinning movement.
Charkha Sangh	: Spinners' Association, the All-India body that Gandhiji had formed in 1925 to provide employment to the starving millions of India.
Chawl	: Locality.
Chaddar	: Bedspread.
Chowpatty	: Public square.
Dal	: Pulse – uncooked or cooked.
Darbar	: Court.
Daridra Narayana	: The God of the poor; symbolically, God in the form of the poor and the distressed.
Devanagri	: Script of national language 'Hindi'.
Dewan	: Adviser, Prime Minister of the erstwhile Princely State.

Dharmaraja	: A prince of virture, the first among the five Pandavas.
Dharmashala	: A charitable travellers' home.
Dhoti	: Indian loin-cloth.
Fakir	: A man of renunciation.
Firka	: Sub-taluka.
Gaddi	: Post-position, throne.
Ghee, ghrit	: Clarified butter.
Goonda	: Miscreant, rowdy, hooligan.
Gujarat Vidyapith	: The National University, Ahmedabad, which Gandhiji founded in 1920.
Guru	: Preceptor, spiritual guide.
Gurukul	: Place of teaching or School
Harijan	: Literally, man of God, the term used by Gandhiji in relation to one-time secluded sections of the society.
Harijan Sewak Sangh	: An association for the service of Harijans which Gandhiji founded in the thirties.
Hinayana	: The doctrinal cult of Buddhism.
Inquilab Zindabad	: Love live Revolution!
Jamia-Millia	: A University in Delhi.
Japti	: Confiscation of property, etc., in defiance of non-payment of taxes, etc.
Jehad, Zehad	: Crusading war in the name of religion.
Jowar	: Coarse tropical grain.
Karma Yogi	: Believer in the path of Karma-action with selflessness.
Khadi	: Hand-spun and hand-woven cloth.
Khadi Mandal	: Organization for the propagation of spinning-wheel.
Khadi Pracharak Mandal	: The organization for the spread and popularization of Khadi.

Khichadi	: A dish of pulse and rice cooked together.
Kisan	: Peasant, agriculturist.
Kshatriya	: One belonging to warrior class.
Kumkum	: A red-coloured dust used as auspicious mark on forehead by Indian women, also being used on ceremonial occasions.
Kurta	: Shirt, here loose garment especially of the North Indian type.
Lathi	: Cudgel, wooden stick.
Maharaja	: The ruler of a former Indian State of bigger territory.
Mahatma	: Literally, high-souled person, a title bestowed on Gandhiji by Indian people.
Mahavidyalaya	: A centre of higher education College.
Mahayana	: Another Buddhist cult laying emphasis on the propagational aspect.
Mal	: A cotton tape used in a spinning-wheel.
Mandal	: Association, gathering
Nawab	: A petty ruler, a landlord.
Palak	: A variety of green vegetable.
Pandal	: Temporarily erected shed for public gatherings and ceremonials, etc.
Paramdham Ashram	: Literally, the abode of higher pursuit, Shri Vinoba's ashram at Pavnar.
Parashuram	: Seer of Ramayana age possessing super-human valour.
Parishad	: Council.
Praja Mandal	: The term then applied to people's organizations in Indian States.
Puni	: Carded cotton roll.
Qaumi Ekta	: Communal unity.
Raj	: Rule, sovereignty, kingdom.

Raja	: A king, ruler, prince.
Rajpramukh	: The titular or rather the constitutional head of the interim Unions of States after Independence.
Rajput	: A warrior, one belonging to the martial race.
Roti	: Indian bread.
Ryot	: People, subject, ruled.
Sanyasini	: Nun, recluse.
Sardar	: Leader, captain, champion.
Sarvarajochhetta	: Uprooter of kings.
Satyagraha	: Literally, insistence on Truth; Gandhiji's weapon of love and truth for mass action.
Satyagrahi	: A believer in Satyagraha.
Sepoy	: Soldier, policeman.
Servants of India Society	: The society founded by the late Shri G.K. Gokhale for preparing lifelong, workers devoted to the cause of Mother India.
Shantiniketan	: 'House of Peace' a University founded by Dr. Ravindra Nath Tagore in West Bengal.
Shawl	: A loose covering over body.
Shravana	: A month of Indian Year.
Sthitaprajna	: The man of equipoised mind.
Swarajists	: Those wedded to Council Entry programme during twenties.
Tahsildar	: Revenue officer of a Tehsil or Sub-division.
Tarka	: The Logic.
Vad	: The second half of Indian month.
Veth	: Forced free labour.
Verandah	: A ground-floor balcony
Vishnu	: The second among the trio of Gods symbolizing protective facet of the Supreme.

Yogi : One who practises Yoga, *i.e.* spiritual, mental and bodily discipline for self-realization.

Zamindar : Absentee landlord

Zamindari : Absentee landlordism

Chronology of Events

1947 Jan.10	: Expressed desire to join the Interim Government.
Feb. 3	: Addressed first press conference as Education Minister.
May 5	: Delivered opening speech at the session of the Standing Committee of the Legislature on Education at Simla.
Oct.10	: Delivered historical speech at Jama Masjid of Delhi.
Dec. 19	: Declared opened the Central Institute of Education.
21	: Delivered Convocation Address at Patna University.
27	: Presided over the Indian Muslim Conference at Lucknow.
1948 Jan 13	: Presided over the 14th Session of the Central Advisory Board of Education in New Delhi.
16	: Opening address at the All India Educational Conference in New Delhi.
March 3	: Speech delivered in the Legislative Assembly in connection with the General Budget–List of Demands for 1948-49 year.
11	: Made statement of Policy for Education in the Legislative Assembly.
August 8	: Speech delivered in the Constituent Assembly (Legislative) on Imperial Library (Change of Name) Bill.
Nov. 11	: Declared opened the Exhibition of Indian Art in New Delhi.
Dec. 27	: Inaugurated the annual session of the Museum Association of India in New Delhi.
28	: Presided over the Silver Jubilee Session of the Indian Historical Records Commission in Delhi.

Index

B

C

D

J

K

L

M

N

O

P

Q

R

S

T

U

The Selected Works of MAULANA ABUL KALAM AZAD

Volume V

(1955)

Chief Editor

Dr. Ravindra Kumar

ATLANTIC PUBLISHERS & DISTRIBUTORS

Published by
ATLANTIC PUBLISHERS AND DISTRIBUTORS
B-2, Vishal Enclave, New Delhi - 27
Phone: 5413460

Sales office
4215/1, Ansari Road, Darya Ganj
New Delhi - 110002
Phone : 3273880

Typeset at
APD Computer Graphics
B-2, Vishal Enclave, N. Delhi - 27

Printed in india at
Mehra Offset Press
New Delhi

To

MOTHER INDIA

Preface

Dr. Shri Ravindra Kumar is an admirer of Maulana Abul Kalam Azad. This is nothing unusual. Maulana Azad had numerous admirers in the course of India's struggle for freedom. The number increased appreciably after India attained freedom. Partition of India was the heavy price India paid for this freedom. Maulana Azad had throughout his whole political life opposed forces which encouraged separatist trends in our national life. It was in the partitioned India that people realised more vividly the soundness of the views Maulana had expressed on the communal problem.

Maulana Azad was among the major figures in our unique struggle for freedom waged under the leadership of Gandhiji. The Selected Works which Dr. Ravindra Kumar has edited bring out the greatness of Maulana Azad in several fields of life. He was most assuredly an outstanding scholar, a great journalist, a matchless orator but with equal ease he was also a great statesman who played a significant role in every crisis which India and, in particular, the Indian National Congress faced time to time in its struggle to make our country free and independent.

He had also his due share in shaping India's destiny in her first decade of Independence. He was an outstanding member of the union cabinet but what was more important was the mature advice he made available to his comrade and fellow warrior Pandit Jawaharlal Nehru as the latter sought to grapple with India's difficult and daunting problems in the first crucial phase of her independence.

Dr. Ravindra Kumar may not yet be a mature scholar but the enthusiasm he had shown in portraying the intellectual and political life of Maulana Azad deserves commendation. The country is still faced with problems which greatly exercised the Maulana's mind. What he thought and said on these problems would still be a source of inspiration and enlightenment to his country in the difficult days through which we are all passing.

SADIQ ALI

Introduction

Maulana Abul Kalam Azad a veteran freedom fighter who strove hard all through his life to maintain the unity and solidarity of the country; a sagacious statesman who knew intimately the feelings and aspirations of the Indian people; a keen and sympathetic connoisser of Indian Art who was anxious to resuscitate its glorious traditions; a discerning philosopher who appreciated the ethos of Indian civilization better than many others; a great patriot who sincerely aspired to see India occupy a place of intellectual eminence in the comity of nations – was eminently suited to lead the country in the field of education, learning and culture. It is clear from all the documents – speeches, correspondence and abstracts of talks etc. included in Volume Five of the Selected Works of Maulana Abul Kalam Azad.

Till he breathed his last on February 22, 1958 he struggled with the problems of education and culture which is clearly stated in the parliamentary documents pertaining to him. Eleven years of his ceaseless struggle to reconstruct the educational edifice of free India, ensured a bright future for the youth of the nation and generations that followed.

The corner-stone of Maulana Abul Kalam Azad's educational policy was his conviction that democracy cannot function without eradication of illiteracy. This supplied the motive power to his efforts in the field of national education. In a press conference on Feb. 18, 1947 he quoted Disraeli' who used to say that 'a democracy has no future unless it educates its masses.'

Addressing the conference on All India Education on January 16, 1948 Maulana Azad pointed out:

"We must not, for a moment, forget that it is a birth-right of every individual to receive at least the basic education without which he cannot fully discharge his duties as a citizen."

Thus the Volume V will throw light on the ideas, works and steps taken by Maulana Azad for the development of a new educational system for our country.

I am thankful to the officials and staff of National Archives of India, specially to its Director Dr. Rajesh Parti, Assistant Director Shri P.R. Malik, Mrs. Manju Sehgal, Mrs. Meena Kapoor, Shri N.P. Sharma and Shri Pramod Mehra, Chairman Shri Sadiq Ali and staff of Gandhi National Museum and Library, New Delhi, Director, Deputy Director and other staff of N.M.M.L., Chairman Shri Babubhai Jashbhai Patel, Secretary Shri Jitendra Desai and other staff of Sardar Vallabhbhai Patel National Memorial, Ahmedabad, officials and staff of Navjivan Trust, Ahemdabad, officials and staff of Kakasaheb Gadgil Pratishthan, Pune, officials and staff of Parliamentary Library and several other institutions for making available to me all records in their possession.

I am greatly indebted to his Excellency, Hon'ble Dr. Shankar Dayal Sharma, Vice-President of India, His Holiness Maulana Syed Abul Hasan Ali Nadvi, Hon'ble Dr. (Mrs.) Najma Heptulla, Deputy Chairperson, Rajya Sabha, Shri A.J. Jalali and Shri S. G. Mohiuddin of Maulana Azad Academy, Lucknow, Shri V.N. Gadgil, Dr. Akbar Ali Khan, His Excellency, Hon'ble Shri B. Satya Narayan Reddy, Governor of U.P. and Shri Nathubhai Naik for their kind suggestions and co-operation in many ways in the preparation of this volume.

My special thanks are due to Dr. Hari Dev Sharma, Mrs. Kamlesh Ravindra Kumar, Dr. Malti Malik and Shri A.K. Awasthi, who inspired me for this task, to Dr. K.R. Gupta and Shri Manish Gupta for undertaking the publication of this series of the Selected Works of Maulana Azad courageously.

DR. RAVINDRA KUMAR

Abbreviations

A.I.C.I.	:	All India Conference on Letters
A.M.U.A.B.	:	Aligarh Muslim University Amendment Bill.
A.M.	:	Ancient Monuments
B.H.U.A.B.	:	Banaras Hindu University Amenedment Bill
C.A.T.	:	Cultural Agreement with Turkey
C.R.C.	:	Cultural Relations Council
C.B.E.	:	Central Board for Examinations
D.A.S.B.	:	Discovery of Ancient Sites in Bikaner
D.S.T.H.	:	Dictionary of Scientific Terms in Hindi
E.C.C.T.E.	:	Election to Committees of Council for Technical Education.
E.S.	:	Exchange of Students
E.T.I.	:	Engineers and Technical Institution
G.G.B.	:	Gol Gumbaz at Bijapur
G.M.B.	:	Gilgit Manuscripts on Buddhism
G.M.H.R.S.	:	Grants to Museums and Historical Research Socieites.
G.U.	:	Grants to University
H.M.H.	:	Historical Monuments on Hyderabad
I.G.	:	Imperial Gazettes
I.N.C.C.U.	:	Indian National Commission for Co-operation with Unesco.
I.O.L.	:	Indian Office Library
I.S.S.A.	:	Indian Students Sent Abroad
J.M.I.D.	:	Jamia Millia Islamia, Delhi
K.M.	:	Karnataka Music
L.D.	:	List of Demands

L.S.S.L.	:	Lawrence Schools at Sanwar and Lovedale
N.A.T.F.	:	National Art Treasurer Fund
N.L.I.	:	National Language of India
N.S.F.A.	:	Night Schools for Adults
O.C.O.M.N.R.S.R.	:	Other Capital Outlay of the Ministry of Natural Resources and Scientific Research
P.C.	:	Princes College
P.M.	:	Protected Monuments
R.S.M.C.	:	Recommendations of Scientific Man-power Committee
R.S.U.	:	Radio Sets from UNESCO
R.S.U.B.E.	:	Rural University of Basic Education
S.A.E.	:	Soviet Art Exhibition
S.C.M.P.E.	:	Symposium on the Concept of Man and the Philosophy of Education
S.C.T.T.	:	Scheduled Castes for Technical Training
S.M.C.	:	Scientific Man-power Committee
S.S.D.	:	Shortage of Schools in Delhi
S.W.T.	:	Symposium of World's Thinkers
T.D.P.L.	:	The Delhi Public Library
T.D.U.A.B.	:	The Delhi University Amendment Bill
T.E.	:	Training of Engineers
T.E.W.	:	The East and the West
T.M.V.	:	Temple of Mathura and Vrindaban
T.S.I.H.R.C.	:	Twenty-eighth session of the Indian Historical Records Commission
U.A.E.A.	:	Unesco Adult Education Adviser
U.C.	:	Unesco Conference
U.S.	:	Unesco Staff
V.B.B.	:	Visva-Bharti Bill
V.C.	:	Vice-Chancellor
V.C.I.U.	:	Vice-Chancellor of Indian Universities

List of Documents

S. No.	Documents	Date
1.	Answers in Parliament to the questions asked about the night schools for adults	05.02.1951
2.	Oral answers in connection with the dictionary of Scientific terms in Hindi	05.02.1951
3.	In connection with the Government College, Ajmer	05.02.1951
4.	In connection with the visit of Dr. Frank C. Laubach to India	21.02.1951
5.	Oral answers to the questions asked in the House of the People regarding discovery of ancient sites in Bikaner	21.02.1951
6.	Regarding the Scholarship Board for Scheduled Castes	21.02.1951
7.	About the History of India	21.02.1951
8.	Speech at the first All India Conference on Letters, held in New Delhi	15.03.1951
9.	Oral answers to the questions asked regarding the Scheme to start a regular School of Fine Arts in Delhi by the Government	19.03.1951
10.	Regarding the Pubilc and Private Institutions	19.03.1951
11.	Regarding the Gilgit Manuscripts on Buddhism	19.03.1951
12.	Regarding the Grants to Museum and Historical Research Societies	24.03.1951
13.	Regarding the Red Fort of Delhi	24.03.1951
14.	About the educational concessions to the dependents of defence service personnel	24.03.1951

Contd.

S. No.	Documents	Date
15.	In connection with the taking over of Vishwa- Bharti	24.03.1951
16.	Welcome Address at the session of I.N.C.C.U.	24.03.1951
17.	Speech in Parliament in connecction with the General Budget – List of Demands and answers to the questions asked in this regard.	27.03.1951
18.	Replies to the questions raised in Parliament regarding Central Relations Council.	28.03.1951
19.	Oral answers to the questions asked in the House of the People about the Scientific Man-power Committee.	28.03.1951
20.	In connection with the Jamia Millia Islamia of Delhi	02.04.1951
21.	Regarding Seleted Trainees etc.	02.04.1951
22.	Regarding Indonesian Students	02.04.1951
23.	In connecting with the Sindhi Script	02.04.1951
24.	Parliament of India: Maulana Abul Kalam Azad and Vishwa-Bharati Bill	07.04.1951
25.	Oral answers to the questions asked in the House of the People about the ancient monuments	18.04.1951
26.	Regarding Indian History	18.04.1951
27.	About the Grants to the University	18.04.1951
28.	About the Imperial Gzaettes	21.04.1951
29.	Regaridng Historical Monuments in Hyderabad	21.04.1951
30.	Regarding U.N.E.S.C.O. Adult Education Adviser	21.04.1951
31.	Regarding the rural University of Basic Education	21.04.1951
32.	In Connection with the Lawrence Schools at Sanawar and Lovedale	21.04.1951

Contd.

S. No.	Documents	Date
33.	In connection with the Symposium of World's Thinkers.	25.04.1951
34.	Regarding the Grants to Universities.	25.04.1951
35.	About Exchange of Students	25.04.1951
36.	Abouth Higher Technical Education	25.04.1951
37.	Maulana Abul Kalam Azad, Indian Parliament and the Benaras Hindu University (Amendment) Bill.	26.04.1951
38.	Oral Answers to the questions asked in the House of the People about Central Board for Examination.	28.04.1951
39.	Speech, delivered by moving the Visva-Bharati Amendment Bill in the House of the People and answers to the questions asked by the Members in this regard.	28.04.1951
40.	Further discussion on the Visva-Bharati (Amendment) Bill.	30.04.1951
41.	Further discussion on Visva-Bharati Bill	01.05.1951
42.	Further discussion on Visva-Bharati (Amendment) Bill in the House of the People.	02.05.1951
43.	Further consideration and adoption of the motion, moved by Maulana Abul Kalam Azad in the House of the People in connection with the Visva-Bharati (Amendment) Bill.	03.05.1951

Contents

Document No. 1

ANSWERS DATED 5-2-1951 BY MAULANA AZAD IN PARLIAMENT TO THE QUESTIONS ASKED ABOUT THE NIGHT SCHOOLS FOR ADULTS

Shri Balmiki: Will the Minister of Education be pleased to state the number of night schools for adults in the Centrally Administered Areas?

The Minister of Education (Maulana Azad): A statement is placed on the Table of the House. [*See* Appendix X, annexure No. 2].

Shri Balmiki: Will the hon. Minister kindly state the expenditure incurred on these schools in the years 1949 and 1950?

Maulana Azad: I am not in a just position to reply that question just now.

Shri Balmiki: Will the hon. Minister kindly state the number of such schools that have been opened in the Harijan Colonies?

Maulana Azad: The schools are opened on no such principles as to the *Mohallas* in which they should be opened and in which not. They are opened in places where facilities exist and their doors are kept open for everyone.

Shrimati Durgabai: May I know whether the schools run by the private agencies in the Centrally Administered Areas receive any grant from the government, and if so,how much?

Maulana Azad: I am unable to furnish details. Certain rules exist in this respect and grants to private schools are sanctioned in accordance with those rules.

Giani G.S. Mussafir: What is the number of such schools in Delhi?

Maulana Azad: The number is 150.

Ch. Ranbir Singh: Will the hon. Minister kindly state as to how many of such schools meant for old persons have been opened in the villages?

Maulana Azad: Perhaps the hon. Member is referring towards 'adult'. Sufficient number of schools have been opened in the rural areas of Delhi.

Shri Gautam: Have the Government any figures regarding the total number of schools needed in the Centrally Administered Areas and the number of schools that have actually been opened, as also the number of schools expected to be opened during the current year?

Maulana Azad: I am unable to state anything in respect of all the places, but so far Delhi is concerned we have had an estimate and we think that by the present rate of progress we shall be able to meet the requirements of the whole of Delhi within the next five years.

Sardar Sochet Singh: May I know whether the students are being coached for any particular examination under the present scheme of Adult Education. I mean whether this education aims at preparing them for the Matriculation, Middle or any other examination?

Maulana Azad: These schools have been opened under the Social Education Scheme which aims at making illiterate persons literate, besides teaching them certain other things as are necessary for raising their standard of life and help in their professions.

Sardar Sochet Singh: Is it not necessary for them to pass any examination?

Mr. Speaker: Order, order. We proceed to the next question.

Document No. 2

ORAL ANSWERS DATED 5-2-1951, BY MAULANA AZAD TO THE QUESTIONS ASKED IN PARLIAMENT

DICTIONARY OF SCIENTIFIC TERMS IN HINDI

Prof. S.N. Misra: Will the Minister of **Education** be pleased to refer to reply to starred question No. 659 asked on 5th December, 1950 and state:

(a) the recommendations made by the Board on Scientific Terminology at its first sitting held on 11th December, 1950, connnected with the preparation of a dictionary of scientific terms and later text books in Hindi; and

(b) What is the estimated cost of the scheme, if any, proposed by the Board?

The Minister of Education (Maulana Azad): (a) The Board has endorsed the views of the University Commission and the Central Advisory Board of Education that as far as possible international scientific and technical terms should be used in all books written in Hindi and other principal languages of India. They have also recommended the appointment of staff consisting of a Director, assisted by scientists representing Physical, Biological and Social Sciences, philologists and technical assistants to prepare dictionaries of Scientific Terminology and to write books in Hindi. For the tiime being the board has recommended that work should be confined to the following 9 subjects:

1. Mathematics,
2. Physics
3. Chemistry,
4. Medicine,
5. Zoology,
6. Botany,
7. Agriculture,
8. Geology,
9. Social Sciences and Administration subjects.

(b) The Board has estimated the cost of the scheme for the first year at Rs. 5 lakhs.

Prof. S.N. Misra: Is it a fact that due to the number of Hindi knowing persons being less on the Board a diffculty is being experienced in carrying on its activities?

Maulana Azad: I think the hon member's information is not correct. On a perusal of the names of the members, he will come to know that the Board consists of a sufficient number of Hindi scholars. While constituting it, it was considered that its personnel should include such persons who should be scholars not only of Hindi but of other Indian languages also.

Prof. S.N. Misra : What is the number of such scholars in the Board?

Maulana Azad : I may read out the list to you:

Dr. S.S. Bhatnagar, Dr. D. S. Kothari, Dr. Beni Prasad, Dr. K.N. Bhal, Dr. J.S. Ghosh, Dr. K. Mitra, Dr. C. R. Reddi, Dr. S.k. Chatterji, Acharya Narendra Dev, Shri Kaka Kalelkar, Dr. Jafar Ali Khan Asar.

Prof. S.N. Misra: Are the Government aware that the Akhil Bhartiya Hindi Sahitya Sammelan has passed a resolution wherein this Board has been severely criticized?

Maulana Azad: It is clear that whenever any such work is undertaken, it becomes very difficult to satisfy all sections of people. All the necessary factors were taken into consideration by the Government in the constitution of this Board and only such persons have been selected as are experts in different branches of Science and also are scholars of the various classical and modern languages of India. The Government are satisfied that this Board as constituted is quite competent for the purpose.

Seth Govind Das: Are the government aware of the work done in this behalf by the Hindi Sahitya Sammelan and similar other organizations and are they considering of increasing the number of members by including representatives of such organizations as have some such work to their credit?

Maulana Azad: The Government are prepared to consider every such proposal and the Board shall surely take advantage of the work done by various organizations in this connection. I may also add that it may not be possible for the members of the Board to do all this work themselves. So various committees will be set up and other capable persons will also be asked to give help.

Seth Govind Das: May I know whether at the time of co-opting members will the Government consult the Hindi Sahitya Sammelan and other organisations about the manner in which this work has till now been handled and the manner in which it should be conducted in future?

Maulana Azad: Yes Sir, I am satisfied that the Board will surely keep all this in view.

Document No. 3

REPLY OF MAULANA AZAD DATED 5-2-1951 IN THE PARLIAMENT TO QUESTIONS RAISED IN CONNECTION WITH THE GOVERNMENT COLLEGE, AJMER BY PANDIT M.B. BHARGAVA

Pandit M.B. Bhargava: (a) Will the Minister of **Education** he pleased to state whether Government have sanctioned the starting of law classes in the Government College, Ajmer?

(b) If so, what is the estimated expenditure, recurring and non-recurring likely to be incurred thereon?

(c) Have such classes been started and if not why not and by which time are the said classes likely to be started?

The Minister of Education (Maulana Azad): (a) Yes, from the session beginning from July 1950.

(b) Total recurring expenditure involved is Rs. 8,900 (approximately). No non-recdurring expenditure is required.

(c) No; because the Agra University expressed their inability to agree to the affiliation of these classes from the session beginning from July 1950 in view of certain technical difficulties. These classes are expected to be started from July 1951.

Document No. 4

REPLIES DATED 21-2-1951 BY MAULANA AZAD TO THE QUESTIONS ASKED IN PARLIAMENT ABOUT THE VISIT OF DR. FRANK C. LAUBACH

Shri Rathnaswamy: Will the Minister of **Education** be pleased to state whether it is a fact that Dr. Frank C. Laubach is visiting India shortly to launch mass literacy campaign?

The Minister of Education (Maulana Azad): No. Sir.

Shri Syamnandan Sahaya: I seek one clarification : whether its answer is in negative or it has no answer at all?

Mr. Speaker: Order, Order.

Maulana Azad: It is without reply.

Document No. 5

ORAL ANSWERS DATED 21-2-1951 BY MAULANA AZAD TO THE QUESTIONS ASKED IN THE HOUSE OF THE PEOPLE

DISCOVERY OF ANCIENT SITES IN BIKANER

Shri Sidhva : (a) Will the Minister of **Education** be pleased to state whether any discovery of ancient sites has been made in Bikaner Division?

(b) If so, what are they and to what age do they belong?

(c) Is the discovery work still proceeding or has it been completed?

The Minister of Education (Maulana Azad): (a) About 70 ancient sites have been discovered in the recent exploration in Bikaner Division.

(b) The site range is date from the 3rd millennium B.C. to the first millennium A.D.

(c) The exploration party worked for two months, November and December, 1950. It is proposed to resume the work next October.

Shri Sidhva: Will the excavation work be continued or will it be stopped?

Maulana Azad: I have just now told you that the work will be resumed in October again. The thing is that we have got a limited staff and they have to do a lot of work. They have to do office work along with the field work. Therefore we arrange in such a manner that every sort of work may continue. The exploration work in Bikaner was started in November and December, and now this work would again be resumed in October

Shri Sidva : Do you get any assistance from the Geologists in this work?

Maulana Azad: Yes, their assistance is sought where it is required.

Shri A.C. Guha: Sir may I know to which age and civilization do these ancient sites belong?

Mr. Speaker: It is more for the scholars to decide that.

Shri A.C. Guha: Sir, the archaeologists must have come to some decision as to the date or the nature of the civilisation to which these belong. Do they belong to the Indus Valley civilization or not?

Maulana Azad: There are about fiften such sites among the discovered ones which seem to belong to Mohonjadaro and Harappa period. There are some sites where such pottery has been found in respect of which it is thought that it belongs to the first century A.D. Anyway the exploration work is still in progress.

Kanwar Jaswant Singh: What is the location of the palce where these sites have been found in Bikaner?

Maulana Azad: There is a certain site in Bikaner where a river has dried up. This is the place where these sites have been found.

Shri Kamath: Is it proposed to start excavation work somewhere near Delhi and New Delhi?

Maulana Azad: No such scheme has come before the Government as yet.

Document No. 6

ORAL ANSWERS DATED 21-2-51 BY MAULANA AZAD TO THE QUESTIONS ASKED IN THE HOUSE OF PEOPLE

SCHEDULED CASTES SCHOLARSHIP BOARD

Prof. Yashwant Rai: Will the Minister of **Education** be pleased to state the total amount spent on scholarships awarded by the Scheduled Castes Scholarship Board to candidates from Punjab during the year 1949-50?

The Minister of Education (Maulana Azad): Rs. 30,716.

Prof. Yashwant Rai: How many students did apply in all?

Maulana Azad: Applications were received from 168 students out of them 53 were accepted and scholarships were granted to them.

Shrimati Velayudhan: Sir, what is the total amount of the scholarships granted and what is the number of scholars who received them.

Maulana Azad: I have just now stated the number was 53.

Mr. Speaker: The question-hour is over.

Shri Sidhva: No, Sir, there is one minute more.

Mr. Speaker: All right, next question, Mr. Kamath, 1631.

Shri Kamath : May I put question No. 1632?

Mr. Speaker : All right.

Document No. 7

REPLY DATED 21-2-1951 BY MAULANA AZAD TO THE QUESTIONS ASKED IN THE HOUSE OF THE PEOPLE

HISTORY OF INDIA

Shri Raj Kanwar: Will the Minister of **Education** be pleased to state:

(a) how far the work of preparation of a comprehensive History of India from the ancient times to the present day has progressed; and

(b) when it is likely to be completed?

The Minister of Education (Maulana Azad): (a) Probably the hon. Member has in mind the history of India, preparation of which has been undertaken by the Indian History Congress, It is expected that four of the proposed twelve Volumes willl be sent to the press during the current year.

(b) It is difficult to lay down any date for the completion of the work. The Editorial Board have, however, fixed a limit of three years.

Shri Hanumanthaiya: Can the English version be read, Sir, because it is an important question and we did not follow the reply?

Mr. Speaker: I have resisted such requests till now. It is now more than two years that we are carrying on like this and in view of the Constitution having come into force now, it is better that such requests are not repeated.

Shri Raj Kanwar: May I know from the hon. Minister of Education the names of the gentlemen who are on the Editorial Board charged with the work of the preparation of this history and the date from which they have taken up this work.

Maulana Azad: I cannot give the names of the members of the Board at this time. But they had begun this work in 1947.

Shri Raj Kanwar: Are any of the editors whole-time employees as well?

Maulana Azad: I cannot give this information.

Shri Raj Kanwar: In how many volumes is it proposed to compile this history, and what amount will be spent on it in the long run?]

Maulana Azad: I have just now stated that they want to publish it in twelve volumes, and out of these four are about to be sent to press. Government cannot tell the amount of expenditure that will be incurred on them. This work is concerned with the History Congress and not with the Government.

Shri Hanumanthaiya: In what language is this history being written?

Maulana Azad: English.

Shri Sidhva: I would like to know from the hon. Minister whether the Netherland's Government have sent some documents regarding the history of India. If so, then to what century do these documents belong?

Maulana Azad: So far as I understand nothing has been sent to this government directly. This information can be had from the Indian History Congress, if any such documents have been sent to them.

Dr. Ram Subhag Singh: Is it proposed to publish this book in Hindi as well?

Maulana Azad: The Congress has decided to prepare this book in English first and then afterwards it would be easy to translate it in the other languages of the country.

Document No. 8

SPEECH OF MAULANA AZAD DATED 15-3-1951 AT THE FIRST ALL INDIA CONFERENCE ON LETTERS

I am glad to welcome you to this first all India Conference on Letters to be held under the auspices of the Central Government. The history of India's achievement in the field of letters extends over millenniums, and is evidence of the innate genius of the people and the encouragement and support extended by enlightened kings and other lovers of letters. These great traditions still remain; but for reasons which are well known, the patronage which in the past was extended to literature by the State has been absent ever since India is free, it is imperative that we try to make up for the lost ground and create conditions in which our languages can develop their innate potentialities and contribute to the heritage of the world.

I may briefly refer to the proposal which was put forward over five years ago by the Asiatic Society of Bengal for the establishment of a National Cultural Trust. This was to be charged with the task of stimulating and promoting the culture of the country in all its aspects. The Society proposed that the Trust should function as an autonomous body and consist of three Academies, *viz*., an Academy of letters to deal with the Indian languages, literature, philosophy and history; an Academy of Arts (including graphic, plastic and applied art) and Architecture, and an Academy of Dance, Drama and Music. It was intended that these Academies should aim at maintaining and improving the standards of achievement in all these fields of culture.

Since literature and culture can flourish best in an atmosphere free from the restrictive influence of officialdom, it was proper for the Asiatic Society to Recommend that the Trust should be an independent body, predominantly non-official in its composition, and operate through its own agencies. In order to giver greater freedom to the Trust and make it independent of annual grants from the Central or provincial Governments, the Society also proposed that an endowment of four crores of rupees should be created. The proposals were referred to the

Central Advisory Board of Education which asked one of its committees to examine them. Accordingly it was recommended that the Central Government should contribute half the amount, while the provincial governments and the Indian States should contribute the balance.

You are all aware that ever since the attainment of independence, the country has been passing through a period of serious stress and difficulty. The aftermath of the partition led to a large-scale uprooting of the population and imposed a severe strain upon the financial resources of the country.World conditions were also such that India had to spend a larger proportion of her revenue of defence than would be necessary in normal times. As a result of these factors it has not been possible for the Government to bring into existence the Cultural Trust as it has agreed to in principle.

As you know, the financial difficulties still continue and it is not certain when the Government will be in a position to carry out in full its programme in respect of the Trust. Nevertheless, a beginning has been made and an all India Conference on Art was held in Calcutta in August 1949, as a result of which an Advisory Body on Art was set up. We have decided to hold the Conferences on Letters and on Dance, Drama and Music during the current year so that the advisory bodies for these subjects may also be set up without further delay. It is in pursuance of this decision that we have met today and I am hopeful that your deliberations will help us in the attainment of our objectives.

I am glad to find this array of non-official talent in this assembly, the more so as the importance of non-official initiative in the fields of culture cannot be over-emphasised. If you look at the agenda, you will find that the first item for your consideration is a proposal for the establishment of an Indian Academy of Letters which will co-ordinate literary activities in all the Indian languages. 'Co-ordinate' is perhaps an unfortunate word, because all literary creation is an expression of the freedom of the spirit and does not lend itself to control or organisation. What, however, an Academy can do is to consider ways and means for the preparation and maintenance of an over-all survey of literature in all the Indian languages so that, through greater knowledge of one another's efforts, literary men and women in all the languages can be spurred to greater activity and help in the creation of a literature which is comparable to that of the advanced languages of the world.

So long as there was an alien Government in the country, the people were suspicious of any governmental interference in the sphere of literature and culture. This was natural, for the people feared that such interference would have political implicaitons. Today, with the establishment of a National Government, there need be no such political fears, and some people, in fact, expect the Government to be entirely responsible for the development of our languages. I would, however, like to state that even a National Government cannot, and should not be expected to develop literature and culture through official fiats. The Government should certainly help both by material assistance and by creating an atmosphere which is congenial to cultural activities, but the main work of the development of literature and culture must be the responsibility of individuals endowed with talent and genius. The scope of non-official activity in these fields is unlimited and can never be over-emphasised.

Throughout the British period, except in a few relatively unimportant areas, no Indian language has enjoyed the status of a State language, nor has any of these languages been used as a medium of instruction in the universities and other higher institutions of learning. Consequently, whatever developments there have been, have been due to their internal strength. The situation has, however, completely changed with the attainment of freedom. An Indian language has attained the status of the national language, and other Indian languages enjoy the status of State languages in their own areas. The Indian languages are also being increasingly used in higher education, and in the course of the next 15 years or so, they will completely replace English as the medium of instruction at all stages of education. The support of the State and use in the universities are factors which help in the growth of a language, and there is no doubt that the Indian languages which have until now developed without any extraneous aids, will now begin a new phase of development.

I have already said that one of the first duties of an Academy of Letters would be to survey and investigate the literature which now exists in all the Indian languages. This is necessary so that we may know exactly what has been achieved in the Indian languages, and what remains to be done. It is obvious that if any language is to attain recognition outside its own domain, it must contain works which are accepted as valuable contributions to human knowledge or culture. For this, it is not enough if a language translates works from other languages. Valuable as such translations are, and greatly as they contribute to the development of a language, they cannot by themselves establish a language as a world language. A language or literature attains that stauts only when it makes some contribution which by its originality or depth of insight or beauty of expression marks an addition to the achievements of man.

The fourteen languages recognised by the Constitution include Sanskirt and Tamil. Sanskrit is, of course, in a class by itself, and is rightly recognised as one of the most developed of classical languages. Tamil also has a rich and ancient literature and its poetry has been and deserves to be translated into foreign languages. We must however, remember that Tamil is really a classical language, and most of the achievements of Tamil which entitle it to recognition belong to a past age.

If, therefore, we leave out Sanskrit and Tamil as classical languages, we must face up to the painful fact that only Bengali and Urdu among the modern Indian languages can claim to some extent international recognition. Urdu, in less than three hundred years, has achieved a progress that is almost phenomenal. Urdu poetry developed suddenly and produced poets who can rank with the immortal poets of the classical languages. Mir Anis can take his place after poets like Valmiki, Homer and Firdausi; Sauda, Mir and Ghalib have composed lyrics that are excellent, judged by any standard. Ghalib, in particular, has reached heights of originality and beauty that rank him with the greatest lyric poets of the world. In prose too, Urdu has, in about a hundred years, produced works in history and literature that have rightly attained international fame. Among the Indian language it is only from Urdu that some works had been translated into English and other European languages more than a hundred years ago. Garcin de Tassy published a French translation of Sir Syed Ahmad's *Asar-al-Sanadid* as early as 1850. Maulvi Nazir Ahmed and Maulana Shibli Numani have also produced works which have been translated and quoted by well-known European scholars. In the third volume of his *Literary History of Persia*, Edward Browne has drawn extensively upon the works of Shibli Numani. In fact, a large portion of this book, particularly the chapter on Hafiz, is almost a translation of Shibli Numani's *Shair-al-Ajam.* Browne has expressed his regret that Shibli Numani's book did not appear ten years earlier, for in that case his first two volumes of *Literary History of Persia* would have benefited by the incorporation of his material and interpretation. It is not only Shibli Numani's work which has attained this status. There are other authors too whose books have been translated into Arabic, Persian, Turkish, Russian and German.

Beisdes Urdu, the only other modern Indian language which has attained international status is Bengali. This is due almost entirely to the genius of Rabindranath Tagore. There is perhaps no language today which has not translated some of the works of Tagore. His name is rightly recognised as among the immortals and on account of him Bengali has an honoured place among the literatures of the world. Similarly, some of Sarat Chandra Chatterji's novels have also been translated into some European languages.

If we exclude Sanskrit and Tamil as classical languages, and leave out Urdu and Bengali, it is a regrettable fact that none of the other modern Indian languages have yet attained world status or made nay contribution to the literature of the world. It is true that Gujarati has one work which has attained international importance, *viz.*, the autobiography of Mahatma Gandhi. Similarly, Tilak's *Geeta Rahasya* in Marathi has also rightly won the appreciation of Scholars throughout the world. But we cannot class a language as a world language on the strength of only one or two books.

I am sure that all the literary figures who have assembled here today will agree with me that we have to pay special attention to the question of Hindi. We have accepted it as our national language, and the Constitution provides that it must take the place of English in 15 years. It is therefore essential that Hindi should develop sufficient strength and wealth to fulfil this important role, and yet we have to admit with sorrow that Hindi has not yet developed a literature which has achieved international standards or recognition. I would like to remove one misunderstanding in this connection. What is called Hindi today must be distinguished from Brij Bhasha and Avadhi. It was in Brij Bhasha and Avadhi that during the 16th and 17th centuries great progress was made under Moghul patronage. From the time of Akbar to that of Shah Alam there was always a Poet laureate in Brij Bhasha at the Moghul Court. It was during Jehangir's reign that Tulsidas wrote his famous work in Avadhi. Brij Bhasha and Avadhi, between them, threw up a galaxy of talents of which some of the most distinguished names are those of Tulsidas, Amir Khusroe, Malik Mohammad Jaisi, Abdul Rahim Khan Khanan, Mirabai, Kabir, Dadu, Ramdas, Shah Barkat Ullah and Abul Jalil Bilgrami.

The poetry of Brij Bhasha attained a high degree of excellence and can rightfully claim a place among the literature of the world. This, however, is quite distinct from what is called Hindi today. Modern Hindi started as a literary language in the beginning of the 20th century and was in fact only a variation of the same language of which the other variation is Urdu. The only difference between the two is that Hindi is more Sanskritic in vocabulary. There is no doubt that a great quantity of literature has been produced in Hindi since the beginning of this century. Many magazines and newspapers have been and continue to be published. Hindi can also boast of translations from almost all the Indian languages as well as from some of the languages of Europe. While therefore the quantity of literature produced in Hindi is extensive, the quality is not yet of a degree which can entitle Hindi to a place in world literature. This is a matter which is of anxious concern to all of us, for a language which we have chosen to be our national language must attain a status commensurate with that dignity. As nationals of India, it is therefore our duty to try to enrich the literature of Hindi and see that really first-rate literature is produced in it.

I have mentioned earlier that apart from Sanskrit, Tamil, Bengali and Urd, there are some important works in languages like Gujarati and Marathi, and one may add Telugu. It is however necessary that all these languages must develop rich literatures of their own so that the contribution of India to world literature may correspond to her past attainments.

I would like to draw your attention to one other problem which the present conference whould consider. Though Hindi has been accepted as the national language of India we have to recognise that it is not the mother tongue of people from the South, the East and the West. Till these areas take up the study of Hindi on an adequate scale and their people acquire facility in the use of Hindi, the problem of our national language is not really solved. We must however, be very careful as to how we proceed in the matter. We must respect the susceptibilities of our brethren from South, West and East India. They should never feel that they are being compelled to accept something against their will. We are grateful to them that they have accepted Hindi as the national language and we must work for the spread and development of Hindi with their willing co-operation. It was in order to tide over the difficulties of the transitory period that it was decided to have an interval of 15 years during which the use of English should continue. That decision should not be lightly changed and we must be careful to avoid doing anything which may create an impression among our brethren from these areas that it is proposed to change that decision without their consent. I would, however, at the same time, appeal to them to remember that if we are to succeed in implementing our decision to substitute English by Hindi after 15 years, the necessary preparation for the change must begin now. I have every confidence that we will receive the co-operation of all Indians – whether they come from the East or West, the North or South – in the proper development of Hindi as our national language.

I would conclude by saying that the question of the national language is not the concern of any particular section or group. It is a matter which vitally affects the whole country. I consider it an accident that the language which was chosen to be the national language was from North India. Under a different set of circumstances, it might have been a language of the South. Since, however, the choice has been made, it is the national duty of all Indians –whether of the South or of the North – to do everything for the development and enrichment of Hindi. I am confident that, with the full co-operation of the North and South, East and West, Hindi will soon develop a literature which will enable it to claim its place among the rich literatures of the world.

Document No. 9

ORAL ANSWERS DATED 19-3-1951 BY MAULANA AZAD TO THE QUESTIONS ASKED IN THE HOUSE OF THE PEOPLE

PUBLIC AND PRIVATE INSTITUTIONS

Shri Raj Kanwar: Will the Minister of **Education** be pleased to state:

(a) Whether there are any recognised public or private institutions in the Centrally Administered areas, in which training is imparted in such fine arts as (i) music both in vocal; (ii) dancing; (iii) painting; (iv) scripture and (v) architecture;

(b) If the reply to part (a) above be in the affirmative, their number, the places where they are located and the amount of financial assistance given by Government to each such institutions?

The Minister of Education (Maulana Azad): (a) and (b). a Statement is placed on the Table of the House. [*See* Appendix XVIII, annexure No. 3.][1]

1. Not included.

Document No. 10

ORAL ANSWERS DATED 19-3-1951 BY MAULANA AZAD TO THE QUESTION ASKED REGARDING THE SCHEME TO START A REGULAR SCHOOL OF FINE ARTS IN DELHI BY THE GOVERNMENT

Shri Raj Kanwar: From the statement given to me by the hon. Minister it appears that Government are giving Financial assistance to four such institutions to the extent of Rs. 100/- per annum to one, Rs. 2,700/- to another, Rs. 15000/- to the third and Rs. 9,200/- per annum to the fourth institution. May I know whether Government have any scheme to start a regular school of fine arts in Delhi, the capital of the country?

Maulana Azad: Government have many such schemes but they are bound by financial difficulties.

Mr. Speaker: I think we better proceed to the next question.

Document No. 11

REPLY DATED 19-3-1951 BY MAULANA AZAD TO THE QUESTIONS ASKED IN THE HOUSE OF THE PEOPLE

GILGIT MANUSCRIPTS ON BUDDHISM

Prof. S.N. Mishra: Will the Minister of **Education** be pleased to state:

(a) whether India's oldest treasures of manuscripts, the Gilgit Papers on Buddhism have been rehabilitated; and

(b) If so, whether it was with the help of foreign experts or laboratory experiments carried out in National Archives?

The Minister of Education (Maulana Azad): (a) The rehabilitation of the Gilgit manuscripts has been taken up and the major items in the collections have been renovated. The repair of the rest is in progress and is expected to be completed shortly.

(b) Foreign experts were consulted but the final process for repairing the pages was evolved as a result of experiments made at the repair shop of the National Archives.

Prof. S.N. Misra: May I know whether any part of it has been deformed during repairs.

Maulana Azad: No. 336 pages have been repaired till now and no repairs of any page have been deformed, and for the rest of the pages it is expected that as a result of the process of repair that has now been evolved no page would be deformed and all will be renovated.

Prof. S.N. Mishra: May I know whether another method of renovating the manuscripts has been discovered?

Maulana Azad : Yes, in the beginning, the usual method was adopted. But this manuscript is not on paper but on bark. Therefore special arrangements have got to be made for that.

Document No. 12

ORAL ANSWERS DATED 24-3-1951 BY MAULANA AZAD TO THE QUESTIONS ASKED IN PARLIAMENT

GRANTS TO MUSEUMS AND HISTORICAL RESEARCH SOCIETIES

Maulvi Wajed Ali: (a) Will the Minister of **Education** be pleased to state the names of the Museums, Historical Research Societies and Cultural or Linguistic Societies, with amounts received by them as grants from Government during the years 1948-49, 1949-50 and 1950-51?

(b) Was any grant given to Assam Museum, Gauhati, Assam *Sahetya Sabham* Jorhat, and *Kamrup Anusandhan* Society, Gauhati, during these years?

The Minister of Education (Maulana Azad): (a) A statement is laid on the Table [*See* Appendix XIXI, annexure No. 4][1]

(b) No application was received from any of these institutions for grants from Central Revenues.

Maulvi Wajed Ali: May I know will the Government consider the applications if received from the institutions in Assam and from those mentioned in section (b) of the question?

Maulana Azad: The Central Government follow special rules for the sanction of grants to these institutions. It will then be considered whether they are covered by those rules or not.

---

1. Not included.

Document No. 13

ORAL ANSWERS DATED 24-3-1951 BY MAULANA AZAD TO THE QUESTIONS ASKED IN THE HOUSE OF THE PEOPLE

RED FORT

Shri B.S. Arya: (a) Will the Minister of **Education** be pleased to state whether it is a fact that the Red Fort of Delhi remains open for the visitors every day during the day time?

(b) If so, do the Government servants employed in the Red Fort get the Sundays off or not?

(c) If they are not given any day off, what are the reasons thereof?

(d) According to the Government holidays list, how any holidays per year, are provided for the Red Fort employees?

The Minister of Education (Maulana Azad): (a) Yes, Sir. It remains open to the visitors from 8 A.M. to 11 A.M and from 4 P.M. to 7 P.M. in summer and from 10 P.M. to 1 P.M. and 3 P.M. to 6 P.M. in winter.

(b) The government servants employed in the Red Fort get two Sundays off in a month.

(c) Does not arise.

(d) The Red Fort employees are given 8 holidays in a year by rotation.

Shri B.S. Arya: Are the Government aware of the fact that the Fort was not closed like all other Government Departments on the days Mahatma Gandhi and Sardar Patel died?

Maulana Azad: I am unable to state anything offhand. It has not come to my knowledge.

Document No. 14

ANSWERS DATED 24-3-1951 BY MAULANA AZAD TO THE QUESTIONS ASKED IN THE HOUSE OF THE PEOPLE

EDUCATIONAL CONCESSIONS TO THE DEPENDENTS OF DEFENCE SERVICES PERSONNEL

Shrimati Velayudhan: (a) Will the Minister of Education be pleased to state whether the Government of India had sent some suggestions to the State Governments regarding the continuance of educational concessions to dependents of Defence Services personnel and if so, When?

(b) What were the suggestions?

(c) Is there any uniformity in the concession enjoyed by these Students, as a result of the recommendation of the Government of India.?

(d) Have Government got any information as to the number of students whose concessions were withdrawn as a result of the suggestions from Government?

(e) How many States have accepted the recommendation *in toto* and what are those States?

The Minister of Education (Maulana Azad): (a) and (b) Yes, Sir. Government made the following suggestions in August 1948:

(i) that no new application for these concessions should be entertained after the 1st October, 1948;

(iii) that concessions once granted should in the case of children and dependents of Defence Services personnel who have been killed or incapacitated as a result of war service be continued until their education is completed to the extent that existing schemes in the State allow; and

(iii) that concessions to children and dependents of other Defence Services personnel should be granted until the end of the particular course, Primary, Middle, High or College, which they were undergoing on October 1st 1948, under the scheme in operation in the States.

(c) to (e). Only eight of the present Part 'A' States replied and they generally agreed with the suggestions made by the Government of India. Information is not available as to the actual concessions afforded by State Governments and the number of persons who ceased to have the benefits. As the Central Government do not contribute any share of the expenses on the grant of these concessions, the matter concerns the States entirely.

Shrimati Velayudhan: I want to know whether prior to the recommendations from the Centre every student who received the concession was allowed to study up to Matric.

Maulana Azad: I have just stated that the Central Government are in no way concerned with this. The concessions in question have been given by the various State Governments. The Central Government, as such, are unable to state anything in the matter.

Shrimati Velayudhan: I also want to know whether those recommendations sent have a uniformity in the giving of concessions.

Maulana Azad: No, Sir, the Central Government did not feel any necessity for this. The matter lay entirely within the purview of the State governments and they were following their own rules. All that the Centre did was to emphasis that no new applications should be entertained after October, 1948.

Shri Rathnaswamy: In the case of failure of the students in the first year are these concessions renewed?

Maulana Azad: I am unable to state anything in this connection. The State Governments must have got their own rules which they might be following in granting such concessions.

Shrimati Velayudhan: I want to know whether the position is that when one student can study up to the fourth class only another can study up to Matric, according to the recommendations from the Centre.

Mr. Speaker: There are no recommendations from the Centre. It is a matter entirely with the State governments. He has made it clear more than once.

Shri Rathnaswamy: May I know whether such students are given any boarding facilities?

Mr. Speaker: We need not go into the details of the question.

Shrimati Velayudhan: May I Know whether the State Governments act according to the recommendations from the Centre?

Mr. Speaker: But he has said there are no recommendations. I think we will proceed to the next question.

Document No. 15

ORAL ANSWERS BY MAULANA AZAD DATED 24-3-1951 IN THE PARLIAMENT TO THE QUESTIONS ASKED IN CONNECTION WITH THE TAKING OVER OF VISHWABHARATI

Dr. M.M. Das: Will the Minister of **Education** be pleased to state:

(a) Whether it is a fact that negotiations are going on between the Union Government and the authorities of *Viswabharati* of Tagore regarding financial commitments involved in the scheme of taking over;

(b) if so, the approximate date when negotiations will end in decision; and

(c) Whether there is any plan or proposal before government to run *Viswabharati* as a separate University run by the Union Government?

The Minister of Education (Maulana Azad): (a) to (c). The attention of the hon. Member is invited to the reply given on the 7th March, 1951, to the Starred Question No. 1935 asked by Shri S.N. Mishra.]

Dr. M.M. Das: In part (a) of my question I have asked about the financial commitments of the Government of India. May I know the exact nature of these financial commitments on behalf of the Government of India so far as the scheme of taking over this institution is concerned?

Maulana Azad: At present the Central Government is giving an annual grant of one and a half lacs of rupees to this institution. In case it becomes a University and the Bill to that effect gets through this house, the Central Government will give an annual grant of four and a half lacs of rupees.

Dr. M.M. Das: I understand that those amounts have been paid to the Institution as recurring grants for running the institution. By 'financial commitments' I mean any compensation to be given or the cost of maintaining a certain standard of the institution.

Maulana Azad: In fact this amount of four and a half lacs of rupees includes expenditure in respect of all such items.

Dr. M.M. Das: May I know whether it is a fact that the government intends to bring forward a Bill declaring this an institution of national importance, and if so, may I know when that Bill will be introduced and what will the main provisions of that Bill?

Maulana Azad: The Bill is at present under the consideration of the Government and we propose to place it before the House at the earliest.

Dr. M.M. Das: I wanted to know the main provisions of that Bill.

Maulana Azad: It is very difficult for me to state anything in this connection at this stage.

Dr. M.M. Das: In view of the fact that the copyrights of the works of Tagore were granted to this institution, may I know whether those copyrights will still remain with this institution?

Mr. Speaker: It is too early to say–let us have the Bill before us.

Shri Chattopadhyay : I want to assscertain the number of arts and science students respectively studying the college section of *Viswabharati*?

Maulana Azad: Just now I am not in a position to reply to this question.

Document No. 16

WELCOME ADDRESS DATED 24-3-1951 AT THE SECOND SESSION OF I.N.C.C.U.

On behalf of the Indian National Commission and myself, I extend a very cordial welcome to Dr. Jaime Torres Bodet, Director General of Unesco, on the occasion of his first official visit to India. The welcome is the greater as we have been expecting him since last year, and the disappointment felt at his inability to fulfil his engagement then has accentuated our pleasure in finding him in our midst today.

We welcome Dr. Bodet not only because he is the Director General of UNESCO, but also because of the personal contribution he has made, both before and since he assumed that office, towards the furtherance of peace through education. His work in rural adult education in Mexico won the appreciation of discerning critics all over the world. Ever since he assumed office as Director General, he has given a new impetus to the programme of Fundamental Education and the service of underdeveloped areas. I have every hope that his present tour of India, Ceylon and Pakistan will establish closer bonds between Unesco and these countries and lead to greater efforts in the cause of education for peace and unity.

Unesco is one of the specialised agencies of UNO which was established to achieve international unity and peace. We must, however, confess that world unity on the political plane is still a distant goal. The world organisations which have been set up to achieve political unity, whether as the League of National or the United Nations Organisation, have not yet achieved anything that can rekindle the hopes of men. UNO, founded to solve all political problems in a spirit of equity by remaining free from entanglement with power blocks, is unfortunately itself becoming a victim of power politics. The conflicts between nations that formerly marked the field of diplomacy are now often displayed in the deliberations of UNO. How can we then hope that UNO will succeed in its aims unless it can disentangle itself from the trammels of political groupings and judge all questions from the point of view of international justice and peace? While aware of the present shortcomings, India is nevertheless a staunch supporter of UNO, for world peace is so precious an objective that we cannot give up any instrument which offers even a remote hope of achieving it. And what instrument of world peace can there be other than UNO? Like the Persian poet Urfi, I feel like saying:

Zi Naqs-i-Tashna-Labee Dan Ba Aql-i-Khesh Manaz
Dilat Fareb Gar Az Jalwa-i-Surab No-Khurd.

'You need not take pride in your acumen if you look at the sands of Sahara and are not beguiled by the mirage of water;
For if you had been indeed thirsty, you would have seen the sand as water.'

If then the hopes of peace held out by UNO prove in the end to be illusory, the illusion is itself so dear to us that we would fain cherish it.

If therefore in this troubled world we can find any gleam of hope for unity and peace, it can be only through the activity of Unesco. Unesco rightly recognises that all conflicts ordinate in the mind of man, and hence it is in the minds of men that the bastions of peace must be built. The emphasis here is on the cultural unity of mankind to which different countries and different peoples have made their contribution. In Unesco one may therefore forget the clashes of Lake Success and live in an atmosphere where representatives who oppose one another in UNO can co-operate in creative effort. I may cite as an instance the political differences which have divided our country from South Africa. India has rightly sought the help of UNO to remove discrimination and racial inequality that prevail in South Africa, but in Unesco we find that the representatives of South Africa co-operate with the representatives of India in advancing the cause of education, science and culture. Education is basic to the creation of an atmosphere in which human beings can meet one another on a plane of friendship and equality, and we are particularly happy that the direction of Unesco is today in the hands of one who had identified himself with the furtherance of these ends.

Mr. Director General, you will perhaps agree with me that men and women of the present generation have been brought up in an atmosphere of such national exclusiveness that they cannot be expected to achieve world unity and world citizenship easily. They have been trained to think on lines which make it difficult to transcend the limitations of race, class or nationality. If therefore we are to achieve world unity, and all agree that without such unity the future of man is dark, all our efforts must be concentrated to educate the future generations for world citizenship. If from their earlier days, the children of today are trained to think of one another in terms of unity and brotherhood, they will, when they grow up, develop an attitude of mind in which the present conflicts will become unnecessary and unreal.

I also hope, Mr. Director General, that you will agree with me that for achieving this end the entire method of teaching history and geography in schools must be changed. Till this has been done, there can be no hope of achieving a real unity of purpose among the peoples of the world and without such unity there can be no world citizenship. The way in which we teach history and geography today not only militates against this objective but is, in a way, not ever founded on fact. This terrestrial globe which nature has created as one has been divided by us for our purposes into different compartments. Not content with this, we have painted the common world in different colours in order to ensure that these divisions are maintained and demarcated them as Asia and Europe, America and Africa. When we teach a child geography, we do not start by saying that he is an inhabitant of the earth, but one the contrary we start by instilling in his mind that he is from Delhi, and Delhi is in India, and India is in Asia, and Asia is in the Eastern Hemisphere. It is only after all these stages have been passed that we at last tell him that he is a denizen of the world. Is it surprising that a child brought up in this way thinks of himself as belonging to the particular spot where he has been born, be it Delhi or Paris, Peking or New York? At most he can transced his provincial and national borders and feel himself an Asian or a European, an African or an American, but the idea of his membership of the human species remains a mere abstraction.

I am sure, Mr. Director General, you will agree that this method of teaching geography must be changed. We must have new maps for children in the elementary stages in which the world will be painted in one colour; we must teach the child that he is a denizen of the world first and foremost, and then go on to tell him that just as a town is divided into different wards for purposes of convenience, but nevertheless the town remains one, so the world is divided into segments like Asia and America, of the world. Just as the ward is again divided into smaller sections and streets, the continents are divided into smaller units and we call them countries, but these countries remain integral parts of the same world.I have no doubt that geography taught in this way will, from their very childhood, establish in the minds of children a sense of belonging to One World.

Like mistaught geography, history mistaught has also become an instrument for the division of making. In our current history books, we are told that men belong to different races and nations. The story of these nations emphasises their internecine conflicts so that the relation between men from different groups is represented as one of hatred and discord. It is inevitable that history so taught must lead to a constriction of the mind, a narrowing of the vision in which the child's identity with his group depends upon its sharp demarcation from all other groups. I sometimes think that it was better when men and women believed implicitly in the story of the Bible, and thought that whatever be the differences between nations and races, they were all the children of Adam and Eve. This concept of common parentage served as a bond of unity in the midst of our many differences and conflicts. In the 19th Century, as our knowledge increased, we started questioning these religious legends. Instead of derivation from common parents, we started to divide mankind into Caucasians and Mongolians, into Aryans and Semetics, and into further sub-divisions within each larger division. I do not know if the story of Adam and Eve is literally true or a Hebrew version of the Chaldean myth, but I have no doubt that it is in essence true: it is a recognition of the fundamental truth that the human race is one in origin and hence all men are akin to one another. Such recognition is not to my mind incompatible with belief in the theory of evolution. One can accept that theory and still hold that all men belong to the same species and differences among them developed on account of differences in environment and other factors. Just as the teaching of geography must be recast to bring out the unity of the world, we must recast the teaching of history to bring out the unity of man.

I would like to refer to the so-called opposition between East and West, or between different races and cultures. Most accounts of such conflicts seem in any case to be based on a misunderstanding of facts. We are told that centuries before the Christian era, the Persian attack on Greece was an attack of the East on the West, and led to a counter-attack by the West led by Alexander. Are these however conflicts between East and West, or campaigns of conquest by individuals who wanted to bring the whole of the known world under their sway? It seems to me that we have thus created needlessly a myth of conflict between East and West extending over millenniums. It seems obvious to me that till we recast the teaching of history and geography, we cannot hope to change the attitude of man. I know that this is no easy task, for even with such reform of the teaching of history and geography, many obstacles will remain. Perhaps the greatest of these obstacles is the cult of narrow nationalism. It is strange that nationalism which developed as a defence against the autocracy of kings has itself become aggressive today. A force for liberation and liberalism in the 19th Century, it has today become an instrument for holding back the progress of man. So intense and pervasive has become its influence that however clearly we recognise the need of world unity and however keenly we desire it, we cannot yet transcend the limitations of nationalism. And yet unless we can go beyond nationalism, the future of man is dark.

Mr. Director General, I am glad to hear that Unesco has already taken steps for reform in the methods of teaching history and geography. I was glad to learn that seminars have been held for the purpose and what is more important, Unesco is undertaking to produce a history of mankind which will emphasis the growth of world unity. I have every hope that this aspiration of Unesco will be translated into reality during your regime, and I can assure you that India, which is one of the founder members of Unesco, will extend all possible help and co-operation towards the furtherance of that end.

I have now great pleasure in requesting the Prime Minister to inaugurate this session of the Indian National Commission.

Document No. 17

SPEECH OF MAULANA AZAD DATED 27-3-1951 IN PARLIAMENT IN CONNECTION WITH THE GENERAL BUDGET – LIST OF DEMANDS AND HIS ANSWERS TO THE QUESTIONS ASKED IN THIS REGARD

Maulana Azad: Sir, I was glad to note that those of my hon. friends who took part in the Debate today realized by themselves that until sufficient funds are made available to the Ministry of Education its hands are tied and it is unable to accomplish tasks which you would want it to accomplish. It is a common axiom that you cannot have it both ways on the one hand you insist that no wood be burnt and on the other you demand that the fireplace be lighted and the meals cooked. Now, you cannot have it both ways. The fireplace can be lighted only if wood is burnt and wood can be burnt only if money is made available for purchasing.

Two years ago I drew your attention to this fact. I did not state simply that I was not satisfied with the way the work of the Ministry of Education was being carried on but, as you might remember, I said I was unhappy about it. The difficulty, however, is that our hands are so badly tied that no step can be taken. Even today one of my friends remarked, "What are you doing? If you were to distribute radio sets in the villages with a great good that would do to the people?" Yes, that is true, but the sets for distribution are not going to drop down from the heavens. That calls for money. Money is the ultimate hurdle in the way of all schemes of which there is no dearth. Let me tell you, our hands are full of schemes but to the extent the hands are full of schemes the pockets are empty of money. What are we to do?

My hon. friend drew my attention to the fact that one of the important items on our programme should have been to utilize for the work of education and social service those of our young people who are studying at the universities for their degrees. This is right. This is very important. Other countries have accomplished that task that way. But, let me remind him that was the very first thing that came to my notice on taking over charge of the Education Ministry. The report made by Sergeants Committee is known to you. In that report the period for the spread of basic education throughout the country was put at 40 years. Hence, immediately on taking charge of the Ministry I appointed the Kher Committee. This Committee laboured for full one year and brought out a scheme. I had also drawn the attention of this Committee to the fact that the problem of teachers formed a formidable obstacle in the way of our work. If we were to start the work of education throughout the country we would stand in need of twelve lakhs of trained teachers. Our training centers are there but considering the speed at which they are working we may not perhaps be able to produce twelve lakhs of trained teachers even in 50 years. How are then we going to resolve this difficulty? Why not consider conscription of youngmen for the purposes of education in the same way as we have it for military service? Why not approach the universities with the request that they might make it compulsory for all those who receive education from the standard of Matriculation onwards to serve as a teacher for at least two years before they are awarded their degrees? During these two years we might, of course, pay them an allowance to help them meet the essential expenses. A sum of forty to fifty rupees might be paid on that account. Kher Committee considered the proposal and accepted it. They included it in their recommendations and formulated a full scheme. According to that scheme we could have compulsory and universal basic education in sixteen instead of forty years, ten years for the junior stage and six years for the senior stage. As for the expense they proposed that thirty per cent. of the expense should be borne by the Provinces, now called States. That is how the scheme could be followed up. The expenditure on buildings should be the least possible. As far as possible we should be able to do with *Kachcha* houses, or thatched shelters or huts.

Babu Ramnarayan Singh (Bihar): Very Good.

Maulana Azad: But then you need money even for the construction of thatched huts. The estimate of expenditure which they had arrived at was very much an underestimate. Were we to put that sixteen year scheme into practice the Centre would have to contribute two crores of rupees at the rate of thirty per cent. while the States would have to pay at the rate of 70 per cent.

For that purpose, we called a Conference of the Education Ministers of the States and placed the scheme before them. They generally agreed with it. Some of the States in particular expressed their full readiness to put it into operation. Uttar Pradesh, Bombay and Madras expressed their readiness to stand 70 per cent of the expense. They offered to initiate the scheme provided the Centre was prepared to meet 30 per cent. of the charge. When things had reached that stage and the budget time approached this scheme was brought up but it was found that not a penny could be spared for the purpose. Consequently, the whole of that scheme is at present lying in the midst of a pile of papers.

The idea of conscription from the universities formed part of that scheme. The idea was welcomed by some Members of the Bombay University. The Vice-Chancellor of the Delhi University assured us that they were prepared to put it into operation if we wanted, but it is a pity we could not initiate the scheme.

Obviously we could not disregard all other parts of the scheme and take up just this one, that is, call up these youngmen from the universities. That would not do. Suppose we were to call them up what were we to do with them? There must, after all, be some plan, some arrangements into which they could be fitted. If there are no such arrangements what is the use of calling them up? And, then you must give them something to live on, at least a subsistence allowance. Even if you were to give them fifty rupees a month per head and if you were thus to employ one lakh of teachers in a year in the whole country you would require 50 laksh of rupees per month, that is, six crores of rupees per annum. Such were the considerations.

Shri Sidhva: Did you or did you not urge upon the Minister of Finance that he should provide for so much money ?

Maulana Azad: Of course I did, I fought for it for three months. It was not the present Minister of Finance but Dr. Matthai.

Seth Govind Das: Let us hope he would do something.

Maulana Azad: For three months I held my ground but without any useful results. Now, this would have entailed for us an expenditure of only two crores in the first year and four crores in the second year and thus it would have gone on for sixteen years. This would, of course, have involved a thrity per cent. contribution from our side and a seventy per cent. contribution from the States and in ten years' time the whole of your country which is blind today would have been blessed with the gift of eyes. But I regret this cannot be done now.

Similarly we drew up a scheme of adult education, which I have started calling by the name of social education. This scheme was formulated on the understanding that the expense would be shared on a fifty-fifty basis, fifty per cent. of the charge to be borne by the Centre and fifty per cent, by the States. We made an effort to set it afoot. With great efforts a sum of reupees one crore was found for the purpose two years ago–a paltry sum when you consider that it was meant to serve for the wholeof India, the whole of the country. We also called a Conference of the States Ministers for the purpose, in order to discuss the scheme. This was done and they were all told to go back to their respective places and set about making the necessary.arrangements. Accordingly, they went back and set about making the necessary arrangements. We had not distributed the amount as yet when we were told all of a sudden that there was a deficit of thirty crores. You might be remembering how the crisis arose and had to be met somehow or the other.

Despite the decision to stop all capital expenditure and to effect a 20 per cent. cut in all other expenditure, I persisted in my refusal for full one month and four times a Cabinet meeting was held to discuss this issue. It is no secret to tell that I had not reconciled myself to that position throughout. But ultimately when the Prime Minister persisted too much and prevailed upon me, there was no help for me but to accept it. What was the result? You can just see for yourself the turn that position had taken subsequently. We asked the States to make necessary preparations which they did and are doing even now. That sum of one crore was reduced to eighty or seventy lacs of rupees by stages. They then put in their demands as they had made the necessary arrangements already. This created a difficult situation for us. Then cam the next year and we thought this time we will be able to have the original sum of one crore doubled to two crores of rupees. I do not know whether you will feel surprised or sorry when I tell you that not to speak of raising it to two crores of rupees, even it has not been possible to maintain the original one crore and it has now been stated that because of the present financial stringency did exist and that it exists even now. This is undoubtedly true. The result was that even that sum of one crore has been stopped. We took recommendations and made necessary arrangements. Now the payments have again been stopped after a few months and there is a categorical refusal that they are quite unable to help us anyway. What can be our reply to it?

An overall provision of 14 lacs of rupees was made towards the Basic Education during the last year for the whole of the country. What has happened to those 14 lacs? The year had hardly run out when a big hurdle came in the way. An attempt was made to reduce this sum of 14 lacs in the name of economy and now, I think barely four lacs of rupees out of them have been left with us. Any way it should suffice to give you a picture of the various difficulties that we are facing in this behalf.

Now if you expect me to express gratitude to such hon. friends who have to-day emphasised here to find somehow or the other a way out to set apart a definite fund for the Ministry of Education then I have only to be excused. If they think that merely a ten minutes' speech will solve the whole problem, then I am constrained to sumbit that such hon. friends are labouring under a great illusion. There will be no outcome of those speeches and after a year even they will forget what they have said here to-day. Again on the occasion of the presentation of the next Budget they will come forward with complaints such as the non-provision of any radio sets or this or that particualr thing. In this way nothing will come out. I therefore, will advise that you should do what I had requested you to do two years back. I may repeat what I had actually told you then. If you really feel that something ought to be done in this behalf, then you should proceed to set up a committee of the House for this purpose who, while bearing in mind constantly the prevailing financial stringency and the consequent diffculties, should explore ways and means to find money for purpose of Education which, if they consider to be so very necessary, will necessitary a reduction in expenditure on other items in case it is decided to make further provisions in respect of some particular item. Without this money cannot be available. What then should be done under such conditions? If you feel this task of national educationl to be of such an importance as should not be ignored on any score whatsoever, then something must be done even though we may be unable to do it as fully as we may wish. We will have to draw a line somewhere and fix a limit upto which we have to spend money during the coming few years and, as such money has to be found somehow or the other–may be it means a reduction in expenditure on other items. This money must be given priority over all others. It was after careful calculations and considerations that we had asked for a sum of 15 crores for the last year. Were it possible to find even these 15 crores for education then all these things to which you have drawn attention, could have been done. After all what ratio does a provision of 15 crores of rupees bear to overall revenue of the country as a whole?

Shri Sidhva: Quite negligible.

Maulana Azad: It is correct to say so. In other words it does not work out even to two per cent. If therefore, you wish that this task of education should be accomplished in right earnest, then you should not feel content with mere speech-making. If you did so, the twelve months will be over very swiftly and by the time the next year's Budget is presented, nothing will have been done with the result that a *status quo* will continue. You know the conditions obtaining in England as to how after the termination of war that country realized the necessity of effecting economy and you know also the extent to which they are actually saving. Despite their decision to effect economy and saving, they have resolved not to enforce that economy in the matter of education and on the other hand, they have increased the provisions from nine millions to twelve millions sterling. Similarly I want that a committee of this House should be set up which should take decisions and its recommendations should be placed before the Government. So if you also want to solve the problem of National Education in the same way, then you should give earnest attention to it and set up a committee for this purpose which should give their opinion after a full consideration of the issue. It may then be more possible to find a way out.

I want to make one or two more submissions But time at my disposal is short an barely ten minutes more are left with me. I therefore, will refer to them very briefly.

My hon. friend Seth Govind Das has drawn attention towards the cause of Hindi but I fail to understand how did such a necessity arise. I say so because only yesterday morning a short while before putting me that question we have had a conversation and I had told him that at the moment there were two basic things which were mot imoportant for the propagation of Hindi. The first of them is that we should try to intensify the propagation in the non-Hindi speaking areas because unless that happens the issue of a national language will remain unsolved. Again the second basic neeed is to write such text books and coin scientific terms in Hindi as to give this language the status it deserves as the medium of instruction for higher education and ultimately replace English so far the Ministry of Education is concerned. I may submit, that ever since we provided in the Constitution that Hindi shall be the national language of the country, my Ministry has started work in that direction and as a first step has entered into correspondence with the States drawing their attention towards this matter. Next so far as the services are concerned, time has come when knowledge of Hindi should be made a compulsory thing. My Ministry has been making constant efforts towards this aspect. You will be happy to know that we have accepted it in principle and we are going to make Hindi a compulsory subject in the Civil Service examinations. The next stupendous task is that of coining suitable technical terms in Hindi. A dictionary should be compiled of all such terms and suitable text books written. You know that Ministry of Education has set up a Board for that purpose which is already working in this behalf. The work, however, is not so simple as to be accomplished immediately. It is bound to take considerable time. But a start in the direction has anyway been made and we hope that with the passing of each day we shall continue to make steady progress in the achievement of our object.

So far as the non-Hindi speaking provinces are concerned only some days ago you might have read in the newspapers that the Education Ministry convened a Conference and one of its sessions was exclusively arranged for the representative of those provinces alone where the mohther tongue is not Hindi. The matter was discussed and they were asked about the difficulties that generally confront them and about the troubles which were likely to come in their way in the adoption of Hindi. The findings of the Conference are before us. We have to consider the whole matter and we want to settle these matters with the Governments of the concerned States. The Central Advisory Board of Education gave full attention to this matter during its last Session. The Education Ministry itself put this matter before the Board and sought its advice as to what further steps should be taken to develop and popularize Hindi. The Board remommended that an All-India Institution, with its headquarters at Delhi, should be established and it should be entrusted with this work. It has made recommendations about ten or twelve things more and has suggested that they should work on those very lines in order to popularize Hindi. The Government are considering these recommendations now. Personally I think that in respect of such a work as that of popularizing a language it would be better if the Government were to give monetary help and the actual work may be carried out by the non-official agencies. Non-official agencies perform such duties more efficiently. But you have to consider it.

One thing more has come before me. There are five divisions in the Education Ministry at present which are further sub-divided into Sections. We want that one Section should be solely run for the purpose of popularizing Hindi in those provinces whose mother tongue is not

Hindi. So far as the Government the Universities and the local bodies are concerned they would continue their work as usual. They would continue to supervise the progress of this work and would continue to submit their reports. If necessary they will tour extensively, so that some spirit could be infused in this work. But the question of staff again comes in the way. I may tell you that only a few months ago we were faced with such a terrible situation that far from expanding our staff we had to consider about its reduction. The question of expanding the staff depends upon the availability of funds. However we are giving thought to the whole subject and we hope that we will carry out the programme. With all that I agree that one wishes that the Education Ministry should have accomplished more. But there is the question of funds, if the funds can be arranged all these works ...

Shri T.N. Singh: I would like to ask one thing and it is that there has been some misunderstanding about Hindi and it would be better if you please remove it. This misunderstanding has been created because some people refer to one of your speeches which ...

Maulana Azad : My friends have already spoken about this thing to which you refer now. I understand that there has been some misunderstanding among my friends with regard to this matter.

It is possible that I may not have expressed my self in detail. When my hon. friend said that his views were different from those of mine, I was expecting that he would put forth his own views which might be different from those of mine. But after some time I heard him expressing those very ideas which I had already expressed. He has said the modern Hindi and modern Urdu both have developed from *Brij Bhasha* and hundreds of years have passed since. My friend is right when he says that many words change their shape and from when one language evolves from another, in this way the languages take a changed form.

Seth Govind Das: I did not say it about Urdu but about Hindi.

Maulana Azad: True, your remark that it has evolved from *Brij Bhasha*, and all other *Prakrit* languages which were in vogue right from the thirteenth century, were about Hindi. There is no doubt in it that the language used in the Ramayana is also Hindi. It is one thousand times Hindi; nay, it is one million times Hindi. But it is not modern Hindi. You have seen that there is no difference of opinion between you and me. Look into my speech and you will find that I have never said that anything written in the *Brij Bhasha* is not Hindi. Surely it has not been written in Chinese. If it is not Hindi, by what name shall we call it; the language used in Ramayana is definitely Hindi. Today we find a lot of difference between English of Chaucer and that of Byron and Tennyson. Who would say that the English language used by Chaucer is not English? We cannot call it Chinese. That is definitely English. But even then it is not modern English, which was used by Tennyson and Byron in their poerty at a later date. So I never meant it even for a singly minute that whatever previous literature we have at this time is not in Hindi, or that Hindi should not be given the right to claim with pride that the language used in the Ramayana and in other literature of this kind, which exists as a classical literature, is not Hindi. I have said to the effect that this has directly descended from that language, but even then we shall have to differentiate between it and the modern Hindi. You have accepted whatever I said there. I did not name Hindi, but modern Hindi. Apparently there is a difference. With all that I do not claim to be a scholar of Hindi. Only those persons can establish their opinion, with respect to this language. If they do not agree to my opinion, there is no reason that I should insist. This is my opinion that Ramayana has no doubt been written in Hindi, but it is not modern Hindi; and we have to make difference between the two. Moreover, if that opinion is wrong, I am prepared to accept the views of those who can give their opinion in this connection.

Shri D.D. Pant (Uttar Pradesh): It is in Pali.

Maulana Azad: Does my hon. friend think that Pali afterwards took the shape of Hindi? I have not got time, otherwise I would have spoken something more. One of my hon. friends has complained that our staff at Washington does not pay due attention especially to the needs of the private students. I may tell you that we have only six persons appointed for this purpose there. According to our original scheme there ought to have been seventeen persons on that staff. Again the question of funds came in and we were not able to appoint seventeen persons. You should know that America is not a small country, it is a world in itself. There are about 1,500 institutions there, which are thousands of miles away from each other; some in the North, some in the South, and some other in different parts of the country. Now if we want to keep ourselves in touch with all those institutions, we apparently require more staff. Because of the financial stringency we could not afford to keep an enlarged staff. We are regularly asking for the reports from those places, and we believe that the men who have been kept there are zealous workers. They try their best to keep themselves in touch with all the students who are there. They also tour and try to remove their difficulties. The persons who approach them, their needs are definitely considered. They arrange for tickets, make arrangements for railway or steamer passages for them, and arrange accommodation for them in case they have not got any. We are regularly receiving reports to this effect. It is possible that some persons may have complaints. But that too depends upon the expansion of our staff.

I shall not take much of your time. But in the end I would again remind you that the coming twelve months will pass swiftly. If this matter is not settled in the manner in which I have requested you, no results whatsoever would be achieved.

Dr. Ram Subhag Singh: May I know your opinion about the various national institutions? What would be the attitude of the Government with respect to the degrees conferred by the Kashi Vidyapith and other such institutions?

Maulana Azad: I have studied the constitution of the Kashi Vidyapith. Perhaps you might be knowing that one of my colleagues has reminded me that it was about two years back when this matter came to my notice and I wrote to my Ministry whether we can consider this matter. When the Ministry made an enquiry, they replied that it was laid down in their constitution that they cannot receive any help from the Government. I again wrote to them saying that they had taken this decision during the British regime. Non-acceptance of any Government aid at that time was quite understandable, but now there was a National Government functioning in the country at present. To this they replied that they have decided it in principle not to take any Government aid. After this the whole matter remained where it was. But I assure you that if any responsible person from that end communicates that they have no such restriction – according to their constitution or that there is some other way – the whole matter will be favourably considered. So far as the question of recognition of their degrees is concerned I may tell you that we have set up a Committee and it is considering this question with regard to all such institutions. You have pointed out that these institutions served a good deal in the days of the struggle for freedom. It is quite true. But when the question of degrees would come, past services would not be taken into account but only standard of education would be taken into consideration. The Committee is doing its work and I hope it will finish its work soon. So far as the Central Government are concerned, they will accept their recommendations.

Some Hon. Members *rose* –

Mr. Deputy Speaker: Hon. Members will see that it is not 3 o'clock and the Demands in respect of the other Ministry have to be taken up.

Shri Sidhva: There is only one point which I wish to raise and that is whether the Finance Minister who is collecting Rs. 38 crores can spare Rs. 1 crore for Education.

Mr. Deputy-Speaker: There can be any number of such questions. Education is such a vast subject, I agree that three hours are not at all enough for discussing such a subject. Even three days may not be enough.

Shri Durgabai *rose* –

Mr. Deputy-Speaker: I cannot get on in this House if every Member gets up and does not care for the Chair. There are a number of ways in which the time could be extended. Hon. Members have not got the courage. Let me not be misunderstood. They can ask the Government to provide even three days or four days. But when Government allots the time Members are not prepared to be in their seats. As between the two what is to be done? I am really surprised, and it is strange, that hon. Members have come in such numbers today. Many a day I have had to sit inside the room, waiting to see whether there is a quorum in the House. If we are insistent upon a larger number of days being allotted I am sure that the Government will certainly be pleased to do so. But we must also reciprocate and see that we take interest. After agreeing to the time allotted there is no use trying to get over it. Let us go according to the time allotted: It is open to the whole House to say that the time allotted is not enough, but not at the fag end. That is what I have to say.

Shrimati Renuka Ray: We should not pass the Demand unless the Finance Minister gives an assurance that the money saved at the recommendation of the Estimates Committee is given for Education.

Mr. Deputy-Speaker: Order, Order. It becomes very delicate for me when my hon. sisters get up from their seats. I will not put the Demands to the vote of the House. The questions is:

"That the respective sums, not exceeding the amounts shown in the order paper, be granted to the President to complete the sums necessary to defray the charges which will come in course of payment during the year ending the 31st day of March, 1952 in respect of Demands Nos. 14, 15, 16 and 17 under the control of the Ministry of Education.

Document No. 18

REPLIES DATED 28-3-1951 IN THE PARLIAMENT BY MAULANA AZAD TO THE QUESTIONS RAISED REGARDING CENTRAL RELATIONS COUNCIL

Dr. M.M. Das: Will the Minister of **Education** be pleased to state the expenditure incurred upto now for the Cultural Relations Council?

The Minister of Education (Maulana Azad): The expenditure incurred for the Indian Council for Cultural Relations uptil now is Rs. 1,24,167.

Dr. M.M. Das: May I know the amount spent during the current year and the amount for which provision has been made for the next year for this Council?

Maulana Azad: I cannot give separate figures for these two items.

Dr. M.M. Das: May I know the purpose for which this Council was formed and the work done by this Council uptodate?

Maulana Azad: The Council has prepared many schemes, some of them have already been undertaken and some are being undertaken. One of the tasks undertaken by it is to make arrangements for the teaching of Sanskrit in such universities of foreign countries where no arrangements for Sanskrit studies already exist and to send Professors of Sanskrit there. In pursuance of that scheme last year we sent a professor to Tehran University, who is teaching Sanskrit there, and his work has generally been appreciated. A Sanskrit Library is also being opened there. In this matter too the Council is helping them. Besides this a quarterly magazine in Arabic language and another in Persian and English is being published for the Middle East countries and this has been very much liked in those countries. Apart from this, the Council has set up a Library of its own and is extending it. The Council is also contemplating to start a South East Asia section.

Dr. M.M. Das: May I know whether an Indian Dance Party was sent to Egypt by this Council on the occasion of the India Festival in Cairo and the whole expense was borne by this Council?

Maulana Azad: Yes, such a party was sent. A part of the expenditure was borne by the Government of Egypt and a part by the Council itself.

Shri K.C. Sharma: Will the hon. Minister be pleased to state how many books the Council has arranged to be written on Indian Culture and Civilization?

Maulana Azad: My hon. friend must know that this Council was set up only one and half years ago. The Council cannot be expected to perform every sort of work within this short period of one and half years.

Shri A.S. Guha: Has this Council established any cultural contacts with the Buddhist countries of South East Asia?

Maulana Azad: I have just now stated that the Council is contemplating to open a South East Asia Section very soon. The object of this Section would be to develop cultural relations with the Buddhist countries of this part of Asia.

Shri A.C. Guha: Is it an autonomous body or a Department of the Government?

Maulana Azad: No. It is not a Government Department. It is altogether an independent body. The Government gives grant to it.

Dr. M.M. Das: In relation to the Indian Dance Party sent to Cairo, may I know the amount of expenditure that was incurred?

Maulana Azad: I cannot mention the exact amount at present. But I think the expenditure incurred would be between ten to fifteen thousands of rupees.

Document No. 19

ORAL ANSWERS DATED 28-3-1951 BY MAULANA AZAD TO THE QUESTIONS ASKED IN THE HOUSE OF THE PEOPLE

SCIENTIFIC MANPOWER COMMITTEE

Pandit Munishwar Datt Upadhyay: (a) Will the Minister of **Education** be pleased to State how many stipends and of what amounts have been provided for in pursuance of the recommendation of the Scientific Manpower Committee?

(b) What institutions have been allotted these stipends?

(c) How many stipendiaries have started working under this scheme and in what establishments and subjects?

The Minister of Education (Maulana Azad): (a) During the years 1949-51, 425 senior Stipends of the value of Rs. 150 per mensem have been instituted for the post-collegiate practical training of graduates in Engineering and Technology and 300 junior Stipends of the value of Rs. 75 per mensem have been instituted for the Diploma holders. The stipends are tenable for a period of two years.

(b) A statement giving the names of educational institutions and the number of stipends allotted to each of the institutions and utilised by them is laid on the Table of the House. (*See* Appendix XIX, annexure No. 35.)[1]

(c) 521 Stipendiaries have started training in the various establishments. A statement giving subjects of study of the stipendiaries and the establishments where they are at present undergoing training is placed on the Table of the House (*See* Appendix XIX, annexure No. 36). [2]

Pandit Munishwar Datt Upadhyay: Are there any arrangements in our colleges and universities to impart such training?

Maulana Azad: In the universities there is meagre arrangement for the practical training. This is why such help has been given to students so that they may undergo training for two years in such institutions where the arrangements for such technical training exist.

Pandit Munishwar Dattt Upadhyay: Are these arrangements for imparting such training confined to India alone or arrangements have been made to send the trainees abroad also for this purpose?

Maulana Azad: No, Sir. So far the arrangements for imparting such training have been made in India only.

Dr. Deshmukh: May I know. Sir, what percentage of the personnel who have been listed in the Scientific Manpower Committee list have been found employment or considered?

Maulana Azad: A Statement has been placed on the Table of the House. If the hon. Minister will take the trouble to study it he will know the details in full.

Pandit Munishwar Datt Upadhyay: Is any aid being given to the Engineering Department of the Hindu University for this purpose?

Maulana Azad: This help has been given to the students and not to the universities. This can be verified from the Statement whether any help has been given to the students of the Hindu University or not.

Pandit Munishawar Datt Upadhyay: I only want to know about the Hindu University?

Maulana Azad: Yes. Help has been given to the students of the Hindu University also.

Pandit Munishwar Datt Upadhyay: How much?

Maulana Azad: I cannot give the figures. You will know every detail from the Statement.

---

1. Not included.

2. Not included.

Document No. 20

ORAL ANSWERS DATED 2-4-1951 BY MAULANA AZAD TO THE QUESTIONS ASKED IN PARLIAMENT REGARDING JAMIA MILLIA ISLAMIA OF DELHI

Dr. Ram Subhag Singh: (a) Will the Minister of **Education** be pleased to state whether Jamia Millia Islamia of Delhi has suffered any damage because of the rioting in the year 1947?

(b) If so, what was the value of the damage done to that institution?

The Minister of Education (Maulana Azad): (a) Books and furniture lying in the buildings of Jamia Millia Islamia, Delhi, were damaged and looted during the disturbances in 1947.

(b) The value of the damage is not known as no report was lodged with the Police and no enquiry was held. According to the statement of the Jamia Millia authorities, the damage amounted to nearly Rs. 5 lakhs.

Dr. Ram Subhag Singh : Are the Government contemplating to give any financial assistance to the Jamia Millia by way of compensation; or has such help been already given?

Maulana Azad: The Jamia did not apply for any such help and as such this question never came up before the Government.

Dr. Ram Subhag Singh: What is the number of those universities of India which suffered losses in the year 1947?

Maulana Azad: The other institutions too might have suffered losses as a result of such disturbances. But it is difficult for the Government to accept the principle of taking the responsibility for such losses upon themselves.

Pandit Krishna Chandra Sharma: Do the Government intend to rebuild the library of the Jamia?

Maulana Azad: Grants are given to the Jamia for educational purposes alone but not grants have been given to Jamia for this purpose so far.

Dr. Ram Subhag Singh: Is it a fact that some financial help has been given to the Jamia by the Toronto University of Canada?

Mr. Deputy-Speaker: How does it arise?

Dr. Ram Subhag Singh: The Jamia Millia was damaged during the riots and the question was whether the Toronto University are going to contribute towards the cost of the reconstruction.

Maulana Azad: I cannot say anything about it.

Mr. Deputy-Speaker: The Government cannot say anything with regard to this matter.

Shri Sonavane: May I know whether Government has accepted the Principle of paying compensation to the parties who have suffered losses due to riots?

Maulana Azad: No, the Government have not accepted any such obligation upon themselves.

Document No. 21

ANSWERS OF MAULANA AZAD DATED 2-4-1951 TO THE QUESTIONS ASKED IN PARLIAMENT REGARDING TRAINEES SELECTED ETC.

The Minister of Education (Maulana Azad): (a) At present the total number of trainees in the Training Centre for the Adult Blind is 101.

(b) The number of ex-servicemen under training in the Centre is 21 and of civilians 80.

(c) The candidates apply for admission to the Superintendent of the Centre and are selected on merit.

Dr. M.M. Das: May I know the annual expenditure incurred by the Government for running this institution?

Maulana Azad: No, I cannot give this information just now.

Dr. M.M. Das: May I know what percentage of the total expenditure is contributed by the Defence Department?

Maulana Azad: It has no connection with the Defence Department now. It is now connected with the Ministry of Education.

Dr. M.M.Das: What is the special kind of training that is being given to these people?

Maulana Azad: A variety of crafts such as music, *niwar* making, cane work, wool spinning, mat making, knitting and typewriting are taught. All these crafts are being taught there.

Pandit Munishwar Datt Upadhyay: Will the hon. Minister be pleased to give the names of the places where all those students, who have received training up till now, have been employed?

Maulana Azad: I require notice for it.

Shrimati Durgabai: I would like to know the number of such persons who have been employed in the government institutions after receiving their training?

Maulana Azad: I cannot give the exact figures just now, but I can say that all those persons who receive training in this institution get employment.

Shri Bhatt: Will the hon. Minister be pleased to state the amount that is being spent on each student per year, and are the expenses so incurred greater or less than what they are in the other institutions?

Maulana Azad: I have just now stated that I require notice for it. The question had nothing to do with the original question. That is why I have not got these facts and figures with me at this time.

Shri R. Velayudhan: May I know whether there is any plan for the placement of the trainees after the completion of their training?

Mr. Deputy-Speaker: All of them have been absorbed, he says.

Maulana Azad: I have just now stated that I cannot give the exact figures. But I understand that the persons who pass from this institution get employed immediately.

Document No. 22

ANSWERS DATED 2-4-1951 BY MAULANA AZAD TO THE QUESTIONS ASKED IN THE HOUSE OF THE PEOPLE

INDONESIAN STUDENTS

Pandit Munishwar Datt Upadhyay: (a) Will the Minister of **Education** be pleased to state how many Indonesian students have been studying in Indian institutions with the Indian Government scholarship and in what subjects?

(b) What is the expenditure of the Government of India under this scheme?

(c) Are there any conditions attached to the grant of stipend, if so, what?

The Minister of Education (Maulana Azad): (a) Ten Indonesian scholars have been studying in India in the following subjects:

Mechanical Engineering	3
Electrical Engineering	2
Chemical Technology	1
Economics and Sociology	1
Arts	2

Three scholars have since left India after completion of their studies and the scholarship of one has been cancelled due to unsatisfactory progress.

(b) Approximately rupees sixty thousand have been incurred so far on this scheme.

(c) None.

Pandit Munishwar Datt Upadhyay: Do any arrangements for the exchange of students between India and Indonesia exist? If so, how many students have been sent to Indonesia and for what subjects?

Maulana Azad: The Government of the Indonesian Republic have expressed their readiness to invite Indian students provided we find any useful educational material there. But the Indian scholars have not so far been sent there.

Pandit Munishwar Datt Upadhyay: Will this system continue in future as well or will it stop with the despatch of the first batch?

Maulana Azad: This is only a four-year scheme, out of which two years have already passed and two years more are left. After that it will be considered whether this system should be continued or not.

Pandit Munishwar Datt Upadhyay: What is the amount of scholarship granted to each of the students?

Maulana Azad: Two hundred rupees plus some help for tuition fees etc.

Shri Rathnaswamy: May I know if any Indian students are given scholarships in Indonesia on a reciprocal basis.

Shri Symanandan Sahaya : Do the Indian students in India in any case get two hundred rupees as monthly scholarship?

Maulana Azad: Keeping in view the present day conditions the hon. member will have to agree that two hundred rupees is not a huge amount. We will have to grant at least this much amount of money to the students who would come from foreign countries to receive higher education here, and for whom we take the responsibility of granting them with scholarships.

Shri Hussain Imam: Was the amount given by the hon. Minister for one year, or for two years?

Maulana Azad: This is four-year scheme. A sum of rupees one lakh to be spent in four years was earmarked for it; out of this amount sixty thousand rupees have already been spent.

Document No. 23

ANSWERS DATED 2-4-1951 BY MAULANA AZAD IN PARLIAMENT TO THE QUESTIONS ASKED IN CONNECTION WITH THE SINDHI SCRIPT

Shri Sidhva: (a) Will the Minister of **Education** be pleased to state whether any orders have been issued to Bombay and other Governments to see that the Sindhi script be substituted by Hindi script?

(b) If so, when were these orders issued and on what grounds?

(c) Have Government received any representation from a large number of Sindhis objecting to the Sindhi script being totally removed from the various languages?

(d) What is the reason for Government coming to that decision to issue such an order?

The Minister of Education (Maulana Azad): (a) Yes, but those orders have since been revised. A copy of the Press note embodying the latest decision of the Government of India to use both Arabic and Devnagari scripts is laid on the Table of the House [*See* Appendix XX, annexure No. 18.]

(b) and (d) The questions do not arise in view of the latest decision.

(c) The Government of India have received a representation from certain members of the Sindhi community requesting that the Sindhi language may be written in Arabic script.

Shri Sidhva: Is it a fact that the Sindhi script was removed before the Press note in reply to my question was issued. I would like to know on whose bidding it was removed, who made this suggestion or made representation to this effect?

Maulana Azad: This issue came up before this government when a very large number of Sindhis migrated to Ajmer and settled there and arrangements had to be made for the education of their children. They had brought books of the primary classes with them and they were all printed in the Sindhi script. The local Government adopted that script. After this a meeting of the Sindhi Sahitya Parishad was held at Bombay and a resolution was passed in that meeting to the effect that for the future the Devanagri script should be adopted for the Sindhi language and a request was made to the Government to publish the Sindhi text books in the Devanagri script for the education of the Sindhi students. The Government considered this proposal and after giving thought to it they arrived at the decision that the said proposal was indeed a good one, and its implementation would lighten the burden of educating the Sindhi students. We have accepted the Hindi language and the Devanagri script as the national language and the national script of India and as such the Sindhi students will certainly have to read Hindi. Now if they learn the Devanagri script writer learning their own mother tongue, it would be an easy task for them to learn Hindi as well; and both the objectives would be achieved side by side without wasting double time for it. Therefore the Government decided to act upon this proposal and the State Governments too were directed to act accordingly in their respective areas. But after this a number of protests from Sindhi people against this decision began to pour in from the various parts of the country and it was pointed out that this was an open violation of the fundamental rights which guaranteed the protection of language and script of every Indian community. Among them the Sindhi Language and Script Association protested most strongly against the decision and also adopted a lengthy resolution in this connection emphasising the fact that the entire Sindhi literature which was written during all these hundreds of years, was in the Sindhi script and now if all of a sudden this script of the Sindhi language was changed the result would be that the new generations would remain totally ignorant about this old literature and in this way a wall of ignorance would be created between them and the old Sindhi literature. The motive underlying the decisions of the Government was not to impose a script on Sindhis against their will. The government have accepted this fundamental principle that the Sindhis alone have a right to take any decision with respect to the script of their language, and the Government would not tolerate it even for a single minute that some script would be imposed upon them. The government had thought that the Sindhi Sahitya Parishad represented the majority opinion of the Sindhis. But now if a section of the Sindhi community is against the decision and is in favour of the Sindhi script, all that the Government could do is to accept both the scripts for the Sindhi language. The children whose guardians want them to get educated through the Devanagri script may be taught Sindhi in the Devanagri script and for those whose guardians favour

Sindhi script, arrangements should be made to teach them in the Sindhi script. Arrangements for the second script can only be made in schools when at least forty student express their desire to receive education in that particular script. The Central Advisory Board of Education has approved this very principle with regard to the question of language and script. For the present this very system will be adopted for Sindhis also.

Nevertheless, the arrangements cannot last for long, The government expects that within the next two or three years the Sindhis of India will have a full chance to arrive at a well balanced decision after considering all the aspects of this important problem. On the other hand the Government too will come to know as to how many of them want to get their children educated through the Sindhi script and how many through the Devanagri script; and then it would be easy for us to arrive at a final decision in this connection.

Shri Sidhva: I do not want to say anything more after this satisactory explanation, but is the hon. Minister aware of the fact that the government of Bombay do not allow the Sindhis to use both the scripts. If it is a fact, then have the Government of India directed them to the effect that both the scripts should be used?

Maulana Azad: The Government of India have sent directions to the State Governments after the press note was issued. It is hoped that the State Governments would act according to the instructions that have been given to them.

Pandit Balkrishna Sharma: Sir, is it a fact that in the year 1872 some Commissioner had invented this script which is now known as Sindhi script? Is it not a fact that History does not mention that fact that there was anything like the Sindhi script?

Mr. Deputy-Speaker: The question hour is over.

Document No. 24

MAULANA AZAD AND VISHVA-BHARATI BILL

Parliament of India
April 17, 1951

VISVA-BHARATI BILL

The Minister of Education (Maulana Azad): I beg to move for leave to introduce a Bill to declare the institution known As "Visva-Bharati" to be an institution of national importance and to provide for its functioning as a unitary, teaching and residential university.

Mr. Speaker: The question is:

" That leave granted to introduce a Bill to declare the institution known as 'Visva-Bharati' to be an institution of national importance and to provide for its functioning as a unitary, teaching and residential university."

The motion was adopted.

Maulana Azad: I introduce the Bill.[1]

1. Was introduced on 28-4-1951.

Document No. 25

ORAL ANSWERS DATED 18-4-1951 BY MAULANA AZAD IN THE HOUSE OF THE PEOPLE TO THE QUESTIONS ASKED ABOUT ANCIENT MONUMENTS

Prof. S.N. Mishra: Will the Minister of **Education** be pleased to State:

(a) Whether the proposal to carry out a survey of ancient monuments in the States of India with a view to picking out monuments to be taken over the Central Archaeological Department has been implemented; and

(b) If not, the reasons for the delay?

The Minister of Education (Maulana Azad): (a) and (b) Yes, Sir. The survey has started.

Prof. S.N. Mishra: May I know in which of the States has this work been started?

Maulana Azad: It is not necessary to name any particular State. The survey work is going on in all the three categories of States, *viz.*, parts A, B and C.

Prof. S.N. Mishra: May I know if any monuments have been selected in this connection and, if so, which?

Maulana Azad: In the case of Part B States, work has been done in Hyderbad, Jaipur and Udaipur. Work has also been done in Madhya Bharat and Travancore-Cochin.

Shri T. Husain: Has Government appointed any additional staff for the purpose and, if so, is there any scholar of Persian and Sanskrit on this additional staff?

Maulana Azad: Yes, The additional post of an Advisor has been created. It was not thought necessary to employ any more additional staff because the staff already there can cope with the work very well.

Shri T. Husain: I wish to know whether the Advisor is a scholar of Sanskrit or of Persian or of both?

Maulana Azad: The Advisor is the same person who has been the Director for several years, *viz.*., Mr. Chakravarty.

Prof. S.N. Mishra: What is the time limit fixed for this work?

Maulana Azad: No specific time limit has been fixed but efforts are being made to finish the work as early as possible.

Document No. 26

ANSWERS DATED 18-4-1951 BY MAULANA AZAD TO THE QUESTIONS ASKED IN PARLIAMENT REGARDING THE INDIAN HISTORY

Shri Sidhva: Will the Minister of **Education** be pleased to state:

(a) whether the Netherlands government have agreed to supply the Government of India with microfilm copies of old records which have any bearing on Indian History;

(b) if so, whether these records relate to any particular period of Indian history and how old are they; and

(c) whether any amount has been paid to the Netherlands government for these microfilm copies?

The Minister of Education (Maulana Azad): (a) Yes, Sir. The Government of Netherlands have agreed to supply the microfilm copies.

(b) These records belong to the Dutch East India Company and mainly cover the 17th and early 18th centuries.

(c) A sum of Rs. 7,503 has, so far been paid.

Shri Sidhva: I wish to enquire whether the historical records which are being sent here by the Government of Netherlands and which are said to belong to the East India Company, in fact belong to the 'Dutch East India Company', or 'East India Company'?

Maulana Azad: They belong to the Dutch East India Company.

Shri Sidhva: Which century, did you say, they belong to?

Maulana Azad: The seventeenth and the eighteenth centuries.

Shri Sidhva: Is it correct that some volumes on Indian history have been prepared by the National Archives of India, and, if so, when are they going to be published?

Maulana Azad: The question does not arise but, all the same, I should like to state that no such history is being prepared by the National Archives.

Document No. 27

REPLIES BY MAULANA AZAD DATED 18-4-1951 IN THE PARLIAMENT TO THE QUESTIONS ASKED ABOUT THE GRANTS TO UNIVERSITIES

Shri S.C. Samanta: (a) Will the Minister of **Education** be pleased to state the amount of recurring and non-recurring grants given to the Universities in the Centrally Administered areas (university-wise) since 1947-48?

(b) Have any special grants or loans been made to the universities during this period?

(c) If the answer to part (b) above be in the affirmative, for what purposes were they made?

The Minister of Education (Maulana Azad): (a) to (c) A statement is placed on the Table of the House. [See Appendix XXII, annexure No. 16.][1]

Shri S.C. Samanta: Has any committee been appointed to review the activities of the Delhi University and other Central universities about their finances and to report on their needs at present and in the future?

Maulana Azad: No. No such committee is there at the moment.

Shri T.N. Singh: I wish to know if any grant is being paid by the Government to our old national universities, such as the Gujrat Vidyapith or the Bihar Vidyapith?

Maulana Azad: No. No grant has been paid to them so far, nor have they applied for it. The case of Kashi Vidyapith did come up before the Ministry two years back but it was found that a provision had come to be introduced into its constitution that no Government aid of any kind should be sought and hence the matter could not go any further.

Kaka Bhagwant Roy: I wish to enquire whether the Patiala government has sent any proposal to the Government of India for the establishment of a university at Patiala and, if so, what are their views on the subject?

Maulana Azad: No. No, such application has been received by us.

Dr. Deshmukh: May I know if the hon. Minister has examined the financial condition of all the Universities in India and is there any proposal to see that all universities attain a certain minimum standards, so far as finances concerned?

Maulana Azad: The hon. Member knows the conditions in which the Government of India finds itself at this time. Hence no such proposal is practicable.

Shri Dwivedi *rose* —

Mr. Speaker: This question is restricted only to the Centrally administered areas.

1. Not included.

Document No. 28

ORAL ANSWERS DATED 21-4-1951 BY MAULANA AZAD IN THE HOUSE OF THE PEOPLE TO THE QUESTIONS ASKED ABOUT THE IMPERIAL GAZETTES

Shri Balwant Sinha Mehta: (a) Will the Minister of **Education** be pleased to state whether Government are contemplating to revise and make the Imperial Gazettes of India up-to-date?

(b) If so, when will this work be undertaken?

(c) If not, do Government propose to publish another such like publication?

The Minister of Education (Maulana Azad): (a) to (c). The attention of the hon. Member is invited to the reply given to Starred Question No. 584 by Shri A.V. Thakkar on the 22nd Feb. 1949. The question of revision of the Imperial Gazette of India can only be taken up when the present financial stringency is over.

Document No. 29

ANSWERS DATED 21-4-1951 BY MAULANA AZAD TO THE QUESTIONS ASKED IN PARLIAMENT

HISTORICAL MONUMENTS IN HYDERABAD

Shri Ganamukhi : Will the Minister of **Education** be pleased to state:

(a) Whether Government are aware that the monuments of historical value in Hyderabad State situated at Kalyani in Bidar district are being neglected; and

(b) whether Government propose to take over these monuments.

The Minister of Education (Maulana Azad) : (a) and (b) No Sir.

Shri Ganamukhi : Are the ancient monuments situated in Hyderabad State, being looked after by the Hyderabad State or by the Union Government?

Maulana Azad : Hyderabad State is responsible for the supervision of the places which the hon. Member has referred. The Government of India takes the responsibility only of such monuments as are considered to be of national importance, and the places referred to are not such.

Shri S.V. Naik : What arrangements the Government are making for Ajanta and Ellora?

Maulana Azad : These have been included in the places of national importance.

Document No. 30

ANSWERS DATED 21-4-1951 BY MAULANA AZAD TO THE QUESTIONS ASKED IN THE HOUSE OF THE PEOPLE

U.N.E.S.C.O. ADULT EDUCAITON ADVISER

Dr. Ram Subhag Singh: (a) Will the Minister of **Education** be pleased to state whether the Government of India have any U.N.E.S.C.O. Adult Education Adviser?

(b) If so, when was that appointment made?

(c) Who is the present incumbent?

The Minister of Education (Maulana Azad): (a) Yes, U.N.E.S.C.O. have placed the services of a consultant on Rural Adult Education at the disposal of Government.

(b) The first Consultant Dr. Spencer Hatch was appointed by U.N.E.S.C.O. in September, 1950 and joined the Ministry of Education on October 11, 1950.

(c) Dr. Mrs. Emily G. Hatch.

Dr. Ram Subhag Singh : Was this Adult Education Adviser appointed by U.N.E.S.C.O. for India or the Government of India itself appointed him?

Maulana Azad: He has been sent by U.N.E.S.C.O.

Dr. Ram Subhag Singh: Whether the salaries of this person and his staff are paid by the Government of India or by U.N.E.S.C.O.?

Maulana Azad: U.N.E.S.C.O. bears the travelling expenditure of the expert appointed by it, in his journey to and from India. But so long as he stays in India, the Government of India have to bear the expenditure incurred in setting up of an office for him and his travelling expenses from one city to another city in India.

Dr. Ram Subhag Singh : And who pays their salaries?

Maulana Azad : The U.N.E.S.C.O.

Dr. Ram Subhag Singh : Previously this post was held by Dr. Hatch. Was it he who appointed Mrs. Hatch or the U.N.E.S.C.O.?

Maulana Azad : The Appointment was made by U.N.E.S.C.O. He had come for six months only. She was appointed to this post when he left this country after the expiry of his appointment period.

Dr. Deshmukh: With what activities Mrs. Hatch is associated at present?

Maulana Azad: A Centre has been opened for Adult Education in Delhi. A house has been rented in Village Alipur, which is at a distance of eleven miles from Delhi, and we are starting a Janta College there. We have made this college the Centre for Adult Education. It is proposed to carry out this on such lines so that this institution may serve as a model institution for the whole of the country. Dr. Mrs. Hatch is working in this very Centre at present.

Dr. Ram Subhag Singh: Before her present appointment was she aware of the conditions prevailing in India?

Maulana Azad: About Dr. Spencer Hatch I know that before getting this appointment he had worked in Madras and Mysore for a long period and he has also the experience of South America. About Mrs. Hatch I am not sure whether she had come to India before her present appointment or not. But she has been carrying on this work in America and is considered an expert there.

Document No. 31

ANSWERS DATED BY 21-4-1951 BY MAULANA AZAD TO THE QUESTIONS ASKED IN THE HOUSE OF THE PEOPLE

RURAL UNIVERSITY OF BASIC EDUCATION

Dr. Ram Subhag Singh : Will the Minister of **Education** be pleased to state if there is any proposal under the consideration of the Government of India to establish a rural University of basic education?

The Minister of Education (Maulana Azad) : No, Sir.

Document No. 32

REPLIES DATED 21-4-1951 BY MAULANA AZAD TO THE QEUSTIONS IN THE HOUSE OF THE PEOPLE

LAWRENCE SHOOLS AT SAÑAWAR AND LOVEDALE

Dr. Deshmukh: (a) Will the Minister of **Education** be pleased to state the number of entitled children in each of the Lawrence Schools at Sanawar and Lovedale in each of the years 1949-50 and 1950-51?

(b) How many of them were free and how many were half-free?

(c) What was the total income and expenditure in each of the above years in each school?

(d) What was the deficit that the Government of India had to meet in each of the years on each school?

(e) How many of these entitled children in each school were sons of Army Officers and how many belong to the Scheduled Castes?

(f) How many of the sons of the Army Officers and boys from scheduled castes were free and how many half-free in each school?

(g) What is the average monthly salary of the Army Officers whose sons obtained concessions?

The Minister of Education (Maulana Azad): (a) to (d). A statement is laid on the Table of the House. [*See* Appendix XXII, annexure No. 40.]

(e) There are no Scheduled Caste members among the "Entitled" pupils. "Entitled" pupils means pupils whose parents have served in the Indian Army and have been treated as British officers or soldiers and who were entitled to admission to the Lawrence Schools at concessional rates prior to the taking over of these schools by the Ministry of Education. These concessions continue in accordance with past commitments.

(f) There were no sons of Army officers in receipt of a freeship at either school in 1949-50 or 1950-51. One son of an Army officer was in receipt of a special half-freeship at Sanawar in 1950-51. There were no

Scheduled Caste boys in receipt of a freeship or half-freeship at either school during 1949-50 or 1950-51.

(g) The information is not readily available. The concessions are according to commitments and based on individual incomes.

Dr. Deshmukh: May I know if it is contemplated by Government that in future whatever concession like freeships or half-freeships may be given, a certain percentage will be reserved for backward class and Scheduled Caste students?

Maulana Azad: Keeping in view the general educational policy of the Government of India it would be difficult to fix a definite number for any particualr community. All concessions must be based on merit alone. We have drawn a Scholarship Scheme for these shcools the object is that the admission to these schools be opened to all and concession should be given to children on merit alone.

Dr. Deshmukh: What is the amount that is proposed to be given by way of scholarships during the current financial year?

Maulana Azad: I cannot disclose that amount just now.

Pandit Munishwar Datt Upadhyaya: Are there any speical rules for admission to these schools or the rules which are applicable to other schools also apply to these schools?

Maulana Azad: It has been declared a public school. A particular rate of fee has been fixed and the admission is open to all. All the benefits with regard to education and training of a residential public school are available here.

Shri J.N. Hazarika: Who appoints the teaching staff of the Sanawar and Lovedale schools? How many Indians are there now?

Maulana Azad: Previously the management of these schools was under the Defence Ministry. After the Independence it was decided that these schools should be declared public schools and their management be taken over by the Ministry of Education. The entire teaching staff of these schools is under the Ministry of Education. The entire teaching staff of these schools is Indian. There are only two Europeans, one is the principal who has been working there since long and the other one is a professor.

Shri Sonavane: May I know whether there are any Scheduled Caste and backward class students in these schools?

Maulana Azad: I have replied it just now.

Document No. 33

ORAL ANSWERS DATED 25-4-1951 BY MAULANA AZAD TO THE QUESTIONS ASKED IN THE HOUSE OF THE PEOPLE

SYMPOSIUM OF WORLD'S THINKERS

Shri S.N. Das: Will the Minister of **Education** be pleased to state:

(a) Whether it is proposed to hold a symposium of World's thinkers and philosophers in New Delhi to discuss the concept of man in Eastern and Western cultures; and

(b) if so, what steps have so far been taken?

The Minister of Education (Maulana Azad): (a) The Government of India have accepted the invitation of UNESCO to hold a symposium on 'the Concept of Man and the Philosophy of Education in East and West' in New Delhi in December 1951.

(b) Details regarding themes of discussion and participants in the symposium are under consideration of the Government of India and UNESCO.

Shri S.N. Das: Has any such list been compiled by the Government of India as may be containing the names of the philosophers and thinkers of other countries?

Maulana Azad: No, we did not feel the necessity of preparing any such list at this time. It has been planned that thinkers of eleven or twelve countries may be invited, half of whom would be from the Eastern countries and the other half would be from the West. So far as the Eastern countries are concerned it is proposed to send invitations to some selected thinkers of India, Ceylon, Japan and if possible to China as well.

Shri S.N. Das : What is the reason that philosophers of only twelve countries are being invited?

Maulana Azad: As a matter of fact some sort of restrictions have got to be imposed on such occasions. The UNESCO has prepared the outline and they thought that if philosophers and thinkers of eleven or twelve counties of Asia and Europe are invited then the purpose would be served.

Mr. Speaker: I find several Members are anxious to put questions. Let the proposal materialise.

Document No. 34

ANSWERS DATED 25-4-1951 BY MAULANA AZAD TO THE QUESTIONS ASKED IN THE HOUSE OF THE PEOPLE

GRANTS TO UNIVERSITIES

Dr. Ram Subhag Singh: (a) Will the Minister of **Education** be pleased to state whether it is a fact that the Punjab University and some other educational institutions which were disrupted owing to partition of the country will be given grants by the Government of India.

(b) If so, have these grants been fixed?

The Minister of Education (Maulana Azad): (a) Yes, Sir.

(b) The Government of India in the Ministry of Rehabilitation have placed at the disposal of Punjab Government a sum of Rs. 14,00,000 for disbursement to the Punjab University and other disrupted educational institutions which have now re-established themselves in India.

Dr. Ram Subhag Singh: Out of this sum of Rs. 14 lakhs how much will be given to the Punjab University?

Maulana Azad: The Ministry of Rehabilitation had placed the entire money at the disposal of Punjab Government. The Government of Punjab spent the money in the manner they liked.

Mr. Speaker: The question is what amount of money was given to the Punjab University?

Maulana Azad: Information was sought from the Punjab Government in this connection, and it was learnt that they had distributed this money in the following manner:

Punjab University: 4 lakhs.

Vedic Research Institute, Hoshiarpur : Rs. 75,000.

For the establishment of some displaced colleges: Rs. 571,540, schools; Rs. 3,12,840.

The balance of Rs. 40,620 was kept for opening two more institutions.

Sardar Sochet Singh : Will the hon. Minister be pleased to state the proposed location of the Punjab University?

Maulana Azad: This information can only be given by the local Government.

Shri A.C. Guha : Has any grant been given to the Calcutta University as that University is also disrupted due to partition?

Maulana Azad : No, this question does not arise with respect to the Calcutta University.

Shri A.C. Guha : Is there any proposal before the Government?

Maulana Azad: No, at present there is no such proposal before the Government.

Pandit Munishwar Datt Upadhyay: Have the Punjab Government also contributed anything towards this fund or the entire amount has been given by the Central Government?

Maulana Azad: I cannot give this information. An enquiry was made from the Punjab Government regarding the manner in which this money was spent. They have given these figures. I cannot give the information as to how much money the Government of Punjab have spent, or not, on this account.

Shri T.N. Singh: I would like to know whether this sum of Rs. 14 lakhs has been spent as non-recurring grant alone or has been used as recurring grant as well.

Maulana Azad: I cannot give exact information. From the figures that have been sent by the Government of Punjab it appears that this money has been spent on non-recurring accounts alone.

Document No. 35

ANSWERS DATED 25-4-1951 BY MAULANA AZAD TO THE QUESTIONS ASKED IN THE HOUSE OF THE PEOPLE

EXCHANGE OF STUDENTS

Pandit Munishwar Datt Upadhyay : Will the Minister of **Education** be pleased to state:

(a) whether the Carnegie Corporation of U.S.A. has made a grant of $150,000 for exchage of students for study;

(b) if so, whether this grant is available for Indian students also; and

(c) what portion of this grant would be available for Indian students and for the study of what subjects?

The MInister of Educaiton (Maulana Azad): (a) We have no information.

(b) and (c) Do not arise.

Document No. 36

ANSWERS DATED 25-4-1951 BY MAULANA AZAD TO THE QUESTIONS ASKED IN THE HOUSE OF THE PEOPLE

HIGHER TECHNICAL EDUCATION

Shri V.K. Reddy: (a) Will the Minister of **Education** be pleased to state what is the amount sanctioned by the Government of India to various universities for promoting higher technical education in 1951-52?

(b) Which Universities have been given such grants and what is the amount given to each of them?

The Minister of Education (Maulana Azad): (a) A sum of Rs. 61.07 lakhs has been provided in the budget estimates for the purposes of grants to Engineering and Technological Institutions including three non-university institutions.

(b) Does not arise as the budget has not yet been sanctioned.

Shri V.K. Reedy: Sir, I could not follow the answer.

Mr. Speaker: He said that a sum of about Rs. 61 lakhs has been provided for in the Budget. As regards (b) he said that the matter is for consideration after the budget is sanctioned and duly passed.

Shri V.K. Reddy: What is the amount granted to the Andhra University for 1950-51?

Mr. Speaker: That does not arise, he said.

Document No. 37

MAULANA ABUL KALAM AZAD, INDIAN PARLIAMENT AND THE BENARES HINDU UNIVERSITY (AMENDMENT) BILL 26-4-1951

The Minister of Education (Maulana Azad) : I beg to move for leave to introduce a Bill further to amend the Benares Hindu University Act, 1915.

Mr. Speaker: The question is:

"That leave be granted to introduce a Bill further to amend the Benares Hindu University Act, 1915."

The motion was adopted.

Maulana Azad: I introduce the Bill.

Document No. 38

ORAL ANSWERS DATED 28-4-1991 BY MAULANA AZAD TO THE QUESTIONS ASKED IN THE HOUSE OF THE PEOPLE

CENTRAL BOARD FOR EXAMINATION

Dr. Ram Subhag Singh : (a) Will the Minister of Education be pleased to state whether it is a fact that the Government of India propose to establish a Central Board for High, Secondary, and Intermediate examinations for all Centrally Administered States as well as for the Andaman and Nicobar Islands?

(b) If so, what are the underlying principles for establishing this Board?

The Minister of Education (Maulana Azad): (a) The matter is still under consideration.

(b) The establishment of one Board for all the Centrally Administered Areas is intended to promote uniformity of standards in these States as well as to raise the standard of Secondary Education.

Dr. Ram Subagh Singh : The medium of instruction being different in the high schools in the Centrally Administered Areas, how far is it proper to constitute a Central Board for holding examinations and setting questions papers for them.

Maulana Azad : The matter is being considered. A conference was convened on the 3rd of March in Delhi to which the Chief Commissioners of all those areas were invited and they were consulted in the matter and they are being considered. I am, therefore, unable to state anything categorically at this stage.

Pandit Munshiwar Datt Upadhyay: May I know whether the Central Government is consulting the State Governments who have had experience of such Boards and are now thinking of having a change in their constitution?

Maulana Azad : The question of consulting the former State Governments did not arise. The Local Governments have been following a set procedure for the conduct of the work so far. Now it is being considered to set up a Board which would help in raising the standard of Secondary Education. It is yet to be decided whether such a step is right or wrong. Everybody concerned would be consulted before arriving at any decision.

Pandit Munishwar Datt Upadhyay : My question is whether those State Governments which have conducted experiments in this regard and who have got such Boards in their respective territories have been consulted? I ask this question because, according to my information, some of the State Governments are already thinking of introducing some changes in them?

Maulana Azad : Their opinions will also be taken into consideration.

Shri Dwivedi : I want to know whether apart from the examination conducted by the Delhi and Ajmer Boards, the Government recognise other examinations of similar standards being conducted in the Centrally Administered Areas till the formation of such Boards?

Maulana Azad : Yes, I understand that apart from Delhi and Ajmer, the existing Local Boards of other Centrally Administered Areas have been recognised for this purpose.

Shri Deshbabdhu Gupta : Will the hon. Minister please state if the majority at the Chief Commissioners' Conference convened recently in this connection, had opposed this proposal?

Maulana Azad : Nothing can be said about this thing at present. The report is still under consideration.

Document No. 39

MAULANA AZAD'S SPEECH DELIVERED BY MOVING THE VISHVA BHARATI AMENDMENT BILL IN THE HOUSE OF THE PEOPLE DATED APRIL 28, 1951 AND HIS ANSWERS ETC. TO THE QUESTIONS ASKED BY THE MEMBERS IN THIS REGARD

The Minister of Education (Maulana Azad: I beg to move:

"That the Bill to declare the institution known as 'Visva-Bharati' to be an institution of national importance and to provide for its functioning as a unitary, teaching and residential university, be taken into consideration."

While moving for the consideration of this Bill, I feel that my task is quite simple and a brief one. I am sure that there is none in the House who is unaware of the importance of that Institution. I also feel confident that everyone of us is fully conscious of the place of honour and the esteem which it has created for itself in the minds of people both within and outside India during the last thirty years. As a matter of fact, by passing this Bill, we are giving it nothing new or anything which it has not achieved already. What is it then that we want to declare by passing this Bill? There are two things, first of these is to recognise that the institution has national importance. Whether we declare it to be as such today or not and whether we acknowledge it or not, the fact remains that this is an institution of national importance. The other object of the Bill is to give official recognition to it as a university. The fact is that ever since Dr. Rabindra Nath Tagore had established this institution in 1921, it has been working as a full-fledged university. Not only in India, but outside also it enjoys the esteem of a university. Scholars and students from all over the world come to Visva-Bharati to carry and spread the impressions gathered from here in all parts of the world. It was,. therefore, only our fault that we had not given it the official recognition so far – a status it had already achieved and has deserved since long. We are giving credence to that status today.

Another consideration that I want you to consider carefully is the general form in which this Bill has been drafted and presented. All along our efforts have been to give this Bill such a shape and include in it only such new things and provisions of law which are absolutely necessary for a university to have. But as far the type of education and system of education in this particular institution are concerned or even as far the general principles of education are concerned, we have been careful to preserve their original character and we have exercised maximum caution not to introduce even a shadow of an alteration. A study of the Bill must have made that quite clear that Dr. Rabindra Nath Tagore, while opening this institution, did not care to adopt the general terms of the existing universities. He had made efforts to adopt Hindi terms for the different posts and the committees in his institution – for instance the word he adopted for the Executive Council is "*Karya Samiti*'. All terms like this have been taken by us as such while within brackets we have given their English equivalents, so that people may not feel any difficulty in understanding them. We have not altered them anyway. Some of the amendments tabled by some hon. friends seek to adopt other terms in place of those which are current at present. But I hope you will agree with me that it is inadvisable to alter the terms which were adopted by Dr. Rabindra Nath Tagore himself. For instance the term *'Karya Samiti'* chosen by him for the Executive Council does not appear as good to certain friends. We can have another word in its place. But I feel that we should not indulge in such an attempt and the words he had selected, should be left unaltered. For some of these words he had given no new equivalents. For instance, he has suggested no equivalent for the word 'principal'. Some hon. friends have tabled amendments in which they have attempted to make the words like *'Vidyapith'* or *'Vidyalaya'* current in place of the word 'university'. I feel this course is also undesirable to adopt. What Hindi words should be adopted for words like 'university', principal and so on, is a matter which cannot be decided here. We cannot coin definite terms on an occasion like this while passing a Bill. This is a job of the experts. You are aware that the Government of India have set up a Board to consider all such technical terms and compile a Hindi dictionary of the same. This is the function of that Board. But for the present we have also left those words which Dr. Tagore himself had left unaltered. Again, we have also adopted those Hindi equivalents which he has used. Similarly a question has arisen regarding the spelling of certain words, for instance of the very name of the institution *viz.,* Visva Bharati. Certain friends think that the letter 'S' having been used in the Bill, it will read as *'Visva'* and not *'Vishva'*. It is not so. It remains still *'Vishva'*. The fact

Seth Govind Das (Madhya Pradesh): As in the case of the word 'Shimla'.

Maulana Azad: In this regard a method of writing Sanskrit or other oriental words has been settled. It has been decided that 's' whenever used for Sanskrit words, will pronounce 'sh' and not 's'. For this very reason from the very beginning 's' and not 'sh' has been used while spelling Visva-Bharati. Similarly there is the word *'Sikhsa Samiti'*. Certain friends want 's' to be replaced by 'sh' there too. I will like to say that it is unnecessary. It pronounces still 'sh' and this is the international method.

Shri Sidhva (Madhya Pradesh): When was this international method settled?

Maulana Azad: It has been in practice since long. I think that the Bengal Education Society had also adopted this method in 1904.

Seth Govind Das: What shall we do when we have to use 's' for instance in the word *'Sansar'*.

Maulana Azad: We place a dot there.

Prof. K.T. Shah (Bihar): The case of 's' pronounced as 'sh' there should be the critical mark of a dash on s, and a critical dot is put on 'S' when pronounced as *Sansara.*

Maulana Azad: Anyhow the Press in which it has been printed possesses this type of letters only. I will therefore submit that it has been printed correctly and the international practice is that the sound of Sanskrit letters, whenever printed, is understood in this very way. According to that practice again it is correct and, as such, we should not alter them. Further ever since Visva-Bharati has been established, its name has been written in this very form and this very spelling was adopted by Dr. Rabindra Nath Tagore himself. We have therefore, decided not to alter it. Whatever be the case, we have made efforts not to alter the objects for which this institution was established or the general educational atmosphere which it has helped to create. The Government of India feel that this institution is Dr. Tagor's present to the nation and as such should be preserved. I recall in this connection what Mahatma Gandhi had told me in 1947. When in January 1947, I took over the charge of the Ministry of Education, Mahatma Gandhi had told me that he had a keep-safe of Gurudev with him. Those who knew Rabindra Nath, generally used to call him as Gurudev. So he had told me that it was precious thing kept with him and that it was his desire to hand it over to the Government of India. I feel a pleasure in having this opportunity, although somewhat delayed, to set the Government of India's seal on the preservation of this institution. I also hope that the House will give me an early opportunity to request it for the passage of this Bill. I do not think there is anything left in the Bill for which it need be circulated for eliciting public opinion or be referred to a Select Committee. The few clauses of the Bill are the same which are normally provided for the administration of any other university. I consider it to be better and, as such, I request my hon. friends that instead of taking much time in the discussion over the Bill it should be passed at the earliest.

Mr. Chairman: Motion moved:

"That the Bill to declare the institution known as "Visva-Bharati" to be an institution of national importance and to provide for its functioning as a unitary, teaching and residential university, be taken into consideration."

Dr. Ram Subhag Singh (Bihar): I am very glad to note that the hon. Maulana Azad has presented a Bill declaring Visva-Bharati an institution of national importance. It is also a matter of a satisfaction that two things of Shri Rabindra Nath Tagore–one the song 'Janganman' and the other Visva-Bharati have–been acknowledged of national importance.

The importance of Visva-Bharati is known all over the world. It attracts students from all parts of the world, more specially from the countries of the East. Some professors, teachers and students come from the Western countries as well. All of us know how highly those professors have spoken of Visva-Bharati in other parts of the world and all acknowledge its importance.

I do not want to say much about what has been provided in this Bill. I agree with the hon. Maulana Azad that no one should have any objection in accepting it and there should be no lengthy debate about the Bill. But there are one or two sections in the Bill, about which I think it necessary to say something. The object with which the late Dr. Tagore had established the University of Visva-Bharati, was to study and do research on the ancient traditions of India, and also to study the culture and civilization of the oriental countries and along with that to make a comparative study of cultures of the countries of the East and West. He had made a good progress in achieving that aim, and he did his best to serve these ends through Visva-Bharati and this institution did make constant progress under his able guidance.

Afterwards, as Maulana Azad has stated, Gandhiji placed the scheme of the noble creation of Gurudev before Maulana Azad and asked him to accept it as a thing of national importance. It is our good fortune that he has presented this Bill and we will always remember him for this.

There is growing need of such institutions these days. The U.N.E.S.C.O. has been established with the object of making a study of the various civilization and cultures of the world. But Gurudev has established this institution thirty years prior to the formation of U.N.E.S.C.O. when the British oppression was in its full swing. All the leaders of the country including Maulana Azad were victims of their oppression and were behind the bars.

However, we are happy that the world recognizes its value and we also acknowledge it as an institution of national importance and it is also possible that after some time the U.N.E.S.C.O. also may recognize it as an institution of world importance.

It gives us great pleasure to know that hon. Maulana Azad has stated that no further modifications will be made in the Bill. But there should also be a provision for removing any defects therein. We should not hesitate in correcting any mistakes of spelling or description in the Bill. But these are insignificant things. My main objection is regarding the special powers which have been conferred on the Visitor.

It is a matter of great satisfaction that the President of India has been nominated as the Visitor to this institution. He has been vested with very great powers. Everybody knows that the President will not act irresponsibly. Whatever he will do, he will do on the advice of various Ministers and the Ministries. The Bill empowers the Visitor to reject the recommendations of *Karma Samiti* or the Education Committee. It is obvious that these Committees will have wider knowledge of that institution. I am not undermining the capabilities of these personalities as I know that our President Dr. Rajendra Prasad and the Minister of Education Maulana Azad are the makers of the destiny of our nation, they have good knowledge of the affairs of Visva-Bharati very efficiently. But this will not suffice as Dr. Rajendra Prasad has not been vested with these powers in his personal capacity. It is possible that hon. Maulana Azad may continue as Minister of Education and Dr. Rajendra Prasad as President for five or ten years, but after the lapse of their terms some other person may become the Minister of Education and someone else may become the Visitor. What would be the situation then? It is possible that the *Karma Samiti* and Education Committee might have wider knowledge than those who might not have studied in Visva-Bharati or in any other national institution. In that case it will not be proper to give more powers to the Visitor. It has been laid down in this Bill:

"Where *Karma Samiti* does not, within a reasonable time, take action to the satisfaction of the *Paridarsaka,* the *Paridarsaka* may, after considering any explanation furnished or representation made by the *Karma Samiti,* issue such directions as he may think fit, and the *Karma samiti* shall comply with such directions."

It is evident from this that the Visitor has been given very wide powers. The present Visitor is the President Dr. Rajendra Prasad and the Minister of Education is Maulana Azad. I am sure hon. Maulana Azad will give true advice and his advice will be in the interest of Visva-Bharati. But it is not certain that Maulana Azad will be succeeded by a man of the same capabilities as the Minister of Education, and the Ministry of Education also may not have thorough knowledge of Visva-Bharati. May be, he may institute an enquiry into the affairs of that institution. But all of us are fully aware of the results of the enquiries conducted by the Government officers. In these circumstances the advice given to the Visitor by the Minister of Education seems to be fraught with dangerous possibilities. I, therefore want, that some of these powers should be curtailed and the Executive Committee should be vested with maximum powers. I agree that the Visitor should be given some powers. There should be such provisions that if three-fourth members of the Executive Committee *or Karma Samiti* do not like the orders of the Visitor, they may reject them. If such provisions are made, I think they will be in the interest of Visva-Bharati.

I am in full agreement with other provisions of the Bill. I hope the hon. Minister of Education will show the same broadmindedness as he has shown in presenting this Bill, in running Visva-Bharati on the same lines as late Dr. Rabindra Nath Tagore had tried to run it. That step would be beneficial not only to Visva-Bharati and to our country alone but to the entire world as well.

I have to say one thing more. Here provisions are being made to accord University status to Visva-Bharati. In this connection I would like to submit that Visva-Bharati should not be allowed to go the way of other universities. Today most of the universities suffer from lack of discipline. These days we find that the students manhandle their teachers and professors. In my opinion it would be a grave mistake to place Visva-Bharati in the category of other universities under the present circumstances. Therefore it is my submission that Visva-Bharati should be run on such lines by which its spirit may remain alive. I am sure that the hon. Minister of Education will make his best efforts for the successful achievement of the objects of late Dr. Rabindra Nath Tagore.

Seth Govind Das: Madam, I too heartily welcome this Bill. To my mind, what is most needed to us after the achievement of independence is that our Bharat may continue to remain a true Bharat. Now that we have achieved independence it is our first and foremost duty to preserve the thoughts put forth by the eminent thinkers of this ancient land, do further research on them and convey a timely and true message to humanity by examining them in the light of ideas represented by other parts of the world.

In the modern age, during the period of our slavery, the credit for bringing about a country-wide awakening or raising the pretige of our motherland high in the world goes to two great personalities–Mahatma Gandhi and Gurudev Rabindra Nath Thakore. In the sphere of literature, all the Indian languages bear the impression of Rabindra Babu's all round genius in some way or the other. There are five branches of literature, namely, poetry, drama, novel, story and essay. In the sphere of all of these five branches of literature – not only in any single language but in all the ten or eleven prominent languages of India – we find a clear impression of the great poet Rabindra's personality. Many a poet and dramatist and novelist and sotrywriter and essayist has drawn inspiration from the *Kavisamrat* Rabindra Nath. Rabindranath's literature has conveyed the fundamentals of the Indian thought to all foreign countries as well.

It was with two objects in view that the Gurudev had established Visva-Bharati. One related to the research of the various aspects of the Indian Schools of thought and the other to its co-ordination with other ideologies of the world. If we go through the hitherto history of Visva-Bharati, it will be known that what we get from Visva-Bharati is otherwise inavailable from any other source. When we were ruled by the foreigners our system of education having been moulded in accordance with Lord Macaulay's objectives was such as only aimed at producing more and more of *Baboos* who might help maintain foreign domination over this country. At that time Visva-Bharati and many other institutions like Visva-Bharati such as Gurukul Kangri etc., came into being in order to enable us to maintain a high level of our cultural life and convey its message to the entire world. The Government of independent India really deserves congratulations for the fact that they, as the hon. Minister of Education said a short while ago, in accordance with the great legacy given to them by the late Mahatma, have brought forward such a Bill after achieving independence.

I may add one more thing in this connection. Even now our system of education is, to a great extent, based on old models. It will, of course, take some time for the recommendations made in the University Commission's Report to be implemented. Therefore, as my friend Dr. Ram Subhag Singh also said just now, we are required to see to it that we are not led away by such emotions and lose the very objectives and ideals with which Gurudev had established Visva-Bharati. While on one hand I welcome the present Bill, on the other hand, I wish to make it clear that we have to be very careful and alive in this regard. Had such a Bill been passed in the life-time of Rabindra Babu, no such care and attention would have been guided by his own personality. Personality is regarded as the greatest thing in the world. But today he is not alive. Unfortunately our country has been constantly losing great men like him. So, as Shri Ram Subhag Singh also remarked, what I am afraid of is lest a day should come when despite the fact that we are today welcoming such a measure, we may begin to feel that by passing such a Bill we had simply hampered the progress of an independent institution like Visva-Bharati. Now that Rabindra Babu is no more with us we are required to pay still more attention to this fact. Some time after the passing of this Bill we should review the whole situation as to how the affairs of Visva-Bharati are being managed; and if, after such a review, any amendment be deemed necessary in the Bill, it may suitably be incorporated.

It is on account of his intelligence that man has achieved the top position among other creatures of this world. Nature has bestowed upon man the power of understanding. This power is developed through education. That is why such an importance is attached to education. It is education alone which makes a man a man. It will be seen that man has reached new heights of development and progress, so much so, that he can go round the entire world in only a few hours. Big dams are being constructed and big factories are going to be established for the production for various innumerable things. What is meant to be said is that man is busy in the production of many a thing. But whereas on the one hand such developments are being made . . . .

Mr. Chairman: The non. Member is aware that many Members wish to speak on this bill. He is dealing with education in a general way. He should particularly confine his remarks to the provisions of this Bill.

Seth Govind Das : Other general things and this Bill are closely related. You will know it, Madam, that there is no restriction on speaking on any Bill. So I was saying that while on the one hand, man makes efforts to make progress, on the other hand, he also makes preparation for destruction of the entire human race. Apart from the fact that we have made Atom bombs and Hydrogen bombs, we have also produced many other destructive things. If we continue to proceed with the production of constructive and destructive things simultaneously, I am afraid, a time may come when some such bomb can be made which may shatter the entire universe into pieces. At this time we need such an education as may rid us of future calamities. India's metaphysicians, saints and sages, philosophers, poets and men of letters had laid down certain doctrines. There is a long tradition behind them. The greatest of their teachings is that the happiness of man and the world cannot be achieved unless man conquers his own self. Although we have made every effort to conquer the world, we did not care to conquer our own selves. Such was the greatest teaching of Mahatma Gandhi as also of Dr. Tagore. Our long tradition has also taught us this very doctrine. Let us not allow our objectives and ideals to perish and let us endeavour to conquer our own selves so that we may help to achieve happiness for the entire humanity. Let this Bill, that has been brought forward by the hon. Minister of Education assist this institution in the achievement of its objectives and ideals. My keen desire is that this Bill may raise the prestige of this institution still higher.

In the end I once again heartily welcome this Bill.

Shri A.C. Guha (West Bengal): I think there is none in this House who will not welcome this Bill with enthusiasm. For those who come from Bengal, this institution was something more than a mere institution. It was the symbol of our culture. Towards the end of the last century Maharishi Devendranath Tagore started a small institution with the name of Santiniketan, "The Abode of Peace". Then from that time it has been developing slowly and gradually. Then came a renaissance movement in Bengal and Rabindra Nath Tagore, or rather the entire Tagore family was the spearhead of that renaissance movement. The Tagore family influenced literature, art and culture, in all its phases and all its aspects.

Shri Kamath (Madhya Pradesh): Politics also.

Shri A.C. Guha : My hon. friend Mr. Kamath asks me to mention also politics. Yes; in politics also. Rabindranath Tagore himself and his brother Jyotindranath Tagore took a prominent part in politics also. Even in those days of turmoil and trouble in the first decade, Rabindra Nath Tagore was in the Bengal political movement.

This institution has been nursed by Rabindranath Tagore carefully and with deep affection. He developed it without any help from the Government, rather keeping it aloof from all Government control and subsidy. During this period, another institution developed in Bengal which also kept itself aloof from all Government control. One of its fundamental principles was that it should not take any Government aid, and should not come under control of Government. I would like to remind Maulana Sahib about 84 that institution also that is the College of Technology of Jadhavpur. I hope Maulana Sahib will also give that institution the charter of a University. That institution also deserve the recognition of the nation when the nation has achieved political independence.

This Bill as it has come before us may have some defects as all human handicrafts much have some defects. But, the Maulana Azad Sahib has appealed to us that we should pass the Bill without making any alterations. In deference to his appeal, most of the Members have agreed not to move their amendments. Naturally, there must have been some defects in the Bill and I hope that with the experience gained through the working of the Act, after some time, government may come before this House with further amendments.

But, there is one thing of which I would like to remind the Government and Maulana Sahib, that by giving the charter of a University we may not petrify the spirit of the University; that by giving the charter to the institution, we may not give it the shape of a stony edifice in the place of the moral and spiritual force that the institution has so long been I appeal to the Government and also to those persons to whom the care of this institution will be given, that they may see to it that the ideal with which Rabindranath Tagore has been working; the ideal according to which he has developed the institution may not be submerged under this edifice of a formal university. It is more than a national institution, it is an institution of much more than national importance as has been enunciated in the Bill. It is an institution, for some years of international importance. It is an institution having a peculiar characteristic of its own. Any one who has gone to that institution can see that the classes are being held sometimes in the open air, without any formal class room and all these things. The institution has been developed deliberately by Rabindranath Tagore with a rural bias and to give it a rural bias, he developed also the Sri Niketan.

Mr. Chairman; May I know whether the hon. Member is likely to take some more time?

Shri A.C. Guha: Yes; I would like to continue tomorrow, I mean the day after tomorrow.

The House then adjourned till Half Past Eight of the Clock on Monday, the 30th April, 1951.

Document No. 40

FURTHER DISCUSSION DATED APRIL 30, 1951 ON THE VISVA-BHARATI (AMENDMENT) BILL

Mr. Speaker: The House will now proceed with the further discussion of the matter to consider Visva-Bharati Bill.

Shri A.C. Guha (West Bengal): The other day I was speaking about the ideal with which Rabindranath Tagore has developed the Visva-Bharati. In this connection, I may give the House a quotation from a letter which Rabindranath Tagore wrote in 1921 to an American friend. He Wrote:

> "To give spiritual culture to our boys was my principal object in starting my school in Bolpur. Fortunately in India we have the model before us in the tradition of our ancient forest schools where teachers, whose aim was to realise their lives in God had their homes. The atmosphere was full of the aspiration for the infinite and the students who grew up with their teachers close by, united with them in spiritual relationship, felt the reality of God, for it was no mere creed imposed upon them of a speculative abstraction ..."

Mr. Speaker : What is he quoting from?

Shri A.C. Guha: From a letter of Rabindranath Tagore about Visva-Bharati instution, he wrote that letter in 1921 to an American Friend.

> "Having this ideal of a school in my mind which should be a home and a temply in one, where teaching should be a part of a worshipful life, I selected this spot, away from all distractions of town, Hallowed with the memory of a pious life whose days were passed here in communion with God."

Here, Rabindranath Tagore referred to his father Maharashi Devendranath Tagore, who established the nucleus of the institution.

> "The first help that our boys set here on this path is from the cultivation of love of nature and sympathy with all living

creatures. Music is of very great assistance to them, the song being not of the ordinary hymn type, dry and didactic, but as full of lyric joy as the author could put in them. You can understand now these songs affect the boys when you know that singing them is the best enjoyment they choose for themselves in their leisure time, in the evening when the moon is up, in the rainy days when their classes are closed. Mornings and evenings fifteen minutes' time is given them to sit in an open space composing their minds for worship. We never watch them and ask questions about what they think in those times, but leave it entirely to themselves, to the spirit of the place and the time and the suggestion of the practice itself. We rely more upon the sub-conscious influence of nature, of the association of the place and the daily life of worship that we live than on any conscious effort to teach them."

This was the ideal with which he established and developed this institution. He did not put in any buildings and other stony edifices for the classes.

The University Commission has recommended that this should be converted into a university and a rural bias should be developed in this rural university. I do not really know whether the Bill that is before the House will really further these ideals and achieve this purpose. Rather I have a doubt that this may give it the formality associated with any other university. One previous speaker mentioned here the functions of the Visitor. To me the functions given to the President of the Republic as Paridarsaka and also those given to the Governor of West Bengal as Rector or Pradhana are too much. These and the provisions about the *Karma Samiti* might give this institution the formal nature of other universities. In the *Karma Samiti* the Visitor may nominate any number of members–no number is fixed. It may develop a sort of officialdom. This has to be guarded against. Of course, we welcome this move of the Government to give this institution the charter of a university; but we must take care that the soul and the spirit with which Rabindaranath developed it are not lost.

Before concluding I would like to refer to the high ideals with which Rabindranath established this institution and the ideals he kept in view all through his life, not only as a philosopher and seer but also as a great organiser and a patriot. He wanted this institution to develop not only in communion with God but also in communion with the people of the locality and in communion with the people of this country and the people of the whole world. This university has naturally, therefore, attracts scholars from outside, As the representative of this University he visited different parts of the world, particularly those neglected places of Asia which had deep and intimate cultural relations with India – Siam, Indo-China, Java, Indonesia and even Persia and as the representative of Visva-Bharati he was the harbinger of the new cultural renaissance of Asia and of humanity. The university attracted scholars from far and wide, and scholars of international repute such as Sylvain Levi (France), Winternitz (Germany), Tucci (Italy) and Yeon Noguchi (Japan). Many other scholars of international fame came to this university and it has already become a centre of international culture and it has already become the centre of communion with entire humanity.

Before concluding, I would like to quote a passage from Rabindranath's own poem –

For friends who do not follow the Bengali poem, I may give here a rough translation of the sentiments expressed in those lines:

Arise! Oh my soul in this holy land.

On this shore of the ocean of Great Humanity of India.

Standing here, stretching out my two arms,

I salute Man the God;

I offer my delightful prayers to him in ecstatic rhyme.

In the mountains – absorbed in meditation.

In the great plains – garlanded by rivers

Like necklace of sacred beads –

We see the holy mother earth

On this shore of the ocean of Great Humanity of India.

Let this institution–the University of Visva-Bharati–worship the great humanity of the world through the humanity of India.

Shrimati Jayashri (Bombay) : I congratulate the Government of their bringing this measure and thus perpetuating the memory of one of the great personalities of the world. This is the most appropriate monument to be raised in honour of Gurudev Rabindranath Tagore, and I take this opportunity to pay my humble homage to that great poet, philosopher and sage of this land. By establishing Visva-Bharati Gurudev aimed at achieving *Visva-Bandhutwa* or international brotherhood. Students from all over the world came to Shantiniketan and they partook of Indian Culture from this institution. I would request the authorities to keep this ideal before them when they take over this big institution. It is something like an oasis in a desert. It helped in giving culture to our rural population. Students from the villages were helped and their cottage industries were also helped by the institution known as Sri Niketan. In this way this institution will continue to help our rural population. I would once again request the authorities to keep this aim in front of their mind when they take over this institution.

Sir, I have brought in a few amendments with the object of changing a few terms here and there which I thought were not quite appropriate in those places. If others are introduced in those places it would be better because if we leave the present ones to remain for long they will become permanent and it will not be possible to effect the change easily afterwards. For instance, for *Karma Samiti* I would suggest *Karvahi* as more appropriate. Also the term "*Artha-Sachiva*" suggests a Finance Minister and I would prefer the term *Koshadhyaksha* which means Treasurer. These are mere changes of terms and I do not insist or persist that they should be accepted now. I would, however, request that they may be kept in mind whenever any changes in the terminologies ar effected.

Will these few words. Sir, I support the Bill.

Dr. R.U. Singh (Uttar Pradesh) : Visva-Bharati was established to discover and bring to light old cultural values and to preserve and transmit the best elements of Indian culture. It was to act as an interpreter of Indian and Asian culture to the rest of the world. In fact, even in the matter of work in the surrounding villages the same purpose was kept in view. In the words of Rabindranath Tagore it was intended "to bring back life in its completeness to the villages, making the rural folk self-reliant self-respectful, acquainted with the cultural traditions of their own country and competent to make an efficient use of modern resources for the improvement of their physical, intellectual and economic conditions."

I was not here the other day when the Education Minister made his speech commending the motion for the consideration of the House. I would like to have an assurance from him that the essential spirit of this institution will be preserved. It would be a matter of regret indeed if the essential character of the institution were to be altered in any manner whatsoever.

In clause 6 as also in clause 2 there are references to the objects but the objects of the institution as such do not find a place even in the

Preamble. I have no doubt that the hon. Minister is aware that if certain things cannot be put in the body of the statute they might very well be put in the Preamble. The objects for which the Visva-Bharati stands are objects which I have no doubt should have found a place at least in the Preamble. In fact sometimes preambles are found to be longer than the statute itself. In this Bill I find a singular lack as regards reference to the objects of the institution which in my view are absolutely necessary. In fact if one looks at clause 6, one finds that the objects of the institution are rather widely defined. In clause 6(a) it is said:

> "The University shall exercise the following powers and perform the following duties, namely:
>
> (a) to provide for research and instruction in such branches of learning as may be deemed desirable and be found practicable and for the promotion of understanding of cultures between the East and the West and for the advancement of learning and dissemination of knowledge generally."

The opening words are "to provide for research and instruction in such branches of learning as may be deemed desirable and be found practicable." I have not the slightest doubt as a student of law that these words are capable of a very wide meaning indeed. Further on these words occur "for the promotion of understanding of cultures between the East and the West and for the advancement of learning and dissemination of knowledge generally."

As I have said, the objects have not been referred to specifically. The institution existed for a specific purpose, it exists for that purpose and I have no doubt that the institution ought to be maintained for that purpose only and the purpose ought not to be widened in its scope at all.

The Central Government are concerned with a number of universities. The Banaras Hindu University and the Aligarh Muslim University they finance partially. They finance the Delhi University wholly. I do not want to make extensive references to the work of the University Education Commission. Every reader of its report is familiar with the recommendations of the Commission. They have proposed, for example, that advanced work should be the concern of the Centre. The Central Government do want to give a lead in the matter of education, more particularly, university education.

What is the kind of university they run. Anyone familiar with the work of Delhi University will say that the University is very ill-equipped, in the matter of equipment as also in branches of learning. I do not think there are many universities which are as poor as the University of Delhi. If the Government do want to do something they might set up an ideal university in Delhi and I think that would be a good example to the States in the country.

I have referred to this only to make the point that the Visva-Bharati ought not be developed into a "general university" or even a university with a cultural bias. The phraseology of the Bill is such that in the absence of any specific words with reference to objects, I am led to the conclusion that there is a possibility that this university may be developed into a "general university" or a university with a cultural bias. I would not even prefer the latter. The work of the Visva-Bharati has been unique. We do not want to multiply universities; the universities that we have should be run efficiently. But the point I wish to emphasise in this connection is that the Visva-Bharati must be kept within the limits of the objectives for which it was founded.

Next, I should like to come to the question of the administrative set-up of the Visva-Bharati. I regret very much that the administrative set-up proposed follows the set-up of most of the universities in India. In fact except for a few clauses here and there, there is hardly a word which could not very easily be found in other University Acts. For that matter anyone familiar with University Acts can trace the phraseology to one University Act or another. In fact the framers have confined themselves to three or four University Acts with which they are familiar and the main Bill seems to be modelled on the Delhi University with some variations here and there. I should have expected that an institution, which is unique in character, which is concerned with the question of culture and which certainly has an ideal different from the ideals of other universities, may have an administrative set-up different from the existing set-up of the Indian universities, even if the present set-up of Indian Universities is a proper one. Even such variations as have been made have not commended themselves to me and I have no doubt they will not commend themselves to any other Member of the House.

I shall first refer to a small matter on the face of it, but really a matter of great importance in the Bill. We find certain Hindi or Sanskrit equivalents given for certain terms which are current in university terminology. For example, for the word Chancellor the word *Acharya* is used and for Vice-Chancellor the word *Up-Acharya*. If one loses at the powers of the *Acharya*, one finds them to be very nearly the same as those of the Chancellor in most of the Indian universities. Though it is not said in express words, it is implied that the real powers so far as the university is concerned will be vested in the Vice-Chancellor, as is the case with other universities.

As to the propriety of the use of these terms I could have very much to say but I will make only a few observations. *Acharya* means ordinarily a person who is endowed not only with knowledge but also with good conduct. He is to set an example to others by his conduct. Originally the term *acharya* meant ordinarily a senior teacher and the term *upadhyay* was used for a junior teacher. Terms do undergo changes in meaning in the course of history and that is what has happened to these terms also to a certain extent. I shall confine my remarks to the term *acharya*. The term *acharya* in current terminology, as it is accepted at the present moment, means professor. There is another sense in which it has been used and that is in the sense of principal. It is I believe in this sense that a well-known and respected Member of this House, Acharya Kripalani, is called *Acharya*, because he was the principal of certain institution; there are others also who are *acharyas* because they were principals. Now we have got these national universities where the term *acharya* is current; modern Hindi terminology also has got this term. I see no reason why the hon. Minister of Education or his advisers should give the term *acharya* a peculiar meaning, more particularly when *acharya*, that is the Chancellor, hardly has any powers under the proposed Bill. The accepted meaning of the term is there, the current meaning of the term is there; I see no reason why there should have been a departure in this regard; if an appropriate term was wanted, the framers weight have used the term *kulapati* for Chancellor and *upakulapati* for Vice-Chancellor. In fact, they could have invented some terms if necessary. I do feel that the use of these terms in the sense in which they have been used is not appropriate and I do hope Government will deem it necessary to make the necessary change.

Another departure from the provisions of other University Acts is contained in clause 27, "Statutes how made." The Department of Education have done borrowings, and as I said earlier, the borrowings are palpable on the face of the Bill itself, but so far as certain very important matters go they have not deemed it fit to do the borrowing and put things in a schedule to the Bill. In clause 27 it is provided that the first Statutes shall be framed by the Central Government. Now, if we analyse any one of the Acts from which the borrowings have been made, say, the Lucknow University Act or the Delhi University Act, there is hardly any such Act in which this kind of a thing is left to the

Government itself. Very important matters are involved here. For example, the question of the composition of the Court, the question of the composition of the executive council, the question of the academic council, the question of the composition of selection to committees, the relationship between the selection committees and the executive council, are some of the matters involved. A great many of the important matters are ordinarily covered by the statutes. Sir, the University Commission have reported on this matter, they have made certain suggestions. It will not do for Government to come forward in this House and say that these important questions will be dealt with in the manner recommended by the University Commission. If my recollection is correct the University Commission report has not come before this House for discussion. In the present case extremely important matters are involved. In fact, a great deal of space in the Commission's report is devoted to the consideration of some of these questions. The House has not discussed this report at all. If the Government come forward and say that the first Statutes shall be framed by them on the basis of the recommendations of the Commission I dare say that is not the correct thing to do, and Parliament will be ill-advised in giving the Central Government power to make the first Statutes dealing with these very important matters. At least some indications should have been given or the views of the House should have been ascertained by Government as to how these matters should be dealt with.

There is another very important matter which has not been covered by the Bill, that is, the question of the appointment of the Vice-Chancellor. I refer to clause 14. All that is said there is:

> "*The Upacharya* (Vice-Chancellor) shall be the principal academic and executive officer of the University, and the terms and conditions of service of the *Upacharya* (Vice-Chancellor) Shall be as laid down by the Statutes.
>
> The *Upacharya* shall exercise such powers and perform such functions as may be prescribed by the Statutes.
>
> The mode of appointment of the successor to the first *Upacharya* shall be as laid down in the Statutes."

Anyone familiar with the difficulties connected with University education will testify to the fact that one of the evils that we have had to face has been in the matter of appointment to this office. The University Commission themselves have reported that there should be only one term, a term of six years, with which some agree and some do not agree.

This very important question is left for decision to Government itself. Government shall also fix what the manner of the appointment of the Vice-Chancellor will be, whether he will be elected by the *Samsad* or by the executive committee, etc. These are some of the extremely important questions around which the question of University education centres at the present moment. There is certainly the difficulty of obtaining suitable personnel, but the statutes should be so framed that evil may, as far as possible, be avoided. Under clause 27 Government themselves will frame the first statutes. I do think that a very important question of principle is involved and I am surprised that the Government of India should have been advised not to take the House into confidence in this matter but to keep the entire thing to themselves as if they are in a position, without proper advice—more particularly the advice and opinion of this House–, to take a decision on some of these important matters. If this Bill must be passed into law early, I do suggest that the hon. Minister of Education place before the House these statutes so that the wishes of the House might be ascertained and the House might, if it considers necessary, alter any of them. I am not in the least in favour of Government being given such powers. I can understand what is called delegated legislation where, mainly, broad outlines are defined and the executive is left to make certain rules within the limits provided by the Legislature. Here even the broadest outlines in most of these matters are not defined in the Bill and the Central Government are seeking power to regulate these matters according to their own light. I dare say this is not quite satisfactory.

Another departure from the administrative set-up of the Delhi University which has been made, relates to what is called the court. The *Samsad* or the court is made the supreme governing body of the University. I am quite aware that in some Universities the court is made the supreme governing body, in some it is not made the supreme governing body. With the knowledge of the working of the Universities with which I am familiar I dare say that in spite of the provision in certain University Acts to the effect that court is the supreme governing body of the University, it does not exercise any such functions at all. Even if in letter the court is the supreme governing body in certain Universities, it is not so in truth.

[SHRIMATI DURGABAI *IN THE CHAIR*]

Take the Benares Hindu University, where the Court is made the supreme authority, I could cite from the records hundreds of resolutions which are to this effect. "This court recommends to the Executive Council . . . : This is the form of the resolutions at the present moment and this has also been the form before. Now, it is said in clause 19:

> "The *Samsad* (Court) Shall, on a date to be fixed by the *Upacharya* (Vice-Chancellor), meet once a year at a meeting to be called the annual meeting of the *Samsad* (Court)."

Then it is provided:

> "The *Upacharya* (Vice-Chancellor) may, whenever he thinks fit, and shall, upon a requisition in writing by not less than one-thrid of the members of the *Samsad* (Court), convene a special meeting of the *Samsad* (Court)."

A body that is scheduled to meet only once a year is made the supreme governing body. The experiment has been tried and in no University the Court, really speaking, exercises any such supreme powers. In the University of Delhi itself as I have already pointed out, the court has not been made the supreme governing body. I do not see any reason why such a departure should be made in the case of Visva-Bharati. I think we might stick to the terminology of some of the Acts from which the borrowing has been made in this Bill and not make the Court the supreme governing body of the University.

Another point which I should like to emphasise in this connection is that all the defects of the existing organisations of the Universities have been maintained in the Bill. I shall refer to some of these only. Let us take clause 3(h) where the word "teachers" is defined. It is said that:

> "Teachers means such persons as are engaged in imparting instruction and guiding students in practical work or otherwise in the University and in the institutions under its control, and includes professors, readers, lecturers, demonstrators and other grades of teachers appointed by the University.

Now, one of the banes of University education in our country has been the numerous grades of teachers that we have. We do not need so many grades. Let us not carry the ideas of Hindu aristocracy into the University teachers' field. We do not need so many grades of teachers, more particularly in an institution whose purpose is to study culture and disseminate it. Why you should have five or six classes of teachers is ununderstandable to me. The maximum that I would propose is two classes of teachers. I would not be prepared to recommend more.

Shri J.R. Kapoor (Uttar Pradesh): Why should there be even two grades?

Dr. R.U. Singh: For the last fourteen years, I have been advocating only one class of teachers in the Universities and if you really want to do something, you must have only one class of teachers. I welcome the suggestion that my hon. friend Mr. Kapoor has made and I should be extremely happy if there is only one class of teachers in the University that we are proposing.

Shri J.R. Kapoor: It was not my suggestion. I only wanted to understand the hon. Member.

Dr. R.U. Singh: Anyway, I now turn to another defect of the existing University administrative set-up included in the Bill. If we look at clause 26, 28 and 30 we find that there are certain matters to be governed by Statutes; some of them to be governed by Ordinances; and some may be governed by what are called 'regulations'. Earlier in this history of legislation relating to Universities in India, most of these matters had been left to regulations. Later on, it was deemed desirable that matters left to be determined by the Universities should be governed either by Statues or by regulations. The Benares Hindu University follows this practice. Let us now look at the various matters to be regulated by Statutes. They are "Designation and powers of the officers of the University; the terms of office and the method and conditions of election or appointment of the officers of the University; the constitution, powers and duties of the authorities of the University; the Institution and maintenance of *Bhawans* (Halls) and *Chatravasas* (Hostels) etc. etc." Then look at the matters to be governed by Ordinaces: "Admission of students to the University; the courses of study be laid down for all degrees and diplomas of the University; the conditions, mode of appointment and duties of examining bodies examiners and moderators etc. etc." I have referred to these just to show that if you look at these matters, you do not find much of a difference between matters which are sought to be governed by Statutes and matters which are sought to be governed by Ordinances. I dare say that if you must have two classes, then have some important matters governed by Statutes and all others by regulations, as is the practice in the Benares Hindu University. Regulations make for easy change and it is desirable that some of these changes are made easy. I have no doubt that best thing that can be done is to go by the present practice that has grown up in some of the Universities and particularly the practice in the Benares Hindu University, namely having two kinds of rules only made by the University, the very important ones contained in the Statutes which are difficult to change and the less important ones governed by regulations. Now, I must come to some drafting matters which have bothered me a little and some of them are extremely serious. First of all, I shall refer to clause 8 which says:

> "Subject to the Ordinances, the University shall be open to all persons irrespective of sex, nationality, race, creed caste or class . . . "

The intention is apparent and this finds a place practically in every Act. The openings words are "Subject to the Ordinances........" and as a student of law, I must say that these opening words give the impression that discrimination on any of these grounds is not ruled out and if it is made then it will be perfectly legal. I have not the slightest doubt about the correctness of this interpretation. I want to ask the hon. Minister of Education as to whether this is intended. What is it you want? Do you want that there should be discrimination, or do you want to have the power to discriminate, or do you want that there should be no discrimination? If Government want that there should be discrimination, then this clause is perfectly all right. If on the other hand they do not want any discrimination, then these opening words "Subject to the Ordinance" must necessarily be deleted. One more remark that I would make in this connection is that if these words are retained, they will defeat the very purpose of the clause. I would appeal to you, for God's sake, for your sake and for the sake of the person whose institution you are now taking under your care, please remove these words.

Mr. Chairman: But does the Statute provide for any kind of discrimination?

Dr. R.U. Singh: I should personally think that no discrimination is desirable. Now, I am reading from the Memorandum of Association of the Visva-Bharati. Poet Tagore was extremely careful to see that discrimination was not there so far as this great centre of culture was concerned. Discrimination is contrary to the very purpose of an institution of culture. In the rules of Visva-Bharati it was provided that the Membership of the Visva-Bharati and of its constituent bodies shall be open to all persons irrespective of sex, nationality, race, creed, caste or class; and no test or condition shall be imposed as to religious belief or profession in admitting members, students, teachers workers or in any other connection whatsoever.

My point of view in this connection is that if discrimination in any form whatsoever is advisable anywhere else, or can be tolerated anywhere else, it is certainly intolerable in an institution of the kind that poet Tagore set up and, as I have pointed out, the Memorandum of Association of that institution did provide that no such discrimination shall be made. So my words to the Government of India are, if you must have the power, or some authority or body must have the power, to make discrimination, within whatever limits that discrimination might be made, please do not have it with reference to the Visva-Bharati.

Now, I shall refer to two or three other important matters. Clause 4 of the Bill relates to incorporation. This is a technical legal matter, but I think I should draw the attention of the House to this. What is incorporated here by this clause is the Chancellor, Vice-Chancellor and the Court. The clause reads:

> "The first *Acharya* (Chancellor) and *Upacharya* (Vice-Chancellor) of the university shall be the persons appointed in this behalf by the Central Government by notification in the Official Gazette, and the first members of the *Samsad* (Court) and all persons, who may hereafter become or be appointed as such officer or members, so long as they continue hold such office or membership, are hereby constituted a body corporate by the name of Visva-Bharati . . . ."

Sound legal practice is to incorporate not only the Court but other bodies also, namely for example in this case, the Academic Council as also the Executive Council. If a reference is made to the Agra University Act, the Banaras University Act, the Lucknow University Act – with the exception of the Aligarh Act – it will be found that what is incorporated is not merely the Chancellor and the Vice-Chancellor and the Court, but also the more important bodies of the University which include the Senate, namely the Academic Council, and the Executive Council, because both of these bodies have got very extensive and important powers. So, I suggest an amendment of this clause; as it stands, it is not quite correct.

In clause 6(3) among the university's powers and duties are to "organise, establish, affiliate, carry on and maintain or dissolve, disaffiliate or give up new branches or associated institutions having objects similar to those of the University." Now, if we look to the preamble, we find that what is sought to be established is a unitary, teaching and residential university.

Mr. Chairman: I think the hon. Member is going into the clause by clause consideration stage. That stage has not yet begun. This is only general discussion.

Dr. R.U. Singh: The power is "affiliate" is inconsistent with the very idea of a residential university and this word is a misfit and must necessarily go.

Clause 28 (k) says that "subject to the provisions of this Act and the statutes, the Ordinances may provide for all or any of the following matters, namely:

(j) the formation of departments of teachers;"

I have heard of such a thing a "Department of Teaching", but I have never heard in my life a "Department of Teachers."

I will close with the observation that the Bill adopts the administrative set-up of some of the existing Universities for an institution of a different character and embodies even their defects; where it differs from them, the departure is objectionable, more particularly in leaving decisions on extremely important matters to the executive which this House ought not to allow. My hope is that the character of the institution will not be altered.

Pandit Kunzru (Uttar Pradesh): I am sure the decision of the Government to treat the Finance Bill as a national University will give satisfaction throughout the country. It would have been a matter of serious discredit to us had we taken no steps to preserve this unique institution.

Madam, I listened carefully to the speech of the hon. the Education Minister two days ago. He gave reasons to justify the introduction of this Bill, but so far as I remember, did not say a word about its provisions. Perhaps, his silence was due to the fact that all important matters relating to the University will be provided for in the statutes. These statutes will, among other things, deal with such important matters as the classification and mode of appointment and the determination of the terms and conditions of service of the teachers of the University, They will also deal with the discipline of the students and so on. They will provide for the manner in which the Vice-Chancellor is to be appointed and his tenure of office.

Now it is obvious these days the manner in which a University functions depends primarily on the Vice-Chancellor who is its chief academic and administrative officer and on the Executive Council which has been called by the University Commission as the pivotal body in this sphere of administration. I share entirely the views of my hon. friend Dr. R.U. Singh with regard to undesirability of giving Government unfettered discretion to frame statutes on which will depend the character of the University. The Bill is just a skeleton. It will be provided with sufficient flesh and blood by the statutes. I know that in the past when new Universities have been established the first statutes have been framed either by the Government, or by a nominated Vice-Chancellor with the approval of the Government. But I suggest another method which will be more democratic and at the same time enable us to see that the statutes that are framed for the Visva-Bharati will take account of the defects that have been found in the working of the constitution and statutes of the other Universities. My suggestion in this connection is that while the statutes may be placed on the table of the House as suggested by my hon. friend Dr. R.U. Singh, they should when framed by Government be examined by a Committee of Members of Parliament, either elected by this House or appointed by the Education Minister. Once such statutes have been laid on the table of the House I am afraid that there will be hardly any possibility of introducing any important change in them. If the opinion of such Members of Parliament as are connected with Universities is to be made use of it is necessary that the statutes before they are promulgated or before they are placed on the table of the House should be examined by such men. I make this suggestion partly because the statutes will deal with all those essential matters on which, as I have already said, the character of the Visva-Bharati will depend. Bt there is another reason also for making this suggestion and that is the recommendations made by the University Commission. The Members who composed the University Commission were undoubtedly men with wide academic and administrative experience of educational affairs, But he would be a bold man who would say that the recommendations made by the Commission to check the abuses that it discovered have the approval of educationists in general. The commission refers to the undesirability of resorting to election for the appointment of a whole-time and paid Vice-Chancellor, and a unitary teaching and residential University must have a whole time and paid Vice-Chancellor. It deplores the open canvassing and the formation of factions that have been the result of the existing system. Its view is that the whole idea of standing as a candidate for the Vice-Chancellorship must be suppressed. And in order to give effect to its idea it suggests that the Vice-Chancellor should be appointed by the Chancellor on the recommendation of the Executive Council; the Executive Council should send up one man to the Chancellor; the Council would be at liberty to consider the name of any person who in its opinion was likely to make an efficient Vice-Chancellor and make only one recommendation to the Chancellor. Now, the method suggested by the Commission is not quite as new as it might appear to be to those unconnected with the later Universities. The procedure followed in the Allahabad University is that the Court is the final authority in connection with the election of the Vice-Chancellor. In the Lucknow University, on the other hand, the Court has no say in the matter. The Executive Council sends up a few names–two or three names, or it may send up only one name, and in practice it has done so. But I do not find, in spite of the prevalence of this method of choosing the Vice-Chancellor that the Lucknow University has come in for any special praise in the Report of the University Commission. It is obvious to every one conversant with the conditions of the Universities in Uttar Pradesh that the method suggested by the University Commission will not cure the evil that it deplored. Some other method must be found of avoiding the difficulties that have arisen and removing politics from educational affairs. I personally think that a better way of dealing with this matter would be to allow the Members of the Executive Council to recommend names either to the Court or to the Chancellor in accordance with the system that prevails in this House in connection with the election of committees. In other words, I mean that the method of proportional representation by means of the single transferable vote should be adopted. And my reason for making this suggestion is that the proposal made by the Commission will not prevent the formation of factions. There will in spite of the proposal be parties in the Executive Council in the University and the party that commands a majority in the Executive Council may nullify the purpose of the proposal made by the Commission by sending up the name of a person, who may not be the most competent man for being appointed as a Vice-Chancellor, but commands the support of this majority. I think that one very good way of preventing this is to allow voting in connection with the selection of the persons to be recommended to the Vice-Chancellor to take place in accordance with the method used in this House for the election of Committees. There is another method too, that is employed by the Delhi University. I am familiar with it because I have something to do along with two other persons in connection with the selection of persons for the post of Vice-Chancellor for recommendation to the President. The system there is that the Visitor–the President is the Visitor–nominates one man and the Executive Council nominates two persons. These three persons recommend three names to the Visitor. There three names are then placed before the Executive Council for their comments, and the

Visitor makes his choice after receiving the opinion of the University. Then there is this danger in the methods used by the Delhi University, that if there are parties there, then the majority party in the Executive Council can send up two names of its own choice, and thus make an impartial selection very difficulty, if not impossible.

I think, therefore, that the suggestion that I have made will meet the difficulty before us more effectively than that made by the Commission.

I shall now proceed to refer to the recommendations made by the Commission with regard to the composition of the Executive Council and the election of representatives of the registered graduates to the Court. The Commission thinks that the composition suggested by it will prevent log-rolling to a considerable extent in future. I think, Madam, that it is necessary to point out two things in this connection. One is that the election of representatives of the registered graduates, not to the court, but to the Executive Council, has been left to the Court without any recommendation with regard to the method by which the Court should elect its representatives. I am sure that those Members of Parliament who are connected with the Universities know that whenever the Court has to send Members–it has to elect members from among the representatives of the registered graduates to the Executive Council – the majority party sweeps the board. If you want that the Executive Council should not virtually be the nominee of any single party then it is necessary to see that the persons to be elected by the Executive Council are chosen in such a way as to make it impossible for any particular party to prevent the election of any person who does not agree with it. Another thing that I should like to point out is that the Executive Council will have to appoint Deans of the Faculties who will be the Members of the Executive Council. Here again, we have to consider how the Deans may be so chosen as to be in accordance with the best interests of the University. In either case, that is, whether the Court is to elect some members from among the representatives of the registered graduates to the Executive Council or Executive Council is to select the Deans of the Faculties, we have to adopt a method of selection that will not place a premium on the formation of what the Commission calls 'factions'. I think that the best way of gaining our object would be to lay down that the election in either case would take place in accordance with the system prevalent in this House for the election of Committees, that is, the system of proportional representation by means of the single transferable vote.

I should like to say one word more before I sit down. The Commission has recommended that the Vice-Chancellor should be elected for a term of 6 years and that his re-election should not be allowed. The Commission is against the re-election of a Vice-Chancellor, I am sure, in order to prevent the formation of parties in the University. It probably thought that if a Vice-Chancellor knew that he could not be elected again, then he would have no interest in forming a party, but the matter, Madam, is unfortunately not so simple as that. We know even now that when parties are formed, they are not formed in the interests of one person only. There may be 2 or 3 powerful men in it and the interests of all of them then will have to be served by the party. If the method that I have suggested is accepted, then, I think there is hardly any fear that the re-election of a Vice-Chancellor would give rise to abuses. If the term of the Vice-Chancellor is made as long as that recommended by the Commission, if the Vice-Chancellor is incompetent, the affairs of the University will continue to be mismanaged for as long as six years. I do not therefore think that so long a term of office is desirable. It may well be for more than three years, which is the term of office in the Allahabad and Lucknow Universities. But I think that till more experience is gained of the working of any method that may be accepted now, the term of office of the Vice-Chancellor should not be more than four years.

I think I have referred to many of the important questions raised by the Bill. But, I should like to say one word with regard to the views expressed by my hon. friend Dr. R.U. Singh on one or two points. He told us that he was of the opinion that there should be no division of the University teachers into grades. He would probably like to have only one grade, all the members in that grade to be on an incremental scale like the members of the Executive and Judicial services. If this is his opinion, I am afraid, I cannot agree with him. It is of the greatest importance in the University that its teachers should keep abreast of current knowledge and should be genuinely interested in carrying on research. If we offer the teachers of a University conditions of service similar to those enjoyed, say, by the Deputy Collectors and Subordinate Judges, many of them may have no incentive to carry on their studies or engage in research work. They may well think that their promotion to the maximum salary fixed for them was almost certain, they may well rest on their oars.

Dr. R.U. Singh: What about efficiency bars?

Pandit Kunzru: I have heard something about the working of efficiency bars to which my hon. friend Dr. R. U. Singh has invited my attention. I have been told by those who are in a position to express a considered opinion on this point, that the authorities find it very difficult to stop the promotion of a man unless he is totally unfit to occupy a higher position that which he already holds. I have no doubt that the position of a Vice-Chancellor or an Executive Council that stops the promotion of a teacher will not be enviable. I think therefore that in the interests of the University, it is desirable to have a certain numbers of grades. What the proportion of posts in each grade should be is a matter of detail, though in my opinion, an important matter, I shall, therefore, not refer to it now.

As regards the number of grades, that too is a matter of detail. My hon. friend Dr. R. U. Singh has a preference for the American system because he received his education in America. Those of us who are more familiar with the British system of education, may well think that the classification adopted not merely in the Universities of Oxford and Cambridge, which may be called aristocratic, but in the newer universities may well be adopted in India too. There should be three grades of teacher: lecturers, readers and professors. I hope that the statutes of the Visva-Bharati will not try to fix a single grade for all teachers.

Another point raised by my hon. friend Dr. R.U. Singh was the different kinds of rules made by the university authorities: statutes, ordinances and regulations. I was rather surprised that a person so well acquainted with the procedure in a number of universities should have asked us to have only two kinds of rules. Why are three kinds of rules needed? There are rules made by the court. Some of them might be said to deal with its own procedure or with minor matters for which the approval of any higher authority is not necessary. These are now called regulations. Other matters which must go before the court and which must receive the sanction of the Chancellor before they can be put into effect are known as statutes. Whether you call the rules made by the court as regulations or any other thing, this essential distinction between them will remain. Where is the harm, then, in calling the more important rules, statutes and the less important rules, regulations?

Now, I will come to the ordinances. Ordinances are passed by the Executive Council. They have to be placed before the court when it meets; but they do not wait for the sanction of the court before they are put into effect. I am sure that my hon. friend Dr. R. U. Singh is not against the Executive Council having the power of passing ordinances. If the Executive did not have this power and if changes could be made only by the court, I do not know whether any university would be able to function properly. I think, therefore, that both in respect of appointments and the rules to be made by the different university bodies, the present classification is not open to serious criticism. But as regards the other matters to which my hon. friend referred and to which I have referred too, they are important enough to require the serious consideration of Government. We cannot take the Visva-Bharati Bill as a thing by itself. I think it is reasonable to assume that any decision arrived at by Government on the important matters referred to by Dr. R. U. Singh and me might well influence other universities. I therefore, press once more on the attention of the hon. Education Minister the desirability, indeed the necessity of appointing a committee of this House to examine the statutes either before they are promulgated or before they are laid on the Table of the House.

Dr. M.M. Das (West Bengal): After the learned and detailed discussion of the legal aspect of this Bill by two of my eminent friends of this house to which we have just listened, I rise to make only a few general observations about this Bill. It seldom falls to the lot of a democratic government to come forward in Parliament with any legislative measure that receives the unanimous and wholehearted support of every section of the legislature. Even in this baby Parliament of ours, just about sixteen months old, hon. Members in charge of Bills have not always found it very easy to pilot their Bills. But to-day our hon. Minister of Education has come forward with a measure to which there is not a single Member of this House who would not give his wholehearted support and approval. Visva-Bharati is a great and unique institution that has been bequeathed to us and to posterity by that great poet, thinker and philosopher–Rabindranath Tagore. The importance and greatness of Visva-Bharati lie in the greatness of its founder. If Visva-Bharati is great, its founder Rabindranath was greater. Visva-Bharati is the manifestation, the concrete shape that the great poet wanted to give to the high ideals that he cherished, preached and practised in his life. It is the embodiment of the spirit of Rabindranath that soared like an eagle high in the sky, shaking off the shackles of narrow conventionalism and the barriers of race, caste and creed. The gospel of truth and love, of world peace, love of humanity and universal brotherhood and the underlying unity and oneness of all that is great and glorious in mankind, these are the ideals which Rabindranath wanted to embody in this institution of his. The world today is riven with anger and hatred. Warring camps are snarling at each other like wild and mad denizens of the jungle. Nations are racing over the production of armaments. Scientists are engrossed in inventing better and deadlier weapons of death and destruction. But in the midst of all this orgy and pestilence of killing and destruction, Visva-Bharati stands as a heaven of peace to mankind. In the midst of this encircling gloom all around us, this institution–Visva-Bharati–stands as a beacon light inviting millions of peace loving people of the world. Madam, Visva-Bharati preaches the gospel of peace and love and Truth that India preached thousands of years ago through the great universities of Taxila and Nalanda. Tagore was the greatest cultural ambassador that India ever produced. A messenger and interpreter of Indian philosophy and culture, his enchanting voice never failed to capture the ear of the world. The message of the Vedas and the Upanishads, the eternal truths of the universe and its Creator which were discovered thousands of years ago by the great sages of this ancient land and which were echoed and re-echoed in the vales and valleys of the Himalayas and in the vast plains and the mightly rivers of this subcontinent have found expression in those exquisite lyrics and verse of Rabindranath Tagore.

Rabindranath is no longer with us. He has joined the band of the immortals. But his work remains. He has bequeathed to us, the citizens of this free country and to posterity, this unique institution which has received recognition from the whole of the world and which has attracted pupils and scholars from all parts of the world. It is a national trust that goes beyond the boundaries of the nation to the whole world. This institution in India should like, our Taxila and Nalanda of yore, bring succour to people who are most in need of it. It is to us the citizens of India, that he has left this institution. It should be our proud and cherised privilege to see that this tender plant does not die for want of nourishment. Let us keep the flame of peace and goodwill burning that this great and eminent son of India has kindled.

Shri R.K. Chaudhuri (Assam): [*Spoke in Bengali*]

Shri Naziruddin Ahmad (West Bengal): On a point of order. The official languages are English and Hindi. One can speak in his mother tongue if he cannot express himself in English or Hindi. Bengali is not the official language, nor the hon. Member's mother tongue. Further he can express himself felicitously in English.

Mr. Chairman: The hon. Member may speak in Hindi . . . .

Shri Chattopadhyay (West Bengal): Exception should be made on this occasion.

An Hon. Member: He can speak in Assamese.

Mr. Chairman: Unless the hon. Member has adopted Bengali also as his mother tongue.

Shri R.K. Chadhuri: I was going to give my reasons for speaking in Bengali. If those reasons are not acceptable to the House then I will speak in any language you will direct me to do. [*Continued his speech in Bengali.*]

Mr. Chairman: Order, order.

Shri R.K. Chaudhuri: I am giving my reasons.

Mr. Chairman; If they are given in Bengali they will not be understood by others. He may give the reasons either in English or Hindi.

Shri R.K. Chaudhuri: Just one sentence more, Madam. [*Continued his speech in Bengali.*]

Dr. Deshmukh (Madhya Pradesh): That is more than one sentence.

Mr. Chairman: I am bound to draw the attention of the hon. Member to article 120 of the Constitution.

Shri R.K. Chaudhuri: If my reasons are not acceptable . . . . .

Mr. Chairman: The reasons given by the hon. Member are not even known to the Chair. I will draw attention to article 120 which says:

> "Notwithstanding anything in Part XVII, but subject to the provisions of article 348, business in Parliament shall be transacted in Hindi or in English."

Shri R.K. Chaudhuri: It was he who gave the national song, *Jana, gana, mana*, which has been adopted by the nation. It was this song which had driven out our enemies from the country in the past and in the near future our soldiers may sing it and their band will play it to drive out the aggressors again.

I have lost the trend of my speech and it will take me some time to continue in English. I shall continue my speech in Hindi.

Today all over India people not only Indians, but those who live outside even those who live in Pakistan, and the great thinkers of the world, who were enamoured on hearing *Gitanjali* in English besides those who know Bengali and those also who did not know it but knew some others languages, all of them today would certainly be congratulating our hon. Maulana Saheb. I also congratulate him. I think we cannot give a proper expression to our delightful feelings even after our repeated congratuatlions. It is a matter of surprise how the Government of India, who from the very beginning has made a very slow progress in each and every respect, because we have witnessed this fact, could act so speedily in this regard. In this matter of far reaching importance for which the entire country would congratulate hon. Maulana Saheb, the Government of India have today shown that they can also adopt speedy measures if and when necessary. But in addition to this I want to submit a few things more. My first submission is that the name of Shri Rabindra Nath Thakur has been given as Rabindra Nath Tagore in the Bill. I wonder wherefrom this name has been taken when all of his books contain the name Rabindra Nath Thakur.

The Minister of Education (Maulana Azad): The name Tagore has become known far and wide and if the name Thakur instead of that is adopted then it would become very difficult for the world to know his identity.

Shri R.K. Chaudhuri: Why, they would certainly recognise it. Did not the people recognise the identity of Maharishi Devendra Nath? I do not know how and wherefrom this word Tagore has been taken. Whatever may be the case, he was not Rabindra Nath Tagore, he was Rabindra Nath Thakur. Yes, of course a European lived as per name Tagore with their family, as member of the same, and his name was Ramsdon Tagore. But on account of this how the name of Shri Rabindra Nath Thakur came to be changed? I want to submit that may the word Thakur be not palatable to the world but in the various laws that would be enacted in our country his name should be written as Thakur and not as Tagore. I do not care whether by the Word Thakur the English people or the Americans would identify him or not, but I am not in the least embarrassed by it. But I do not like that in the legislation, that is being enacted, the name of great personality of India should be written in the English style. I abhor the very idea even.

Mr. Chairman: It is quite true that the entire world writes Tagore instead of Thakur.

Shri R.K. Chaudhuri: The world used to write in its own languages. But I can produce a thousand books written by Shri Rabindra Nath wherein the author's name is written as Rabindra Nath Thakur.

The Minister of State for Finance (Shri Tyagi): What is written in English?

Shri R.K. Chaudhuri: My second objection is that the amount you are granting is very meagre. The hon. Minister should bear it in mind that when Shri Rabindra Nath Thakur was alive there was no dearth of money at all. Money flowed to him from all parts of the world. With the help of that money he used to run this University. Now he is no more. Mahatma Gandhi also, who could have collected money for it, is no more. Now we have our Pandit Jawaharlal Nehru and our Deputy Leader, if these two would not take the necessary amount of money from the Government then this University cannot function properly. I know that they have asked for five lacs of rupees and that amount has been sanctioned. I do not allege that whatever they asked has not been given to them. They have of course asked this money as a loan. But when you have resources at your disposal then why instead of donating money, you want to give it as a loan to them? I say, why do you like to make the University a debtor? It is not proper to make it a debtor, when you have money why do you give it in the form of a loan? Why do you not give them a substantial grant? I am sure you were certainly prepared to give them a grant of five lacs of rupees, but our hard-hearted friend, who is certainly hard hearted, I mean to say, Shri Mahavir Tyagi has put some obstacles in that matter. He has now become Deputy Finance Minister. He must have insisted upon the full grant not being given just now but to wait and see the future developments. The matter would be reviewed afterwards. If it would seem necessary the loan would be remitted because if this will not be done the Uttar Pradesh people would take exception to it on the grant that a similar amount has not been granted to Uttar Pradesh. He must have insisted on giving the money as a loan in the first instance, and if not recovered it would be remitted later on. The Grant should not be given just now. I think this is the reason why the full amount has not been given.

Shri Tyagi: This is not true.

Shri R.K. Chaudhuri: It may not be so. It can be said that neither Shri Mahavir Tyagi nor Shri Deshmukh raised any objection to that effect but it is a decision of the Cabinet. But in my opinion Shri Deshmukh would not have raised any objection for this petty amount being given as a grant. It can only be the work of our friend Shri Mahavir Tyagi. This is my opinion and I cannot say whether it is true or nor.

Mr. Chairman: He said that it is not true.

Shri R.K. Chaudhuri: I do not want to take more time. I have no capacity too to speak any further in this language. I did not want to speak in English on this matter and whatever knowledge I had of Hindi has been exhausted.

Dr. Deshmukh: There can be no two opinions that the hon. Maulana Sahib has done the most opportune thing in bringing this Bill before the House for converting the Visva-Bharati established by the celebrated poet of India into a University. There can also be no two opinions that this institution called the Visva-Bharati should be declared by means of this Bill as an institution of national importance. There is perfect unanimity in this House in the matter, and as has been said by my friend who has just sat down everybody in the whole of India would be glad to see that this old institution which has been reared and nurtured by one of the greatest sons of India is going to be placed on a permanent footing.

This is certainly a unique institution but my regret is how far the uniqueness of this institution is going to be maintained. It was with this point in mind that I had given notice of a dilatory motion for reference of the Bill to a Select Committee. Already there are more than 100 amendments suggested to this Bill and there are many comments offered so far as the organisation and constitution of the University are concerned. I would not refer to such unimportant matters as to whether a particular individual designated by a particular name has got sufficient authority or more authority, nor do I wish to go into the details of the comparative powers of the Executive Council and the Academic Council. I wish to say a few words on the main idea behind the Bill and behind what was Visva-Bharati created by Rabindra Nath Tagore.

Before I do so, however, I would like to congratulate the government on their proceeding on the right lines in recognising what is valuable in the national life of the country from the point of view of education. I am sure this Bill will be followed soon by a Bill which will convert the Jamia Millia Islamia into another University. While the Government is thinking of these things. I would like them, as has been suggested by some other Members, to make a survey of similar institutions–of course, not so famous or probably not conducted or guided by such celebrated persons as in this case, probably started and maintained by persons who have not put in such a high degree of sacrifice as was done by sponsors and workers in these institutions; but there are throughout the length and breadth of this country many institutions which have been conducted probably by lesser men, of lesser merit and lesser learning but nonetheless having a place in the national life of India, institutions which have really served the people from many points of view in the field of education. I hope as time goes by and we recognise the importance of the role of social and educational workers in our national life, a survey would be taken of what other institutions there exist and what financial and other aid they require. It is an accident.

Madam, that you are in the Chair just now, but it not merely because you are sitting in the Chair that I wish to make a particular reference to your own institution on which you have spent many years to rear and develop it. There are many other persons like that who have taken a great part in the field of women's education as well as rural education. When Government is kind enough to recognise these bigger efforts and to assist them deservedly with lakhs of rupees of funds, I hope they will also assist these smaller institutions with as much aid as is possible for them to give.

Coming to the structure of the Bill I must say that I am totally disappointed. I have not only had the experience of being a member of various executive councils of Universities, I have also had the good fortune of belonging to not less than six Universities all over the world, three in India and three in England. I have therefore some knowledge of not only the structure of Universities but of the way in which a University works. And my prejudice against the constitution of the Visva-Bharati into another kind of University of the very same type as exist in India is based on experience and intimate knowledge of the working of these universities. That is the reason why in my opinion the conversion of the Visva-Bharati into such other University is not very desirable. Because what we are creating is a sort of a hum-drum institution which is daily being debased all over India. There is neither any cultural advancement nor any encouragement to culture and learning to speak of. Most things are done in a sort of a routine manner on the basis of very common considerations. And if we retain the structure of the Bill, I am afraid the idea with which the Visva-Bharati was created will not have much of an opportunity to develop. I would like to read – I am glad no other Member has read it – what was the conception of Rabindranath Tagore in establishing this institution. I am sorry to say that none of the important things which were the objects in creating and establishing Visva-Bharati find any place whatsoever in the structure of the Bill. Not only that, I go further and say that if you have the organisation you are suggesting in the Bill there can be no scope whatsoever – I say it deliberately, purposely and understanding fully what I mean – for any of the objects which were before Rabindranath Tagore being achieved. The main object of Rabindranath Tagore was "to study the mind of man in its realisation of the different aspects of truth from diverse points of view." Where is the "mind of Man" in this Bill and where is any mention of "truth" let alone its various aspects? Then, the second object is "to bring into more intimate relation with one another through patient study and research the different cultures of the East and the basis of their underlying unity." The third object is "to approach the West from the standpoint of such unity of life and thought of Asia." There is some mention of "bringing together the cultures of the Eat and the West," but I assure you, Madam, that under the structure of a University there can be no place whatever for this object because the more learned and the more cultured will never approach such an institution where everything has to be governed by Ordinances, statutes and regulations; everything has to be done by means of Selection Committees and by advertisements. I am sure there are ample Universities which are doing these things however excellent. My point is that Rabindra Nath Tagore's Shanti Niketan was intended to be a place where only the really learned would enter and not the certificate-*wales* and the Matriculates (even if all of them stand in the first class) and others who go there only to obtain some sort of a Degree and nothing more. May I ask the Maulana Saheb whether a University which is brought under a Statute like this can ever be a place of the type we want and Rabindranath Tagore worked for? In our Universities as they have been constituted and are working at present, there is very little room of anything being done which is of real value and intended to uphold a lasting purpose. In the old structure of the Visva-Bharati, there was no idea of any Degrees. It was understood that it was the one cultural centre which was going to be all-important in the whole of the East.

Maulana Azad: We are not going to create new university through this Bill which need recommendations regarding all these things. We are giving this institution of "Visva-Bharati", that was established some thirty years back the statutes of a university.

Dr. Deshmukh: I am fully aware of what the Maulana Saheb is intending. I am merely explaining what the consequences would be if we give our intention to this particular shape. Advisedly, some room has been kept so that some of the things that have been going on the Visva-Bharati may continue, but this cannot be incorporated in the sort of structure which we are giving to the University under this Bill. Irrespective of the financial assistance we give. I would much rather have liked to make this a real centre where the learned people of the whole world would be able to assemble. In the whole of India, there are dozens of universities and every year or two new ones are coming up. But if we really want to preserve the spirit of the Visva-Bharati, then I would have liked smaller Bill which would give ample scope to the persons who are conducting it. Government should also take steps to see that the most learned, the most devoted and the most cultured people find a place in the Visva-Bharati without having to apply for a particular post or asking for a particular salary. This was the original idea with which the institution was started.

The Maulana Saheb has pointed out that we are merely recognising what exists at the present moment. After all, it should not be forgotten that a number of years have passed since the great poet died and therefore, it is possible that lesser lights who have continued the institution might have thought somewhat like this. Along with the high ideals if we cater also for the common run of students we shall attract larger numbers. This may very well be due to the fact that they are not able to keep up the original inspiration, at least spread the theme of the institution as much as possible and try to bring many more students in it. That precisely is the reason why I say that this is not in consonance with the original objective. What will happen, if this Bill is passed can easily be imagined. We shall certainly have hundreds of students who will be studying all sorts of subjects. There will be people offering various subjects and getting their B.As., M.As. and Ph.Ds. probably. But can the Maulana Saheb point out to me a provision whereby this Visva-Bharati will be anything distinct or different from other Universities? I am afraid that the whole paraphernalia of the present Universities based on an imitation of foreign Universities will be strengthened and perpetuated. There is nothing original, nothing that is really in consonance with the ideas of the founder. Time and again, the University Commission has pointed out that we have many Universities which have done very good work, but they are all hackneyed. They have persisted in a particular pattern where there is no scope for originality or Indian culture or Indian genius to prosper and progress. This the Commission has pointed out in more than one place. They have said that if we have new Universities, they should be based on some new and original pattern. They have asked us not to go on repeating what has been done before. I would like to read only one or two passages. One passage reads thus:

> "The full genius of a country can develop only with freedom to create variety. Our University system has not had that freedom. Foreign control could best be maintained by regimented uniformity. Something new and different might threaten control, and therefore was to be looked upon with suspicion. This regimented uniformity, which originated

> partly in bureaucratic unimaginativeness, and partly as an administrative convenience whereby a foreign ruler could maintain control with a small administrative staff, because it is all we have known in our Universities, has become a habit of mind of Indian higher education. It is not inherent in the nature of good education. Repeatedly we have received suggestions that uniformity and standardistation be increased, as though they were prime educational values.

With the requirement which has existed of an academic degree as a condition for appointment to any responsible position in the government service, this demand for uniformity had a very practical, if unwholesome basis. We have recommended that, except in some of the professions, this requirement be abolished. With that action taken, such need for uniformity will no logner exist ....."

Mr. Chairman: Is it necessary to read those recommendations when they do not relate particularly to this University? I think the hon. Member would expect other hon. Members to have read the report.

Shri Kamath (Madhya Pradesh): We have not read it. He is perfectly relevant.

Dr. Deshmukh: I will not read much, but it is very relevant and establishes a very important point. I want to point out by reading out certain passages how some of the Members of the University Commission who are actually responsible for this Bill have really not followed their own advice given in the report. Another paragraph that I would read runs thus:

> "Each of the institutions we have described, beginning and working against great odds outside the University system has made and is making a significant contribution to our national life, but at least up to the recent past under extreme financial privation and hardship. Each of them, so far as it meets the fundamental requirements of our constitution for equal treatment and opportunity for all classes and communities and so long as it maintains acceptable quality in its work should receive grants of aid on a par with other recognised colleges and universities and should be given University status if that is desired. Such support and recognition should be granted without infringement upon the freedom and initiative of the institution."

I would only read one more passage, Madam, which is very telling:

> " A live, progressive society must rely, not upon rules of uniformity but upon live, competent judgment of actual merit. To deny capacity for such judgement is to deny possession of the capacity and integrity necessary to encourage the full cultural and spiritual resources of the country. The University Grants Commission in deciding the degree of recognition and support to be given to any institution should be governed, not by the likeness of that institution to others of a standard type, but by its judgment or whether that institution is making a substantial contribution to the economic, intellectual, cultural and spiritual life of India. By such encouragement of quality with variety, the educational resources of India will be enriched."

If as against these findings and these recommendations, we have a University, as suggested in the Bill, it will only be another teachers' paradise, an industry where the degree-holders will be manufactured for being job-hunters. We have already made much progress in the establishment of institutions of this nature. We may even create many others of the same kind but not the Shanti Niketan. I would really want the Shanti Niketan to be a place of pilgrimage, of a real centre of culture where the most learned not only in India but all over the world will have a free scope for living and being provided for, a place worthy of India's past traditions. India is the centre of the Orient. Nowhere can the philosophy of the Orient be nurtured in a better way than in India. It is our great fortune that a man of the stature and learning of Rabindranath Tagore should have been born in our country and reared that Institution. It is up to us to continue that great and inspiring work of his and not turn it – as I have said –into an industry where graduates and post-graduates will be produced. That might be a very attractive idea – I do not quarrel with it. But it could very well be separated. There could be a University which may be started in the name of poet Tagore in that very place. But the original idea of the mind being nurtured and where the various aspects of truth will be studied and discussed, where the cultures of not only the East and the West, but of all the nations of the world would be brought together where the synthesis of human welfare and human philosophy would be evolved, should be kept separate. I fear that the way in which this Bill has been framed leaves very little scope for it.

I would even now request the Maulana Saheb to consider this aspect of the matter. It is a great fortune of ours that a man of his learning, though he has no university education, is sponsoring this Bill.

It is one of our greatest fortunes I say, because he alone has the learning and culture to sponsor a Bill which seeks to perpetuate the memory of Rabindranath Tagore. I have not the slightest desire to stand in the way of the passage of this Bill. I know Maulana Saheb wants to leave India within a few days. So he is very keen that this should be passed quickly. But the considerations which I have urged should, I think, incline him to the view that there is necessity of really revising the ideas behind the constitution of this Bill. I am afraid Maulana Saheb has not had the time to pay more attention to the points that I have urged.

I was really sorry that my hon. friend Pandit Kunzru did not refer to these fundamentals. He instead, busied himself only with matter of lesser importance. I feel very strongly that the spirit of Shantiniketan must be preserved. That spirit is likely to be killed if we super-impose it with an organisation which will not foster culture. As a matter of fact university education and cultural education are two different things, and very little is being done in our universities for the development of culture. Our universities merely copied the foreign universities without the soul being there. They have merely copied them in the outer structure. If you want to do that in this case as well, I am sure inspiring ideas will not have any scope there.

I do not grudge the money being paid. I want as much money as my friend, Mr. Rohini Kumar Chaudhuri wants to be paid. But let it be utilised for the original idea which poet Tagore had in mind and not merely to produce graduates, post-graduates and L.L.Bs., who can be produced anywhere else. In fact I wanted to move a motion for the reference of this Bill to a Select Committee, but I do not wish to do so and annoy Maulana Sahib. But I hope he will not misunderstand me – I am sure nobody has misunderstand me – because it is not my idea to delay the passage of this Bill. But I want that something really worthy of the name of Rabindranath Tagore should be created and not an institution which is prototype of the other universities.

Mr. Chairman: May I suggest that we may now hear Maulana Sahib. We have already had sufficient discussion. This Bill is not a controversial Bill at all. If hon. Members agree I would like to call upon Maulana Sabib.

Maulana Azad : Those of my friends who have taken part in the present debate have tried to shed light on the various aspects of education and some of them have even broached the subject relating to the recommendations of the Universities Commission. With regard to the present Bill, however, particular stress has been laid on two matters, *viz.*, powers of the Visitor and the framing of the Statutes. I shall, in my speech, confine myself to these two matters alone. So far as the Visitor's powers are concerned the power that has been vested in is not really of a novel character. It is the same kind of power as is provided in every University Act in some form or the other. The university is an autonomous body. As soon as an Act is passed it starts the work of its internal administration in accordance with that Act. There is no external interference with its work. But the need has been felt in every University Act for the provision of some avenue for reform and correction in case of an emergency. If a time comes when the administration of the university is in danger of a break-down or the standard of its education deteriorates to the extreme there must be some authority that might supervise its interests in that contingency and be of help. This is borne out by a glance at the Indian Universities Acts. According to the practice that has been followed heretofore this power was vested in the Chancellor, or the Lord Rector. In universities where the highest office was that of the Chancellor, who used to be either a Governor or the Governor-General this power was reserved for the Chancellor as in the case of the Calcutta University, the Delhi University and other old universities. In the case of those universities where the right to elect the Chancellor has been vested in the Court and a higher office of Lord Rector has been provided for the relevant Acts vests these powers in the Lord Rector, as in the case of the Aligarh University. As the Universities Commission has made a recommendation that the office of the Visitor should now be assigned to the President of the Indian Union the Government has is this Bill appointed the President to be the Visitor and vested in him just those powers that have hitherto been vested in the Chancellor or the Lord Rector. No new power has been conferred nor has any new supervision been imposed. Just have a look at the Acts of Delhi, Aligarh, Banaras and other Universities and then say which is the new power that has been vested in the Visitor which you regard as excessive. What then, is this power? Is it the kind of power that seeks to interfere in any way with the internal administration of the University? Not at all. It is just a kind of check that has been provided to serve in case of special emergency (which need never arise). If, God forbid, an occasion were to arise when those entrusted with the administration of the affairs of the University act with wilful neglect in the discharge of their duties and the advice and the warning by the Visitor fail to produce any satisfactory results it would become essential, under the circumstances, in order to save the University from falling a prey to various evils, that the Visitor should adopt proper measures for conducting an enquiry and then send his findings to the University. It is hoped that this action on the part of the Visitor should prove effective in putting matters right but if the conditions deteriorate so much that even that action does not prove effective then the final decision shall lie with the Visitor and it shall be binding on the university.

If we are going to do away even with this healthy provision for reform in case of emergency I should like to know what other course can be adopted to meet an abnormal situation. The need of such a provision has been felt in the case of every University Act and it is essential with a view to safeguard the future of the Visva-Bharati that the Visitor be vested with special powers to cope with a special emergency.

Viewed from practical point of view this does not in any way affect the internal administration of the university whose functions will not be interfered with. It remains completely independent in all its affairs. A 'watchful eye' has been provided only to serve for unusual circumstances (which, it is hoped, may never arise). If, however, an emergency does arise at some time this eye would be open to watch things, it would not remain closed. I feel that much amount of watchfulness is unavoidable.

The second point that has been very much stressed by my friend, Dr. Kunzru, is that the Statutes should also have been framed and presented along with the Bill at the same time so that the House might have been afforded an opportunity of studying them and that they might even now be placed on the table of the House. The government would have been pleased to do so could the Statutes have been framed immediately but as this could not be done it was not considered necessary to postpone the presentation of the Bill on that account. This is not the first occasion that the Statutes have not been presented along with a University Bill. Many a time before now has also the same procedure been followed. The Bill is passed and the Statutes are left to be passed later on at leisure. The Statutes do not have the same value as the sections of an Act. They are passed on the basis of the Act and have just as much scope as is permitted by the Act. They are not enduring like the Act but are subject to continual change and the University is empowered to insist on a change in them. If it has not been possible to frame them immediately along with the Bill I fail to understand how it affects our task prejudicially and why it should come to be considered that our debate on the Bill would remain inconclusive without them.

Let me also make one more clarification. I have considered all the amendments that have been put in. Out of them I would accept seven. As for the rest I hope they would not be pressed. I have again considered the amendments that seek to modify that spellings of the words "Visva-Bharati" and "Shiksha-Sammelan". I have decided that if the Government Press has such 'S' founts as are provided with the sign which makes them pronounce as 'sh' the letter 'S' in words like 'Visva-Bharati' etc., shall remain, being in accord with the international practice, but if the 'S' with the sign be not available these words would employ 'sh' so that there may not be any possibility of an error.

Out of the seven amendments that I have accepted the first one is that of Prof. K.T. Shah. It purports to say that in clause 5 where it is mentioned with regard to the employess of the University that ......

Mr. Chairman: I should say it would be more proper for you to make those observations at a later stage when we come to the clause by clause consideration.

Maulana Azad: I thought that I might, to save time, clarify the position at this stage. However, let it be postponed till the clause by clause consideration.

Mr. Chairman The question is:

> "That the Bill declare the institution known as 'Visva-Bharati' to be an institution of national importance and to provide for its functionoing as a unitary, teaching and residential univeristy, be taken into consideraiton."

The motion was adopted.

Caluse 2. (*Visva-Bharati as an institution of national importance*)

Prof. K.T. Shah (Bihar): I beg to move:

For clause 2, substitute the following:

> "*Declaration of Visva-Bharati as an institution of national importance* – The Rabindranath Tagore Visva-Bharati is and shall be recognised and maintained as an institution of national importance."

Shri R.K. Chaudhuri: My submission was that if you substituted 'Rabindra Nath Thakur' in place of 'Rabindra Nath Tagore', then there would be no difficulty in it.

Maulana Azad : No. I am of the opinion that he is better known to the world by this very name. But I think there would be no objection to it if the word "Thakur' is written within brackets after the 'Tagore' wherever it occurs.

Prof. K.T. Shah: Madam, I am so sorry I was not able to catch your eye during the course of the general discussion, and urge points in the course of that discussion which now I will have to put forward in the form of amendments.

You will recognise, and I hope the House will agree that apart from indulging in general declamation, I at least have tried with some other friends to make my suggestions concrete in the form of amendments. It is, therefore, not that I want only to show off the defects or the shortcomings of this organization of the framework as it is put before you, but I rather desire to show ways and means, in a definite form in which this organization can be, and, in my opinion, ought to be improved.

The form and structure for this University is a kind of a shell, a mere mould, in which your trying to put the real thing that seems to me without life. Here is an instance in which, I think, it is important that the attention of the House and of the hon. Minister should be drawn to the desirability of associating the name of the original founder with the name of the University as a whole. I have put forward this amendment, and will, if permitted, speak on that at the time when it comes upon clause 1 and the preamble to that clause, and to the whole Bill. But, even at this stage, I should like to say that when you distinguish this University from all other universities of the country, by specifically calling it an institution of national importance, – not only do I not disagree with it, I fully endorse it, – I should like to emphasise that. Just because you make it a university of national importance and declare it formally to be so, it is of the utmost necessity that you should also see to it that somehow this University does stand out as unique and different from the other institutions of higher education that you have in this country.

I am afraid I must associate myself with the many other speakers who have time and again mentioned that by giving the form and structure of the kind that you have provided in this Bill, you are really not showing the objects, the ultimate aims that the great founder had in mind when he established this institution. I think it is proper that the mechanical shape, such as it has, should also embody, as far as it can, the spirit.

I would, therefore have liked to see this matter being referred to some Select Committee which would have thrashed out the whole question from all angles. After all, if you have waited so long, even after the publication of the report of the University Commission, if you have waited for so long as 30 years after the foundation of the institution, is it really very hard, is it really very difficult that we should not wait a little longer and properly consider this instrument of national importance, as we declare it to be, formed in a proper mould, in a very attractive and ornamental casket if you like, that may attract the attention of the whole world?

A previous speaker has said that after all, the great man who founded the institution has gone from our midst; and it would be now in the hands of perhaps relatively smaller men. For that reason, it is still more important that, if you insist upon this declaration statutorily, by a solemn act of this legislature, that this is a university of national importance, I urge, and urge with all the emphasis that I can command, that this is one of those amendments, which, along with others that I have ventured to submit, should be accepted, and every endeavour should be made to see that this deserves your claim, your own boast that this is a university of national importance apart from the many –I hope nobody will take offence at my descripion – departments of higher education which are so many mechanical factories producing out graduates or post-graduates, Doctors of law, Doctors of medicine, Doctors of literature, and so on.

I have tried to scrutinise the Bill in every clause, and sentence and of this proposal, and I am sorry to say that there is hardly a particular in which this can really claim to stand out as a university distinct from all others, unique in its own way, and therefore deserving to be called an institution of national importance, to which not only we in every corner of the country, but the whole world may look forward with some hope, as it were, for a regeneration of mankind, at any rate, as a spiritual refuge. There is nothing, for instance, in this University – again I will come to that when those amendments are taken up by – which even the students and teachers could be included in the body corporate that you create by your Act. You are careful, or careless, to leave that out even from a mere mention. A University without its teachers and without its students is not even a mere husk or a shell.

That this Bill should bring before us an organization which merely gives it a name and a form, or certain catch-words which are used in a university constitution is, to me, a matter of great regret. I trust that those in charge of this Bill will not think that the real purpose that they themselves have in view, with which we are all heartily associated, would be effectively served by undue haste in a matter of this character. The Maulana Sahib is going away, but he is also going to return. We have every hope, and I am certain that he will return after six or eight or twelve weeks. If this matter could be properly considered in every clause, every sub-clause and every letter and sentence of it, then, I think it would be worthy of the great name which we are seeking to commemorate, and the institution and the inspiration that we are trying to build up today. It is not in a sort of a patronising attitude, and I hope no one has that, with which we are giving this institution national importance. The institution has its own importance. We are only recognising it today. Let us not give our recognition in a very inadequate, insufficient and perhaps even in a misleading form.

Dr. Deshmukh: It is a vulgar shape.

Prof. K. T. Shah: Therefore, in so far as this is a mere repetition of the many other mechanical factories which you call Universities, but which in my humble opinion, are nothing else than departments of Government, I repeat, you are not showing it the importance that it deserves. I have, therefore, – apart from the general arguments that I have urged, – sought to place before the House an amendment of the form and structure that you seek to give to it, so that somehow, in some manner that we can devise, it would stand out as a differnt, distinct and really a unique, as also a national institution, in which there will be no room for provincialism there will be no room for sectarianism, and, may I say, there would not be even room for nationalism. It would be an universal institution for the whole of mankind, in which not only an Indian, be he a Bengalee, or a Gujarati, a Hindu or a Muslim, but every one in the world can take pride. Then only can we call it in this country an institution of "national importance". This is a suggestion, therefore, Madam, which I trust, the sponsor of the Bill will not turn down with contempt, but will at least give consideration even if he is not prepared to accept it at this moment.

Mri Chaiman: Amendment moved:

For clause 2, substitute the following:

> "*Declaration of Visva-Bharati as an institution of a national importance.* –The Rabindranath Tagore Visva-Bharati is and shall be recognised and maintained as an institution of national importance."

Pandit Thakur Das Bhargava (Punjab): I am in full agreement with the amendment moved by Prof. Shah. With the same purpose I had also given notice of one or two amendments which related to Clauses 1 and 2. There is no doubt that whatever homage we may pay to our revered Shri Rabindra Nath Tagore, we cannot do him full honour. He was not one of those persons who are born for a particular country, but he was one of those who are born for the whole world. The institution which is connected with his name is not a national institution, but that is an international institution. The Objects given in the Bill lay down that this institution is going to be established with the purpose of evolving something that may bring a synthesis of the East and West which the world needs so much today. No doubt in our hearts we may feel proud that this is our national institution; but in fact it is an international institution, for *Visva* means the whole world, not a nation. The present generation is familair with the name of Tagore and of *Visva-Bharati* and knows what work has been done there. But how would the coming generations not born in his time and unfamiliar with his name, know what *Visva-Bharati is?* Anybody may give any name to a thing belonging to him, for instance, a poor man may call his wife begum. But what would others think of it? The chords of our hearts that are touched at his name, the thoughts that come to our mind by his name, would not come into being without the mention of his name. If his name would not be there before the coming generations they will form various other impressions about it. But if his name also goes with this, then although posterity may forget the name of *Visva-Bharati*, it will remember the name of Shri Rabindra Nath Tagore and will cherish the ideals of which he was the spokesman and interpreter. Hence I submit that in order to perpetuate a thing, it is necessary to give it a proper name. You may take anything. We give good names to human beings so that they may acquire good qualities which those names denote. Its very purpose is defeated by not uniting his name with this institution. The coming generation will take it as an ordinary university. As a matter of fact, as Shri Shah said, I also wanted to speak in detail over this Bill. I find that the same Ordinaces, Regulations and Statutes are contained in this Bill also as are found in any University Act. So far as its constitution is concerned, it should have been a unique thing solely for itself and for which it could be said that whatever was there was not to be found elsewhere. But it has not got that spirit. I fear, for this reason, lest in the times to come the spirit which inspired the creation of this institution may not die. What has been put in the Bill will not help to evolve that spirit, and create that thing in the country which our revered Tagore wanted. Hence it is my submission that the name of our revered Tagore sould not be alienated from something with which he was so intimately connected. If his name also goes with it, the world would look to it with a different view. Hence I submit that so far as this amendment is concerned it would do no wrong. By this we would not be doing honour to him but this will bring honour to the University and to ourselves. If you will accept the name, it would be very effective and the thoughts that would come into the minds of the people at his name will increase the utility of the University.

Some of my friends still express the opinion to send the issue to a Select Committee. I also agree with it, I would invite the attention of Maulana Sahib towards this. Were I allowed to speak, I would also have spoken about it, but I feel that it should go to Select Committee. It is a noble conception of Maulana Sahib that it should be a singular thing, without a parallel. As such it must have been sent to a Select Committee. I would submit that even now, if it is not too late, it may be sent to a Select Committee, where its shortcoming may be removed. That would be a very desirable thing.

Mr. Chairman: Does the hon. Minister accept the amendment of Prof. K.T. Shah?

Maulana Azad: None can differ on his objective that his name and memory should be perpetuated. But we have to see whether this thing fits in the present context or not. I think that the dignified position of Tagore is above that. It would be a very cheap memorial to perpetuate his memory if we are to make this institution serve as a memorial to him.

Secondly it is an open secret that this institution is the creation of Shri Rabindra Nath Tagore. I do not think the people would forget him if his name is not associated with this institution. Anyhow I cannot accept this amendment.

Shri Kamath: What does hon. Education Minister say about the amendment of Pandit Thakur Das Bhargava?

Mr. Chairman: May I know what Mr. Kamath wants to say?

Shri Kamath: I was referring to the suggestion made by Pandit Thakur Das.

Mr. Chairman: But Pandit Thakur Das Bhargava has not moved his amendment.

Shri Kamath: I agree, but what about his suggestion?

Pandit Thakur Das Bhargava: But I have suggested to the hon. Minister that the Bill Select Committee to effect improvements.

Mr. Chairman: But we are now far ahead of that stage. Does the hon. Member press his amendment?

Prof. K.T. Shah: Yes, Madam.

Mr. Chairman: The question is :

For clause 2, substitute the following :

> "*Declaration of Visva-Bharati as an institution of national importance.*– The Rabindranath Tagore Visva-Bharati is and shall be recognised and maintained as an institution of national importance."

The motion was negatived.

Mr. Chairman: The question is:

"That clause 2 stand part of the Bill".

The motion was adopted.

Clause 2 was added to the Bill.

New Clause 2A

Prof. K.T. Shah: I beg to move:

After clause 2, add the following new clause:

> "2A. The Visva-Bharati shall be a unitary, residential and teaching university, providing instruction, training and guidance in research."

This is a description of the University which is implicit as it is claimed to have been in the mind of the author also. I am, therefore, only trying to bring it out and make it concrete in so many words, so that there will be no misunderstanding about it.

In this conncetion, as also in connection with the whole Bill, may I say, without the least desire to offend any body or his susceptibilities, that the Bill seems to have been drafted in a great hurry. Many essential and important matters have received scant attention, and not even copying seems to have been done correctly, not only in the transliteration of Sanskrit words, but also elsewhere.

However, my point is with reference to the kind of fear which the hon. Maulana Saheb was pleased to express that some day, perhaps, a situation may arise when the intervention of an outside authority like the Visitor may be necessary. I want to guard against any such occurrence as far as possible by a definite provision in the Act itself, whereby the nature and form of the University cannot be misunderstood. This institution has been, and must remain, a unitary institution. The power of affiliation given in a later clause would be out of place in an institution which claims to be a unitary institution. Anybody who has any experience of the working of universities in this country would realise the force of this argument. He would realise how the possibility of regional right to affiliate would militate against the spirit and function of a University of the type that Visva-Bharati claims to be. It is, therefore, important to emphasise even in the Act, recognising the University as a unitary University.

Secondly, it is a residential University, which also entails a number of other features, consequences and implications which I would try to bring out later on in connection with the other parts of the Bill. Though I am conscious that they will of course be rejected by the House, nevertheless I feel that I would have done my duty in drawing attention to these matters. This University cannot but be only a residential university in view of the peculiarity, the distinctive character and greatness of this institution, where the teacher and the student come much more into personal contact than in the mass-producing factories that go by the name of universities and colleges elsewhere, the residential character of this institution is of the utmost importance both to the teachers and the students. There is, therefore, nothing improper, nothing out of the way or inconsistent with the conception of this university, as embodied in this Bill, in insisting that it shall be a residential university and it is described as such in the Act itself.

Finally, that it is a teaching university......

An Hon. Member: Cheating university?

Prof. K. T. Shah: Not cheating but teaching! Here I need go no further than point out that it has been the nature of this institution ever since it was founded and this Act does not try to change it. There is, therefore, nothing wrong in recognising that which you yourself are doing, and by calling it by these three adjectives, that I would like to use in the new clause that I have suggested, we are not doing any violence whatsoever to either the letter or the spirit of your Bill. It is simply recognising the facts as you youself are presenting them, and, therefore, calling this institution a unitary, teaching and residential University.

And if it is a teaching university, it cannot be teaching only either in primary or in elementary subjects, and, therefore, I insist it must be a teaching University in the sense of instruction, if you like, but also in the sense of training and in the sense of guidance in research. The research that this University can and should do, in my opinion, will transcend the ordinary material spheres, in which alone we are inclined to consider research possible. The question now is to regard research in objective science, which are the most productive from the mammon-worshipper's point of view to be research proper. But here is a type of research, or at least a possibility of research, which will not yield dividends in terms of money; but which will certainly go a long way to reinforce your claim that this is an institution of national importance.

It is for such reasons that I am explaining every word in the clause that I have suggested. I would insist that research should have no less a place – research, whether by students or by teachers, whether by the executive authorities of the University or even by the general component governing body of the University, – it should be a very important part. It should be, therefore, included in the basic description of this institution. Hence the new additional sub-clause that I have suggested.

Mr. Chairman: Amendment moved:

After clause 2, add the following new clause:

> "2A. The Visva-Bharati shall be a unitary, residential and teaching university, providing instruction, training and guidance in research."

May I know whether the hon. Minister is going to accept the amendment?

Maulana Azad: No, I do not agree with it, I think it to be quite unnecessary.

Mr. Chairman: The question is:

After clause 2, add the following new clause:

> "2A. The Visva-Bharati shall be a unitary, residential and teaching university, providing instruction, training and guidance in research."

The motion was negatived.

Clause 3 – Definitions

Prof. K.T. Shah: I beg to move:

After part (d) of clause 3, insert the following new part:

> (dd) "College" means an institution, affiliated to, constituent of or recognised as such by the University, imparting instruction, giving training, or guiding research in any branch of knowledge and learning, Art or Science."

There is a later amendment also.

Shall I move that also?

Mr. Chairman: Yes.

Prof. K.T. Shah: I beg to move:

After part (f) of clause 3, insert the following new parts:

"(i) (ff) 'Deans' are presiding officers of Faculties; "

(ii) (ff) 'Faculties' means subjects, or groups of subjects for study or research, as provided by the Statutes by the University."

(iii) (fff) 'Government' means any Government established under the constitution in India, and may include a Municipal Corporation, a District Board, or any other local governing body or authority."

The next amendment of mine is No. 21. I beg to move:

After part (g) of clause 3, the following new part be added:

"(gl) 'students are members of the University residing and taking instruction or training or guidance in research in the University."

Mr. Chairman: Does Pandit Bhargava move his amendment?

Pandit Thakur Das Bhargava: No.

Mr. Chairman: Does Prof. Shah wish to speak on his amendments?

Prof. K.T. Shah: Yes, Madam. In these three amendments, I am trying to correct the omissions in which this Act seems to abound. The Act speaks more than once of "Colleges" without giving any definition of that very important term in the Definitions section.

I do not know whether the institution as such being a unitary teaching institution, really needs a separate and distinct organisation of the kind we generally associate with the term College. Nevertheless, because the Act itself does speak in a certain sense of the term Colleges, and there is no definition of that term in the Bill the chances are that needless misunderstanding may be created. Hence the necessity of introducing a clear definition of the term college. The framers of the Act have thought it necessary to put in a definition of the term Halls.

Mr. Chairman: Order, Please. I see quite a number of hon. Members speaking loudly, so that the hon. Member who is speaking is not properly heard.

Prof. K.T. Shah: It is not so necessary to be heard, because they all know that my amendments are going to be all negatived; and they have already made up their minds about the passing of the Bill. But if notwithstanding that, I speak, I do so only because I have an unfortunate sense of duty for drawing the attention of the House to some points, and placing it on the records of this house that these matters were drawn attention to, whether at the time my hon. friends discover their mistake I am alive or not.

The point I was making was that because the Act itself has used a clear definition of the term 'Bhawan' which is a sort of a secondary College, and which is outside the teaching institution, I do not see any reason or justification why we should omit the definition of the term College proper. Any institution which gives instruction or guidance in research should be specifically recognised in the Act.

The definition includes three words which are however to be taken with some reservation. I have, following the usual practice, included affiliated Colleges, constituent Colleges, and recognised Colleges. These words I have used advisedly, because constituent institutions are part and parcel, the integral, essential ingredients, so to say, of the University. Though they are included in the University, they are only particular aspects or particular shapes or particular forms through which the University activities occur.

The *Affiliated College*, and still more, the recognised College, is a different category of institution altogether. An affiliated College may or may not be within the territorial jurisdiction or area of the University. In case like the one we have before us though the territorial jurisdiction is defined and fixed, it is possible, — it is conceivable at any rate, —that institutions may be established, other than those now in existence, by some other bodies, or by some other individuals, which want to share in the spirit of this institution; without becoming part and parcel of the University as a whole in the form of constituent Colleges. I have, therefore, provided for the possibility of affiliation, hoping, however, that this power will not extend outside the territorial jurisdiction and that it would be confined to the territorial limits of the University; and that, therefore, any other institution seeking to establish a College in this part will do so only with a view to sharing the spirit of the University, and otherwise maintaining and conducting its affairs itself.

The third is a "recognised institution". Now a "recognised institution" may be outside the limit of the University itself; and yet the University may be empowered – as this University in a later clause is empowered – to recognise those bodies which are carrying on sympathetic activities or mutually complementary and supplementary activities. There is, for instance, many a field or research in which a single institution may not be able to cope with, or provide all the necessary material. For such case it may be quite necessary and quite desirable to establish a line of co-operation. The line of co-operation will, however, be feasible only if you have power to recognise work done in those institutions outside the University. Hence, by means of this definition, I try to include also recognised institutions within the scope of the University. They are certainly not an integral or essential part of a University that the constituent colleges may be. I repeat that it would not have been quite necessary to give this particular definition had the term "college" not been used elsewhere, in other parts of the Act. The idea is there, and it is necessary to give it a special definite form. That is my justification.

In regard to the definitions of "Deans" and "Faculties" they are not specifically mentioned or at least not clearly. But they are part and parcel of a University organisation almost everywhere in this country. Inasmuch as you have just copied the organisation of Universities in other forms in this country, it is but right an proper that you follow it to its logical conclusion, I presume, therefore that the power given by statute to the universities to set up facilities or to create bodies like 'Boards of Studies' would be utilised. And if you do utilise it, then it is necessary that you have some presiding authority. Hence the "Faculties" and "Deans" are, I think, complementary parts, the necessary corollaries of the establishment of the University that you have designed here.

Last of all comes the word "Government". That word may cause some misconception. I should like, therefore, to make that word clear also. Particularly in the matter of grants, it is possible that not only confusion may occur, but there may be some overlapping, some unnecessary clashing of interests which ought to be avoided.

I have, defined, Government, therefore, as widely as it is possible to do, including not merely the Central, but also the State, Governments. A power or discretion is also provided whereby semi-governmental bodies like municipal corporations, or district boards, or other statutory authorities like a port trust, let us say, or other universities, may also be included. Much of the work of the University, as is claimed here, may have to do with the local bodies. At any rate they may prove to be of great value in giving guidance and assistance in research matters; and if so, it is but right and proper that the University should be benefited and should be assisted by these bodies as well. The Central Government's assistance is clear, though not adequate, as stated in the aims and objects. It is a curious peculiarity of this legislation that such an important thing as the financial provision of the university is put up into a sort of an appendix at the tail end of the Bill in a memorandum, and is not included integrally, specifically, in the body of the Bill as it ought to have been, in my opinion. Such as it is, however, the Central Government is prepared to make grants, and the State Governments, for example, West Bengal, may, and I hope, will make grants. Other bodies may be interested in making grants for specific work or taking the assistance of the University. I therefore, think it necessary to have a clear definition in the definition clause of the term "Government". I am therefore submitting that these definitions are important and must be included in the definition clause.

Mr. Chairman: Amendments moved:

After part (d) of clause 3, insert the following new part:

"(dd) 'College' means an institution, affiliated to constituent of or recognised as such by the University, imparting instruction, giving training, or guiding research in any branch of knowledge and learning, Art or Science;".

After part (f) of clause 3, insert the following new parts:

"(i) (ff) 'Deans' are presiding officers of Faculties;

(ii) (fff) 'Faculties' mean subjects, or groups of subjects, for study or research, as provided by the Statutes by the University;

(iii) (ffff) 'Government' means any Government established under the constitution in India, and may include a municipal corporation, a district board or any other local governing body or authority;".

After part (g) of clause 3, add the followin new part:

"(gl) 'students' are members of the University residing and taking instruction or training or guidance in research in the University."

Maulana Azad: I tried a good deal and heard the entire speech of my friend, but I could not agree with this point that 'Government' 'Student', 'Dean', 'college' and other such words need be defined.

Mr. Chairman: May I know whether the hon. Member is pressing his amendments?

Prof. K.T. Shah: Yes.

Mr. Chairman: The question is:

After part (d) of clause 3, insert the following new part:

"(dd) 'College' means an institution, affiliated to, constitutent of or recognised as such by the University, imparting instruction, giving training, or guiding research in any branch of knowledge and learning, Art or Science;".

The motion was negatived.

Mr. Chairman: The question is

After part (f) of clause 3, insert the following new parts:

"(i) (ff) 'Deans' are presiding officers of Faculties;

(ii) (fff) 'Faculties' mean subjects, or groups of subjects, for study or research, as provided by the Statutes by the University;

(iii) (ffff) 'Government' means any Government established under the Constitution in India, and may include a Municipal Corporation, a District Board or any other local governing body or authority;".

The motion was negatived.

Mr. Chairman: The quesion is:

After part (g) of clause 3, add the following new part;

"(gl) 'students' are members of the University residing and taking instruction or training or guidance in research in the University;".

The motion was negatived.

Mr. Chariman: The question is:

"That clause 3 stand part of the Bill."

The motion was adopted.

Clause 3 was added to the Bill.

Clasue 4 – Incorporation

Prof. K.T. Shah: I beg to move.

In clause 4, after the word "membership" insert the words "as well as the teachers and the students in the University."

That is the amended clause would read as follows:

"The first *Acharya* (Chancellor) and *Upacharya* (Vice-Chancellor) of the University who shall be the persons appointed in this behalf by the Central Government by notification in the Official Gazette, and the first members of the *Samsad* (Court), and all persons, who may hereafter become or be appointed as such officers or members, so long as they continue to hold such office or membership, as well as the teachers and students in the University, are hereby constituted a body corporate by the name of Visva-Bharati, and shall have perpetual succession and a common seal, and shall sue and be sued by that name."

Here also I think it is a question of principle so far at any rate as my view of this Bill is concerned. I consider that a University without Teachers and Students is no University at all. You may recognise all the officers as you have done, and their successors as you have done. But they will be all empty and without any avail so long as the Teachers who make the University, who give it its tone, its spirit, and the students who take the benefit of it, and who are, so to say, the future torch-bearers, are omitted. I think if your idea of the University is – as I hope it was the idea that the great poet had in mind – to perpetuate the real spirit of Visva-Bharati, if you really want the University not to be a mere official appendage of so many nominees of Government, if you want that the University should really be made of the actual workers and beneficiaries of the University, namely its teachers and students, you ought to have no logical reasons to object to my amendment – you may have every other excuse. I have no objection But if you really abide–as you claim to – by the spirit of this institution, then I submit that there is no alternative but to accept this, namely to include all the teachers and the students in the body corporate of the University, who will form the soul, the limbs, so to say of the University.

Maulana Azad: No, I do not agree with it.

Mr. Chairman: The question is:

In clause 4, after the word "membership" insert the words "as well as the teachers and students in the University."

The motion was negatived.

Mr. Chairman: The question is :

"That clause 4 stand part of the Bill."

The motion was adopted.

The House then adjourned till Half Past Eight of the Clock on Tuesday, the 1st May, 1951.

Document No. 41

FURTHER DISCUSSION ON VISHVA-BHARATI BILL, DATED 1-5-1951

Mr. Speaker: The House will now proceed with the further consideration of the Visva-Bharati Bill. Clauses 2 to 4 were disposed of yesterday; we have not to take up clause 5. But before that, I find that there is an amendment by the hon. Member Dr. Punjabrao Deshmukh to a new clause 4A.

Dr. Deshmukh (Madhya Pradesh): Sir, I have this morning given notice of a similar amendment to clause 6 (k); and the hon. Minister is prepared to accept it.

Mr. Speaker: So the request comes to this that instead of moving this amendment at this stage as clause 4A, he wants to move it as clause 6 (k) and as he has tabled a new amendment he wishes the period of notice to be waived. I will allow him to move it; but he will please remind me when we come to clause 6 (k).

Clause 5 – Effect of incorporation etc.

Mr. Speaker: In regard to the amendment of Prof. K.T. Shah, I understand that Government are agreeable to accept his amendment in a different form. Does the hon. Member wish to move his amendment in that case?

Prof. K.T. Shah (Bihar): If the substance is there, I do not care to move mine.

Mr. Speaker: At any rate, let him see Government's amendment, and if it is acceptable to him, he may move it in the amended form.

Prof. K.T. Shah: In the government's amendment, as far as I can see, the crucial point, namely, that the terms and conditions of service cannot be varied to the prejudice of an employee during the period of his employments, does not seem to have been covered correctly.

Mr. Speaker: Instead of discussing the merits of the relative amendments, he may move his own and the Government may accept or reject it.

Prof. K.T. Shah: I beg to move :

After the first proviso to Clause 5, add new proviso:

"Provided further that during the currency of a contract of service and specifically made for a definite term, the terms and conditions of such a contract shall not be varied to the prejudice of such a contract employee without his consent."

The amendment, I think, hardly needs any special commendation from me. It is a simple principle which has been even embodied in our Constitution. I hope that the hon. Minister will accept at least the principle of my amendment, and give effect to it as he thinks proper.

Mr. Speaker: Amendment moved;

After the first proviso to clause 5, add new proviso:

"Provided further that during the currency of a contract of service and specifically made for a definite term, the terms and conditions of such a contract shall not be varied to the prejudice of such a contract employee without his consent."

Maulana Azad: So I have agreed to it in principle; but no doubt there is some change in its wordings.

Mr. Speaker: What is the position now? Are Government anxious to have this clause amended as proposed by them?

Maulana Azad: Yes.

Prof. K.T. Shah; The amendment that is given to me reads:

In the proviso to clause 5, for "Provided that if the University decides to alter the terms and conditions of service of any such employee" substitute "Provided that it shall be lawful for the University to have the terms and conditions of service of any employee not employed for a specified period altered, and where it decides to do so."

This does not include the object I have in view. The proviso means that if a party is not employed for a specified period, then it is lawful for the University to alter his terms; if he is employed for a specified period, then they may alter by payment of six months' salary, which I suggest is not in accordance with the constitutional principle of not varying a contract within the currency of the contract to the prejudice of the employee.

Maulana Azad: I can accept it in the form in which it has been presented now. But I am unable to accept it in the form in which you have presented it.

Mr. Speaker: I am just trying to see what is the difference between the two amendments. It appears that the amendment as suggested by the hon. Minister improve the position of the employees who are taken for a specified period. Now, the hon. Member will see that the proviso stands like this at present:

> " Provided that if the University decides to alter the terms and conditions of service of any such employee, a fresh contract shall be executed for the purpose ..."

Now this will cover both cases: cases of contract for a specified period, or cases where there is only a contract without mentioning the period. In both cases the University will be entitled to proceed under this clause as it stands. Now, in the proposed amendment by Government the proviso is:

> "Provided that it shall be lawful for the University to have the terms and conditions of service of any employee not employed for a specified period altered, and where it decides to do so..."

it follows that a fresh contract shall come in.

Therefore the class of contracts entered into for a specified period is altogether excluded from revision. That is, I think the effect of the amendment.

Pandit Thakur Das Bhargava (Punjab): The purpose of the two amendments is quite different. One refers to a set of circumstances in which a specific period of an employee's contract is there. The other relates to a set of circumstances in which the period is not specific, as in the amendment of the Government. So the two things are quite different.

Mr. Speaker: I do not mean to say that the two are not different. I am merely trying to see for myself as to how far the amendment is an improvement in the one case and is not so in the other. Prof. Shah's amendment says that "during the currency of a contract of service and specifically made for a definite term, the terms and conditions of such a contract shall not be varied to the prejudice of such a contract employee without his consent." So the protection that Prof. Shah's amendment gives is in respect of employees having contracts for a definite term, and the protection does not extend to other employees who are not there for a definite period. If the Government amendment is looked at, it practically means the same thing: "Provided that it shall be lawful for the University to have the terms and conditions of service of any employee, not employed for a specified period altered". Therefore, negatively so far as employees employed for a specific period are concerned, they are not to be touched.

Pandit Thakur Das Bhargava: Therefore, I submit the two are quite different.

Mr. Speaker: And where it decides to do so, a fresh contract can be made. Let us first look at the proviso as it stands and let us see what it really tried to enact. The existing proviso says, "Provided that if the University decides to alter the terms and conditions of service of any such employee, a fresh contract shall be executed" and then the other things follow. Now, the question is, is it necessary to give any protection to an employee? for the purpose of giving protection to contract employees, the proviso as it stands makes no distinction whatever between ordinary contract employees and employees under contracts for a specific period. The proviso, as it stands before the House, treats both kinds of employees on the same basis.

Prof. K.T. Shah: As it stands.

Mr. Speaker: Yes, I am trying to clarify the position as it stands, because it is only in that light, that we can understand the implications and meanings of the amendments. Now, Prof. Shah's amendment says "Provided further that during the currency of a contract of service and specifically made for a definite term, the terms and conditions of such a contract shall not be varied. etc." So his proviso limits the protection that he wants to give, only to employees whose contract is for a specific period. In respect of contracts which are not for a specified period, he is not concerned.

Let us examine as to whether the Government amendment effects that or something else. If it effects that, I am sure Prof. Shah will have no objection to accept that. The Government amendment is to replace some words by other words, and the proviso as amended by the government amendment would read thus:

> "Provided that it shall be lawful for the University to have the terms and conditions of service of any employee, not employed for a specified period, altered and where it decides to do so etc."

Now, clearly, this amendment does not touch, so far as alternations of conditions are concerned, those who are employed for a specific period. The important words in the amendment are "not employed for a specified period." So it gives the liberty to the University to alter the terms and condition of contract employees who are not employed for a specific period. That is how I understand this amendment. Now it is for hon. Members to consider, but I see practically no difference between the two. The hon. Minister will please correct me if I am interpreting the thing wrongly.

Pandit Thakur Das Bhargava: The two amendments apply to alternative conditions. The Government amendment says if the employment is not for a specified period, it applies only then, whereas Prof. Shah's amendment applies only when the employment is for a specified period. Thus they deal with alternative things, not with the same thing.

Mr. Speaker: I am unable to follow the distinction. My only point is that the Government are not trying to touch at all, as Prof. Shah wants to, employees under a specified term of contract. That is the effect of the amendment. It is my own view of the matter. It is for hon. Members to consider.

Prof. K.T. Shah: The right of the University to alter the terms and conditions of service of all employees, whether employed either under general regulations or even by contract generally, is not questioned by me. What I am questioning, and what the amendment of the Government is not providing for, is the right of an employee of the University employed on a special contract for a specific term not to have the terms and conditions varied to his prejudice without his consent. If he consents, then, of course, the question would not arise. But if he does not consent, the Government amendment will simply give him six months' salary, whether or not he is agreeable.

Mr. Speaker: If that is the term of the contract, certainly the University is entitled to put an end to it.

Prof. K.T. Shah: But the employee may be willing to continue.

Pandit Thakur Das Bhargava: Clause 5(iii) deals with such cases where the terms of employment are not going to be changed. According to the Government amendment they are going to be changed if it is not for a specified period.

Dr. S.P. Mookerjee (West Bengal): May I say a few words on the merits of the clause? As you, Sir, explained, the clause as drafted authorises the University to offer new terms of service to all its employees and, if the employees are not willing to accept them, to give them compensation of salary for a period of six months. Now, Prof. Shah wants that the cases of those who enjoy contract service for a fixed period should be protected and that, if their conditions of service are altered to their prejudice, that can be done only with their consent. The amendment as now proposed by the hon. Minister from one point of view is not quite appropriate, because it says that the services of those who hold their period of service for a certain number of years cannot be touched at all. It is not a question of touching them to their prejudice. Even if you want to *improve* their conditions of service, from the way in which the amendment has been drafted the University will be prevented from doing so. That obviously is not the intention of the Hon. Minister. But in the way in which it has been drafted, the result might be that. I personally do not see why ....

Maulana Azad: It has been realized that there would be no need for any change or modification wherever such conditions prevail.

Mr. Speaker: It involves some general points of contracts and hon. Members will see that it refers to all services and even though the expression used is "person employed", it mostly deals with the academic staff. Then we have to see the general law of contracts. These are contracts which are not specifically enforceable, and therefore, if a University does not agree to a revised term—it is not that it is barred from agreeing, that is how I look upon it – the concerned staff or the particular professor may go out; but if the University thinks that he is well worthwhile, it will be entitled to re-employ him. Will that not be the position? It is not that the University cannot revise, there is no point in that.

Dr. S.P. Mookerjee: It would be much simpler to decide to the main question at issue. Is it the intention of the Government that the University should be permitted to alter the terms and condition of service of any employee to their prejudice? Usually that is not the case. Take the large number of employees under Government after Independence. The general position was accepted that without the consent of any employee the terms and conditions of none of them would be prejudicially altered. Why not accept that principle that in offering revised terms and conditions of service to any employee, the terms and conditions will not be altered to the prejudice of any employee. A simple amendment like that will meet everybody's case. In fact, knowing as I do the affairs of Visva-Bharati, the salaries and the terms and conditions which are at present open to its employees are not extravagant or as favourable as under Government service. So, it will be nobody's intention to alter them prejudicially to the interests of the employees. If there is any chance, their prospects would be further improved. So we are more or less having an academic discussion. I suggest that we may leave the clause as it is. It amply protects the interests of the employees. In one particular case a particular professor gets six months and then goes away, buf if you want to make it clear, I suppose you do not want that the University should be entitled to alter the terms and conditions prejudicially to the interests of any employee. I suggest that you may make that clear.

Maulana Azad: There is no need for it. But as you have suggested I would certainly draw your attention to the fact that the form in which it exists is enough, and there is no apprehension like that.

Mr. Speaker: Then I put the amendment to vote. I take it that Government do not propose any amendments.

The question is:

After the first Proviso to clause 5, add new Proviso:

> "Provided further that during the currency of a contract of service and specifically made for the a definite term, the terms and conditions of such a contract shall not be varied to the prejudice of such a contract employee without his consent."

The motion was negatived.

Prof. K.T. Shah: Are government not moving their amendment?

Mr. Speaker: No.

"That clause 5 stand part of the Bill."

The motion was adpoted.

Mr. Speaker: Prof. Shah has got to move an amendment inserting new clause 5A.

Prof. K.T. Shah: I beg to move:

After Clause 5, insert new clause:

"5A. *Objects of the University*–

The objects of the ....

Dr. Deshmukh: May I point out to my hon. friend that a very similar amendment is going to be moved to clause 6. It makes no difference where it comes exactly and that amendment is going to be accepted by Government. If any observations are to be offered by Prof. Shah, he can make them then. I may tell him that the proposal is to embody all the objects as embodied in the Constitution of Visva-Bharati by Dr. Rabindranath Tagore himself. I think that will probably incline my hon. friend not to move his amendment at this stage. If he is not satisfied with the objects as are put in, then he might move his amendment.

Mr. Speaker: Which amendment is he referring to?

Dr. Deshmukh: I gave notice of that amendment this morning. Clause 4A is the same as proposed by the addition of clause 5A. I think the hon. member has got a copy of it. It is exactly the same as given in the Visva-Bharati and the author is Dr. Rabindranath Tagore himself.

Prof. K.T. Shah: I have not read the amendment properly but if this is drawn up by Guru Dev himself and is going to be accepted by Government, I do not presume to be much wiser than him and I therefore do not move my amendment.

Mr. Speaker: I think it is word for word the same.

Dr. Deshmukh: Exactly.

Mr. Speaker: The hon. Member will see that the amendment originally tabled is about the insertion of a new clause 4A and is the same as his amendment which he proposes as a new clause 5A. Is he satisfied that both are identical?

Prof. K.T. Shah: I find that the last item (d) in my amendment is similar and therefore I will not press it any further.

Mr. Speaker: It is going to come as amendment to caluse 6 (k). So then he is not moving clause 5A.

Prof. K.T. Shah: I agree.

Clause 6 — Powers of the University

Mr. Speaker: Then we come to Prof. Shah's amendment No. 29 in the list.

Prof. K.T. Shah: I have several amendments on this clause. It would save the time of the House if you permit me to take them all together and speak on them generally and not moving those which are not necessary and so on.

Mr. Speaker: Will he kindly give me the numbers?

Prof. K.T. Shah: They are Nos. 29, 36, 37, 40, 42, 43, 45, 46, 47, 48, 49.

Mr. Speker: Amendments moved:

(1) In the marginal heading of clause 6 after "Powers" insert "and Duties."

(2) In part (b) of clausee 6,–

  (i) after "to" where it occurs for the first time, insert "establish and"; and

  (ii) omit all the words after "Bhavans (halls)" where it occurs for the second time.

(3) In part (c) of clause 6, omit "affiliate."

(4) In part (e) of clause 6, after "industries" insert:

"help in the spread of elementary education and adult literacy particularly amongst scheduled tribes and backward classes or areas."

(5) In part (f) of clause 6, after "to" where it occurs for the first time, insert:

"organise periodical and public tests of attainment or proficiency of students, whether by examinations or otherwise."

(6) In part (f) of clause 6, omit "hold examinations and"

(7) In part (h) of clause 6, —

(i) after "Statutes" insert "consider, adopt or reject, but not amend"; and

(ii) after "Ordinances or" insert "consider and adopt or reject but not amend".

(8) In part (i) of clause 6, —

(i) after "receive" where it occurs for the first time, insert "and accept";

(ii) after "donations" where it occurs for the first time, insert "and endowments";

(iii) after "benefactions" where it occurs for the first time, insert "or grants"; and

(iv) after "properties" insert :

"on trust or otherwise, for any object not inconsistent with the objects of the University."

(9) In part (j) of clause 6, for "to deal with" substitute "hold, administer and deal with or dispose of".

(10) After part (j) of clause 6, insert

(i) "(jj) to affiliate, recognise or aid any college, school or other educational institution, in any part of the country outside the territorial limits of the University, subject to such procedure as may be prescribed by Statute;"

(ii) "(jjj) to make provision for the residence, physical training, moral welfare, and discipline, conduct and behaviour of the students in the University;"

(11) After part (j) of claue 6, insert:

"(jj) to suggest, whenever so found necessary and recommended to the Samsad by the Karma Samiti of the University and adopted by the Samsad, amendments to this Act which are calculated more effectively to promote the objects of the university."

Prof. K. T. Shah: I will be very brief on this matter. A good many of these amendments are amendments rather of form, or verbal changes, than basic principles.

The principle, however, that I am trying to emphasise, for instance, by my first amendment in this list, No. 29, is to add "duties" to powers, with a view just to empahsise that there should be no absolute power, that power, if it is absolute, is corrupting, and that, therefore, powers must be associated with duties.

It is one of the misfortunes of this age that we are all anxious to insist more and more upon "rights" than upon obligations, powers than duties. We are, therefore, apt to overlook our responsibilities in the desire only to grab power. I would therefore say that in a body like this University, it is of the utmost importance that this emphasis should be laid, namely, on responsibilities at least co-equal with powers if not even more. For, it has a constitutional responsibility, it would be in a much better position to inculcate that sense of responsibility, and that sense of civic responsibility which it is the function of the University to implant in the growing mind. I therefore, commend that particular amendment to the House.

Next, amendments Nos. 36 and 37 are relatively minor amendments, and I do not propose to take the time of the House on them. I only seek by them to remove the power of "recognising" or "affiliating" colleges outside the jurisdiction and halls from this clause, but which I give in a separate amendment later on, with a view to maintain the national character of this institution. I give that with certain safeguards and for certain reasons so that the national character of the institution is in no way upset.

The next amendment No. 40 is really intended to coordinate the entire system of education, from the basic or primary stage right up to the post-graduate or research stage. As such, the University would be a single entity in my conception, and not merely truncated as it were the top layer for only the uppermost purpose. I agree that that also is a matter of outlook rather than of any vital importance. If you think that a stage demarcated in this manner is important, and the University should not be burdened with the primary and other stages of education. I would particularly not insist upon that. I have, however, explained my objective in putting that here.

The next amendment is a little more important in the sense that it deals with a fundamental principle. We are inclined to have an excessive weight attached to examinations, which are merely mechanical arrangements for testing the attainment or proficiency of the pupils. I am suggesting, however, periodical tests, besides examinations, which may be other than the mechanical tests which our universities have so far followed. They are tests more of the ability to reproduce a dead-and-gone knowledge, so to say, by way of answers to set printed questions than any original expression of the alumnus himself. Accordingly, I feel that it would be much better if a provision is inserted in the Bill, in this clause dealing with the powers of the University, to permit the University to apply other than ordinary examination tests, such as we are familiar with, and such as have been condemned as unreliable and hardly at all correct in the estimate they give of the persons who are certified as a result of these examinations to obtain certain degress or diplomas. This is, therefore a little more important matter with me than the others which I have just now mentioned.

The next amendment is a mere verbal change rather than involving any question of principle, to which therefore, I will not refer in detail.

In the distinction that I have made regarding statutes, ordinances and regulations, a certain matter of principle is involved in connection with the powers of the various coordinate bodies, statutory themselves, namely, the Karma Samiti (Executive Council), Samsad – the court or senate as we call in other Universities – and Siksha Samiti (Academic Council). These are different bodies making their regulations under different styles. They must each have a degree of autonomy and effectiveness each in itself.

There are certain powers, reserved in the other Universities Acts, for the supreme governing body the Samsad, to consider the ordinance as well as regulations of the two other bodies. They cannot be amended, but they could be considered and rejected, or if you like, referred back for recosideration. They cannot be amended on the spot, apparently for the reason that the considerations which weigh with these two bodies for preparing them in that particular form are not always properly understood by the thrid body, namely, the Court. They are consequently given the power to consider, but not to amend. They can reject or accept.

Similarly, with regard to regulations, I trust that this distinction between the three coordinate bodies of the University, namely the Court or Samsad, the Karma Samiti and Siksha Samiti, will be appreciated and the suggestion implicit in my amendment would be accepted.

The other amendments in regard to receipt and acknowledgment of donations, endowments, and so on, I would not like to stress, because they are relatively of a verbal character or of minor effect.

The one amendment which, however, is most important in my opinion, is amendment No. 49. But, before that, I would deal with No. 48 which tries to give the power to recognise institutions, whether within the territorial limits of the university or outside, for the purpose of coordinating, co-operating in research, or for the purpose of maintaining the national character of this institution. The power which I have by an amendment removed in the earlier general clause, I am specifically giving under certain conditions which would be in consonance with the general character of the institution as devised in this Bill, and I hope that it would also be acceptable.

The one amendment to which I attach the greatest importance is the last one in this series, namely, No. 49. That is:

After part (i) of clause 6, insert:

> "(ii) to suggest, whenever so found necessary and recommended to the Samsad by the Karma Samiti of the University and adopted by the Samsad, amendments to this Act which are calculated more effectively to promote the objects of the University."

I shall tell you why I insist upon this particularly. In the first place, it is necessary that the University should have a certain autonomy in making suggestions for its own reform. It is common practice everywhere that whenever a measure of this character, or an amending Bill is brought, even in a provinical or state legislature for the reconstitution or reform of an existing University organisation, or its distribution or division, or creation of new Universities, the old, existing University has the right to review, crticise, and suggest improvements in the Bill as proposed by the local legislature. I am, therefore, giving a similar right to this institution, not merely to consider, and, on its own initiative, propose changes which it considers necessary as a result of the experience gained, but also to consider those that may be proposed to the Government, in regard to its constitution.

It is, I believe, admitted by all, without any disrespect to the draftsmen of this Bill, that this Bill has been so hurriedly and clumsily drafted, that there are many places in this Bill – I am sorry I have not been myself able to complete my scrutiny of all the clauses – which need drastic improvements, at least so far as the language is concerned. And rather than move the machinery of the whole government, or the whole legislature to make those necessary changes afterwards, by this amendment I am suggesting the principle of autonomy in the university, that is to say, its own right ot suggest – the necessary amendments which by experience it is found unavoidable and indispensable for the more effective working of the university machinery.

The procedure by which this can be done is also laid down, namely, that the suggestions for reform and for improvement have to come from the Karma Samiti or the Executive Council which has obvioulsy greater experience of both the administrative and the academic sides. If it is found necessary to propose changes, they are submitted, first to the Samsad or the Court, which is the supreme authority and the spokesman, so to say, of the University and, in my opinion Parliament cannot recognise any other than the Court of the University to speak on behalf of the University.

These amendments or suggestions for improvement placed before the Samsad must be considered by the Samsad, and, if adopted, and in so far as they are adopted, with whatever modifications they think proper, those amendments should be suggested to the Government for being given effect to by amendments of the existing legislation. I think there ought to be no objection to this amendment being accepted, because it does nothing more than recognise the autonomy of the University and only permits the University from its own experience to suggest improvements which after experience it thinks necessary in its constitution and should be given effect to. It does not take away the power of Parliament. If there are larger principles involved which the University authorities have not taken into consideration, of course, Parliament is at liberty to negative or modify the suggestions of the University. But in so far as these amendments are initiated by the University, I think this is a healthy principle and should be accepted.

Mr. Speaker: May I know the reactions of the hon. Minister?

Maulana Azad: Sir, I do not want to go into details. But the proposals which have been submitted by my friend cannot be accepted. The amendments go against the very principle on which the Bill has been framed. These amendments aim at interfering in the method of teaching and the mode of examination of the institution. They go into the question whether it would affiliate any outside institution or not. We have left all these things to the institution and do not want to interfere in it. We have taken only those very things which are essential to take at the time of establishing an university. So I am unable to accept all these amendments.

Dr. S.P. Mookerjee: On the merits of the amendments proposed by Prof. Shah, I would say that perhaps it would be undesirable to go into minute details in the Bill itself. Clause 6 (k) as it stands already says :

> to do all such things as may be incidental or conducive to the attainment of the object of the University or any of them."

And many of the matters which Prof. Shah has raised will obviously come under this sub-clasue (k).

I would like to raise one or two points with regard to clause 6. First of all, I would like to have a clarification as regards the exact meaning and significance of sub-clause (c) and also what exactly it means. It is stated:

> " The University shall exercise the following powers and perform the following duties, namely :
>
> (c) to organise, establish, affiliate, carry on and maintain or dissolve, disaffiliate or give up new branches or associated institutions having objects similar to those of the University".

We speak of "new branches" but new branches of what? Does it mean new branches of knowledge or new branches of the University? And what is meant by "associated institutions"? If they are institutions similar to Visva-Bharati and which obviously are not under the control of Visva-Bharati, you cannot dissolve them or maintain them. So some clarification as to what exactly is meant in sub-clause (c) is necessary.

Maulana Azad: It is possible that new branches may be opened after some time. Its door has been kept open and not closed.

Dr. S.P. Mookerjee: If they are associated institutions which are under somebody else's control, you cannot dissolve them. Perhaps this sub-clause requires some re-drafting.

There is one rather important principle – and I am sorry I have not given notice of an amendment in this respect – to which I would like to refer. It relates to clause 6(b) where the University is given power to maintain colleges and Bhavans or halls or recognise colleges and Bhavans. But what exactly will be the position of the schools at Santiniketan? This Bill obviously covers the cases of colleges which means institutions after the matriculation stage. According to the Secondary Education Bill which has been passed in West Bengal will come under the control of the Board. Then what happens to the schools situated in Santiniketan? I am definitely of the view that this Bill will never succeed and Visva-Bharati will never succeed unless you allow Visva-Bharati to maintain its own schools right from the kindergarten stage. There is a new type of secondary education which has been imparted at Santiniketan which in fact, was a special gift of Rabindranath Tagore. That is how Santiniketan's activities started. Unless the child is taken up at the very initial stage it will be impossible to maintain Visva-Bharati at the proper standard. We cannot do that if we allow the University control only over the colleges. I know the Education Minister's intention is all right. He wants Visva-Bharati to prosper according to the ideals of its founder. If that is his intention and the intention of Parliament and of the whole country, I suggest Government might have a small amendment and add "schools" also so that the position may be clear beyond any doubt whatsoever.

Maulana Azad: College and Bhavan are there. You want that 'school' should be added to it.

Dr. S.P. Mookerjee: Yes, we may add the word "schools" after the words "to maintain" in clause 6(b).

If you have schools under the Secondary Education Board following different curricula and different syllabi and adopting different types of examinations, then Visva-Bharati will never prosper. You must trust the University to admit students right from the child stage up to the highest stage. Then you can build up one organic whole according to the ideals which pervaded the establishment of this institution. I would, therefore, ask the Education Minister to accept this suggestion of mine.

Maulana Azad: This Bill has been prepared in consultation with the Visva-Bharati authorities and they did not lay any emphasis on schools. But I know that education of school standard is also being given there and I have no objection if word 'school' is added to it.

Dr. Deshmukh: I would like to say a few words on this suggestion made by Dr. Mookerjee. This change suggested is very necessary and desirable not only from the point of view of existing schools in Santiniketan but also those which the University will recognise and which it would thus be legally entitled to maintain. Schools will include certain other institutions also such as a school of economics and such like things. We know that certain authorities and Universities prefer to call them schools. These also will be covered if we have the word "schools" added on. There is much to be said in favour of this amendment that has been suggested.

Mr. Speaker: Dr. Mookerjee may now formally move the amendment.

Dr. S.P. Mookerjee: I beg to move:

In part (b) of clause 6 after "to maintain" insert "schools".

Pandit Maitra (West Bengal): And the word "schools" will also cover the institutions referred to by Dr. Deshmukh.

Dr. S.P. Mookerjee: That will be a "faculty".

Maulana Azad: The meaning of "School" would be taken as such.

Mr. Speaker: Amendment moved:

In part (b) of clause 6, after "to maintain" insert "schools".

Shri Barman (West Bengal): The point is that otherwise the schools will come under the University of Calcutta. Here we are making a provision that the schools within the Visva-Bharati will be under the University of Visva-Bharati. But the State Legislature wants that all the schools within the Province will come under the Calcutta University whereas here you are making another provision. Will not the two provisions of the State and the Centre clash?

Mr. Speaker: The point is clear, to my mind at least. This is only an enabling or authorising provision. It vests the University with the authority to start schools, if it likes, and the University can give recognition to it. The State will not feel itself concerned unless the University goes to the State for getting the recognition of their schools.

Dr. Deshmukh: It excludes the jurisdiction both of the Calcutta University as well as the State Government.

Mr. Speaker: I do not know whether jurisdiction is excluded in the sense that the University in future will not have the right to approach the State or the Calcutta University. This is an enabling provision and the University may cater to education as best as it likes.

Mr. Speaker: The question is:

In part (b) of clause 6 after "to maintain insert " schools".

The motion was adopted.

Shri Jhunjhunwala: The word "schools" should also be inserted after the word "recognise" in conformity with the insertion of the word "schools" after the words "to maintain".

Dr. S.P. Mookerjee: I agree with him, Sir. I beg to move:

In part (b) of clause 6, after "or-recognise" insert "schools".

Mr. Speaker: The question is :

In part (b) of clause 6, after "or recognise" insert "schools".

The motion was adopted.

Mr. Speaker: I have not yet put to the House the amendments of Prof. K.T. Shah. In between, this discussion came and as the amendments were agreed to on all hands I thought I might dispose of them. Unless anybody wants to speak on the amendments, I shall put them immediately to the House. (*Interruption*) I am not disposing of all the amendments to clause 6. I am only taking up the amendments moved by Prof. Shah. They are Nos. 29, 36, 37, 40, 42, 43, 45, 46, 47, 48 and 49. Of these amendments. No. 29 is, I think, unnecessary, because we are not treating marginal headings as part of the clause. They are left to the draftsman. I have not made it a practice of including them as amendments and putting them to the House. The other amendments are before the House to vote upon.

Shri Kamath (Madhya Pradesh) : All of them together, Sir?

Mr. Speaker: They were all moved together, they are correlated and discussed together. .....

Shri Kamath: It would be a new procedure.

Mr. Speaker: It is not a new procedure. I allowed them to be moved together. But if the hon. Member wants I have no objection to putting them separately: it would mean more time.

Maulana Azad: He has himself moved them together.

Shri Kamath: That is quite right, but if he has to give vote only on one then?

Mr. Speaker: The question is:

(2) In part (b) of clause 6,–

(i) After "to" where it occurs for the first time, insert "establish and"; and

(ii) omit all the words after "Bhavans (halls)" where it occurs for the second time.

The motion was negatived.

Mr. Speaker: The question is:

(3) In part (c) of clause 6, omit "affiliate".

The motion was negatived.

Mr. Speaker : The question is :

(4) In part (e) of clause 6, after "industries" insert:

"help in the spread of elementary education and adult literacy particularly amongst scheduled tribes and backward classes or areas".

The motion was negatived.

Mr. Speaker: The question is:

(5) In part (f) of clause 6, after "to" where it occurs for the first time, insert:

"organise periodical and public tests of attainment or proficiency of students whether by examinations or otherwise".

The motion was negatived.

Mr. Speaker: The question is:

(6) In part (f) of clause 6, omit "hold examinations and".

The motion was negatived.

Mr. Speaker: The question is:

(7) In part (h) of clause 6, –

(i) after "Statutes" insert "consider, adopt or reject, but not amend", and

(ii) after "Ordinances or" insert "consider and adopt or reject but not amend".

The motion was negatived.

Mr. Speaker : The question is:

(8) In part (i) of clause 6, –

(i) after "receive" where it occurs for the first time, insert "and accept",

(ii) after "donations" where it occurs for the first time, insert "and endowments",

(iii) after benefactions" where it occurs for the first time, insert "or grants"; and

(iv) after "properties" insert:

"on trust or otherwise, for any object not inconsistent with the objects of the University".

The motion was negatived.

Mr. Speaker: The question is:

(9) In part (j) of clause 6, for "to deal with" substitute "hold, administer and deal with or dispose of".

The motion was negatived.

Mr. Speaker : The question is

(10) After part (j) of clause 6, insert:

(i) "(jj) to affiliate, recognise or aid any college, school or other educational institution, in any part of the country outside the territorial limits of the University, subject to such procedure as may be prescribed by Statute;"

(ii) "(jjj) to make provision for the residence, physical training, moral welfare and discipline, conduct and behaviour of the students in the University;"

The motion was negatived.

Mr. Speaker: The question is:

(11) After (j) of clause 6, insert:

"(jj) to suggest, whenever so found necessary and recommended to the Samsad by the Karma Samiti of the University and adopted by the Samsad, amendments to this Act which are calculated more effectively to promote the objects of the University;"

The motion was negatived.

Mr. Speaker: All the amendments are lost but the procedure has been very correct!

[MR. DEPUTY-SPEAKER *in the Chair*]

Shri B.K. Das (West Bengal): I beg to move:

In part (a) of clause 6, after "East and the West" insert:

"in furtherance of the object which was defined by the motto 'yatra visvam bhavaty eka-nidam' (where the whole world finds its shelter) given to it by the founder President (Pratisthata Acharya)".

With this amendment the sub-clause will read thus:

"to provide for research and instruction in such branches of learning as may be deemed desirable and be found practicable and for the promotion of understanding of cultures between the East and the West in furtherance of the

> object which was defined by the motto 'yatra visvam bhavaty ekanidam' (where the whole world finds its shelter) given to it by the founder President (Pratisthata Acharya)".

I felt that sub-clause (a) as it stands was inadequate to express the ideal that the Poet had set before Visva-Bharati. So I thought it necessary that the motto that he gave to Visva-Bharati which was expressive of the whole idea and the imagination that was behind the institution, should be embodied as a part of this sub-clause and I hope this will be acceptable to the hon. Minister.

Maulana Azad: The form in which he has presented this thing in his amendment is not to my mind a fact. So far as I know Dr. Rabindra Nath Tagore had not adopted this as a motto. In fact it is only a quotation from the *Upanishadas*, and there is no doubt in it that it is very good quotation. He had set up this tradition to chant these words in the beginning of all the meetings that were convened there. I was quite prepared to take these words in the Bill, but now this amendment which has been moved contains all the objectives that were set up by Shri Rabindra Nath Tagore himself. After this I will assure my friend that there is no need for it now.

Mr. Deputy-Speaker: Does the hon. Member want to press the amendment?

Shri B.K. Das: No, Sir. I do not press it.

Dr. Deshmukh: I beg to move:

For part (k) of clause 6, substitute:

> "(k) to do all such things as may be necessary, incidental or conducive to the attainment of the objects of the University, in particular the attainment of the objects set out in the First Schedule for which institution known as Visva-Bharati was founded by the late Rabindranath Tagore or any of them."

Then consequential to this I will read out another amendment which is No. 5 in this morning's list. Therein we will have all the objects as have been embodied in the original constitution of Visva-Bharati. I will read out that portion from the original constitution of Visva-Bharati. But, I think, it is perfectly in order to take up the First Schedule at this very stage because otherwise it may not be understandable.

Mr. Deputy-Speaker: There is already a Schedule. This amendment will now become the First Schedule and the present Schedule will become the Second Schedule.

Dr. Deshmukh: Yes.

Mr. Deputy-Speaker: Why not we wait until we reach clause 44?

Dr. Deshmukh: Then this amendment will not be understood.

Mr. Deputy-Speaker: He may refer to that amendment but not move it at this stage.

Dr. Deshmukh: When the Schedule is part of a clause, without reference to it the House will not be in a position to follow its purport.

Maulana Azad: Sir, I also think that it should go in the Schedule, but because this is a part of it, therefore, it should be read there.

Mr. Deputy-Speaker: Then let it not be after clause 44.

Dr. Deshmukh: I beg to move:

Before the existing Schedule, insert new Schedule as the First Schedule, and renumber the existing Schedule accordingly:

"THE FIRST SCHEDULE

[*See* Section 6 (k)]

(The objects for which the late Rabindranath Tagore founded the Visva-Bharati at Santiniketan).

(i) to study the mind of Man in its realization of different aspects of truth from diverse points of view,

(ii) to bring into more intimate relation with one another, through patient study and research, the different cultures of the East on the basis of their underlying unity,

(iii) to approach the West from the standpoint of such a unity of the life and thought of Asia,

(iv) to seek to realise in a common fellowship of study the meeting of the East and the West, and thus ultimately to strengthen the fundamental conditions of world peace through the establishment of free communication of ideas between the two hemispheres, and

(v) with such ideals in view to provide at Santiniketan aforesaid a Centre of Culture where research into and study of the religion, literature, history, science and art of Hindu, Buddhist, Jain, Islamic, Sikh, Christian and other civilisations, may be pursued along with the culture of the West, with that simplicity in externals which is necessary for true spiritual realization, in amity, good-fellowship and co-operation between the thinkers and scholars of both Eastern and Western countries, free from all antagonisms of race, nationality, creed or caste".

An Hon. Member: What about the concluding words?

Dr. Deshmukh: I am sorry to say that it has not been found necessary or possible to include the last words found in the constitution of the Visva-Bharati because they are likely to raise certain contentions and differences of opinion. My agreement with the hon. Minister is that I should not insist upon the inclusion of the last words, that is :

> " and in the name of the One Supreme Being who is Shantam, Shivam, Advaitam".

The reason is that this was more or less a tenet of the Brahmo Samajists and to that extent it probably refers more especially to a particular section who believe in that particular sectarian part of religion or non-religion, whatever, it is, and I agree fully with the hon. Minister – although I was very keen at first to include those words. The House does, I believe, wish to make it a point to have nothing which refers to a group of persons and which is not acceptable to everybody. Especially when we have everything else that precedes these words, I think the meaning of all that we mean and the implications are absolutely apparent and therefore I hope the House would not insist upon the inclusion of these last words.

I would like to say a few words on this amendment. Yesterday I had expressed my dissatisfaction at the way in which the Bill was framed and I had also ventured the view that the spirit of Santiniketan and the Visva-Bharati, as the whole of India understands it, will not have really fertile ground to grow and prosper. By accepting this amendment a very large portion of our objection has been removed. Even so, I would have liked these objects to be embodied in the body of the Bill in clause 6 or elsewhere and not by way of a mere Schedule. I would have at least liked it to come at the beginning and not at the end of clause 6, but my consolation is that this is an advantage as against the utter omission of these objectives. So long as they are there I hope there will be some sponsor or worker in the field, some Vice-Chancellor, Some *pradarshak* or some Rector or Visitor who will bear these objects in mind and who will aspire or strive to give effect to them. Even at this stage I would have liked that the whole University, the whole institution, was confined to nothing else but these objectives because in my view these objectives are not only broad enough, comprehensive enough and complete in themselves but they are really worthy of being embodied in any charter or in any constitution of an institution of this nature and quite self-sufficient in themselves.

That would be a sufficiently hight ideal to strive for. No recognition, affiliation of any school or college and no conferring of degrees of the ordinary sort was necessary. The ideal that I would strive for as a result of the Santiniketan would be to create a haven, a sanctuary for saints, sages, the learned, the searchers after truth, philosophers, *Nayyayikas*, the Buddha bhiksus, the Jain philosophers, the Chinese monks, the Christian bishops, the Jewish rabbis and last but not the least, the Maulvis, the Maulanas, the Shastris and the Pandits. Even at this stage, I would urge that this institution confined only to these objectives should be regarded as one of the greatest national importance. Probably, twenty years ago we did not need such an institution so much. But under the present circumstances when the whole world is going mad after armament and destructive instruments of all kinds, only India can give a message to the world. Here we have an institution created by such a high personage as Rabindranath Tagore. What would be nobler than to construct something towards which the whole world can look for inspiration and guidance? I would much rather like that rupees ten crores out of the Gandhi Memorial Fund are set apart for this purpose, and instead of having the authority and control in the hands of the Government of India I would much rather prefer that the Government of India gave another rupees five crores and created a National Trust over which no Government will have any supervision or control. The whole world is agitated today and wants to strive to establish peace. If we throw open this institution to the whole world, we would probably get Rs. 50 or 60 crores from the free nations all over the world and will be able to build something which is so grand and noble that the whole world may derive benefit from it. The U.N.O. has come and gone. (*An Hon. Member*: Not gone yet). Certainly, the way in which it has worked does not justify our hope that it is going to be of any use in the maintenance of world peace. It has already been failing in its duty and India has only complaints to make about it and nothing very much to gain from or congratulate the U.N.O. for. Hence, the necessity of building up this institution founded by Rabindranath Tagore is all the more. We can create through it a world force of thought and philosophy and dissuade the nations of the world from running a mad race of destruction which threatens one day to consume humanity. I would really have preferred not to make this institution a humdrum sort of an institution which we are doing at present. All the objects embodied in the Bill may be very good, desirable, advisable; but they can be easily separated and only the ideals laid down by Rabindranath Tagore should have been kept, because apart from anything else he insisted not merely on a particular plan of work but he laid emphasis on "the simplicity of the externals." He knew that the soul of philosophers and thinkers could not properly be housed in huge structures of cement, concrete and steel. It could only prosper if the surroundings answer the urges and stirrings of great soul. That is why he deliberately used the words "simplicity in externals". He did not want surroundings of a very mundane nature which may spoil the harmony of the atmosphere of this place. I have no doubt he was right. Once you pass this Bill, all this will go. As soon as you create a University, you will want laboratories; hostels; buildings which modern science and modern living require. All the ideals for the fulfilment of which Rabindranath Tagore spent his whole life, all the things that constitute the kernel of the whole thing, may very well be missing from the institution as it will grow up under this Bill. It is from that viewpoint that I was urging that the original ideal and objectives were quite sufficient and there was no need to bring in any extraneous matters. If it was necessary that the leaders of this institution should have sufficient opportunity and powers to look after the students who are admitted then let this be created into a separate University to which the West Bengal and Central Governments may give whatever funds they want, but for the administration of this institution there should be a National Trust over which no Government can have any control whatsoever. The people who are prepared to devote themselves to this institution should be completely free and independent to carry on its activities in any way they like.

I would not like to say anything more. I am thankful to the hon. Minister for accepting at least the incorporation of these objectives in the body of the Bill. I hope the House will also accept my amendment.

Maulana Azad: As a matter of fact when we prepared the draft of the Bill we were taking all these objectives in it. But after this when this draft came up for consideration, it was thought that it was not at all necessary because we were introducing a Bill for an institution which was already existing–the institution of Visva-Bharati established by Shri Rabindra Nath Tagore, which we have accepted as an institution of national importance; it only means that we have accepted the mode of its working as well as its objectives and that we are simply maintaining it. But when I saw that many of our friends were of the opinion that the objectives as laid down by Shri Rabindra Nath Tagore should come in it in one form or the other I readily agreed to it because the Government too agreed to these objectives. So I accept it.

Mr. Deputy-Speaker: Amendments moved:

(1) For part (k) of clause 6, substitute:

"(k) to do all such things as may be necessary, incidental or conducive to the attainment of the objects of the University, in particular the attainment of the objects set out in the First Schedule for which institution known as Visva-Bharati was founded by the late Rabindranath Tagore or any of them."

(2) Before the existing Schedule insert new Schedule as the First Schedule, and renumber the existing Schedule accordingly:

"The First Schedule

[*See* Section 6(k)]

(The objects for which the late Rabindranath Tagore founded the Visva-Bharati at Santiniketan):

(i) to study the mind of Man in its realization of different aspects of truth from diverse points of view,

(ii) to bring into more intimate relation with one another, through patient study and research, the different cultures of the East on the basis of their underlying unity,

(iii) to approach the West from the standpoint of such a unity of the life and thought of Asia,

(iv) to seek to realise in common fellowship of study the meeting of the East and the West, and thus ultimately to strengthen the fundamental conditions of world peace through the establishment of free communication of ideas between the two hemispheres, and

(v) with such ideals in view to provide at Santiniketan aforesaid a Centre of Culture where research into and study of the religion, literature, history, science and art of Hindu, Buddhist, Jain, Islamic, Sikh, Christian and other civilisations, may be pursued along with the culture of the West, with that simplicity in externals which is necessary for true spiritual realization, in amity, good-fellowship and co-operation between the thinkers and scholars of both Eastern and Western countries free from all antagonisms of race, nationality, creed or caste."

Shri Kamath : I beg to move:

In the amendment moved by Dr. Deshmukh, in part (v) of the First Schedule, at the end, add:

> "and in the name of the one Supreme Being who transcends all such differences and antagonisms."

Shri Harihar Nath Shastri (Uttar Pradesh): Compulsory recognition of God.

Shri Kamath: The amendment moved by my hon. friend Dr. Deshmukh is a laudable and worthy amendment in connection with this Bill. Before I come to my own amendment I will say a word or two with regard to the amendment moved by Dr. Deshmukh. In the last part, that is (v), I find that Zoroastrian culture or religion has been omitted. The famous Jana Gana Mana of Gurudev definitely and explicitly refers to Zoroastrain along with the other religions mentioned there.

I therefore, suggest that the word "Zoroastrian" also be added to the other words included here. Hindu, Buddhist, Jain, Islamic, Sikh, Christian etc.

Dr. Deshmukh: It comes in the "other civilizations".

Shri Kamath: It should not be because India has been a meeting-ground of all the civilisations, including Parsi or Zoroastrian and it should find a place along with the others mentioned here.

Then the word "Buddhist" may be correctly spelt. It is wrongly spelt here. That is, however, a minor thing which I leave to the draftsman.

Coming to the amendment moved by me just now, I fail to see why this very vital part of the objectives as contemplated, as envisaged by Gurudev Tagore should be at all omitted from this new clause. Dr. Deshmukh did not give, to me at any rate, very convincing reasons for the omission suggested by him. After all what are we doing in this Bill? We want to keep alive the spirit, the tradition and the entire atmosphere that was created therein by Gurudev from as long back as 1902. It may be that some of us may have our own creed, may have our own religious point of view; but the Bill concerns itself solely with the Visva-Bharati at Santiniketan and if we are honest and true to the memory of Gurudev we should keep alive that spirit. The very inspiration of Santiniketan came to Gurudev from an Upanishadic hymn, and it was only after he attained to the sense and the intuitive knowledge of the Infinite and the Supreme Being that he took steps to constitute or establish the Visva-Bharati at Santiniketan. It may be that we are a secular State. But I am afraid that we are making a fetish of the secular State. What we should do in this connection today is to see how far we are going to preserve, maintain and promote the spirit that animated Gurudev. We are taking into our custody, under our protection the Visva-Bharati University at Santiniketan. But what is the use of taking only the externals without the spirit, the inner spirit that animates the whole structure, the whole institution. If we throw out this thing, it would only mean that we are taking the shell without the kernel and I for one would go so far as to suggest that we shall be false to the memory of Gurudev if we delete this important part of the objectives as envisaged by him. I would even say that it would be an insult to the memory of Gurudev who among the very few, handful of thinkers, brought about a spiritual renaissance which was followed subsequently by a political renaissance. Just because we hold certain different views, we should not insult the memory of Gurudev. I, therfore, suggest that if you really want to maintain and promote the spirit that animated Gurudev when he founded the Visva-Bharati at Santiniketan, you would do well to include this particular part of the objectives which had been omitted by Dr. Deshmukh. If we do not do that we miss the whole tenor, the whole spirit of the life of Gurudev. He moved and lived and had his being in God and it is no exaggeration to say that he was a man of God and he walked with God. If we are going to keep alive his institution, his Visva-Bharati, are we to do it by imposing, or thrusting, our own predilections and prejudices into that University? Or are we here to promote his ideals and nurture them as he would have wished us to do? If you are not prepared to promote the spirit that animated him, better wash your hands of this University and this Bill. I, therefore, move that at the end of part (v) the following be added:

> "and in the name of the One Supreme Being who transcends all such differences and antagonisms".

I am not particular about including the words "Shantam, Shivam, Advaitam" because they are in Sanskrit, and may not quite fit in here.

Mr. Deputy-Speaker: Is not "Siksha Samiti" Sanskrit? Many Sanskrit words have been used here.

Shri Kamath: But not in this particular amendment, Sir. I may even stop with "One Supreme Being". I do not want to add anything further, I have no time to suggest any amendment because Dr. Deshmukh changed it at the last moment. I would therefore suggest that the words "and in the name of the One Supreme Being" be added.

Mr. Deputy-Speaker: What is the reaction of the hon. Minister ? Is there any objection on the ground of the Constitution?

Maulana Azad: Sir, I would tell you that there is no question of objection at all. Nobody is against it if work is done in the name of God. But we have to see whether anything befits a particular place. The purpose was that the objects of the 'Visva-Bharati' as laid down by Shri Rabindranath Tagore should be kept. So much so that all those things have been covered. And now in the end he had kept these words; just as it is a rule with the Mohammedans to chant the words "*Bismillah-ul-rehmanurahim*", in other words they invoke the name of God before they begin any work, and indeed it is a good thing. But now when you are framing an Act and are keeping its objects in its Schedule, I would like to draw your attention to this fact that this thing does not suit there, is not befitting, and so I differ on this point.

The second thing in it is that where the words Hindus, Buddhists, Sikhs, Jain and all other names have been mentioned, mention of Zoroastrians too should have been made in it. It is all right. There was no difference on this point. But we are laying down that thing here which Shri Rabindra Nath Tagore had himself kept in it. He did not think the necessity of mentioning it because he put down the words "Christians and other civilizations" after it and as such all these come in the words "other civilizations". Therefore I think that it should be kept in that very form in which it has been laid down.

Mr. Deputy-Speaker: Amendment moved:

In the amendment moved by Dr. Deshmukh, in part (v) of the First Schedule, at the end, add:

> "and in the name of the One Supreme Being".

Shri Kamath: That is enough.

Mr. Deputy-Speaker: The other words are omitted. He need not leave it to me. If he wants, I will place that also before the House.

Shri Kamath: It may be omitted. This will do.

Shri Jhunjhunwala (Bihar): I also want to move an amendment that the wordings should remain as it was proposed first in the body of Dr. Deshmukh's amendment and that no word should be taken out of it.

Mr. Deputy-Speaker: That is the words "*Shantam, Shivam, Advaitam*"?

Shri Jhunjhunwala: Yes, Sir.

Mr. Deputy-Speaker: Then somebody must move it.

Shri Jhunjhunwala: I beg to move:

In the amendment moved by Dr. Deshmukh, in part (v) of the First Schedule, at the end, add:

> "and in the name of the One Supreme Being who is Shantam, Shivam, Advaitam."

The hon. Minister of Education while moving this Bill in Parliament said that through this Bill he simply wished to give national importance to Gurudev's trust, Visva-Bharati. The hon. Maulana Sahab disclosed that Mahatma Gandhi, a few days before his death, had asked him to assume responsibility of Gurudev's trust. I regret to say that I had not gone through the entire Bill until the hon. Minister declared that he was bringing this Bill in accordance with Gandhiji's desire. But later when I read this Bill in detail I felt none of these two things was there. It appears that he wants to adopt it by only giving it a form of university. Had this Bill been allowed to remain in the form in which it was brought, it would have pained me, for within only a few days the great spirit that was animated by Gurudev would have disappeared from Visva-Bharati and the institution would have become like those universities about which Mahatma Gandhi used to say that they were only meant for producing clerks and such other persons who got employed in the then imperialistic Government. Mahatma Gandhi wanted these universities to be inspired by that spirit. I was expecting the hon. Maulana Sahab to make such provisions in the Bill as might enable the other universities to be inspired by such spirit of Gurudev. But, as I mentioned earlier, the Bill did not have any such provision. Yesterday when my friend Dr. Deshmukh dealt with some points in his speech, the hon. Maulana Sahab and other supporters of this Bill probably realised that it was necessary to add that clause to this Bill. Again, this morning when I went through this amendment, I felt satisfied for, after all, some scope had been provided for inculcating that spirit. But I am at a loss to understand why my friend Dr. Deshmukh is deleting from his amendment the very spirit of it. It is by no means an ordinary thing. Now-a-days a general tendency is found among us, be it due to any fear or the habit of appeasing others, that we do not have enough courage to utter the real truth. We even do not dare to utter truth in the spirit of truth. We are afraid to call a spade a spade. We merely pretend outwardly to bring a unity between the philosophies and religions of all other countries but do not make sincere efforts to achieve that end. When it comes to maintaining the real spirit which obtains in every religion, we propose its omission without effecting any change in other remaining things. I will, therefore, suggest with all the force at my command that if in the name of Gurudev any task is to be performed or any university is to be established, the spirit that animated Gurudev should be kept alive. In the absence of that spirit, it would be better to withdraw the Bill itself than to do such a thing in the name of Gurudev after deleting its very spirit. I for one would go so far as to say that by doing so they are instead of looking after his sacred trust are betraying it. This is not good. If we really wish to bring the Bill in keeping with the spirit of Gurudev, let us have courage enough to declare that they have no right, whatsoever, to delete that spirit. I did not know whether or not these words were contained therein and, as such, I had to enquire of my friend, the hon. Shri Panjab Rao Deshmukh, whether these words were there. Now that it has been ascertained that these words were there, I think this Bill should not be passed by us till of course, these words are not included.

Mr. Deputy-Speaker: Amendment moved:

In the amendment moved by Dr. Deshmukh, in part (v) of the First Schedule, at the end, add:

> "and in the name of the One Supreme Being who is Shantam, Shivam, Advaitam."

Prof. K.T. Shah: I have accepted in general the substitution of this for the objects clause that I had proposed myself. The necessity of a definite objects clause appeared so very great in my eyes that I was surprised that the draftsman had omitted it altogether. I am glad, however, that subsequently good sense has prevailed, and for once at least, the infallibility of this Government has been recognised as not to be so universal as it is claimed to be; and that amendment of their own proposals is possible, of course, by those whom they inspire or who inspire them. I am glad, therefore, that the objects clause is to be added specifically, and it is to be added in the name of the original founder of this institution.

I agree that there may be difficulties with regard to the last words in this objects clause as drafted by Gurudev for reasons which we now generally combine in the words 'Secular State'. For my part I feel that there may be some force in it. But if you claim that these objects are as drafted and maintained by the founder and if you demand our support for this, then I am moving my motion. If you demand my support on the ground that they are those drafted by Gurudev himself, then I submit it is a sacrilege for you to omit those very words with which you may not agree and if you are going to keep his very words, then you have no right to commit this sacrilege. Whatever my personal opinion may be, I am prepared to accept this in substitution of the amendment drafted, provided you give them in the full text and not take liberties with them. I refer for example to the omission or the absence of the two items which I particularly mentioned in my objects clause, namely the need for discipline and the mutual co-operation and this I cannot press for the simple reason that this form is much superior and much wider and therefore, I take it that it would include also the aim that I had in my mind, when I suggested the amendment in my words. I repeat that if you put all the amendments and demand support from this House on the ground that they embody the founder's spirit and his essence and his own soul. I suggest that you have no right to mutilate them in the manner that you are doing. I submit, therefore, that the addition proposed by my hon. friend Mr. Jhunjhunwala should also be included in the amendment and on that condition, I am willing to forego my amendment.

Dr. S.P. Mookerjee: The amendment which has been proposed by Dr. Deshmukh will clear up certain doubts which were in existence in the minds of Members of this House and indeed in the minds of many people outside. Knowing as I did the intention of the hon. Minister, I had during the last few weeks, personally discussed with many people whom I met when they expressed their misgivings as regards the ultimate results which may follow the establishment of a statutory University at Santiniketan. The fear generally expressed was that the University might become just a stereotyped institution of the like that we have in different parts of the country. I know that the Maulana Sahib was anxious from the beginning, as in fact he has made it abundantly clear today, that the intention of Government is to maintain intact the great ideals for which the founder stood. For that reason the clarification of the objectives in the words of the founder himself is essential. I knew personally how the mind of Rabindranath Tagore worked with regard to Government control and Government interference regarding Visva-Bharati. As you know, Sir, years ago the institution at Santiniketan was completely independent and I vividly remember the day when he came to meet my revered father who was then incharge of the affairs of the Calcutta University and made a suggestion as regards possible co-operation between Calcutta University and Visva-Bharati, maintaining intact the complete academic freedom of Visva-Bharati. Although the

Indian Universities Act did not make such co-operation possible, yet a certain device was made and Visva-Bharati has worked during the last 30 years as an institution where work of a special kind was being accomplished and at the same time its students were being permitted to sit at the examinations of the University of Calcutta. Rabindranath's great fear was that if the University came under official control, then its very propose would become difficult of accomplishment. In fact, as he said in one of his great speeches, its soul was likely to be destroyed. Those wo are acquainted with his great writings know of that story which he wrote of a bird which was kept in a golden cage, beautifully served but not allowed to go out of the cage and how money was lavishly spent on the maintenance of the golden cage which was studded with jewels and how fruits not fresh from the nature's garden but artificial food-stuff were brought into the cage so that the bird might develop its own life as the king thought it should. Later on everyone was anxious about the external features of the cage but the poor bird had died and no one took any notice of it. That is how he described the stystem of education prevalent in this country. He abhorred nothing more than external restrictions and regimentation. It is for this reason that we have to be extremely careful that the objectives of this University should be very clearly laid down by statute and also a constitution should be given to it which would enable it to function properly and make it impossible for any Government to interfere with its internal working.

Speaking about the objectives, I greatly welcome that the very words that the poet used should form part of the statute. Like Dr. Deshmukh, I would have very much liked if this clause had gone into the body of the Act itself and not relegated to the schedule. If you want to do a thing, do it properly; do it with grace; do not do it with any mental reservation whatsoever. What was the hesitation in putting those words in the Act? I have not been able to discover any reason. Again, while you put it in the schedule, you deliberately omit the last few words. Why have you done it? I have been asking myself, and I would appeal to Maulana Sahib to look into the matter more carefully and if possible revise the decision which he has taken on behalf of Government. What is it that we are afraid of? Is it because we have said that ours is a secular State, we should not mention Supreme Being anywhere in any constitutional document?

Dr. Deshmukh: Without any name: He is not called a Deva or Allah.

Dr. S.P. Mookerjee: That was what I was going to say. Apart from the mere mention of the Supreme Being, as the Maulana Sahib put it before us, just now, is it really necessary that these particular words should remain there? I would like to address myself on this point. First of all, as has been emphasised by one or two speakers, it is not for us to edit the objectives of the founder. We have no right to do that. If you say that you do not accept the objectives, do not pass the Bill, and say Government is not prepared to pass the Visva-Bharati Bill on the model that Rabindranath Tagore thought should be its objective or ideal.

Secondly, apart from the theoretical approach to the problem, to my mind, it is vital that these words should be there. Now, look at the clause as it stands minus those words. It refers only to the external activities concerning the study of religions, art, culture, architecture, philosophy, literature of so many great civilisations and an effort to discover a unity amongst them. That will be the external activity of scholars and professors and others who would be prepared to work in this great untrodden field. But, with what mental objective will this work be carried on? Knowing the little that I do of the writings and intentions of Rabindranath Tagore, the great stress which he laid at every stage was not merely on the material pursuit of these great studies, but also the spirit in which those studies should be undertaken. It is this spiritual background which it was his dream and ambition to bring into the orbit of the University. That must be the chief characteristic of an institution like the Visva-Bharati. Otherwise, it is meaningless. You can have other Universities where similar formal studies will be made, studies of comparative religion, of comparative art, comparative literature, comparative architecture and so on. But, the new element in the study of these, where Hindus, Muslims, Christians, Sikhs, Jains, and people drawn to Santiniketan from all parts of the civilised world would meet and discuss amongst themselves the great principles underlying their own studies, will be the spirit in which these studies will be undertaken and that is one of the very important objectives of this University. Therefore, I would most humbly request the Education Minister that he should make no effort to edit the objectives.

As I read the amendment of Dr. Deshmukh, I find he simply says the objectives as were declared by Rabindranath Tagore be embodied in the Schedule – we are not doing anything more and anything less. Therefore, if you try to edit or omit a portion which in my humble opinion is a vital portion, I believe, it will be doing an act of sacrilege.

I know Maulana Sahib's intention as he has made it abundantly clear in respect of a number of amendments where he did not take up any formal attitude at all. Quite rightly and as becoming a scholar and thinker of his eminence he was prepared to come forward and say that in respect of all these matters, it was his desire that the University should reflect the ideals and thought of Rabindranath Tagore. For this reason, I very strongly urge that the objectives should be left exactly as they were pronounced by the founder without any alteration whatsoever.

As I said that the condition of success of a University at Santiniketan will not only be the acceptance of the objectives for which the University stood, but, also the giving of a constitution which will enable it to function properly. Here, I am not without misgivings. When I look at the structure of the constitution, frankly speaking I do not like the large powers of control which have been vested in the Visitor. Who is this Visitor? The President of the Indian Republic. Will he act on his own responsibility? Obviously not. He will have to act on the advice of the Education Minister and his advisers. This means that you bring this institution practically into the arena of party and political controversy. I am not suggesting that the Government should have no control whatsoever. So far as the general financial administration of any institution goes, obviously, when the State grants goes, obviously when the State grants funds for the purpose of working it, it will be its duty to ensure that the money given to the institution is properly spent and spent for the purposes for which the grant was made. Even with regard to academic policy, it may be the responsibility of the Government periodically to have examined the working of statutory institutions in order to find out whether the purposes for which such an institution had been established were being properly carried out, a responsibility which could only be undertaken by persons who are competent enough to sit in impartial judgment over the activities of such an institution. That happens in England which very zealously guards the freedom of its Universities, where Royal Commissions sit from time to time in order to find out how the working of the institutions is going on and how far they advance the national interests. But, you have proposed to clothe the Visitor with powers to approve of the statutes and also with the overall power to supersede any ordinances which will lay down conditions for study and research, etc. vesting of such complete arbitrary powers including the vetoing of ordinances, is not desirable and not consistent with the spirit of the scheme itself. I shall not go into details. When those clauses come up for discussion, I hope we will have a further opportunity of discussion and we may make suitable changes with the help and under the guidance of the Education Minister himself. Here is a case where there is complete agreement on all sides inside the House and also in the country generally. This great experiment that Rabindranath Tagore made unaided, unhelped, and for which no support came from his countrymen in the days of its beginning, is today receiving statutory recognition at the hands of our Government and at the hands of our Parliament. I believe that that is a great advance, for which the Education Minister will legitimately feel proud. But, I would humbly request you not to do anything which may not only destroy, but even impair the efficiency of this institution or make the attainment of the objectives for which the founder stood difficult. A few days ago, it was given to me, and you were also there, to see the Sri Aurobindo Ashram at Pondicherry, call it an international University, where work of a different kind is being done. A great experiment is being made, not according to the stereotyped work with which we are familiar. There will be nothing but good to the country and to the civilised world if such institutions are given statutory recognition and State patronage, and given the fullest freedom to carry on their activities in a manner which will not only redound to their credit, which will not only advance the great objectives which their illustrious founders have had, but also do credit to the entire civilised humanity.

And lastly, as Rabindranath Tagore always used to say freedom must be the very breath and life of this institution. We should do nothing to destroy that freedom or do anything to regiment the working of this institution. I am fully aware that even though you may pass this Bill, and you lay down with clarity the conditions for keeping its constitution free and unfettered, everything will ultimately depend on how far Visva-Bharati succeeds in collecting within its doors the right type of men and women to carry out the work of the institution. Theirs will be a great responsibility. And if Visva-Bharati attracts the men and women of the right type – and they are not easily available – they by their concerted and united efforts and harmonious endeavours can succeed in making this Bill actually effective. It is only then that our purpose will be served. That is a responsibility which we are throwing on Visva-Bharati; and I have not the least doubt in my mind that with the co-operation of all, although it is situated in one corner of India, with the co-operation of all people from all parts of India and the great thinkers and savants from the different parts of the world, we will be able to make this institution worthy of its name.

Pandit Thakur Das Bhargava: Sir, I congratulate the hon. Maulana Azad on his agreeing to accept the amendment moved by Dr. Deshmukh in deference to the wishes of many Members.

As I have said before this Bill does not contain in a large measure the real idealistic concept of Dr. Rabindra Nath Tagore. I am completely disappointed to see that the real idealistic concept, which we had expected has not been included in it. We had expected that the memorial which is being established for perpetuating the memory of the greatest sage of our times would contain something unique as compared with other universities just like its name *Vishva* (world). We had great expectations, specially, when the mover of the Bill is himself a renowned literary figure and can well realize the relative importance of different things. But I have not the least hesitation in saying that I have been greatly disappointed to read it. I find the same statutes, regulations, ordinances and spirit in this Bill which is found in other universities. I thought that the whole Bill will be in keeping with the idealistic concept of Dr. Rabindra Nath Tagore as put forward by Dr. Deshmukh and will empower the university to be a self-governing unit in its internal affairs. As I go through the Bill I find that the education committee has not been empowered to frame ordinances or statutes, and in reality, even the power of framing regulations has not been conferred on it as the word 'authority' is mentioned there. I am simply surprised to read the powers which have been conferred on the Visitor and I wonder whether this university is supposed to spread the spirit of various religions in the world or is simply a university similar to the Banaras Hindu University or the Aligarh Muslim University.

Yesterday, the hon. Maulana Azad had stated that this is a peculiar type of university where pupils are imparted education under the shade of trees and there is no abundance of cement and steel in it. But, in this Bill, I find only cement and steel. I do not find the spirit which should have been there. Yesterday, I had apprehended that this Bill, which we have introduced, is defective from the very beginning and a thing which is based on wrong principles cannot be amended. But I am pleased today to see that those living words of Dr. Rabindra Nath Tagore have been incorporated in it and they are a redeeming feature of the Bill and I hope that if not today, a time will come when somebody will give real shape to these words. He will establish a unique university in this country for the benefit of the world. After studying this source of truth, all the great religious leaders of the world will be in a position, to say that though the political U.N.O. is in Lake Success but the spiritual

U.N.O. is in India and it is in this very university. I want that the university which is being established after the name of Dr. Rabindra Nath Tagore should become the spiritual university of the world with such powers as to be also to enlighten the whole world. But that spirit is lacking in the Bill.

After this, I come to the second point and would like to say that I am fully conscious of the difficulties of hon. Maulana Azad and the Cabinet. I can well understand the reason why they cannot include these three words in the objectives of the Bill. The three words are: *Shivam, Shantam* and *Advaitam*. May I ask those persons the reason of their emphasis as to why these three words must be included in the Bill? Shakespeare has also said "what is there in a name.' Will you be able to lessen the effect of other words if you put the whole objective minus the words 'in the name of so and so'? I think, you cannot. I think even if these three words are not included in it, we cannot lessen the living force of them. Now, the question is whether any defect crops up by excluding those words. Shri Jhunjhunwala has just said that the concept remains incomplete. But as far as I am concerned, I have no objection in their being included in the Bill *i.e. Shivam, Shantam* and *Advaitam*. They are not against any religion. I am not prepared to admit that these words offend the spirit underlying the various objectives of different religions. Shri Kamath has strongly protested against the exclusion of these words. In spite of these opinions, I am aware of the difficulties of the Government and they can say that different meanings can be attached to the word '*Advaitam*'. *Advaitam* means that there is nothing similar to it. Sir, you yourself are a learned scholar of Sanskrit and very well know the different meanings attached to this word. But, you may be aware that there is a different doctrine of *Advaitam* as well which is not followed by everybody. Today we are establishing an university of national importance, where it has been laid down that the underlying spirit of all the religions will be taught, it is possible that it may be so misconstrued in relation to some such doctrine that people may have objection to it. After all, why should we do something like that. In reality, according to my belief, there should not be any objection to the inclusion of these words. But I do not want that anything should be done in the name of Gurudeva, which anyone may object to on the ground that doctrinism has crept into it. There are people who do not believe in *Advaitvat* and are followers of other religions, they may say that there is doctrinism in it. Atheists can object to it even when there is no doctrinism in it.

My second objection is that Shri Kamath wants to include Zoroastrianism in it. But I want to say that that is also included in it. He says that it is a very sacred word. I admit that it is a sacred word and we have many interpretations of it but I say even according to his own logic he should not have any objection to the exclusion of these three words. I can well understand the mentality of others that all their words should be included in it. They want that not a single word should be excluded and I sympathise with their mentality, but why those people who want to add more words to it should raise any objection regarding its exclusion. At the same time, I am not prepared to criticise the objection of Maulana Azad. He has a great responsibility on his shoulders. He is going to establish something of national importance. Suppose, if anybody says that the word *Advaitam* includes doctrinism, then hon. Maulana Azad will have to answer it. Therefore, I want to submit that if these three words are excluded from the objectives of the Visva-Bharati neither it will have any material effect on it nor any defect will crop into it.

Sir, with your permission, I want to say a few words on the amendments moved in respect of this clause, so that I may not have to take the time of the House afterwards.

First of all Sir, I would like to invite your attention to a word that occurs in (a):

> "The University shall exercise the following powers and perform the following duties, namely:
>
> (a) to provide for research and instruction in such branches of learning as may be deemed desirable and be found practicable..."

I very respectfully submit that there is absolutely no need of the words "may be found practicable". Firstly, I say that all those things for the development of which the University has been established are related to the soul and are divine and hence there is no need of the word 'practicable'. Secondly, when the word 'desirable' is there, I think it will be impractical and meaningless to retain the word 'practicable', which takes away the very sense of that word.

Similarly in (c) the word 'or' should not be there. It says "..... to organise, establish, affiliate, carry on and maintain or dissolve, disaffiliate or give up new branches.....". So the meaning of the word 'or' here in "or give up new branches" is beyond my comprehension and I also do not follow what is meant by 'branches'. I think there should be 'and' for the word 'or' here and it is necessary to change it.

Then I come to (d). It is written therein:

> "to co-operate with educational or other institutions in any part of the world having objects wholly or partly similar to those of the University by exchange of teachers, scholars and generally in such manner as may be conducive to their common objects".

I would humbly submit that this word 'conducive' should not be there but the words 'which should advance those objects' should replace the words 'may be conducive' because co-operation with other university only means that both we and the other universities should be mutually benefited by each other. But 'conducive' would mean simply following them. I think their wish is to advance the objects.

I submit these few amendments to hon. Maulana Sahib and if he is pleased to accept them he may do so, otherwise I am not going to press them.

Now, I would like to draw his attention to Article 28 of the Constitution. We do not know about the funds of Visva-Bharati, whether the Government would bear its entire expenditure or it shall have its own funds. According to the provisions of this Bill, the financial commitment is very small. It is to the extent of only a few lakhs. If the aim is to have Visva-Bharati as a separate University and not to make it a Government institution, then I submit that the inclusion of these words will not be against Article 28 (2) of the Constitution.

According to Article 28(1) "No religious instruction shall be provided in any educational institution wholly maintained out of State funds". So, if Visva-Bharati is recognised as a Government institution, this objection can be raised under Article 28(1) which says that nobody can be forced to provide religious instruction in such an institution. But if this institution is not such a Government institution, then it comes under 28 (2) of the Constitution which says:

> "Nothing in clause (1) shall apply to an educational institution which is administered by the State but has been established under any endowment or trust which requires that religious instruction shall be imparted in such institution".

So, If this institution is not maintained wholly out of State funds and if it has its own old funds also, then it comes under Article 28 (2) and religious instruction can be imparted in it. Of course, it can be required to impart only that type of religious instruction which is in accordance with the objects laid down for it. If this institution only receives some aid from the Government and is not run wholly out of State funds, then I do not think there can be any difficulty in the inclusion of these holy words. Since such questions can be raised here. I have therefore suggested that it should be made sufficiently clear whether it comes under clause 1 or clause 2 of Article 28. Of course, I am fully aware that the difficulty with our Government is that they are wedded to secularism and hence they do not want this thing. I have given expression to all points of view so that the whole matter may be clear. Even those who want this amendment to be accepted, do not wish that *Advaitvad* should form part of the instructions in this institution. If it is not concerned with *Advaitvad*, then it would only mean that the name of God should be included in it. The name of God is sacred to all sects and religions mentioned therein. If these words do not propagate *advaitvad*, I would respectfully submit that there should be no difficulty and hesitation, in including these words and in associating them with the University. I would also submit that more light should be thrown on this subject and the hon. Members wishing to speak on it should examine and see whether the inclusion of these words does or does not involve any doctrines. If it does not, my views on it will be different from what if it does.

In reality, it is a matter which should have been referred to the Select Committee and the Bill should not have been considered here in the way it is being done. I am really sorry for that. Many more things would still be coming up on which differing opinions will be expressed by the hon. Members. I would like to submit that the Bill can be much improved upon if it is still referred to the Select Committee. I think there should not be any hurry in the case of such a sacred Bill as the one before us.

Several Hon. Members *rose* —

Mr. Deputy-Speaker: So far as the amendment of Dr. Deshmukh is concerned it has been accepted by the hon. Minister and enough has been said about it.

Shri A.C. Guha: (West Bengal): There are two amendments to that.

Mr. Deputy-Speaker: Yes. I know: one by Mr. Kamath and the other by Mr. Jhunjhunwala. They have also been spoken to at length. I will ask the Minister if he is agreeable, in which case (*Interruption*). So far as interpretation is concerned everybody knows it. There are a number of clauses in the Bill and there is no doubt that it is an important matter. But much depends upon the attitude of the hon. Minister. If he does not agree I will put it to the House straightway.

Prof. S.L. Saksena (Uttar Pradesh): Can we speak afterwards?

Mr. Deputy-Speaker: We are not bound by any rule *(Interruption)* Mr. Guha has already spoken on this amendment.

Shri A.C. Guha: Not on this amendment but in general.

Mr. Deputy-Speaker: There are a number of other clauses on which the hon. Member may throw sufficient light. Let us now hear the hon. Minister.

Maulana Azad: Sir, I have already spoken on the subject.

Shri Syamnandan Sahaya (Bihar): Sir I wish to submit a few things to the hon. Minister. From the speech which the hon. Minister of Education made the other day it appeared that it was the intention of the Government that this Bill should fully reflect the wishes and ideas of Shri Rabindra Nath Tagore. In fact that is the reason why it was thought necessary to give it such a status as to make it an institution of national importance. I hope the hon. Minister of Education still maintains that stand. It is under these circumstances that an effort is being made to retain something that was a part of the creation of Dr. Rabindra Nath Tagore. What possible objection can the Government have to that?

Maulana Azad: This portion is not included therein. The objects as outlined by him do not include this last line. This is obvious. If I say something and also say that I do so in the name of God, the expression 'I do so in the name of God' would not become a specific part of my speech. It was on that basis that I said that it was difficult for that expression to be accepted. I would very strongly appeal to the hon. Members to think over it a little cool-headedly. You are at this time framing an Act for a university and are stating the aims of that University. Now, nobody would question that '*Advaitam*' or the 'One Supreme Being' is a very auspicious name, but, then, you have to consider if it really fits in at the place where it is sought to be brought in, whether it would be suitable in this context. The objectives as outlined by Shri Rabindra Nath Tagore close with the words 'Creed and Class'. After that follows the expression: 'In the name of the one Supreme Being'. This last phrase has nothing to do with all those objects and its elimination does not affect them in any way.

Now, in view of the context in which he used that expression, it was all right for him to do so. But now when you are laying down the aims of a university the use of this expression in that context would not by any means look appropriate. It would look like a superimposition. As you know personally I should not have the least objection to it since it conforms to my faith but then, it does not fit in here. Hence I would respectfully submit that this should not be pressed and that, as suggested in Dr. Deshmukh's amendment we should close with the words 'creed and class'.

Mr. Deputy-Speaker: Now instead of the amendment to clause 6(k) moved by Dr. Deshmukh, Government itself has tabled an amendment in greater detail including the words 'yatra visvam bhavaty eka-nidam'.

Maulana Azad: No, this has not been pressed and has been withdrawn.

Pandit Malaviya (Uttar Pradesh): I should like to make an appeal to the hon. Minister of Education on this point. I have not taken part in the discussion of this Bill very deliberately because it is a matter which has been more or less settled between the Government and those who are incharge of the Visva-Bharati today. Therefore, I did not think it would be right for us to say anything about it. Though I have grave doubts whether it will be a step in the right direction to change the Visva-Bharati into another stereotyped University of which we have several others in the country, I have not said anything about it. But, it seems to me that there is a misconception or misunderstanding about these three words, "Shantam, Shivam, Advaitam". Those who would like to give it a philosophical or a spiritual or religious meaning by suggesting that it refers to *advaitavad*, it seems to me, are very far from the correct position.

Maulana Azad: I have no such misunderstanding.

Pandit Malaviya: Dr. Rabindra Nath Tagore was well-known for his spiritual and religious views which did not subscribe to any of the known *darshanas* of the Hindu belief. He had his own outlook, an outlook of cosmopolitan, cultural oneness of the various religious faiths and beliefs, and when he used these three words, I believe, he wanted to indicate clearly that he was thinking of a Supreme Being who was different from the concept of any particular sect or community or faith or dogma. He said Shivam, he said Shantam, he said Advaitam. Even in the *darshanas*, advaitam will not be found anywhere to be the name of God. *Advaitavad* tells of the relation of the *Paramatma* and the *jivatma* and other spiritual and metaphysical concepts. It does not denote God. What Rabindra Nath wanted to indicate probably was that the Supreme Being that he was thinking of was the one common basis of thought among all religions, all philosophies and all faiths; not one or the other but that which is advaitam, that is not which there can be no second or exception, to which there can be no rival or contradiction, no matter whether. He was denoted by one name or the other by the name of God or of Allah, of *Paramatma* or of Zoroaster. That was perhaps the idea behind these three words and I feel we will be doing a very grave injury to that idealistic concept of Poet Tagore if we remove those words. Not only that I beg to submit respectfully that we will be doing an injustice to the concept of our state which we have now under our Constitution, namely, a secular state, if we remove these words; because it might indicate that we are not prepared today to say that this state has a non-partisan spirit. Where the question of the concept of a Godhead comes in this state can only think of a Godhead which is common to all faiths and to all peoples and all sections and not one which is narrowed down to philosophic limitations or to faiths or to creeds or to dogmas. I think therefore that it would be in the fitness of things if we allow these three words to stand where they are because nobody who has known Rabindra Nath Tagore, nobody who has heard him, nobody who has read him, nobody who has had the benefit of coming into contact with him can doubt that nothing would be farther from his mind and nothing would be farther from his whole life than to think of a dogma or of a faith, or to think of one God as distinct from another God. His words truly indicated his catholic spirit and I feel that we shall be doing him an injury, and, also an injury to all the ideals and objectives which the hon. the Education Minister has said he wishes to inculculate, if we remove these three words. It would be open to grave misunderstanding besides the fact it will mutilate and undo a beautiful piece which was put down as the beacon light of his institution by that great Poet who was not only a great leader of thought in this country but also a great leader of thought in the whole of the mankind of his age. Both from the point of view of the objective we have before us, it will be, I submit, good for its to retain those words.

Prof. S.L. Saksena: I was very glad when this Bill was introduced to fulfil one of the trusts which Mahatma Gandhi had taken from the great Poet and which he bequeathed to the Government to fulfil. This Bill has been criticised on the ground that it does not breathe the spirit in which the great Poet conceived the Visva-Bharati. On this particular clause, I see that objection has been taken to the last line. I confess that I am really shocked. It may be on personal sentiment, but I do feel that the omission does a great injury to our sentiment. If there was any one who can be described as foreign to narrow-mindedness, it was the great Poet Rabindra Nath Tagore. I consider this particular work of his art as a great poem in prose and to delete one particular line on the grounds which have been given is, I feel, a sacrilege. The words "Shantam, Shivam and Advaitam" are interpreted today to refer to God and tomorrow the words Satvam and Ahimsa given by Mahatma may be interpreted to describe God. These words are used because they are annonymous with God. If we interpret the words *Shantam, Shivam* and *Advaitam* in this context as having any smell of sectarianism, then I shall say that there is nothing in this world which can be non-sectarian. Whatever the difficulties of the hon. Maulana may be, I want to tell him how the country will interpret the omission of this line. On reading the University Commission Report, I am glad that the hon. Maulana has put down in the Bill some of the words which are given in the Report as being the words of the great Poet. The same words which describe the objective of the Santiniketan are given here, but I wonder whether by omitting this particular line we shall be able to fulfil the sacred trust left to Mahatma Gandhi by the Poet and which he has transferred to the shoulders of the great Maulana. The Maulana is a great theologian; he is a great philosopher; he has stated that he has no misunderstanding about the import of these words. Then, why object to them? I was pained to hear the speech of my hon. friend Pandit Thakur Das Bhargava. He wanted to omit the words *Shantam*, *Shivam* and *Advaitam* because they had a narrow and sectarian meaning. I think my hon. friend Pandit Malaviya has done a great service by telling us that these words are not conceived with any narrow spirit. They are as wide as the Universe and they describe God, which not even an athiest can object to. *Shantam* means peace; *Shivam* means good; *Advaitam* means a being to whom there can be no second. Who is there in this world, even if he be an atheist, that can object to these words? To omit this line will be a sacrilege. It will be a shock to the whole country. It will be misinterpreted, I therefore pray to the hon. Maulana not to omit these words. They are an essential part of this great poem in prose which the great Poet wrote. They are the embodiment of the objects of the University. If we do want this Bill, let us pass it in the spirit in which the Poet conceived the Visva-Bharati. Let us not tinker with it. I know that the hon. Maulana is not narrow-minded. He has not misunderstood these words. Perhaps, he has been persuaded by friends like my hon. friend Pandit Bhargava. But I would like to tell him that the omission of these words will be misinterpreted by the country. Their inclusion will not be misunderstood, it will add strength to the secular character of the country. Therefore, these words should remain.

Mr. Deputy Speaker: Does the hon. Member feel that Santiniketan should have *Shantam*?

Prof. S.L. Saksena: Yes, Sir. When you are describing it, you must describe it properly. This is the essence of God and peace.

Shri A.C. Guha: I have no fascination for taking any oath in the name of God or of any denominational religion or creed. If from that viewpoint this particular portion is deleted, I have no objection; but if it is deleted on the ground that it smacks of something denominational or sectarian then I think this House should take objection to it. This is an institution to perpetuate the memory of the great founder, Poet Tagore. If, anybody would care to study the philosophy of Tagore, I would ask him to read his *Religion of Man* and his latest book *Manusher Dharma*. In these works, the Poet has given his own idea of world philosophy and the philosophy of life. If the Poet believed in any religion, it was the philosophy of the cosmic force. Whatever objection has been taken to this particular portion has been taken due to a confusion of Advaitam with *Advaitavad*. *Advaitavad* is quite a separate idea. But the idea here is: *Shantam*, that is, peace; *Shivam*, that is good; and *Advaitam*, that is, who is without an equal, without any duality. So, there is nothing to identify it with the famous Hindu philosophy of *Advaitavad* propounded by Shankaracharya.

One of the reasons given for its omission by Dr. Deshmukh is that it represents the creed of Brahmo Samaj. Brahmo Samaj is a theistic society with its doctrine of *Satyam, Sivam* and *Sundaram*. But we have *Shantam*, *Shivam* and *Advaitam* which is not to be found as a rigid doctrine or formula in Hindu scripture.

Then, if we take the Supreme Being in the sense of theism, then also it will be admitted that. He is Peace, Good and without any Duality. If we take it in the sense of Upanishadic Absolute–the Brahma–then also nobody can take objection that the Absolute Brahma is Shantam, peace, is good and without any duality.

If we go farther to the philosophy of Rabindra Nath Tagore himself, he believed in the Supreme Cosmic force leading to Peace, Good and Unity. Whether that Supreme Cosmic force is the Rita of the

Rig Veda or the Tao of the Chinese Laotze,– it is undoubtedly the force of peace, good and of non-duality. If we delete this portion on the ground that it gives an idea of sectarian philosophy, I think it would be doing injustice to the great founder of the institution and to the institution itself. Otherwise, I would have no objection to delete it. As I have stated before I have no particular fancy to take any oath in the name of God. But if it is done on the ground that it implies sectarianism, it would be doing injustice to the founder of the institution. I would, therefore, beg of the Maulana Sahib to accept this amendment.

As for the amendment suggested by Mr. Kamath, I do not think Zoroastrianism need be added. If you do that then there will be so many other doctrines *e.g.* Confucianism left out.

If there is one institution in this country or in the whole world which has tried to transgress all sectarianism, all creed and all denominational religion, it is this great institution. I, therefore, hope that the Maulana Sahib will agree to accept the objective *in toto* as the great founder of the institution had in view.

Shri S.P. Mishra (Uttar Pradesh): Sir, I want to express my ideas regarding the controversy now raging over the retention of otherwise deletion of the words *'Shantam', 'Shivam'* and *'Advaitam'*. In the conflict-torn world of today, we see a most horrible threat of war being held out in the very name of peace. It is in the name of peace that Russia is strengthening her armed might today and it is in the name of peace again that the nations in the Anglo-American Bloc are organising themselves. Gurudev had held that education should be of *'Shantam'* (*i.e.* sober) character and placable in form; yet he never entertained the view that the peace generated by it be something like the peace of the grave. Such type of peace is not wanted. He wanted that it should be *'Shivam'* (*i.e.* benign), it should be prosperous peace and wherein welfare of all is assured. Further it should not be a peace which may turn the human beings into a mere band of idlers; rather it should call upon them to strive constantly towards common prosperity. When again the words 'conducive to welfare' were used, a possibility of controversial interpretation was not ignored and hence the inclusion of the word *'Advaitam'* to remove any such possibility. To promote that spirit of team-work without any caste or creed considerations, it was provided that after the bell had gone in the evening, the Hindus may perform *Sandhya*, the Christians may go to their Church for prayer and the Muslims may recite their *'Namaz'*. But when they have to receive education which aims at peace – not the peace of the grave but a real prosperous and sober peace which aims at the well-being of the whole universe, then from this viewpoint we realize that the whole aim of education can be stated in these only three words which have the entire meaning latent in themselves. While, therefore, professing respect for the ideal and sentiments of the late Gurudev and while guarding against any slip, which may tend to disrespect those sentiments, we are really not only disrespecting those ideals by doing this thing but, in fact, we are also unconsciously changing them altogether. It thus becomes tantamount to killing the very soul while attempting to protect the body. I will, as such, very respectfully emphasise upon the hon. Minister of Education that the words '*Shantam*', '*Shivam*' and '*Advaitam*' do not represent any particular religious sentiments or doctrines but they are, the gist of all those doctrines and ideals which were propagated by Gurudev in his life-time and bearing which in his mind, he had founded and built up Visva-Bharati. If he looks at it from this viewpoint, he will feel no difficulty in accepting this amendment. In conclusion, I will like to request him again to accept this amendment.

Maulana Azad: Sir, once more I wish to make my firm stand against the addition of the last part quite clear. Just now some hon. friends in the course of their speeches have tried to make out that the idea underlying is not a sectarian one and that it is, on the other hand, quite lofty. I hold that there was, at least, no necessity of its mention at this stage. I know that Shri Rabindra Nath Tagore himself held very lofty ideas on this issue and if I were asked to state my belief in God, then I too will refer to what is written in this line. Further I cannot think for a moment that there can be any other idea which is at once more lofty and is based on more broadminded considerations or is even better in some other way. The issue before us at the moment is not what this idea is like. The real issue is whether or not it should be incorporated in an Act which is intended to govern the management of a university and further whether or not it is consistent with the declared objects of the Bill. Once more I will draw your attention to the fact that it is inconsistent with the objects of the Bill under discussion. The point at issue is not the character of the idea. I have already said that it is a very lofty one. Nothing more lofty or better could be said in the course of a debate on a philosophical or religious subject. I, of course, feel that the context in which you want to use it, is not a correct one. The context in which Dr. Tagore had then used it was a correct one in those times. He could use it then and he had described his objective in the word 'Supreme Being'. But now that you want to use it in a schedule which is sub-divided in heads (i), (ii) and (iii) it simply does not look nice. But alongwith you should not think for a moment that I am under some misunderstanding regarding the issue. Personally I too entertain this very belief.

Dr. Ram Subhag Singh (Bihar): When it is already incorporated in the objects of Visva-Bharati and when you entirely agree with it, then it is not proper to delete it from there and then why it is actually being deleted?

Maulana Azad: The objective has been stated above and ends with the reference to caste and creed and this sentence in question is only a concluding one, when we generally utter the words "in the name of God" or "In the name of the Divine Being". They, therefore, do not form a part of the objects proper.

Dr. Ram Subhag Singh: The issue involved herein is not God. It concerns the objects of the Visva-Bharati. The report submitted by the University Commission also contains a reference to that. Its deletion will, in effect, mean to throw off the very ideals for which Visva-Bharati was established.

Maulana Azad: It is not the position. I will again bring it to your notice that it has nothing to do with this issue. The object of the university ends with the words "all religions and all civilizations and irrespective of caste and creed". Only thereafter the words like "In the name of Divine Supreme Being which is" occur which do not form a part of the objects themselves. Further, as I have stated that personally I look at this issue from this viewpoint and I hope you will also agree with me.

Mr. Deputy-Speaker: In all religions God means the same thing. All the religions are mentioned here.

I will now put the amendments to the vote of the House. I will first put Mr. Jhunjhunwala's amendment.

The question is:

In the amendment moved by Dr. Deshmukh in part (v) of the First Schedule, at the end add:

> "and in the name of the One Supreme Being who is *Shantam*, *Shivam*, *Advaitam*".

I think the 'Ayes' have it.

Maulana Azad: The question is whether these words are suitable at this place or not. In my own opinion it is not essential to keep it here.

Mr. Deputy-Speaker: The hon. Member was under a different impression. I will put it again.

Pandit Thakur Das Bhargava: Before you are pleased to put it to vote, may I suggest that this matter may be left over till tomorrow so that Government may consider the position and see their way to accepting it. We do not lose anything by postponing. And this is a very important matter. So I suggest that you may be pleased to have the voting tomorrow.

Shri Kamath: On a point of order, Sir, You have already put it.

Mr. Deputy-Speaker: If the House so desires it can stand over.

Shri Kamath: No standing over.

Mr. Deputy-Speaker: The hon. Minister has not made a suggestion to that effect. If it is for Government to consider the matter, the suggestion must be accepted by Government. But there does not seem to be any indication of it. Therefore I shall put the question.

Pandit Malaviya: I think the House has expressed its opinion in the matter. Personally I did not say either 'Aye' or 'No'. But the House has expressed its opinion. I suggest no division need be called and the matter may now be left to the Government. They may do in this matter as they think fit.

Mr. Deputy-Speaker: The House must decide this matter.

Pandit Malaviya: May I once more suggest, if it is yet possible to do so, that there be no division on this point, and may I suggest that it may be left to the Government to let them do as they wish in this matter?

Pandit Thakur Das Bhargava: My suggestion is that the voting may take place tomorrow because by that time the Government may be able to accept it.

Mr. Deputy-Speaker: At this stage I have only to put it to the vote of the House, unless there is an agreement that it should stand over or the Government gives an indication.

The question is:

In the amendment moved by Dr. Deshmukh, in part (v) of the First Schedule, at the end, add:

> "and in the name of the One Supreme Being who is *Shantam, Shivam, Advaitam*".

The House divided : Ayes, 34; Noes, 84.

Division No. 2

AYES

Asawa, Shri
Barman, Shri
Birua, Shri
Chattopadhyaya,
Choudhri, Shrimati Kamaja
Das, Shri B.K.
Das, Shri Sarangdhar
Ghule, Shri
Guha, Shri G.S.
Gupta, Shri M.L.
Jangde, Shri
Jhunhunwala, Shri
Kamath, Shri
Kriplani, Acharya
Kriplani, Shrimati Sucheta
Maitra, Pandit
Malaviya, Pandit
Misra, Shri S.P.
Mookerjee, Dr. S.P.
Naik, Shri S.V.
Ramachar, Shri
Sahaya, Shri Syamnandan
Saksena, Prof. S.L.
Shah, Prof. K.T.
Shukla, Shri S.N.
Singh, Capt. A.P.
Siva, Dr. M.V. Ganagadhara
Sondhi, Shri
Tek Chand, Dr.
Upadhyay, Shri R.C.
Vaidya, Shri K.
Vaidya, Shri V.B.
Verma, Shri M.L.,
Velayudhan, Shri R.

NOES

Ali, Shri A.H.S.
Ansari, Shri
Arya, Shri B.S.
Azad, Maulana
Balmiki, Shri
Bhagat, Shri B.R.
Bhatt, Shri
Borooah, Shri
Brajeshwar Prasad, Shri
Buragohain, Shri
Chaliha, Shri
Channiah, Shri
Das, Shri Jagannath
Das, Shri S.N.
Deogirikar, Singh
Deshmukh, Dr.
Deshmukh, Shri C.D.
Dholakia, Shri
Diwakar, Shri
Dixit, Shrimati
Dwivedi, Shri
Faizpur Ali, Maulvi
Gadgil, Shri
Galib, Shri
Gopalaswami, Shri
Hazarika, Shri J.N.
Hyder Hussain, Shri
Iyyunni, Shri
Jagjivan Ram, Shri
Jain, Shri A.P.
Jnani Ram, Shri
Kaliyannan, Shri M.
Kanaka Saba, Shri
Keskar, Dr.
Kidwai, Shri
Krishnamachari, Shri T.T.
Kunhiraman, Shri
Meeran, Shri
Menon, Shri Karunakara
Mirza, Shri
Mishra, Prof. S.N.
Mohiuddin, Saikh

Mr. Deputy-Speaker: Anyway it is not accepted by the Government.

I shall put it to the House :

The question is :

In the first proviso to clasue 8, for "authorities of the University," substitute "Karma Samiti".

The motion was negatived.

Pandit Thakur Das Bhargava: In my amendment No. 56 I want the insertion of the words "and if they are minors, their guardians". The consent of the minors means nothing and it is the consent of the guardian which matters.

Mr. Deputy-Speaker: It always means the consent of the guardian.

The question is:

" That clause 8, as amended, stand part of the Bill".

The motion was adopted.

Clause 8, as amended, was added to the Bill.

Clasue 9 —*Teaching at the University*

Mr. K.T. Shah: I beg to move:

In clause 9,—

(i) omit "recognised";

(ii) after "teaching" insert "training, or research in";

(iii) omit "at";

(iv) omit "and" occurring after "Statutes"; and

(v) after "Ordinances" insert "or Regulations".

There is some mistake. The word "at" must be substituted by "in". Instead of "at the university" it would be "in the university."

The net effect of these amendments would be that all teaching, not only recognised teaching, but all teaching in the University shall be conducted ......

Maulana Azad: You want to omit the word 'recognised', it is quite all right I accept it.

Prof. K.T. Shah: And "at" should be changed "in".

Maulana Azad: Yes.

Prof. K.T. Shah : Then I wanted to add the word "Regulations". The words "Statutes and Ordinances" are there already but I want to add "Regulations" also. Usually rules made by the academic council are known as "Regulations" and as teaching comes in the sphere of the academic council and as professors and others will be regulated by ordinances and the general policy by statutes we must have regulations for teaching.

Shri Santhanam : If the hon. Member sees clause 30 such a matter does not appear to come under regulations at all and that is why it has been omitted in this caluse. A careful scrutiny of clause 30 will show that regulations have no place here.

Prof. K.T. Shah : Actually "regulation" itself has not been properly defined.

Shri Santhanam : Teaching is done by ordinances. Regulations refer to procedure of committees and such other matters.

Prof. K.T. Shah: All right. I will not press for "Regulations".

Mr. Deputy-Speaker : Evidently they want to earmark particular power to particular authorities, and therefore advisedly the words "Statutes" and "Ordinances" have been used.

Pandit Kunzru (Uttar Pradesh) *rose—*

Mr. Deputy Speaker : Amendment moved:

In clause 9,—

(i) omit "recognised" and

(ii) for "at" occurring after "teaching" substitute "in".

The motion was adopted.

I need not place the other parts before the House.

Prof. K.T. Shah : No.

Mr. Deputy-Speaker: Did the hon. Member, Pandit Kunzru want to say something?

Pandit Kunzru: All that I wanted to say was that I did not agree with Prof. Shah and that I agreed entirely with what fell from the lips of my hon. friend, Mr. Santhanam.

Mr. Deputy-Speaker: The question is:

In clause 9,—

(i) omit "recognised" and

(ii) for "at" occurring after "teaching" substitute "in".

The motion was adopted.

Mr. Deputy-Speaker: The question is:

"That clasue 9, as amended, stand part of the Bill."

The motion was adopted.

Clause 9, as amended, was added to the Bill.

The House then adjourned till Half Past Eight of the Clock on Wednesday, the 2nd May, 1951.

Document No. 42

FURTHER DISCUSSION DATED 2-5-1951 IN THE HOUSE OF THE PEOPLE ON VISVA-BHARATI (AMENDMENT) BILL

Mr. Speaker: Clauses 2 to 9 have been disposed of. I shall now take up clause 10.

Clause 10. – *[The Paridarshaka (Visitor)]*

Prof. K.T. Shah (Bihar): I intend to move all the amendments to the clause standing in my name.

Pandit Thakur Das Bhargava (Punjab): I do not propose to move any of my amendments but I would like to speak on the clause.

Mr. Speaker: Prof. K.T. Shah's amendments are Nos. 60, 62, 63, 65, 66, 67. He may move them.

Prof. K.T. Shah: I beg to move:

(1) At the commencement of sub-clause (2) of clause 10, insert the following:

> "On a formal representation being made to him by any body, authority, or teacher in the University."

(2) In sub-clause (2) of clause 10, after the word "University" where it occurs for the second time, insert the words "or its general or financial administration."

(3) In sub-clause (3) of clause 10, after the word "give" insert the words "at least one clear month's".

(4) In sub-clause (3) of clause 10, after the words "to be made" insert the words "giving the names and addresses of the person, or persons he has appointed to make the inspection or conduct the enquiry".

(5) In sub-clause (4) of clause 10,—

(i) for the words "may address" substitute the words "shall forward to".

(ii) for the words "with reference to the result" substitute the words "the report together with his own views thereon";

(iii) after the brackets and words "(Executive Council)" insert the words "the report of the inspection or inquiry and".

(iv) Omit all the words after the brackets and word "(visitor)" where it occurs for the second time.

(6) In sub-clause (5) of clause 10,—

(i) after the word "shall" insert the following,—

> "place before the Samsad all the papers and documents mentioned in the preceding sub-sections, together with its own suggestions regarding the action it thinks proper and necessary to take in the matter, and shall";

(ii) after the brackets and word "(Visitor)" insert the words "the opinion of the Samsad, together with its directions on the";

(iii) Omit the word "such" occurring after the brackets and word "(Visitor)"; and

(iv) for the word "as" substitute the word "which".

I will explain each amendment, and put in its proper place in the clause where it occurs. But before I do so, I should like to say that, on principle, I am opposed to the idea of a Visitor in a corporation or a public body like a University and particularly a University of this character. By general agreement a University is regarded as an autonomous body, and it should be an autonomous body in the best interests of learning and advancement of science, art or literature. That being the premise I think the introduction of any external agency, such as a *Paridarshaka*, or Visitor, offends against the very idea of an autonomous corporation like a University. As such it ought – even if there were no other ground at all, – be objected to.

As a matter of history it would be within the knowledge of many Members of the House that the idea of *Paridarshaka* or Visitor in Indian Universities was not included in the first constitution of the oldest Universities in India; and it was not till the time of Lord Curzon that suspicions, perhaps in the minds of the then authorities of the official world so developed regarding the teaching in the Universities, that they thought it necessary to have an overriding authority included in the constitution. Where, therefore, the then authorities felt the Universities were developing a line of independence inconvenient to them, they could check it in time. In many Universities, Sir, historic struggles have occurred with regard to the provisions of the Indian Universities Act of 1902 (or was it 1904?), wherein the representatives of the Indian people, the then members of the senates of those

Universities, strongly protested against the officialising tendency visible in introduction of changes of this character.

The very presence of an outside authority like the Visitor, and that, too, the head of the State, is an indication, to my mind, an index of an attitude of suspicion with which the activities of a body like a University were being viewed. In the official mind the very idea of a perfectly free atmosphere for the cultivation of knowledge, for the advancement of science, for the advancement of thought even, is viewed with suspicion. For those who are interested in maintaining the existing order it is always inconvenient that progressive elements, or elements which may not be satisfied with the mere *status quo*, should be allowed that freedom, that fullness of independence which may prove inconvenient, which may be upsetting their settled order of things.

The origin of the idea of a Visitor – and I have no doubt that the origin at least was no other than the one that I am describing – even this origin of the presence of a *Paridarshaka* or Visitor must be necessarily objected to now, in these days when we claim that, not only are the people and the Government one and their interests identical, but that according to the Constitution and according to the frequent professions of the leaders of Government, we have every desire to provide the fullest freedom for the advancement of thought, of learning and science. In an institution of this character, particularly where even in the official days, the original idea of the institution and the founder of the institution, were synonymous with the atmosphere of freedom that Gurudev stood for, and that he in his various activities symbolised to the chagrin of the then powers that were, the presence of a Visitor cannot but be an anachronism, an obstruction and an absurdity. In his various activities such, for instance, as his surrender of his title to the Government was acting in a manner repugnant to all their own professions of freedom in a civilised society, the Poet symbolised an idea of academic freedom which the provision of an official Visitor cannot but obstruct. I say in a corporation of this character, in an institution of this origin and nature the presence of an outside agency, like the *Paridarshaka*, is not only an index of suspicion towards the possible development of this University, or of the activities of this University, but is a negation of your own professions, and an indication that you are feeling uneasy with regard to the growth of free sentiment, free thought in an institution with the traditions such as this institution has.

It is an irony, Sir, that a Government, composed of freedom-lovers such as our present leaders are, should have thought fit to include – and, in my opinion, it is a stigma utterly undeserved – a provision like this in a corporation like the Visva-Bharati, that we all unanimously claim was the dream of a great soul in our country, and whose constitution, whose entire purpose and object should be left as free and uncontaminated and undefiled by our provisions as possible.

On principle, therefore, I would object, and would have suggested the complete deletion of this clause. At the time of the general discussion, this matter was also referred to by several speakers who objected as I do to this clause. In his reply to the objections raised by several hon. Members, – I was not among them – to the very fact of there being a visitor, the hon. Minister said that it is conceivable that there might arise occasions when an outside, independent authority such as the President, may be necessary to give an impartial decision when questions of the character envisaged arise.

I have, of course, no objection to the President giving an impartial decision. What I object to is that the President is not likely by himself to act entirely on his own authority. He would necessarily be advised by his constitutional advisers, probably the hon. Minister of Education for the time being. It is not unlikely that the advice of the hon. Minister of Education may be such and the President may be made to act upon that advice to such an extent, that the basic interests of the institution may suffer. The points, therefore, made against the inclusion of the Visitor have not in my opinion been answered by the hon. Minister of Education.

Even supposing that it is conceivable that in a situation of this character that he dreads some difficulty may arise, there is always the Parliament to save it. The Parliament, which passes this legislation, can also alter it, and can also provide further safeguards. Personally, I have no such apprehension. But if you genuinely fear apprehensive on this score, why do you forget that there is such a body as the Parliament of India always available in a moment of emergency when it arises in an institution of, as you call it, "national importance". If you fear the infusion of party sentiment, and even if Parliament is guided by Party motives at a time when the amendment of this Act becomes necessary to its mind, that party motive will be in the ordinary arena of party politics, and will not involve the high dignity and prestige which must necessarily be associated with the name of the President. From the propriety of the matter also, I would say that the presence of the Visitor is highly objectionable and at any rate of the constitution of the President into a Visitor is indefensible.

Lest, however, this may be regarded as merely a negative attitude, I am trying to make, by my amendments, the provision as harmless as possible, though I fear that it might not entirely neutralise the evil effect of having the President as the Visitor. The first amendment I have suggested would make the President unable to act, except on a representation being made by anybody or authority of the University. Of his own accord the President will not be able to intervene as he is allowed to do in the section as it stands. Only they know the shoe best who wear it and feel where it pinches. In the event of a representation being presented to the Visitor by some responsible body like the Court, the Executive Council, the Academic Council, or even a teacher, then only he will go into the matter. Past experience shows that if intrigues occur in a University, as they do elsewhere, they centre more or less round personalities. I have, therefore, suggested that the invitation for intervention should be made by some responsible body or authority which would include, of course, the Executive Chiefs, the Acharya, the Upacharya or even an aggrieved individual, like a teacher. These terms are specifically defined in the Act. I am, therefore, importing no outside notion in proposing this amendment. I am confining, be it noted, the right to make such a representation inviting intervention of the President only to three categories, and not extending it to outsiders or even to all the officers of the University. That is as far as my first amendment is concerned.

As regards my next amendment, I do not wish the right of inspection and enquiry on the part of the Visitor to be a very wise one. I do not want him to set up a roving Commission, as it were. The right must be definitely restricted, although some attempt is made to restrict it in the present sub-clause itself, I would urge the addition of the words "the general and financial administration". The Visitor should have no right to interfere in purely academic matters. For example, he should have no right to go into complaints about the honesty of the conduct of examinations, or the propriety of certain courses, or the composition of certain syllabi, or the prescription of standards of attainment, or of textbooks. He is entitled morally to intervene, to safeguard the general administration of the University; and because Government make a financial grant, he is entitled to intervene in financial matters. But he should not intervene on the purely academic side even if there is a request.

I have not altered or touched the other things mentioned in this sub-clause, because I take it that they must also be considered from the general or financial point of view. The addition of these two words towards the end will necessarily limit or restrict the function of the visitor in interfering with the University administration to the financial and administrative side only. The academic side should be sacrosanct and free from any such intervention.

My next amendment is:

> "That in sub-clause (3) of clause 10, after the word 'give' the words 'at least one clear month's' be inserted."

That I take it, is so obvious that it ought not to require any special commendation from me. The present sub-clause runs:

> "(3) The *Paridarshaka* (Visitor) shall in every case give notice to the University of his intention to cause an inspection or inquiry to be made, and the University shall be entitled to be represented thereat."

It does not specify the period of notice. I suggest that there must be some definite minimum period, at any rate, fixed by the Act itself of which notice must be given, so that the various authorities of the University concerned, and the various members of the University, may have time to take counsel together, and be in a position to say whether there is any justification whatsoever of intervention of the kind demanded by the Visitor.

I have not gone into the details of the notice, but it is obvious that the notice should not come during the vacation period, when ordinarily the bodies of the University would not be functioning, when many of the members may be absent from headquarters. But I take it that those familiar with the working of the Universities and their habits would see to it that the provision is not abused in a manner as to take undue advantage, or indirectly to undermine the very working of the University.

My next amendment is No. 65.

Mr. Speaker: But that is a consequential amendment.

Prof. K.T. Shah: It relates to the "giving the names and addresses of the person or persons he has appointed to make the inspection or conduct the enquiry." It is necessary for the University to know who are going to conduct the inquiry, if the inquiry is going to be conducted at all. Even if it is made at the invitation of the University Authorities, it is but proper that the party, the Visitor, if he conducts the enquiry should let them know who are the people who are going to conduct the enquiry and what are their addresses. I would, therefore, not dwell much upon it.

The next Amendment is a little more substantial. The first portion of it runs:

"That in sub-clause (4) of clause 10, —

(i) for the words 'may address' the words 'shall forward to' be substituted."

Mr. Speaker: Is that also not more or less consequential?

Prof. K.T. Shah: As it is, it is discretionary: I would like to make it compulsory–"*shall* forward it to the parties concerned". There should be no discretion allowed to him. Nor should he be given any grounds for excuse. My whole idea is to reduce his intervention to the minimum, and to neutralise the virus of that intervention as much as I can.

The next portion of my amendment is:

"That in sub-clause (4) of clause 10, –

(ii) for the words 'with reference to the result' the words 'the report together with his own views thereon' be substituted."

The "result" may be stated in a nutshell– that such and such person is to be dismissed, or that such and such a person is to be compensated, etc. It need not give the reasons. The result would mean only the final conclusion, as I read or understand that term. If a university is to be regarded as an autonomous body, I consider it necessary that the Visitor shall forward to the University authorities through the Vice-Chancellor, his whole report, the report of the enquirers or investigators or inspectors, and his own views thereon. He must not spring a surprise upon them. He must not, in my opinion, sit in judgment upon the University, after the University authorities have communicated their views on the matter; and then he, as it were, sits as a Supreme Court Judge on the total material before him and give his own verdict thereafter. It is not in consonance, in my opinion, with the dignity of the University or of the President.

In so far as you want the President as a Visitor, to be really a friend and well-wisher of the University, in so far as you want the President or the Visitor to act as a peace-maker, as it were, one interested in the smooth-running of the University, I think it but right that even when an occasion arises when he must make an enquiry at the request of the University authorities, or individually, he should forward a complete report of the Inspection, or Inquiry, together with such views as he has formed, to the University. Until the University is in possession of his own mind and how it works upon the information laid before it. Until and unless the University comes to know the reasons for the report or the result put forward, I am afraid the university bodies will be at sea as regards how and in what manner the Visitor will take action thereafter. They would be all the time on their trial, and would not know how to shape their own reply or rejoinder on a matter like this. After all the intervention of the Visitor will not be a common occurrence: it would be very extraordinary. It means, therefore, that the University would be on tenter-hooks and would be anxious to know as to how the matter has developed. It is, therefore, of the utmost importance, in my opinion, not only that the University should know all the reasons and the complete text of the report and the working of the mind of the Visitor himself. I am not taking away – please note – the right of the Visitor to have, as it were, the last word in the matter. Only, I do not want the Visitor to act as a supreme authority, a supreme appellate authority at a premature stage.

The next part of the amendment is:

> "(iii) after the brackets and words '(Executive Council)' the words 'the report of the inspection or inquiry and' be inserted."

Now the communication must be made to the *karma samiti*, of which, of course, the Vice-Chancellor is a member. Usually the President or Chairman guides the *karma samiti* and therefore he would in the normal course give his advice to the *karma samiti* when it meets and considers the report, together with the reports of the *Paridarshaka*.

The next amendment is:

> "all the words after the brackets and word '(visitor)' where it occurs for the second time be omitted."

Now, I want, by this amendment, that the Executive Council also should, at the first moment when it considers the report and the views of the Visitor, be free to take any line of action it thinks proper. The Vice-Chancellor also should not prejudice, so to say, the opinion of the *Karma Samiti* or the Executive Council by giving his own views. He will have every time, occasion and opportunity to do so when this *Karma Samiti* sits formally as a body and considers the report. He will be a member of the body, and he will have every opportunity and right to guide the deliberations, if he thinks proper, as to what is the particular line of action to be adopted in reply to the report that is given.

My next amendment deals with sub-clause (5) and runs:

> "after the word 'shall' the following be inserted, namely:

> 'place before the Samsad all the papers and documents mentioned in the preceding sub-sections, together with its own suggestions regarding the action it thinks proper and necessary to take in the matter, and shall'."

By this amendment the final power is sought to be given to the supreme University authority, namely the Samsad, as to what reply should be given and what line of action should be adopted in dealing with the report that the Visitor has sent to the Vice-Chancellor. The *Karma Samiti* is therefore to meet after considering the report, to report itself to the Samsad. A formal meeting of the Samsad should be called. That should consider the report and the advice, if any, of its own *Karma Samiti* and then make a final reply to the Visitor. Not any other body but the Samsad, the supreme governing body of the University, should be, and should alone be, the body to give the Visitor its answer on the matter. I, therefore, provide that, not the *Karma Samiti*, not the Vice-Chancellor, but the Court, in proper meeting assembled, shall consider the report, and shall give its advice or opinion to the Visitor, in reply to the Visitor, as it were, defending the University, explaining the University's line of conduct, justifying it, if necessary, and even turning the tables where and if it should be necessary on an unfounded or irrelevant investigation that may have been conducted.

It is true that the University is to be represented at the enquiry. But I am not quite clear in my mind as to what these words mean, namely that the University shall be represented thereat. Does it mean that it will be allowed to be heard or does it mean that it would be included in the personnel of the Committee or it would be included in the personnel of the enquirers? I am not quite clear as to the meaning, reading the words as I do. It may be clear to the draftsmen. It is not clear to me.

I would, therefore, like the hon. Minister when he replies to it to make it clear as to what is included. If it is a mere question of the representative being present – as a prisoner at the bar – it is incompatible with the dignity of the University to be treated, even before the matter is fully discussed, as if it was an accused person. I think the right of the University to be included in the personnel should be made beyond doubt. But in that part I have advisedly not made a suggestion by way of amendment, because I want to give the benefit of the doubt – whether they give me or not – of the best of intentions, and I beg the hon. Minister to make it clear that what is meant by this is that the University's representative shall be on the Committee which conducts the enquiry so that it will be in a position to give a proper advice even at that stage of the proceedings. Even if you do not make it a member of the Enquiry Committee, you must at least give it the position of some sort of advisers or assessors in the matter. You have, therefore, to make it clear that the words in the sub-clause relating to the representation of the University before the Committee of Enquiry must be placed beyond a shadow of doubt.

The last thing is:

> "after the brackets and word '(Visitor)' the words 'the opinion of the Samsad, together with its directions on the' be inserted."

The opinion of the Samsad would be forwarded to the Visitor, and also the Samsad's own indication of the line that should be followed in the matter. This is in consonance with my idea, and logically follows from my promise that the University is an autonomous body. The Visitor has brought to its notice some flaw, some defect, some shortcoming, some ground for complaint in its working, and, therefore, has placed the same before it, through unimpeachable authority, after proper enquiry, at which the University was represented and now the supreme governing body of the University is called upon to give its own line of action. When the supreme governing body takes a line which may be prejudicial or which may not appear to be a proper line, perhaps the Visitor has authority to say the last word. But all these stages in my opinion must be gone through if you want that the Visitor should remain.

I repeat – I will not be tired of repeating – that the very presence of the Visitor is an eye-sore to me. It is an offence to the idea of an autonomous body like a University – and a University of this tradition, of this origin, of these memories. I think, therefore, you should withdraw that clause altogether. But if you must have that clause, if you must inflict this stigma, if you insist on this suspicion in the working of the University. I beg you to make it as innocuous as possible. I beg you to maintain the integrity and autonomy of the University, its dignity and self-respect, to the maximum degree possible, and allow the Visitor to function only as a sort of *amicus curiae*, a friend of the University, and give it proper advice, after independent enquiry, on which the supreme governing body of the University has been represented, and which in the fullness of time may give its own line of action. We cannot assume that the Court of the University will be composed of such partisans, such perverts, as would simply insist obstinately upon their view, and would not listen to the good advice that may come from a friend of theirs. I at least refuse to believe that in respect of any University, much less of a University with these traditions. I trust, therefore, that the various parts of my amendment will be accepted and that the clause will be modified accordingly.

[MR. DEPUTY-SPEAKER *in the Chair*]

Mr. Deputy-Speaker: Amendments moved:

(1) At the commencement of sub-clause (2) of clause 10, insert the following:

"On a formal representation being made to him by anybody, authority, or teacher in the University."

(2) In sub-clause (2) of clause 10, after the word "University" where it occurs for the second time, insert the words "or its general or financial administration".

(3) In sub-clause (3) of clause 10, after the word "give" insert the words "at least one clear month's".

(4) In sub-clause (3) of clause 10, after the words "to be made" insert the words "giving the names and addresses of the person, or persons he has appointed to make the inspection or conduct the enquiry".

(5) In sub-clause (4) of clause 10, —

(i) for the words "may address" substitute the words "shall forward to";

(ii) for the words "with reference to the result" substitue the words "the report together with his own views thereon";

(iii) after the brackets and words "(Executive Council)" insert the words "the report of the inspection or inquiry and".

(iv) Omit all the words after the brackets and word "(Visitor)" where it occurs for the second time.

(6) In sub-clause (5) of clause 10, —

(i) after the word "shall" insert the following:

> "place before the Samsad all the papers and documents mentioned in the preceding sub-sections, together with its own suggestions regarding the action it thinks proper and necessary to take in the matter, and shall";

(ii) after the brackets and word "(Visitor)" insert the words "the opinion of the Samsad, together with its directions on the";

(iii) Omit the word "such" occurring after the brackets and word "(Visitor)"; and

(iv) for the word "as" substitute the word "which".

Pandit Thakur Das Bhargava: Sir, I have carefully heard the discussion on Prof. K.T. Shah's amendment and so far as principles are concerned I conform with them. Yesterday, I had submitted that the constitution of Visva-Bharati as it has been framed would not fulfil the objects which we had cherished to achieve from Vishva-Bharati. The constitution embodied in the Bill is in a way against the central conception of Visva-Bharati. Sir, if you will only look to the powers given in this Act to the *Karma Samiti*, the *Shiksha Samiti*, the *Samsad* and the *Paridarshaka*, you will find that the *Shiksha Samiti* which is the very life of a University has in reality been rendered a lifeless body in the Bill. So far as education or allied matters are concerned, the *Shiksha Samiti* should have been given full powers. But in the present Bill the *Samsad* has been declared to be the body competent for making Statutes, Ordinances and Regulations. *Samsad* would make Statutes but the draft will be prepared by the *Karma Samiti*. It has also been mentioned that the *Samsad* will have the right to prepare the draft if it so desires, but usually the draft will be prepared by the *Karma Samiti* and *Samsad* would pass it into a Statute. Similarly, other Ordinances related to education, which are of really very important nature, will be made by the *Karma Samiti* and the draft of that will be prepared by the *Siksha Samiti*. The *Sikhsa Samiti* has no power to pass any Ordinance; it will only prepare the draft. After the draft has been prepared, the *Karma Samiti* will give it the final shape. I want to submit that clauses 28 and 29 of this Bill are so worded as to have become difficult for the common man to understand. It will be seen from the powers of the *Karma Samiti* which it possesses over the drafts of the *Siksha Samiti* under clause 29 that the *Karma Samiti* in many cases can to a great extent turn down the proposals of the *Siksha Samiti*. Nevertheless, however, there is an appellate authority, a revision authority, and if the *Paridarshaka* so desires he can make changes in the Ordinances made under the authority of both the *Siksha Samiti* and the *Karma Samiti*. Therefore in this Bill the *Paridarshaka* is not merely a constitutional head or a figure head as Prof. Shah thinks, but he has got dictatorial powers. He can do anything, he can make it or mar it. Such are the powers that have been vested in the *Paridarshaka* regarding ordinances.

I would like to draw your attention in this connection to clause 28 which says:

> *28. Ordinances*.– Subject to the provisions of this Act and the Statutes, the Ordinances may provide for all or any of the following matters, namely: –
>
> (g) the conditions of residence of the students of the University and the levying of fees for residence in *Bhawanas* (Halls) and *Chatravasas* (Hostels) and of other charges.
>
> (i) the maintenance of discipline among the students of the University......".

There are many matters in which very large powers have been given to the *Paridarshaka*. Thus he has also got powers with regard to Statutes. He can, by his inspection, twist anything as he likes according to his desire. And if things are not done to his liking, he can demand explanation, I think that the scheme of Visva-Bharati Bill is such that if the *Paridarshaka* were merely a constitutional head, the amendments of Prof. K.T. Shah would have been suitable. But in the present structure of the Bill the *Siksha Samiti* has been given the least powers while the *Karma Samiti* possesses the powers of the *Samsad* and above all dictatorial powers have been given to the *Paridarshaka*. Indeed, the whole scheme of the Bill needs be changed; otherwise all these amendments are rendered inaffectual. The Bill, as it is, gives, on one hand, so large powers to the *Paridarshaka* that he can do whatever he likes and under clause 10 can cause an inspection or enquiry to be made by some other person and also give his opinion on the report when it is submitted to him, and, on the other hand, he has not the power to make an inspections himself– cannot understand how these two things are logically consistent.

The Minister of Education (Maulana Azad): It provides both the things – he may do the inspection himself or get it done through somebody else.

Pandit Thakur Das Bhargava: I would submit that I have read the clause 10 and the wordings there are not consistent in themselves. It says:

> "The *Paridarsaka* (Visitor) shall have the right to cause an inspection to be made by such person or persons as he may direct to the University....."

Maulana Azad: I have understood the point. It is not intended to be an ordinary section. The Visitor will interfere only if there arise some special occasion necessitating the Visitor's intervention. For this purpose he has been given the right to appoint some eminent educationists of the country, in whom he has confidence.

Pandit Thakur Das Bhargava: I have no doubt that as the hon. Maulana Saheb has explained, the purpose is to set things aright through some other person. But I want to submit that the Universities of today as also the students are not like those of the olden times. The students of today strike every now and then, run away from the examinations, leave the examination papers unfinished, often quarrel with their teachers and sometimes even murder them. Hence it was necessary that in the present times the *Paridarshaka* should have been empowered to inspect himself. I think that the original idea of the hon. Maulana Azad was very good that the *Paridarshaka* should himself have the right of inspection. I had tried to bring about a small change which is noted in the amendment numbers 60 and 64, that if any such opportunity arises, if any situation like that occurs, the *Paridarshaka* may personally go there and put everything in order. I think if this power is added no harm is going to be done. The logical conclusion of the powers that have been given will be that he himself could go and set things aright. That is the impression of the hon. Maulana Saheb also and I would urge upon him to bring it into effect by considering over these two amendments and accepting them so that his impression that the *Paridarshaka* could personally go there and clear the issue, may be rendered practically possible. The *Siksha Samiti* should also be given more powers to enable it to function as an autonomous body. In my humble opinion it was not proper to have given such powers to *Samsad*, *Karma Samiti* and *Paridarshaka*. But you have the right to change the whole scheme of the Bill and give effect to the amendments put forth by Prof. K.T. Shah. So far as my amendment goes, if the structure of the whole Act is all right, the *Paridarshaka* should logically be given this power.

Maulana Azad: But there is no restriction about it. When he has been appointed a Visitor, there is no handicap for his intervening when he deems it necessary. When he thinks it desirable he can himself set aright the matters and such a situation can also arise when he may appoint some other person. There is no such restriction in it.

Pandit Thakur Das Bhargava: I fully agree with the hon. Maulana Saheb that such an occasion would be rare when a personal intervention may be necessitated. But with the existing wordings in clause 10 it would not be correct to say that the right of personal inspection is included in the powers vested in him. In this connection I beg to submit that if a particular procedure of doing something has been prescribed by law, that thing can be done only in that prescribed manner and not otherwise. It is a point of law regarding which if any authority is required in support I can in support of it cite High Court and other authorities. Take for instance the case of the confession of a criminal. The manner of writing the confession has been laid down in section 164 of the Criminal Procedure Code. But if that is not written in the prescribed manner and if the criminal himself writes the whole confession then that statement would be invalid. It is a principle of law that when you have laid down some power, it must also be seen that they are given effect to. I would submit that your real purpose with which I am also in full agreement cannot be fulfilled by clause 10. I would therefore request that with the inclusion of these few words:

> "Shall have the right to inspect or cause an inspection to be made"

your purpose as well as ours would be served; otherwise, if you do not do it, there would be left a lacuna regarding personal intervention in rare cases.

Dr. S.P. Mookerjee (West Bengal): This clause, from some points of view, is one of the most important clauses in the Bill. I do not wish to say much on the general question of policy of giving large powers of inspection to the visitor, who happens to be either the Head of a State or the Head of the Indian Union. We will have to work for creating conditions in an atmosphere of freedom. Of course, the Government is responsible not only for finding funds, but also for ensuring that the universities get a machinery which will enable them to perform the functions which are allotted to them by the statute. Here, the powers which are given to the President as visitor are extremely wide in character. The powers given here include not only the right to insepct or order inspection regarding administrative and financial matters, but regarding academic questions also. I would like to suggest for the consideration of the hon. Minister a compromise which I think should meet the exigencies of the situation. Obviously, when grants are made to a university, it should be somebody's business to see that so far as administration and financial management of the university go, there is nothing that can be complained against. If the visitor feels that occasionally enquiries should be made or if complaints are made against such administration justifying an enquiry, let us have a provision of this type enabling the visitor to direct inspection regarding every academic matter which may come within the purview of a univesity, and then also to be the final deciding authority as regards the implementation of any recommendation which may be made by such a committee of enquiry, I think, is extremely harmful for the proper development of such a university as we are contemplating. It practically means that the entire academic policy of the university under the law may be subject to directives which may be issued by the visitor. Of course, the hon. Minister may say that these are intended for really emergent occasions. If such an emergent occasion should arise when a university, such as the Visva-Bharati, is found to neglect the academic responsibilities which are entrusted to it, then, the university, which is a creature of statute, may be dealt with in so many other ways. You can stop the grant; you can amend the law; you can influence the decision of the university through pressure of public opinion. I would therefore suggest this to the hon. Minister. I am not suggesting any formal amendment because I am leaving the matter in the hands of the Education Minister. If he is prepared to accept this idea, then his advisers and draftsmen may prepare a proper draft amendment of this clause so as to keep the powers of inspection in the hands of the Visitor in regard to administration and financial matters; but with regard to academic matters, let the Visitor have the power to bring to the notice of the university any matter concerning its academic activities, and to make any suggestions for their improvement if such suggestions are really called for. Obviously, if we follow such a procedure, then, any university worth its name, specially one of the character that we are contemplating will not do anything which may go against the real academic needs of the country or of this special institution. I would beg of the hon. Minister not to endow the visitor with such wide powers so that on any and every matter concerning the university he may direct an enquiry and also force the results of such enquiry and his decisions thereon upon the university. So far as I have been able to find, sir, such a drastic procedure is not in existence anywhere. The universities in England enjoy a special autonomy and they are extremely reluctant to part with such autonomy even though they are in receipt of large funds from the Government. As you know, the University Grants Commission is working in the U.K., consisting of distinguished educationists and other administrators, and by co-operation and understanding with the universities, they are able to influence the working of the universities in a way which is fully consistent with national interests. Also, the right vests in the Parliament of England to appoint a Royal Commission from time to time if such an occasion arises for enquiring into the affairs or activities of particular universities. Of course, we are working under a different pattern. I hope gradually our universities will be completely free from any sort of control or interference from Government. I am not saying this because Government interference is bad as such; but we are visualising the development of our country on democratic lines and naturally the powers of Government will vest in parties which may be ruling over the destinies of the country for the time being. It is of the utmost importance that our universities should function as really independent organisations where the teachers and the workers will be entitled to express their view points on matters which concern their academic activities and also on matters of national importance completely free from fear or from expectation of favour. That is also the policy which the hon. Minister has in view. The compromise which I am suggesting, I think, will meet both the points of view. If the hon. Minister is agreeable, then, instead of continuing the discussions now on this clause, he may instruct his advisers to prepare a draft which may be brought into the House half an hour later. Meanwhile, we may continue with the other amendments.

Mr. Deputy Speaker: Are there such far-reaching powers given in the Benares Hindu University Act?

Dr. S.P. Mookerjee: I have not been able to find any such provision.

Mr. Deputy-Speaker: In the Aligarh University Act?

Dr. S.P. Mookerjee: I have not seen the Aligarh University Act. But, I have seen the recommendations of the Radhakrishnan Commission which make no reference to them.

Maulana Azad: Sir, I may tell for your information that these powers have been given in this as well.

Dr. S.P. Mookerjee: I do not know if a proposal has been made for amending the Act in this manner. In any case, so far as the Visva-Bharati is concerned, it is functioning on a different plan altogether, and it cannot be the intention that the Visitor should be clothed with such large powers.

Maulana Azad: So far as I understand what has been said by the hon. Syama Prasad Mookerjee, it is that so far as the powers of the Visitor are concerned, he can use them for inspection and enquiry purposes and for other similar things of the University. But for other things he would only send his opinion to the academic council, and it would not be that his decision would be final. This is the only difference. Keeping this principle in view I am prepared to consider this suggestion.

Mr. Deputy-Speaker: Then, let the discussion on this clause stand over.

Shri Kamath (Madhya Pradesh): Is it going to be held over?

Mr. Deputy-Speaker: Yes; I shall proceed to clause 11.

Clause 11– [*The Pradhana (Rector)*]

Dr. Deshmukh (Madhya Pradesh): I do not wish to move my amendment; I will speak on this clause.

Mr. Deputy-Speaker: Why not the hon. Member reserve his observations to some other clause? They are all so intimately connected that if the hon. Member wants to make a few observations he can make them in connection with any other clause. Why not I put this clause now to the House?

Some Hon. Members: There are other amendments to this clause. Prof. Shah has some.

Mr. Deputy-Speaker: Very well.

Prof. K.T. Shah: I beg to move:

For clause 11, substitute the following:

> "11. The Pradhan (Rector). – (1) Whenever the Samsad finds it necessary so to do, it may by a resolution, passed by not less than two-thirds of the members present and voting at a meeting of the Samsad convened specially for the purpose, resolve to institute the post of a Rector of the University.
>
> (2) The Rector shall be elected by the Samsad, at a meeting of that body called specially for the purpose, and by a majority of not less than two-thirds of all the members present and voting at the meeting, from amongst the names submitted by the *Karma Samiti* for the purpose.
>
> (3) Within three months after the Samsad has resolved to institute the post of the Rector, the *Karma Samiti* shall prepare and submit to the Samsad a panel of no more than three names for election by the Samsad as Rector.
>
> (4) The Rector shall hold office for three years from the date of his election, unless earlier resigned, or removed from his office by a resolution of the Samsad passed by not less than three-fourths of the total members of that body present and voting at the meeting.

> (5) The Rector shall have power to supervise the administration of the University and for that purpose do all things necessary, call for any document, report, or officer for any explanation he finds necessary on any matter relating to the University."

Sir, this section, like the preceding one, is objectionable on principle, at least in my view. It is part, of course, and parcel, of the Government's attitude in the matter of officialising this University and departmentalising it completely. In one case you put the Head of the State, or rather the Head of the Union, as the Visitor, and endow him with very wide powers of intervention at any time and in any matter relating to the University, and the University is reduced to a mere skeleton without life, purpose, or soul. In the next case, you create the Head of the State in which geographically the University is situated, the Rector, both equally objectionable.

The term Rector, in its origin, is ecclesiastical. It really means someone who maintains discipline, someone who keeps you in order, so to say, someone, therefore, who is a kind of a dictator in your University. To have a dictator in the University is not a desirable thing in itself; but to have a dictator of the kind you want to create in the University from the official world, and to make the Governor of West Bengal *ex-officio* Rector is, to my mind, negativing the very idea of this University.

This is, of course, I repeat it again, in tune with the idea that the Government seems to have. Everywhere they want to have someone, for the miserable pittance of two or three lakhs that they are pleased to give this University as against a Trust or Endowment or Foundation of Rs. 15 crores or so that my hon. friend mentioned as being necessary for carrying out the functions of this University in a fitting manner. To quote a Biblical idiom – you want to sell the heritage of this University for a mess of pottage. Government gives two or three lakhs of rupees; and for that consideration you give wide powers to the Head of the State, and to the Governor of West Bengal who apparently does not even have any connection with the University. You want to make him the Rector entrusted with very considerable powers in his own sphere.

Rectors in British universities free from Ecclesiastical influence are selected from amongst men of eminence and have a nominal connection with the university concerned. The Rector of the University of Glasgow, of Edinburgh or of Aberdeen has a very limited connection with the university. They are really "*nam-ke-raste*". These people as it were, add ornaments or dignity to the bodies of which they happen to be life-long members. Here, of course, the office is to be co-terminous with the period for which the Governor happens to be the Governor of West Bengal. I think, therefore, that on principle this is objectionable and for my part I would like deletion of the clause.

Once again, however, with the desire that is characteristic of me, to be as reasonable as possible. I am trying not to negative it altogether but to meet as much as I can the opposite side if only they would be reasonable at all. I have, therefore, suggested to give the power to the University, if they so think, to have a Rector if they think one necessary.

For that purpose, the procedure I suggest is as follows: In the first place, let their supreme governing body resolve that there shall be a Rector, that the post of Rector shall be instituted. If they consider, from a variety of reasons, all bearing upon the University's needs and not from outside considerations, that it is necessary to have, after the Acharya and the Upacharya, a Rector, let them make that post a paid one or an honorary one just as they think it proper. But the initial step, the first *demarche*, should be that of the University's supreme governing body – the Samsad. The Samsad should resolve that there shall be a Rector. And lest there should be any misuse, lest there should be occasion for wire-pulling or intrigue, I provide for a specific majority, that it should not be a chance or scratch vote. It must be a decision after due consideration, and after deliberately and properly thinking out the needs, requirements, and the duties, powers and functions and terms of office and all that.

The next step is: when the resolution is passed to institute the post of Rector. Having instituted the post the next step is to appoint the person.

I suggest that the appointment must be by election by the body which institutes the post. That the election should become a matter of intrigue, I further provide that there shall be a panel of names regarded fit for this post, to be prepared by the Executive Council – the *Karma Samiti* – and presented to the electing body – the Samsad. This is a guarantee that the Executive Council will consider much more the fitness and the propriety and the suitability of the individual suggested to be the Rector, and to be really of the University, for the University and in the University, and really choose the man most suitable.

Lest, however, the University's Executive Council be also misled. I provide that the election by the Samsad, from amongst the names suggested by the *Karma Samiti*, must be by a very specific majority of two-thirds of those who are present and voting at a meeting specially convened for the purpose. The members will have notice that this item is on the agenda, so that as many of them as possible would be present and there would not be a chance vote, or an election by a mere nominal majority.

The term of office of the Rector I prescribe is not only definitely three years, but I provide for the contingency that he might resign. It does not follow necessarily that the post is permanent. It may be instituted, in the first instance, for two or three years as the case may be. If an incumbent, at any given time resigns, dies, or is removed from office, the same procedure may be followed or the post kept vacant as the Samsad may like. The important point is that it is not an *ex-officio* post which will always be filled, whether an individual is competent or incompetent, or whether he desires to have any connection with the University or not. This is the tradition of the old British Government in India which I think, the sooner we depart from the better for the University, I would, therefore suggest here as in the previous case that the University should not be tied to the official leading strings, and that for no consideration whatsoever.

The right of removal is the crux of applying the principle, as I view it in this. The right of removal must be vested in the Samsad so that the Rector does not consider himself apart from, or independent of, the University. The Governor of West Bengal must not consider himself and conduct himself as something not belonging to the University, something quite apart from and independent of the university. The Rector chosen by the University, or elected by the University authorities by a given procedure, should not be so independent, indifferent, or careless about the University's opinion. Even if such a person should feel or act in any manner that may seem objectionable, the proper University authority, the supreme governing body should have the right to remove him.

The right to remove in my opinion is a much more important sanction in the hands of public bodies than the right to appoint. The right to elect does not give a charter of misbehaviour for the period of election. I hope and trust that all those of us who want to have elective offices, all those who claim to possess the confidence of our electorates or our people, should also bear in mind the responsibility, *viz.* that the election, once completed, does not give us a right to misbehave for the period of election. We must feel responsible for every moment. And in order that the responsibility should not be forgotten or lost sight of, even by a person of the level of the Rector of the University, I suggest that the right to remove him should be provided for. He must not be made in any sense utterly independent of the University. I know that the right can possibly be misused. I have, therefore, suggested that the removal resolution cannot be passed except at a meeting specially convened for the purpose, and by a three-fourths majority. Whereas in the previous case I was content with providing for a two-thirds majority, so that no injustice may be done or there may be room for intrigue, here I ask for a still larger majority for similar reasons. The right to remove is important as well as needed. Let me give an example. Supposing he is found drunk at his post. There must be some power or authority to remove him, to bring him to book or call him to account and then remove him. This is too big an office for ordinary disciplinary action to be effective. You may take disciplinary action against a member of a party, and threaten him with removal. But a Rector of the University must not be threatened with mere disciplinary action of this kind; nor must we give him the position of snapping his fingers at the University. The disciplinary action must be one and one only, namely his removal from the office.

I hope I have made out a sufficiently good case in the place of the *ex-officio* Rectorship of the Governor of West Bengal.

Mr. Deputy-Speaker: Amendment moved:

For clause 11, substitute the following:

"11. *The Pradhan* (*Rector*)-- (1) Whenever the Samsad finds it necessary so to do, it may, by a resolution, passed by not less than two-thirds of the members present and voting at a meeting of the Samsad convened specially for the purpose, resolve to institute the post of a Rector of the University.

(2) The Rector shall be elected by the Samsad, at a meeting of that body called specially for the purpose, and by a majority of not less than two-thirds of all the members present and voting at the meeting, from amongst the names submitted by the *Karma Samiti* for the purpose.

(3) Within three months after the Samsad has resolved to institute the post of the Rector, the *Karma Samiti* shall prepare and submit to the Samsad a panel of not more than three names for election by the Samsad as Rector.

(4) The Rector shall hold office for three years from the date of his election, unless earlier resigned, or removed from

his office by a resolution of the Samsad passed by not less than three-fourths of the total members of that body present and voting at the meeting.

(5) The Rector shall have power to supervise the administration of the University and for that purpose do all things necessary, call or any document, report, or office for any explanation he finds necessary on any matter relating to the University."

The amendment is self-explanatory and after the lucid exposition by the Mover I do not think it is necessary to have a discussion. (*Interruption*) Hon. Members have a right to speak on any amendment and we have so many clauses and amendments. However, I would like to limit the speeches to five minutes.

Shri Kamath: It is a new rule you are promulgating for discussion on a Bill.

Mr. Deputy-Speaker: It is not a rule but only a desire.

Shri Kamath: Sir, there is much to be said for the amendment just moved by my hon. friend Prof. Shah. The House will see that even as regards the Acharya and Upacharya (The Chancellor and the Vice-Chancellor) the successors to the first Acharya and Upacharya will be elected, by the Samsad in the case of the Acharya, and in the case of the Upacharya the Board of appointment shall be as laid down in the statute. I am referring to clause 13 and 14 of the Bill.

The House will also see that the power to make statutes has been conferred on the Samsad, that is the University Court. The only exception, so far as I can see, to this very sound provision as regards election to the various offices of the University, is this office of the Rector or *Pradhan*, who throughout will be the Bengal Governor *ex-officio*.

The Constitution lays down that the Governors shall be nominees of the President, that is to say, the President acting upon the advice of his Council of Ministers at the Centre. Therefore the *Pradhan* of Vishva-Bharati is going to be always a nominee of the Central Government. I for one am afraid that this provision stipulating that the Rector will be the Governor, in other words the nominee of the Central Government or the President, militates against the spirit of freedom from interference and control of Government, which ought to pervade a true university, particularly a university that has been nurtured on spiritual foundations by Guru Dev. I fail to see why when even in regard to the Chancellor and the Vice-Chancellor the power has been conferred on the Samsad to elect them–I am referring to the successors to the first Acharya and the Upacharya–the Rector alone should be the Governor of West Bengal *ex-officio*. My friend Prof. Shah has in his lucid speech made it clear why it is desirable and necessary that the Rector or *Pradhan* of Vishva-Bharati should be elected by the Samsad, as he seeks to do in his amendment.

Mr. Deputy-Speaker: What are the powers of the Rector?

Shri Kamath: I am coming to that also presently, namely the second point adverted to.

It is strange that the Bill is completely silent on the powers and functions of the Rector. The only reference is the one line reference to the *Pradhan* that so-and-so shall be the Rector of the University. Throughout this Bill of over 44 clauses and laying down as it does the powers, duties and functions of the various bodies and other officers of the University, it is strange indeed that the Bill should be completely silent as regards this particular matter. If he is going to be a mere ornamental officer, if this Rectorship or *Pradhan's* office is going to be an ornamental office, even then I feel that the *Samsad*, the University Court must have the power to elect him just as that power has been conferred on that court so far as the *Acharya* and the *Upacharya* are concerned. I would therefore ask the Minister to tell us whether he has at all tried to consider what exactly the functions, powers and duties of this Rector will be and why he has thought it fit to make him a nominee of the Central Government, of the President, always and why a different mode has been adopted or prescribed for the appointment of the *Acharya* and the *Upacharya*, that is to say by the Samsad "as laid down in the statute", – the statute itself to be made by the Samsad. This is the only exception to the rule which so far as I can see militates against the spirit of a true University and especially of a University of the Visva-Bharati type. I therefore support the amendment moved by my friend, Prof. K.T. Shah and earnestly appeal to the House to give consideration to this matter and see that the *Pradhan* of Visva-Bharati does not continue to be a nominee of the President.

Dr. Deshmukh: In my view there are too many persons concerned with the administration of this University. We have the Visitor, then we have the Rector and then the usual Chancellor and Vice-Chancellor are there. As has been pointed out by my friend already no functions have been assigned to the *Pradhan* except to give him certain rights of nomination contained in clause 18 (xv), which reads: "*persons* nominated by the *Pradhan* (Rector)". Now, in the statement of objects and reasons in paragraph 4 it has been stated:

> "4. It is, therefore, proposed to make such a declaration and have the Visva-Bharati constituted as a Central University. The constitution that is proposed to be given to Visva-Bharati is in conformity with the recommendations made by the University Education Commission with such modifications as are considered necessary to preserve the tradition and special features of the institution."

I would like firstly to point out that the University Commission never recommended a constitution like the one proposed in the Bill. In fact it visualized something much simpler. Secondly, I have the University Commission's report before me and I do not find anything therein suggesting the appointment or any recommendation with regard to the office of the Rector as has been suggested here. I therefore urge that this unnecessary office may easily be done away with. After all, we will have to have somebody as a Chancellor and if we look to the report of the University Commission on this point it will be found that the Governor is suggested as more or less the usual person who will be the Chancellor. In paragraph 40 on page 421 the Commission says:

> "Present practice varies but in most provincial universities the Governor of the Province is *ex-officio* Chancellor. This arrangement has worked well, especially in Province with only one University. Where there are several universities in one province the Governor himself may feel that he cannot give to all of them as much personal contact as is desirable. This is a question which should be settled by each Province (or State) for itself."

So far as the Chancellor's office is concerned we will have either the Governor or somebody else chosen by the Samsad. Then what would be the necessity for the Rector's office? As has been pointed out no functions are to be performed by him, and since this is a Central University and since we propose that the President should be the Visitor with extensive powers. I think the policy should be to minimise these officials and not to increase them because it does create more complications which should be our policy to avoid.

I am not moving an amendment but I think this is a superfluous office which could easily be dropped. In any case the Governor of the State would be there in some shape or the other and even if he is not there since it is a Central University there would be no harm. I suggest that the Chancellor, the Vice-Chancellor and the Visitor should be the only officers of the University. And since the drafters of the Bill themselves could not assign any function to the Rector's post, it is quite obvious that it is being left to the Samsad to find out what functions he should perform and to search out what he should do. It is no good having an office first and then finding out work for the holder of that office. It would be much better to decide the functions that a person should perform and then to make provision for his appointment.

Shri Indra Vidyavachaspati (Uttar Pradesh): I want to submit to the hon. Minister of Education, something about the amendment which is before the House. In spite of there being no hope of this amendment being carried through, it is my submission to him that for the preservation of the institution, for which he is enacting this law, it is essential that the proposed post of Rector should be omitted. I quite agree with this part of amendment that there should be no *ex-officio* Rector and there is no necessity of giving this place to the Governor of West Bengal. Not only it is unnecessary but also it may prove harmful. Our aim is to preserve this national institution, which has been giving a good lead to other institutions of the country, and not to close it. When you will enact similar laws and grant charters to other national institutions, the aim of those will be the preservation and development of these institutions and not their suppression and annihilation. The hon. Minister of Education stated earlier that by enacting this law he wants Visva-Bharati to continue as it is and to preserve its spirit. I tell you from my own experience of long association with the national institutions that if this institution could continue for so many years even without the Government aid, and could keep up its spirit, the only reason is that it was not under the control of the Government. Its freedom was the protector of its spirit. Now, when we have our National Government, it is natural that the Government should realise that they have got to preserve the national institutions. As you are affording legal protection to Visva-Bharati today, similarly you can extend the same protection in future to other institutions also. The aims and objects of such protection would be to preserve the spirit of those institutions, which so far has been preserved due to their freedom. If you curtail their freedom and exercise rigid control on them, their spirit cannot be preserved. There is a great drawback in this Bill that there would be too many officers to exercise supervision over it and the problem of its control would become cumbersome. It is indeed very good that you have appointed the President as the Visitor of this institution. He has been vested with great powers. He can appoint any Government servant or outsider to inspect that institution if he so likes. You have made provision for the Governor of West Bengal and also for the inclusion of the Minister of Education of that state in the court of that institution. You may just think how this institution will be able to develop itself having so many officers to supervise it? How it can have initiative and how it can maintain its freedom? I am of the opinion that it would be the best course to drop the post of Rector. If you are keen on keeping this post, then this also can be held by the President himself. Both the offices of Visitor and Rector can be held by one man. The more you increase the number of posts, the more difficulties will be faced by that institution.The Chancellor of a University is the life and soul of a University. I am of the view that it would be better if the President is appointed Visitor and Chancellor both. In Delhi University, the work is going on very smoothly as both the posts are held by the same person. This is a good example for us to come to the conclusion that only one man should hold both these posts. The appointment of two persons will destroy the very spirit of that institution. I would request the hon. Minister of Education that it would be the limit of red-tapism if we burden this institution of national importance and of an independent character by appointing so many officers. There is a Visitor, A Rector and one Superintendent, whom will they consult? This will simply create more difficulties in future. When you have appointed the President as the Visitor of the Institution, there is no need to appoint the Governor of West Bengal as the Rector and there is no necessity of creating any other post. Not only that it will have no advantages at all but on the contrary it will be detrimental to the interests of the institution. I am suggesting it for the sake of independence of this institution not to keep any provincial control on it otherwise it will lose its national character. By introducing this Bill you are aiming to give it an international importance, and do not confine it to India only. Then why do you involve the Governor of Bengal in it. His appointment will serve no purpose. If you were to appoint the Governor of Bengal as its visitor and do not appoint the President on that post, then it may have some meaning but the Governor of Bengal should not be appointed when you have already appointed the President. My submission is that the hon. Minister of Education should give due consideration to it. Perhaps our Prime Minister is the present Chancellor of this institution, I would request him to think over the situation if two officers were appointed over the Chancellor how would that Chancellor be able to perform his duties as a Chancellor, as also a Vice-Chancellor as Vice-Chancellor. Therefore if you want to protect all the independent institutions, you should keep in view that there should not be too many officers, otherwise their very spirit would die and with it their physical existence too. There are so many big universities functioning in our country, how could these small institutions function in comparison to them. Such institutions can only run on the strength of their independence and spirit. Therefore, you should do away with this control and drop the idea. No doubt you can move amendments with respect to other provisions, but this must be deleted.

Maulana Azad: The purpose of this provision was that as the institution is located in Bengal so Government of Bengal, which is taking interest in this Institution may continue to do so in future also. That the Governor of Bengal should be appointed at this post was settled in consultation with the authorities of Visva-Bharati.

Shri Kamath: Now this institution has attained the national importance.

Maulana Azad: No doubt it was assumed the status of national importance, but at the same time the Rector has not been given special powers. You may study it thoroughly and see as to how far he can interfere into the affairs of the institution. Whatever has been laid down in the Bill, has been done, keeping in view the unique position of Visva-Bharati, otherwise it is a good as a paper scheme. All these powers have been vested in the President. The Provision has been laid there only with this idea in view that Bengal also should have some say and interest in it. It does not effect the powers of the Visitor in any way and therefore I think that this provision should remain.

Shri Kamath: What are his functions?

Maulana Azad: Practically the Bengal Governor would be connected with this institution in an honorary capacity. There is no special function assigned to this post.

Shri R.K. Chaudhuri (Assam): What are his functions?

Mr. Deputy-Speaker: The functions are to have an eye upon the institution. The question is:

For clause 11, substitute the following:

> "11. *The Pradhan (Rector)*– (1) Whenever the Samsad finds it necessary so to do, it may, by a resolution, passed by not less than two-thirds of the members present and voting at a meeting of the Samsad convened specially for the purpose, resolve to institute the post of a Rector of the University.

(2) The Rector shall be elected by the Samsad, at a meeting of that body called specially for the purpose, and by a majority of not less than two-thirds of all the members present and voting at the meeting from amongst the names submitted by the *Karma Samiti* for the purpose.

(3) Within three months after the Samsad has resolved to institute the post of the Rector, the *Karma Samiti* shall prepare and submit to the Samsad a panel of not more than three names for election by the Samsad as Rector.

(4) The Rector shall hold office for three years from the date of his election, unless earlier resigned, or removed from his office by a resolution of the Samsad passed by not less than three-fourths of the total members of that body present and voting at the meeting.

(5) The Rector shall have power to supervise the administration of the University and for that purpose do all things necessary, call for any document, report, or officer for any explanation he finds, necessary on any matter relating to the University."

The motion was negatived.

Mr. Deputy-Speaker: The question is:

"That clause 11 stand part of the Bill."

The motion was adopted.

Clause 11 was added to the Bill.

Clause 12. – *(Officers of the University)*

Amendment made:

After part (iii) of clause 12, insert the following new part:

"(iiia) Karma-Sachiva (Registrar)".

—[*Shri B.K. Das*]

Prof. K.T. Shah: I beg to move:

Renumber clause 12 as sub-clause (1) of that clause and add the following sub-clause as sub-clause (2):

"(2) All the officers mentioned in sub-section (1) shall be elected by the Samsad of the University in such manner as may be prescribed in that behalf by the Statutes:

Provided that the Statutes may lay down different periods for the duration of the different officers."

What I want to bring out is the elective character of these officers. The term is used in this Bill rather indiscriminately. In one place the word 'appoint' is used and in another the word 'elect' is used. I think it is but proper that we should have uniform phraseology and this should relate to the elective character. If you leave these things to be determined by statutes, as you have provided here, I have no objection. But I do want to stress the elective character of these officers. They are a part and not apart as it were from the University bodies with which they have concern. They should be properly elected according to the procedure provided by the statute and there should be no question of appointment or selection. The principle of election is the most important thing to my mind. Secondly, the mode or procedure of election shall be also determined by statute. I can conceive of the term of office of a Vice-Chancellor being different from that of the Chancellor and similarly the term of office of the Artha Sachiva may be different from that of the Karma Sachiva whom we have added just now. But I want that all these people should be elected and hold office during the term to be prescribed by the statute.

I commend the amendment to the House.

Mr. Deputy-Speaker: The question is:

Renumber clause 12 as sub-clause (1) of that clause and add the following sub-clause as sub-clause (2):

"(2) All the officers mentioned in sub-section (1) shall be elected by the Samsad of the University in such manner as may be prescribed in that behalf by the Statutes:

Provided that the Statutes may lay down different periods for the duration of the different officers."

The Motion was negatived.

Mr. Deputy-Speaker: The question is:

"That clause 12, as amended, stand part of the Bill."

The motion was adopted.

Clause 12, as amended, was added to the Bill.

Clause 13. – [*The Acharya (Chancellor)*]

Shri Biswanath Das (Orissa): I have given notice of an amendment to this clause.

Mr. Deputy-Speaker: But it was given only at 10-30. At any rate is the hon. Minister prepared to accept it.

Maulana Azad: No. I do not agree to it.

Mr. Deputy-Speaker: Then there is no point in moving it.

Dr. Deshmukh: Sir, this article refers to the election of the Acharya (Chancellor) and it is provided that the successors to the first Acharya shall be elected by the Samsad (Court) in the manner prescribed by the Statutes.

Now, Sir, although it is left to the statutes to determine as to how the Chancellor shall be appointed, I submit, Sir, that there is every reason why it should be indicated in the Act itself as to how the Chancellor shall be elected.

So far, under the British Rule the Chancellorship of a University always went to the Governor of the province and the provision here for the election of an Acharya is evidently due to the fact that the West Bengal Governor has been given some other office and, therefore, the Chancellor has got to be elected. I have no quarrel with the powers of the Samsad of electing a Chancellor, but whether it should be merely left to the choice of a court or whether the selection should not be a matter of some concern to the Central Government who have taken over this institution of national importance is a question which has been agitating my mind. I should really have thought that the Minister in the Centre or the Government of India should have some say not only in regard to the appointment of the Acharya, but also of the Upacharya (Vice-Chancellor) with a view to seeing that a suitable person is elected. Wherever you may look our experience is that the method of election has not been very happy in all such cases. So far as this question is concerned, the University Commission has made certain recommendations. They were not absolutely convinced about the method of election, but they think that these officers should continue to be elected. They have, however, suggested that the election should be left to the Executive Council, that is the *Karma Samiti* must take the responsibility of sending up only one name and that should be the name which should be accepted by the Chancellor for appointment. If we do it so far as the Vice-Chancellor is concerned, I think, Sir, it should be done with regard to the Chancellor also. My suggestion, therefore is that it should be laid down in the body of the Bill itself that the Samsad should recommend about five names and the freedom of appointing a particular person who would be best suited to carry on the traditions and the work of the University should be left to the Central Government.

I hope you will permit me to offer some remarks so far as the Vice-Chancellor's appointment is concerned for which I have given notice of an amendment.

Shri Biswanath Das: I had given notice of an amendment to omit sub-clause (4) of clause 13. I am sorry, Sir, I was absent during the discussion of this most important Bill. But I feel very strongly that the Universities should not have the power of conferring honorary degrees.

It has become a rather very unfortunate part of the activities of our Universities to go about begging for conferring honorary degrees on personages, however eminent they may be. These degrees mean nothing for persons of eminence like our hon. Education Minister or our leader Pandit Jawaharlal Nehru. Is it, on the other hand, a recognition of the University that confers degrees on them? Why should the Universities be so very anxious to run after politicians and educationists for conferment of honcrary degrees upon them? It took my life away when I read comments of a daily newspaper which stated succinctly: "Why wait on deputation for conferring degrees? Why not all the universities come to one place and then confer degrees on gentlemen of respect and repute?" Sir, that is the position with regard to the conferment of degrees.

Sir, this reminds me of the glorious traditions of our universities of yore. You look into Maha Bharata, Bhagavata, or Ramayana. You see what glorious traditions our universities set up. You read of King Parikshit who goes to a university as an ordinary citizen without any pomp or glory. He goes there, passes remarks and quick comes the reply from a *vidhyarthi*.

Mr. Deputy-Speaker: How does the omission of this clause improve the position?

Shri Biswanath Das: If you omit this clause, the University at least will be spared of the privilege of conferring honorary degrees and give up sycophancy. That is what I want to plead with the hon. Minister for Education as also with the hon. Members of this House.

Mr. Deputy-Speaker: Does the hon. Member think there must be a positive prohibition otherwise?

Shri Biswanath Das: I do not want any prohibition. I want that this clause may be omitted so that this University, which is a University of international reputation, will be spared from that blessing, which I consider a misery, for any University to have the right or the privilege of conferring an honorary degree on any individual. I am very sorry that the Government of India have not found their way to come forward with amending Bills to save the reputed Universities of Banaras and Aligarh from the shackles of official interference. Now that this University was free from these shackles, you have brought in many. Why put a further humiliation on it by conferring this so-called 'power'? It is not a power. I join issue that in these hard and difficult times this is no privilege either. This is a positive danger – danger to the freedom of the University, danger to the reputation of the University, danger to the sanctity of the University and for what it stands for. Time there was when our Universities did not care to confer degree for the man and his culture was gold, for all that. But now unfortunately you want them to have a stamp and you authorise the University to give the mark. By all means give it, if you so desire. But do not go further than what is absolutely necessary. Gurudev stood for a very high ideal. It reminds me of the days when reference was made by the Indian National Congress to Gurudev regarding *Vande Matharam*. He withstood like a rock against public opinion from Bengal, which was all against him. He ruled out of order certain passages in it without caring for the public opinion of the people of Bengal. That is the sturdy independence which was displayed by the founder of this great University to which you want to give statutory recognition. I appeal to you and to the hon. the Education Minister to do nothing to impair that independence which he so scrupulously maintained and the spirit which he inculcated in the minds of his followers. Under these circumstances I appeal to the hon. the Education Minister to see that not only sub-clause 4 is wiped off but also the sub-clauses in clause 26 connected with the conferring of honorary degrees are also wiped off. If you want to respect the honour, the dignity, I should also add the honesty, and the independence of these Universities, I think, it is better that Visva-Bharati and with it all the other Universities be saved from these 'powers'.

Babu Ramnarayan Singh (Bihar): It is the way of the world that if every person may go on earning an honest living, none would be put to any difficulty. The root cause of all the conflicts in the world at present is the increasing number of such persons as depend on other's alms. I strongly support the proposal of Shri Biswanath Das challenging the practice of conferring honorary degrees. People should receive degrees only after undertaking some sort of studies and passing certain examinations meant for the purpose. A person may or may not deserve it but he should not be decorated with an honorary degree in any case. If such a practice prevails, I may say, our freedom will be lost. Many things are being said with respect to Visva-Bharati University. It would have been quite in fitness of things if Visva-Bharati would have been kept quite independent. But I find that the Governor of Bengal and also our President have already been involved in this institution and it is just possible that some others may also be involved. To my mind the better course would have been to vest the University men themselves with all the power and the degrees would have been conferred on the deserving candidates alone. I am totally opposed to conferring any honorary degrees and I, therefore, submit to the House to do away with this practice. As I said earlier just as one should not depend on other's alms, in the same way degrees should also be conferred on only such persons as really deserve them or pass some examinations by labouring hard. If certain thing is achieved after begging for it, it does not do any good but on the other hand, it only tends to bring some harm. The same thing can be said in respect of honorary degrees as well, for in this way even the non-deserving persons also get them. So I once again support the amendment and sincerely hope that the hon. Minister, who himself is a hard-worker, will not like the practice of conferring honorary degrees and will accept this amendment.

Maulana Azad: If my humble opinion is asked in this connection, I have no hesitation in saying that I am opposed to conferring honorary degrees and I do not like such a practice. Particularly in view of the way in which these degrees are being abused in our country, I am doubtful if any person, whosoever, can like it. May I tell you why this provision was made in this Bill. Visva-Bharati is an institution which can be said to be an international university in the true sense. We are going to give it a form of university only today but as a matter of fact it has been functioning as a University since the very first day. Shri Rabindra Nath Tagore had himself called it an international university. It is possible that some great men from big universities and institutions of foreign countries may come here and pay a visit to this institution. Under these circumstances, this institution may feel the desirability of conferring some degrees on such persons. So we should look at this provision with these things in view. Should no such provision be made, it would not be possible to get an opportunity to confer degrees on these distinguished visitors. I believe probably such an opportunity will only do good to the institution itself. I wish to make it quite clear that it is merely in view of its international status that this provision has been made. This provision does not lay down compulsion, it merely provides if such a proposal is made it will be necessary for the Chancellor to confer the honorary degree. That is why such a provision has been made here. In view of its international aspect, it would be better if the practice of conferring honorary degrees is not done away with.

Shri B.K. Das (West Bengal): Was not an honorary degree conferred on the poet himself?

Maulana Azad: I do not know.

Mr. Deputy-Speaker: There are no amendments to this clause.

The question is:

"That clause 13 stand part of the Bill."

The motion was adopted

Clause 13 was added to the Bill.

Claue 14 was added to the Bill.

Clause 15 was added to the Bill.

New Clause 15A

Amendment made:

After clause 15, add the following new clause:

"15A. The *Karma-Sachiva* (Registrar) shall act as the Secretary to the Samsad (Court) and the *Karma Samiti* (Executive Council) of the University and shall perform such functions as may be prescribed by the Statutes and the Ordinances and the manner, the terms and conditions of the appointment of the *Karma-Sachiva* shall be laid down by the Statutes."

—[*Shri B.K. Das*]

New clause 15A was added to the Bill.

Clauses 16 to 19 were added to the Bill.

Clauses 20 and 21

Prof. K.T. Shah: Here I should like to point out one thing. On a previous occasion I had suggested in an amendment that along with the word 'powers' the word 'duties' should be added. I was then told that it was a question of drafting. I again point out that in this clause the heading reads thus: "Powers and duties of the Samsad" and the words "powers and duties are included together. Therefore, I hope it would not be within the sole and absolute discretion of the draftsman to take or not to take it.

Mr. Deputy-Speaker: Have we not passed that clause?

Prof. K.T. Shah: It was left as a matter of draftsmanship when I suggested that the word 'duties' should be there along with the word 'powers'.

Mr. Deputy-Speaker: The draftsman will take note of that. The question is:

"That clauses 20 and 21 stand part of the Bill."

The motion was adopted.

Clauses 20 and 21 were added to the Bill.

Clauses 22 to 25 were added to the Bill.

Clause 26 — *(Statutes)*

Amendment made:

In part (c) of clause 26, after the words "powers" insert the words "functions and duties".

–[*Shri B.K. Das*]

Shri B.K. Das: I am not moving my amendment No. 89 in the list but I may point out that on a previous occasion, we have inserted the word 'employees' instead of 'servants'.

Maulana Azad: I do not see any particular reason to change it. After all we all are public servants.

Mr. Deputy-Speaker: The question is:

"That clause 26, as amended, stand part of the Bill."

The motion was adopted.

Clause 26, as amended,was added to the Bill.

Clause 27– (*Statutes how made*)

Dr. S.P. Mookerjee: I beg to move:

For sub-clause (1) of clause 27, substitute the following:

"(1) The first Statutes shall be framed by the First Acharya (Chancellor) and shall be subject to the approval of the *Paridarshaka* (Visitor)".

I have to submit, Sir, that the hon. Minister is willing to accept this amendment. It has been suggested to me that it would be better if we only say "by the First Chancellor". He will of course appoint a committee for the purpose.

Mr. Deputy-Speaker: Amendment moved:

For sub-clause (1) of clause 27, substitute the following:

"(1) The first Statutes shall be framed by the First Acharya (Chancellor) and shall be subject to the approval of the *Paridarshaka* (Visitor)".

Pandit Kunzru (Uttar Pradesh): Are Government accepting this amendment, Sir?

Mr. Deputy-Speaker: Yes.

Pandit Kunzru: I am very glad to note that the Education Minister has at last been good enough to realize the desirablility of the Statutes being framed, not by the Central Government autocratically, but by those connected with the University, that is going to be established. As the future administration and character of the University Visva-Bharati will depend almost entirely on the Statutes, it is of the utmost importance that they should be made in such a way as to take account of the experience of other universities and also bear in mind to what extent the recommendations made by the University Commission should be modified in their application to the Visva-Bharati.

Mr. Deputy-Speaker: The question is:

"(1) The first Status shall be framed by the First Acharya (Chancellor) and shall be subject to the approval of the *Paridarshaka* (Visitor)".

The motion was adopted.

Mr. Deputy-Speaker: The question is:

"That clause 27, as amended, stand part of the Bill."

The motion was adopted.

Clause 27, as amended, was added to the Bill.

Clause 28. — (*Ordinances*)

Shri Venkataraman (Madras): I only wanted to suggest that after the words "the admission of students to the University" in sub-clause (a), the words "and the qualifications for such admission" be added. It is a suggestion which, if acceptable to the hon. Minister, may be considered.

Mr. Deputy-Speaker: His point seems to be that ordinances should provide for qualifications also.

Maulana Azad: But admission covers qualifications as well.

Mr. Deputy-Speaker: All right; admission includes qualifications also.

Amendment made:

"In part (e) of clause 28, after the word "conditions" insert the word 'and'."

— [*Shri B.K. Das*]

Shri B.K. Das: I do not want to move my next amendment. But, I may just point out that the conditions of residence of the students of the university have been laid down, but no provision is made as regards the appointment of provosts and superintendents. The creation of such posts is not prevented; but I think it will be better if it be put down here definitely.

Maulana Azad: It is not needed. It can be done.

Mr. Deputy-Speaker: Here is a clause (1) which says "any other matters which by this Act or the Statutes are to be or may be provided for by the Ordinances." Any other thing as may be necessary, will be done. The question is:

"That clause 28, as amended, stand part of the Bill."

The motion was negatived.

Clause 28, as amended, was added to the Bill.

Clause 29. — (*Ordinances how made*)

Amendment made:

98. In part (b) of the proviso to sub-clause (1) of clause 29, after the word "conditions" insert the word "and".

– [*Shri B.K. Das*]

Dr. S.P. Mookerjee: I have got two amendments. I beg to move:

(i) In sub-clause (4) of clause 29,–

(a) after the words "meeting to cancel" occurring in line 3, insert the words "vary or revise"; and

(b) for the words "be void" substitute the words "will stand varied, revised or cancelled as the case may be".

(ii) In sub-clause (5) of clause 29, after the word "Ordinance" occurring in line 4, insert the words "on the ground that it is inconsistent with or repugnant to the provisions of the Act".

The Bill provides that if an Ordinance is proposed, it goes to the court or samsad. Under sub-clause (3) the samsad may consider the proposal. Under sub-clause (4) the samsad has the right to cancel a particular ordinance by not less than a two-third majority. I enquired of the hon. Minister what exactly are the rights of the samsad: can it only approve or cancel or can it also vary or revise? Suppose, it cannot vary or revise, and it decides to cancel, there will be a deadlock. There is no provision in the Bill to provide for such a contingency. But, I was assured by the hon. Minister that when an ordinance will be placed before the court, the court may also vary or revise. So, I suggest that that may be made absolutely clear. When the ordinance goes to the court, it may do one of four things: either approve or vary or revise or cancel; in the case of the latter, it must be done by not less than a two-third majority. That is one aspect of my amendment.

Mr. Deputy-Speaker: I think "cancel or modify" any such ordinance, would be better.

Dr. S.P. Mookerjee: Yes; modify may be accepted.

The other is about the powers of the Visitor.

The Minister of State for Transport and Railways (Shri Santhanam): In that case, the latter half should also be suitably modified.

Dr. S.P. Mookerjee: That would be consequential.

The other amendment is about the powers given to the Visitor, regarding approval of the ordinances. According to the Bill, ordinances deal with academic matters. In the opinion of some of us, the Visitor should not be given large powers to cancel any ordinances or direct the university to accept whatever he decides. Here, the powers of the Visitor will be limited to two items: first, if the Visitor considers that there is any matter which is inconsistent with the Act or is repugnant to the Act, then his decision shall be final and he can cancel any ordinance and that cancellation shall be binding. The second is, under sub-clause (7) if there is a difference of opinion between the executive council and the academic council regarding the justification of a particular ordinance, then, that matter will have to be finally decided by some one and that may be left to the Visitor to decide as proposed in the Bill. These are the purposes for which I am suggesting these amendments, which the hon. Minister has seen and his advisers also have looked at from the drafting point of view. They may be accepted.

Shrimati Renuka Ray (West Bengal): I have an amendment to sub-clause (5).

Mr. Deputy-Speaker: Let me dispose of sub-clause (4). I shall come to that presently.

Maulana Azad: As I have just now said to my friend, there is absolutely no restriction in the sub-clause 4. But if they would like to make some amendments they cannot do so; on the other hand if they want some safeguards they can have them with the help of two-third majority. But if they want that we should make it more clear, I will have no hesitation in doing so because I agree with its principle. But at the same time it would be better if its working would be left to the draftsman.

Shrimati Renuka Ray: I want to change a word in sub-clause (4).

Mr. Deputy-Speaker: What is that?

Shrimati Renuka Ray: After the word "meeting" in the third line, substitute the following:

> "to modify or cancel any such Ordinance and such Ordinance shall from the date of such resolution, stand modified or cancelled accordingly."

Shri Sondhi (Punjab): Where is the amendment? Sir, amendments of which notice has not been given and which have not been circulated are being moved and accepted.

Shrimati Renuka Ray: It is a very slight modification that I am suggesting.

Shri Venkataraman: Probably it would be better to have the words "as the case may be" at the end.

Mr. Deputy-Speaker: I have got the amendment here and I shall put in the proper form. The question is.

In sub-clause (4) of clause 29 for all the words occurring after the word "meeting" in the third line, substitute the following:

> "to modify or cancel any such Ordinance and such Ordinance shall from the date of such resolution stand modified or cancelled, as the case may be."

The motion was adopted.

Mr. Deputy-Speaker: Then we come to sub-clause (5) and Dr. Mookerjee has already moved his amendment. He has suggested a modification and Shrimati Renuka Ray wants substitution.

Shrimati Renuka Ray: I am not moving my amendment. If Dr. Mookerjee will accept a little change in his own amendment, I will not move mine. I want the words "if the Ordinance is repugnant or contravenes any of the provisions of the Act" to be added.

Dr. S.P. Mookerjee: The language will be looked into by the draftsmen; that is what the hon. Minister has said.

Mr. Deputy-Speaker: If this is agreed to. I shall put it accordingly to the House.

The question is:

In sub-clause (5) of clause 29, after the word "Ordinance" occurring in line 4, insert the words "on the ground that it is repugnant to or contravenes any of the provisions of this Act".

The motion was adopted.

Shri A.C. Guha (West Bengal): I do not like to move my amendment, Sir; but I say that in view of the changes now made in sub-clause (4) and (5) sub-clause (6) also requires re-drafting. Otherwise the President will have power to suspend any of the Ordinances.

Dr. S.P. Mookerjee: That is not necessary. The consideration of the matter by the Visitor may take not more than a month only. Even if he decides not to approve of any Ordinance on the ground that it is repugnant or contravenes any of the provisions of the Act, he will require some time and the maximum time given is one month. And so far as the powers are concerned, they are limited under sub-clause (5).

Shri A.C. Guha: Well, if it is not considered necessary by the Government I do not press it.

Mr. Deputy-Speaker: The question is:

"That clause 29, as amended, stand part of the Bill."

The motion was adopted.

Clause 29, as amended, was added to the Bill.

Clause 30 to 43 were added to the Bill.

Mr. Deputy-Speaker: No amendments are moved to clause 44?

Dr. S.P. Mookerjee: I have suggested an amendment which the hon. Minister has kindly agreed to accept. Clause 44, as you will find Sir, is an important one which gives the power to remove difficulties. First the Court will have to be constituted, also the other bodies; and this power was given in the Bill to the Central Government. I have suggested – and the hon. Minister has kindly agreed to this suggestion – that these very important powers should really vest in the Visitor and not in the Government and the Visitor should act in consultation with the Vice-Chancellor of the University so that the academic aspect of the matter may be properly kept in view.

Amendment made:

In clause 44, for the words "the Central Government" substitute the words "the *Paridarshaka* (Visitor) in consultation with the Vice-Chancellor".

–[*Dr. S.P. Mookerjee*]

Mr. Deputy-Speaker: The question is:

"That clause 44, as amended, stand part of the Bill."

The motion was adopted.

Clause 44, as amended, was added to the Bill.

Mr. Deputy-Speaker: Now I had overlooked it. Dr. S.P. Mookerjee has to move his amendment regarding a new clause after clause 33.

New Clause 33A

Dr. S.P. Mookerjee: Yes, I shall move it now, though it concerns more the Finance Minister than the Minister of Education. I beg to move:

After clause 33, insert the following new clause:

> "33A. There shall be paid from out of the Consolidated Fund of India a sum of not less than Rs. 4 ½ lacs and such additional sums as may be required for revenue and capital expenditure and recommended by the Central Government."

The Government has made the following note, on page 16 which embodies the memorandum attached to the Bill, dealing with the financial provisions:

> "The new University will also require a maintenance grant to the extent of Rs. 4 ½ lakhs per year."

And it also says that certain capital grants and some interest free loans will have to be granted to the University in order to enable it to carry out its activities. The last paragraph in the financial memorandum states:

> "No specific reference to the grants proposed to be paid by the Central Government has been made in the draft Bill."

I do not wish to make a long speech. The provision of a statutory grant for a university is a very necessary factor not only for the purpose of enabling it to carry on its activities but also for clothing it with the necessary security and freedom. I do not wish to embarrass the Government by suggesting a higher grant than what the Government has already agreed to accept. I think from every point of view, even as a gesture, it will be a good thing if the Finance Minister agrees – I am sure the Education Minister will not object to it – to make a statutory provision in favour of Visva Bharati. There is no additional obligation on the Government to pay more than 4 ½ lakhs which Government has decided to pay to the University and it is only making a statutory provision, so that there may not be any ambiguity and the University may be given full security and freedom to carry on its activities.

Shri Santhanam: May I suggest that the latter half of the amendment is wholly out of order. It suggests that such unlimited amounts as may be recommended by the Central Government may be paid. The first half of the amendment may be all right if the hon. Finance Minister agrees. But no payment can be made without express provision by law. If it is sanctioned by Parliament it will come under the Budget. The latter part of the amendment is out of order.

Dr. S.P. Mookerjee: It is only a technical point. To satisfy him I can say "approved by Parliament".

Shri Santhanam: If it is approved by Parliament crores may be paid. It is wholly unnecessary. The Parliament has precisely the power of disposal of the Consolidated Fund. When a thing is approved any amount may be paid.

Mr. Deputy-Speaker: This Parliament passes the legislation. So far as particular legislation is concerned power is given to Government to make a grant. They will make the provision.....

Shri Santhanam: Specific provision may be made, not provision for an uncertain amount. So far as that is concerned it depends on the Government to make a recommendation and the Parliament may approve. We cannot make a law that in future the Central Government may make a recommendation and the Parliament may sanction an uncertain amount.

Mr. Deputy-Speaker: Apart from the question of taking the Minister by surprise I do not think there is any technical objection. It is Parliament that passes the legislation and empowers suitable grants to be made by the Central Government. No doubt the Central Government would include it from year to year.

The Minister of Finance (Shri C.D. Deshmukh): I am afraid this will be a very unusual kind of provision. It is likely to prove an embarrassing precedent. Also I am not sure if in actual practice it will serve any useful purpose. Our general experience has been that the minima are never possible to adhere to and it may be that the needs of the University will require larger sums (*Interruption*). I do not know but it may work that way, not necessarily but that is the general experience. You may cast your mind back on the grants with which the various universities started and compare them with the grants they are getting now. There is a general tendency that way. I do not think it serves any practical purpose and I think it is likely to prove in other respects an embarrassing precedent. I am sorry I am not able to recommend its acceptance to my hon. colleague.

Maulana Azad: I can say this much that there are three central universities of Banaras, Aligarh and Delhi which receive grants from the Central Government. No amounts have been specified for them in the Acts concerned.

Dr. S.P. Mookerjee: It was suggested by Mr. Santhanam that the latter portion may be omitted and the amendment confined to the first part, which is already covered by the recommendation in the Financial Memorandum.

Shri C.D. Deshmukh: I did not confine myself to the second part at all. I confined myself more to the first part.

Mr. Deputy-Speaker: The grant proposed to be paid by the Central Government has not been made in the Bill itself.

Shri C.D. Deshmukh: That is intentional, because all the grants are not statutorily provided for.

Dr. S.P. Mookerjee: There are some which are provided for.

Shri C.D. Deshmukh: I am not aware: I cannot think of any precedent for this. I do not know if my hon. colleague is aware of any grant which is provided statutorily as a minimum grant for a university.

Shri Santhanam: The amendment cannot be moved without the recommendation of the President.

Mr. Deputy-Speaker: So far as the recommendation is concerned I have my doubt. I would like to hear the Finance Minister about this matter. If Members will refer to the Bill this matter has been recommended. (*Interruption.*) Order, order. Hon. Members must have the patience to hear me. This Bill involves commitment by the Central Government of expenditure from out of the Consolidated Fund. In the Financial Memorandum which is under the rules attached to a Bill specific reference is made to this and therefore the President has given his sanction for the consideration of this Bill to the extent of 4 ½ lakhs. He wants to introduce the sanction granted by the President as a clause in the Bill. I do not think the sanction stands in the way.

Pandit Kunzru: I think the President alone has the privilege of recommending to us provisions for money grants. I do not think that it is in the power of any private Member to bring forward a provision asking Parliament to make a grant, simply because its principle has been approved by Government. Government must not merely approve of the principle but also come forward with a motion asking for a grant of the money by Parliament. Apart from this I think the suggestion made by my hon. friend Dr. Mookerjee should not be accepted. There are many central universities and not one of them gets its grant except in the ordinary way: that is by inclusion in the Education budget. This gives an opportunity of considering, if we so desire, the affairs of these universities. But if the grant is to be paid out of the Consolidated Fund there will hardly be any discussion on it. I think this is highly undesirable. I know that many years ago it was desired that the Bose Institute should be placed in this position, namely that it should get its grant out of the Consolidated Fund. That is, the grant should not be open to discussion by the Legislative Assembly.

Shri Sondhi: That is a non-voted grant.

Pandit Kunzru: It should become a non-voted grant. Happily this proposal was never placed formally before the Government. I am surprised that so experienced a Parliamentarian as my hon. friend Dr. Mookerjee should have come forward with this proposal. I respect his love for the Visva-Bharati. Perhaps he thought it his duty as an admirer of Guru Dev, who was the founder of the University to come forward with this proposal. I entirely agree with the Finance Minister that the acceptance of this proposal would create an undesirable precedent and further would place undue restriction on the power of Parliament to discuss a grant before voting on it. I am therefore strongly opposed to it.

Shri C.D. Deshmukh: I wanted to point out that apart from anything else the notice of this amendment has been too short. I understand it was not circulated at all and in a matter like this one ought to set a precedent, which would make for safety, that it should have been properly circulated so that we should have time to consider it. Then, the point that you made, sir, that it has been referred to negatively in the sense that we have not made a provision, that is to say we deliberately came to the conclusion that it would not be appropriate to make a provision, if a provision is to be made I consider that it does require the recommendation of the President – under rule 84 of the Rules of Procedure the recommendation of the President has to be attached to the amendment. From that point of view also I do not think it is possible to accept that amendment.

Maulana Azad: I beg to submit that it is not needed at all so far as the interests of the Visva-Bharati are concerned. Some of my friends have just now reminded me that there are three universities which are connected with the Centre. These are Banaras, Aligarh and Delhi. I can say this much that no provision whatsoever has been made for any specific amount in all the Acts which relate to them. It was proposed in the beginning to sanction a sum of rupees three lakhs for them per year, but now a sum of rupees twenty lakhs to twenty-two lakhs is being sanctioned for them every year in the Budget. And I do not think that you are doing anything against their interests if you do not specify any amount in the Act which you are going to pass within a few minutes; I think there was no question about it too. Besides it this amendment has come all of a sudden. Before this neither any notice was given of it nor was it ever seen.

Dr. S.P. Mookerjee: I have no desire to embarrass Government in any way. The principle of making statutory grant is nothing new – it has not been flung upon the House or anybody else – but I quite appreciate the difficulty that the Finance Minister and the Education Minister pointed out. I do not wish to press the amendment. The matter may be examined by Government independently.

Schedule

Mr. Deputy-Speaker: Very well. Now we shall take up the Schedules. We have already adopted yesterday a motion to add a Schedule on clause 6. That will be the First Schedule and the Schedule to clause 7 which I shall now put to the vote of the House will be the Second Schedule.

Shri Kamath: There is a new word in this Schedule, Sir, which is unknown to me at least. It says:

> "The area known as Santiniketan in the District of Birbhum in West Bengal, *admeasuring* 11.5 square miles....".

It says "admeasuring"......

Shri Venkataraman: Admeasuring is a word known to everybody.

Mr. Deputy-Speaker: Both mean evidently the same thing. The question is:

"That the Schedule stand part of the Bill."

The motion was adopted.

The Schedule was added to the Bill.

Clause 10. – [*The Paridarsaka* (*Visitor*)] — *contd.*

Mr. Deputy-Speaker: Clause 10 was held over. Has any agreement been arrived at?

Dr. S.P. Mookerjee: Yes, I am moving an amendment in that connection. I beg to move:

For sub-clause (6) of clause 10 substitute the following:

> "(6) When the *Paridarsaka* (Visitor) has, in pursuance of this section, addressed the Upacharya (Vice-Chancellor) in connection with any financial or administrative matter relating to the University and the Karma Samiti (Executive Council) does not, within a reasonable time, take action to the satisfaction of the Paridarsaka (Visitor) in respect thereof, the Paridarsaka (Visitor) may, after considering any explanation furnished or representation made by the Karma Samiti (Executive Council) issue such directions as he may think fit and the Karma Samiti (Executive Council) shall comply with such directions."

Some Hon. Members: This amendment has not been circulated.

Pandit Kunzru: We should have a copy of that amendment before us before any discussion takes place.

Mr. Deputy-Speaker: I shall read it slowly so that Members can write it down. We held over clause 10 so that Government may look through it. If further time is to be taken up things will not proceed. Hon. Members, I suppose, have paper and pencils.

Shri Kamath: We are not being supplied with pencil and paper nowadays.

Mr. Deputy-Speaker: They are usually supplied.

Shri Kamath: We have not got them now.

Maulana Azad: It is an amendment on which agreement has been reached.

Prof. K.T. Shah: Sir, if the agreement is only to be between the hon. Minister and Dr. Mookerjee, and the rest of the House does not know it then I do not know....

Mr. Deputy-Speaker: That is not the intention. Agreement means agreement of the whole House. All that the hon. Minister says is that on behalf of the Government he agrees to the amendment. Now I will read the amendment slowly for hon. Members to follow it :

"(6) When the Paridarsaka (Visitor) has, in pursuance of this section, addressed the Upacharya (Vice-Chancellor) in connection with any financial or administrative matter relating to the University and the Karma Samiti (Executive Council) does not, within a reasonable time, take action to the satisfaction of the Paridarsaka (Visitor) in respect thereof, the Paridarsaka (Visitor) may, after considering any explanation furnished or representation made by the Karma Samiti (Executive Council) issue such directions as he may think fit and the Karma Samiti (Executive Council) shall comply with such directions."

Shri Santhanam: There is hardly any difference – the original clause seems to be as a good as the amendment.

Dr. S.P. Mookerjee: My friend, Professor Shah said that the draft as proposed is not entirely acceptable to him. Nor is it to me, but this is the amendment which Government is prepared to accept in order to accommodate the various points of view which were expressed on the floor of the House. If hon. Members would refer to clause 10 as it stands, they will find powers are given to the Visitor to direct an inquiry to be made or inspection to be made into all affairs of the University and such affairs may relate to its buildings, library, equipment, any institution maintained by the University, exmainations, teaching and other work conducted or done by the University. Once that inquiry is ordered then the University will also be entitled to be represented thereat. Later on, the visitor may address the Vice-Chancellor with reference to the result of such inspection and enquiry and call for the comments of the University. After receiving the comments, the Visitor may, according to the draft as it is before us now, direct that certain changes should be made or that certain steps should be taken by the University and such directions shall be entirely binding on the University. Some of us had felt that this clause should not be there at all, and that the President should not be given such wide powers of inspection at all. It is felt by others that even if the powers are given, they should not relate to academic matters at least, which means that the enquiry must be confined to administrative or financial matters alone. This amendment which is acceptable to the Government provides that while the Visitor will have the right to direct an enquiry to be made into all matters, administrative, financial or academic, without any restriction being put upon his discretion, the final directives which may be issued by him to be binding on the University will relate not to academic matters but only to financial and administrative matters. In other words, if any proposals are made relating to academic questions, those proposals will be sent to the University and the University will be asked to consider them. How far they can be implemented will be a matter for the University to decide. To that extent, we have made a positive gain. The visitor will not have the power to give any final directions to the University regarding academic matters. If the powers of the Visitor could be removed altogether, even in respect of the enquiry to be made, it would be perhaps acceptable to Prof. Shah and others, but the Government feels that the right to order an inspection need not be curbed but the final decision to implement conclusions in respect of academic matters may be left to the University. This may not be a cent. per cent. compromise.

Pandit Thakur Das Bhargava: What about Section 29 which deals with Ordinances?

Dr. S.P. Mookerjee: The hon. Member was not here; there also a very important change has been accepted.

Pandit Thakur Das Bhargava: I was here and I know how far it has been amended. But still, you can amend and cancel.

Dr. S.P. Mookerjee: No. With regard to Ordinances, let us be very clear about one thing. The only power which the Visitor will now have will be in respect of two things. One is that if there is any Ordinance proposed which is repugnant to the Act or which contravenes any of the provisions of the Act, then obviously the Visitor may say that such an Ordinance shall be void. It is nobody's case that the University may be given the liberty or the licence to do things repugnant to the Act which Parliament is passing. The second thing is that if there is a difference of opinion between the Academic Council and the Court, then somebody has to decide. There should not be a deadlock. There the power has been given to the Visitor to intervene, but if all the bodies of the University can come together and agree on some formula, then obviously the Visitor will not interfere. Then, with regard to the right of inspection, under clause 10, although inspection may cover all matters, the right to issue final directives is confined only to administrative and financial matters and does not extend to academic matters. Speaking from the University's point of view, I think this is a substantial change and if later on the powers and abused either by the Visitor or by the University then the Parliament is here wide awake to its responsibilities and it can do whatever it lives at any stage.

Mr. Deputy-Speaker: Amendment moved:

For sub-clause (6) of clause 10, substitute the following.

"(6) When the Paridarsaka (Visitor) has, in pursuance of this section, addressed the Upacharya (Vice-Chancellor) in connection with any financial or administrative matter relating to the University and the Karma Samiti (Executive Council) does not, within a reasonable time, take action to the satisfaction of the Paridarsaka (Visitor) in respect thereof, the Paridarsaka (Visitor) may, after considering any explanation furnished or representation made by the Karma Samiti (Executive Council) issue such directions as he may think fit and the Karma Samiti (Executive Council) shall comply with such directions."

Maulana Azad : I accept it.

Pandit Kunzru: I want to say a word with regard to the amendment proposed by Dr. Syama Prasad Mookerjee. His amendment, if accepted by the House, would enable the Visitor to issue directions to the Vice-Chancellor with regard to the carrying out of the recommendations made by the Committee of Enquiry appointed by him only in respect of financial and administrative matters. But I see no reason why the power of the Visitor to issue instructions to the Vice-Chancellor should be confined only to such of the recommendations of the enquiry committee as are concerned with financial and other administrative matters. It is quite possible that the standard of teaching in a University may go down; it is possible that the examinations may be made so easy as to make its degrees almost entirely worthless. We know that at least in the case of one.....

Mr. Deputy-Speaker: I am afraid the hon. Member was not here when.....

Pandit Kunzru: I was here throughout.

Mr. Deputy-Speaker: Order, order. A number of amendments were moved by Prof. Shah and following that speeches were made. Dr. Mookerjee also spoke on this matter and wanted to introduce an amendment. Considering the volume of opinion, Government thought that they must go half-way. Not that I am objecting to the hon. Member speaking on this matter now. But I thought that it was agreed that in academic matters the Visitor ought not to have such extraordinary powers. The hon. Member may go on if he likes.

Pandit Kunzru: I was present here when this was done.

Mr. Deputy-Speaker: It would have been better if the hon. Member had intervened then and tried to shape or influence the opinion of Government.

Pandit Kunzru: But I was not given an opportunity to intervene: things were managed so quickly. The matter was postponed for further consideration till a draft in the proper legal language had been placed before the House. So this is the first opportunity that I have of expressing my opinion on this matter.

I was saying, Sir, that we know that at least in the case of one University the Government was compelled to institute an enquiry into its affairs, not on financial or administrative grounds, but on academic grounds. Such a thing may happen again. I hope it will never happen in the case of the Visva-Bharati. But Visva-Bharati too is a human institution. Its affairs too may need to be looked after by sympathetic supervisors sometimes. And if we are prepared to allow the Visitor to issue instructions to the Vice-Chancellor in respect of financial and administrative matters, there is no reason why we should doubt his *bona fides* when after making a proper enquiry on which the University will be represented he tells the university that he feels satisfied that its academic affairs are not being properly managed and that certain steps must be taken in order to bring them into order. In the absence of this power the Visitor or the Government will be able to intervene in two ways: either an Act will have to be passed by Parliament authorising the Visitor or the Central Government to issue instructions to the Visva-Bharati in respect of academic matters, or the grant will have to be stopped in order to compel the Visva-Bharati to improve its academic side. Now, is it desirable, Sir, that either of these extreme steps should be taken? I think it would be a lesser evil if the Visitor continued to enjoy the powers proposed to be conferred on him by the Bill before us rather than drive Government to any of the alternatives, mentioned by me, in an emergency. I do not think therefore that the amendment put forward by my hon. friend Dr. Syama Prasad Mookerjee ought to be accepted by this House, and I cannot congratulate the hon. the Education Minister on having been in a hurry to accept the suggestion made by Dr. Mookerjee on the spur of the moment.

Dr. S.P. Mookerjee: Not on the spur of the moment, and not suggested by me alone but by so many Members.

Pandit Kunzru: My hon. friend Dr. Mookerjee has great experience of administrative and academic affairs of a big University and what he says is entitled to our respectful consideration. But I venture nevertheless to submit that on the grounds that I have placed before the House his amendment should not be accepted. There is time yet for the Government to reconsider its position. I repeat that it would be much better to allow the Visitor to be invested with the powers proposed to be conferred on him by the Bill rather than make the change proposed by Dr. Mookerjee and then compel Government either to stop the grant to the Visva-Bharati or to get legislation passed in order to bring its academic affairs into order.

Prof. K.T. Shah: It was on account of my amendment that the change was necessitated and the clause was held over and therefore I may be allowed to say a few words.

I am not going to say a word about Dr. Kunzru's remarks, because there seems to be a radical difference of opinion. He does want to have the Visitor and plenary powers to the Visitor, whereas I do not want the Visitor at all. So there is no argument about that.

As regards the amendment, let me say at the outset that it may be an improvement up to the point it goes, but it does not explicitly remove the academic matters from inspection or enquiry by the Visitor at all. My understanding was that these matters would be completely taken out of the powers of the Visitor, to order an enquiry or make an inspection or make suggestions.

I recognise the distinction, now made. The distinction made is that in the first case, that is to say, in respect of financial and administrative matters, which may be within the legitimate purview of the Visitor, when they do not take action within a certain time to his satisfaction, the Visitor may issue directions and they will have to be binding. In the second case they would be merely in the nature of a suggestion. I see the distinction. But I do not see the distinction represents agreement, so far as Dr. Mookerjee and myself are concerned. I want academic matters to be completely removed, and an express statement to be included in sub-clause (1) that these inspections shall be confined only to administrative and financial matters.

If a mere suggestion is to be made by such an exalted personage as the Visitor of this University, who will be the President of the Union, these suggestions will have the force, if not of command, of very weighty recommendations and as such they cannot be lightly ignored. I do not regard even that as a desirable feature in a University constitution. That an outside authority, acting on its own – I had made the suggestion that his action should be at the request of the University which is not included – should make even suggestions on academic matters is objectionable on principle, and to that extent, therefore, this does not represent what I thought would be the accepted idea of the Government.

Pandit Malaviya (Uttar Pradesh): I should like to submit in this matter that the question of academic or other control, which Government should exercise over universities is a matter of far-reaching importance. The tendency all over the world is that while grants are to be given by Governments to universities, they must have some machinery, some method of ensuring that the grants which the Government makes to those universities are spent correctly and are utilized for the purposes for which they are made. To that extent, there is provision for control and inspection and all that. Beyond that, even if there is some technical provision for the interference of the administrative set-up in university affairs, the tendency everywhere is, not to welcome that and not to allow that and particularly in the matter of academic affairs. I submit, that the universities should be trusted to look after their own standards and not only by themselves; there is an institution like an Inter-University Board in India in which every university is represented and which meets from year to year to discuss and decide about common problems, about matters of standards, policy, etc. Even then, if there are to be universities with different standards, it may not, after all be any great catastrophe. We know in America there are so many universities about which – it is not a concealed fact – official lists are given saying that these are Grade A Universities, these are Grade B Universities and these are Grade C Universities etc. That helps in the spread of higher education and I submit that if higher education is to be worth the name, the less of Government interference, the less of Government control, the less of enquiry and inspection from the administrative machinery of the day– after all, all this means interference by the Government–the less of it there is, the better will be the chances of the growth of real higher education in this country (*Hear, hear*). The proposal which has been accepted by Government is in the right direction. I do not wish to go into the larger question of the powers which the Visitor will have, of instituting inquiries and all that. On the one hand, I am anxious that the University should work and function in the most correct manner and should always be open to criticism and visits and inspection by all those who may be interested in them because there is always a desire on the part of Universities to set right any mistake, any shortcoming which may be there, but on principle.........

Pandit Maitra (West Bengal): There is also the Central Advisory Board of Education which meets every year in different sub-committees.

Pandit Malaviya: So far as principles are concerned, I think the progressive nations all over the world, in England and in America are more and more insistent that grants should be given to universities. Sir, the Cambridge and Oxford Universities receive grants from the British Government which sometimes equal to 75 per cent of their total expenditure. But there is a University Grants Commission in England – and our Universities Commission also strongly suggested it – and it confines its activities to inspection and visits, and they are very frequent to see that the grants which are given to those universities are properly utilized for the purposes for which they are made. That is a very different matter. Therefore, I think – the financial matters and even administrative matters are there – that it will be in the right direction if academic matters are left out. I should have preferred that they should have been left out altogether even in the earlier clause. If they are not left out there, at least they should be left out in this clause which has been accepted by the Government, which I feel is in the right direction and I hope the amendment will be carried.

Shri Syamanandan Sahaya (Bihar): Sir, enough has been said on this subject already and there is hardly any time now. Even then, I thought an amendment like the one which is proposed by Dr. Mookerjee deserved my support and that of this House. I was surprised, to say the least, to hear what I heard from Pandit Kunzru. In fact, one of the merits of this amendment is that it is perhaps the golden mean between the extreme views of Pandit Kunzru and those of my hon. friend Prof. Shah. Pandit Kunzru has mentioned about the powers of interference which in certain circumstances he considers necessary, by the Paridarsaka. One has to make a choice in academic matters as to whether such a power, however necessary, must lie in the hands of one person even as high as the Paridarsaka or in the hands of the different bodies which constitute a university. I have no doubt in my mind that on a careful consideration it will be agreed that in academic matters, the powers ultimately must lie in the hands of the different bodies constituting the university. With regard to powers of inspection and ordering of enquiry left in the hands of the Paridarsaka, even in regard to academic matters, my hon. friend Prof. K.T. Shah gave away his case when he said that the recommendations of the Paridarsaka will in any case be weighty recommendations. I see no reason why they should not be weighty. After all, if the President of the Indian Union feels that in a certain university certain recommendations have to be made in the interest of the University and the country, it is as well that he should do so in the larger interests of the country and it is as well that the recommendations should be considered weighty enough. Therefore, I extend my wholehearted support to the amendment and I hope the House will accept it.

Shri Kamath *rose* —

Mr. Deputy-Speaker: We have had enough discussion on this....

Shri Kamath: When I was about to speak, you said that the clause had been held over.

Mr. Deputy-Speaker: Hon. Members can insist on their rights.

Shri Kamath: I rose to speak then and you said that the clause had been held over. It was an assurance given by you, Sir.

Mr. Deputy-Speaker: All right. Mr. Kamath.

Shri Kamath: The voice of Pandit Kunzru who has been nurtured all his life on liberal traditions, and who has been an advocate, I almost said apostle, of liberty and freedom, sounded strange in the House today. If his views are accepted in their entirety, it will mean that Government would be invested with the power to interfere with the working of this university at every step and at every stage. It has been observed by a philosopher that that Government is best which governs least. Whatever may be said for that in other spheres of governmental activity, at least in the educational sphere, so far as universities are concerned, I wholeheartedly agree with that observation of the philosopher, and Government should interfere the least. I therefore would have wished that even this unfettered right conferred on the Paridarsaka, the right to cause inspection or enquiry, should not have been unrestricted or unfettered. It has been the tendency of the Government, especially during the last four or five decades, or two or three decades to be more exact, to interfere in every sphere of human activity, right from food to God. The Upanishadic sage said, "Annam Brahma".

Mr. Deputy-Speaker: How is God a human activity?

Shri Kamath: Without God, there is no human activity at all.

Shri Naziruddin Ahmad (West Bengal): God is everywhere.

Shri Kamath: Without God, you would not be there, Sir, and we would not be here.

I was saying that this tendency has been on the increase of late, I mean this tendency to interfere with the universities, and some governments in Europe and also in Asia have tried to make universities centres of their own propaganda, for propagandizing their own ideology. I believe Germany and Italy tried to do it in the third and fourth decades of this century and also in Moscow I believe there is a tendency in this direction. And recently in the papers we read that Peking Government had stepped in and tried to dictate to a certain ancient university in that land. I do not suggest that our Government or our Paridarsaka are cast in that mould or want to arrogate to themselves the right and the power to interfere in any manner they like in our universities, particularly in Visva-Bharati which was founded, nurtured and brought to this stage by Gurudev Rabindranath Tagore. But, Sir, the danger is always there and with due deference to the President, the Paridarsaka and the Ministers who will guide him and advise him in all matters, there is no guarantee that the future Paridarsaka or the future advisers will be of the same calibre or of the same type. As Sardar Patel used to say, there is nothing permanent in this transistory world. We wish the Paridarsaka and our Ministers were permanently here, but there is a God above who guides the destinies of the world and in His wisdom He may ordain otherwise. Therefore, Sir, as we in this Parliament desire to legislate for as long and as far as we can see, and make provisions for emergencies that might arise, I say that this right to be conferred on the Paridarsaka to enquire into the affairs of the University without any invitation or request made to him from the University is a dangerous provision, and to my mind it is an objectionable provision. The Minister has agreed to the amendment moved by Dr. Mookerjee – I had almost said, agreed in a half-hearted manner to the amendment – but clause 10 as it stands is very defective and dangerous. I only pray to God that he may vouchsafe wisdom to the Paridarsaka and his advisers here not to interfere at their sweet will and pleasure, not to interfere in the sacred precincts of learning according to their whim, fancy or caprice, but to do so only when really and truly the situation demands it, when there is real dissatisfaction within the University and that state of affairs has been conveyed to them from a reliable and competent quarter. Otherwise, I for one am afraid that this provision is likely to be abused by the Paridarsaka, and human nature being what it is, I should not be surprised if the advisers of the Paridarsaka, if not to-day, at some later stage try to make even this Visva-Bharati University, whose heritage we all know so well a centre for the propagation of their own ideology or any particular idea that may catch their fancy at any time.

Yesterday this House voted down a suggestion for the incorporation of the words *"Shantam, Shivam Advaitam"*, or the Supreme Being. Suppose in the near future this is taken up, and if some professor or *Adhyapak* or anybody else in the University teaches in the name of the Supreme Being that is *Shantam, Shivam and Advaitam*, am I to take it that the *Paridarsaka* or his advisers who have been invested with absolute power under this section will interfere even in that matter?

Mr. Deputy-Speaker: Not under the amendment.

Shri Kamath: They can interfere certainly and that is derogatory to the spirit of Visva-Bharati. Clause 10(2) gives the Paridarsaka unfettered right to inquire into any matter at any time and without giving any reason whatsoever. Therefore even at this stage I would request that Prof. Shah's amendment be accepted. I would however, omit the word "teacher" from the amendment and have it only as "On a formal representation being made to him by any body or authority in the University." Only then should the power of the Paridarsaka be exercised in the matter.

Mr. Deputy-Speaker: The question is:

For sub-clause (6) of Clause 10, substitute the following:

> "(6) When the Paridarsaka (Visitor) has, in pursuance of this section, addressed the Upacharya (Vice-Chancellor) in connection with any financial or administrative matter relating to the University and the Karma Samiti (Executive Council) does not, within a reasonable time, take action to the satisfaction of the Paridarsaka (Visitor) in respect thereof, the Paridarsaka (Visitor) may, after considering any explanation furnished or representation made by the Karma Samiti (Executive Council) issue such directions as he may think fit and the Karma Samiti (Executive Council) shall comply with such directions."

The motion was adopted.

Mr. Deputy-Speaker: Does Prof. Shah want to press his amendments?

Prof. K.T. Shah: Yes, Sir.

Shri Santhanam: When we have passed this amendment, the other amendments cannot arise.

Mr. Deputy-Speaker: Instead of giving a ruling I shall take the vote of the House. The hon. Member has raised the point that the other amendments are barred.

Pandit Kunzru: Prof. Shah's amendment is totally inconsistent with the amendment just now accepted.

Prof. K.T. Shah: There are other parts to the amendment.

Mr. Deputy-Speaker: I shall put to the House No. 60.

Pandit Kunzru: May I suggest that No. 60 cannot be put to the House.

Mr. Deputy-Speaker: I cannot agree with the hon. Member. It only says with that the initiation of proceedings by the Visitor may be made under certain restrictions.

The question is:

(1) At the commencement of sub-clause (2) of clause 10, insert the following:

"On a formal representation being made to him by any body, authority, or teacher in the University,"

The motion was negatived.

Mr. Deputy-Speaker: The question is:

(2) In sub-clause (2) of clause 10, after the word "University" where it occurs for the second time, insert the words "or its general or financial administration".

The motion was negatived.

Mr. Deputy-Speaker: The question is:

(3) In sub-clause (3) of clause 10, after the word "give" insert the words "at least one clear month's".

The motion was negatived.

Mr. Deputy-Speaker: The question is:

(4) In sub-clause (3) of clause 10, after the words "to be made" insert the words "giving the names and addresses of the person or persons he has appointed to make the inspection or conduct the enquiry".

The motion was negatived.

Mr. Deputy-Speaker: The question is:

(5) In sub-clause (4) of clause 10,—

(i) for the words "may address" substitute the words "shall forward to".

(ii) for the words "with reference to the result" substitute the words "the report together with his own views thereon".

(iii) after the brackets and words "(Executive Council)" insert the words "the report of the inspection or inquiry and".

(iv) Omit all the words after the brackets and word "(Visitor)" where it occurs for the second time.

The motion was negatived.

Mr. Deputy-Speaker: The question is:

(6) In sub-clause (5) of clause 10, –

(i) after the word "shall" insert the following:

"place before the Samsad all the papers and documents mentioned in the preceding sub-sections, together with its own suggestions regarding the action it thinks proper and necessary to take in the matter, and shall";

(ii) after the brackets and word "(Visitor)" insert the words "the opinion of the Samsad, together with its directions on the";

(iii) Omit the word "such" occurring after the brackets and word "(Visitor)"; and

(iv) for the word "as" substitute the word "which".

The motion was negatived.

Mr. Deputy-Speaker: The question is:

"That clause 10, as amended, stand part of the Bill."

The motion was adopted.

Clause 10, as amended, was added to the Bill.

Clause 1. — (*Short title and commencement*)

Prof. K.T. Shah: I beg to move:

"In sub-clause (1) of clause 1, after the word "the" insert the words "Rabindranath Tagore".

I do not want to make any remarks on this part, I will do so on the Preamble. I commend this amendment to the House.

Maulana Azad: It is unnecessary, because when we see Tagore's place in the world, it is felt that this Bill does not lack in any way if his name is not mentioned in it.

Mr. Deputy-Speaker: The question is:

"In sub-clause (1) of clause 1, after the word "the" insert the words "Rabindranath Tagore".

The motion was negatived.

Mr. Deputy-Speaker: Then Pandit Thakur Das Bhargava's amendment is barred, Shrimati Raiji's amendment refers only to a question of spelling, Shri Hazarika's amendment is also barred. The question is:

"That clause 1 stand part of the Bill."

The motion was adopted.

Clause 1 was added to the Bill.

The Title was added to the Bill.

Enacting Formula

Prof. K.T. Shah: I beg to move:

After the long title of the Bill, add the following Preamble:

> "Whereas it is right and proper to recognise and perpetuate the work and teachings of the poet and philosopher, Dr. Rabindranath Tagore, and to set up and maintain a fitting memorial to his life of dedication to the cultural revival of this country;
>
> And whereas the late Dr. Rabindranath Tagore founded an institution known as the Tagore Vishva Bharati at Shantiniketan in the district of Birbhum in West Bengal, donating all his land and property in that area, and endowing that institution with the whole amount of his Nobel Prize as well as the income from all his copyright works, the objects of which are such as to make the institution one of national importance."

The point that I would like to make is a very simple one. I would associate officially in the title of the University the name of the founder. There is no dispute, there is no suggestion that anybody else but Dr. Rabindranath Tagore is the founder of this University. There are plenty of precedents whereby the names of founders or even donors have been associated with the Universities in this country as well as abroad. You have the famous Smithsonian Institute of America. Most people do not know who Smithson was who founded the Institute. He was a chemist who gave some funds for its foundation, he did not live to see the Institute inaugurated that but for Government intervention, the University would not have come into being. His only service was the donation, whereby his name has been perpetrated. Similarly, in the case of the Cornell University......

Mr. Deputy-Speaker: In India you have got the Annamalai University.

Prof. K.T. Shah: That is all the more reason why we should incorporate the name. The Cornell University was also founded by the grant of land. The donor did not survive, but his successors founded the University in his name. In this country, we have the recently established Sayyaji Rao University. The Annamalai Universtiy also was founded on a donation. The Osmania University also is in the same footing. It perpetuates the name of the Osmanias.

Shrimati Renuka Ray: In any case, the name will be there when one reads clause 2.

Prof. K.T. Shah: My point is why not perpetuate the name here? If you do not want it, you can reject it. That is not my concern.

Shri Santhanam: We have passed clause 2 which says all that the hon. Member wants. We have also adopted a convention that we will not accept amendments to the Enacting Formula.

Mr. Deputy-Speaker: As Mr. Santhanam has pointed out, is not this covered by clause 2?

Prof. K.T. Shah: Everything is not covered. Clause 2, I may humbly submit, is really a part of the Preamble, namely, it recognises only perfunctorily the original foundation by the Poet to which also full justice is not done. I want this institution to be associated with the name that everybody knows and not merely that the name should be known by reading clause 2 of this Act. I have given some illustrations to show how Universities are known by name. In my opinion, this Visva-Bharati also should be known by the name of Poet Tagore.

Mr. Deputy-Speaker: But the House has rejected that amendment.

Prof. K.T. Shah: That is so far as Tagore Visva-Bharati is concerned. It was only consequential in that clause 2. Here, the Preamble is distinct and separate and I submit that any decision of the House previously does not bar my moving an amendment to the Preamble. Nor is my amendment out of order. (*An hon. Member*: Read it.) I wanted to read it, but the Chair declared that it should not be read. May I read it, Sir?

Dr. S.P. Mookerjee: May I make an appeal to the Chair that we should discuss this particular matter with all solemnity? The name of the University was given by the Poet himself and if we really want to honour it, it would be much better to keep it as Visva-Bharati as the Poet himself had styled it and not change it in any way whatsoever.

Mr. Deputy-Speaker: On a point of order, after the Constitution has come into force, we have not been having any Preambles. Therefore, I rule this amendment which relates to the "Preamble" out of order. The hon. Member should not refer to ancient practice; let us follow the recent practice. The question is:

"That the Enacting Formula stand part of the Bill."

The motion was adopted.

The Enacting Formula was added to the Bill.

Maulana Azad: I beg to move:

"That the Bill, as amended, be passed."

Mr. Deputy-Speaker: I find several hon. Members want to speak. I shall adjourn the House now.

The House adjourned till Half Past Eight of the Clock on Thursday the 3rd May 1951.

Document No. 43

FURTHER CONSIDERATION AND ADOPTION OF THE MOTION, MOVED BY MAULANA AZAD IN THE HOUSE OF THE PEOPLE ON 3-5-1951 IN CONNECTION WITH THE VISHVA BHARTI BILL

Mr. Speaker: The House will now proceed with the further consideration of the Visva-Bharati Bill.

Motion moved:

"That the Bill, as amended, be passed."

I would like to invite the attention of the House to the third reading motion and the speeches thereon. I see so many are anxious and eager to catch the Speaker's eye to have an opportunity to speak. I have no objection to give an opportunity to the largest number possible, but I may say, this House has discussed the motion for consideration for two days – that means a general discussion on the Bill – and then the clauses were taken up and it took three days to complete the clause by clause reading. So five days have been taken up over this Bill. Presumably everything that could be said has been said....

Pandit Kunzru (Uttar Pradesh): We have had three days.

Mr. Speaker: I am speaking with reference to the records. On the 28th April we started at about 12-15 – it may not be one day – then on the 30th we took the whole day – of course the question hour is always excluded – then we considered it on the 1st and 2nd May....

An Hon. Member: Four days.

Mr. Speaker: Whatever it may be, whether it is four days or five days practically every clause has been discussed threadbare....

Dr. Deshmukh (Madhya Pradesh): Not threadbare.

Mr. Speaker: It may not be to the satisfaction of individual Members but it is to my mind. Therefore, I would request Members to be short in speeches. It is no use repeating again the arguments or the aspects advanced during the earlier stages. Otherwise the alternative will be for the Chair to close its eyes. I would request hon. Members to be short over this, because they are also very anxious to see the session coming to an end. They are enquiring how long they are going to sit and I have said it is entirely in the hands of Members to bring the session to a close. Hon. Members will bear in mind the whole picture of the business before the House; they have to adjust accordingly. I might also invite attention to rule 95 which says:

> "The discussion on a motion that the Bill be passed shall be confined to the submission of arguments either in support of the Bill or for the rejection of the Bill. In making his speech a member shall not refer to the details of the Bill further than is necessary for the purpose of his arguments which shall be of a general character."

Dr. Deshmukh: We will obey that.

Mr. Speaker: I know, if Members are not prepared to co-operate, I shall have to give them time to argue as to whether they are in order or not. It is not my purpose to prevent them from arguing anything, but the purpose is to see that we take a reasonable overall view of the business of the House and finish the arguments briefly. Lengthy arguments are not necessarily convincing arguments.

Shri M.A. Ayyangar (Madras): I do not wish that this Bill should be concluded without a glowing tribute to the wisdom of the hon. Prime Minister and also the hon. Minister who is incharge of this portfolio, for having given statutory recognition to a unique experiment that was started by the late Rabindra Nath Tagore. He was rightly called a *Maharishi*. India had a unique kind of life, knowledge of which, according to the intentions of the *Maharishi*, must be spread out to the rest of the world, a world where conflicts are arising almost every day; he wanted from that Visva-Bharati to spread that knowledge which will avoid all conflicts in future. As the name implies, Visva-Bharati was established in Santiniketan in the district of Birbhum. I understand Birbhum to mean *Veera Bhumi* where in the midst of conflict Rabindra Nath Tagore chose Santiniketan which is the embodiment or abode of *shanti* or peace. That is exactly what is needed in the world of today where conflict is ruling everywhere, where conflict has entered the soul of man. In the midst of conflict the spirit must be so evolved that the inner nature is conquered. It is for this that the *Maharishi* in the midst of fight established Shantiniketan or the Abode of Peace. The knowledge that will be disseminated from this instituion will be only for a particular place like Bengal nor even for the whole of India but for the whole universe. Therefore, the Poet rightly called the institution "Visva-Bharati". He has given it the name: Where the whole universe becomes one abode. That is a true interpretation of our ancient culture and philosophy. India may not be as progressive economically as the rest of the world, but it has got an indestructible soul. This University is a grand experiment and this message will go forth to the rest of the world. A man who says that another person is a friend of his and yet another is an enemy of his – such a man has a very small mind. To a man with a large heart, the whole world is his family. This Visva-Bharati is intended to create messengers of peace, who will take their proper places among the nations of the world and see to it that the law of the jungle no longer prevails in human relations. In the *Bhagavad Gita*, the whole of mankind is divided into two categories, the *Asuraprakriti* and the *Devaprakriti*. We have evolved from the *Asuraprakriti* and we must become *Devaprakritis*. We must become angelic. For that purpose, non-violence – *Ahimsa* – must be placed in the forefront of all human relations and that is why the Poet said *Shantam*, that is, *Ahimsa*. Whether the words *Shantam*, *Shivam* and *Advaitam* are incorporated in the text of the statute or not, I am sure that this spirit will be disseminated from here. We are trying in this University to evolve a harmonious religion. Researches will be made here into the unity of all religions. He who has got a large heart and has studied all religions will certainly find that there is an essential unity in all religions. The differences are more apparent than real. Persons are wanting who emphasise this aspect of essential unity. Unfortunately, they are exploiting religion for various political purposes. I am sure this University will preach the essential unity among all nations and bring about that peace for which Mahavir laid his life, for which the great Buddha also strived from end to end, and for which the Mahatmaji also laid his life. I am sure this experiment will thrive and this spirit will prevail in it. The western materialistic world has conquered outer nature. It has developed instruments to fly to the top of the skies; to dive deep into the deepest waters; to run faster than sound and mind. But it has not conquered inner nature. If we attempt to teach anything at all to the world, it is the conquest of the inner nature. If the true spirit of *Ahimsa* prevails and there is peace in our hearts, then the rest of the outer nature is conquered by itself.

So far as *Shantam* is concerned, we always desire peace. It is bad that we should eschew the word *Shantam*. That proposal does not appeal to me. But whether we use it or not, the name of this place is itself Shantiniketan – the Abode of Peace. You cannot erase it, just as you cannot erase the lustre from the sun or the moon. Just as the sun and the lustre are indivisible and one, so also, whether you call it lustre or not, the glow will be there.

So far as *Shivam* is concerned, it ought not to be identified with Shiva.

Dr. Deshmukh: Does this exposition come under the rule you have read out, Sir?

Mr. Speaker: Let the hon. Member proceed. I am giving him a little more time to conclude.

Shri M.A. Ayyangar: I am finishing, Sir, I am only anxious that this University should be that kind of *Gurukul* which we all desire to establish. We did not conquer outer nature. We did not conquer the Asian continent by mere conquest in the accepted sense of the term. We brought our culture to bear upon people. We have and had no territorial ambitions. We have always wanted more to give than to take. If a man delights in giving, there would be no quarrel in this world. This is what our savants have preached. I expect that this spirit will breathe in this University. I agree with the wisdom of this Government in giving it a statutory basis.

So far as *Shantam* is concerned, Mahatmaji often said that he did not want the peace of the Corpse; he wanted the peace of the living. In *Raghu Vamsa* it is said....

Mr. Speaker: He is now going into an irrelevant discussion.

Shri M.A. Ayyangar: I am trying to anticipate those who might say that this whole Bill should be dropped because this particular line "*Shantam, Shivam* and *Advaitam*" is not included. I want to submit that even without it, this Bill goes a long way. We are creating a new era. Our children will be taught more to respect others' wishes and sacrifice for them than for their own comforts and conveniences. If such people are manufactured in this University, there will be an end to all wars.

So far as *Advaitam* is concerned, it says that God alone is the Supreme Being. That is what exactly is conveyed by *Allah-o-Akbar*.

Mr. Speaker: We are entering into something which is irrelevant at this stage of the discussion. The hon. Member may support the Bill generally, and even there I think he has sufficiently supported it by now. He may close by saying that he supports the Bill.

Shri M.A. Ayyangar: I do support the Bill. I do want this Visva-Bharati to spread a message in the world and what is that message? It is the message of *Ahimsa*, prosperity, universal love and affection and universal brotherhood. That message is the essential unity of all religions; the fact that God is one and indivisible; that humanity is one and indivisible. That is the message we want this University to spread to the four corners of the world.

Yesterday, it was said that there might be interference with this University. I am sure that with the assurance of the hon. Education Minister there would be no pin-pricks. Like the *Maharishis*, those in charge of this institution should be allowed to evolve a religion, a new mode of life, an Aryan mode of life of which everyone must be proud. I have great pleasure, even at the sacrifice of some time of the House, to support the third reading wholeheartedly. I am sure that this institution will be worked in the spirit in which it was founded and in which it is sought to be continued.

Prof. K.T. Shah (Bihar): I rise to oppose this motion. That is not because I do not wish the Visva-Bharati to be recognised as an institution of national importance. That is because the Bill as it stands, even with the few amendments that have been grudgingly accepted, fails to embody the spirit that ought to breathe through it. The hon. Mr. Deputy-Speaker has reconciled himself to the mutilation of the objectives as defined by the founder, perhaps in his enthusiasm to support the motion and perhaps as he loyally must. But for my part, I think it is one of the biggest reasons why this motion should not be passed and the Bill should be reconsidered. The Bill is hedged round and restricted in such a manner that it cannot fulfil the objectives which you profess that it is going to fulfil.

My second reason is a little more personal, though it is not associated with myself. By a reference to a recent practice, my amendment for the association of the name of Tagore was not admitted yesterday. I feel that if for on other reason, at least for the reason that we are not associating the name of Tagore in the very title of the University, we ought not to pass the Bill in the form in which it is now before the House.

An English poet spoke of the then politician or writer, Bacon: "See how Bacon shines the greatest, wisest minister of mankind". I trust that this Parliament should not be exposed to a criticism of this character that we failed, that we grudged to associate the name of the greatest founder who gave all his property – endowed it with the Nobel Prize, endowed it also with all the income from his copy-right and also devoted the best years of his life to enthuse the spirit, to make it the living orgnism. We hope that it would be continued in the same spirit perhaps, but not under this constitution. I trust that even now, even at this late hour, wisdom will prevail and that the Bill will be amended still further. After rejecting this motion in such manner that at least these two points will be included, I wholeheartedly support this Bill.

Dr. Deshmukh: While speaking on the motion for consideration, I had voiced my disagreement with the proposal embodied in the Bill, more or less for the same reasons which have been expressed by my hon. friend Prof. K.T. Shah and some other hon. Members of this House. One of the things which I pointed out was that this organisation of a University was unsuited to the ideals and objects which Rabindra Nath Tagore had placed before himself and for which essentially this institution was meant. I had also pointed out that the University Commission had repeatedly said that the pattern of Universities hereafter should be something new, something original and should not follow the patterns which have been followed so far.

I would like to read only a few sentences from a book written by Mr. Arthur E. Morgan, one of the Members of the University Commission. That will show how utterly unsuited the present pattern of the Universities is for the needs of India and especially in a place like Shantiniketan. Besides what has been stated in the course of the Report, these are very pertinent observations: "In some respects the Universities of India are not in the main current of the national life." Secondly, he observed after having gone round India and having seen so many experts and heard their evidence: "A stranger might never have learnt from those hearings that a village exists in India". He came into contact with University people and the evidence that was placed before him gave the impression that if one was a complete stranger, from the learned expositions and submissions of these people, one can think that there was nothing like a village in India. This is also a very important quotation: "The pattern and culture of the Universities are from a foreign land and are not rooted in the native soil." I know the respect with which Mr. Morgan is held and that was the reason why we called him all the way from America to give us his advice so far as the structure and the future organisation of our University education was concerned. This is what he has said.

So, I submit that the hon. Minister was not well advised in keeping the scheme which is identically the same as of other Universities that exist in India and my complaint is that it is not in this atmosphere that the spirit of Poet Tagore can survive, much less progress and thrive.

I would have very much liked that this place was kept free from these rules and regulations. As I said in my second speech, I would have liked this place to be created into a spiritual U.N.O. where all those who are learned and cultured in the world may assemble and guide the destinies of the world and promote peace more effectively than the American U.N.O. which has unfortunately already become a battle-ground of wits for outwitting the other side. Even now there is an opportunity before us to make this sacred place in India into a sanctuary for the learned of the world, of every religion, of every inclination, so that the world may be guided better.

Dr. S.P. Mookerjee (West Bengal): Although there may be room for difference of opinion as regards some of the provisions of the Bill, I rise to give my whole-hearted support to the measure as has been amended by the House and which is now going to be passed. There could be no legislative enactment which is not capable of improvement. But what are the essential features of this Bill which we are about to pass?

First of all, the great objective for which the founder stood has found a place in the Bill. No doubt a few expressions have been omitted which many of us would have liked to have found a place in the Bill. Their omission has been most unfortunate. But I do not think it is going to make much practical difference, because both the Government as also every section of the House have declared that it is the intention of all that this University should develop not on the ordinary pattern, but on the basis which the founder had made his own.

Secondly, so far as the constitution is concerned, we have merely laid down the bare outline of the constitution. Now, here a note of warning has been sounded and I would like to emphasise that point of view. When the status are framed we have to take good care to see that we do not build up this University on the pattern of the existing Universities. Sir, as you will recall, the Bill as originally drafted laid down that the first statutes shall be framed by the Central Government. On my amendment this clause has been altered and the responsibility for framing the first statutes has been placed on the first Chancellor who is no other than Shri Jawaharlal Nehru. He is the present Chancellor and I believe it is the intention that he will continue to be the first Chancellor of the University. I would, therefore, especially appeal to him that while the first statutes are drafted he will see to it that they are not modelled or copied *verbatim* from the statutes which are now in existence in relation to ordinary Universities in India. That is a very important point. If we fail to draw up these statutes properly we will not be able to implement the provisions of this Bill. It is not for me to suggest what procedure he should adopt, but if I may make a general suggestion, I would propose that he should appoint as Chancellor a small committee which should include representatives of Visva-Bharati and within a month or so the statutes can be properly drafted which he can examine and then place before the Visitor for formal approval. We have just given a bare outline in this Bill as to how the constitution should be drawn up, but much more remains to be done and that will depend on the manner in which the statutes are drafted.

The next point is about the possibility of Government interference. Now we have been able to amend the original provisions to a considerable extent. I do not mind what exactly the provisions of the law are; it all depends on the spirit in which a particular enactment is actually worked. Now the intention of all, whether belonging to Government or outside, is that the fullest possible freedom should be given to those who are incharge of the affairs of this University to carry on their activities, consistent with the objectives of the founder. I would, therefore, specially request the Education Minister not to interfere with the detailed working of this institution. That also is a very important consideration. Freedom is the essential condition on which such an institution can grow. Let us not make mistake about one point. This was a new experiment which Rabindra Nath Tagore made in the field of education. His efforts were greatly doubted by his contemporaries within the country. But when recognition came from savants and people who knew about new experiments in education outside India, then many people in India started being attracted to this institution. Now let us not try to develop education on one and a single pattern. We have some Universities also which are being modelled on different lines. Here is a new experiment, consistent with our genius and aspirations, which can be very fruitfully pursued and which, luckily today, has found the seal of approval from the hands of the Government of the day. I think if we proceed on sound lines we will be able to show results which will not only do credit to this country but which will help in solving many intricate problems which face human civilization today.

I would make an appeal to the Finance Minister. Powers have been taken over by Government in this Bill in respect of many matters, but there is no provision in the law as to whether Government is going to make any financial assistance or not, although an assurance has been given by the Education Minister and the Finance Minister that funds will be forthcoming. That is a consideration which I hope will be constantly kept in view by the Finance Minister.

One other thing I would like to mention before I conclude. While framing the statutes one has to take care to see that all those rigid conditions which are attached to the appiontment of Professors and others and also to erection of buildings and other formalities should not be included in the working of Visva-Bharati. It is not necessary that every Profeessor should draw a salary of Rs. 1,000 or Rs. 1,200. People who are drawn to Visva-Bharati are very eminent men who have practically devoted their life to that institution and are satisfied with a subsistence allowance. If any attempt is made by the Central Government to have standardised scales of pay for the staff because members of the staff of other Universities are not satisfied with less, that I think will be a mistaken idea. I am not suggesting that they should be starved. Everyone who works there must be given conditions of service which will enable them to live properly. But it is not necessary that we should standardize their salaries. Similarly with regard to buildings we do not want large buildings there. We have spent lakhs and lakhs on palatial buildings elsewhere. Those who have visited Visva-Bharati know how many classes are held in the open garden. When I was delivering my address at the time of the last convocation, in the absence of Shri Jawaharlal Nehru, it was held in the mango garden and it was a delightful and inspiring atmosphere. It was one of the many innovations of the Poet, under the inspiration of his great father. Let us not try to interfere with such liberties that such an institution has been enjoying. These are the special features of Visva-Bharati. Although, they may be external features and characteristics, yet they are very valuable as they are indicative of its peculiar attitude towards many problems which face that University. We must be able to preserve them intact and develop them in the future.

With these words I give my support to the Bill as amended.

The Prime Minister and Minister of External Affairs (Shri Jawaharlal Nehru): In view of what my hon. friend just said I should like to make clear, if there is any doubt about it, the attitude of Government in this matter. Also, I possess, without being worthy of it, another capacity and that is the Chancellorship of Visva-Bharati. We have looked upon this not only as a very great institution but as a very special and uniqe institution, and we are particularly anxious, if I may say so, that our Education Department should not try to bring about any regimentation of it in line with others. The chief business of the Government of India or the Education Ministry will be to help it to develop on its own lines naturally to see that any falling off in standards, according to its own standards, does not take place, or any deterioration so far as we can help it – but generally to allow it to develop according to its own genius or according as far as possible, to the vision that the great Poet had. And I entirely agree with Dr. Mookerjee when he laid stress on certain factors which may be called external if you like, but, nevertheless, which must have a very powerful influence in moulding the student there and creating a new environment, whether it is teaching in the mango grove or doing anything like that. I do attach great importance to it and I entirely agree with him that we should not spend our money on a large number of brick structures as we unfortunately still do in making our buildings, whether it is educational buildings or other buildings, and have little left to carry on the work in those buildings. I might mention that some time ago instructions were issued by the Govt. on this very subject, that we should try to forget brick and mortar as far as possible in buildings and have our schools, colleges and institutes in sheds, in thatched huts if necessary so as to utilise the money to greater advantage for the present.

One thing else, As I said, I feel a little embarrassed at having to occupy a position like that of the Chancellor of Visva-Bharati. Because whatever virtues I might possess. I am painfully conscious of a lack of virtue in so far as the qualities for a Chancellorship of such an institution are concerened, apart also from the fact that I am rather fully occupied otherwise, and can give very little time to it. But whether I give much time to it or ont, I have all along felt not only a very deep interest but a very special obligation to the memory of the Poet and, if I may say so, it was due to a promise I made to him – or rather to my acceptance of his direction in this matter – that I feel that I ought to do my utmost for the growth of this magnificent idea to which he gave birth.

Shri Naziruddin Ahmad (West Bengal): I accord my humble and whole-hearted support to the Bill. But in doing so I have to express my regret as to the manner in which a large number of substantial amendments were accepted on the floor of the House. I am not much in conflict with amendments themselves, but what I do wish is that when such important amendments have to be accepted they should rather be done in a Select Committee and outsdie the Huse. It is often very difficult for individual Members of the House to follow the course of the debates when amendments of a serious nature are accepted off-hand in the House.

Then again I am not very much in favour of loading a Bill, much less an educational Bill, with pious sentiments and idealism. To a certain extent they detract from the attention that should be paid to the working of the University rather than to the ideals incorporated in the Bill.

The last matter which I should mention would be about the amendment to introduce the Almighty God into a Schedule. The House by a large majority voted it down. I should submit that the reason of the majority should be more apparent to the minority than it apparently is. I believe that the view of the majority was that God is everywhere. He is omnipresent and is all prevading; and by the very nature of things, it must be assumed that he is also already in the Schedule; and I thought the majority should therefore protest against the attempt of the minority to confine the Almighty within the confines of a narrow Schedule. That is, I believe, the logic of the opposition by the majority.

The Minister of State for Parliamentary Affairs (Shri Satya Narayan Sinha): I beg to move:

"That the question be now put".

Mr. Speaker: The question is:

"That the question be now put".

The motion was adopted.

The Minister of Education (Maulana Azad): I have nothing new to state at this stage. All necessary points have been stated by me earlier. While introducing the Bill I had assured the House on behalf of the Government of India that it was not being introduced to give Visva-Bharati the status of an ordinary university. I had been said that the objects of the Bill is to preserve and promote the ideals for which that great Institution was established. Further I had then referred to what had transpired between me and Mahatma Gandhi in January 1947 at the time I took charge of this Ministry. He had told me that Gurudev had left a great trust with him which he was going to entrust me thereafter. The Government of India, by introducing this Bill, had tried to preserve that trust and the passage of this Bill, does not mean at all that any dishonesty will be practised instead of making efforts for its preservation or that any attempt will be made to change the very ideals for which this University had stood all along. Doing that, I feel, will instead of preserving it mean sheer dishonesty and a betrayal of the trust.

That is all, I have to add nothing further. I feel thankful to hon. friends whom I had appealed not to press unnecessary amendments which they have withdrawn.

Mr. Speaker: Before I put the motion to the House, I will put a small formal amendment to vote.

The question is:

> "That the clauses of the Bill be re-numbered consequential upon the insertion of new clauses in the Bill."

The motion was adopted.

Mr. Speaker: The question is:

> "That the Bill, as amended, be passed."

The motion was adopted.

Who's Who

Abbas, Tayabji	: Former Judge, Baroda State, joined national liberation movement (1916); became President of Kaira District Congress Committee.
Anney, M.S.	: Reputed nationalist leader, some time member of Viceroy's Council; was elected President of the first Session of All India Hindu League, held at Lucknow in 1935.
Azad, Abul Kalam	: Nationalist and front ranking freedom fighter; was the Editor of 'The Vakil of Amritsar' Al-Hilal', 'Al-Balagh'; was elected President of Indian National Congress in Delhi (1923) and in Ramgarh (1940); was appointed Education Minister in free India's first Cabinet (1947) headed by Jawaharlal Nehru.
Beasant, Annie	: A leading social reformer; was the founder of Indian Home Rule League; elected twice President of Indian National Congress.
Benarji, W.C.	: Liberal Congress leader of Bengal; was elected first President of Indian National Congress (1885).
Bhopatkar, L.B.	: A Prominent Congress Worker of Poona.
Boulay, James De	: Member Incharge of Home Department Political, Government of India (1918-20).
Curzon, Lord	: Governor-General of India (1905), was responsible for the division of Bengal.
Das, C.R.	: Renowed Swarajyaist leader of Bengal; was elected President of Indian National Congress at Gaya in 1922.

Desai, Bhulabhai J. : Leader of Congress Party in Indian Legislative Assembly (1946); was appointed a Member of Congress Working Committee several times between 1934-46; marvellously pleaded for I.N.A. Convicts (1946). His parleys with Liaqat Ali Khan, when the Congress leaders were in Jail, regarding the future set up for national government had been one of the reasons for Congress High Coomand's cool attitude towards him.

Despande, G.R. : A close devotee of B.G. Tilak and prominent figure of Maharashtra.

Gandhi, Kasturba : Devoted wife of Mahatama Gandhi, the father of Nation.

Gandhi, M.K. : Supreme leader of national liberation movement (1920-47); was elected President of Indian National Congress (1924); was the Editor of 'Young India' and 'Navjivan' (1920-1930), 'Harijan' (1933-48), Harijan Sewak (1933-1948) and author of 'Hind Swarajya'; participated in the Second Round Table Conference held in London in 1931.

Gokhale, D.V. : An eminent Parliamentarian of Maharashtra.

Gokhale, G.K. : One of the founder leaders of the Indian National Congress (1885); was nominated to the Central Legislative Council (1906); was founder of Servants of India Society; visited England in 1906 to discuss the Education Policy for India; was elected President of Congress in 1905.

Hakim Ajmal Khan : Veteran freedom fighter and Congress leader of Delhi; was a prominent figure of Non-cooperation and Khilafat Movement (1920); was appointed a Member to the Working Committee of Indian National

		Congress (1920, 1923 and 1925); was elected President of Congress, in 1921 at Ahmedabad.
Jaykar, M.R.	:	A moderate leader of Bombay and leading lawyer; was an expert in Constitutional matters.
Jinnah, Mohammad Ali	:	First Governor-General of Pakistan (1947); was the Vice-Chancellor of Osmania University; elected a Member to the Indian Legislative Assembly in 1930 and 1934.
Kelkar, N.C.	:	A close associate of B.G. Tilak and well known Swarajyaist leader; was elected to the Indian Legislative Assembly in 1924.
Khaparde, G.S.	:	An ardent follower of B.G. Tilak; was a member of Imperial Legislative Council; became Vice - Chairman of Indian Home Rule League in 1918.
Kher, B.G.	:	A leading Congressman of Bombay, became the Premier of the state in 1937 and the Chief Minister in 1946.
Liaqat Ali Khan	:	A Prominent leader of United Provinces Muslim League; was appointed Finance Member in the Interim Government (1946) headed by Jawaharlal Nehru; elected leader of All India Muslim Parliamentary Party (1946) and became first Prime Minister of Pakistan in 1947.
Malviya, M.M.	:	Front ranking Congress leader was elected President of the Indian National Congress in 1919.
Mavalankar, G.V.	:	Leading freedom fighter of Gujarat; was a Secretary to Gujarat Sabha (1920), became President, Indian Legislative Assembly (1946), and Speaker, Lok Sabha (1958).
Mehta, Firozeshah	:	Founder leader of Indian National Congress; was elected President in its Surat Session held in 1907.

Minto, Lord : British Viceroy to India since 1908; became popular for his reforms scheme of 1909 which was known as Marley-Minto Reforms; introduced Separate Electorate System for Hindus and Muslims.

Misra, Gokaranath : Prominent Congress leader of U.P. 1916-20 and General Secretary of the Party in 1919-20.

Mohammad Ali : Prominent figure of Non-cooperation and Khilafat Movement (1920); was elected President of Indian National Congress at Kokanada in 1923; Edited 'Comrade' and 'Hamdard' newspapers (1910-20); presided over the Session of All India Jamiat Ulama - i -Hind (1929); was appointed Inspector of Schools of Rampur (1903-1904); was the author of 'Political Problem of India'.

Mukhtar Ahmed Ansari : Patriot and nationalist; was a front ranging Congress leader of Delhi; elected President of Indian National Congress in 1927; participated actively in the Non-cooperation and Khilafat Movement (1920) and Salt Satyagraha (1930); was nominated to the Working Committee of Indian National Congress in 1919, 1922 and 1930.

Nehru, Jawaharlal : Noted freedom fighter, was President of Indian National Congress (1929, 1936 and 1946), became first Prime Minister of free India (1947); was the founder of All India Kisan Sabha, Bharat Krishak Samaj and a number of organisations.

Nehru, Motilal : A well known Barrister of Allahabad; was a prominent figure of Congress Party, was elected to the Indian Legislative Assembly in 1924 and also President of Indian National Congress in 1928.

Pal, B.C. : Prominent Congress Swarajyaist leader from Bengal; was the Editor of 'New India' (1901) and 'Bande Mataram' (1904).

Patel, Vallabhbhai : Great freedom fighter; was organiser of 'Nagpur Flat Satyagraha' (1923), Borsad Movement (1924) and Peasants Agitation of Bardoli (1928); was elected President of Indian National Congress at Karachi in 1931; became Deputy Prime Minister in the first Cabinet (1947) of free India, headed by Nehru; was elected Chairman of Congress Parliamentary Board in 1934, 1937 and 1946.

Patel, Vithalbhai J. : Top ranking Congress leader of Gujarat; was a Barrister of Bombay High Court (1908 – 1914); was elected to the Legislative Council of Bombay (1913), Imperial Legislative Council (1919) and the Indian Legislative Assembly (1924); became President of Bombay Municipal Corporation (1924) and the first Indian Speaker to the Indian Legislative Assembly (1925 – 30).

Plato : Great Greek Philosopher (about 500 B.C.), was author of the 'Republic', 'The Laws' and 'The Statesman'.

Prasad, Rajendra : A prominent Congress leader and constructive worker of Bihar; was elected President of Indian National Congress (1935); was appointed a member to the Working Committee of Indian National Congress several times between 1922 and 1949, Congress Parliamentary Board (1937 and 1947), Food and Agriculture Minister in the Interim Government headed by Nehru (1946); was elected Chairman of Indian Constituent Assembly (1947) and the President of Indian Republic in 1950, 1952 and 1957.

Rai, Lajpat : Popularly known as 'Punjab Kesari'; was elected President of Indian National Congress in Calcutta in 1920, a front ranking Congress leader from Punjab and social reformer.

Rajagopalachari, C.	:	Front ranking Congress leader of Madras and a Gandhian thinker, twice premier of Madras State (1937 and 1946); was appointed Governor for West Bengal (1947), Governor-General of India (1948) and Minister of Home Affairs in 1950; was well known for his suave diplomacy and cruditness; founder of Swatantra Party of India.
Raj Bahadur	:	Noted freedom fighter of Rajasthan, was appointed a Minister in the Cabinet by Mrs. Indira Gandhi.
Ramatirtha, Swamy	:	A prominent scholar of Hindu philosophy; was a follower of Adventism; visited United States and other Western countries several times.
Roy, M.N.	:	Thinker and well-known freedom fighter from Bengal; was a Congress leader who participated in Communist International held in Moscow in 1920; was defeated by Maulana Abul Kalam Azad for Congress President's election in 1940 at Wardha.
Saminullah Khan	:	Prominent Citizen of Dacca and the founder of All India Muslim League in 1905.
Shauqat Ali	:	Elder brother of Maulana Mohammad Ali; was a prominent figure of Non-Cooperation and Khilafat Movement; was appointed to the Working Committee of Indian National Congress between 1920 and 1930.
Shibli, Nomani	:	Well-known spiritual leader from Lucknow; was a scholar of Islamic philosophy.
Shivaji Maharaj	:	A Great Maratha Sardar of 17th Century.
Spoor, Ben C.	:	A member of British Parliament in 1918.

Swamy Dayanand Saraswati	:	Founder of 'Arya Samaj' and the author of 'Satyartha Prakash' ; was a great reformist and scholar of Vedic Philosophy.
Syed Ahmed Khan, Sir	:	Muslim reformist and the founder of Scientific Society of Ghazipur and the Muslim College of Aligarh; was the editor of 'Tahzeeb-ul-Akhlaq'; was nominated to the Indian Legislative.Council (1878); was author of a number of books including 'College of 'The Indian Revolt', 'The Asbab Bagawaat-e-Hind', 'Present State of Politics' and 'Loyal Mohammadans'.
Tara Chand	:	Noted educationist; was secretary and adviser, Union Ministry of Education; was appointed Ambassador to Iran in 1951.
Tegore, Devendra Nath	:	Father of Ravindra Nath Tagore and a well-known Social reformer of Bengal.
Thakkar, A.V.	:	Noted Gandhian and constructive worker of Gujarat, was closely associated with the Servants of India Society.
Tilak, B. G.	:	Great Congress leader from Maharashtra; was a prominent figure of Swadeshi Movement (1905); was the editor of 'Maratha' and 'Kesari' and was imprisoned several times during national liberation movement of India.
Tyagi, Mahavir	:	Prominent Congress of U.P. ; was appointed a Minister of State in the Union Council of Ministers by Pandit Nehru.
Vivekananda, Swamy	:	Great thinker, scholar of Adventism and Hindu Philosophy ; was a staunch follower of Swamy Ramkrishna 'Paramahansa' and founder of the 'Ramakrishna Mission', visited U.S.A. several times.
Vyas, Jaynarayan	:	Leading Congressman of Rajasthan; was the Premier of the State in 1946.

Glossary

Ahimsa : Non-violence, Mahatma Gandhi's weapon of love for mass action.

Ashram : Literally, hermitage, a place for penance and spiritual pursuit.

Begar : Forced labour.

Bhagvadgita, The : The song celestial, highly philosophic poem laying emphasis on the selfless views of life and action.

Bhakta : Devotee, disciple.

Bhartiya : Indian.

Brahmin : One belonging to the priestly class.

Chaddar : Bedspread.

Charkha : Spinning-wheel.

Charkha Jayanti : Yearly celebration of spinning movement.

Charkha Sangh : Spinners' Association, the All-India body that Gandhiji had formed in 1925 to provide employment to the starving millions of India.

Chawl : Locality.

Chowpatty : Public square.

Civil Disobedience Movement : Satyagraha Movement of Mahatma Gandhi to resist British rule in India.

Constructive Programme : Eighteen-fold programme of Mahatma Gandhi for resurgence of India.

Dal : Pulse cooked or uncooked

Darbar : Court.

Darindra Narayana : The God of the poor; symbolically, God in the form of the poor and the distressed.

Devanagri	: Script of national language 'Hindi'.
Dewan	: Adviser, Prime Minister of the erstwhile Princely State.
Dharmaraja	: A prince of virture, the first among the five Pandavas.
Dharmashala	: A charitable travellers' home.
Dhoti	: Indian loin-cloth.
Fakir	: A man of renunciation.
Firka	: Sub-taluka.
Gaddi	: Post-position, throne.
Ghee, gjrot	: Clarified butter.
Goonda	: Miscreant, rowdy, hooligan.
Gujarat Vidyapith	: The National Universtiy, Ahmedabad, which Gandhiji founded in 1920.
Guru	: Preceptor, spiritual guide.
Gurukul	: Place of teaching or School.
Harijan	: Literally, man of God, the term used by Gandhiji in relation to one-time secluded sections of the society.
Harijan Sweak Sangh	: As association for the service of Harijans which Gandhiji founded in the thirties.
Hinayana	: The doctrinal cult of Buddhism.
Inquilab Zindabad	: Love live Revolution!
Jamia-Millia	: A University in Delhi.
Japti	: Confiscation of property, etc., in defiance of non-payment of taxes, etc.
Jehad, Zehad	: Crusading war in the name of religion.
Jowar	: Coarse tropical grain.
Kaira Satyagraha	: No-tax campaign of the Peasants of Kaira District in 1918 against the Bombay Government, it was the second campaign (after Champaran) of

	Mahatma Gandhi in India against the British Rule and the first of Sardar Vallabhbhai Patel.
Karma Yogi	: Believer in the path of Karma action with selflessness.
Khadi	: Hand spun and hand woven cloth.
Khadi Mandal	: Organization for the propagation of spinning-wheel.
Khadi Pracharak Mandal	: The organization for the spread and popularization of Khadi.
Khichadi	: A dish of pulse and rice cooked together.
Kisan	: Peasant, agriculturist.
Kumkum	: A red-coloured dust used as auspicious mark on forehead by Indian women, also being used on ceremonial occasions.
Kurta	: Shirt, here loose garment especially of the North Indian type.
Kshatriya	: One belonging to warrior class.
Lathi	: Cudgel, wooden stick.
Maharaja	: The ruler of a former Indian State of bigger territory.
Mahatma	: Literally, high-souled person, a title bestowed on Mahatma Gandhi by Indians.
Mhahavidyalaya	: A Centre of higher education, College.
Mahayana	: Another Buddhist cult laying emphasis on the propagational aspect.
Mal	: A cotton tape used in a spinning-wheel.
Mandal	: Association, gathering
Nawab	: A petty ruler, a landlord.
Namaskar	: Respectful salutations.
Palak	: A variety of green vegetable.
Pandal	: Temporarily erected shed for public gatherings and cremonials, etc.

Paramdham Ashram : Literally, the abode of higher pursuit, Shri Vinoba's ashram at Pavnar.

Parashuram : Seer of Ramayana age possessing super-human valour.

Parishad : Council.

Praja Mandal : The term then applied to people's gatherings and ceremonials, etc.

Puni : Carded cotton roll.

Qaumi Ekta : Communal unity.

Raj : Rule, sovereignty, kingdom.

Raja : A king, ruler, prince.

Rajapramukh : The titular or rather the constitutional head of the interim Unions of States after Independence.

Rajput : A warrior, one belonging to the martial race.

Roti : Indian bread.

Ryot : People, subject, ruled.

Resolution on forced labour : This resolution was passed in the first Gujarat Political Conference, held at Godhra in October 1917 under the Presidentship of Mahatma Gandhi. In the resolution "It was the custom of Government Officers when touring in the district to extract work from certain section of the people, and often not to pay for it. The village carpenter, for instance, would be called upon to make the wooden pegs for the officers' tents, the potter to provide earthen vessels and even to fetch water in them, the barber to tidy up and to do the lamps, the sweeper to sweep and to take and fetch message, the grocer to supply all foodstuffs, and the peasants to arrange bullock carts for transporting the Saheb's luggage from one camp to another. The petty officers of the village had to remain in attendance throughout the period of the officer's stay and in addition, to look after the needs of the shrishteder (the judicial clerk) and other clerks. It was rarely that all this work and supplies were paid for and on top of it all, all these men had to remain in attendance for hours, and sometimes for days, on end. After the Home Rule League was established, vigorous agitation was started to an end to this pervicious system." Lokamanya Tilak was also present in the Conference.

Rowlatt Bill : In this Bill the Government had been provided a number of special powers for arresting and detaining, without trial, persons suspected of anti-government activities.

Sanyasini : Nun, recluse.

Sardar : Leader, captain, champion.

Sarvarajochhetta : Uprooter of kings.

Satyagraha : Literally, insistence of truth, Mahatma Gandhi's weapons of truth and love for mass action.

Servants of India Society : A band of people pledged to serve the country in a constitutional way. This society was organised by the Great Leader of Maharashtra Mr. Gopal Krishna Gokhale.

Shantiniketan : 'House of Peace' a University founded by Dr. Ravindra Nath Tagore.

Shawl : A loose covering over body.

Shravana : A month of Indian Year.

Sthitaprajna : The man of equiposied mind.

Swadeshi : Country made.

Swaraj : Self-rule, according to Mahatma Gandhi's conception, social, economic and political independence in the true sense of term.

Swarajist : Term used for those who wedded to Council Entry Programme after Civil Disobedience and the Khilafat Movement.

Tahsildar	: Revenue officer of a Tehsil or Sub-division.
Tarka	: The Logic.
Talati	: The Talati is a village revenue officer, concerned with collection of land revenue.
Taluka	: Taluka or Tahsil is an administrative unit of varying sizes, but usually extending over a few hundred square miles in area and containing a number of villages and one or two towns of population exceeding 10,000.
Talukdar	: A land-holder.
Vad	: The Second half of Indian month.
Veth	: Forced free labour.
Verandah	: A ground-floor balcony
Vishnu	: The second among the trio of gods symbolizing protective facet of the supreme.
Yogi	: One who practises Yoga, *i.e.* spiritual, mental and bodily discipline for self-realization.
Zamindar	: Absentee landlord
Zamindari	: Absentee landlordism

CHRONOLOGY OF EVENTS

(1951)

1951 March 15	:	Inaugurated First All India Conference on Letters in New Delhi.
March 24	:	Presided over the Second Session of the Indian National Commission for Cooperation with Unesco.
March 27	:	Speech delivered in the House of the People on General Budget – List of Demand for 1951-52 year.
April 17	:	Introduced Vishva-Bharati (Amendment) Bill in the House of the People.
April 26	:	Moved for leave to introduce the Benares Hindu University (Amendment) Bill in Parliament.
May 3	:	Got the motion adopted in connection with the Vishva-Bharti (Amendment) Bill, in the House of the People.
June 7	:	Addressed the Unesco Conference in Paris.
August 18	:	Declared opened the Indian Institute of Technology at Kharagpur.
August 25	:	Moved for leave to introduce the Benares Hindu University (Amendment) Bill and Aligarh Muslim University (Amendment) Bill in Parliament.
September 22	:	Formally inaugurated the Vishva Bharti as a Central University.
September 27	:	Introduced Aligarh Muslim University (Amendment) Bill in the House of the People.
October 27	:	Inaugurated the Delhi Public Library.
November 3	:	Presided over a meeting of the Vice-Chancellors of the Indian Universities, held in New Delhi.

December 13	:	Inaugurated a Symposium on the concept of Man and the Philosophy of Education in the East and the West in New Delhi.
December 26	:	Inaugurated Twenty-eighth Session of the Indian Historical Records Commission at Jaipur.
	:	Elected Deputy Leader of Congress Parliamentary Party.

Index